The Early State

New Babylon

Studies in the Social Sciences

32

MOUTON PUBLISHERS · THE HAGUE · PARIS · NEW YORK

The Early State

Edited by

HENRI J. M. CLAESSEN
PETER SKALNÍK

MOUTON PUBLISHERS · THE HAGUE · PARIS · NEW YORK

This publication has been made possible by a grant given by the Netherlands Foundation for Pure Scientific Research

ISBN : 90 2797904 9
© 1978, Mouton Publishers, The Hague, The Netherlands
Printed in Great Britain

Preface

The idea of undertaking the arduous venture to produce a volume on early states gradually developed after the *IXth International Congress of Anthropological and Ethnological Sciences*, held in Chicago in September 1973. Here the future editors met almost incidentally during the session on West African Culture Dynamics. In the course of brief meetings in the hotel, alternately drinking coffee and beer, we discovered each other's interest in early states. So in subsequent correspondence we agreed upon the usefulness of bringing together a collection of contemporary analyses in connection with this subject.

In the course of 1974 we agreed upon the broad plan for a book, on the basis of which we invited a large number of scholars to participate. The criteria we used in selecting these scholars were, in fact, determined by a mixture of considerations. We aimed at as wide as possible a range of cases — wide from a geographical as well as a historical point of view. Then, we also tried to draw our collaborators from a variety of disciplines. So we looked for anthropologists, archaeologists, historians, sociologists and political scientists. At the same time we tried to bring together colleagues from different ideological backgrounds — a difficult undertaking indeed. Fortunately, the response was most encouraging. Hence, in April 1975 a general *Letter of Information* was sent to those who had accepted our invitation. This letter set out a number of details of the plan for the book, while a fairly detailed list of questions to be discussed in the case studies was enclosed with it. Our contributors were requested to pay special attention to these questions in order to enable a comparison of the data. The reason for this was that we wished to arrive at a synthetic approach to the available data.

Apart from the case studies, we felt that some theoretical chapters would be needed, in which a sample of recent theories and viewpoints would be presented. We were fortunate enough to find Professor Ronald Cohen (Northwestern University, Evanston, USA), Dr. Anatolii Khazanov (Academy of Sciences, Moscow, USSR) and Professor Lawrence Krader (Free University, West Berlin) prepared to accept our invitation to write these chapters.

In the course of the preparations, several colleagues who had initially accepted our invitation were obliged, for different reasons, to withdraw from the project. This, together with the rather arbitrary way in which we had selected our authors, in the end led to a fairly random selection of early states for our sample.

During the *34th Annual Meeting of the Society for Applied Anthropology* in Amsterdam in March 1975, both editors had an opportunity of discussing the progress of the work with Dr. Donald V. Kurtz (University of Wisconsin, Milwaukee, USA) and Dr. S. Lee Seaton (Bowling Green State University, Ohio, USA), who wrote the chapters on the Aztecs and Hawaii respectively. Here we also met Professor Lawrence Krader with whom we discussed a number of problems in connection with our intended volume. We again profited from his wise advice in several subsequent meetings with him (Berlin, Rome). In Prague, we discussed the plan with Dr. Jan Pečírka (Charles University, Prague), Dr. Timoteus Pokora and Dr. Josef Kandert (Náprstek Museum, Prague). Dr. Pokora later wrote the chapter on China, and Dr. Kandert the chapter on the Zande.

Henri Claessen organized a seminar on *The Formation of the State* at the Institute of Cultural and Social Studies of the University of Leiden in the fall of 1975. In this seminar Dr. Jac. J. Janssen (Institute for Egyptology, University of Leiden), Dr. Henri B. Teunis (Institute for Mediaeval History, University of Utrecht) and Dr. Martin Doornbos (Institute of Social Studies, The Hague) participated. The first mentioned two scholars contributed the chapters on Egypt and France respectively to this volume. Dr. Doornbos, at a later stage, gave helpful criticism of the volume. Our contacts with our other contributors were only by letter. Though written contacts are usually more awkward than personal ones, we nonetheless had some most pleasant experiences in this way.

In October 1975 and May 1976, Henri Claessen visited Prague in order to enjoy a few days of close contact and collaboration with Peter Skalník. Both trips were financed by the Institute of Cultural and Social Studies of the University of Leiden.

Here the original plan was amended and adapted to suggestions received and experiences gained. Without wishing to underestimate the contributions of others to the development of the project, we would like especially to mention those of Professor Ronald Cohen, Professor Herbert Lewis (Madison, University of Wisconsin, USA), Dr. Anatolii Khazanov, Dr. Natalia Kochakova (Academy of Sciences, Moscow, USSR), Dr. Guram Koranashvili (Georgian Academy of Sciences, Tbilisi, USSR) and Dr. Donald V. Kurtz, with whom, notwithstanding the language barrier, we had some most fruitful discussions about the many problems involved.

By the spring of 1976 practically all the case studies and the theoretical chapters had reached the editors, and it was possible for the work on the comparative part to start. Drafts of the relevant chapters written by the editors were sent, upon completion, to all participants in the project, who were invited to comment upon them. To say that their comments, additions and suggestions were interesting would be an understatement. If our chapters have any value at all, this is due to the participants' critical, and above all stimulating remarks.

Not only the participants to the project have reacted to our ideas. Other colleagues have provided comments, ideas, criticism and stimulation as well. We should mention with special gratitude Martin A. van Bakel, and Piet van de Velde (both of the Institute of Cultural and Social Studies of the University of Leiden), who, from the very beginning, have aided our efforts with their patient attention, encouragement and critical comments. Professor Patrick E. de Josselin de Jong of the same Institute has provided comment on one of our chapters. He was also most active in procuring funds for travel and other expenses incurred by the Dutch editor. Professor M. Estellie Smith (SUNY, Oswego, New York, USA) wrote us some most stimulating letters and drew our attention to literature unknown to us. Dr. Lucien Bäck (The Hague) most carefully read all the editors' drafts, and we gratefully acknowledge his influence. Dr. Jan Pečírka (Charles University, Prague), Dr. Susan Drucker-Brown and Professor Meyer Fortes (both of the University of Cambridge, UK) served the Czechoslovak editor with their kind advice as so many times before. Professor Romila Thapar (Jawaharlal Nehru University, New Delhi, India) most willingly read and commented upon one of the chapters. Dr. Simon Kooijman (State Ethnographical Museum, Leiden) most carefully read and commented upon the chapters regarding Polynesia. Dr. Myron Aronoff (Tel-Aviv University, Israel) gave valuable comments upon our ideas and methods.

The volume is divided into three parts, viz.:

I. A *theoretical* part, or *Thesis*, which contains a general introduction to the problem, the working hypotheses, and chapters by Cohen, Khazanov and Krader.

II. The *case studies*, or *Antithesis*, constituting the main part of the volume. Here the twenty-one cases are arranged in alphabetical order, according to the names of the states.

III. A *comparative* part, or *Synthesis*, in which the editors attempt to draw general conclusions from the data of the case studies. It contains first a discussion of the structural characteristics of the early state, and next a functional/processual synthesis of the data with regard to the way in which the early state functioned. In a further chapter the early state is placed within the general framework of the development of social forms. The volume closes with a chapter summarizing the main conclusions of the *Synthesis*.

For it to have been possible for a volume like this, to which scholars from so many different countries have contributed, to be presented in readable English in the end, we are indebted to Miss Maria van Yperen, of the Royal Institute of Linguistics and Anthropology in Leiden. She has corrected the manuscript patiently and with an amazing gift for understanding each author's intentions.

We owe a great debt of gratitude to the Netherlands Foundation for Pure Scientific Research, which generously provided Peter Skalník with a grant enabling him to stay in the Netherlands for half a year to finish the editorial work. The same Foundation also aided the final publication of the volume by providing a subsidy for the printing costs.

We are most grateful to the Board of the Institute of Cultural and Social Studies of the University of Leiden which, by giving its consent for grants to be made available on two occasions, not only made possible Henri Claessen's two visits to Prague, but also the language-editing of the text and the typing of the manuscript. Without these grants we would never have been able to complete the work. That Henri Claessen was able to receive half a year's leave to edit this volume was possible only thanks to the ready cooperation of his colleagues in the Anthropology Department, who took over his teaching and administrative duties during that period.

The unenviable job of typing and retyping the manuscript was undertaken by Mrs. Ria Boss-Bakkers, who did so in a most competent and cheerful way, assisted for sometime by Miss Joyce van der Smitte. The artwork was drawn by Mr. Paul Bijvoet.

We owe a final word of thanks to Iet Claessen and Dagmar Skalníková. That they, throughout the three years of preparation of this volume, succeeded in convincing their husbands that life is always more than just science is not the least of their merits.

Wassenaar, The Netherlands   Henri J. M. Claessen
January 1978   Peter Skalník

List of Contributors

Claessen, Henri J. M. *University of Leiden, The Netherlands*
Cohen, Ronald *Northwestern University, Evanston, Illinois, USA*
Gurevich, Aron Ia. *Academy of Sciences, Moscow, USSR*
Janssen, Jac. J. *University of Leiden, The Netherlands*
Kandert, Josef *Náprstek Museum, Prague, Czechoslovakia*
Khazanov, Anatolii M. *Academy of Sciences, Moscow, USSR*
Kobishchanov, Iurii M. *Academy of Sciences, Moscow, USSR*
Kochakova, Natalia B. *Academy of Sciences, Moscow, USSR*
Koranashvili, Guram *Academy of Sciences, Tbilisi, USSR*
Krader, Lawrence *Free University of Berlin, W. Berlin*
Kurtz, Donald V. *University of Wisconsin, Milwaukee, USA*
Lewis, Herbert S. *University of Wisconsin, Madison, USA*
Maretina, Sofia A. *Academy of Sciences, Leningrad, USSR*
Pokora, Timoteus *Prague, Czechoslovakia*
Schaedel, Richard P. *The University of Texas, Austin, USA*
Seaton, S. Lee *Bowling Green State University, Ohio, USA*
Sedov, Leonid A. *Academy of Sciences, Moscow, USSR*
Seneviratne, Sudarsan *Jawaharlal Nehru University, New Delhi, India*
Skalník, Peter *formerly Comenius University, Bratislava, Czechoslovakia*
Steinhart, Edward I. *The University of Texas, Austin, USA*
Teunis, Henri B. *University of Utrecht, The Netherlands*
Vansina, Jan *University of Wisconsin, Madison, USA*

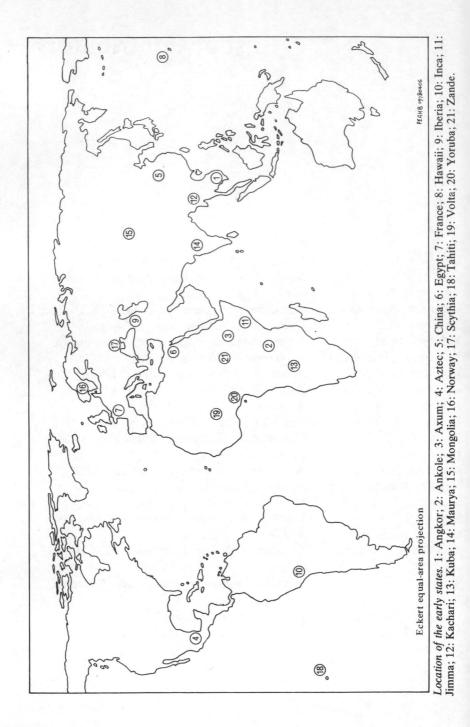

Location of the early states. 1: Angkor; 2: Ankole; 3: Axum; 4: Aztec; 5: China; 6: Egypt; 7: France; 8: Hawaii; 9: Iberia; 10: Inca; 11: Jimma; 12: Kachari; 13: Kuba; 14: Maurya; 15: Mongolia; 16: Norway; 17: Scythia; 18: Tahiti; 19: Volta; 20: Yoruba; 21: Zande.

Contents

PART ONE

Thesis

Part One was written with the intention of introducing the reader to the study of the early state. Chapter 1, particularly, was written by the editors to fulfill this aim. Their preliminary definitions, standpoints, hypotheses and questions are presented in this chapter. It is, however, not the traditional introduction to a collection of essays, which summarizes the ideas expressed in case studies. To the contrary and in keeping with the aims of the volume, chapter 1 discusses a number of basic theories relating to the early state and in this way presents a critical basis for the evaluation of the case essays. The ideas in it are of a preliminary character, to be checked against the antithetical force of the data expounded in Part Two. The chapter was originally written before the case studies reached the editors.

The three theoretical essays which follow chapter 1 not only present arguments but also add new ideas to the editors' hypotheses. Together with chapter 1, they balance the fresh data presented in Part Two. This theoretical approach in Part One leads to a presentation in Part Two of the data on particular early states.

1   The Early State: Theories and Hypotheses

HENRI J. M. CLAESSEN and PETER SKALNÍK

The state is a social phenomenon which first appeared only several thousand years ago. Many theories have been evolved up to now to account for its origins and subsequent development. The question has been approached by all kinds of scholars: philosophers, historians, political scientists, and in later times also archaeologists, sociologists and anthropologists. All these people have tried to illuminate the problem from their own particular point of view. An extensive literature exists, and every year new interpretations are added to the already vast body of material.

Among the most important obstacles preventing students from gaining a firm grasp of the subject are the following three.

(1) There does not exist any *definition* of the state that is accepted by the entire community of scholars. This naturally leads to a situation whereby almost every scholar evolves his/her own definition, which invariably differs slightly from the already existing ones, although some of them can be said to form 'schools' with a similar approach. This way it is virtually impossible to arrive at synthesis.

(2) In a number of cases, theories concerning the *character* of the state in various epochs are based on insufficient or premature data. The scholars concerned usually succeed in proving that their theory is correct for the cases they have studied, but when one tries to apply these theories on a world-wide scale, their inadequacy soon becomes apparent.

(3) Particularly, much confusion is found in the theories on the *formation* and *early development* of the state.

The present volume is concerned mainly with the third question. Its object is (1) to bring together a number of case essays based on advanced contemporary research on 'early states', and (2) to check some existing theories against the data of these case studies in order to establish a firm ground on which to base new viewpoints on the origin and early development of the state.

What are the basic programmatic principles of the editors as regards the study of the early state which served as guidelines for the present volume?

Firstly, we believe in a dialectical relation between factual data and theory. We share the conviction that

> the assumption that there exists a realm of facts independent of theories which establish their meaning is fundamentally unscientific. Science proceeds by challenging the deceptive obviousness of everyday observation and commonsense. (Blackburn 1972: 10).

Theory, on the other hand, cannot be created without close reference to empirical data. Neither the positivistic nor the theoreticistic extreme is very attractive to us.

Secondly, we are convinced that the state as a product of social relations must not be reified, personified or sacralized. We agree with Radcliffe-Brown that it is *not*

> an entity over and above the human individuals who make up a society, having as one of its attributes something called 'sovereignty', and sometimes spoken of as having a will or as issuing command (1940: xiii).

The state is an organization, *a specific kind of social organization*, expressing a specific type of social order in a society. It is

> a collection of individual human beings connected by a complex system of relations. Within that organization different individuals have different roles, and some are in possession of special power or authority (Radcliffe-Brown, ibid.).

Thus the term state gives expression to the existing relations in a society and to ideas pertaining to power, authority, force, justice, property and many other phenomena.

The state is a specific, historically limited type of human organization. As Engels succinctly put it almost one hundred years ago:

> The state .... has not existed from all eternity. There have been societies which have managed without it, which had no notion of the state or state power. At a definite stage of economic development, which necessarily involved the cleavage of society into classes, the state became a necessity because of this cleavage (1972: 232).

Being the product of a divided society, i.e., the society of political economy, the state organization would obviously wither away once the conditions which gave birth to it were overcome.

Although the time of existence of the state in comparison with the stateless phase in the evolution of mankind is brief out of all proportion, it has nevertheless gone through several different stages of development. It is appropriate to draw a rough distinction between two categories of states here. On the one hand, there are the complex, modern industrialized and developing states, and on the other the more or less simple non-industrialized states of the pre-capitalistic epoch.

The present volume will be concerned with what we have called the 'early state', which is supposedly typical of the initial stage of the evolution of the pre-capitalist non-industrial state. It will concentrate on the question of the transition between the 'primary' and 'secondary' social formation (Marx), characterized by specific, unique kinds of relations between the various producing communities, emergent class division and the presence of the early state. This concentration on the early state does not imply, however, that the views developed here are without relevance for the understanding of the modern industrialized type of state, or for the problem of the state in general.

Recent comparative studies (cf. Krader 1968; Claessen 1970) have demonstrated that the structure, functioning and evolution of early states of all times and places show marked similarities. These findings give us reason to believe that it may be possible to develop a generally acceptable definition of the early state and to infer some of its basic characteristics. Obviously only the case essays in the second part of the volume and the comparative chapters in its third part will be able to establish whether, and to what extent, the supposed categorical unity does exist. Up to that point this unity and similarity in structure, functioning and evolution of early states will be assumed by way of a working hypothesis.

1. THEORIES

In this section we will present a rather brief survey of some theories on the origin and early development of the state. Over the years numerous views and theories have been formulated on this subject. Service, in his recent book (1975, chapter 2) gives an interesting summary of a number of these theories, while Krader (1968, chapter 1), d'Hertefelt (1968) and Carneiro (1970) have also dealt with them. Therefore the present section can be restricted to a discussion of only a few modern theories, selected on the basis of their relevance to the problem of the early state.

A survey of theories might start with Rousseau's *Du contrat social*, published in 1762. The ideas formulated in this essay formed a point of departure for numerous theories and debates. Notwithstanding this, Rousseau in many respects also formed the close of a specific period of thinking; a period that had begun long ago, when Hobbes wrote his *Leviathan* (1642) in defense of the claims of absolute rulers, to which Locke replied with his *Two treatises on government* (1690). A period in which Montesquieu wrote *Lettres persanes* (1721) and *De l'Esprit des*

Lois (1748), and Vico published his *Principi di una Scienza Nuova* (1744). Even so, Hobbes was not the initiator of this debate, for Jean Bodin (1583) had already discussed the origins of the state as resulting from conflict (as Ibn Khaldun had done in the Muqäddimah (1377) two centuries earlier) in his *Les six livres de la République*, and Machiavelli had written *Il Principe*, formulating principles of government in 1532. Principles which had, in fact, been put into practice already before him by rulers like Louis XI of France (cf. Kendall 1971).

One thing all these scholars had in common was that their data were extremely limited. They mainly theorized from a self-conceived past to a wished-for future, or tried to explain only half-known phenomena with data that were totally inadequate for that purpose (cf. Fortes and Evans-Pritchard 1940: 4).

For the beginning of an empirical kind of analysis of the origins and early development of the state one must look back to a not too distant past. Though already Maine, Comte and Spencer had shown some interest in the subject, the first thorough discussion of it is found in Friedrich Engels, who based his work on historical and anthropological data. In 1884 he published *Der Ursprung der Familie, des Privateigentums und des Staats*, in which he on the one hand summarized Morgan's *Ancient society* (1877) and on the other added important supplementary information in the field of politics and economics based mostly on Marx's excerpts from Morgan's book as well as his other excerpts (cf. Skalník 1973a; Krader 1972, 1973, 1975). In Engels' view the state came into being when the necessity to protect a developing private property arose (Engels 1964: 121). This involves that the state was evolved in order to preserve a class society. In his own words (1972: 231):

> As the state arose from the need to keep class antagonisms in check, but also arose in the thick of the fight between the classes, it is normally the state of the most powerful, economically dominant class, which by its means becomes also the politically dominant class and so acquires new means of holding down and exploiting the oppressed class. . . .

The point of departure of Engels' theory was the idea that formerly there existed only common ownership of the means of production (for a critical evaluation of this point of view cf. Firth 1972: 17 ff.). The progressive social division of labor, called forth by the growth of population and the increasing diversification of the means of subsistence, made an ever-increasing production necessary. A product of this was a surplus which could be appropriated to cover the needs of those who no longer participated in food production (Engels 1964: 178 ff.). A solution to this problem, according to Engels, was found in amongst other things the development of slavery. This view was a result of Engels' concentrating mainly on what he conceived of as the optimum, i.e., the European historical development (cf. Godelier 1970: 99–100; Ecsedy 1972; Skalník 1973a; Krader 1975: 279–280).

In his earlier work, *Anti-Dühring* (1877/78), however, Engels discussed another possible way in which a class society and the state might have developed. Here he suggested a gradual change of 'functional' power into 'exploitative' power. This particular process of class formation and the development of the state was considered by him more universal, embracing most European states (except for the countries of classical antiquity). As Krader wrote in 1975 (p. 275):

> The servant of the community becomes the overlord; tribal chiefs, with the transformation of society from primitive to class society, become transformed into rulers. The oriental despotism is the crudest form of the State ... (which) fulfills the peace-keeping function within the society, the war-making function without, and control of the water supply. The independence of social functions as over against the society by these organs [of defense, ed.] was, developed into dominance over the society (id. p. 274; cf. Engels 1939: 197–199, 201).

The influence of military force, of war and conquest, played a considerable role in Engels' views on the origin of the state, the same holding true for the 'managerial' role of functionaries (cf. also Godelier 1970: 100–102; Khazanov 1972: 146; Krader 1973: 150). As has been shown by Koranashvili (1976: 39–40), Engels' theory of the rise of the state in the Orient (as expressed in *Anti-Dühring*) was multicausal, since he considered the emergence of a surplus product, the growth of population, and closer contacts between agricultural communities as important factors. A small stratum of functionaries regulated these factors jointly, and in this way exercised 'functions useful for society', which were based upon the existence of private ownership of land or other wealth. However, in *Der Ursprung* he stressed slavery as the main cause of the division of society into *classes* (the 'second way' in *Anti-Dühring*). Here the population no longer was divided according to the criteria of free/unfree, or ruler/ruled, but those of exploiting/exploited became essential. In *Der Ursprung* the case of the Germans served Engels as counter-evidence, thus evoking the discussion on force in his earlier book. The German state was born directly from the conquest of foreign territories, a situation for which the clan organization did not provide the means of domination. Here, in fact, lay the roots of the often contested hypothesis of the emergence of the state via the chiefdom type, called by Engels 'military democracy' (see Khazanov 1974).

In *Der Ursprung* Engels clearly gives preference to the process of economic stratification. Important economic functions tended to become herditary in certain families. A class of merchants developed, characterized by Engels as 'veritable parasitic plants', whose members, while 'skimming the cream of the production', rendered only minor services in return, and in this way gathered enormous riches, which gave them great influence in society, and made possible their ever-growing influence on production (1964: 185 ff.).

Using data from Greek, Roman and German history, Engels outlined how class formation, and with it state power, came about, thus giving rise to the necessary political apparatus to guarantee the lasting supremacy of the dominant class. For, as Engels argued:

> society had involved itself in insoluble self-contradiction and is cleft into irreconcilable antagonisms, which it is powerless to exorcise. But in order that these antagonisms, classes with conflicting economic interests, shall not consume themselves and society in fruitless struggle, a power, apparently standing above society, has become necessary to moderate the conflict and keep it within the bounds of 'order'; and this power arisen out of society, but placing itself above it and increasingly alienating itself from it, is the state (1972: 229).

Notwithstanding his somewhat rhetorical style, Engels here points to a very important relationship, namely that between the development of private ownership and social classes on the one hand, and the origin of the state on the other.[1] Studies by Fried (1967), Godelier (1969, 1970), Khazanov (1971, 1972, 1974, 1975), Terray (1975), Eder (1976) and many others, show that this relation was not such a simple causal one as Engels made it out to be, and as some recent authors, such as Semenov (1974) or Hindess and Hirst (1975), seem to think. The discussion in the third part of the present volume may possibly give some more insight into this important problem.

Another important problem in this connection is that of the relationship between the concept of the early state and the so-called Asiatic mode of production. Karl Marx, and to some extent also Engels (*Anti-Dühring*), in his consideration of the historical development of India, China, Persia and other Islamic countries, has stressed, mainly since the 1850s, the special character of the state in these non-European regions. He particularly emphasized the dichotomic relation between agricultural communities and the state organization, occasioned by the necessity of constructing and maintaining irrigation systems. Marx discovered that the exploitation of the producers living in village communities was not based on the existence of private ownership of land, but mostly on allegiance to a deified and despotic ruler who personified the state. This prompted the provision of regular or irregular tribute in kind, labor or even money. The state revenues were also claimed as remuneration for the imaginary or real protection of communities and/or trade, as well as for organizing water works. Marx considered this type of state as decisive for the character of the first form of class society; in point of fact it represented, according to him, the transitional stage between the primitive (primary) and the civil (secondary) social forms. He designated this form of organization the

Asiatic mode of production (cf. Marx 1859, 1953, 1964; Vitkin 1972; Skalník 1975; Krader 1975: 118 ff.). It represented, according to him, the first 'progressive' epoch in the economic formation of society or civilization, the beginning of the society of political economy (also called civil, civilized or political society by Marx).

Marx's excerpts of the works of Morgan, Maine, Phear, Lubbock and Kovalevsky were not published until recently (cf. Gamaiunov 1968: 270, 343–412; Krader 1972, 1975: 196). They were, however, partly used by Engels in his *Der Ursprung* (1884) after Marx's death, although he did not use the concept of the Asiatic mode of production (see Krader 1975: 271–280; Bäck 1976).

Nevertheless, the idea that early forms of state organization displayed certain universal features, resembling those found by Marx in the Orient, has generated lively debates among both adherents and opponents of Marx's concept in the past four or five decades (e.g., Wittfogel 1957; Skalník and Pokora 1966; Pečírka-Pešek 1967; Tökei 1969; Godelier 1969; Vitkin 1972; Koranashvili 1976). Some of the adherents have succeeded in developing Marx's ideas further into a more or less universally applicable theory (espccially Krader 1975). According to this, irrigation works and despotism are only secondary traits, however, while the basic class opposition between village communities with communal land tenure on the one hand, and the state organization with political, ideological and economic power on the other, provides the core of this theory.

However, the theories of Marx and Engels on the origin of the state and the character of its early forms received little attention in the circles of nineteenth and early twentieth century social scientists. This is explained partly by the fact that the often savage and caustic style of the works of both was little appreciated by the bourgeois-oriented scholars of the time, and partly by the fact that interest in an evolutionistically oriented school of social science at the end of the nineteenth century rapidly waned. New ideas in anthropology and other disciplines, based mainly on fieldwork, replaced evolutionism, which became a focus of anthropological interest again only in the second half of this century (cf. Harris 1968).[2]

That is not to say that the question of the origin of the state and its further development no longer received any attention at all. On the contrary, shortly after 1900 the German sociologist Oppenheimer, following Gumplowicz (1899), put forward his well-known *conquest theory* (Ueberlagerungstheorie) to deal with the problem (Oppenheimer 1909). Though intended as an historical analysis, the work was, in fact, evolutionistic in its approach. There are broad resemblances with Engels' views. For Oppenheimer, too, the state was an instrument of oppression, designed to confirm social inequality. In his view, however, this inequality originated in the conquest and subjection of one people by another. This subjection — and here again Oppenheimer comes very near to Engels' views — had no other purpose than the economic exploitation of the defeated (1932: 6 ff.). Thus conquest lay at the root of the state. Pastoral peoples especially, who combined organizational abilities with mobility and effective striking-power, were able to defeat and subject the more sluggish agriculturalists. The latter, remaining in the same place, accepted their subordination and paid tribute to the conquerors. The organization needed to accomplish this was the *state* (Oppenheimer 1932: 42).

Oppenheimer's views came to be severely criticized. In 1922 Lowie put forward his objections in a number of articles, later brought together in the form of a book (1927). Here he showed that (a) conquest did not always lead to state formation, (b) some states seemed to have developed without the aid of conquest, and (c) the conquering people of Oppenheimer's theory must have already possessed some kind of stratification. This led him to the conclusion that conquest cannot be the only mechanism responsible for state formation. Lowie in his turn proposed that the *association*—i.e., a number of people acting together voluntarily — might have led to the formation of the state. As an example he mentioned the 'clubs' of the Plains Indians. These played a leading role in the organization of the buffalo hunt and displayed great power during the hunting season. A centralized power could have developed from this type of association. However, Lowie did not elaborate this suggestion. Recently M. G. Smith tried to explain 'political change' exclusively from the essentially similar political phenomenon which he called 'corporation' (1974: 165–204).

In spite of all the criticism, the conquest theory had many adherents. Thurnwald (1935) elaborated and improved the theory, mainly with the aid of African data. Westermann (1952) also made extensive use of the conquest theory to explain state formation in Africa. There seem to be no objections to the view that the development of the state was deeply affected by conquest in some cases, but as a general explanation this theory is rather unsatisfactory. We know of too many cases in which internal development led to the emergence of the state, or in which peaceful contacts between neighboring peoples resulted in its formation (cf. Lewis 1966; Cohen 1974).

When in the years after the Second World War evolution became a focus of interest in anthropology again, the interest in the origin and development of the state also became prominent once more. Among the evolutionists, primarily Steward (1955) tried to reconstruct a sequence of stages of the evolution of communities from the hunting and gathering level to the state level. Though Steward sometimes had to do violence to his data to squeeze them all into the same theoretical mould, it should be said that the results of his efforts seem quite trustworthy (cf. Harris 1968; Carneiro 1973).

The stages he distinguished were:
(1) hunting and gathering; (2) incipient agriculture; (3) formative period (of the state); (4) regional florescence; (5) initial conquests; (6) dark ages and (7) cyclical conquests.

Steward then established that the states he had investigated were all situated in arid or semi-arid areas (1955: 199). Perhaps he intentionally restricted the results of his research to only these areas. Later research proved that his theory could be applied on a much wider scale. But, as Carneiro suggests (1973: 94 ff.), this course might have led the multilineary-oriented Steward too near to a unilinear kind of evolutionism.

Be that as it may, the mechanisms that made possible the major leaps forward in the evolutionary process was, in Steward's opinion, *irrigation*. For irrigation needed organization, power, and coordination. It opened up the possibility of the large-scale concentration of people, and in the end supposedly led to state formation. Though conquest played a role in at least two of Steward's stages, he did not mention this as a causal factor. In his approach, conquest was an effect rather than a cause of development.

It was Wittfogel (1957) who most ardently defended the view that irrigation — under specific conditions (1957: 18) — led to the development of the state. In his opinion the effective management of large volumes of water made an efficient organization indispensable. Once this organization existed, a 'hydraulic economy', characterized by the division of labor, intensive cultivation and cooperation on a large scale (1957: 22), and in which the state eventually assumed the managerial role, inevitably developed. When all is said and done, the same criticism applies to both Steward and Wittfogel: the suggestion that irrigation is the cause of state formation has not been proved to be of nomothetic value. There are many examples of state organization without irrigation works, and conversely irrigation not leading to the development of a state at all (cf. Claessen 1973).

This is *not* to say that the existence and development of irrigation works does not exercise any influence on the growth of political organizations. The organization and control of irrigation systems is often closely allied to political power (Smith 1969; Downing and Gibson 1974), while also the interference of political leaders with irrigation systems frequently leads to an intensification of (already existing) despotic, bureaucratic, or managerial tendencies (cf. Mitchell 1973). As regards influence on the development of state systems, however, this theory seems inadequate (cf. Adams 1966: 68, 76; Krader 1975: 290).

Some authors, including the archaeologists Childe and Adams, have suggested that an urban type of society and the state developed simultaneously. In a number of cases they have been able to demonstrate this simultaneousness of development (Adams 1966; Childe 1950; Redfield 1953). It remains to be investigated, however, to what extent the rise of cities may have been an indispensable concomitant of the formation and further development of the state. In addition, the question of how sedentary the population should be for it to be able to evolve a state organization should be raised. It is closely connected with the problem of the state among nomadic peoples [cf. Krader's and Khazanov's (Scythia) contributions to this volume].

In 1967 Fried published his study entitled *The evolution of political society*. He distinguished the following stages in this evolution: (1) egalitarian, (2) rank, (3) stratified, and (4) state society. For the present discussion especially the two last-mentioned stages are of importance. In his view

a stratified society is one in which members of the same sex and equivalent age status do not have equal access to the basic resources that sustain life (1967: 186).

The state he defined as:

. . . the complex of institutions by means of which the power of the society is organized on a basis superior to kinship (1967: 229).

This definition is somewhat divergent from the main line of his argumentation where he suggests that the state is the organization developed to maintain, if necessary, by force, the unequal access to the basic resources. Where this power did not develop, the situation of unequal access to basic resources could not persist. Examples of a return to simpler forms of social organization due to lack of power are presented by Leach in his analysis of Kachin societies (1954).

According to Fried (1967: 191), stratification appears the moment that communal property of the means of production is replaced by private ownership. This formulation comes rather near to the above-mentioned ideas of Engels. The most important factor responsible for this transition, in the view of Fried, was a growing population pressure on the resources (1967: 204).

Yet population increase is not necessarily an immediate cause for changes in the social structure. As long as there is an abundance of land the dispersion of population seems the easiest solution, and the need for change of the social system will be but limited (cf. Stauder 1972; Harner 1975). However, when there are no more opportunities of extending the territory, population increase *may* lead to pressure on the resources. As a consequence of this, certain groups of people may attain a more favorable position with respect to the means of subsistence than others, and in that case stratification may follow (cf. van Bakel 1976).

Kottak (1972) tried to test Fried's theories by applying them to the development of the state in Buganda (East Africa). He showed, through partly hypothetical arguments, how factors such as increasing population, changes in the means of subsistence, and the development of a market economy went hand in hand with the development from a rank to a stratified type of society and finally to the state.

Convincing though his arguments may seem, more definite corroborative evidence for Fried's hypothesis is called for (cf. Service 1975: 44 ff., 90 ff., 284 ff.). This question will for the greater part be discussed later, in the third part of this volume. An exception will be made for the factor of population pressure, which is cited by several other scholars as well. As early as 1956 Schapera, who based himself on South African data, suggested that a growing population called forth a more complex and more powerful political system (1956: 219 ff.). This idea did not draw much attention at the time. In 1968 Stevenson tried to show that there exists a causal relationship between the density of population and the degree of social stratification. Though he was able to demonstrate an obvious correlation he did not succeed in developing the latter into a causal relationship.

More attention was given to Carneiro with his *A theory of the origin of the state* (1970a). In this article he, too, made *population pressure* the prime mover of evolution towards statehood. His theory, however, is much more sophisticated. He combined population pressure with *war and conquest*, and argued that these factors were mechanisms that would produce the state only under specific conditions. These conditions were either *environmental circumscription* or *social circumscription*. The first condition was met where a growing population lived in a confined area, delimited by mountains, jungles, deserts, or seas. Social circumscription was a situation whereby a tribe living in an area without natural boundaries was surrounded by other tribes, so that extension of the territory was impossible for that reason. In these cases population growth developed into population pressure. Thus, after a certain period there inevitably came a moment when the only way of extending the tribal territory was by conquest, meaning war with neighboring tribes. The conquered party had but one chance of survival: submission to the conquerors and paying whatever tribute was exacted. At the end of this process the whole of the circumscribed territory would have been brought under the sway of one particular dominant ethnic group, of which the survivors of the vanquished peoples became subjects.

One might ask how, in this new system, the problem of population growth was solved after the casualties of war had been made up for by new births. Carneiro does not answer this question, but only remarks that the subdued will have had to produce more food than before (1970a: 735). This may no doubt have been possible for a while.

Recently the archaeologist Webster (1975) proposed certain modifications of Carneiro's theory, which, on the whole, seem very sound.

He stressed the fact that even the *threat* of war

produces a potent environment for evolutionary change by rendering ineffective many of the internal constraints on socio-political evolution otherwise present in ranked societies (1975: 467).

In his opinion this would lead to a more *stable leadership* (at least in
some cases). The position of the chief would then become stronger. As
a second effect he points to the possibility of the incorporation of
smaller areas into the territory of a given chiefdom. These would form
a kind of *capital resource* for the chief, his rights with respect to such
conquered lands not being restricted by all kinds of mutual obligations.
With the aid of these funds the ruler would then be able to *pay his*
supporters (mercenaries, councillors, servants). This might also give rise
to the development of *patron–client* kinds of relations (Webster 1975:
468; Mair 1962). The strengthening of the position of the managerial
groups in the societies concerned might in fact trigger off the development of a state organization (cf. Bigelow 1969).

Cohen (1974) also discusses the relation between war and the origins
of the state at length. In his words (1974: 173) 'Warfare does help to
create the centralized state' (cf. also Danilova 1968). This body of
hypotheses seems quite convincing. However, their nomothetical
value, like that of other plausible theories, remains to be tested against
the case studies in the second part of this volume (cf. Service 1975:
44).

The argument of population pressure is also advanced by Polgar
(1975: 15 ff.). Though he agrees in some respects with Carneiro, he
believes that population pressure only starts *after* the process of
stratification has begun. Polgar argues that (1975: 8)

...each step towards centralization of economic and political power, influenced the producers to create more of a 'surplus' — that the producers
responded to this coercion by increasing the number of their children, i.e.,
their domestic labor power, as well as intensifying their use of the land.

While appreciating this statement, one should bear in mind that a
greater number of children will only offer advantages for production
after a lapse of some years, and that until that blessed moment arrives,
the parents will have to work harder than ever. However, in view of
the almost natural unwillingness of man to produce more than is
needed (cf. Sahlins 1972), the idea that the institution of some form of
political or religious leadership is a necessary condition for the production of a surplus seems plausible.

The widely held idea of a *correlation* between population size and
complexity of the social and political organization can be accepted as
correct, but, as Polgar remarks, this is not a *causal* relation. To verify
this, one has only to look at the *temporal sequence*. Some archaeological data at least seem to point in the direction of socio-political
changes occurring *before* population growth (Polgar 1975: 10; cf. also

Wright and Johnson 1975: 276). This is the reverse of what Boserup asserts to be the case in her well-known hypothesis (1965).

This discussion about correlation and causality in some way resembles the often heated debates generated by Sahlins' *Social stratification in Polynesia* (1958). Sahlins only demonstrated, in fact, that there existed a close connection between the complexity of the social system and the size of the surplus produced. Though the word 'surplus' also gave rise to a fierce debate (cf. Orans 1966), it was impossible to explain away the fact that people often eat food they have not produced themselves, however. In a later work Sahlins more or less reformulated his earlier views, stating that

> too frequently and mechanically anthropologists attribute the appearance of chieftainship to the production of surplus. In the historic process, however, the relation has been at least mutual, and in the functioning of primitive society it is rather the other way around. Leadership continually generates domestic surplus. The development of rank and chieftainship becomes *pari passu*, development of the productive forces (1972: 140).

The idea that the more complex kind of political and economic organization develops in a mutual interaction situation is pragmatically attractive. It would render unnecessary the search for a specific prime mover.

Still further removed from materialistic explanations are the views put forward by Goldman (1970), who uses the concept of status rivalry as the motor behind the evolution of social systems. The confrontation between people with ascribed and achieved status leads, according to him, to the gradual development of more complex social forms. Unfortunately he is unable to provide sufficient evidence to show that this development really did take place (cf. Claessen 1974).

There remains to be discussed one other recent theory. It was advanced by Service in his *Origins of the state and civilization* (1975). After several introductory chapters, Service presents a number of case studies, and ends his book with two chapters of conclusions. The first of the concluding chapters is called 'negative', the other 'positive'. His ideas are in essence the opposite of the theory that economic inequality is essential to the development of political power structures (1975: 290). Service points to the fact that in the beginning political leadership is connected with personal qualities, and not with economic differences (cf. Ecsedy 1972: 195).

The emergence of this type of leader is often accompanied by the development of reciprocal and redistributive actions (Service 1975: 292; Van Baal 1975). Service then adds: 'The leader's position is *strengthened* [our italics] by his doing the job well and fairly' (1975: 293). The great problem becomes however, how such 'charismatic positions' could have been transformed into 'offices'. Where heredity evolved, a solution to this problem presented itself. For in this way inequality became *institutionalized*. As long as the communities in question are characterized by a relatively peaceful, theocratic mode of rule, they are qualified by Service as *chiefdoms*. Where 'secular sanctions', backed by force, or the threat of it, are developed, the *state* makes its appearance. Service suggests that the field in which these secular sanctions first emerged in society was that of lese-majesty (1975: 295). Amending Carneiro's theory of circumscription he points to the fact that what was perhaps more important than war was that (1975: 229): 'the benefit of being part of the society (which) obviously outweighed the alternatives'. This is, in fact, an elaboration of the above-mentioned idea with regard to the chief doing his job 'well and fairly'. This relatively peaceful picture is corrected in part by Service's emphasis on the otherwise harsh conditions of life for the lower castes in early states (1975: 301).

Service's views are indeed quite far removed from the theory that the state originated in social conflict. It is interesting, therefore, to list here some of the arguments he puts forward against this view. First of all, he points to the lack of data testifying to the existence of a group of merchants who had important private dealings in the known early states or late chiefdoms (1975: 283). Next, he discusses the often defended notion of economic stratification — 'the unequal access to the basic resources' — and, though he accepts at least the possibility of the existence of economic inequality, he emphatically rejects the idea of *exploitation* of the disadvantaged groups. Depending on the definition of this concept, however, it is possible to demonstrate exploitation even in lineage-based societies, as Terray has done (1975: 106–111). As for his final argument against the conflict theory, it is that there is no evidence for class conflicts found in early states.

To summarize: the theories concerning the origins and early development of the state are predominantly concerned with its origins (emergence, formation, rise, appearance). Less attention is paid, however, to the subsequent development of what is called the early state here.

The theories discussed above may, in very broad terms, be divided into two categories, viz. those according to which:

(1) the state is based on social inequality, and

(2) the state is based on some form of 'social contract'.

Although these categories are not absolutely mutually exclusive, they are considered as qualitatively different here.

To be more specific, the views of Engels and Fried clearly belong to the category according to which the state develops as an organization for the maintenance of a situation of social inequality, with emphasis on the economic aspect. Both Engels and his followers (e.g., Hindess and Hirst, Terray), as well as Fried and Kottak have put forward a number of arguments in support of their point of view.

Among the adherents of this thesis may also be reckoned Steward, Wittfogel, and Goldman. In their case, however, emphasis is placed on ecological and organizational features.

While, from Engels to Goldman, the state was regarded as resulting mostly from *internal* developments, other scholars, also belonging to the first category, have advanced theories according to which the state originated from *external* factors. Oppenheimer, Thurnwald, and later Carneiro, for example, claimed that conquest and war led to the subjection and exploitation of one people by another, this giving birth to a state organization to maintain the existing state of inequality. As a prime cause Carneiro mentioned population growth and subsequent pressure on the resources.

The second category of theories is represented particularly by those of Lowie and Service. Though these authors do not deny the existence of such factors as inequality or exploitation, they nonetheless believe that the state emerged and developed as a pragmatic or useful association of people or social group, which benefited from cooperation and effective central government.

It would be premature at this stage to make definite evaluative statements about the theories discussed above. They will have to be tested against the data brought together in the second part of this volume.

2. HYPOTHESES

In the simplest terms every state may be viewed as an organization comprising three main components: *a number of people, a certain delimited territory,* and *a specific type of government.* Correct as it may be, this characterization is far too broad to be useful, because it applies to any community, including stateless societies (cf. Mair 1962). Therefore, a further specification of the components will be inevitable.

The first component in need of elaboration is *a number of people.* It is impossible to give even the vaguest estimate of the minimum number of people that is necessary for the existence of the state. Birdsell (1973: 337 ff.) has demonstrated that, as soon as a group of people exceeds the number of 500, a government based on face to face relations only will no longer be possible, and some form of organization will become necessary — unless fission takes place. However, to infer from this figure the minimum number of people needed for an early state seems impossible for the moment (cf. Adams 1975: 252 ff.).

Discussing the concept of *territory*, Nadel (1942: 69) points out that citizenship of a state is determined by 'residence or birthright in the territory'. It appears that the concept of territory in early states is rather vague, and embraces first and foremost the relationship between a given population and its territory. It can be noted how in most early states the rule over a particular territory is closely related to the rule over the people living in it (cf. e.g., Skinner 1964: 107; Beattie 1971: 166; Trouwborst 1973). On the other hand, as Sahlins (1968: 5 ff.) points out: 'The state and its subdivisions are *organized* as territories — territorial entities under public authorities'. Thus the concept of 'territory' seems to cover something more than just a piece of land on which people live. Therefore a necessary addition to the component of territory seems to be that the early state extends its sway over people who either have residence, or have been born in its territory.

About the *government* of the state Nadel says that it has to be centralized, maintaining law and order, and excluding independent action by its citizens (1942: 69). The analyses of Krader (1968) and Claessen (1970) point in the same direction, viz. a governmental nucleus, formed by the sovereign, his councillors, ministers, etc., is present in all cases. In addition, in the states analyzed by these authors there was at least the pretention of the maintenance of law and order. This implies, at any rate in theory, that the sovereign, or the central government, has the power to make rules and laws, or to issue decrees and impose decisions which must be obeyed by the population as a whole, and disobedience of which is punished (cf. Radcliffe-Brown 1940; Weber 1964; Cohen 1970: 489; Service 1971).

Government, being one of the key features and functions of the state organization, can be divided into two main components: *power* (partypolitical aspects), and *administration* (cf. M. G. Smith 1956, 1960: 15–39).

To begin with power, this is, in principle, the capacity to influence decisively the choice of behavioral alternatives of someone else. This can be achieved in various ways: by moral persuasion, by threats, by physical force, by control 'over some set of energy forms' (Adams 1975: 12), or simply by giving the other person the feeling that the wishes or laws of the central authority are in conformity with the norms and values of his own society.

Power, according to this view, is a broad concept with many facets, ranging from brute force to the stimulation of the enthusiastic compliance with the wishes of those in power. This may be represented in the form of a *continuum*, with 'force' at one extreme and 'authority' at the other. Swartz *et al.* (1966: 14 ff.) have distinguished power into a 'coercive' and a 'concensual' type. These terms can be used interchangeably with those of 'force' and 'authority' developed in the above view. It is interesting to note that Swartz in a later study (1968: 33 ff.), also works with a continuum, of which 'coercion' and 'legitimacy' are the two opposite poles. He likes to speak of the *degree of legitimacy* of a government, thus implying that every government somehow has to find a solution to the problem that not always all people are convinced of the acceptability of laws and commands. In fact, this will be but seldom the case (cf. Wertheim 1971).

This legitimacy is usually based upon ideological conviction and persuasion. Though the state power is usually recognized and accepted by the majority of the population, the rulers will have to organize its ideological support and often manipulate this for their own ends. That a government will try to prevent 'independent action by its citizens' seems quite obvious. When a government is no longer capable of maintaining its power, and where separatist tendencies have free rein, there is no longer any real *central* government, and hence no longer a real state. An implication of this viewpoint is that the government of a state has to be *independent.* However, in some cases apparently independent early states pay some kind of ceremonial tribute to the sovereigns of other states. As long as this obligation does not lead to interference in the internal or external affairs of the early state in question, there is no reason to consider these states as being *non*-independent. A state will therefore be considered as independent if its independence is *de facto.* This implies that the state will also have to have the power to defend its integrity against threats from outside.

Administration is the management of state affairs or the executive apparatus of a state government, that manages these affairs. The latter usually takes the form of a hierarchy of officials, the top functionaries of which are concentrated in the capital (or governmental center). Ideally, the apparatus serves the aims of the decision-makers. However, it is possible for the apparatus under certain circumstances to seize more or less independent power in the state.

Taking into consideration the fact that the state can be characterized briefly as the organization designed for the regulation of social relations in a society divided into at least two main social groups, a discussion of the phenomenon of *social stratification* seems to be in place at this juncture (cf. Sahlins 1958; Maquet 1961; Fried 1967; Holý and Stuchlík 1968; Tuden and Plotnicov 1970; Plotnicov and

Tuden 1970; Claessen 1970; Smith 1974; Service 1975). Generally speaking, social stratification denotes that a specific population is divided into different, fairly broad, more or less stabilized categories showing a mutual hierarchical order and based on property, status and/or power (cf. Sahlins 1958: 1–3).[3] Though Smith (1974) views stratification 'neutrally' as 'the (institutionalized) restriction of access to positions of varying advantage' (p. 151), and suggests that it is 'political in base and ultimately rests on force' (p. 153), the real stratifying factor in the eyes of most scholars is *unequal access* to the means of production in a given society. To some of these scholars this aspect is of so great importance that they regard it as the decisive prerequisite for the emergence of the state. Following Engels (1964: 189), they argue that the state exists mainly as an organization for the maintenance of this inequality (cf. Nadel 1942: 69; Fried 1967: 225 ff.). Hindess and Hirst, in a recent publication (1975: 28 ff.) emphatically repeat this view, making the existence of mutually *antagonistic social classes* (based on economic inequality) the keystone of their argument. There seems to be no objection to the view that one of the characteristics of the state — and perhaps the most important one — is the existence of classes. However, there is an obvious difference between:

A stratified society... in which members of the same sex and equivalent age-status do not have equal access to the basic resources that sustain life (Fried 1967: 186).

and a society where

.... coercive apparatuses are organized and co-ordinated as an apparatus for the maintenance of exploitative relations of production between a class of laborers and a class of non-laborers (Hindess and Hirst 1975: 34).

The two quotations refer to two different, mutually rather distant stages in the evolution of society. The transition from the one to the other may take a considerable amount of time. The analysis of this transition is one of the main subjects of the present volume.

The importance of the said difference was clearly realized by the Soviet medievalist Neusykhin (1898–1969) who coined the term 'barbarian kingdoms' for those organizations representing the stage where the class division was not yet sharply defined, and where 'the political power of one class or stratum over the other social strata' has not yet reached full development (Neusykhin 1967: 80–81; cf. also 1974: 167–209, 225–233). The view that an incipient class society is not identical with the state, but is separated from it by a long period of evolution, is also expressed by Khazanov. This scholar argues at length that one must inevitably allow for a long 'epoch of class formation', a period in which the incipient class society gradually evolved the institutions of the state (1971: 73 ff., 1972, 1974: 141, 145, 1975; cf. also Terray 1975: 96, 100).

These views have received implicit support in recent publications by a number of Soviet scholars, who have introduced the term *gosudar-stvennoe obrazovanie* or 'state-like formation', under which 'barbarian kingdoms', 'African kingdoms', etc., can be subsumed (cf. Tomanovs-kaia 1973). Ol'derogge, basing himself on Engels' definition of the state as 'the organization of class supremacy', rejected the applicability of the term *state* to many African cases (Ol'derogge 1970, Tomanovs-kaia 1973: 280, and note 16, p. 283). It is apparent, however, that the term 'state-like formation' is only a temporary solution, and probably too cautious a one.

The fact that many scholars have had considerable difficulty in drawing the dividing-line between the state and the non-state is a result of their failure to understand that the transformation was not an abrupt mechanical one, but, on the contrary, was an extremely lengthy process. A process characterized by the development of a distinct socio/political organization which we propose to call the EARLY STATE.

One may suggest the following *working definition* of the early state: the early state is the organization for the regulation of social relations in a society that is divided into two emergent social classes, the rulers and the ruled.

From the discussion in the preceding paragraphs the following main *characteristics* of the early state can be inferred:

(1) There is a sufficient *number* of people to make possible social categorization, stratification and specialization.

(2) Citizenship is determined by residence or birth in the *territory*.

(3) The *government* is *centralized*, and has the necessary sovereign power for the maintenance of law and order, through the use of both authority and force, or the threat of force.

(4) It is *independent*, at least de facto, and the government possesses sufficient power to prevent separatism (fission), and the capacity to defend its integrity against external threats.

(5) The productivity (level of development of the productive forces) is developed to such a degree that there is a *regular surplus* which is used for the maintenance of the state organization.

(6) The population shows a degree of *social stratification* that emergent social classes (rulers and ruled) can be distinguished.

(7) A *common ideology* exists, on which the legitimacy of the ruling stratum (the rulers) is based.

This does *not* imply that all of these characteristics must have played a causal role in the development of the early state. It is quite possible that conversely some of them developed as a consequence of evolution towards the state.

Now, whenever a polity ('the widest-scaled network of authority relations, affecting a set of interrelations among roles', Cohen 1970:

488) can be described as possessing the characteristics outlined above, the early state stage will have been reached. This statement implies that the early state need not necessarily be *pristine* in the sense in which Fried (1967: 231 ff.) used this term. It also implies that a given society may reach the early state level more than once. Analyses of actual state development clearly show that certain societies did, in fact, reach the state level several times, with periods of centralization alternating with periods of disintegration (Egypt and China are well known examples; cf. also Steward 1955: 185 ff. and Service 1975: 225–264). Moreover, there is the old evolutionistic question of the relation between invention, technology and organizational advances (new ideas) on the one hand, and the development from the chiefdom level to the state organization on the other, which is discussed on a higher level by Adams (1975). He stresses the possibility of development towards the state from the chiefdom level, as well as the reverse process of development from the state to the chiefdom. Unfortunately in this dialectic of 'back and forth' movement he seems to overlook the essential qualitative differences between the chiefdom and the state, as he uses mainly structural and quantitative criteria.

In this connection, the formulation of a working definition of chiefdoms seems not out of place. Taking Service's definition (1975: 16) as point of departure, it may be formulated as follows.

Chiefdoms are socio-political organizations with a centralized government, hereditary hierarchical status arrangements with an aristocratic ethos but no formal, legal apparatus of forceful repression, and without the capacity to prevent fission. These organizations seem to be universally theocratic, with submission to authority taking the form of that of a religious congregation to a chief-priest (for 'aristocratic ethos' cf. Goldman 1970: xv-xxi).

The chiefdom is far more highly developed than the simpler types of political organization led by 'big men', or comparable leaders.

To reach the early state level is one thing, to develop into a full-blown, or *mature* state is quite another. An often long and complex evolutionary process separates these two stages. Hence in the various societies that can be classified as early states, the degree of complexity, the extent of the territory, the size of the population, and the degree of power of the central government may differ considerably. Several scholars, irrespective of their methodological approach, have already made this point (cf. Gluckman 1965: 83 ff.; Claessen 1970: 311 ff.; Goldman 1970: 541 ff.; Carneiro 1970b: 845). So it may be useful to distinguish — again by way of working hypotheses — three *types* of early state, viz.:

    (1) the inchoate early state;
    (2) the typical early state;
    (3) the transitional early state.

The following criteria, evolved mainly on the basis of earlier research by the editors (Claessen 1970; Skalník 1973b), may be of help in distinguishing these types. They are a further specification of the seven (hypothetical) characteristics of the early state defined above.

The *inchoate* early state is found where kinship, family, and community ties still dominate relations in the political field; where full-time specialists are rare; where taxation systems are only primitive and ad hoc taxes are frequent; and where social differences are offset by reciprocity and close contacts between the rulers and the ruled.

The *typical* early state exists where kinship ties are counterbalanced by territorial ones; where competition and appointment to office counterbalance the principle of heredity of office; where non-kin officials and title holders begin to play a leading role in government administration; and where ties of redistribution and reciprocity still dominate relations between the social strata.

The *transitional* early state is found where the administrative apparatus is dominated by appointed officials; where kinship influences are only marginal aspects of government; and where the prerequisites for the emergence of private property in the means of production, for a market economy and for the development of overtly antagonistic classes exist. This type already incorporates the prerequisites for the development of the mature state.

The principal aim of the present volume can now be described as the testing of the basic hypotheses concerning early states, set out above. The essential questions to be answered are:

I. What are the general characteristics of the early state? To what extent are the seven postulated characteristics applicable?

II. What is the minimal definition of the early state?

III. What types of early state can be distinguished, and what are their distinguishing features? Is the division into the three types, inchoate, typical, and transitional useful?

IV. Which was the most likely process of state formation, and to what extent is it in conformity with either of the two opposed categories of theories distinguished above?

The questions that have arisen in the course of the section on theories can be summarized as follows.

(1) What can be said about the existence and role of social classes in the evolution of the state?

(2) Is it possible to ascribe the characteristics of the Asiatic mode of production to all, or only some, of the early states?

(3) What was the role of conquest in the rise and further development of the early state (assuming that neither the conqueror nor the conquered already had a state organization)?

(4) What role did war and other types of *external* conflict play in the evolution of the early state?

(5) What was the influence of population growth and/or pressure on the development of the early state?

(6) What kind of a correlation existed between the development of trade and markets and the emergence of the early state?

(7) What were the methods of resolving *internal* conflicts in the early state?

(8) What kind of a correlation existed between the development of the early state and the rise of cities and urban life?

The theoretical chapters by Cohen, Khazanov, and Krader following below are intended to highlight a number of difficulties and problems connected with the subject of the early state. Thus they may show, together with the present introductory chapter, how wide and varied is this field of study. Their statements and questions will be tested together with the hypotheses put forward in this chapter.

FOOTNOTES

[1] It is interesting to note that already the early Buddhistic treatises on society pointed out that private ownership of land led to social inequality and to the necessity to maintain law and order (Rhys Davids 1965, IV: 77–94). The same is true of early Islamic writings.

[2] Lenin's revolutionary attempt at a theory of the state (1917) was based for the greater part upon an analysis of Engels' *Der Ursprung* and some works of Marx's.

[3] Fallers (1973: 3–29) suggested a total abandoning of the term 'social stratification', and the adoption of the multifaceted concept of *inequality*, whereby the 'stratum' and 'class' reduction might be avoided.

REFERENCES

Adams, Richard N. (1975), *Energy and structure: a theory of social power.* Austin: University of Texas Press.

Adams, Robert McC. (1966), *The evolution of urban society.* Chicago: Aldine.

Baal, J. van (1975), *Reciprocity and the position of women.* Assen: Van Gorcum.

Bäck, Lucien (1976), *Zum Entstehen einer Klassengesellschaft. Textkritische Untersuchung zu ethnologischen Studien in den Werken von Karl Marx und Friedrich Engels.* Berlin: Dissertation Manuscript.

Bakel, M. A. van (1976), Bevolkingsdruk en culturele evolutie [Population pressure and cultural evolution]. Ms., Leiden.

Beattie, John (1971), *The Nyoro state.* Oxford: Clarendon.

Bigelow, R. (1969), *The dawn warriors.* Boston: Little, Brown.

Birdsell, Joseph B. (1973), 'A basic demographic unit', *Current Anthropology* 14: 337–356.

Blackburn, R., ed. (1972), *Ideology in social science: Readings in social theory.* London: Fontana Books.

Boserup, Ester (1965), *The conditions of agricultural growth*. Chicago: Aldine.
Carneiro, Robert L. (1970a), 'A theory of the origin of the state', *Science* 169: 733–738.
— (1970b), 'Scale analysis, evolutionary sequences, and the rating of cultures', in: *A handbook of method in cultural anthropology*, ed. by R. Naroll and Ronald Cohen, pp. 834–871. New York: Natural History Press.
— (1973), 'The four faces of evolution', in: *Handbook of social and cultural anthropology*, ed. by J. J. Honigmann, pp. 89–110. Chicago: Rand Mc-Nally.
Childe, V. Gordon (1950), 'The urban revolution', *Town Planning Review* 21: 3–17.
Claessen, Henri J. M. (1970), *Van vorsten en volken*. [Of princes and peoples.] Amsterdam: Joko.
— (1973), 'Despotism and irrigation', *Bijdragen tot de Taal-, Land- en Volkenkunde* 129: 70–85.
— (1974), 'Review of: I. Goldman, Ancient Polynesian society', *Bijdragen tot de Taal-, Land- en Volkenkunde* 130: 180–184.
Cohen, Ronald (1970), 'The political system', in: *A handbook of method in cultural anthropology*, ed. by Raoul Naroll and Ronald Cohen, pp. 484–499. New York: Natural History Press.
— (1974), 'The evolution of hierarchical institutions: a case study from Biu, Nigeria', *Savanna* 3: 153–174.
Danilova, Ludmila V. (1968), 'Diskussionnye problemy teorii dokapitalisticheskikh obshchestv' [Problems under discussion in the theory of the precapitalistic societies] in: *Problemy istorii dokapitalisticheskikh obshchestv* ed. by L. V. Danilova. Vol. I. Moscow: Nauka. Also published as: Controversial problems of the theory of precapitalist societies. *Soviet Anthropology and Archaeology* 9: 269–328 (1972).
Downing, Th. E. and Gibson, McGuire eds (1974), *Irrigation's impact on society*. Tucson: University of Arizona Press.
Ecsedy, Cs. (1972), 'Some questions on the political evolution of the traditional state in Africa, south of the Sahara', *Neprajzi Értesitö* 54: 189–215.
Eder, Klaus (1976), *Die Entstehung staatlich organisierter Gesellschaften. Ein Beitrag zu einer Theorie sozialer Evolution*. Frankfurt/Main: Suhrkamp.
Engels, Friedrich (1877/78), *Herrn Eugen Dührings Umwälzung der Wissenschaft. (Anti-Dühring)*. Marx-Engels Werke 20, pp. 5–303.
— (1939), *Herr Eugen Dühring's revolution in science (Anti-Dühring)*. New York: International Publishers.
— (1964), *Der Ursprung der Familie, des Privateigentums und des Staats*. Bücherei des Marxismus-Leninismus, Band 11. Berlin: Dietz.
— (1972), *The origin of the family, private property and the state*. Edited with an Introduction by Eleanor Burke Leacock. London: Lawrence and Wishart.
Fallers, Lloyd (1973), *Inequality. Social stratification reconsidered*. Chicago and London: University of Chicago Press.
Firth, Raymond (1972), 'The sceptical anthropologist? Social anthropology and Marxist views on society', *Radcliffe-Brown Lecture* 1. London: Oxford University Press. Repr. in: *Marxist Analysis and Social anthropology*, ed. by M. Bloch. London: Malaby Press (1975).
Fortes, Meyer and Evans-Pritchard, E. E., eds (1940), *African political systems*. International African Institute. London: Oxford University Press.
Fried, Morton H. (1967), *The evolution of political society*. New York: Random House.

Gamaiunov, L. S. (1968), 'O vypiskakh Karla Marksa iz rabot po Vostoku' [On Karl Marx's excerpts from the works on the Orient], Narody Azii i Afriki 2: 137–147.

Gluckman, Max (1965), Politics, law and ritual in tribal society. Oxford: Blackwell.

Godelier, Maurice (1969), 'La notion de "mode de production asiatique" et les schémas Marxistes d'évolution des sociétés', in: Sur le 'mode de production asiatique', ed. by Roger Garaudy, pp. 47–100. Paris: Editions Sociales.

— (1970), Préface, in: Sur les sociétés précapitalistes, ed. by Maurice Godelier, pp. 13–142. Paris: Editions Sociales.

Goldman, Irving (1970), Ancient Polynesian society. Chicago: Chicago University Press.

Gumplovicz, L. (1899), The outlines of sociology. Philadelphia: American Academy of Political and Social Science.

Harner, M. J. (1975), 'Scarcity, the factors of production, and social evolution', in: Population, ecology and social evolution, ed. by Steven Polgar, pp. 123–138. The Hague: Mouton.

Harris, Marvin (1968), The rise of anthropological theory. London: Routledge and Kegan Paul.

d'Hertefelt, M. (1968), A concept of government. Cahiers Économiques et Sociaux 4: 329–345.

Hindess, B. and Hirst, P. Q. (1975), Pre-capitalist modes of production. London: Routledge and Kegan Paul.

Holý, L. and Stuchlík, M. (1968), 'Analysis of social stratification', in: Social stratification in tribal Africa, ed. by L. Holý, pp. 7–65. Prague: Academia.

Kendall, P. M. (1971), Louis XI. London: Allen and Unwin.

Khazanov, Anatolii M. (1971), 'Les grandes lignes de la formation des classes dans la société primitive', in: Problèmes théoriques de l'ethnographie, pp. 66–75. Moscow: Academy of Sciences.

— (1972), 'F. Engels i nekotorye problemy klassoobrazovania' [F. Engels and some problems of class formation], in: Problemy etnografii i antropologii v svete nauchnogo nasledia F. Engel'sa, ed. by Iu. V. Bromley, A. I. Pershits and S. A. Tokarev, pp. 134–161. Moscow: Nauka.

— (1974), 'Military democracy' and the epoch of class formation' in: Soviet ethnology and anthropology today, ed. by Yu. Bromley, pp. 133–146. The Hague: Mouton.

— (1975), 'Razlozhenie pervobytnoobshchinnogo stroya i vozniknovenie klassovogo obshchestva' [Disintegration of the primitive communal order and the origins of class society], in: Pervobytnoe obshchestvo, ed. by A. I. Pershits, pp. 88–139. Moscow: Nauka.

Köbben, A. J. F. (1970), 'Cause and intention', in: A Handbook of method in cultural antropology, ed. by R. Naroll and Ronald Cohen, pp. 89–99. New York: Natural History Press.

Koranashvili, Guram V. (1976), Problema dokapitalisticheskikh obshchestvennoekonomichekikh formatsii v istoricheskom materializme [The problem of pre-capitalist socio-economic formations in historical materialism]. Tbilisi: Tbilisi University Press.

Kottak, C. P. (1972), 'Ecological variables in the origin and evolution of African states', Comparative Studies in Society and History 14: 351–80.

Krader, Lawrence (1968), Formation of the state. Englewood Cliffs: Prentice Hall.

— (1972), *The ethnological notebooks of Karl Marx*. Assen: Van Gorcum.
— (1973), *Ethnologie und Anthropologie bei Marx*. München: Hanser.
— (1975), *The Asiatic mode of production*. Assen: Van Gorcum.
— (1976), 'Social evolution and social revolution', *Dialectical Anthropology* 1: 109–120.
Leach, E. (1954), *Political systems of highland Burma*. London: Athlone.
Lenin, V. I. (1917), *Gosudarstvo i revoliutsiia. Uchenie marksizma o gosudarstve i zadachi proletariata v revoliutsii*. [State and revolution. The teachings of Marxism on the state and the tasks of the proletariat in the revolution.] Polnoe sobranie sochineni, vol. 33.
Lewis, Herbert S. (1966), 'The origins of African kingdoms', *Cahiers d'études Africaines* 23: 402–407.
Lowie, Robert H. (1927). *The origin of the state*. New York: Harcourt Brace.
Mair, Lucy (1962), *Primitive government*. London: Pelican Books.
Maquet, J. J. (1961), *The premise of inequality in Ruanda*. London: Oxford University Press.
Marx, Karl (1859), 'Vorwort', in: *Zur Kritik der politischen Oekonomie*. Marx-Engels Werke 13.
— (1953), *Grundrisse der Kritik der politischen Oekonomie* (Rohentwurf 1857–1858). Reprinted as:
— (1964), *Pre-Capitalist economic formations*. With an Introduction by Eric Hobsbawm. London: Lawrence and Wishart.
Mitchell, W. P. (1973), 'The hydraulic hypothesis. A reappraisal', *Current Anthropology* 14: 532–535.
Morgan, Lewis H. (1877), *Ancient society*. Cleveland: World Publishing Company.
Nadel. S. F. (1942), *A black Byzantium. The kingdom of Nupe in Nigeria*. London: Oxford University Press.
Neusykhin, A. I. (1967), Dofeodal'nyi period kak perekhodnaia stadiia razvitia ot rodo-plemennogo stroia k rannefeodal, nomu (na materiale istorii Zapadnoi Ievropy rannego srednevekovia) [The Pre-feudal period as a transitional stage in the development from the clan-tribal order toward the early feudal one (based on materials from the history of western Europe in the early Middle Ages)], *Voprosy Istorii* 1: 75–87.
— (1974), *Problemy ievropeiskogo feodalizma* [Problems of European feudalism]. Moscow: Nauka.
Ol'derogge, D. A. (1970), 'V. I. Lenin i problemy vozniknoveniia gosudarstva' [V. I. Lenin and the problems of the emergence of the state], in: *Kratkoe soderzhanie dokladov godichnoi nauchnoi sessii Instituta etnografii AN SSSR*, pp. 5–7, Leningrad.
Oppenheimer, Franz (1909), *Der Staat*. Frankfurt am main: Mohr.
— (1932), *De Staat*. Utrecht: Bijleveld.
Orans, Martin (1966), 'Surplus', *Human Organization* 25: 24–32.
Pečírka, J. and Pešek, J., eds (1967), *Rané formy civilizace* [Early forms of civilization]. Prague: Svoboda.
Plotnicov, L. and Tuden, A., eds (1970), *Essays in comparative social stratification*. Pittsburgh: University of Pittsburgh Press.
Polgar, Steven (1975), 'Population, evolution, and theoretical paradigms', in: *Population, ecology and social evolution*, ed. by Steven Polgar, pp. 1–25. The Hague: Mouton.
Radcliffe-Brown, A. R. (1940), 'Preface', in: *African political systems*, ed. by M. Fortes and E. E. Evans-Pitchard, pp. ix–xxiii. London: Oxford University Press.

28 Henri J. M. Claessen and Peter Skalník

Redfield, Robert (1953), *The primitive world and its transformations*. Penguin Books (1968).
Rhys Davids, T. W., ed. (1965), *Sacred books of the Buddhists:* IV. London: Pali Text Society.
Sahlins, Marshal D. (1958), *Social stratification in Polynesia*. Seattle: University of Washington Press.
— (1968), *Tribesmen*. Englewood Cliffs: Prentice Hall.
— (1972), *Stone age economics*. Chicago: Aldine.
Schapera, Isaac (1956), *Government and politics in tribal society*. London: Watts.
Semenov, Iu. I. (1974), 'On Northwest Coast society', *Current Anthropology* 15: 400.
Service, Elman R. (1971), *Primitive social organization*, 2nd edn. New York: Random House.
— (1975), *Origins of the state and civilization*. New York: Norton.
Skalník, Peter (1973a), 'Engels über die vorkapitalistischen Gesellschaften und die Ergebnisse der modernen Ethnologie', *Philosophica. Zborník Filozofickej Fakulty Univerzity Komenského* 12–13: 405–414.
— (1973b), 'The dynamics of early state development in the Voltaic area (*West Africa*)'. Unpublished C Sc. Dissertation, Charles University, Prague. Abstract of it forthcoming in: *Political Anthropology and the state of the art*, ed. by S. Lee Seaton and Henri J. M. Claessen. The Hague: Mouton.
—(1975), Review of M. A. Vitkin 'Vostok v filosofskoistoricheskoi konceptsii K. Marksa i F. Engel'sa', *Political Anthropology* 1: 88–90.
Skalník, Peter and Pokora, Timoteus (1966), 'Beginning of the discussion about the Asiatic mode of production in the USSR and the People's Republic of China', *Eirene* 5: 179–187.
Skinner, E. P. (1964), *The Mossi of Upper Volta*. Stanford: Stanford University Press.
Smith, M. Estellie (1969), 'Technology and social control'. *Paper* presented at the 68th meeting of the AAA, New Orleans.
Smith, Michael G. (1956), 'On segmentary lineage systems', *Journal of the Royal Anthropological Institute* 86: 39–80.
— (1960), *Government in Zazzau*. London International African Institute.
— (1974), *Corporation and society*. London: Duckworth.
Southall, Aidan (1965), 'Critique of the typology of states and political systems', in: *Political systems and the distribution of power*, ed. by Michael Banton, pp. 113–138. ASA monographs 2. London: Tavistock.
Stauder, Jack (1972), 'Anarchy and ecology: political society among the Majangir', *Southwestern Journal of Anthropology* 28: 153–168.
Stevenson, Robert F. (1968), *Population and political systems in tropical Africa*. New York: Columbia University Press.
Steward, Julian H. (1955), *Theory of culture change*. Urbana: University of Illinois Press.
Swartz, Marc J., ed. (1968), *Local-level politics*, Chicago: Aldine.
Swartz, Marc J., Turner, V. and Tuden, A., eds (1966), *Political anthropology*. Chicago: Aldine.
Terray, Emmanuel (1975), 'Classes and class consciousness in the Abron kingdom of Gyaman', in: *Marxist analysis and social anthropology*, ed. by Maurice Bloch, pp. 85–135. ASA Studies 2. London: Malaby.
Thurnwald, Richard (1935), *Die menschliche Gesellschaft in ihren ethnosoziologischen Grundlagen*. Vol. 4. Berlin: De Gruyter.

Tökei, Ferenc (1969), *Zur Frage der asiatischen Produktionsweise*. Neuwied und Berlin: Luchterhand.

Tomanovskaia, O. S. (1973), 'Izuchenie problemy genezisa gosudarstva na afrikanskom materiale' [The study of the problem of the genesis of the state, based on African material], in: *Osnovnye problemy afrikanistiki*, ed. by Iu. V. Bromley, pp. 273–283. Moscow: Nauka.

Trouwborst, A. A. (1973), La base territoriale de l'état du Burundi ancien. *Revue Universitaire du Burundi* 1: 245–254.

Tuden, A. and Plotnicov, L., eds. (1970), *Social stratification in Africa*. New York: Free Press.

Vitkin, M. A. (1972), *Vostok v filosofsko-istoricheskoi konceptsii K. Marksa i F. Engel'sa* [The Orient in the philosophical–historical conception of Karl Marxs and F. Engels]. Moscow: Nauka.

Weber, Max (1964), *Wirtschaft und Gesellschaft*. Studienausgabe. Köln/Berlin: Kippenheuer und Witsch.

Webster, David, (1975), 'Warfare and the evolution of the state: a reconsideration', *American Antiquity* 40: 464–470.

Wertheim, W. F. (1971), *Evolutie en revolutie. De Golfslag der emancipatie* [Evolution and revolution]. Amsterdam: Van Gennep.

Westermann, D. (1952), *Geschichte Afrikas. Staatenbildung südlich der Sahara*. Köln: Greven Verlag.

Wittfogel, Karl A. (1957), *Oriental despotism. A comparative study of total power*. New Haven: Yale University Press.

Wright, Henry T. and Johnson, Gregory (1975), 'Population, exchange, and early state formation in southwestern Iran', *American Anthropologist* 77: 267–289.

2   State Origins: A Reappraisal[1]

RONALD COHEN

1. INTRODUCTION

Give or take a few multi-national corporations, the state is the most powerful, continuously authoritative, and most inclusive organization in the history of the species. Even a relatively small and weak state has the universally acknowledged right, if it wishes, to expropriate holdings of the largest and most powerful multi-nationals in the world. Evolution doesn't stop of course; imperialism, groupings of nations, and actual federations may develop on the way to global political and social organization (Naroll 1967). For now, however, and for the forseeable future true sovereignty stops with national state boundaries so that these units remain the largest scaled political organizations that continuously act and react as corporate entities on the world scene.

How and under what conditions such powerful and ubiquitous structures evolve has fascinated scholars for a long time. So far, however, many of the major theoretical thrusts have been based on lack of agreement about what a state is, about what it does, why or how it develops, and what utility, if any, it has for its members. This in turn stimulates the well-known cacaphony of academic voices in which researchers from differing traditions speak past each other to 'true believers' in their own specialties, or of their own ideological persuasion. This essay attempts to go beyond such polemics and commitments to an examination of factors clearly associated with state foundation. My goal is to assess some modest generalizations that provide a synthesis of present views rather than heightening the enthusiasm of adversaries or previously enshrined positions and disagreements.

In what is to follow I shall discuss the definitional problem and then examine in turn ecological and demographic factors, external relations, internal organization, and finally cultural factors associated with the rise of early states. In my view the process is systemic and multi-causal. Each set of factors, or any particular factor, once it develops, stimulates and feeds back onto others which are then made to change in the general direction of statehood. Although its roots may be multiple, once a society or group of them start developing toward early statehood the end result is remarkably similar no matter where it occurs. Why such convergence occurs and is part and parcel of state formation is the major goal of this paper.

1.1. *Definition of the State*

Let me start by saying what the state is not. This will allow us to look at some 'classic' approaches and compare them. The state and society are not synonymous. To suggest that some sense of 'collective will' or any degree of political activity and social control signifies statehood is to beg the question. If we accept the position of Koppers (1963) then all human groups controlling or occupying a territory are to be seen as states whether they be hunting tribes or empires. This leaves the explanation of early centralized governments unanswered, indeed unasked. The problem of varying degrees of socio-political complexity is not resolved by using similar terms for significantly different organizational forms. Equating the state to any or all political organizations makes the worthwhile point that all humans try to live their lives within some form of social order, that includes variations in power, authority, and a system of values that prescribes some and proscribes other activities. However, because all societies have organized social and political behaviour does not mean that all have similar forms within which it takes place.

The state is not necessarily a stratified multi-ethnic community or society in which one ethnic group dominates the other. Thurnwald (1935) saw ethnic stratification and its correlated socio-political and economic organization as the basic ingredient of the state.[2] Pre-nineteenth century Hausa, the various Yoruba states, Pabir, and Zulu in Africa, or the Hawaiians, Fijians, and Tongans in the Pacific are only a few of the possible examples in which ethnic stratification is not a diagnostic feature of the state and its origins. Early states in which members of non-ruling ethnic groups have both high and low places in the polity are common. Furthermore, just as the Saxons eventually merged with the Norman conquerors of England, so too early states often witnessed the ultimate fusion of ethnically stratified groups associated with a new ethnicity that expresses the emergent culture of the state.[3]

In a more general sense, however, social stratification is a universal correlate of early states. From Rousseau to Marx and Engels, through to contemporary writers such as Fried (1967), early states are defined as governmental systems of control in which ruling groups use and create the state as a means for maintaining themselves in power over other subordinated classes in the society. In his *Discourse on inequality*, Rousseau argues that the state ('civil society') was conceived of originally by the rich man to protect himself against those who could attack his position. The state therefore, he says, destroys liberty, supports the inequality between rich and poor through fixed laws of property, and in so doing puts the ordinary citizen into 'perpetual labor, slavery and wretchedness' (Harmon 1964: 302). Marx and Engels, especially the latter (Engels 1891), derive the state from comparative analysis. Like Rousseau they see it as a correlate of class formation (stratification) in which the upper class owners of the means of production interact to develop a system that protects the interests of the privileged class (Krader 1968: 25). Fried takes the same position when he theorizes that the state i.e., centralized government, emerges inevitably out of social stratification or institutionalized inequality in which not all persons in society have equal access to those resources that sustain and enhance life (Fried 1967: 186).

Since this functional quality (ruling group domination by use of the state) is a universal feature of early states it is difficult to quarrel with this position. But as a causal theory it is not subscribed to universally. Some theorists (e.g., Service 1975) interpret the same evidence in quite different terms. Instead of seeing stratification as a *cause* of early states they see it as a *result*, while the original causes lie in the functional benefits derived by the citizens by their acquiescence to state power. In this view the essential feature of state formation is not the coercive power of the ruling class, but the widespread support for its legitimacy — even when its socio-economic system involves exploitation by the ruling class.

Other definitions tend to lump as many correlates together as possible, turning the definition of an early state into a generalized model of a particular form of political system. Such seems to be the goal of Murdock's (1959: 37) eighteen diagnostic features of African 'despotisms' which Lenski (1966: 157) cites approvingly as a set of features found as well in most other early states. Krader (1968: 27–8) does essentially the same thing giving to the state a large array of features all of which are descriptive generalizations about a complex type of socio-political system. Any of these detailed propositions can be challenged. Early states do not for example universally practice human sacrifice (Murdock 1959: 38), nor do they necessarily demand that members either accept state sovereignty or reject it leaving no middle ground (Krader 1968: 27).

Furthermore, such definitions tend to obscure the search for origins. Both Murdock's eighteen features and Krader's long list of traits provide no clue as to how such complex systems could have evolved. Here the Marxist position seems more satisfying. The state and the protection of inequality are interwoven theoretically into a process that forces history to move toward despotic centralized control. Why inequality should have been so well engrained before the state and why the state emerges when it does, however, are not really very clear, nor predicated by such theorizing, instead we are presented with historical details in terms of a 'class struggle' leading invariably to the state.

Hobhouse *et al.* (1915) were possibly the first contemporary writers to define the state as a hierarchical and centralized authority system in which local entities lose their autonomy and become districts whose heads are subordinated to the center. Nadel (1942: 69–70) has a particularly lucid presentation of this viewpoint in which he conceives of statehood as a political system having: (1) centralized government, (2) territorial sovereignty, and (3) a ruling group with separate training, recruitment, and status. With a few correlated additions this is the same definition used by Fortes and Evans-Pritchard (1940) in their classic division of African polities into state and non-state systems, and by Julian Steward (1949) somewhat later in his attempt to see universal patternings of culture growth and state formation in semi-arid regions of the world. Service (1975) in his recent work agrees with this position and adds, as did Fried (1967), the monopoly of the use of threat as a use of force.

Related to this approach but distinct from it is the information-systems definition used by Wright and Johnson (1975: 267) in their work on state origins in Mesopotamia. Working with records of transactions between differentiating settlements in a region these authors conceive of the state as a total decision-making organization in which specialized administrative centers make decisions affecting the actions of lower level settlements and their activities. The organization must have three or more levels of hierarchy to function in a state-like manner in which information is stored, processed, summarized and transmitted so that information at the top affects behaviour at lower levels of hierarchy.

The information transactions are however all in the economic sector of the region. These researchers assume therefore that growing coordination of economic activity in a hierarchy of differently sized settlements is an indicator of similar developements in the governmental sector of society. Unfortunately, the exact correspondence between the economic and political organization is not clear in their work.

What is clear from all of these structural definitions that stress the organizational attributes of states is a research strategy. In effect, all of these approaches agree that what creates supra-local authority and centralized control also creates early states. As Service (1975: 272) points out, this still leaves a problem since it does not distinguish clearly between chieftaincy and statehood — between centralized polities that are more and those that are less complex.[4] States are centrally organized hierarchies, but this classification includes types of polities that are often considered to be pre-state systems.

In my view, chieftaincies are sufficiently different from states to warrant separate classification. The key diagnostic feature is fission. All political systems up to the time of the early state, have as part of their normal political and demographic processes, inherent tendencies to break up and form similar units across the landscape. Barnes (1967) has aptly called this the 'snowball' effect in which the polity builds up to a critical size, then splits up, over succession disputes, land short-ages, or other reasons, into smaller units that in turn grow again toward their own break-up thresholds. The state is a system that overcomes such fissiparous tendencies. This capacity creates an entirely new kind of society. One that can expand and take in other ethnic groups, one that can become more populous and more powerful without necessarily having any upper limits to its size or strength. Only the state among all known human political systems is capable of such growth in size and power.

Early states refer to the first beginnings of centralized polities whose mode of production is pre-industrial. Many features of pre- and post-industrial states are similar. For example both have to solve problems of regime change, and both must coordinate center-periphery relations. However, industrialization requires such massive shifts in population and social organization, such as the development of large-scaled urban masses, trade unions, the regulation of economic activity, access to life sustaining resources through salaries, among many other features, that it is necessary to conceive of industralized states as a separate kind of society, with distinct political problems, and adaptive solutions.

The institution that has the primary task of maintaining such con-tinuity in early states is the bureaucracy. By this I mean a set of officials, priests, nobles, slaves, eunuchs, and their sub-organizations who manage the administrative machinery of the state hierarchy. They oversee the royal succession which often threatens civil order, and they serve as an official and generally privileged class who maintain and enforce relations between peripheral sections of the state and the royal capital.

Chieftaincies also have office holders who help the chief carry out governmental functions. However, at this level of political develope-ment each nodal point in the structure of the polity is an exact replica of that at the center. If and when pressures build up for the pyramidal structure to break each piece is already equipped with the same set of officials as its parent polity. In the early state, on the other hand, many officeholders at the center carry out unique duties not shared by anyone else. There is generally a state religion focussed on the royal court and its functions. Leaders of local segments may have their own officials, but these do not carry out the elaborate and complex duties and court procedures practiced in the capital.

In summary then, the early state is a centralized and hierarchically organized political system in which the central authority has control over the greatest amount of coercive force in the society. Sub-units are tied into the hierarchy through their relations to officials appointed by and responsible to a ruler or monarchical head of state. These officials maintain the adminstrative structure of the system and attempt to ensure its continuity by having among them a set of electors who choose and/or legitimate a new monarch. For purposes of convenience I shall use 'state' in the remainder of this essay to mean 'early state' as contrasted to industrial states.[6]

1.2 *Correlates and Causation*

The definition given above is structural. It distinguishes the state from other political systems by viewing it as specific set of hierarchical relations involving an accepted and traditional system of unequal power distribution, albeit an evolving one. As I have said elsewhere (Cohen 1973: 871), making a taxonomy of political structures creates a central problem for political anthropology and provides it with an agenda for research. The taxonomy explains very little by itself. However, it does force us to ask how the differences come about, and what effects they have on the people who live within them. In effect then, the definition isolates an entity, and it is this entity whose origin we seek.

The correlates of statehood are widely known. A ruling class under a monarch that is privileged and wealthy in relation to the rest of the population from whom they get most of their wealth is an ubiquitous feature of early states. This is associated with urbanism, architectural expression of class differences and the semi-differentiation of upper class generally urban culture from that of others in the state who carry on with local cultural practices derived from their pre-state adaptation as locally autonomous polities. The society is also differentiated by occupation, ethnicity, and rural or urban residence into peasants, craftsmen, traders, priests, nomads, diviners, entertainers, and many others. This requires a complex system of trade, markets, and a revenue system by which the state drains off income in currency and kind in order to maintain itself and its armed forces. The upper class also enjoys luxury goods brought to the state through a well-developed system of long distance trade. A complex set of legal–judicial procedures develops to mediate disputes between various elements using the political structure as a system of judicial hierarchy and appeal. Foreign relations are maintained with surrounding polities who are often made to pay tributes if the state is the most powerful among a set of societies within a region. States therefore have sovereign territories in which members are citizens under its laws, and spheres of influence in which some lesser power is exerted. If this latter quality is present we shall refer to it as hegemony in contrast to sovereignty which operates within states. Hegemony differs from soverignty in that a state has total authority over all citizens within its sovereign rule, while final life and death sanction are left in the hands of local rulers of groups over whom it exercises hegemony. Revenue collections, trade, military service, law, and a generally increased use of communications, all place a premium on accurate forms of record keeping. It is not surprising then that record keeping develops widely as a correlate of early state formation.

To search for specific causes among all these developements, is in my view a fruitless even a spurious question (cf. Adams 1975: 243). Each of these features, and many more enable the other to emerge and to select from among all possible solutions the centrally organized structure of the state. The structure requires these correlates, and the correlates enable the structure to continue, *or to emerge.* The process is systemic, and self-limiting.[7] No matter how or where it starts, functional requirements force the development of the above correlates. Early states are self-limiting in their variance. Why this should be so will become clear in what follows when we look more closely at the pre-conditions and developmental pathways taken by the early states as they evolve out of previously uncentralized systems.

2. FACTORS AFFECTING THE RISE OF EARLY STATES

2.1. *Location*

In his massive work on Mediterranean history Braudel (1972) argues that the physical environment, as well as the demographic and socio-cultural forces dependent upon it underlie the specific historical developments of the region. But if we generalize and ask whether locational and geographical factors per se have some systematic relationship to early states, the matter becomes murky. What specific qualities of the environment should we look at? Food supply, other resources, and location have all been suggested by Braudel. Food supply is usually thought of in terms of the carrying capacity of the land, defined as the maximum ability of an environment to continuously provide subsistence at the level of culture practiced by the inhabitants (Allan 1949; Cook 1972: 25). However, as Hayden (1975) and others (Street 1969: 105) have noted this feature of the environment is difficult to measure accurately because (1) it is almost impossible to calculate the food potential of a region, (2) technology *potential* is at present not known or understood for different cultures and (3) the resource environment varies significantly through time in any one place.

Hayden's (1975) suggestion that we use mortality rates due to food shortages as a threshold measure of environmental pressure is provocative, but involves some formidable problems. How can we obtain mortality rates for Sumeria, ancient China, or the Western Sudan over the last millennium? If such information could be obtained for early states it would be possible in effect to measure the Toynbean challenge, and to assess whether variations in periodic food shortages stimulated, or were at least associated with, consequent socio-political developements. At this point it is sufficient to note that no study that I am aware of has made detailed comparisons of early states in areas with, and those without regular food shortages, using specific and measurable indicators to isolate the effects of carrying capacity on state formation.

Nevertheless, the location-environment argument lives on. Lenski (1966: 161) has correlated state formation with environment in pre-colonial Africa. His data indicate that ninety-two per cent of all 'lesser and major' states in a sample of thirty-eight are located in areas other than the rain forest. He concludes that this reflects the difficulties such societies encounter in transportation (1966: 162). The forest restricts the capacity of the central government to move men and goods throughout the realm. In other words, the forest maintains local autonomy and is a major obstacle to state organization. Lenski may have a point for the African materials, but when necessary such obstacles have been overcome by technology. An obvious example is the massive and carefully tended bridges developed by the Inca in order to connect their capital to the peripheral regions of the state. Certainly if we map pre-colonial state development, as Beals and Kelso (1975: 572) have done, there is very little correlation with environmental features except a marked lack of state development in extreme climate zones, and for North America in general. The distribution seems to argue for six separate regions of state development (1) a continuous band across Europe, North Africa and the Nile

Valley, the far East and South Asia including India, China, and Japan; (2) a middle American development including both Mexico and Yucatan; (3) a south American development in the high Andes; (4) a West African Zone; (5) an East African zone in the lake region and the Ethiopian highlands; and (6) a Polynesian zone. States may, and probably did develop independently within these zones, but contacts and diffusion within them are also well documented. It is hard to imagine what such widespread regions have in common geographically that could have stimulated state formation.

On the other hand, no matter what the soil-type or the climate (outside of the extreme latitudes), being in a zone of state-building seems to have been a prime factor in developing such traits. In this sense pure location, but not the physical conditions of the environment are important predictors. Such societies felt the effects of statehood before others. Ultimately however, all societies have been incorporated into states or become centrally organized themselves (and begun to absorb others).

Finally there is the locational factor of trade. Ports of trade and termini at the ends of trade routes are clearly correlated with early state development. In cases such as Benin, Dahomey, and the city states of the Mediterranean we have documented evidence that trading communities attract population and become centralized polities earlier than many other areas in their hinterland. There is little doubt that geographic features such as good harbors, settlements at the mouths of rivers, or nodal gathering and/or resting points on well-worn trade routes have attracted population and contributed to the development of early states. In examining the African material Gluckman (1965: 143–4) concluded that only at salt and jade mines and along major trade routes do chiefs' powers become more permanent. This is the main thrust of Braudel's (1972) argument as well. Although he is sensitive to the effects of mountains, plains, and prevailing winds, it is the geographical (and other) features supporting the rise of towns that he feels provide the most penetrating insight into Mediterranean history. But again geography does not clarify the whole story or even its most important parts. The trade route, or one city and its routes often compete and win out over another (Braudel 1972: 278). It may help, but the understanding of state formation is not to be found solely in the wind, the rain, and the location.

3. DEMOGRAPHY

With the possible exception of warfare, population pressure, or an increase in population density is one of the most widely noted features of state formation. The idea goes back at least to Spencer (1897) and was central to the work of V. Gordon Childe (1936). More recently, Boserup (1965) has traced the effects of increased population on the political organization of Europe and on subsequent developments in technology that led to decreased fallow periods and increased productivity which in turn supported larger populations. Lenski (1966: 145–6) notes that pre-state societies are all below a level of 1500 persons per settlement while early states contain on the order of 200 times more people, along with much higher densities per square mile.

Causal mechanisms for the increase are twofold, rising birth rates and the circumscription of population within a confined space. Harris (1971: 223) has tried to compute overall world population before and after the spread of food production. He suggests a pre-neolithic world-wide increase of possibly five persons per year which rose to 625 per year after the inception of the neolithic. More convincing evidence comes from Lee (1972) whose data support the notion that with less wandering, less carrying of young children from place to place, Bushman women reduce the artificially maintained longer periods between pregnancies with little or no extra input of effort:

> sedentarization alone may trigger population growth, since women may have children more frequently without any increase in work on their part, and without reducing their ability to provide for each one (Lee 1972: 342).

Althabe (1965) working with pygmy groups in Cameroon has also noticed that sedentarization is associated with larger families. Archaeological evidence (Struever 1968; Smith and Young 1972) indicates more sites containing larger populations within similar sized land surfaces in areas where the neolithic replaces hunting and gathering.

Once mankind took on food production there is therefore good evidence that his population began expanding. But how does this lead to the state? After all, the inception of the neolithic is removed from state foundations by large and significant gaps of time. Indeed, many food producing groups have remained in autonomous settlements, or nomadic pastoral groupings until the founding of modern states. Carneiro (1970) has theorized that when the normal expansion of population is circumscribed by geographic, or possibly other forces, the tensions and conflict associated with increased pressure on resources produces differential access to valued goods and tendencies to centralized control, and coordination of the population. Steep-sided Peruvian valleys, desert-rimmed rivers like the Nile, or places where a people live in relation to rich resources given their particular technology would tend, under this theory, to restrict migration out of the region. This increases population density and leads to enhanced power for leaders.

Empirically, these theories fit well with observations made by Netting (1972) among the Kofyar of the Jos Plateau in Nigeria. This author (Netting 1969, 1972) has found that increased pressure on land resulting either from increased density or the shrinkage of available farm plots leads to more individual land holdings and more intensive agriculture. This in turn is associated with higher land values, more strictly demarcated boundaries, elaborated rules of ownership and inheritance, increased inter-personal conflicts, and disputes over property.

> The largest Kofyar chiefships in which a species of paramountcy united a number of adjacent villages were found in the plains where population density was highest and competition for arable land keenest (Netting 1972: 235).

Netting then tries to generalize this finding across a series of cases elsewhere (Ibo, Tiv, Jukun, and Alur). Unfortunately, there is no information on the correlation of population pressure to centralization for these other societies so that he winds up with only one case (Kofyar) in which the data support his argument. The point is crucial. For though he can show how these African societies build centralizing tendencies onto previously autonomous local settlements — as indeed others have done (Horton 1971; Cohen 1974) — he is unable to attribute these comparable developments to population expansion or pressure, as is called for by the theory.

The theory that population pressure contributes to the formation of states rests therefore on the widely documented observation that population expands in size and density per settlement as well as numbers of settlements per region once man becomes a sedentary food producer. Thus population expands, and along with increased scarcities due to rising pressure on resources it forces leaders to increase their control over the social organizations they participate in (Adams 1975: 149). Taken on its face value the theory seems plausible and not too surprising. Long term trends do in fact show invariant relations between population increases and centralization of authority.

Nevertheless closer inspection of data, and well designed attempts to test the relationship are beginning to create second thoughts. Dumont (1965: 320–321) in a detailed comparision of political development in the Valley of Mexico and Mesopotamia concludes that population pressure is a necessary but not sufficient condition for state formation. His data do not support the notion that 'nucleation' (i.e., increased organizational complexity and coordination between differentiation settlements) develop in response to prior or correlated pressures on resources. After reviewing the theory and looking at a number of independent cases of state formation, Service feels that it is *organization* not population pressure that provides the means and impetus to statehood (1975: 276–278); for him population growth and food scarcities are 'enablers' not causes of social complexity. Instead, he compares population pressure to emphasis on 'economic surplus' which may have been due to the inception of tributes rather than to any measurable increase in productivity. In other words, it is not pressure on resources, but 'the intensification of demand' (Cowgill 1975: 513) by increasingly hierarchical authority systems that reorganizes society, giving it the appearance of being larger and/or providing the conditions for further growth in more densely packed settlements.

Possibly the most elegantly designed test of the population pressure theory has been that of Wright and Johnson (1975). Using the size of settlements per period and comparing organizational development in three areas of southwest Iran these researchers have demonstrated a consistent tendency for population *decline* immediately prior to state formation. They theorize, but cannot as yet demonstrate, that such declines in population are probably associated with unsettled conditions, conflict, warfare, and possibly an influx of nomads into the area. This alternate hypothesis must wait for future testing, meanwhile the population theory seems to have suffered badly at the hands of the facts.

We can on this basis formulate a synthesis. As man changes over to reliance on storeable and renewable food resources population becomes more sedentary, and begins to increase at a much more rapid rate than before. This occurs well before statehood, and continues on after states are formed. Data are lacking that clearly relate such population increase to state formation. However, some research supports the notion of population increase *prior* to chieftaincy (Harner 1970), and *after* states emerge (Wright and Johnson 1975). Population increase does therefore produce some competition between independent settlements, and can underlie the growth of chieftaincy, as Netting's (1972) data indicate. Statehood is dependent on other factors; it is an organizational capability that allows for the coordination of large numbers of settlements, or nomads. Therefore, it creates conditions for a greater size of social unit, but does not in and of itself depend upon such an increase in order to come into existence.

A methodological point is of crucial importance. If we correlate population size with degree of political complexity, we obtain results. However since the political units are increasingly inclusive it is important to use population per region or number of settlements per region, i.e., overall density within the region circumscribed by the state-to-be. Increased social complexity may well involve a redistribution of the population into variously sized settlements with little or no overall change, in the short run. Urban centers may for example depopulate nearby rural areas leaving the regional population size unchanged.

A related ethnographic point about the size of social units is rarely ever noticed. Sedentarization is associated with an increased demand for persons among kin groups, settlements, and domestic units. Althabe's (1965) case study of the change over from hunting and gathering to agriculture indicates an associated increase in polygyny, larger families, and more authority for adult men. He also notes a change from sister exchange to bridewealth as the means of obtaining wives. Extra people can be a burden in a hunting camp, but mean more labor, more followers and supporters, as well as more prestige and power in a locally autonomous community of food producers. Sedentism creates a new value for children, wives, and indeed on any or all means by which local groups can increase their size. Thus from the neolithic onwards *person acquisition* by social units becomes an important feature of social life. This leads to increased birth rates, to adoption, polygyny, bridewealth, clientage, fostering, and even to forcible capture and enslavement of strangers who are then used to add size and strength to local groups.

Population size of local groups can be manipulated as a function of local organization, before states or chieftaincies emerge. The operational process set in motion by sedentarization is not simply a matter of birth rates. Instead a wider system of population growth begins to appear in which local groups prosper through attracting or capturing, or leading people from elsewhere. Settling down means that populations are not spread evenly over the landscape. Social, political, economic, and ecological forces now act to create coalescing, albeit fissioning groups whose size is part of their success. Population and state formation are, then, related but not demographically as theory would suggest. Instead they are linked by the needs of groups for extra members, and for the needs of local populations to coordinate larger numbers of people per social and economic unit. Organizational changes that accompany the inception of food production also create institutions such as lineages, villages, age set systems, or big man systems, in which hierarchy and the numbers of persons per group become accepted and valued aspects of group life.

4. EXTERNAL RELATIONS

The relations between pre-state polities may stabilize or at least be satisfactorily handled within the social and economic organizations found at this level of evolutionary development. On the other hand, changing relations between polities can create selective pressures that are responded to by the development of more centrally organized hierarchies. Long distance inter-polity trade, warfare, peaceful inter-polity alliances and hegemony, and symbiotic relations between groups having different ecological adaptations all contribute to the emergence of centralized polities. At the present stage of knowledge, however, it is not clear exactly how these factors operate in response to differing conditions. Let us look, briefly, at each of them.

4.1. *Inter-polity Trade*

As already noted, writers like Polanyi (1957), Gluckman (1965) and Braudel (1972) have described the relations between trade, especially long distance trade and the rise of early states. Long distance trade involves transporting goods between regions so that trader-transporters have peaceful access to separate polities. In West Africa the port of Whydah situated at an access point to both the sea and the open savanna developed as a powerful trading center. Its concomitant growth as a politically powerful state is quite clearly related to its function as a trading entrepot between Europeans and Africans, especially during the slave trade (Polanyi 1966). Further east Dike (1956) has shown how attempts to control the slave trade in the Niger delta led to more centralized political organization in that region. In East Africa, Abrahams (1967) described the same process among Nyamwezi chiefs who increased their power in order to control trade between hinterland groups and Arabs on the coast. Hickerson (1962) mentions more complex organization developing among the Wisconsin Chippewa which he attributes to their desire to control trade between the Europeans to the east and the Sioux to the west.

In my own research on pre-colonial kingdoms in northeast Nigeria, it is clear that many articles of long distance trade were distributed by monarchs in the region and that these monarchs were deeply involved in such trade.

The causal relationship of long distance trade is however not a simple one. After carefully measuring the quantity of inter-regional trade in Mesopotamia, Wright and Johnson (1975) conclude that such trade did not increase in volume until long after the founding of the state. Conversely, material from coastal West Africa (Dike 1956; Polanyi 1966; Horton 1969) suggest the opposite. The answer lies in a set of intervening factors. If a pre-state polity or a group of them lies on or at a nodal point in an increasing long distance trade, then this environmental feature exerts pressure on the local leadership to increase their power and stabilize control over the trade. To do this they need greater military capability and full-time officials who can coordinate the increased managerial functions associated with the trade (cf. Wright and Johnson 1975: 277). The results of such increased organization are the well-known trading states and ports of trade in which commerce and government are intimately linked. Conversely, however, if the pre-state polity is not located at a crucial nodal point along a developing trade route, as with many of the states of the Western Sudan, long distance trade has little or no causal significance for the rise of states. In early Mesopotamia trade does increase through time — but not until *after* the founding of the state (Wright and Johnson 1975: 279). In effect then, long distance trade is both a cause and an effect of state formation, depending upon factors other than the trade itself.

Local trade within a region is almost by definition closely associated with the founding of states. Differentiation in society, and the supra-local coordination capabilities of central authorities make for an increased flow of goods and people throughout the state, especially to and from the capital. This both reflects and supports the capacity of a central authority to sustain itself and even to store or house food stuffs against future shortages.

4.2. *Warfare*

Warfare is said to be a cause of statehood, and a result. Spencer (1897) suggests that the organizational capabilities demanded by warfare, its hierarchy and central command spread from the military to society. Warriors become kings and bring military discipline to government. The rise of the Mongol empire under military leaders is a good example of the process. Gearing (1962) describes increases in Cherokee political centralization as the result of increased warfare brought on by the incursions of the American colonists. When one group successfully conquers another, as with the Normans in early England, or the Kanuri in fifteenth century Bornu (Cohen 1975) then the conquerors must devise a system of administration to coordinate their rule over the area.

More recently Otterbein (1970) has tried to test this idea. He argues (1970: 23–28) that successful warfare requires high degrees of subordination i.e., obedience to leaders. He finds that subordination is widespread among the military organization of uncentralized societies. It is almost universal among centralized ones at both the military and governmental levels. Therefore 'subordination within the military leads to subordination within the political community...' which supports further development of the military (Otterbein 1970: 28).

Although these data are suggestive, the research design is too weak to carry the weight of the argument. Subordination exists across many facets of uncentralized social and political life — in hunting, religious ceremonies, family life, rites de passage, and so on. Why must we attribute increased subordination in government to only one institution at the pre-state level and test only for that feature while disregarding others? Furthermore centralization is just that, i.e., more integrated control and subordination of all aspects of social life including the military. It is the integration of social units that requires explanation not subordination which is present both before and after centralization has developed.

Another group of scholars (Bagehot 1872; Andrzejewski 1954; Fried 1967; Vayda 1968; Service 1975) suggest that societal evolution comes first, and then provides a basis for the increased scale, frequency, and success of warfare. Citing specific cases they note that a more disciplined, more organized polity produces larger armies, better defense against warring neighbors, and it stimulates the use of warfare as a form of inter-societal relations. More specifically, warfare between raiding nomads and outside predators, as described in Lattimore's (1940) work (cited in Service 1975) on northwest China leads to the strengthening of defences and the emergence of a more centralized polity among the sedentary peoples being threatened. Finally, warfare among roughly equivalent neighbors gives people an appreciation for the protection that centralized leadership affords (Service 1975: 299). In effect, Service concludes that people accept more centralized polities because of the utility of such a system in the face of outside dangers.

The approach being taken here is more synthetic and systemic. This leads me to assume that any or all events and activities leading to more centralization of authority and supra-local coordination through hierarchical control tends to pressure a pre-state system towards greater centralization. Although its causal connections to state formation are complex I believe warfare is such a factor. It is complex because under certain conditions it does *not* give rise to states, under others it does, and under still others it follows as a capability or result of state formation.

Let me illustrate this briefly with some examples from my own research. In the Lake Chad area of the fourteenth and fifteenth centuries, the leading Magumi clan was forced to leave the Kanem area to the northeast of the Lake. After much wandering about on the Bornu plain to the west of the lake they and their followers settled on the south bank of a river that protected them from desert raiders. Previously they seem to have been a semi-Islamized, semi-nomadic clan group with a chiefly lineage living among other clans organized in a similar manner. Although clans and lineages within them were ranked, there seems to have been little centralized bureaucracy, no permanent capital, and a not very complex set of ideas about administration.

On the Bornu plains they eventually built a walled city, to protect themselves against the local peoples, who seem to have lived in localized autonomous villages. Slowly, using their superior cavalry, and military strategy the people of the walled city, or Kanuri as they came to be called, subdued group after group of the plainsmen. Those who refused, ran away, or were killed, or were taken as slaves. At the same time (fifteenth century) the people of the city started to develop ways and means of administering these semi-subject peoples. As the Magumi chief evolved into a true despotic monarch, trusted relatives, and officials of the royal court were given specific villages, or gained the rights over them, as their own particular responsibility. By the end of the sixteenth century the Bornu plain was witness to a powerful kingdom under its royal capital of Birni Gazargamo. Out on the plains local cultures still flourished but more and more of the people, who remained in the area came to be thought of, and to think of themselves, as part of a larger state. In some areas the tie remained tenuous, in others it became a new identity that tied them and their descendants into this emergent Muslim kingdom of the Sudan.

It is not clear exactly why the original Kanem chieftaincy broke up. Oral tradition has it that there was an elongated set of succession struggles over the chieftaincy, and between the leading lineage and its clan (Magumi) with one of its own previously separated segments (Bulala). This latter conflict was due to leadership rivalry, population pressure on resources, desire to control trade routes to the Mediterranean or a combination of all of these. The result is however quite clear. The losing, and previously dominant or 'owner' clan did finally leave Kanem in defeat to wander in, and finally settle on, the Bornu plain (Cohen 1967; Smith 1971).

Here then is a sequence in which warfare plays a dominant role. A chiefly system breaks up, not an unusual occurrance. One of the segments departs to find a new home. In doing so they find themselves among peoples who are less equipped militarily. This accident plus their sense of cultural and religious superiority, triggers off a rapid series of important effects. Within a century they had built the beginnings of a great walled city, using complex imported architectural techniques, and a continuing set of trade and religious ties to other great centers of the Muslim world. They imported and developed even more military techniques and weaponry, and most important of all they began experimenting, developing, and importing techniques for administering a progressively more subject and finally an hierarchically organized and stratified multi-ethnic citizenry.

Obviously, warfare is not the whole story. But it played a significant role in turning a loosely organized, probably semi-nomadic people into a centralized, pluralist, monarchical state. In effect and contrary to Service's conclusion (1975: 270), this does seem to be anthropological evidence for the possibility that conquest can, under the proper circumstances stimulate a developmental trajectory that leads to the founding of a true state. The reverse is also true. There are many accounts in West Africa (Forde and Kaberry: 1967) of 'successor' states in which an already centralized governmental regime moves elsewhere, conquers an area, then uses this new area as its sovereign territory. Thus warfare and conquest do, as Service suggests (1975: 270), follow state formation. However, in special circumstances, the reverse is also true.

Increased conflict, warfare, or raiding, in an area also sets up tendencies towards centralized government. Again, however, no simple direction of change is apparent. Service (1975: 259, 271) notes that defensive measures taken against raiding nomads in northwest China, and Mesopotamia, stimulated the growth of walled towns, intensified agriculture and the rise of powerful centralized governmental systems. Thus nomads raiders do not necessarily take over from sedentary agriculturalists as Ibn Khaldun suggested, but they may stimulate political development. In the Kanuri case cited above, raids for slaves, plunder, and subjugation of the Bornu plains stimulated three possible reactions, all of which occurred. People could run away and set up villages elsewhere out of reach, generally in hilly more forested areas where cavalry were less effective. They could develop new defensive techniques such as walled, more densely populated towns and new military tactics such as the use of bee hives thrown into a cavalry charge, or stone walls built across narrow valley floors. Or they could remain on the plains and become part of the growing power of the Bornu state.

All of these occurred. Ultimately Bornu produced a ring of small statelets around its borders as a secondary reaction to its own formation as a state, and its raiding activities among neighboring especially non-Muslim peoples. Thus warfare, and defense against increased warfare can propel previously uncentralized autonomous villages into larger, stratified, and centrally organized polities (Cohen 1974; f.c.).

And that's not the end of it. Pastoral nomads in conflict with sedentary agriculturalists can take over an area and create a new state. In Sokoto (Nigeria) and other areas of Hausaland, Fulani nomads were interacting with sedentary centralized governments. For reasons of religious reform, increasing competition for water and land, and antagonism towards Hausa domination, the pastoral Fulani organized, clan by clan under a religious leader and overthrew the Hausa states in a *jihad* or holy war. Statehood had already developed in the area. However, they were a stateless people who took on more centralized organization for military and religious reasons. At the far reaches of this vast movement some 500–600 (805–965 km) miles away to the east, Fulani nomad lineages and clans came into conflict with local non-state agriculturalists over access to pasturage, increased tributes, and their own alien status in the Benue Valley (Abubakar 1972). In the early to mid-nineteenth century these Adamawa Fulani organized under a leader, founded the Fombina emirate of Yola and created an hierarchical adminstration out of previously segmenting, locally autonomous, nomadic clans. The new state was allied to other states but emerged as an autonomous centralized polity within the Caliphate of Sokoto.

The common factor here is competition between nomads and agriculturalists, a sense of cultural and religious superiority on the part of the nomads that rationalized the warfare as a *jihad* or holy war. Ethnic solidarity united hitherto segmented nomads into large-scaled fighting forces against small locally autonomous villages in one case, and against city-based states on the other. It is also possible that the early Sokoto conflict was exacerbated by drought conditions that increased the competition between nomads and agriculturalists.

This discussion clarifies Otterbein's (1970) findings that military successes are not correlated with degree of political complexity, as well as the more recent and much more sophisticated replication of his results carried out by Naroll and Divale (1976). Cultural, social, and political complexity are related to military *capability*, and none of these is necessarily related to territorial change which is what these authors use to measure warfare. [Ninety per cent of territorial change in the Naroll-Divale (1976: 180) sample was the result of warfare.] On the other hand, military capability is an organizational variable. It is therefore trivial and possibly tautological to theorize that increased organizational effects in the military are correlated to the same capacity in the political realm. The above discussion of cases indicates that the important variable is not the military per se but *significant increases in interpolity conflict* as measured by factors that show increased aggressive violence into interpolity relations. It is the change that brings response, not warfare itself. The suggested correlation does not assume any specific cause or effect relations since warfare can both stimulate and result from state formation.

4.3. Ecological Conditions

Although it is not often noted, changing ecological conditions can drastically alter relations between groups leading to tensions, conflicts and a tendency for increased organization. Thus in the case described by Abubakar (1972), Fulani who came southwards to the Benue Valley came from poorer to better soil conditions and to areas where their cattle products were less desirable. They had therefore to trade cattle, give cattle as tributes at ceremonies, and provide sexual access to their women for those owning pasturage areas. This provoked

increasing hostility and helped to unify the Fulani against the agriculturalists. Other variables are at work here as well. In a personal
communication on this point Robert M. Netting cites previous work by
Derek Stenning and notes that pastoralists who move to better pasturage areas tend to sedentarize because they have year round pasturage.
However their cattle increase rapidly and this produces conflicts with
local indigenous peoples over land use. This puts pressure on the
nomads to solidify a defensible land base and to diversify their holdings into agriculture (Netting: personal communication).

Balanced symbiotic relations between groups who produce different
goods can change to the disadvantage of one of the parties. If this
continues without redressing the balance it can create conflict and help
to unify those who have lost out because of changing conditions
(Cohen f.c.).

4.4. *Tributary or Client State Formation*

The local leadership of the non-state polities surrounding a state can
increase their power and authority by becoming the representative of
their people to their powerful neighbor. Early states often ask their
neighbors for annual tributes, or for safe-conduct for their commercial and military expeditions. Leaders who take on such tasks increase
their power. As already noted, defensive reactions to a large state can
create a more compact, often walled set of settlements surrounding the
state. Defense and increased population size lead to more disputes
which tend to over-load the leadership turning them into full time
mediator–decision-makers. Neighbor states with friendly relations then
often pay tributes to several large polities simultaneously (Cohen
1971). Claimants to the throne of the tributary may seek support from
the surrounding larger states so that internal conflicts are reflected 'big
power' support (Cohen 1971). Sometimes as well, especially if the
tributary's subordination is vital to the interest of the larger state, a
consul is placed there who reports directly to the more powerful
neighbor. The consular tributary is semi-independent and has many
more degrees of freedom than internal segments of the state itself.

Due to weakness in the larger state, growing power in a tributary,
alliances with more powerful neighbors, the ambitiousness of local
leaders, or opportunism by a consul seeking to set up his own kingdom, such tributaries may achieve independence, switch their subordination elsewhere, or rise up after the defeat of their originally dominant neighbor. Statehood then creates hierarchies among neighboring
states and societies that are inherently unstable given the fact that the
inequalities of power among all states and societies in a region do not
remain the same over time.

In summary: the external relations of one polity to others in a region is a potent force in helping to produce early states. Warfare, conquest, trade, ethnic and ecological competition for dominance in an area, superiority of military technology, defensive reactions to raiding, the desire of tributaries to break away, have all contributed to greater degrees of centralized power and the growth of hierarchical early states.

5. INTERNAL FACTORS

Until quite recently the most widely used paradigm for internal changes in society that lead towards the formation of early states has been some variant of a marxist approach. Although it is more apparent in archaeology with the work of Childe (1936), Fried's (1967) position rests squarely on marxist theory. By defining statehood as a system of specialized institutions that maintains social stratification (Fried 1967: 235) he basically accepts the class basis of early states, even though he introduces a series of independent variables whose changing nature are associated with the development of stratification. Service (1975: 284–5) on the other hand, after a careful survey of case materials from around the world finds little or no support for the notion that early states originate from the efforts of powerful groups in society using coercive force, or its threat, to protect their proprietary and unequal rights over resources. Once it comes into existence, as an evolved form of socio-political organization, the early state is clearly stratified, and a ruling class does, ubiquitously, have unequal access to coercive power and wealth. It would seem, therefore, that marxist theory describes the *results* rather than the causes of state formation.

The problem lies in the confusion between cause and effect. To make Marxist theory into a truly causal analysis we must hypothesize, a conspiracy theory of history in which an upper-class-to-be has planned or worked at the creation of the early state. It is in this sense that Service is right. Early states rarely emerge out of class conflicts unless we stretch that concept to include any or all possible conflicts at any level between any groups within society, which is confusing. Furthermore in many if not all of the early states so–called horizontal class distinctions are cross–cut by vertical groupings based often as not on conflicting ties of ethnicity, clientage, trade, and kinship, that relate groups and factions at the top to large segements of the population. We must therefore look elsewhere, both within the society and beyond it, for the causes whose effects Marx analysed into class–based statehood.

Here, I follow Krader (1968), Horton (1971), and Service (1975) in looking at those features of pre–state societies that are already pre-adapted for development into more complex systems. In my view, the fundamental feature is that of property which provides basis for the later development of unequal access to resources. Food production as compared with hunting and gathering is based on the continuous relations (lasting more than individual spans) of collectivities to renewable resources such as srops and herds. Such property relations are defined as a group's traditionally recognized, legitimated, and defenable resources such as crops and herds. Such property relations are Notice here the similarity of this definition to Fried's concept of stratification (unequal access to resources). Property which is inherent in the Neolithic makes stratification inevitable. Although some very loose and viable ideas of territory, water holes, personal tools, nets, etc. are present among hunters and gatherers this new idea concentrates on continuous relations between a group and its means of sustenance. In so doing it becomes the basis for a new society and polity.

The new society emphasizes the continuity of relations between groups and their resource base. It also relates property–owning groups to one another in locally autonomous polities until internal conflicts and pressures on resources splits the group up so that sub-groups hive off to exploit less crowded environments nearby. The polity is divided into descent groups and households, or groups of these that have some formal linkage to one another as members of wards, villages, clans, and so on. The important point as seen in Althabe's (1965) work on the sedentarization of hunters and gatherers is that extra persons become valuable. Polygyny, children, and bridewealth instead of exchange marriages, become much more common, all reflecting a desire for more persons per household and per family. Once humans settled into food producing communities the number of persons per household is an important predictor and indicator of its success as a productive and a political sub-unit in the locally autonomous polity. Therefore, as we have seen, it is at this level — well below that of the state — that humans developed person acquisition institutions such as clientage, fostering, adoption, pawning, and slavery. Food production forces property relations on the species, because it is based on resource utilization of longer duration than human life spans, while simultaneously and correlatively providing advantage to larger local property-owning groups. In evolutionary terms these bedrock correlates of food production are a constant basis for inequality within and between polities. Unequal access to resources is therefore an unalterable and inevitable accompaniment of mankind's adaptation to food production especially agriculture.

As Fried (1967) and others point out rank differences among pre-states are widespread. Permanent offices for local headmen, lineage elders, ward heads, faction leaders, or Big Men, are a universal features of such societies. There is in effect a permanent authority structure that creates a localized hierarchy. Recruitment to office varies from highly ascribed primogeniture within one special lineage group to the very open competitive form found in New Guinea. There are shrine priests, hunt leaders, advisers to the headman, youth leaders, war party leaders, often with special titles signifying their offices.

The localized autonomy is rarely made up only of descendants of the founding group. Strangers, as individuals and groups join and form later comers, as opposed to owners-of-the–land (in West Africa). Or groups in the community are ranked in terms of their recognized proximity in descent terms to a founding ancestor (in the Pacific Islands). Thus community-wide differences, although not great, stabilize and carry with them some notion of higher or lower status depending upon birth into a particular segment. At the same time cross-cutting institutions such as age sets, elders councils, religious cults, secret societies or communal work groups develop and knit various segments of the local polity together. Service (1975: 76–77) describes how within a region, groups of such villages can interrelate socially and economically with one original one coming eventually to dominate the area. On the other hand, the fact that until very recently there have been regions where small locally autonomous groups still prevailed, e.g., West Africa, New Guinea, or the Amazon Valley indicates that stratification and supra-local authority structures among such local polities are not inevitable consequences of their adaptation.[8]

Polity fission is the leitmotif of social life in such groups. The local community expands in size until it is too large for local land holding. People must travel further and further to their fields — so they simply hive off and form a new community elsewhere. Or else some of the excess population is drained off through migration to nearby centers. Often there are internal conflicts over political office, or land holding, or the attribution of misfortunes such as sickness, death, or crop losses to a particular group, who then leave to set up their own polity elsewhere. Rarely, with agriculturalists, possibly more so with pastoral peoples, there are open exploitable territories in all directions. In this case biological increase allows the group to spread out over the landscape as their genealogies proliferate. Whatever the specific reasons, the hierarchical, inegalitarian, tendencies inherent in the organization of local autonomies are held in check by the continuing fission of such polities which is their dominant response to land shortages and internal conflicts. This keeps each polity at a relatively low level of hierarchy and makes its fissioning the most important feature of its socio-political adaption. Strathern (1972) describes the process succinctly for New Guinea in the following words:

> Within groups expanding in size there are opportunities for new big-men to
> obtain followings, increase their power, and create new group segments. At
> the same time other groups are declining, and their members eventually
> disperse or are swallowed up by more powerful hosts or neighbours. But
> competition between big-men, or the development for other reasons of
> internecine disputes, splits the successful groups apart again, so that groups
> size returns to a previous level; and the positive feedback process can then
> begin again (1972: 230).

With a few changes here and there to include lineages and lineage
head-men this passage describes my own experience with the development of traditionally autonomous (Bura) villages in Nigeria,
although whether lineages get 'swallowed up' or ranked varies in
relation to a range of well-known factors (Middleton and Tait 1958;
Horton 1971).

Homeostatic relations are, nevertheless, tightly confined to a narrow
range of determinant conditions. There must be sufficient land to
expand into, and/or the population must remain stable or declining.
More generally the resource base must continue to support such a
proliferating population. There must be no obvious need to control a
special resource, like water, or nodal points on an expanding trade
route. There must be no need to defend the local autonomy from
conquest or even total destruction by neighbours who use warfare as
an instrument to gain political control of a region either for their own
use, or to incorporate the group into an expanding state. If any of
these conditions are not met, then evolutionary trends are immediately
set in motion.

Given such 'normal' features of geography, demography, and inter-
polity relations, the surprising feature of evolution is not the formation
of early states but those seemingly homeostatic situations in which the
society has been held back from developing such institutions. I would
hypothesize that a number of counter effects have slowed the process
down. First population growth is kept artificially low by disease, out-
migration, or widespread infertility. In West Africa for example neo-
nate deaths approach fifty per cent or more, and there are well-known
regions of female infertility that stretch across large bands of territory
(Adadevoh 1974). Secondly, there is the possibility that the population
has only recently changed over from hunting and gathering to a
food-producing way of life. Thus, evolutionary processes of state-building
have not had enough time to manifest themselves among local socio-
political systems. Bragginton (1975) posits this to be the case among
many of the Highland New Guinea groups. Thirdly, I would suggest
that localized autonomies considered on a world-wide scale are at the
peripheries of states. There they have developed through the sedentarization of hunting bands (Althabe 1965), or through having pushed

into more inaccessible forests, mountains, and deserts (Lathrop 1968). The seeming homeostasis of their political evolution is simply a fiction of ethnographic reporting. They are, and always have been, evolving and adapting to local conditions. Today they are parts of nation states and the incorporative plans of central governments committed to economic and social developement. State-building is a continuing process.

Given this explanation for the so-called survival of non-state systems, and given the fact that in an unknown number of cases food producers were forced back into hunting and gathering ways of life,[8] what internal factors help to create and adapt non-state societies to complex centrally organized political units?

The step to chieftaincy is an easy one. These are simply localized autonomies that come to recognize the superior authority of one of their own in a grouping of small polities. The group still breaks up regularly, and it may only use the chief for some judicial, ceremonial, and foreign relations functions. Otherwise each constituent polity still manages its own affairs. Each segment of the chieftaincy has all the necessary offices and functions to become an independent unit whenever it feels powerful enough to break away. Bureaucratic offices are often held by the kinsmen of the chief. In other cases local leaders are made to pay annual tributes and to support the central chief for purposes of warfare and defense. Vansina (1966: 247) has noted that in either case such sub-groups may and do break away to become independent polities, especially when the central chieftaincy is weakened by succession struggles.[9]

Both of these structures lead to problems. If local segment leaders are recruited from the chiefly lineage, and then their offices become hereditary, or if they are chosen from among indigenous leaders, then either way their interests are directed over time to local concerns as opposed to giving support to the central authority. There is no way except through force to subdue the sub-chiefs. Chieftaincy as a system constantly proliferates but has few means to maintain control. At the same time power is, in effect, dissipating outwards from the central authority. The centrifugal character of such systems can be held in check if and when each generation of new chiefs has the right to fill subordinate posts with kinsmen more closely related to himself. Working with a number of such systems over time, Vansina (1970: 177) concludes that once the chief starts down the road to more central control one of two structural consequences occurs. Either chiefs fail to enhance centralization and the chiefship breaks up, or they succeed and the use of close relatives gives way to the use of non-royal kinsmen, and even non-kin. This moves the system towards a centrally appointed bureaucracy whose only means to success and position is the loyality and obedience of its member-officials to the central ruler. Kinsmen are never fully subordinate, since they are, potentially, rivals for chiefly power. When chiefs with the requisite political skills, in the midst of circumstances that favor greater degrees of organization succed in changing the rules of recruitment, then the system begins to evolve towards statehood.

The circumstances favoring such an internal change are those selective pressures already discussed such as warfare, circumscription, defensive reactions, and so on. Faced with such pressure a polity must evolve a more organized hierarchical system, if it is to survive as an autonomous unit. Otherwise it will be incorporated into a neighboring polity, be forced to flee in more or less segmented pieces, or be wiped out.

Translated into everyday life such pressures involve an increased scale and/or frequency of conflict. Ecological circumscription, or defense against outside raiders in walled towns, lead inevitably to more intensive agricultural practices, which in turn means more conflict over land use and ownership (Netting 1972). Sometimes as with the Alur, internal conflicts produce the recognition that more centralized leadership as practiced by neighbors is a desirable goal (Southall 1956). Even without such neighbors to emulate, increased conflicts between local communities enhance the power of local leaders, along with the solidarity and size of settlements. Because Harris' (1965) data are so instructive on this point let me briefly summarize. She notes (Harris 1965: 188–9) that the degree of inter polity conflict and competition is directly associated with the enhancement of chiefly authority among three different sets of named Mbembe villages. Set A (Osopong) with low intervillage conflict, low conflict with Ibo attackers, has high intervillage marriage rates, low degrees of authority for local chiefs, and high population density (250 per mile^2). Set B (Okum) experiences numerous attacks from outside groups, lives in larger more compact villages, has many fewer marriages between villages, low overall population density (77 per mile^2) and much *more* authority for local chiefs who represented their settlements to others. Set C (Adum) has probably experienced a longer period of attacks from outside, has had much intervillage hostility and the competition for scarce resources and chiefs who represent their group and coordinate the entire set of villages for common defense. Although it did not occur, Set C, it seems to me, is on the verge of unifying under a central paramount chief — or of breaking up.

Conflict tends to enhance hierarchical control through the increased use of the leadership. However, pre-state autonomies and chiefship can only tolerate a certain as yet not clearly stipulatable level of conflict before they must break up or develop new integrative institutions. Once the conflict involves a major segment of the polity which refused to recognize the authority of local leaders, splitting is inevitable. The data on this point are now clear and unequivocal. Pre-state polities fission as part of their normal political process. States do not.

States emerge therefore in situations in which break-up is impossible or unacceptable. Whatever the reason, the impossibility of fission means that a quantum increase of political activity must be initiated by the traditional authorities. By handling more disputes, organizing more communal activities, being consulted on more occasions, by representing the polity to others more often, by handling and redistributing the fruits of long distance trade, by carrying out more and more elaborate ceremonies for the public welfare, the leadership must spend more and more time carrying out its political and administrative duties. By fulfilling such functions for more groups, more often in an expanding non-fissioning polity they *ipso facto* have more power and more authority than before when major issues were settled periodically through fission.

But notice what has happened. *The polity centralizes in response to an increased administrative work-load by the leadership.* No class conflict is involved; no exploitation of the ruled by the rulers. The actual shift to the state and to more centralized control is instead the result of increased needs by the populace for functions that leaders already perform (cf. Service 1975). Later, once the increased activity and functions are routinized, and their new power achieves symbolic and cultural expression, then we can speak of a stratified ruling class that has unequal access to resources.

Stratification and the struggle between classes of people that lead to state formation fit much more closely into Ibn Khaldun's classical theory. When pastoral nomads and agriculturalists interact over time, competition for control over water and other resources leads to state-building based from the beginning on ethnic distinctions. When the groups first begin to interact conflicts are avoided by joking relationships between individual nomads and agriculturalists that help them to create symbiotic relations between the two ecologies. Ultimately, the conflicts become greater than the benefits to be derived by maintaining the visitor–stranger lower status for the nomad. Nomads, organized along lines of clanship and segmentary descent may then organize and unify large numbers of warriors against a common foreign enemy (Cohen 1975).

Leadership for the nomads can come from a variety of sources. Clan groups and/or lineages among them may have been ranked in the pre-state society so that a chiefly person, with the proper political skills can take advantage of the situation and move towards greater power for himself, his family, and his descendants. Throughout the Islamic world there has been a tendency for religious leaders, or scholar–priests to be resorted to as mediators and/or rallying points to bring previously disunited groups together (Evans-Pritchard 1949; Abubakar 1972). They have little or no responsibilities to cattle and are therefore freer to go from one nomad group to another preaching unity and warfare as a solution to increasingly difficult relations to sedentary agriculturalists (Cohen 1975).

Once the nomad clans are united and coordinated for warfare they are generally superior in numbers, weaponry, and taste for battle compared with local sedentary agriculturalists. In many places e.g., Baluchistan (Salzman 1971), or the western Sudan (Abubakar 1970) the victorious pastoralists, often semi-sedentary, already use nomads as a mobilizable force to control the locally autonomous or small chieftaincy agriculturalists. The new leaders, from the nomad groups, and their followers establish a sedentary base, often a walled town. As a class they form a ruling elite over those nomads who are still pastoralists, and the indigenous agriculturalist. The central town becomes a citadel out of which a state begins to form. Spooner (1969: 148–9) in discussing how this occurred in Baluchistan notes that the nomad conquerors soon came to derive their income, as rulers, adjudicators and insurers of nomad rights by extracting tributes from the agriculturalists. Nomads served primarily as a source of military power and only secondarily as a source of pastoral products. At first the leaders are identified with the interests of the nomads, but Spooner (1969) follows Ibn Khaldun in noting that, ultimately, they shift and take on the interests of agriculturalists, as they themselves become more sedentary. The dynastic family had fought and led the nomads to ensure their rights to pasturage and water. After a period of sedentism and leadership however they begin to shift their interests to lands, crops, and peasants. In Baluchistan, and in the western Sudan it led to a series of walled towns.

> It takes time before the dynastic family becomes actually settled, but the forts are a tangible symbol for all three classes (settled nomads, agriculturalists, and pastoralists) of the growing ties between the dynastic family and the settled people (Spooner 1969: 148–9).

Establishing centralized control is not all smooth sailing. Abubakar (1970: 215ff.) notes that once the Fulani nomads of nineteenth century Fombina emirate state had established their domination over the local agriculturalists, the unity of the movement began to break down along typical segmentary lines of clanship and lineage. Only through the use of force, and the creation of a set of permanent central officials at Yola, the Fombina capital, along with the moral and religious sanction of the Caliphate at Sokoto was the leader and founder able to hold the newborn emirate together. Ultimately Fulani clan segments at the peripheries provided local Muslim leaders. The emir developed a non-kin set of administrators at the center, while the indigenous agriculturalists formed a non-Muslim under-class articulating into the state by relations between their own village headmen, and Fulani members of the ruling group acting in the name of the emir (Cohen 1975).

In more general theoretical terms, whether the state emerges from a clash between nomads and agriculturalists over control of local resources, or from agriculturalists becoming progressively more circumscribed, or from defensive reactions against outside enemies, the results are remarkably similar. Fission as an inherent quality of political life must be overcome and the continuity of a particular authority structure must be assured. To do this the authorities obtain vastly increased military capabilities by uniting related segments whose combined warrior manpower is relatively large. At the same time some form of permanent managerial–bureaucratic functions emerge that become more specialized. As we have noted the operational step to more specialization is simply more time spent at carrying out administrative–judicial functions occasioned by greater utilization of leaders judicial and other functions as well as the increased coordination of political and economic activities.

The early state emanates outwards. However they got into this position, as conquerors, lineage heads of the leading clan, heads of a leading village becoming an urban trading and/or administrative center, or whatever, the leading family and within it the royal person, form the central focus of the system. Surrounding the monarch and his royal relatives are a court of nobles, priests, slaves and foreign representatives who serve as advisers, administrators, war leaders, adjudicators, and record-keepers of the realm. Various sectors of the population differentiated by occupation may be represented as well. Often as not these groups are also based on common residence and/or descent so that widespread principles of representation can be used for such syndicalist purposes. As we have seen these officers emerge from a number of possible backgrounds in the pre-state system. No matter what their provenience, the state requires such functionaries on a permanent basis. Without them, or with too few of them with too few powers, the state founders and probably splits at the first sign of trouble, internal rivalry, or succession strife over the throne. The court must articulate the administration with the people and the territory it controls. There are several ways to do this, depending upon local history. But whether sub-groups and territories are consolidated or dispersed under center officials who administer them, whether nomad groups are linked directly to the throne, or to local peripheral lords, some linkage system between the center and the masses of the people defined in sub-group and territorial terms must emerge. This provides an appellate court system, a revenue collection and warrior-raising system, or in more general terms an information system that provides the basis for state sovereignty.[10]

Once the early state emerges, once people have recognized, or fail to oppose successfully, the growth or imposition of the centrally organized hierarchy, then the authority structure of a polity has differentiated out from more generalized diffuse background. It is now possible for the ordinary person, the noble, the slave, anybody, to relate to it as a subject, or more generally — as a citizen. Before the state, absorption into a polity meant cultural absorption as well. This is necessary because membership in the same polity meant in effect acceptance of membership in closely related local groups. Hierarchy solves the problem by inventing citizenship — the common membership, in and subordination to a central government that provides a means of mediating between different cultural groups. Once government structures specialize out as specific full-time occupations, then everyone has a role within this differentiated aspect of social life. Statehood implies then not just specialized rulers, but specialized citizen–subjects whose interaction with government, can from this point on in human history become itself an object of evolution.

This depiction should however not be taken too literally. The stability of early states is a relative matter. Compared to localized autonomies or chieftaincies they are significantly more stable. However, the rise of powerful neighbor states and of a number of sources of internal conflict may result in their weakening or splitting. Contending royal candidates for the throne supported by officials and would-be officials in their entourage can turn an interregnum into a civil war that produces a rash of such struggles (Goody 1966). Either a strong party and its candidate then wins out, or the state splits up, loses territory at its borders, or is subdued by an outside power who is often supported by one of the internal candidates. Trade routes can shift taking away a basic source of wealth for a state formed originally to control the trading center. A weak administration faced with serious external and internal problems produces an opportunity for neighboring states and internal rivals. Statehood does not insure internal peace. What it does is to override previous instability by a new form of organization that does not include break-up as part of its political process.

6. CULTURAL FACTORS

6.1. *Technology*
There is no evidence that the formation of early state systems follows

in any invariant way the developement of improved technology. Although improved technologies emerge, or are often associated with centralized government, few of these if any consistently appear as predictors, enablers, or triggering devices for the onset of early statehood. By improved technology I mean ways and means of achieving goals through reduced amounts of per capita human effort. Such improvements do occur in association with statehood in production, transportation, information processing, architecture, and scientific knowledge. However, with the possible exception of warfare capability most of these improvements do not occur prior to the founding of states (c.f. Goody 1971).

Basic tools, for production in agriculture and craft work, show no systematic improvement before and immediately after state formation. The plow and other forms of machinery do not universally either precede or necessarily follow state formation. On the other hand the specialization occasioned by state formation especially in the urban centers allows for concentrated use of tools for specific purposes. This concentration, in which not everyone uses a similar set of tools, produces the enabling social basis for technology developement. Society first, however, has to be organized economically, and politically so that such specialists are encouraged and supported.

The same generalization applies to other types of technology. As we have seen, only when society has differentiated and developed coordinating, managerial–bureaucratic offices, is there a capacity for long distance trade with improved transportation techniques, record-keeping and writing, complex architectural forms, as well as complex measurement devices. All of these indicators of 'civilization' are the results of early state formation. Once developed they increase the capacity of the state to supply its needs, and stabilize its authority. But the authority system and its bureaucratic officialdom are the true causal agents of later technological improvements. It requires control over large masses of labor to build monuments, roads, bridges, and canals.

In dealing with this same problem Adams (1975: 287) notes that the

process whereby centralized units exposed through a multiplication of their numbers is a coordinate process, but one that does not suggest any great changes in the kind of technology.

He cites Carneiro (1969) to indicate that although technological capability is increasing quantitatively, there are few if any really outstanding qualitative innovations that go along with early state formation. Only later as states develop and apply role specialization to increasing their control over resources, only then does technology begin to take off.

The one possible exception is warfare. Certainly, it too develops rapidly once states appear on the scene. All early states must at regular

intervals defend themselves, put down rebellious tributaries, or van-
quish rival states. Cavalry, cross-bows, horsed chariots, gunpowder,
and a host of other technical devices develop rapidly after the inception of states. Similarly with military strategy, which becomes a very
conscious specialization once monarch's have the ability to field large
armies. Thus, as with other forms of technology, warfare is stimulated
by statehood. However, in cases of state-building where two non-state
polities compete for local control, as with nomads and agriculturalists,
then superior military technology becomes crucial in giving the victory
to one or the other party. The conquest state does occur, and it
depends at least to some extent upon the military technology of the
victors. Otterbein (1970: 44–8) goes over this point, demonstrating a
correlation between weaponry and political centralization which is
mediated by the degree of professionalization in the military (1970:
48). However, since a professional soldiery is often the result of
political centralization, it is clear that although military technology
affects state formation, it is also affected by it in a feedback process of
developement.

Irrigation is a special problem. Wittfogel's (1957) original hypothesis
that large-scaled irrigation works lead willy-nilly to statehood has been
reportedly discredited (Woodbury 1961; Adams 1966; Claessen 1975).
Nevertheless, a modified version is now being revived in which irrigation serves to intensify or help in the developement of centralization
(Claessen 1975: 56). The mechanism seems to be one already discussed above. As Hunt and Hunt (1974: 154) note, scarcity of water,
irrigation works, and a conflict-resolving political hierarchy interact to
produce (a) more conflict and (b) greater use of the conflict-resolving
institutions. As with land shortages, or constriction behind defensive
walls, increased disputes lead to increased power for the political
hierarchy through enhanced judicial and managerial functions. Thus
irrigation may intensify centralization, if other factors are present,
(water scarcity, increased number of disputes, and a political hierarchy
responsible for settling conflicts). A number of scholars have therefore
begun to revive interest in the impact of irrigation (Downing and
Gibson 1974; Claessen 1975).

6.2. *The Evolution of State Religion*

In pre-state societies the authority system is closely linked to religious
beliefs and practices. Commonly, a local headman or the local elders
mediate between the living and the dead to further the welfare of the
community. The headman often protects his people against witches
disease, infant mortality and other misfortunes. When adjudication

becomes difficult, he may resort to trial by ordeal in which spiritual forces exercise judgement, or rely on specialized diviner–advisers who help with the decisions. It is not surprising therefore that when the power and authority of the local headman is increased so that he is consulted by, and administers the affairs of, a group of local polities as their chief, then his supernatural powers, and the need for their enforcement, increases in scale and degree of control over people and things.

Compared with less hierarchical systems chiefs and monarchs perform more elaborate rituals at religious ceremonies. Bloch (1974) points out that increased ritualization of behavior is in effect an increased elaboration of authority. Ritual by its repetitive nature in collective situations emphasizes and is in fact a rigid imposition of rules for behaving so that the entire congregation acts out, and accepts, the authority of those in charge of the ritual performance. In this sense, says Bloch, ritual is culturized and symbolic authority. As such it supports authority. Thus, to increase the ritual associated with a local headman's office, is to increase or to substantiate an increase in his authority.

And this is in fact what happens. Netting (1972) had noted that the Kofyar chiefships increased their authority over adjacent communities due to land shortages, increased elaboration of land ownership rules, and the overloading onto the most competent adjudicators of the disputes resulting from increased conflicts. As this occurs the supernatural powers of headship increases, as do the rituals associated with the office. Each supports the other and provides legitimacy for the increasing power of the chief as his services are required more frequently by the people.

As we have already noted, the increased functions of a political office draw to it greater amounts of power and authority. Once this occurs the emergent office is associated with more ritual and more supernatural powers. The important point is that such supernaturally enhanced powers are already part and parcel of localized leadership patterns among pre-state polities. State formation and chiefship simply elaborate these cultural features along with the developement of political aspects of the role.

The exact forms of such rituals and powers vary, although some are widely distributed. Out of the respect felt for a local headman evolves a reverence for the person of the chief and an awe for the early monarch. His body, his person, once he is in the office, are equated with the power of the overall coordinated polity. Ordinary people must approach him with care using symbolic gestures of inferiority. To touch his head, the seat of his wisdom, is widely considered taboo. Special rituals of approach to his person develop. In the western Sudan he is

kept behind a curtain or even caged so that no one can come too close
to the royal presence. In many places he periodically recreates the
fertililty of the land, and offers sacrifices at the graves of the royal
ancestors not just for his own lineage or village, but now for the entire
realm.

Adjudication and warfare practices often stress, at least in the oral
traditions, some belief in the supernatural powers of the chief. He
miraculously settles difficult cases. And he has magical means of aiding
his armies to win battles, sieges, and raids against enemy groups. The
gods, ancestors, and spirits aid and help to make him an intermediary
between men and the mystical forces that control the universe.

Connected to the same evolutionary sequence is the development
of royal regalia as well as elaborate installation and burial rituals.
Sacred symbols of office, a drum, a staff, a stool, or neck rest, and
sacred, secret objects that are part of the paraphernalia of headman-
ship elaborate rapidly in association with the emergence of chiefly and
royal office. These objects symbolize the authority of the central ruler,
as well as the continuity of the state above and beyond any single
incumbent's lifetime. Succession involves custody of these objects or
their use by the holder such as a Queen Mother (Cohen f.c.) to
legitimate the new ruler. Succession and royal burial are special events
developed out of the death of local leaders, but elaborated upon
enormously so that the process of installation elevates the incumbent
above his fellow royals, into leadership of the state. Death involves
placing the leader among his royal dynastic ancestors where he can be
appealed to, and interceded with by succeeding monarchs.

Some writers (Service 1975; Adams 1975) see in these developments the association of early statehood with 'theocracy', or 'divine
kingship'. Certainly, all early states have rulers ubiquitously believed
to have supernatural powers, to stand close to the royal ancestors and
to intercede between man and the gods for their people. Nevertheless,
what should not be forgotten is the fact that such features are simply
the elaboration of the religious functions performed by local leaders in
pre-state systems. Divine kingship is a particular form of such generally enhanced supernatural status in which, as in ancient Egypt, the
ruler qua ruler is a god in his own right. Although, not a widespread
practice it is a particular outgrowth of the more ubiquitous form of
state religion practiced by early states.

In more generally applicable terms the state develops a theology to
support its authority system giving it a legitimacy that is omnipotent
and supernatural. As the power and authority of the leader is increased, through the increased demands placed on his office by his
people, so too are the religious and symbolic meanings and beliefs
which enhance and explain his power to others inside his society and

beyond. What was previously a set of beliefs concerned with fertility of land and people, of rectitude sanctioned and defended by the people, the ancestors, and the spirits of a locality, now becomes state religion whose avowed purpose is to provide sanctions for the legitimacy of the ruler, his duties to his people and they to him, and for his capacity to contact and intercede with the supernatural for their benefit.

6.3. *The State as Emergent Ethnicity*

The pre-state chieftaincy and locally autonomous polities are culturally homogeneous. People may come from elsewhere, local groups may be absorbed, there may be, indeed there usually are, different cultural strands woven into the life of the polity. However, at any one time there are widespread commonalities of language, culture, values, ecology, technology, family life, religion, and socialization. Differentiation occurs as segments break off and spread over the landscape. In general, common ethnicity is wider scaled and more inclusive than political unity.

Once the state emerges multi-ethnicity becomes possible, even inevitable. Ethnic groups can maintain semi-separate existence within a state and tie themselves by various means into the central governmental structure. The ethnic group itself may be associated with a locality, or with one or more occupations or it may be dispersed and be adapting variously to its incorporation. Clearly, the degree to which the ethnic groups are restricted socially, politically, and economically will predict to their degree of continuity as differentiated segments within the state. The important point is the capacity of the state to absorb people by establishing, in effect, a separate means by which they relate to the authority structure. As we have seen statehood involves not simply subjects, but *citizens* — persons with stipulated rights and duties to a complex governmental apparatus, no matter what their cultural, economic, and social relations may be to others in and out of the state itself.

This does not mean that citizenship is invariant or unchanging. Early states developed a range of techniques for incorporating new groups and for maintaining flexible relations to specific segments of the polity. Nomads are often linked by ethnic or clan ties while sedentary groups may use territorially-defined units (Cohen 1971). The Inca relocated villages from royal provinces to freshly conquered ones often taking some or many of the conquered population and distributing them elsewhere (Moore 1958: 103). Furthermore, power, especially in the central governmental administration was usually restricted to a political class often of similar ethnic background, with the possible addition of slaves, eunuchs, and royal clients who shared the elite sub-culture.

Once the state emerges as an organization of center and periphery groups, then membership is itself a selective pressure operating to create common ethnicity. Membership in a common political hierarchy, military obligations, economic ties within the state and a host of factors that increase contacts across ethnic groups — all tend towards pan-ethnic cultural ties. For trade, lingua franca develop, the state religion dominates even if local religions are allowed to continue. Laws that allow the state to mediate between groups having their own local customs become the 'law of the land'. Common citizenship creates the basis for an evolving state culture. Thus evolution is not simply a tendency to heterogeneity. Indeed, as Carneiro (1975) has pointed out, the number of states decreases through time.

The shape of the emergent national culture is determined by so-called 'greater' and 'lesser' traditions. The greater tradition is that of the capital and its ruling group. Lesser traditions are those of local peoples. The 'greater' tradition is associated with power, wealth, and urbanism. It spreads slowly outwards mixing with local cultures to create, ultimately, the national identity. However, differences in ecology, e.g., nomadism, deep and solidary local roots, immigration and incorporation of new cultural groups restrain homogeneity. National cultures are constantly being infused by foreigners who join the state as citizens and retain important elements of their own. Thus national cultures grow, influenced by elite cultures. At the same time forces of differentiation continue, so that homogeneity is never achieved because citizenship is never based solely on culture. England took centuries to develop the Englishman. Just as the process seemed to succeed, the empire collapsed, and non-English people started immigrating and becoming citizens. This has produced new variations within the polity and tendencies, ultimately, towards a new and different national culture for the English nation.

For the early states the most ubiquitous cultural feature is the emergence of a two-class system of rulers and ruled. However it came to power, the ruling group is differentiated culturally. In caste systems such as India, or Rwanda the sub-groups may be multiple. Nevertheless, the ruling group forms a clearly defined, culturally distinct entity. They may on closer inspection be cut up into royals, slave-bureaucrats, fief holders, the military, priests, and so on. From the standpoint of a national culture however, all are either rulers or ruled. The culture then creates a class system by lumping ethnic groups among the subject-citizens into one overall group of 'commoners' and a complementary ruler group of government functionaries or 'nobles'.

The capability to solidify, organize, and coordinate human activity on a permanent basis beyond ethnicity is the enormous adaptive leap taken by the founding of states. Tendencies to state cultures emerge, but contrary forces of differentiation are not controlled by statehood And this capability of uniting humanity beyond local loyalties of culture beyond process of differentiation and past history is an idea whose implications and possibilities have yet to be fully taken advantage of by the species.

6.4. *Political Culture and Statehood*

Hierarchy, respect for leaders, and positive values associated with inequities in power and authority are increasingly present in pre-state societies, especially chiefly systems. However pre-state systems also stress the possibility that achievement, personal political skill, and success will create many followers for an ambitious man. Such political systems generally provide some place in the local or chiefly set of offices for 'big men' or those with 'influence'. Egalitarianism is woven deep into the strands of such societies. Many may strive, achieve, and be admired for it. But always within limits. Too much success, or even overly consistent failure can be attributed to malevolent forces, believed to be brought to bear on the unfortunate by the overly successful few. At the political level, a leader must strive to assure everyone his due. To use authority in unwarranted ways leads to loss of support and therefore of power. In pre-state societies every man is potentially a chief (LeVine 1966).

However, once the early state appears the ethic of egalitarianism tends to weaken drastically. Hunting and gathering are dominantly egalitarian; pre-state food producers maintain concepts of hierarchy and egalitarianism in tension. States on the other hand elevate hierarchy to a dominant pre-eminent place in society. The permanence of centralized governmental systems places inequality at the heart of the society and it triumphs as the most important element of political culture. A sixteenth century court scribe in the Western Sudan caught this flavour when he wrote that people with a bad monarch were infinitely better off than one who had no ruler at all (Fartua 1928).

The details of political culture focus on the value of superior–subordinate relations. Achievement in early states does not occur through open individualistic striving against an abstract standard of excellence (McClelland 1961). Instead there is a constant emphasis placed upon the potentialities of deference. Household heads, local leaders, nobles, and above all else the ruler himself are seen as beneficent, father-like, protectors who provide security and a position in the society with access to the necessities of economic, social and political existence. The primary importance of hierarchy, of personal superior–subordinate dyads is reflected in the writing of Ibn Khaldun, and of almost all social scientists who have described pre-industrial state systems (Nadel 1942; Smith 1960; Cohen 1967). Fallers (1973: 170) puts well for the Baganda kingdom:

> ... terms which emphasize the personal (superior–subordinate) tie between the individuals concerned rather than simply differences in rank, are almost universally used today ... in modern economic and political relations as well as in more traditional contexts ... it is through such ties of a patron–client nature, Baganda believe, that a person gets ahead in the world. A popular proverb says ... "The obedient servant carries his master's crown into battle". Faithful service is rewarded by the opportunity to acquire wealth and glory. A master seeks in his servant ... loyality, and ... obedience. Conversely, a servant seeks a master who is kind and who is "favored by his superiors".

This type of generalization which can be repeatedly found in early state descriptions gets to the essence of the political culture — the set of values and symbols that prescribe the proper way to behave in a polity. For the most part, service in the bureaucracy is not paid for by salary. Instead, loyalty and obedience to superiors are rewarded by allowing the subordinate to achieve greater access to power and authority. The system of hierarchical networks is supported by a cultural system that places enormous stress on loyalty, obedience, and the rewards to be obtained from it. Simultaneously, of course, the political culture also stresses the wisdom of kindness, generosity, and the protection of subordinates by superiors. Careless, arrogant, miserly superiors lose subordinates, and therefore power and authority, which is most often operationalized in terms of numbers of subordinates. A good leader is a 'river to his people', and when he is, they flock to his banner.

Such a cultural stress emerges as the need for, and creation of, hierarchy occurs. At first, cultural materials already to hand are used, albeit in new ways, to represent the new relationships. Leaders are viewed as 'the father of us all' as well as 'lions' or 'elephants' to symbolize a new and magnified status in relation to ordinary people. First fruits given to a ward, lineage, or village head, evolve into annual tributes to a chief, and then a royal leader. The Nyakyusa age-mates of a new chief pay his bridewealth for the two great queens who will produce the next generation chiefs. They are not his lineage mates for whom it is customary to contribute bridewealth. Instead, they are using bridewealth as a symbol of their solidarity with the chief. A primary mode of kinship obligation is being extended symbolically to show how leaders and subjects are mutually involved in each other's fate. In later stages of state developement, such payments to superiors represent the benefits to be derived from citizenship and the obligations due to the political hierarchy.

Socialization into early state societies stress autonomy training significantly less often than in non-centralized systems (Barry and Paxson

1971). Children are taught the value of deference, of giving respect to superiors, and the necessity of utilizing subordination as a form of currency to obtain a proper place for themselves in the society. But this goes back to the need for larger more coordinated social units that develop along with agriculture. Authority and discipline are important aspects of food production. With person acquisition comes more authority and a greater emphasis on subordination. In other words, although personal autonomy is present and emphasized at pre-state, post-hunting band levels, subordination and its value is also well-established once sedentarization and food-production develops, in which large and hierarchically organized households are the basic unit of society. Thus subordination, discipline, loyalty, and negative evaluations of autonomy are positively correlated with political complexity. Once the forces of external and internal change occur then values of subordination already present in post-neolithic society support these changes by placing ever-more emphasis on hierarchy, giving it greater and greater amounts of pay-off as a value to be replicated through child-training. Hierarchical control creates a demand for a political culture that enhances its legitimacy and emphasizes its benefits. Not too surprisingly, early states invariably produce such an ideological support system.

7. CONCLUSION

The state is a specifiable variety of political systems distinguishable by its centralized bureaucracy and dominant control of force by the central authority over subordinate segments of the society. Compared with others this definition has the heuristic value of providing a place for the state in an overall roster of political structures whose relations to one another form a description of the political evolution of mankind. It assumes (a) that the structure of authority is a highly determinant quality of political activity and its organization, and (b) that forces selecting for changes in authority are the basic causes of political evolution. At a more detailed level this means we can find answers to the emergence of such systems by asking about the sorts of sequences and events that produce the differences between two large classes of centralized polities, chieftaincies and states. This difference, as discussed here rests on the observed fact that state structures enable the system to override fissionable political forces that up until then could not be contained so that polity break-up is a statistically normal part of pre-state political life.

The emergence of state structures has been theorized to have been selected for by population pressures, long distance trade, location, warfare, conquest, defense, internal strife, or the benefits to be derived from more permanent forms of centralized control. Closer examination of both theory and data indicates that none of these factors is sufficient or even consistently antecedent to state formation. In many instances factors claimed to cause the state, e.g., a desire by the ruling class to exert control over access to scarce resources, are consequences rather than antecedent correlates of this evolutionary sequence. We therefore agree with writers like Wright and Johnson (1975) who conceive of the process as a systematic one. Whatever starts the sequence off tends to change other qualities of political, social, economic, and cultural life so that from a number of different starting points, following different trajectories of change, very comparable results ensure.

Why this convergence has occurred in political evolution is an interesting question and one not often addressed by researchers whose overgeneralized and event-based cause–effect theories tend to obscure this issue. The position taken here leads to the conclusion that once a society starts to change its authority structure towards greater permanency and stable supra-local hierarchy, then the political realm itself becomes an ever-increasingly powerful determinant of change in the economy, society, and culture of the system. The entire process is a large-scale feedback system in which multiple possible sets of causes in the ecology, economy, society and intersocietal environment may singly or in combination produce more permanent centralized hierarchies of political control. After this initial impetus, the hierarchical structure itself feeds back on all societal factors to make them more closely into an overall system that supports the authority structure. This is why early states so far removed from one another as Inca Peru, ancient China, Egypt, early Europe, or pre-colonial West Africa have so many striking similarities of organization, culture and society. The form of the state once it evolves becomes an *emergent* selective force in the evolution of human society. Its needs and its survival create pressures that are satisfied by adapting the rest of society—religion, values, local organization, ethnic identity, and socialization—to state structure.

FOOTNOTES

[1] This paper is part of a longer term project involving field work in northeastern Nigeria as well as an extensive review of cases already available in the literature. The writer is grateful to the National Science Foundation, and the National Endowment for the Humanities for their financial support for the work. Professors George Dalton and Chris Boehm read previous drafts of this paper and made a number of helpful criticisms.

[2] Thurnwald's (1935) definition was based on the conquest theory of state origins—the historical process which he, and many others, posit as the underlying cause of the ethnically stratified nature of early states.

[3] See below. In India and U.S.A. where social and ethnic stratification is well-developed in the past, and in Israel and South Africa where it still is, it is inevitable that

unless state-wide ethnicity develops in future, then these states will be enmeshed in irreconcilable conflicts.

[4] Wright and Johnson (1975) suggest that a two-level hierarchy is more likely to be a chieftaincy, while three-level ones are states. Why this should be so is not very clear as yet in their work, and does not necessarily apply to complex African chieftaincies such as the Azande.

[5] Wright and Johnson recognize this quality but do not make it a central feature of their definition. They note that the processing of large amounts of information by a 'control hierarchy . . . undercuts the independence of subordinates.' (1975:267).

[6] The distinction is not as clear as it should be. Many states today are hardly industrial. Nevertheless they have taken on the outward governmental forms of such polities. In my view they are still classifiable as 'industrial' since they are committed to this mode of production and to the transformation of society associated with it. Their strategy is to use the political sector of the state to create the desired changes elsewhere in the community.

[7] C.f. Wright and Johnson (1975 : 284). These authors have tested the relationship of single variables to state formation and rejected all such hypotheses. This leads them to propose multi-variate systemic methods and theory for future research.

[8] Lathrop (1968 : 26) suggests that upriver Amazon horticulturalists were pushed out of good soil areas near the river in the thick, less fertile forests by militarily superior later comers. Once they moved they adapted to hunting and gathering, keeping at the same time many traces of their previous horticultural phase.

[9] Vansina (1966) describes these societies as 'kingdoms' whereas under the system of classification being used here they would be 'chieftaincies'.

[10] Whether the state also provides the basis for the coordination of an economic system is not clear. Certainly, the capital city can be seen as a market for goods from the peripheries. However, trade does not necessarily have to flow up and down the lines of political hierarchy. Villages at the peripheries of the Sudanese states traded with other villages, with the capital of their own state, and with people from other states. Tributes of course, followed the political hierarchy, but this is more accurately seen as revenue or taxation.

REFERENCES

Abrahams, R. G. (1967), *The political organization of Umyamwezi*. Cambridge: Cambridge University Press.

Abubakar, Sa'ad (1970), *The Fombina emirate 1809–1903*. Unpublished Ph.D. dissertation, Ahinadu Bello University, Zaula, Nigeria.

— (1972), 'The establishment of authority in the upper Benue basin', in: *Savanna* 1, 1, 67–80.

Adadevoh, K. B., ed. (1974), *Sub-fertility and infertility in Africa*. Ibadan: Caxton Press.

Adams, Robert McC. (1966), *The evolution of urban society*. Chicago: Aldine.

Adams, Richard N. (1975), *Energy and structure: a theory of social power*. Austin: University of Texas.

Allan, William (1949), Studies in African land use in northern Rhodesia. in: *Rhodes Livingstone Papers* 15.

Althabe, G. (1965), 'Changements sociaux chez les Pygmées Baka de l'Est Cameroun', in: *Cahiers d'Etudes Africaines* vol. 5, no. 4.

Andrezejewski, S. L. (1954), *Military organization and society*. London: Routledge and Kegan Paul.

Bagehot, Walter (1872), *Physics and politics: Thoughts on the application of the principles of 'natural selection' and 'inheritance to political society'*. Reprinted 1956. Boston: Beacon Press.

Barnes, J. A. (1967), *Politics in a changing society: a political history of the Fort Jameson Ngoni*. 2nd edn. Manchester: Manchester University Press.

Barry, Herbert, III and Paxson, L. M. (1971), 'Infancy and early childhood: cross-cultural codes', in: *Ethnology* 10: 466–508.

Beals, Kenneth L. and Kelso, A. J. (1975), 'Genetic variation and cultural evolution', in: *American Anthropologist* 77: 566–579.

Bloch, Maurice (1974), 'Symbols, song, dance and features of articulation: is religion an extreme form of traditional authority?', in: *European Journal of Sociology* 15, no. 1: 55–81.

Boserup, Ester (1965), *The conditions of agricultural growth*. Chicago: Aldine.

Bragginton, Joan (1975), *Patterns of interaction in the Beha valley: a study of social organization in the eastern highlands of New Guinea*. Unpublished Ph.D. dissertation Northwestern University (Anthropology).

Braudel, Ferdinand (1972), *The Mediterranean and the Mediterranean world in the age of Philip II*. 2 Vols. Translated by Siân Reynolds. New York: Harper and Row (published originally in France 1966).

Carneiro, Robert L. (1969), 'The measurement of cultural development in the Near East and Anglo-Saxon England', in: *Transactions of the New York Academy of Sciences*, 2nd ser. 31 (8): 1013–1023.

— (1970), 'A theory of the origin of the state', in: *Science* 169 (3947): 733–738.

— (1975), 'The principle of mutual exclusion in the evolution of states'. *Paper* delivered at the American Anthropological Association meetings, San Francisco. (December).

Childe, V. Gordon (1936), *Man makes himself*. London: Watts.

Claessen, Henri J. M. (1975), 'Despotism and irrigation', in: *Current anthropology in the Netherlands*, ed. by Peter Kloos and Henri J. M. Claessen. pp. 48–62. Leiden.

Cohen, Ronald (1967), *The Kanuri of Bornu*. New York: Holt, Rinehart & Winston.

— (1971), 'Incorporation in Bornu', in: *From tribe to nation in Africa*, ed. by R. Cohen and J. Middleton. Scranton: Intext (Chandler).

— (1973), 'Political anthropology', in: *Handbook of social and cultural anthropology*, ed. by J. J. Honigmann. Chicago: Rand MacNally.

— (1974), 'The evolution of hierarchical institutions: a case study from Biu, Nigeria', in: *Savanna* 3, 2, 153–174.

— (1975), Origins of the state: a controlled comparison. *Paper* delivered at American Anthropological Association meetings, San Francisco. (December).

— (f.c.), 'Oedipus, rex, and regina: the Queen Mother in Africa', in: *Africa*.

Cook, Sherburne (1972), 'Prehistoric demography'. *Addison-Wesley Modular Publication* 16.

Cowgill, George L. (1975), 'On causes and consequences of ancient and modern population changes', in: *American Anthropologist* 77: 505–525.

Dike, Kenneth O. (1956), *Trade and politics in the Niger Delta 1830–1885*. Oxford: Clarendon Press.

Downing, Th. E. and Gibson, McGuire, eds (1974), *Irrigation's impact on society*. Anthropological Papers of the University of Arizona, no. 25. Tucson: University of Arizona Press.

Dumont, Louis (1965), 'Population growth and cultural change', in: *Southwestern Journal of Anthropology* 21 (4), 302–324.

Engels, F. (1891), *The origin of the family, private property and the state*. Reprint edn, 1972. New York: International Publishers.

Evans-Pritchard, E. E. (1949), *The Sanusi of Cyrenaica*. London: Oxford University Press.

Fallers, Lloyd (1973), *Inequality: social stratification reconsidered*. Chicago: Univeristy of Chicago Press.

Fartua, Ahmed Ibn (1928), *The Kanem wars of Mai Idris Alooma*. Translated by H. R. Palmer in Sudanese memoirs Vol. I, Lagos: Government Printer. (London: Cass 1967).

Forde, D. C. and Kaberry, P. M., eds (1967), *West African kingdoms in the nineteenth century*. London: Oxford University Press.

Fortes, M. and Evans-Pritchard, E. E., eds (1940), *African political systems*. London: Oxford University Press.

Fried, Morton H. (1967) *The evolution of political society*. New York: Random House.

Gearing, F. O. (1962) 'Priest and warriors', in: *American Anthropological Association Memoir* No. 93.

Gluckman, Max (1965), *Politics, law and ritual in tribal society*. Oxford: Blackwell.

Goody, Jack R., ed. (1966), 'Succession to high office', in: *Cambridge papers in anthropology* no. 4. Cambridge; Cambridge University Press.

— (1971), *Technology, tradition, and the state in Africa*. London: Oxford University Press.

Harmon, M. Judd (1964), *Political thought from Plato to the present*. New York: McGraw Hill.

Harner, M. J. (1970), 'Population pressure and the social evolution of agriculturalists', in: *Southwestern Journal of Anthropology* 26: 67–86.

Harris, Marvin (1971), *Culture, man and nature*. New York: Crowell.

Harris, Rosemary (1965), *The political organization of the Mbembe*, Nigeria. London: HMSO.

Hayden, Brian (1975), 'The carrying capacity dilemma: an alternative approach', in: Population studies in archaeology and bioligical anthropology: a symposium, ed. by Alan C. Swedlund, in: *American Antiquity*, Vol. 40, no. 2, pt. 2, memoir 30, 11–21.

Hickerson, H. (1962), 'The southwestern Chippewa: an ethnohistorical study', in: *American Anthropological Association Memoir* 92.

Hobhouse, L. T., Wheeler, G. and Ginsburg, M. (1915), *The material culture and social institutions of the simpler peoples*. London: Chapman and Hall.

Horton, Robin (1969), 'From village to city-state', in: *Man in Africa*, ed. by M. Douglas and P. Kaberry. London: Oxford University Press.

— (1971), 'Stateless societies in the history of West Africa' in: *History of West Africa*, ed. by J. F. A. Ajayi and M. Crowder, vol. I. London: Longmans, pp. 78–119.

Hunt, Eva and Hunt, Robert C. (1974), 'Irrigation, conflict and politics: a Mexican case.' in: *Anthropological papers of the University of Arizona*, no. 25: Irrigation's impact on society, ed. by T. E. Downing and M. Gibson, pp. 129–157. Tucson: University of Arizona Press.

Koppers, W. (1963), 'L'Origine de l'état'. *VI International Congress of Anthropological and Ethnological Sciences* 1970. (Paris 1963) Vol. 2, 159–168.

Krader, Lawrence (1968), *Formation of the state.* Englewood Cliffs: Prentice Hall.

Lathrop, Donald N. (1968), 'The "Hunting" economies of the tropical forest zone of South America: an attempt at historical perspective', in: *Man the hunter,* ed. by Richard B. Lee and Irvin DeVore. Chicago: Aldine.

Lattimore, Owen (1940), *Inner Asian frontiers of China.* Paperback ed. 1962. Boston: Beacon Press.

Lee, Richard B. (1972), 'Population growth and the beginnings of sedentary life among the Kung Bushmen', in: *Population growth: anthropological implications,* ed. by B. Spooner. Cambridge: MIT Press.

Lenski, G. (1966), *Power and privilege: a theory of social stratification.* New York: McGraw Hill.

LeVine, R. F. (1966), *Dreams and deeds.* Chicago: Aldine.

Lowie, Robert (1927), *The origin of the state.* New York: Harcourt, Brace and World.

McClelland, David C. (1961), *The achieving society.* Princeton, N.J.: Van Nostrand.

Middleton, J. and D. Tait. (1958), *Tribes without rulers.* London: Routledge and Kegan Paul.

Moore, Sally Falk (1958), *Power and property in Inca Peru.* Westport, Conn.: Greenwood Press.

Murdock, G. P. (1959), *Africa: its peoples and their culture history.* New York: McGraw-Hill.

Nadel, S. F. (1942), *A black Byzantium.* London: Oxford University Press.

Naroll, Raoul (1967), Imperial cycles and world order. *Papers* Peace Research Society International, Vol. V.

Naroll, Raoul and Divale, W. T. (1976), 'Natural selection in cultural evolution: warfare vs. peaceful diffusion', in: *American Ethnologist* 3, 1, 97–129.

Netting, Robert McC. (1969), 'Ecosystems in process; A comparative study of change in two West African societies', in: *Ecological essays* ed. by David Damas, Natural Museum of Canada Bulletin 230. Ottawa: Natural Museum of Canada.

— (1972), 'Sacred power and centralization: aspects of political adaptation in Africa', in: *Population growth: anthropological implications,* 214–244, ed. by Brian Spooner. Cambridge: MIT Press.

Otterbein, Keith (1970) *The evolution of warfare.* New Haven: HRAF Press.

Polanyi, Karl (1957), *Trade and markets in the early empires.* Glencoe Ill.: Free Press.

— (1966), *Dahomey and the slave trade.* Seattle: University of Washington Press.

Salzman, P. C. (1971), 'Adaptation and political organization in Iranian Baluchistan', in: *Ethnology* 10, 4, 433–444.

Service, Elman R. (1975), *Origins of the state and civilization.* New York: Norton.

Smith, H. F. C. (1971), 'The early states of the central Sudan', in: *History of West Africa,* ed. by J. F. A. Ajayi and M. Crowder, Vol. I: 78–119.

Smith, M. G. (1960), *Government in Zazzau.* London: Oxford University Press.

Smith, Philip E. L. and Young, T. Cuyler (1972), 'The evolution of early agriculture in greater Mesopotamia: a trial formulation', in: *Population growth: anthropological implications.* Cambridge: MIT Press.

Southall, Aidan (1956), *Alur society*. Cambridge: Heffer.
Spencer, Herbert (1897), *Principles of sociology*. New York: Appleton-Century-Croft.
Spooner, Brian (1969), 'Politics, kinship and ecology in southeast Persia', in: *Ethnology* 8, 2, 139–152.
Steward, Julian (1949), 'Cultural causality and law: a trial formulation of the development of early civilizations', in: *American Anthropologist* 51 (1): 1–27.
Strathern, Andrew (1972), *One father, one blood: descent and group structure among the Melpa people*. London: Tavistock.
Street, John (1969), 'An evaluation of the concept of carrying capacity', in: *Professional Geographer* 21: 1–4.
Struever, Stuart (1968), 'Woodland subsistence-settlement systems in the lower Illinois valley', in: *New perspectives in archaeology*, ed. by S. Binford and L. Binford. Chicago: Aldine.
Thurnwald, Richard. (1935), *Die menschliche Gesellschaft*. Vol. 4 (the state). Berlin-Leipzig: De Gruyler.
Vansina, Jan M. (1966), *Kingdoms of the savannah*. Madison: University of Wisconsin Press.
— (1970), 'Cultures through time', in: *A handbook of method in cultural anthropology*, ed. by R. Naroll and R. Cohen. New York: Natural History Press, 165–182.
Vayda, A. P. (1968), 'Hypotheses about function of war', in: *War: the anthropology of armed conflict*, ed. by M. H. Fried, Marvin Harris and F. R. Murphy. New York: Natural History Press, 85–91.
Wittfogel, Karl A. (1957), *Oriental despotism*. New Haven: Yale University Press.
Woodbury, R. B. (1961), ' A reappraisal of Hohokam irrigation', in: *American Anthropologist* 63, 3: 550–560.
Wright, Henry T. and Johnson, Gregory (1975), 'Population, exchange, and early state formation in southwestern Iran', in: *American Anthropologist* 77: 267–289.

3 Some Theoretical Problems of the Study of the Early State

ANATOLII M. KHAZANOV

The concept of the early state and its social equivalent the early-class type of society has recently become fairly widespread. But up to now it is still not thoroughly understood, and there are still many vague and uncertain points about the problem of the early state. Considering the extremely limited space available in an article, the main objective of the present one will be only to formulate some of the more important questions in connection with the comparative, theoretical study of early states. Only in some cases shall I try to delineate the possible answer to these. Many other important questions will not even be brought up.

1. THE EARLY STATE—WHAT IS IT?

Of course, any pre-industrial state is 'early' in comparison with modern states. Hence, in my view, a more closely defined and restricted use of the term is desirable. The early state, then, is more correctly speaking the earliest and truly pristine type of state, the immediate successor to the disintegrating primitive society.[1] Early states marked a new stage in the historical development of mankind, and constituted the first link in the longer or shorter chain of statehood continuity in one region or another. In this respect we can consider early states as distinctive not only from modern states, but also from the ancient states (e.g., the Greco-Roman states of antiquity), where the latter marked the next, higher stage of development.

But if the starting point of the early state can be determined with comparative ease—though even here this is easier in theory than in practice—the definition of its terminal point is a much more difficult task. The only possible way to go about this is by isolating a number of peculiarities or distinctive features of, and processes associated with, the early state; in proportion as these features and processes were discarded, the states in question were becoming more developed, i.e., ceasing to be 'early'.

In order to be able to define these peculiarities and processes it is well worth looking briefly at the early states at the very moment of their birth. At that particular moment they represented a rather unsteady kind of polity, preserving many characteristics from a previous developmental phase and with a complex and unstable social structure and different kinds of relation of dependence, no single one of which definitely or irreversibly predominated over the other, but with an advancing civilization.

Perhaps these are the most common, or possibly even the universal characteristics of the early state. And evidently the basic tendencies associated with the development of such states were the effort to discard their primitive inheritance on the point of social and political structures, the strengthening and institutionalization of their governmental structure, the stabilization of the social composition of the society, the crystallization of specific types of relation of dependence, of which one might finally emerge as the leading one, and the stimulation of the development of civilization.

Only after these processes had completed themselves did the early states cease to be 'early'. But the demarcation of the actual borderline dividing the early state from the 'non-early' one in a given period or place is the task of the researcher investigating concrete examples of these types of state.

2. IS THE EARLY STATE UNIVERSAL?

The question here is whether every newly developing state will always take the form of the early one. This may seem a pointless question, since at first glance the universality of the early state seems to be predetermined by its aspect of primacy. Indeed, one may well debate about when the phase of the early state ended in Egypt, ancient Mesopotamia, or China, but the pristine states which emerged in these regions were unquestionably early ones.

Nevertheless, it is worth distinguishing briefly between the different variants of the state foundation, because the variations frequently pertain not only to internal development, but also to the external influences to which the relevant states were open. In this connection it is necessary to distinguish between pristine states and secondary states.

Not only pristine states were early ones, but also those created under the influence of already existing ones, as a form of response to the offered challenge by these, especially where the former preserved their own characteristics, were early states. For example, one may easily observe an obvious and direct connection between the time of formation of the state in one or another region of the ancient Orient and its proximity to already emerged states. But all of the states which were formed one after another there—Akkad, Elam, Mari, Assur, Mana, Urartu, Media, Persia and others—were early states for a longer or shorter period, either till their downfall, or, sometimes, until the processes of their own internal development, accelerated by external influences, were sufficiently realized.

Unquestionably, early states also came about as a result of conquering of already existing states, even such well-developed states as the Roman Empire or China, by the barbarians (i.e., tribes and peoples belonging to the pre-state level, namely that of chiefdoms or stratified societies). Time was needed to reorganize the socio-economic structure of these barbarians, or to synthesize the two systems, if such synthesis resulted in a new type altogether.

Yet another case was that of the conquest of the more developed state by the early one and the subsequent integration of their respective socio-economic structures (e.g., the Arab conquests under the first caliphs, or the Mongolian conquest of Iran). In this specific case the early states remained 'early' only for a short time, during which the conqueror's structures were not yet totally transformed. These latter three types may be designated as *secondary* early states.

Nonetheless, the states founded as a consequence of the expansion or colonial policies of more developed states—which hence represented a kind of secondary developed states—were definitely not early ones, even at the very time of their origin (e.g., Livonia in the Middle Ages, or the U.S.A.). Nor are the states created in the post-colonial period early. Their societies witnessed the disintegration of traditional structures during the preceding colonial period (e.g. Nauru or even Papua New Guinea), or they are on the whole a product of colonialism (e.g., Mauritius and Guyana).

Thus, it cannot be said that any state which comes into being will necessarily take the form of the early one, this being dependent on the different ways in which it may come about and develop.

At the same time it can be assumed that many specific traits and characteristics of every early state were conditioned not only by particular internal but also by external circumstances surrounding its origin. This problem has not yet been sufficiently investigated even on the regional level, however.

3. THE LEVEL OF ECONOMIC AND TECHNOLOGICAL DEVELOPMENT

Even if it cannot be said that every emerging state will inevitably take the form of the early state, we may still consider the latter as representing a necessary stage of a universal development in the sense intended by Carneiro (1973: 97–100). That is why we would do well to query whether there ever was such a thing as a single, distinctive level of economic and technological evolution marking this type of state.

Obviously, the existence of a productive economy is always a major precondition. Hunters, fishermen and food-gatherers could never and nowhere found states of their own. Even stratified societies, like those of the Indians of the northwest coast of North America, were rare exceptions among them.

Within the framework of a productive economy, however, any other limitations are evidently non-existent. The early states of Oceania were essentially still at the stage of the Stone Age; those of the ancient Near East emerged during the Chalcolithic period; of the Balkan Peninsula in the Bronze Age; and of the rest of Europe and Subsaharan Africa only in the Iron Age. The systems of production in the early states also varied widely, ranging from swidden agriculture to pastoral nomadism. The suggestion that irrigation was the primary condition of the emergence of pristine early states has been refuted by archaeological evidence from Mesoamerica, China and other regions.

It seems more fruitful to consider the problem of the economic and technological level of early states from another point of view. This level had to be sufficiently high to provide a certain minimum surplus for the social division of labor and other phenomena connected with the origin of the state to be possible. This minimum surplus could be ensured within different systems of production and technological development, however, depending on local conditions.

There was even less question of a uniform economic and technological level upon attainment to which the early state would inevitably give way to a more advanced type of state. In all likelihood there was no close link between the level of economic and technological development and socio-political structures, at least in the pre-industrial era. The fairly advanced states of antiquity gave way to the early states of early medieval Europe. But all attempts to prove any considerable economic and technological difference between them have failed (Gurevich 1971: 158–159).

It is further interesting to find out what kind and degree of economic development the early states had undergone. It seems that they made more rapid technological advances in handicraft production than in agriculture or animal husbandry. As a matter of fact, one cannot even say with certainty that the total output and, all the more so, the per capita output increased substantially after the early state came into being. Furthermore, it should be taken into consideration that if such an increase still did take place, it was achieved through expansion of production itself, that is to say, through improved cooperation (e.g., in irrigation) and/or organization, rather than as a result of technological advances (e.g., improvement of agricultural implements) (Childe 1952: 10; Steward 1955: 200, 207). However, this may hold more or less true not only for early states but also for many other kinds right up to modern times.

Yet another question arises in connection with this problem, namely, whether there were any specific environmental factors and productive systems (or economic systems) that were more conducive to the further development of early states than others. Obviously, this question can be answered in the affirmative. For example, it will be impossible for states which are based on pastoral nomadism, unlike those based on plow agriculture, to advance beyond the early state level (Khazanov 1975: 251 ff.). Another possibility worth considering is that in some early states irrigation was in certain respects not only a factor stimulating advancement, but also stagnation.

In other words, there are limits to the development of any given society within the framework of one and the same productive system. Having reached these, the possibilities of further development become inversely proportional to environmental dependence.

4. SOME QUESTIONS CONCERNING THE FORMATION OF EARLY STATES

These questions form part of a general theory of the emergence of the state. In connection with early states I would like merely to point out certain aspects deserving considerable further attention.

The formation of the state is inseparably linked with the processes of social stratification and the origin of classes which took place in disintegrating primitive societies. The principal feature or essential corollary of these processes was the gradual rise of a ruling stratum which controlled production and the distributive mechanisms of the society in question.

The conditions sine qua non for this were the development of a regular surplus and conditions for its realization and distribution, which were met through the social division of labor and exchange in the broadest sense (including reciprocity and redistribution).

A regular surplus, rare exceptions aside, developed as a by-product of the neolithic revolution. But the important point to note is that not only the pace of economic and social development but also specific characteristics of social differentiation in different societies were determined by the simultaneous operations of a whole set of different factors, including social, historical, environmental, economic, technological, demographic, and other circumstances. That is why there was no clear-cut and direct correlation between even the productive capacity of a given society and its advancement along the path of social stratification.

Carneiro (1970) has rightly criticized the 'automatic theory' of the origin of the state, according to which the development of agriculture automatically brought about a surplus of food and subsequently, after some intermediate stages, the birth of the state itself. He emphasized the fact that agriculture did not always necessarily produce a surplus. A surplus itself, moreover, need not always automatically lead to the formation of the state. For example, a society might stagnate on the chiefdom level, or even a lower one.

There was, by no means, absolute determinism in the processes leading to the formation of social classes. They possessed a certain reversibility depending on different internal and/or external factors. They could be speeded up, slowed down or interrupted, remain static or even cease, and be revived again, depending on various local conditions. The preconditions for the emergence of social classes were the same for all spontaneously developing societies, but its concrete mechanisms varied.

The conditions for social and economic inequality and exploitation, originally represented by primitive, insufficiently differentiated forms, arose after it became possible for the output to be divided into essential supplies and a surplus. At the same time, the necessary conditions arose for the divorce of managerial and administrative functions from productive ones. This was one of the most important results of the social division of labor, reflected in the growing complexity of social structures and productive processes.

Two stages of disintegration of primitive societies—represented by rank societies and stratified societies respectively—are now often distinguished by scholars (Fried 1960: 716–722). This approach does justice to the gradualness of the rise of a ruling stratum. But should we always divide this process into only two stages, or may they possibly be more or less numerous? And what is more, should we attach universal importance to each of these stages? As far as I can see, this problem remains as yet unsolved.

In general two trends can be distinguished in the process of class formation. The first of these is connected with the control and coordination of political and economic activities by the ruling stratum, which among other effects resulted in the latter gaining access to the total volume of surplus products and the appropriation of this surplus from its producers. The second depended on the acquisition of a surplus by the direct exploitation of the producers (in particular slaves), which was more or less derived from the means of production.

Judging from the Near Eastern, African, American and even the Oceanic evidence, the first trend was the basic one in the formation of early states. We should next inquire when exactly the second trend might become dominant. It may well be that the latter manifested itself later than the former. For example, it is now clear that the Mediterranean states of antiquity, which were marked by slave ownership on a vast scale, were by no means the truly pristine states of that region. They had been preceded by early states based on different systems of dependence and exploitation.

Much attention has been given recently to the environmental and ecological circumstances which favoured the rise of a ruling stratum and the emergence of the state.

In particular, some scholars concentrating on this problem are of the opinion that irrigation and the necessity of flood control were the decisive factors in the emergence of all truly pristine states, i.e. those states which developed spontaneously. In this case irrigation is suggested to be not a productive or economic precondition for state formation, but an organizational and political one.

This representation seems rather exaggerated, however. The earliest states did, in fact, come into being in irrigation areas, but the origin of the irrigation schemes here preceded that of the state. In other regions early states, including the pristine ones, were far from always connected with this type of agriculture at all.

The conquest theory of the origin of the state in all its variations and modifications likewise is unable to convince us. Conquest could mark the origin of early states, could stimulate this, and, finally, could determine specific local variations. But the relevant internal conditions, i.e., a sufficient level of development of both conquerors and conquered, also had to be present for this.

One should look for the determinant of specific forms of political organization—i.e., of the later states—in the governmental structure of the relevant pre-state societies, which underwent a certain degree of transformation and were supplemented by newly risen institutions. What determined the specific form of this kind of organization in its formative period? Certainly, this always appears to be again a combination of a great many different factors, varying according to local conditions. Their comprehensive analysis must remain a task for future scholars, however.

For example, it is worth noting that the gradual rise of a ruling stratum engaging in managerial–bureaucratic activities was accompanied by a differentiation of the governmental structure and its division into several sub-structures. The principal ones among these were the administrative–managerial, religious–ideological and military sub-structures. Although this division sometimes was not so much personal as functional, nevertheless in many societies of the state-formation level one can distinguish three more or less separate occupational groups in this stratum, viz. the 'managers', 'priests' and 'military leaders'. The influence and authority of these groups during this transitional period varied with different societies and were perhaps of some importance for the shape of the relevant future states.

In any case, the public authorities during the period of transition to a state society were growing more and more independent of the commoners. The ruling stratum was concentrating more and more of the power extracted from the rest of society in its hands. And eventually this resulted in the origin of the state.

5. THE CONTINUITY WITH THE PRE-STATE SOCIETY

Already, on account of their nature, the pristine early states possessed a number of traits inherited from the preceding pre-state phase. This continuity can be traced in the social composition of the societies in question, in their respective forms of dependence and exploitation, in the continued importance of kinship ties in the social life, in the types of local structure and institution as well as the latter's functioning, and so on. Quite possibly, one may posit as a general rule that many traditional systems, after the foundation of the early state, underwent certain modifications in accordance with the new conditions rather than collapsing or being abolished.

Perhaps two kinds of continuity should be distinguished here. The first is of a local and regional character and connected with the specific characteristics of the societies in question. The second involves the more general trends of historical development. A specific form of division of labor in governmental structures, special types of family and community, variations in the importance of kinship ties in social and government structures, or the more or less active role played by the state itself in the direct appropriation of surplus products provide examples of locally conditioned continuity observable in actually existing early states. But the existence of a community per se, the continued importance of kinship ties, or the prevalence of free commoner strata which were observable in most, if not all, early states provide significant examples of the second kind. The task of future investigations will have to be to define in detail the two kinds of continuity, to determine their concrete limits, and to isolate the factors conditioning them.

6. THE SOCIAL STRUCTURE OF THE EARLY STATE

Local variations notwithstanding, there are two main features characterizing the social structure of early states, viz. plurality of social strata and instability, both vertical and horizontal. These features are distinguishable at all levels of social structure. Every society possesses these distinctive features to a greater or lesser extent, however; it still being problematic whether there is any marked difference between the early state and other pre-industrial types of state. But we should also observe that in the early state class formation had not reached its completion, class structures had not yet become stabilized, and social, economic, legal, and other gradations did not mutually coincide. Appointment vs. heredity—that was the essential opposition characterizing early states as well as, incidentally, many later kinds of state.

For example, one may distinguish such occupational groups in the composition of the ruling class as 'managers', 'priests', and 'military leaders'. The 'managers' can further be provisionally divided into an 'aristocracy' and a 'bureaucracy'. Of course, such a functional division is not a unique feature of the early state, nor is it a monopoly of the early state. But the social structure of precisely the early state was the most heterogeneous, and the different groups of its ruling class were the most isolated the one from the other, and, as a result, not infrequently struggled for power. Besides, it must be taken into account that such a functional division in the early state was often supplemented by ethnic, kinship, and other forms of division.

At the same time a comparatively numerous stratum (or strata) of economically still-independent commoners enjoying personal freedom and which would be considered as a leftover from previous times existed in early states. But this stratum was eroded from above and more especially from below, and the commoners' rights were gradually restricted and reduced. Some of the commoners moved upwards to join the ruling class, but many more of them descended to the dependent strata, or perhaps even the entire commoner stratum itself grew more and more into a dependent stratum. The different categories or strata of dependent people with varying degrees of restriction of freedom made up the bottom of the social structure of all early states. The composition of these strata often became even more complex as a result of the absorption of conquered groups. The formation of the dependent class or classes had likewise not yet reached completion in the early state.

There is yet another question that deserves special consideration. To what extent can we speak of an open character (or, conversely, a closed character) of the principal strata and classes in early states? Were there any important differences in vertical social mobility with more developed states of the pre-industrial era? There is the interesting hypothesis put forward by Claessen (1975: 46) that the more developed the state organization and the greater the social complexity the greater will be the vertical social mobility. But when dealing with this problem one should, perhaps, also pay attention to other variables such as the role of wars and conquests, the importance of the genealogical principle in the functioning of the society in question, the specific characteristics of the social structure (e.g., the existence of castes, which is putting obstacles in the way of vertical mobility even in modern India), and so on. The horizontal corporate ties seem to me especially important in this connection. It is true that even in medieval Western Europe, where they were fairly developed, the rate of vertical mobility, as Bloch (1936) and other scientists (e.g., Perroy 1961) have demonstrated was quite high. But in Byzantium, where these ties were weak, vertical mobility was still greater (Kazhdan 1968: 49ff.).

However, there was another trend observable in early states which opposed vertical mobility, namely, the tendency towards stabilization of the composition of the principal strata and classes. It was connected with horizontal mobility, viz. the gradual elimination of the divisions between different groups and strata located close to each other on the scale of social gradations. But whether this tendency reached any degree of completion in the early state still remains an unsolved question.

7. FORMS OF DEPENDENCE AND EXPLOITATION

It is impossible to define any early state simply as an 'early slave-owning' or 'early feudal' or any similar such state if one views it not retrospectively but, rather, statically. It is precisely in the early state that different forms of dependence and exploitation exists side by side, without the distinct and irreversible prevalence of any one of these. Such types of relation and institution as slavery, bondage, clientèle, tributary, compulsory labor, different kinds of taxation, etc., can all be observed among them. Most, if not all, forms of dependence and exploitation in the early states went back to the preceding pre-state phase, however. Moreover, some of them, for example, the tributary relation, may be considered as sufficiently undifferentiated to imply various possibilities of exploitation.

But one characteristic of most, if not all, early states deserves special attention because it may well turn out to be one of their distinctive features. I am referring here to the significant role played by the early state itself in the direct exploitation of the producers through taxation, compulsory labor and other obligations. This characteristic is commonly considered as peculiar to so-called 'Asiatic societies'. But all early states possessed at least some characteristics relating them to these latter. In many respects the early states were the direct predecessors of 'Asiatic societies', being only less developed. In the course of their further development one particular form of dependence and exploitation would as a rule become dominant. Accordingly, the society ceased to be an early class society and the state, as it became more developed, ceased to be an 'early state'. In other words, France under the Capetians was a feudal and not an early state. The kingdom of Clovis, on the other hand, was an early state, in particular because any feudal elements it possessed were potential rather than actual, being only one of several possible tendencies of development.

8.   FORMS OF POLITICAL ORGANIZATION

According to the fairly popular belief, despotism was the most widespread form of political organization in early states (Wittfogel 1957). In that case despotism is often understood in the sense of absolute and unrestricted power, at any rate in theory. Perhaps, with reference to early states, one may put special stress on the unlimited right of disposession of public resources, including human, and on the direct control of the production processses.

But in point of fact this problem is not so simple. There were many early states whose governments cannot be qualified as despotic ones. For example, the states founded by pastoral nomads had all the characteristics of early states. But the governments of such nomadic states did not interfere directly in production, while supreme power was considered as belonging to the whole of the ruling clan. From this stemmed the institution of 'appanage' (or, to use the Turko-Mongolian term, 'ulus') or the principle of power-sharing, whereby every member of the ruling clan was entitled to administer a certain nomadic group as well as part of the conquered agricultural area. Another example is provided by early-medieval Western Europe, which also lacked despotism. Even in ancient Mesopotamia, which seems in some respects to represent a classic example of despotism, absolute royal power only arose under the Dynasty of Akkad and reached full development under the Third Dynasty of Ur. The previous city states are defined with some reservations by specialists even as monarchies (D'iakonoff 1959: 145–147).

That is why the assumption that despotism was the first and earliest form of state power is questionable. Moreover, the beginnings of despotism may perhaps in some cases be regarded as a borderline case, dividing early states from more developed ones.

I would like to stress above all, however, that there was no direct connection between early states and despotism. It may well be that development towards despotism was the most widespread tendency in the early states, but it was not the only one. In my view, European history, both ancient and medieval, in general testifies this clearly enough. It is most important to determine the factors promoting the emergence of despotism. These factors are not yet clearly understood in their essence.

Obviously, irrigation in particular and public works in general cannot provide the sole explanation. I would advance the hypothesis that the emergence of despotism was conditioned by deeper and broader processes connected with the requirements and difficulties of social integration,[2] with certain peculiarities of particular social and political structures, and also with specific processes of the formation of the early state.

Perhaps the specific forms of political organization of both early states and pre-state polities depended in many respects also on the participation of different groups of the ruling strata in government and the historical background of these. Let us consider a number of variants as examples.

The first variant is characterized by lack of differentiation of governmental functions at the top level. The paramount chief, later the king, was usually simultaneously principal priest and military leader. Differentiation, total or partial, of these functions seemed to occur on the lower levels. As a rule the priesthood was not a hierarchical, closed corporate group. Nor was there a distinct military group, isolated from the bulk of the population. It is true that warfare could favor an improvement in the social positions of certain individuals and their incorporation into the ruling stratum or class. But in my view, Carneiro (1970) exaggerates in supposing that warriors, along with the ruler and his kinsmen, always formed the nucleus of any upper class.

The primacy of the traditional kinship system and its influence on the fulfilment of managerial governmental functions are most typical of the variant under consideration. Many African, and especially Polynesian, societies may be regarded as concrete examples of it.

The characteristic feature of the second variant consists in the especially strong position of the priesthood, organized as a hierarchical corporation and clearly distinguished from other ruling groups. But here also government functions at the top level were not completely differentiated. The society was ruled by a paramount chief-cum-priest, later the king–priest, emphasis being placed on the latter's sacred and even divine origin. Sometimes priests would even pretend to the supreme power, although theocratic forms of government were rather rare.

Apparently, the priesthood grew powerful and influential as soon as it came to regulate the production cycle, and/or to control basic communal resources or if the temporal aristocracy was unable to keep the people united.

The third variant is represented by the gradual rise of a military aristocracy that had been ousting aside the traditional aristocracy from power. The factors which favored the increasing influence of such military groups are quite obvious. These were above all the growing importance of warfare in the life of the society and, accordingly, the growing importance of military organization. As a result, military occupation grew into a profession and such a new institute as the military corporation (bodyguards) came into being. This contributed to the concentration of power appropriated from traditional institutions in the hands of military leaders. And so the descendants of military leaders developed into true monarchs and despots no more seldom, if not more often, than the descendants of paramount chiefs.

Thus the political organization of early states could develop along different lines and assume different forms.

9. EARLY STATES AND CIVILIZATION

From the beginning of the eighteenth century many scholars have identified the state with a specific civilization. But strictly speaking this identification is not quite correct. Civilization is a broader concept than the state. Aside from the latter it also embraces a written language—a 'new instrument for the transmission of human experience and the accumulation of knowledge' (Childe 1957: 37), and the existence of towns—'a community that comprises a substantial proportion of professional rulers, officials, clergy, artisans who. . . . live on the surplus' (*ibid*). The obvious fact is that the contemporary state, like any more or less developed state of the past, presupposes a civilization. Aristoteles' Ζῷον Πολιτιχόν stands first and foremost for a person living in a Greek town, i.e., city-state.

But did all early states reach the level of civilization? This question is not as self-evident as one may imagine; it at any rate deserves discussion.

It is true that the earliest states of Mesopotamia already possessed a written language and towns. Many early states of Africa, America, and Oceania, or those of the nomads of the Eurasian steppes, on the other hand, did not have a written language at the moment of their emergence. And many of them lacked towns; unless ruler's headquarters could be considered as such. In principle, the primitive or early state was not inconceivable without a written language and towns.

Therefore the assertion is quite justified that the development of civilizations took place, or, more correctly, proceeded and was finally completed, precisely in early states.

This fact is not surprising. I have stated above that there was diversification and differentiation of government structures in early states. The same can be observed as regards their settlement systems and communications (written language).

10. THE TYPOLOGY OF THE EARLY STATE

The creation of a typology in itself—typology for the sake of typology—is senseless. The point of view from which it is approached is all important.

The classifications of early states may vary widely, depending on what principles of classification—territorial, temporal (e.g., ancient vs. medieval early states), synchronous, diachronous (one such classification distinguishing between inchoate, typical and transitional early states being proposed by the editors of this volume), or even retrospective, according to what development potentials were later realized— are used. The last of these is inadmissible in anthropology, because this science usually lacks the diachronous approach and, moreover, because the spontaneous development of the societies studied by it was interrupted in modern times. In historiography, on the other hand, this principle of classification is quite acceptable.

Synchronous classifications themselves may vary, furthermore, depending on similarities or differences in systems of technology and production, governmental structures, and so on.

11. THE COURSE OF DEVELOPMENT OF EARLY STATES

Thus all early states have some characteristics in common. These are connected first and foremost with their stage of development and their heritage from previous stages of development. At the same time there is not, nor ever was, any typological unity among them.

The further development of the early states at the same time implied their further divergence. Classes and estates interlinked by specific forms of dependence and exploitation took form within their framework. Correspondingly, the early states became 'Asiatic', slave-owning, feudal or otherwise; likewise with different forms of political organization, ranging from despotic, constitutional and absolute monarchical, tyrannical and oligarchic to democratic rule. On the other hand, not one developed state could ever take the form of what is designated by Malinowski and Krader as the 'tribal state' and 'tribal consanguinal state' for instance (Krader 1968: 4).

But the factors determining the actual course of the further development of the early states, and what is more the specific form each took in the course of this process, still remain virtually uninvestigated. The only fact that seems more or less certain is that of the impossibility of a single universal explanation. Obviously, we must always take into account the joint operation of a whole set of determining factors, both internal and external. Quite a different matter is that, of these factors, some might be more important than others.

FOOTNOTES

[1] All societies of the pre-state level are provisionally designated as primitive by the author, although the societies in question varied markedly in complexity and degree of development.

[2] Marx remarked that a despot personified the social unity.

REFERENCES

Bloch, Maurice (1936), 'Sur le passé de la noblesse francaise', in: *Annales d'Histoire économique et sociale*, no. 40.
Carneiro, Robert L. (1970), 'A theory of the origin of the state', *Science*, 169.
— (1973), 'The four faces of evolution', in: *Handbook of social and cultural anthropology*, ed. by John J. Honigmann, Chicago: Rand McNally
Childe, V. Gordon (1952), 'The birth of civilization', in: *Past and present* no. 1.
— (1957), 'Civilization, cities and towns', in: *Antiquity* no. 121.
Claessen, Henri J. M. (1975), 'From rags to riches and the reverse—Rule and reality of vertical social mobility in six states' in: *Rule and reality*. Essais in Honour of André J. F. Köbben, ed. by Peter Kloos and Klaas W. van der Veen. Amsterdam: A.S.C.
D'iakonov, I. M. (1959), *Obschestvennyi i gosudarstvennyi stroi drevnego Dvurech'ia* [Social and governmental organization of ancient Mesopotamia]. Moscow: Nauka.

Fried, Morton H. (1960), 'On the evolution of social stratification and the state', in: *Culture in history*. Essays in Honor of Paul Radin, ed. by Stanley Diamond. New York: Columbia University Press.

Gurevich, A. J. (1971), *Genezis feodalizma v Zapadnoi Evrope*. [Genesis of feudalism in western Europe.] Moscow: Nauka.

Kazhdan, A. P. (1968), *Vizantiiskaia kul'tura (X-XII V)*. [Byzantine Culture in the 10th-12th centuries.] Moscow: Nauka.

Khazanov, A. M. (1975), *Sotsial'naia istorija skifov. Osnovnyea problemii razvitiia drevnikh kochevnikov evraziiskikh stepei*. [Social history of the Scythians. Main problems of development among the ancient pastoral nomads of the Eurasian steppes.] Moscow: Nauka.

Krader, Lawrence (1968), *Formation of the state*. Englewood Cliffs: Prentice Hall.

Perroy, E. (1961), 'Social mobility among the French noblesse in the later Middle Ages', in: *Past and Present* no. 21.

Steward, Julian (1955), *Theory of culture change*. Urbana: University of Illinois Press.

Wittfogel, Karl A. (1957), *Oriental despotism*. New Haven: Yale University Press.

4   The Origin of the State Among the Nomads of Asia

LAWRENCE KRADER

1. THEORY OF THE STATE IN GENERAL

1.1. The state is the product of that society which is divided into two classes of people; a class composed of those directly engaged in social production, and a class of those who are not so directly engaged. The social product is conformably divided into two parts; a part which is applied to the reproduction of the direct producers as a social class, and a surplus which is appropriated to the maintenance of the class of those whose relation to production in the society is other than direct. The direct producers in the society do labor, work and toil both for themselves and for these others, whose relation to social production is either indirect or non-existent; it is these others that the social surplus adverts. The state is the organization of society for the regulation of the relations both within and between the social classes. Yet the relations of the two social classes to the state differ; it is in the interest of that class in the society which appropriates the social surplus produced that the agencies of the state are active. The class-divided society is composed of the rulers, who have appropriated the social surplus, and the ruled, who are the direct producers in the society.[1]

1.2. The social class of the direct producers has no immediate interest in the formation of the state. On the contrary, as we shall see, the social class maintained a number of archaic collective institutions, which had been evolved long before the formation of the state; these institutions, as gentes, sibs, clans, kin village communities, continued to exist among them long after the state was formed as the overarching power in the society. These institutions of the collectivity had long maintained the functions of keeping the peace, resolving conflicts both within and between the clans and villages, etc., attacking and defending in war, and continued to do so after the formation of the state. The agencies of the state, when established, took over these same functions of the administration of justice, conduct of war and diplomacy; at this point the interests of the social classes were divided. The archaic collective institutions had formerly resolved conflicts or maintained the peace internally in the interest of the social whole, in this case the whole community, clan or tribe. The agencies of the state now defended, warred, both in the interest of the state and that of the social whole. It is a double interest, conflicting internally within itself; on the one side, it is the interest of the state as the representative of the social class in whose interest it is organized, on the other, the interest of the social whole.

1.3. The state is formed by and out of the relations of these classes in society to one another and to the social whole: it is formed as the society is divided and internally opposed. It is not formed by the ruling class, for that class has to be established in the first place by the process of social division in order to fulfil its ruling function. It would be an error to take the interest of the ruling class to be the process of formation of the state itself, for that class did not form the state in its own interest. On the contrary, the interest of the ruling class emerged out of the formation of the ruling class. The two are mutually supportive, and reinforce each other; they are not identical. To hold that the ruling class formed the state in its own interest would be a teleological interpretation of history.

1.4. It is sometimes held that the state is identical with the society in which it is found, that the state is composed directly of people. This usage merely multiplies terms without necessity. The state is neither identical with human society in general nor with any particular society. It is not identical with a class-divided society. The state is the organization of a particular kind of society, which is a class-divided society. The state is, in its abstract meaning, the principle of organization of that society; concretely, it is the organization itself. We will consider its further concretion below.

1.4.1. Human societies have been classified according to habitat, whether tropical, desert, temperate or polar; they have been classified according to their mythologies, whether solar or lunar; they have been classified as matriarchal or patriarchal. Here one principle will be applied: human societies are of two types, on the one hand they are non-divided, forming an undifferentiated whole; on the other they are divided into classes according to the relations of the members of the society to social production, to the surrounding nature and to the technology of the society. The non-divided, undifferentiated society is primitive society, the divided society is civilized society, or civil society, it is the society with the state, or political society. Primitive society is founded on primitive economy, primitive relation to nature and technology, whose principle is that the unit of production coincides with the unit of consumption; the relations of production are such that each works for the other, and this work relation is reciprocated by the other. Civil society is founded on the division and opposition between the social classes, whereby one of these classes labors and works in society and on the natural surroundings, both for its own maintenance and for its reproduction as a class; at the same time it labors and works for another social class, which labor and work is not returned. The latter is the principle of non-reciprocity; it is the principle of political as opposed to primitive economy; it is that on which the state is founded, and is presupposed by the latter.

1.4.2. The society with the state is a small part of the number of societies of the human kind, and covers an extremely small time period of the entire history of humanity. It is a recent phenomenon, perhaps no more than 5,000 years old, but has engulfed virtually the entirety of the human kind during the few millennia since its inception. It has come to dominate the history of mankind because no power on earth is comparable to it. There have been those in the past, such as Eduard Meyer or Wilhelm Koppers, and in the present, such as E. A. Hoebel, who would make the state identical with human society as a whole.[2] Not only is this the multiplication of terms without necessity, as in the preceding case; it further confuses the issue of government versus the state. The element of self-government may be found in any human society, however informal that government may be. The mode of government of the Eskimos, Pygmies, Andaman Islanders, Tierra del Fuegians, is informal, discontinuous, detectable with difficulty, and scarcely vested, but it is government, and as such is concerned with the resolution of conflict, maintenance of internal and external peace of the society and the conduct of war.[3]

1.5 In the society with the state the distinction between authority and power is made. Power lies with the organization of society that has centralized its internal means of regulation and control; authority lies with the people as a whole. (This distinction was affirmed by Cicero, in ancient Rome.) The centralization of the power in turn is negated in civil society. On the one hand, it is there negated by the division and opposition between the social classes that make it up; an external negation. On the other hand, it is internally negated by the opposing interests of the individuals within the ruling class who make it up. These latter individuals have in common their private interests as a class, which is their class interest, and the individuals are class-individuals. These class interests come into conflict with each other. The means of social regulation by the state are directed to the overcoming of the oppositions between the social classes as they are to the overcoming of the oppositions between the individual interests within the ruling class. Social organization is thus made into political regulation and control of the society in this case; it is above all regulation and control through the political economy. The opposing interests between and within the classes that make up the society of the political economy are the subject of political regulation and control.

1.6. The state is the formal organization of the society of political economy; the informal elements of the organization of the human being and human society fall outside its purview. The human individual exists only as a formal being in relation to the state; the human individual extrudes the formal being, as the legal person, civil person, persona civilis or moralis, Rechtsperson, etc., to meet the relation required of and to the state. The human society extrudes the formal side of its organization as the state to define and relate to the legal or civil personality of the individual human being.

1.6.1. The state is the formal organization of class composed and class opposed human society. On the one side, we have seen, it is the abstract principle of this formal organization, whether it be the society of the Asiatic mode of production, of the slave or servile modes of production, or that of the modern society of production of capital. On the other side, the state is concretized in particular states, ancient and modern.

2. THE STATE IN NOMADIC SOCIETY

2.1 The nomadic societies of central and middle Asia developed the state, both in its abstract and concrete forms, in the course of their history over the past three millennia. The states of these nomads first appeared during the first millennium prior to the modern era on the margins of the history and territory of the agricultural peoples of China, India, Persia. It is sometimes maintained that the Turks, Mongols and other nomads of inland Asia had not developed the state. That they had developed the state a thousand or more years after the agricultural peoples had done so is clear; that they had developed the state in relation to, and in opposition to the state formation of the agricultural peoples no less so. But this is not to say that the nomads developed no state at all. On the contrary, they developed the state, at first as a marginal and emergent historical phenomenon in Eurasia and in Africa, and later developed it into a fully fledged element of the history of these regions of the world.

2.2. In order to comprehend the place of the nomads in world history, it is first necessary to grasp the division of labor in society between nomads and agricultural peoples, which will be here set forth in the light of the history of east and central Asia. The nomads of central Asia made their historical appearance in the confederation of the Hsien Pi during the latter part of the first millennium before the modern era, in conflicts with the Chinese of the early Ch'in Dynasty. The records from the annals of this early Chinese dynasty mention briefly their relations to the nomads. At a later time, during the course of the first millennium of the present era, the relations were made firm, were deepened and extended between the Chinese on the one side, the Turks, Mongols, Manchu on the other.[4] With the subsequent development of writing among the latter, we have come to have not only the viewpoint of the ruling class of the Chinese but also that of the nomads.

2.3. The inhabitants of the Mongol steppes during the past two millennia have been sometimes Turks, sometimes Mongols. Their main economic basis has been pastoral nomadism. It is sometimes claimed that they also practised agriculture. It is difficult to deny this, but that is not the point. The inhabitants of Mongolia, such as have been already mentioned, were mainly pastoralists, supplementing their subsistence with a minor amount of agriculture, and by exchanging their pastoral (also hunting and gathering) products for the products of their agricultural neighbors. The forces that held the Tatars to their major economic concern, pastoralism, were both internal and external. The internal force was the weight of tradition, or customary practice; the external was the weight of production by their agricultural neighbors and exchanges made with them. The transcontinental network of exchanges held both sets of practices in place.

2.4. Behind and underlying this exchange network lies a vast system of the division of labor in society in Asia, such as is comprehended with difficulty within European history, extending quantitatively and qualitatively beyond European historical experience and categories of history. The nomads of Asia lived and still live in tents, being without fixed abode, breeding domesticated livestock in herds, primarily sheep, goats, cattle (bovine), horses, camels and moving with them from one pasture to the next, according to the season. They exchanged the surplus products of their nomadic life with those of the agricultural peoples, on the one side livestock on the hoof, also the products thereof, wool, peltries, leather, felt, for agricultural products on the other. The Chinese exchanged their products such as rice, tea, cotton, to meet the wants of the nomads. The nomads met the wants of the Chinese, providing sheep flesh for their diet, cavalry for the armies, post horses, ceremonial steeds, transport camels.

2.4.1. In other parts of Eurasia there is a division of labor within the village, or within the producing unit, whether the country, province or the nation as a whole, whereby the exchange of herding for agricultural products is carried through. In northern China and neighboring central Asia, however, there has been a great specialization of social production on either side of the Great Wall of China, whereby the nomadic Turks and Mongols have had a major concern in stockbreeding, and but a minor concern in agriculture, and the Chinese, predominantly agricultural, devoted only a small part of their social labor and land to cattle, camel, sheep or horse-raising. Each side was dependent to this degree on the exchange of the indigenous product for that of the other.

2.4.2. Agricultural production is intensive, pastoral extensive. The herds of the nomads extend over vast areas; agricultural production by comparison is concentrated. In consequence, the same number of people live by pastoral production in a territory which is 100 times greater in extent than that of the agriculturists. The nomadic peoples of Turkestan, in middle and western Asia, have a pattern that is neither as extremely specialized as the pastoralism of Mongolia nor as diversified as the European. The traditional European maintained rural economy was maintained by agricultural and animal husbandry practices generally within the village, from the Iberian Peninsula to the Alps and Russia. The Kazakhs and Uzbeks of middle Asia, traditionally pastoralists, had an appreciable, if limited, amount of agriculture in their winter camps and pastures. These peoples, together with the neighboring Kirgiz, Turkmens, were engaged historically in exchanges of their pastoral product, with their agricultural neighbors, just as were the Mongols. The social division of labor in traditional european practice thus fell within the ethnic groups. In western Asia the social division of labor was maintained between the ethnic groups; in eastern Asia this was developed into a greater extreme of division among the 'ethnies' than in western Asia.

2.5. This vast, continent-wide exchange system in Asia was frequently interrupted; it was defective. The institutions which were engaged in the exchanges were not well or efficiently developed, as contrasted to the world-wide oil, coal, steel, cotton, rice, meat, wool markets of the modern period of the production of capital. The interruptions of the great exchanges produced raids and wars; indeed they led to conquest of either side by the other, thence to conquest dynasties which appear from time to time in Chinese history: the T'o-pa Wei, Chin, Liao, Yuan (Mongol) and Ch'ing (Manchu). Attention has frequently been drawn to the wars of conquest between nomadic Tatars and Chinese. This is an abnormal condition. Customarily, the Chinese and the nomadic Tatars exchanged surplus products with one another, they did so over a period of thousands of years.

2.6. The Turks and Mongols had a class-divided society during the period of our concern. The social class of direct production—the herdsmen and their families—were engaged, in part, in the production of their own maintenance, and, in part, in the production of a surplus. A part of this surplus was adverted for the purpose of exchange. These immediate producers—*arat* in Mongol—at the same time produced a surplus which was applied in part to the maintenance, in traditional times, of their ruling class: the *Khans*, the military leaders, the ministers, courtiers and retinue of the princes or *Khans*. The ancient and modern Tatars were alike divided into two social classes; the class of herdsmen, who were direct producers, in society, and the class of aristocracy, or nobility for whom a social surplus was produced. We have seen that the social surplus was circulated in two directions: to the neighboring agricultural peoples and to the ruling class of the Tatars. The product of the exchange from the agricultural side was, in turn, adverted in part to the common people and in part to the ruling class: silks, jewels and other sumptuary wares went to the use of the ruling class, the aristocracy, while tea, rice, etc. were consumed by both classes in society. Slaves are also found in the old, or traditional Tatar polity, but their economic importance was minor.

2.7. The ancient Hsien Pi had a ruling stratum of princes, or aristocracy. Whether they actually formed a social class or not is difficult to tell from the written record, which has come to us only from the Chinese side. The chiefs of the Hsien Pi may have been the leaders of a confederation of tribes, or, alternatively, they may have been an actual ruling class. If the former then we have a case of an emerging state, a state *in statu nascendi*. If the latter, then the state was already in being. Without stirring up this problem of the early form of the Tatar polity, we note that the state amongst these peoples has undergone its historical development. It is of interest to observe that the state amongst them can be traced from its early beginnings, in the period of its coming into being, through its full historical fluorescence during the past 2000 years among the Turks, Mongols and Manchus (who were originally nomads of a different type from the others).

2.7.1. The historical records of Blue (Kök) Turks, the Orkhon and Yenisey Turks, the Mongols and the Manchus provide good accounts of the formation of particular states among the nomadic peoples. The best known of these, in the European accounts, is that of the Mongol empire of the twelfth–fourteenth centuries. The Mongol society at the beginnings of this period, in the twelfth century, was already a society divided into hereditary classes. The father of Chingis Khan, Yesügei Bagatur, belonged to the lower stratum of the nobility. Mongol society was divided into social classes of rich and poor, Chingis Khan himself in the course of his life passed from the extreme of poverty to that of wealth. During this period, the classes in Mongol society were stabilized and the oppositions between them were carried forward, principally in the same form, with certain modifications to be mentioned below, down to the beginning of the twentieth century.

2.7.2. The Mongol empire in that period was founded on the conquests effected over neighboring parts of eastern, southern and western Asia and eastern Europe by the Mongol state. That state was the product of a class-divided society, the classes of the society having mutually opposed relations to the means of production. On the one side, there were the direct producers in the society, the herding people and their families; these had been organized from time immemorial into kin-villages, lineages and clans. The '*Secret history of the Mongols*', a document compiled in the thirteenth century, traces the genealogy of the emperor, Chingis Khan, over twenty-four generations: the Secret History composes the transition from myth to history, and from the transition of the Mongols prior to the formation of the state. The twenty-four generations of the genealogy are not to be taken in the literal sense, in which five centuries of human history are covered, but indicate that the transition had been made by them from a primitive forest people to the pastoral society of the steppes, with a political economy and the state. At the same time, the social organization of kin-village communities, clans and clan confederations was maintained by them from the pre-historical period through the empire of Chingis Khan, recorded in the Secret History; this organization survived even into the twentieth century, although it was much disrupted latterly. The folk–historical element of the Secret History bears both upon the ancient past and the recent history of the Mongols.

2.8. The social class of the Mongol herding families maintained its traditional communal and consanguineal organization down to the period of state formation among them, and indeed long after the first introduction of the state, after the stabilization of the relations between the social classes, and indeed even into the period of its disruption of traditional economy and society in the early twentieth century. The institutions of collective life survived among the clans of herdsmen. The institution of individualism was developed but in a very minor degree among this class.

2.9. The ruling class of traditional Mongol society, on the contrary, was formed early in the lines of individualism: central to this formation was the figure of the *Khan*, who personified the state. Chingis Khan gathered about himself, in the last decades of the twelfth and the beginning of the thirteenth centuries, warriors who had given up their occupation as herdsmen, had been torn forth from their kin-villages. They swore their allegiance to the *Khan*, served him as soldiers, advisers, ministers, and bore a personal relation to him, which was formalized as the relation of *nöxüt,* 'friends'. Much has been written about the *nöxüt,* retainers of the emperor. It has even been thought that they were feudal lords. That, of course, they were not. They took their oath as the followers of the *Khan,* and stood in a relation that was bound to his person. They maintained a private relation as the intimates of the emperor: each side knew the strengths and weaknesses of the other. This is the subjective aspect of their relation. Objectively, their relation was a formal one: it is a relation to the state personified in the *Khan;* the oath of allegiance was to the personification of the state. The state is the sum of the formal relations of the individual human being, just as it is the sum of the formal relations of the society. For their service to the state, the retinue received great rewards, and punishments as great for their disservice, for negligence, misfeasance, malfeasance or non-feasance in office. It is for this public career that they had formally broken with their birthright. They were the broken men on the one side, the men torn forth from the villages on the other.

2.10. These retainers were individuals, their individuality was expressed within the framework of the thirteenth century Mongol society and state. The brief statements of the Secret History recount their names, their characteristic traits whether bravery or cunning, and the particularities of their relations to the *Khan,* whether of jealousy, generosity, zealous service, fear or pride. The Secret History is an account in the service of the state, and the individualism is that of the ruling class in that service and in self-service. This contradiction was no more overcome in the history of the particular form of the state among the Mongols than it was in the history of the particular form of the state in nineteenth century European capitalism. At that later time, the ideology of individualism achieved one of its high points of expression in philosophy, romance, poetry and song, again centered on the figure of the emperor (Napoleon and Napoleonism!). Yet one of the functions of the state is to contain the extreme forms of individual interests as they conflict with each other within the ruling class.

2.11. The formation of the state is therefore asymmetrical in the history of the Mongols, as it is in the history of the states of Europe, Africa and elsewhere in Asia. On the one side, the tradition of collectivity is carried forward in the communal organization of the villages and clans of the Mongols; this is characteristic of the herdsmen, laboring among the herds. On the other side, individuality is developed among the warriors, the great men, ministers in the service of the prince, as it is among the nobility and the princes themselves.

2.12. We have said that a modification was introduced into the Mongol class structure. Following the conversion to Buddhism in the late sixteenth century, many herdsmen entered into the service of the Buddhist lamaseries, serving there not as monks or disciples, but as herdsmen. These families of herders no longer served the traditional princes and clan chiefs, but labored in the monasteries, tending, herding, milking, shearing wool, making butter, or kumys, etc. Their relations were new, and at the same time traditional. The lamaseries profited from the surplus produced, exchanged and sold by the herdsmen. The herdsmen paid a form of tithe or tribute to the lamaseries, but were freed from imposts to the secular authorities by this means. They were bound to the service of the lamaseries, just as the traditional herding families were bound to the service of the princes, *noyot*. Both forms of labor in the Mongol society were unfree.

2.13. The theory has been circulated about that the Mongol *arat* were feudal serfs. This may be true, but if so, then feudalism is thereby given a different interpretation and meaning. The feudalism of the European model, in the Middle Ages, had a number of characteristic features in common with the Mongol. Each society was divided into classes, each had formed a state. The state sovereignty in each was acknowledged, personified in a ruler, or overlord. Social labor in both cases was unfree. The laboring class in each society produced a surplus that was appropriated by the ruling class, the surplus being in the form of surplus labor or a surplus product which was extracted in kind: money played virtually no role whatsoever in either case. The ruling class in Mongolia, as in European feudalism, was an aristocracy, the overlord was a prince, king or emperor, frequently elected by his retainers, the broken men in both societies. The overlord had a personal relation to his vassals, in the European society, to his retinue in both. They stood, in one sense, in relation to him as clients to patron.

2.13.1. The differences between traditional Mongol and European feudal society and the state are likewise striking. All Mongols, commoners and nobility had a common descent. This was not so in European feudalism, where it was a grave insult to impute common blood to a noble family. The opposition between town and countryside, as between the product of town industry and the product of the land, which was present in European feudalism was absent in the traditional Mongol economy. In both the traditional Mongol economy, and in that of European feudalism, a surplus was extracted from the direct producers, as we have seen. That surplus was appropriated, whether in labor or in kind, by the representatives of the ruling class, acting at once as landowners and as landlords in feudal Europe. As landowners they extracted the surplus, whether in labor or in kind, in their private capacity as groundrent; as landlords they extracted the surplus labor or surplus product in their public capacity as tax. Rent and tax coincided in feudal Europe during the Middle Ages, the relation of landowner and landlord coincided, the public sphere was non-different from the private sphere. In traditional Mongolia, the private and public spheres were *at first* non-different, rent and tax coincided, landowner and landlord were one and the same person. But during the nineteenth and twentieth centuries, an important distinction is to be noticed in the traditional herding economy of the Mongols. The secular princes had private herds as opposed to the herds of the state treasury; the relation of the herding families of the commons to the one differed from the relation to the other. Social labor of the Mongol herdsmen in the private capacity, *xamjilga*, in the service of the prince, was distinct from the social labor of the *arat*, which was neither distinctively public nor private. It was, in either case, bound labor, unfree labor.

2.13.2. In fine, what is shared between the Mongol society in its traditional form and European feudal society is not in any way specific to the two of them, but is shared with society in ancient Rome, and in the traditional civil society and the state in Africa. These questions first have to be resolved if feudalism is to be imputed to the medieval Mongol society.

2.14. The traditional Mongol nomadic society was a society with a form of political economy, civil society and the state. The economy underwent an inner evolution, particularly in regard to the appropriation and distribution of the surplus produced in the society. That surplus, at first non-different private and public, later came to be differentiated as private on the one side, public on the other, in one sector of the economy, while at the same time, the non-difference of the two sides was maintained in another sector of the Mongol economy. It has been sometimes held that the surplus produced in political economy and society is not different from that produced in primitive economy and society. Thus, in the latter 'something extra, for a guest, or for a feast' is offered in proof that the surplus is found in both primitive and political economies. That is not relevant to our matter, for in primitive economy no differentiation is made between production in the family and production in society, just as no differentiation is there made between the division of labor in the family and the division of labor in society. In political economy, on the contrary, a family may produce and set aside for a guest or a feast, but this surplus is distinct from the production in society of surplus value as surplus labor or product. The distinction between the two forms of surplus was maintained in traditional Mongol society, just as the division of labor in the family was distinct from the division of labor in society, in the form of the division of labor between the agricultural and pastoral societies. These differentiations were maintained in traditional Mongol political economy and society, where they continued to exist side by side from the era of the Mongol empire down to the beginning of the twentieth century.

2.15. The state among the nomads underwent its inner evolution.

Consider the beginnings of the state in the first millennium before the present era among the nomads of Asia: There it is barely evolved. The records pertaining to its existence are few, the nomads themselves had no writing, their state was ephemeral, and soon disappeared from view. The state among the later nomads was more stable, and, from the beginning of the first millennium of the present period on, was almost continuously in existence. The history of the state among the nomads is epitomized in the history of the indigenous written records and of script among them. (The relation between the formation of the state and the development of script, of writings, is not a chance correlation, but a coordination with interacting consequence in the service of the former.) The script and records of the ancient Uygurs, the 'runic' inscriptions of the Orkhon and Yenisey Turks, the writings of the Mongols in the scripts which are derived from the Indo-Tibetan ('Phagspa, Indic Devanagari) and from the Uyguric, the Manchu records in a script derived from the latter; all these together make up a thesaurus of the activities of the nomadic state in the first and second millennia of the present era. The nomads evolved the state in relation to the more stable and continuous, more advanced, more ancient, more 'civilized' state of their agricultural neighbors. The two sides together formed a great, barely integrated, defective economic and social unity in the past, which was composed of an interconnected network of economic, political and bellicose relations, that of the specialized agricultural and herding peoples. This network spread over the larger parts of eastern central, western and southern Asia, determining the formation of the state as abstractum in its several parts, and as concretum in the history of the particular peoples; agricultural on the one side, nomadic on the other.[5]

2.16. Historically, the state was not discovered by the nomads of central and middle Asia, nor was it invented by them: the state is no one's discovery, no one's invention. The state is the product of particular social conditions, whereby society, divided into opposed social classes, produces a central organism of political authority within its midst: the entity in its abstract form which arches over the entire society. Concretely, historically the state controls and regulates the relations between and within the social classes by means of particular agencies. The state is not for this control and regulation; that is a false teleology. The state is the abstract expression of this centralized control and regulation. The means for that control and regulation are the concrete social agencies of extraction of surplus labor and surplus product from the immediate producers in society, the distribution thereof, the collection of rent and tax, juridical administration, military and police actions, the maintenance of record and archives, post and communication at home and abroad. The state in concrete historical form was developed among agricultural people in the Old World and the New, and among nomadic peoples of Eurasia and Africa. The state is older, more stable, associated with more complex development and undertakings among certain agricultural peoples in ancient Egypt, China, or Persia than among nomadic peoples. Yet it is false to consider the latter as the reflex of the former, or as merely occupying the interstices between the agricultural spaces. On the contrary, the state, in its inner nature, form, content and function is the same abstract entity throughout its various concrete historical changes in external form.

3. COMMENT ON THEORY AND METHOD IN THE ORIGIN OF THE STATE AMONG THE NOMADS

The history of nomadism and of the state among the nomadic societies of Asia is complex, for, just as there are many nomadic societies, so there are many histories, which are in interaction with each other and with neighboring agricultural and hunting societies. In order to elucidate the historical process of state origin and formation, one may take as the point of departure those societies wherein the state has not been formed historically by inner moments, or insufficiently formed, e.g., among the Tuvinians; or one may take as the point of departure those societies in which the state has been formed by inner moments of their history, e.g., the Kök Turk, the Orkhon and Yenisey Turks, the Mongols. It is from the latter history that the analysis made here has taken its point of departure. The formation of the state has been led from its foundation in history, the formation of the opposed social classes in the nomadic societies. Plainly, one does not start with the history of those nomadic societies in which the state has not been developed, if one proposes to write the history of the formation of the state: on the contrary, classless societies are introduced into the analysis in order to demonstrate the presence or absence of the historical conditions necessary for the phenomenon under investigation.

Next, the hypothesis is sometimes advanced that the state, if formed among nomadic societies, is formed only in conjunction with the formation of the state among the agricultural societies. Such a hypothesis is founded on the theory of diffusionism, which has little to offer to the present stage of the discussion of the theory of the state and the history of the same. The state was first formed in Asia, in all probability, first among the agricultural peoples. The nomadic societies stand in both direct and indirect relation to this early state formation. However, to limit the discussion to these historical phenomena is to focus attention only on the surface, the superstructure, and to withdraw it from its proper object, the foundation. The presence of class-divided societies among nomadic Turks and Mongols in ancient and medieval times is historically attested; these societies have formed the state among themselves. The historical moments of state formation among them, issuing from the formation and opposition of the social classes there, as between the common herding families on the one hand, and the nobility on the other, are different from the historical moments of state formation among the agricultural Chinese, Persians, or peoples of India. The first thing to be said therefore is that the state in nomadic societies had a different historical origin and course than that among agricultural peoples. The second is that all these historical phenomena are variants of a single institution, the state, whose variant forms are in interaction with each other and with the whole.

The theory of the origin and nature of the state in general has been well developed in the nineteenth and twentieth centuries. The historical process of state formation among the nomads of central and inner Asia in particular has been brought out by orientalists and ethnologists in the same time period. Here the general theory and the particular historical process are brought together.

FOOTNOTES

[1]   The nature of class interest and class oppositions is a matter that must be explored in another context. The relation of individuals of the ruling class to the interest of this social class and to the state will be considered in the following pages.

[2]   There are those such as David Easton and A. R. Radcliffe-Brown who would suppress the idea of the state by the elimination of the term. Their main reason appears to be that the term has proved too complex. This is the opposite of the multiplication of terms without necessity: it is its diminution or reduction, likewise without necessity. The fact that a term has been misused, or that its object is too complex is no reason in itself to discard it.

[3]   Government is one of the functions of the state. There is, however, a contradiction between government and the state, for justice is a concern of government, it is not the concrete concern of the state. The universal rule of law within the confines of a governing body is contradicted by the concerns of the state which lead to the universal rule of law within these confines when it is in the interest of the agency of the particular state to do so. The state in the abstract is concerned with justice as abstractum.

[4]   These Tatars are social groups which comprise the Altaic language community. Among them are the Uygurs, Kök Turks (Blue Turks), Orkhon and Yenisey Turks, T'o Pa, T'u-chüeh, Yüehchih, Kyrgyz, Jou-Jan (Juan-Juan?), Mongols proper, Naiman, Kereit, Kara Kitan, Pohai, Chin, Liao, Manchus. They were commonly termed Tatars, singly or collectively. The Hsien Pi were perhaps a confederation of the ancestors of some of these, together with non-Altaic speakers whose descendants live in Siberia, or lived there.

[5]   This network was, to begin with, an exchange system of the specialized farming and herding production unities. The social division of labor between them was integrated in a

great market and tribute system that spread over the entire continent. The evolution of the market system over the world to the point attained in the present capital market can be traced. The religious, political, etc., systems over Asia reinforced this defective unity of exchange.

REFERENCES

The line of development of the theory of the state runs from G.W.F. Hegel to Karl Marx.

Source materials and references for positions set forth above will be found in various publications of the present writer.

Krader, Lawrence,

I. *Theory of the State in General.*
— (1968), *Formation of the state.* Englewood Cliffs: Prentice Hall.
— (1974), *The ethnological notebooks of Karl Marx.* Assen: Van Gorcum, 2nd edn.
— (1975), *The Asiatic mode of production.* Assen: Van Gorcum.

II. *The State in Nomadic Society.*
— (1952), 'The cultural and historical position of the Mongols', in: *Asia Major* 3: 169–183.
— (1955), 'Qan-Qagan and the Beginnings of Mongol Kingship', in: *Central Asian Journal* 1: 17–35.
— (1972), *Peoples of Central Asia.* Bloomington and the Hague, 3rd edn.
— (1963), *Social organization of Mongol-Turkic Nomads.* Bloomington and the Hague.
— (1955), 'Feudalism and the Tatar Polity', in: *Comparative Studies in society and history* 1: 76-99.
Here the theory of the state among the nomads by usurpation, propounded by Wilhelm Radloff, *Aus Sibirien*, 2nd edn., Leipzig 1893, is considered, likewise the theory of feudalism among the Mongols by B. J. Vladimirtsov, *Sotsial'nyi Stroi Mongolov.* Leningrad 1934. On the personality of Chingis Khan cf. V. V. Barthold, *Turkestan down to the Mongol invasion.* London 1928. Ch. 4. On the work of the orientalists Radloff and Barthold, v.: *The International Encylopaedia of the Social Sciences.* New York 1968 (s.v.).

PART TWO:

Antithesis

The chapters in this part form the core of the volume. Written by specialists from various countries and with various scholarly backgrounds, they offer a random sample of data on a number of early states, presenting the most current research achievement in this field. Due to a number of factors beyond the control of the editors several areas where early states developed are not covered by the articles in this volume (e.g., the Mediterranean basin, the Middle East, Slavic Eastern Europe, Japan) but we think it possible to consider the sample presented in Part Two sufficiently strong to be a counterpoint, a kind of antithesis, to Part One, and as such to serve as a base upon which the evaluation and the synthetical discussion of Part Three can rest.

5   Angkor: Society and State

LEONID A. SEDOV

From the purely chronological point of view the Angkorian period in the history of the Khmer people can hardly be called 'an early childhood'. The appearance on the historical map of the, in many respects, unique and, in others, typical state of Angkor was preceded by a prolonged formative period of emerging statehood of the Khmer tribes that began in the first century A.D. and eventually culminated in the establishment of the early state in its purest form that was Angkor. This process cannot be described in any detail here for reasons of space and because of the scarcity of data in general. It seems useful, however, to sketch at least a picture of what went on in the territory of the future state of Angkor during this period.

1. HISTORICAL BACKGROUND

The beginning of the new era finds the Khmer tribes at the stage of the Iron Age culture. The population, sparse as it is, is made up of tribal clan communities with strong internal kinship ties and living relatively isolated from each other, though mutually at peace.

This situation changed radically after the coastal regions in the Mekong Delta came under the influence of the highly developed Indian civilization. Indian immigrants, colonists and traders brought with them their own ideas of government, 'customs and fashions', and religious symbolism. They acquainted the aborigines with various new techniques, including methods of land reclamation, and with handicrafts and the art of war. However, the main changes in the life of the people of this coastal region were connected firstly with the introduction of writing, that major tool of civilization, and secondly with the drawing of the coastal communities into the broader sphere of international trade. These two factors radically changed the nature of the existing community of agriculturists and hunters transforming it into a *nagara*, or clan community with a state-like character. Trade and the crafts serving this trade became the chief occupation of the populace of this *nagara*. And the war craft acquired a place of honor among the other crafts, corresponding to a similar place of honor of the slave trade in the commercial structure.

We shall not dwell on the social characteristics of the *nagara*, referring the reader to the work by M. Kozlova, L. Sedov and V. Tiurin for this (1968, pp. 524–28). For our present purpose it is necessary only to say a few words about the nature of the relations between the *nagara* and the periphery which as yet lacked a state organization. This periphery served as the chief source of slaves, valuable commercial commodities and, partly, foodstuffs. At least, that is what Chinese travellers of the period stated in their reports (Giteaux 1958; Malleret 1960). All these commodities were secured in the form of tribute or as war spoils and prisoners. Only in this sense can we speak of a Funan military expansion and of the emergence of the first 'empire' on Cambodian soil. What, in fact, it amounted to was the domination of trade routes, or in other words the subjugation of other competing *nagaras*, and the political and military exploitation of the inland areas.

The impact of the *nagaras* on the life of the interior regions, with their clusters of relatively small, autarkic communities, would not have been so radical if it had not been for the slave trade, that is, military plundering. It was precisely this plunder that stimulated the creation of a political and military apparatus of resistance among the peacefully stagnating communities of the interior. In the space of 300 years primitive state formations cropped up where once peripheral 'wilderness' had been, enabling the communities in question to defend themselves against Funanese slave raiders. The process was facilitated by the migration of some Funanese to the interior regions, which played the same role as the earlier migration of Indians had played for Funan itself. At any rate the conquerors of Funan — the Chenla kings Bhavavarman and Chitrasena — were such immigrants (Pelliot 1903). The wish to profit from the wealth of a refined but ageing Funan played no small part in the newer states' thrust forward.

The center of gravity gradually shifted to the interior. New states no longer were based on trade, like Funan; nor were they as yet of the 'irrigation' type, like Angkor. Chenla, which had gained in strength and vigor in the course of her struggle with Funan, continued the policy of outward expansion, that is, of plundering other communities.

Formally these communities were incorporated into the new 'empire', but in actual fact they preserved their autonomy. Precisely this situation characterized Isanavarman's state, which astonished even the sophisticated Chinese with its splendor, but proved only an ephemeral phenomenon existing for no more than fifty years. Descriptions left behind by the Chinese help us to discern in Isanavarman's state an overgrown tribal confederacy (comprising about 20,000 people), having come to specialize in the business of war ('all the inhabitants of the country bear weapons and armour so that the slightest quarrel will end in bloody fighting') and subjugating thirty other large tribal units of which it is known that they continued to be ruled by their own rulers (Hervey de Saint-Denys 1883). It seems that the use of slave labor assumed larger proportions in Isanavarman's state than in Funan. At any rate, the development of construction in stone attests to this.

The dominance of Isanavarman's clan over other tribes and clans, based as it was on purely military and political superiority, without being strengthened by other factors, could not be stable. In fact, for the subsequent 200 years we see incessant warring between kingdoms or principalities which in actual truth were neither but were all exactly the same kind of tribal communities passing through an identical process of 'primitive' state formation and plunged in a situation of war 'of all against all'. Similar periods of intertribal warfare can be observed in ancient Egypt during the period of internome wars preceding the establishment of the southern and northern kingdoms, and in China during the so called 'Warring States' period.

The intestine strife as well as external (Javanese) aggression made the problem of integrating the warring communities into a unified state especially pressing. Such unification was besides more or less natural given the ethnic similarity of the communities, their linguistic affinity and the homogeneity of the environment and of their socioeconomic level. However, all previous attempts at achieving unity by strictly political and military means had failed. Only Jayavarman II managed to find a new basis for integration on which his successors could gradually build a mighty centralized state. This integrative basis was the cult of *devaraja*, of the phallic symbol of the king and the kingdom in which were welded together the Indian religious symbolism, high in ascendancy from the heyday of Funan, and local practices such as the worship of land elevations, faith in the mystical connection between the tribal head and the fertility of the land, and the ancestor cult. The king's personality became sacral to an extent unknown to the rulers of the pre-Angkorian states or communities. The authority of Jayavarman, ruler of a small territory to the northeast of Lake Tonlé Sap that he was, was also greatly enhanced due to special political circumstances, to his bold challenge to the Sailendra kings of Java and to his proclaiming himself *chakravartin*, or universal monarch. These steps brought him wide renown.

But an especially important feature of Jayavarman's policy was that, unlike the earlier claimants to the emperorship, he began to integrate the most influential clans into the unified political system, admitting their prominent members to the ruling elite and transforming clan communities into so-called *varnas* and temple communities (Sedov 1965). Thus, the central cult of the king was supplemented with those of the magnates and their ancestors, and theocratic and state functions came to be closely interwoven. This process is clearly discernible from the famous Sdok Kak Thom inscription (Finot 1915), describing the rise to power of the clan of the king's *purohita* (chaplain) Sivakaivalya. At the end of the process in the twelfth century, there were some 20,000 statues of divinities in the country (Coedès 1941), or in other words, conjecturally about 3,000-3,500 temples, all fulfilling important ritual, administrative and economic functions. That is how the local integration of self-sufficient, archaic agrarian communities ('communal microcosms') was realized (Marx 1881: 405–20).

Unification of the country continued along the lines laid down by Jayavarman in the reigns of his successors, Indravarman and Yaśovarman. Under them the king's power received an even more solid basis of legitimacy due to clever dynastic marriages which allied the clan ruling at Angkor both to the 'lunar' dynasty that has reigned over Funan and to the 'solar' race of kings that had ruled in Sresthap-ura; undoubtedly a holy place for all Khmer tribes from time im-memorial (Porée-Maspero 1950). Finally, one of the major factors in the succesful integration was the drawing of the economic sub-system of the society into the integrative process. It was Indravarman who laid the foundations for the irrigation system of Angkor, thus providing for the rapid economic development of the region. Irrigation furnished the state with a large reserve of newly reclaimed lands which it could distribute among its staunchest supporters, and concentrated in it a new and important social function—the construction and maintenance of an extremely complex hydraulic system—which at the same time provided an additional basis of legitimacy.

Thus the social and political system of Angkor had assumed definite form. We shall now pass to a more detailed description of the system.

2. THE KING

It is logical first to characterize the apex of the state hierarchy, that is, the king's authority. As we have already said above, Angkorian kings were deified and shown divine honors by the fear-stricken populace, which believed in their miraculous powers. It should be noted, however, that this divine character was at first assigned not so much to the actual occupants of the throne as to the royal power as such; the kings themselves coming to be regarded as personified gods only later (Dupont 1946). It was believed that the king's power resided in the royal *linga*, the symbol of masculine generative power in the form of a phallic image. In the *linga* kings merged with Siva, as it were. This idea is most clearly expressed in the inscription of Práh Nôk, in which a general addresses King Udayadityavarman II (1050–1067) as follows: 'let me present the trophies to your invisible 'I' that is Siva residing in the golden linga' (Barth et al. 1885–93: 166).

The idea of the merging of the king's power with that of the gods of the Indian pantheon (Siva, Vishnu, or Buddha) was introduced by Jayavarman II, assisted by the Indian *brahmana* Hiranyadama. This priest initiated a special rite consisting in part of the recital of appropriate Tantric texts and special sacrifices. Later, each successive monarch had to be confirmed in office, and his mystical divine power was conferred upon him by the royal chaplain (*purohita*), whose post was hereditary in one of the *brahmana* clans. It should be emphasized that during their lifetime Angkorian kings were considered not so much as gods, but rather as mystical intermediaries between gods and men. According to a popular legend transmitted by Tcheou Ta-kouan, the king was obliged to sleep every night with a nine-headed serpent — the owner of all the land — who appeared to him in the form of a woman. The king could not shirk this responsibility even once, as this would have brought down great harm to the people. The kings were not held to be descendants of gods, but were believed to become gods (or merge completely with gods) posthumously.

If, symbolically, the royal power was embodied by the *linga*, practically, it was represented in the royal clan. As opposed to certain textbook notions of the unlimited despotism of oriental monarchs, the royal power of the Angkor rulers was greatly restricted by tribal and clan traditions and norms. The clan as a whole fulfilled the function of a stabilizing core for the Angkor ruling elite. Along with every other noble clan, the royal clan was vitally concerned with its numerical growth. That is why the rule of hypergamy obtained with respect to such clans. Accordingly, married women belonging to a noble clan remained in it together with their husbands of more humble origin and their children. We see princesses' husbands appointed to the highest state functions alongside princes and relatives of the queen. This particular method of recruiting the top echelons of the power structure was noted by Tcheou Ta-kouan who wrote: 'In the majority of cases princes are appointed to the higher posts, or those appointed bring

their daughters to the king's harem' (Tcheou Ta-kouan 1951: 14). In
the majority of genealogies of noble families that have come down to
us in the inscriptions, the progenitors were relatives of the kings' wives
(or concubines raised to an alleged status of legal wives by their
descendants).

Stable as a whole, due to its numerical strength and cross-ties with
other grand families, the royal clan proved less monolithic during
periods of change at the top. Because of the coexistence within it of
two different principles of inheritance — namely the matrilineal and
the patrilineal one — the clan often became split after the king's death,
with the various factions engaging in a bitter struggle over the vacant
throne involving wider strata of the population. Of the twenty-seven
kings of the Angkorian period, eight came to power subsequent to a
contention with another claimant. A direct transfer of power from
father to son is recorded in nine cases out of thirty-two (Chenla and
Angkor), while of this number only twelve kings were former royal
princes. In almost as many cases (eight) the power passed to brothers
or cousins (the Old Khmer did not make a difference between brothers
and sister's children, and designated both by the same term) (Coedès
1964: 157 n. 3), or to a wife's nephew, to grandsons or even to
husbands of first cousins once removed. The choice among these many
candidates was determined 'by their age and virtue'. Matrilineal descent was especially important and the authors of royal genealogies
attached prime importance to the elucidation of the origins of kings'
mothers and wives.

Some kings backed their claim to the throne exclusively with their
wives' genealogies. Thus Suryavarman I emphasized the fact that his
wife Viralakśmi belonged to Indravarman's clan, and Jayendravarman
claimed a right to the throne as the husband of Indravarman I's
daughter, Jayendradevi.

The high social status of women and their position in the power
structure corresponded with their role in matters of descent and
inheritance (Sedov 1966: 44–46). Chinese writers noted that Cambodian women sometimes were famous for their knowledge of astrology
and political sciences and that some held high offices, including that of
judge. The Lovêk inscription informs us that one of the wives of
Radjendravarman II, named Prana, served under his son Jayavarman
V as chief of the latter's staff of private secretaries.

Because of the enormous tension around the problem of the succession and the dangers posed by the numerous male claimants, Angkorian kings sought support and protection from the female members
of the court, who acted as a kind of counterweight to the explosive
male environment. The harem was of particular importance as a
symbol of royal prestige and an instrument of the king's power. In

addition to five wives, one of whom was the principal one, kings had from 3,000 to 5,000 concubines and maids of honor. The harem was recruited from among the daughters of dignitaries and officials of all ranks, and hence fulfilled the function of a link between the king and the aristocracy of the royal service clan, being a symbol of the kinship between them, as well as a kind of hostage institution. Besides, the king's entourage included from 1,000 to 2,000 female courtiers possessing the exclusive right to enter the inner palace chambers. The king's personal guard was also made up of women bearing spears and shields.

Angkorian kings (except those of the latter period of the empire) would take this entire retinue with them on their regular tours of inspection of the country and on pilgrimages to distant shrines. Every temple and *aśrama* had special royal bedchambers serving the king as temporary residence during such tours. Special officials responsible for their maintenance and security (*chmam vrah krala phdam*) are mentioned recurrently in the inscriptions.

The construction of roads for the sake of efficient tax-collection and military movements also remained one of the major preoccupations of monarchs. By the time of Jayavarman VII the country possessed a well-developed network of highways running on a level above that of the floodwaters, crossing rivers by means of stone bridges, and provided with inns at ten-mile intervals (Parmentier 1936).

The utmost attention was paid to the security of the king. Neither armed guards nor the divine aura surrounding the person of the king were considered sufficient protection. So one of the inscriptions informs us that though the king (Yaśovarman I) 'knew everything that is knowable .... he used spies' eyes to protect himself from possible attempts on his life' (Barth et al. 1885: 413, 425). Generally speaking, the actual relationship between the king and the people and the king and his courtiers was far removed from the paternalistic ideal as formulated in Indian theories of the state and reflected in Khmer panegyrics to their kings (Sahai 1970: 33–34).

3. THE NOBILITY

In spite of its numerical strength, power and key position in the state structure, the royal clan naturally did not constitute the sole component of the ruling stratum. The above-mentioned process of integration of rural communities into a unified state system was completed by the tenth century, with the establishment of a system of rural communities, that is characteristic of an early class society. In Angkorian Cambodia this system took the specific form of a combination of *varnas*, *vargas* and religious institutions (temples and *aśramas*).

Rural communities continued to form the foundation of the society, though in the course of the integration process they had lost their territorial clan nature whereby a large stretch of territory was occupied by a group of people belonging to one and the same kinship group, and had become territorially more restricted extended family communities (Maretin 1974: 60–66). The different territorial units now became administrative divisions of the state (*praman, visaya* or *deśa*) ruled and taxed by the center though preserving certain vestiges of communal self-government. The clan unity had been destroyed and various clans (*kula*) now saw themselves divided into different branches inhabiting territories lying far apart from each other and integrated into a new system of more limited territorial ties. However, clan ties had not lost all their importance, the clans, even in this divided and 'dismantled' form, preserving their individual organizational structure and rules and customs governing the relations between clan members. At the lower level of the village (*sruk, grama*) the kinship structure remained altogether intact, each village being an extended family settlement. As a result, the society came to resemble a piece of fabric, with the vertical clan ties, forming the warp and the horizontal neighborhood ties, interwined with the thread of administrative subordination, the weft.

In the formation of the vertical structure the differentiation of clans into noble ones, belonging to the *varna* category, and common ones, named *vargas*, was of a decisive importance. *Varnas* were those clans that possessed the hereditary privilege (and obligation) to delegate certain of their members to fulfil particular secular and sacerdotal functions in the capital. It should be noted that the word *varna* was used indiscriminantly to designate an individual clan endowed with such a privilege, as well as the entire corps of individuals and clans exercising these particular functions. This ambiguity sometimes makes the interpretation of some of the inscriptions quite difficult. Thus the inscription on the Kómpong Thom stele (Coedès 1942: 62–68) tells of the creation of two new *varnas* by King Jayavarman V on the occasion of his completing his studies in 974. The relevant decree instructs the royal preceptor (*Vrah Guru*) to select from among the priest-representatives of the already existing seven *varnas*, two groups of twenty persons each to be made the founders (*Mula*) of the new *varnas*. The newly created *varnas* were given 'villages, lands and paddy-fields' in ownership, and were exempted from all obligations other than that of sending śivaite priests (*pamnvas*) into the royal service. 'Those of the priests who will distinguish themselves by their bearing, high morality and exemplary conduct will be appointed to *acharya* (teacher) posts in the capital', says the inscription. It can be concluded then, that in Jayavarman V's time there existed seven such priviliged, hereditary functional bodies, each representing an unknown number of individual clans, and that then two more such bodies were established, each representing twenty clan branches (in accordance with the number of founders stipulated by the king). In later inscriptions we often come across representatives of these two *varnas* in high offices in the capital, the royal service (*rájakárya*) being at once a privilege and an obligation.

We furthermore learn that the women belonging to these new *varnas* were obliged to marry only men from thc three highest *varnas*, supplying the court with the three topmost categories of officials, who had a parasol with a golden handle as their insignia. From what we know of the Angkorian system of titles (Sedov 1967: 107–108) we may conclude that only three of the seven *varnas* existing before the reform produced officials with the title of *mratan* or higher. The reform raised the number of these *varnas* to five. Taking the figure twenty as the hypothetical average number of clans represented in each *varna*, we can conjecture that the ruling stratum of Angkor was made up of about 100 clans. The rank and file of these *varnas* remained in agriculture, and only the chosen higher representatives served in the capital or in prominent local functions. They were known by the general designation of *tamrvác*, meaning 'inspectors' or 'overseers'. The famous oath of officials under Suryavarman I (Coedès 1951: 205–216) lists about 200 names of *tamrvác* with the titles of *mratan* and *mratan khlon*, which means that each clan of the *varna* rank delegated about two of its members to the corps of titled officials. These dignitaries did not receive regular salaries, but, only periodically, gifts from the king, including lands, villages, serfs (*khnum*) and various valuable objects. The chief source of their livelihood was constituted by their clan lands, worked by their rank and file kinsmen. This arrangement is mentioned clearly in the Sdok Kak Thom inscription (Finot 1915: 90), which speaks of people serving the king and depending on the resources of their clan (*anak, vrah rájakáryya gi ná ayatta kulopáya*). The titled officials were regarded as the heads and guardians of their repective clans. Many names of officials are followed by the name of their relevant clan villages (e.g., *mratan Sri Víraparákrama sruk Karom Thnal* (Coedès 1951: 213)). In their capacity as clan guardians the court officials were designated *anak sanjak* (Sedov 1967: 163). The *varna's* property often took the form of the property of a clan temple, where an ordinary clan member served as priest. The patrons of such temples were also high court dignitaries. For example, it is recorded about Suryavarman I's general Sri Nrpasimhavarman that he came from a lineage 'from time immemorial famous for its devotion to Siva's lotus-like feet, and therefore enjoying in perpetuity the possession of its clan town of Graiveya, rich with sacrifices to Siva' (Coedès 1953: 243). The concern with the maintenance of clan temples, which constituted the foundation for the well-being of the entire clan, is reflected in a passage of the oath to Suryavarman I, viz: 'If we are unwaveringly constant to the oath, may His Majesty give orders for the upkeep of the religious foundations of our localities and the provision of our families with all the necessary means'.

Although the *varnas* of lower status than the above-mentioned five did not supply titled nobility, they also enjoyed certain special rights. The *varna* of the goldsmiths (*cámíkarakára*) evidently constituted a kinship-cum-professional group of such a privileged kind.

The majority of the population was organized in common, un-privileged clans, called *vargas*. Many of these, like the *varnas*, sent into the state service professionals of specific occupations, which were hereditary per *varga*, such as artisans of various kinds, shepherds, gardeners, court servants (e.g. parasol bearers), entertainers, and so on.

4. THE COMMONERS

Such was, so to speak, the vertical structure of Angkorian society. It was knit together by clan relations from top to bottom. We shall now take a look at the horizontal structure. On the horizontal plane—the territorial one—a cluster of village communities, tightly cemented by territorial neighborhood ties and state administrative bonds, came into being. In each of the territorial communities segments of various clans, *varnas* as well as *vargas*, existed side by side and entered into complex relations with each other, with other territorial communities and with the unifying totality, namely, the state. We shall now try to outline these relations.

The clan segments were headed by clan elders designated by the Sanskrit term *mula*, meaning 'the root'. Usually, this was a hereditary type of function descending from the founders of the clan branch in question. Thereupon, these segments became divided into secular and religious divisions. The guardian-founder, who settled a given segment in a certain area, also as a rule founded a clan temple and decreed which division of the segment had to 'enter religion', i.e., become the hereditary priests of that temple. The temples in many instances were exempted, wholly or partially, from state duties and were drawn into a different system of economic ties, namely, with the central temples. The priests fulfilled not only religious but also, probably, arbitrarional functions (Sedov 1969; Coedès 1964: 117).

The secular division of the clan was headed by *mulas* and other elders known as 'the first among the people', or *puruśapradhana*

(Sedov 1968: 78). From their midst local dignitaries, designated by the term *valadhyaksa* ('overseers of the people') and *sresthin* ('the first', 'the best') (Sedov 1967: 108–109), were appointed by a procedure combining the principles of election, heredity and appointment. This stratum was semi-communal and semi-governmental. At any rate, the government did its best to integrate it into the centralized apparatus with its system of titles and insignia. Of these people Tcheou Ta-kouan wrote that 'below those who have a parasol with a golden handle, there are those who have a parasol with a silver handle; there are also those who use a silver palanquin . . . . Officials entitled to a silver parasol are called *sseu-la-tin* (śresthin)' (Coedès 1918: 9). For Tcheou Ta-kouan, accustomed as he was to the bureaucratic institutions of his native country, there was nothing about them that made them any different from ordinary officials (Tcheou Ta-kouan 1951: 13–14). It should be remembered however, that his evidence relates to the late thirteenth century, when clan and kinship ties had already become substantially transformed in the course of the evolutionary process.

On the lowest step of the hierarchy under discussion there were the village notables (*amcas*, or *mai-tsie*, as Tcheou Ta-kouan called them, regarding them also simply as local clerks) and elders (*grammavrdhi*) (Sedov 1967: 109). Higher up there were 'population chiefs' (*Khlon vala*) subordinated to the regional chief (*khlon visaya*). To the same rank belonged the numerous lesser treasury officials, tax-collectors and administrators of duties and obligations such as the *khlon karya, khlon glan, khlon bhutaśa*. They were subordinated to higher state officials responsible for taxes and revenues namely the *tamrvac rajakarya* (Sahai: 71–84). These in their turn were employees of the relevant central departments (for example, the central court department, *vrah sabha*, or the central department of stored goods under the *khlon glan*, this time not the local but the principal one). The departments were subordinate to the king and his five (or four) ministers (Migot 1960: 40; Wales 1934: 79) fulfilling the function of general counsellors without specialized tasks.

The members of the clan who 'had entered religion' and become the personnel of the clan temple had their own administrative organization. It comprised the *khlon vnam* (literally, 'the chief of the mountain'), known also by the names of *adhikarinah, kulapatir, purohita* or *bhagavan* (in the case of *aśramas* the head was also the teacher of holy texts or *adhyapaka*) as well as numerous priests (*hotars* or *smins*) and financial administrators similar to the secular ones (*khlon glan*, superintendents of the fields or *khlon ksetra*, etc.). The fields belonging to such a temple were either divided up between the personnel or were worked as a single complex of 'cult fields', producing sacrificial rice for distribution among the personnel (Sedov 1963: 78). The lands were worked by serfs or *khnum* belonging to the temple. The *khnum* had their own 'food fields', which they received from the temple (as the Trapan Don On inscription shows, the fields were not sufficient for their subsistence), or they lived entirely on a share of the harvest which in its totality belonged to the temple. About sixty per cent of the rice they produced was consumed by the temple and only forty per cent by the *khnums* themselves. The standard amount consumed by them was about 400 g. of husked rice a day, as against 3 kg. a day by the priests (Sedov 1967: 172–173).

Once a clan temple was exempted from the majority of state duties it entered into a relationship of economic and, probably, administrative dependence on one of the central temples. In the tenth and eleventh centuries there were about ten such temples in the country. They were semi-state institutions fulfilling important economic functions alongside the religious ones (we use the word 'semi-state' because all the higher positions in these temples were also the prerogative of certain noble families). Their economy was closely interwoven with the state economy, in the sense that they developed large specialized industries supplying the state with particular products (e.g., the Vrah Pulinn, or 'Holy Island' supplied the state with butter). Their own requirements were met mainly by their own lands and *khnums* (e.g., the Ta Prohm temple had about 6,000 *khnums*), about one fifth of their needs being supplied by the dependent clan temples and other agricultural communities. State subventions were also provided but they were disproportionately small.

The tribute paid by clan temples to central ones was generally limited in extent, and, in fact, almost nominal, amounting to an average of 100 kg of rice a year, or 5.5 kg per member of the clan temple, including *khnums*. The figure is negligible in comparison with the clan temple's average annual consumption of 4 tons. But there were also cases of clan temples paying the central one a tithe (Coedès 1953: 130). It is also possible that the contributions of products other than rice were more considerable. There are instances known of corvée being exacted, whereby the people affiliated with clan temples were obliged to work the fields of the central temple (Práh Vihar). It is worth noting that even temples belonging to the king's kinsmen were not exempt from such corvée (Coedès 1954: 219–223).

The civil obligations of clan temples, if the latter had no immunity, were much more burdensome. We can deduce the extent of these obligations from the Phnom Bakhen inscription, which says that one third of the rice offerings of the clan temple of Rudraśrama went to the commissioner of state revenues. Other inscriptions are also eloquent in this respect. One of them says that a family to which a temple belonged had to fulfil certain civil duties (*thve rajakarya*). Another inscription stipulates that four *aśramas* belonging to the clan of Yogiśvarapandito need not render services to local authorities (*anak ta khlon visaya*), which represented a partial immunity, but were subordinated to the state tax-inspectors (Sedov 1968: 167–169).

The total corpus of the inscriptions does not provide us with exact data on the nature and extent of the duties to which clan temples and peasant communities were liable. Broadly generalizing, state duties fell into two categories, namely, gifts in kind (*cancula*) comprising agricultural and manufactural products of various kinds and the obligation to work on state construction projects or do military service (*karya, nar*). The primary state duty was connected with rice production. Here also, two forms of civil obligation existed; that is, the payment of tax in kind (*sru*) and corvée (*vriha*). Such obligations as supplying butter (*puryyan*), performing labor on the orders of local authorities (*visaya*), doing guard duty (*kandvar cralo*), and working on construction projects (*bhutaśa*) are often mentioned in the inscriptions (Sedov 1968: 149–152). Service at the court and the exercise of lower administrative functions were also compulsory. Special officers called *khlon kanmyang pammre* were responsible for the recuitment of young men for court service.

Not only free commoners but also *khnums*, including those owned by clan temples, could be summoned to work for the state or serve in the army. This fact is attested by, among other things the smaller number of men than women occurrring on the lists of temple *khnums*. Still, it is evident that the greater part of the state duties rested upon non-temple communities, the temple communities being immune from these and having obligations towards certain central temples. This relationship is expressed with especial clarity in the Pràsàt Kantop inscription (Coedès 1952: 126–132), saying that the lands and *khnums* which *sten* Mahendrani received from his clan (*gotra*) and passed on to his children and grandchildren, so that his progeny might continue to fulfil their civil obligations (*thve vrah rajakarya*) and provide their own livelihood (*aras*), were different from those presented to the Sivalinga temple, the clan temple of the same clan (L.S.), which was responsible to the Sivapada temple, one of the central temples (L.S.).

5. ECONOMY

The labor of free commoners constituted the main source of the social wealth of the Angkorian state, but not the only one. Throughout the whole period the unfree population or *khnums* played a major role in production. Being prisoners-of-war and their descendants, they differed little from slaves legally speaking and occupied an intermediate position between slaves and serfs in terms of the form of their economic exploitation. *Khnums* possessed no legal personality (though their names are sometimes mentioned among the witnesses in connection with the demarcation of field boundaries (Finot 1928)) nor legal families, and could be sold, hired and inherited. They were exploited mainly through corvée in temple fields, where they worked in groups of three to five headed by overseers or *amrahs*. However, they resembled serfs in that they were allowed to own personal effects and even plots of land that might be sold or otherwise transferred together with their tillers. Towards the end of the Angkorian period a tendency towards a narrowing of the difference between common community farmers and *khnums* was noticeable. Gradually a homogeneous stratum of unfree peasants was emerging (Kozlova et al. 1968: 532).

The Angkorian period of Cambodian history was one in which the development of productive forces reached a climax that has not been surpassed till modern times. The blossoming of Angkorian civilization, which left behind numerous testimonies of highly developed techniques of stone construction and the large-scale organization of labor for the building of roads, bridges, water reservoirs, and religious and public works, had as its basis an advanced rice-growing economy of the irrigation type. The productivity of the average agricultural worker was fifty per cent higher than at present. Considering the fact that the personal consumption of the semi-slave laborers was extremely low, and the labor intensiveness per unit of production was less than in later periods (the Khmers of Angkor harvested two or more crops a year), we can understand what was the source of the colossal labor reserves and wealth that brought eternal fame to the rulers of Angkor and the civilization they represented (Sedov 1967: 172, 179).

It can be said that in comparison with later periods, Angkorian society was characterized by a much greater use of simple cooperative labor methods on the societal or the temple level. No division of labor had as yet evolved, and no intensive domestic industry for the market existed. The division of labor was only just making its appearance in autarkic peasant and temple communities. Skilled craftsmen, not engaged in agriculture, served the court as well as their communities. The towns were not centers of trade and industry, but rather administrative and cultural focuses, thriving due to heavy extortions from agriculture and the corvée labor of mobilized peasants. Architectural masterpieces were not so much the products of individual masters perfecting their methods and techniques from generation to generation as the results of a 'generalized craftsmanship', i.e., the work of the mass of unskilled villagers torn from their fields and families to toil under the overseers' lashes. This arrangement on the one hand provided for large-scale mobilization of labor, and on the other 'restrained the human mind within the smallest possible compass, making it the unresisting tool of superstition, enslaving it beneath traditional rules depriving it of all grandeur and historical energies'. (Marx 1858: 135).

This feature of the relations of production reveals itself in the construction techniques. The basic principle of construction involved the production of coarse stone masonry, with blocks of stone of varying sizes being hewn and trimmed right in their place of installation. This method corresponds best of all with a situation whereby the majority of workers are unskilled laborers, with only small numbers of trained specialists serving as team-leaders and executing the exterior decorations. Being permanent agriculturalists, the workers had no interest in perfecting their building techniques and had no opportunities for such perfecting, since participation in construction work was episodic in their life. The outstanding scholar of Khmer material culture, G. Groslier, noted that Angkor builders did not know what might be called the 'art of construction' (Groslier 1921: 174, 178). In the course of five centuries of active construction the techniques of construction underwent no evolution and mistakes arising from lack of knowledge of the nature of stone as a building material were recurrently repeated.

Monetary dealings were on the low level corresponding with the above-described conditions. Coins were not minted in Cambodia until the sixteenth century (Migot 1960: 251). Gold and silver in different units of weight and valuable objects (vessels, ornaments, etc.,) were among the standard articles of exchange in transactions. However, other commodities such as rice, cloth, cattle, butter and *khnums* also played a role. Land was often bought and sold, though not in the form of private property for in most cases the parties to such transactions were groups of kinsmen, and the deals were subject to the strict control of both the communities and the state. The state in particular tried to prevent excessive enrichment of its members. Typical were such formulas as the one in the Pràsà Càr inscription, relating to the sale of part of their lands by the branch of a clan or *varga* of boxers to a high dignitary in exchange for silver, cloth and salt, whereas a declaration was made to the court confirming the transaction to the effect that

> all the wealth derived from the *mratan khlon* is necessary to us in order to fulfil our state duties (*thve vrah rajakarya nu gi*) and the rest for our subsistence

(Sedov 1968: 83). Sometimes the sale of land was to some extent symbolic, masking something like a commendation. The sellers preserved their rights to the land, though also certain obligations to the temple which bought the land were imposed upon them (Sedov 1967: 148–49).

6. LAW AND ORDER

As we have already said, the most important function of the Angkorian state system was that of integration. Accordingly, the legal
apparatus was one of the most highly developed components of the
state structure. Angkorian epigraphs bear no evidence of the existence
of any clearly formulated laws or law codes. The king was the highest
court of appeal. As Tcheou Ta-kouan attested, 'all differences between
the people, however slight, are always placed before the king'. But the
king's decrees were not laws in the full sense of the word, and were not
binding on his successors, except morally or for religious reasons.
There are cases of kings, after their accession to the throne, giving
orders for all the ordinances of their predecessor to be committed to
writing, and for all those left unexecuted to be given effect.

Besides these collections of ordinances (as a source for case-law),
another source of law was provided by the Indian *dharmaśastras*,
which Khmer court officials appealed to in trying cases. The inscriptions reflect a close knowledge of the *dharmaśastras* on the part of
Khmer jurists (Sahai 1970: 87–111). 'The reader of the *dharmaśastras*'
was a permanent member of every court, whose duty it was to find
relevant Sanskrit texts. It can be said that India supplied Cambodia
with the general ideas regarding the essence of law as well as the
organizational aspects of jurisdiction. This explains why the terms in
connection with legal processes were usually derived from Sanskrit.
But legal cases were as a rule substantially conducted in Old Khmer.

Legal cases reached the king by way of many intermediate stages
and authorities. According to the Tûol Pràsàt inscription, appeals to
the court were drawn up in the form of Sanskrit verses (Coedès 1942:
97–114). They were first put before the central court of justice (*vrah
sabha*) and the inspectors of morals (*gunadosadarsins*), and only after
that before the king for his final judgement. From Rajendravarman II's
till Djayaviravarman's time the king's tutor (*Vrah Guru*) invariably
participated in jurisdiction. Besides the central court, or *vrah sabha*
there were local courts in the provinces and villages such as for
example, the village court of the Varada *sruk* (Coedès 1954: 292). The
main task of the courts, as can be inferred from the inscriptions,
consisted in the adjudication of land deals and the demarcation of
boundaries. The parties involved paid the members of the court a fee
in kind. The function of arbitrator, examiner and bailiff was also
fulfilled by special officials, called *khlon samtap* (Sedov 1969), either
on a federal or a local level. They were assisted by lower clerks or
ranvan.

The actual trials presupposed a complicated procedure of interroga-
tion of witnesses either in court or on the spot. The subsequent court

decision was then announced to the people concerned, the elders and village heads being summoned especially for this purpose. All the pertinent documents were kept at the central court of justice, in the so-called hall of *brahmanas* and with the officials of the section of holy ablutions (Sedov 1967: 124–125).

The Angkorian state had no codified system of penalties. The only documents representing any kind of attempt at such codification were Jasovarman's statutes on monasteries, in which a system of fines for offences committed at *aśramas* was outlined. A salient feature here is a grading of fines, corresponding with the rank of the offender: nobles had to pay more for the same kind of offence than ordinary people. Other documents emphasized the impartiality of the court and the equality in law of all subjects before the king (Majumdar 1944: 90). Only *brahmanas* enjoyed immunities from certain kinds of punishment (Sahai 1970: 95–96).

The punishments themselves were extremely cruel. In the inscriptions of the tenth century we often come across mentions of floggings. The violation of land rights was punished by mutilation or torture. A group of people guilty of abducting female *khnum* belonging to a temple were sentenced to fifty stick strokes across the face (Coedès 1954: 49–67). Capital punishment took the form of burying the convicted person alive (Tcheou Ta-kouan 1951: 22–23).

As the emphasis fell on the development of internal functions those aspects of statecraft with a more outward orientation were less advanced. S. Sahai notes that the wars conducted by the Angkor Khmers were aimed not at the annexation of neighboring states but at their submission, as had been laid down in the so-called *dharmavijaya* policy (1970: 129–130). That is why the army as an instrument of conquest and occupation was underdeveloped serving instead the purpose of raiding neighbors and repulsing their retaliatory raids. The army had no professional generals. Its leaders—the *senapati* and *mahasenapati*—were the king's relatives (often the king's brothers), high officials and even high-ranking priests. It is worth mentioning that the *varnas*, i.e., priviliged clans, did not supply hereditary military officials. Among the *vargas*, i.e., lower ranking clans, we find at least one hereditary military corporation, namely, that of boxers. In times of war an army was raised by conscripting men from the communities as well as *khnums* (Sahai 1970: 135). Peasant draftees received a rudimentary military training. On the bas-reliefs of the Bantay Chmàr temple a scene of a mock lance fight is depicted, the lances being provided with buttons at their points. Khmer soldiers used very primitive weapons, mostly a lance and a shield, while a belt was their only clothing during fighting. In the view of the Chinese, the Khmer army knew neither strategy nor tactics (Tcheou Ta-kouan 1951: 34).

The inscriptions record the recurrent participation of army detachments in internal struggles and conflicts and in the suppression of revolts and mutinies of noblemen. There were times when the army played a key role by taking the side of one or another claimant to the throne. The army was also used for dealing with popular uprisings (e.g., the Bharata Rahu uprising (Coedès 1929: 297–330) and the insurrections in Malyang province in 1182 (Majumdar 1955: 203)). Generals who won a victory over a rebellious nobleman received the land and other property of his clan into their ownership (Coedès 1953: 233). However, military leaders, especially those in charge of provincial military garrisons, could themselves pose a threat to the central authority (Sahai 1970: 151).

Angkorian kings often led their troops personally. The inscriptions reflect their direct involvement in battles. It seems that the practice of a single combat between rival kings in front of their armies was sometimes observed. The outcome of such a combat could be decisive for the entire battle (Sedov 1967: 68–69).

Before the commencement of a war or a campaign sacrifices were made in temples. So the Práh Nôk inscription informs us of the gifts of General Sangrama to Siva on Mount Prithuśaila on the eve of his army launching an attack upon rebel forces. The rich gifts he made consisted of gold, silver and elephants. After winning a victory he again came to the temple with part of his spoils (Barth et al. 1885: 166).

These are the very bare outlines of the structure of the society and state of Angkor. The most characteristic feature of this structure was the recent integration of independent clan communities into a strong, centralized body, together with the preservation of mighty clan traditions and ties. The key position of the temples in this structure is also worth noting. Accordingly we are inclined to consider Angkorian society as representing a definite phase in a developmental process which may be termed 'state-centered'. The phase itself may be named 'communal–theocratic'.

REFERENCES

Barth, A. and Bergaigne, A. (1885–1893), *Inscriptions sanscrites du Cambode et du Campa.* Paris: Imprimerie Nationale.
Boisselier, J. (1966), *Le Cambodge.* Paris: Editions A. et J. Picard.
Coedès, G. (1918), 'Une nouvelle inscription du Phiamanàkàs', in: *Etudes Cambodgiennes* 14. *Bulletin de l'Ecole Française d'Extreme Orient* (*BEFEO* 18, 6: 9 ff.)
— (1929), 'Nouvelles données chronologiques et généalogiques sur la dynastie de Mahîdharapura', in: *BEFEO* 29: 289 ff.
— (1937), *Inscriptions du Cambodge.* III, vol. 1. Hanoi, Coll. de Textes et Documents sur l'Indochine.
— (1941), 'La stèle de Práh Khàn d'Angkor', in: *BEFEO* 41: 255 ff.

— (1942), *Inscriptions du Cambodge*, Vol. II, Hanoi.
— (1951), *Inscriptions du Cambodge*, Vol. III, Paris.
— (1952), *Inscriptions du Cambodge*. Vol. IV. Paris.
— (1953), *Inscriptions du Cambodge*. Vol. V. Paris.
— (1954), (1) *Inscriptions du Cambodge*. Vol. VI. Paris.
— (1954), (2) 'La stele de Tûol Rolom Tim. Essai d'interpretation par la langue Bahnar d'un texte juridique khmèr du Xe siècle', in: *Journal Asiatique* 242: 49–67.
— (1964), *Inscriptions du Cambodge*. Vol. VII, Paris.
Dupont, P. (1946), 'Les débuts de la royauté angkorienne', in: *BEFEO* 46: 119 ff.
Finot, L. (1915), 'Notes d'épigraphie', in: *BEFEO* 15: 19 ff.
— (1928), 'La stèle du Pràsàt Trapan Run', in: *BEFEO* 28: 58–80.
Giteaux, M. (1958), 'Aperçu sur la civilization du Fou-nan', in: *France-Asie* 5: 147–148.
Groslier, G. (1921), *Recherches sur les Cambodgiens, d'après les textes et les monuments depuis les premiers siècles de notre ère*. Paris: A. Challamel.
Hervey de Saint-Denys (1883), *Ethnographie des peuples étrangers à la Chine... (Méridionaux) de Ma Touan-Lin*. Paris.
Kozlova, M., Sedov, L. and Tiurin, V. (1968), 'Tipy ranneklassovykh gosudarstv v iugo-Vostochnoi Asii', [(Types of early-class states in Southeast Asia)] in: *Problemy istorii dokapitalisticheskikh obshchestv*. Moscow: Nauka.
Majumdar, R. (1944), *Kambujadeca*. Madras: Asia Pub. House.
— (1955), *Ancient Indian colonization in South-East Asia*. Baroda.
Malleret, L. (1960), 'l'Archeologie du delta du Mékong', in: *Publications de l'EFEO* 43: t. II. Paris.
Maretin, Iu. (1974), 'Obschina sosedsko-bol'shesemeinogo tipa u minang-kabau (Zapadnaia Sumatra)' [Extended family type of community among the Minangkabau, western Sumatra] in: *Sotsial'naia organizatsiia narodov Azii i Afriki*. Moscow: Nauka.
Marx, K. (1858), 'Britanskoie vladychestvo v Indii' [British rule in India], in: K. Marx and F. Engels, *Sochineniia*, vol. 9. Moscow.
— (1881), 'Nabroski otveta na pis'mo V.I. Zasulich' [Drafts of a reply to V.I. Zasulich's letter], in: K. Marx and F. Engels, *Sochineniia*. Vol. 19. Moscow.
Migot, H. (1960), *Les khmèrs des origines d'Ankor au Cambodge d'aujourd'hui*. Paris: Le Livre Contemporain.
Parmentier, H. (1936), *L'Art en Indochine*. Saigon: Ardin.
Pelliot, P. (1903), 'Le Fou-nan', in: *BEFEO* 3: 248 ff.
— (1925), 'Quelques textes chinois concernant l'Indochine indonisée', in: *Etudes Asiatiques* 2: 243–263.
Porée-Maspero, Ev. (1950), 'Nouvelle étude sur la Nâgí Somâ', in: *Journal Asiatique*: 241–267.
Sahai, S. (1970), *Les institutions politiques et l'organisation administrative du Cambodge Ancien*. Paris: EFEO.
Sedov, L. (1963), 'K voprosu ob ekonomicheskom stroe ankorskoi Kambodzhi IX-XII vv.' [On the question of the economic order of Angkorian Cambodia in the ninth to twelfth centuries], in: *Narody Azii i Afriki* n. 6.
— (1965), 'K voprosu o varnakh v angkorskoi Kambodzhe', [On the question of *varnas* in Angkorian Cambodia] in: *Kasty v Indii*. Moscow: Nauka.
— (1966), 'Kamni Ankora' [Steles of Angkor], in: *Asia i Afrika Segodnia*, n. 5.

Sedov, L. (1967), *Angkorskaia imperia* [Angkorian empire]. Moscow: Nauka.
— (1968), 'La société angkorienne et le problème du mode de production
    asiatique', in: *La Pensée* 138: 71–84 (reprinted in Garaudy, R. (ed.) *Sur
    le'mode de production asiatique'*, Paris: Editions Sociales, (1969: 327–343).
— (1969), 'O vysshem dukhovenstve angkorskoi Kambodzhi' [On the higher
    clergy in Angkorian Cambodia], in: *Epigrafika Vostoka* 19.
Tcheou Ta-kouan (1951), *Memoires sur les coutumes du Cambodge*. Traduits et
    annotés par P. Pelliot. Paris: Maspero.
Wales, H. Q. (1934), *Ancient Siamese government and administration*. London:
    Harrap.

6   Ankole: Pastoral Hegemony

EDWARD I. STEINHART

Ankole, or Nkore as it was known before European contact corrupted its pronunciation and its traditions, lies in the southwest of the Republic of Uganda, south of the equator and north of the international boundary with Tanzania. For 300 years before the establishment of those boundaries, Ankole was one of over twenty polities which we term the interlacustrine kingdoms. Nestled between Lakes Albert, Edward and Kivu to the west and the broad expanse of Lake Victoria to the east at an altitude of from 4,000 to 6,000 feet (1,220 to 1,830 metres) these Bantu-speaking kingdoms developed in pristine isolation from the main areas of state development in the ancient world.

Both the pristine nature and high degree of political development among these societies has led ethnographers and historians to engage in considerable speculation on the origins and dynamics of Ankole and the other states of the lacustrine zone. Most ethnographic observers of Ankole (Roscoe 1923; Gorju 1920; Oberg 1940; Stenning in Richards 1960; and Elam 1974) have stressed the highly centralized political system centering on the *Mugabe* or king and the rigid caste-like divisions which set cattle-keeping Hima over agricultural Iru and assumed that the state originated in conquest by the intrusive Hima. In contrast, the leading historical observer has described precolonial society as open, socially and politically mobile, even as 'a capitalist society' in which 'the form of capital was cattle' (Karugire 1971: 66). It is possible to reconcile these extremely divergent descriptions by placing the Ankole social system in a dynamic historical perspective. Such a perspective can be obtained through the use of a Marxist analysis derived from the application of the concept of Asiatic (or tributary) modes of production to the examination of the formation and development of Ankole's political economy.

The distinctly African or more precisely lacustrine mode of production is understood here as being based upon the super-imposition of a state and ruling class drawing support not only from the surplus of the dominant form of village-organized production collected as tribute but from the exercise of a monopoly over *some strategic goods* produced or controlled outside the village economy (cf. Hobsbawm 1964: 33–38). For West Africa and the Sudanic zone this support was often obtained from the monopoly by the state and ruling class of precious metals and the international commerce based on the trade for those metals (Coquery-Vidrovitch 1966). In the lacustrine zone, no such monopoly of trade or metals was established or possible. Indeed, what long distance trade in scarce commodities there was appears to have been controlled by the agricultural classes as a supplement to village food production and crafts. What was both possible and perpetuated by the ruling class in lacustrine society was a monopoly of the pastoral resources of the country-grazing land and water for the extensive herds of cattle which were the sole possession of those herdsmen, collectively known as Hima. It is this pastoral monopoly which gives the Ankole kingdom its peculiar political and social structures and which ultimately produced a distinctive lacustrine mode of production within the general type of tributary modes of production.[1]

1. ORIGINS OF ANKOLE

Ankole, or Karo Karungi (The Beautiful Place), was most probably settled by groups of pastoral herdsmen who migrated from Karagwe just south of the Kagera River during the last half of the fifteenth century and established a dynasty which continued to reign in the area until the abolition of kingdoms by the Uganda constitution of 1967. This 'invasion' was led by the semi-legendary 'conqueror', Ruhinda from whom the Hinda kings of Ankole, Karagwe and several other societies of the Tanzania–Uganda borderland trace their descent.

Prior to the Hinda invasion, Nkore had been a remote district on the marches of the 'empire' of the Bacwezi. The Bacwezi are so fully legendary that their existence as real men has been seriously doubted by some scholars (Wrighley 1958). Reputed to be great bearers of culture, particularly the culture of herdsmen, they are believed to have vanished from the face of the earth during a time of troubles in the fifteenth century. The reality of Bacwezi rule, despite its ardent critics and more ardent proponents, was almost certainly little more than the dominance of a pastoral clan and their close followers over a vast, thinly populated and sporadically administered region. This entire region of southwestern Uganda became subject to rival claims to power in the wake of the collapse of Bacwezi dominance. Much of this region fell to 'invaders' from the north known as Lwoo who established a series of states under Bito dynasties centering on the empire of Kitara and claiming legitimacy through descent from the soon-to-be deified Bacwezi (Cohen 1968). In the south, states formed as a reaction to the Lwoo 'invasion' and dominance in the north. Groups of Hima pastoralists fleeing the collapse of Bacwezi rule began to establish their own dominion over the southern marches. Ruhinda and his followers were the most successful of these wandering herdsmen.

According to legend, Ruhinda was a descendant of the last Bacwezi ruler, who, fleeing from the chaos of the collapsing empire, entered northern Tanzania by one of several routes remembered in local traditions. He began to conquer and displace the pre-existing Bantu agricultural authorities having his first major success in Karagwe (Katoke 1971b: 524–29). From Karagwe, Ruhinda led his pastoral followers north across the Kagera River and at the flight of the previous rulers, established his second kingdom in Ankole. He eventually returned to Karagwe and further conquests, leaving his son, Nkuba, to rule Ankole in his behalf.

Such in brief outline is the Ruhinda legend upon which the authority of the Hinda rulers of Ankole rests. What can we suppose forms the historical basis for this epic of conquest? First, we can take as fact the migration of pastoral clans from the heartland of the disintegrating Bacwezi empire. The evidence is strong that a man called Ruhinda led such a cluster of pastoral Hima. His conquests, in the Buhaya and Ankole area, however, may require some re-examination.

It has been argued that the political and social structure of pastoral dominance resulted from the military successes of the herdsmen in establishing a despotic state over the vanquished farmers of the region (Krader 1968: 43–51. It has been counterargued that the pastoralists, rather than introducing statecraft along with pastoral dominance, inherited a rudimentary state system from the Bantu speaking cultivators who preceded them as rulers of these kingdoms (Katoke 1971a: 514 and 1971b: 518–21).

Both theories are suspect. First, both presuppose a reasonably developed area of agricultural settlement in Ankole and neighboring Tanzania. This is highly dubious. The original area of Ankole, little more than the present county of Isingiro in the southeastern corner of modern Ankole district, is even today a dry, sparsely populated, and little cultivated region. The bare and blackened hills of the late dry season are testimony to the discouragement offered to cultivation and the predominance of the interests of the herders, waiting for the first rains to bring a new growth of sweet grasses for their cattle. If Isingiro supported agriculture[2] in the fifteenth century it was on a very marginal scale and with little possibility of it undergirding a developed political system. Those agriculturalists who did reside there at the time of Ruhinda's 'invasion' were probably organized on the basis of small clan-based villages with little or no centralized authority. Secondly, no memories of major battles, negotiations or other signs of conquest or displacement of a previous state are extant. The fall of a major Bantu agricultural state to invading herdsmen, the first premise of either the conquest theory or the Bantu-state theory, seems to me to be unsupportable. What then was the nature of Ruhinda's invasion and conquest?

Rather than picturing Ruhinda as a general at the head of a conquering army it would probably be best to see him as the leader of a lineage of herdsmen, armed with the usual complement of spear and shield. Perhaps he led a cluster of lineages in search of water and pastureland. Spearheaded by the young warriors, but including the elders, the women and children, such a cluster might attract a following of non-kin dependants who being without cattle or status would accept the clan names of the leaders of the pastoral clans along with the status of personal servants.[3] A few hundred people and their cattle guarded by the warriors from hostile predators and raiders moved into an essentially empty land, scattering the few farmers who might oppose them (Karugire 1971: 141–42). Establishing their claim to the pastures and water sources required little force and, in all likelihood, no claim was ever made to authority over the farming folk who were displaced or marginalized, not ruled. No conquest and no pre-existing state, indeed, no state at all was found or created. Settled around the core lineage (not *yet* a dynasty) of the leading warrior, Ruhinda, the herdsmen went about their business of being fruitful and multiplying, filling the new and beautiful land with herds and herdsmen. Ruhinda himself (assuming he personally led the warriors as legend asserts) returned soutward to Karagwe and a further round of 'conquests' leaving Ankole to his kinsmen and followers.

It is difficult to ascertain what the relations between the pastoral and agricultural populations of the region might have been at this early stage in the evolution of Ankole society, but a few speculations and extrapolations may be permitted. First of all, it appears certain that relations were minimal.[4] The herding group organized around the kraal and extended lineage must have been very close to self-sufficient, while the few farmers of the area probably lived in village communities which were fully self-supporting if allowed the peace and freedom to cultivate. This autonomy and self-sufficiency were based on the isolation and separation of the two economies; itself a function of the smallness of numbers of both groups in the area of pastoral settlement and the distinct life styles and routines established by each group within its respective ecological niche (Oberg 1943).

The cultivators operated small family farms, probably similar in terms of the daily and seasonal routine and division of labor of those worked by neighboring agricultural peoples such as the Chiga (Edel 1957), Amba or Konjo (Taylor 1962: 82–85, 93–94), who remained free of pastoral dominance. The basic division of labor by sex and age and the object of agricultural pursuits on family-owned plots was subsistence production, not the creation of a surplus for consumption outside the family unit (Taylor 1962: 103–107; Oberg 1938 and 1943). Agricultural life was bounded by its own religious and ritual practice (Williams, 1936) which was outside the purview of the pastoralists. Craft and trade specialization were practiced on a part-time basis by a wide range of agriculturalists. Iron work, basket weaving and the manufacture of tools and implements from wood, gourds and the like was not the basis for the emergence of a class of artisans nor for the development of a major system of exchange among farmers or between farmers and herders (Good 1972; Kamuhangire 1972).

Thus, what evidence we have about the early years from later observation of the agricultural sector supports the notion that cultivation was an independent pursuit, free from pastoral interference or prestations and practiced in essential isolation from the activities of the pastoral sector. Yet much of the ethnographic literature is replete with images of a servile people, considered the servants (*bairu*), slaves and serfs of their pastoral lords and identified with the entire farming population known as Iru (Bairu is the common plural form). Where and when did this image develop?

In the Ankole of the seventeenth century, the personage of the Iru may have hardly existed at all. Instead, the pastoral group practiced a kind of family herding which allowed little scope for the use of servile labor. The extended lineage of the Hima provided all the labor necessary to the husbandry of their extensive herds of long-horned cattle. They were able and courageous in defense of their herds and quite sophisticated in the practice of veterinary medicine. Indeed, there existed in Ankole down to the present century a general taboo which restricted the work that non-Hima might do around the cattle kraal. Even such menial tasks as the collecting of dung and sweeping of the cattle kraals were the exclusive activity of the pastoral group (Oberg 1938; Karugire 1970). The practice of herding in Ankole led to a life of isolation, migration and independence (Oberg 1943). The cattle keeper was devoted to his herd, which he led about the countryside in search of grazing land and water. There was little time in his daily or seasonal routine to extract tribute or labor from a subordinate class of sedentary farmers, regardless of the organizational or military superiority of the herders. Only a much closer contact and the emergence of a leisure class among the herders would permit such exploitation as the image of the Iru implies. At this early period, what few servants may have existed were probably the handful of dependants who followed Ruhinda's group into the country and a few members of the farming families shattered and displaced by the invading herdsmen.

2. THE PERIOD OF INCUBATION

Between the establishment of the Hinda regime under Ruhinda and his son, Nkuba, and the first half of the eighteenth century, 'nothing of importance seems to have taken place', according to S. R. Karugire (1971: 150), Ankole's leading historian. Indeed, he goes to pains to explain why traditions from this period are so sparse. Forgetfulness over a long period, the tendency not to record the unremarkable and the day to day domestic events in favor of the dramatic doings in international affairs and the general smallness and lack of consequence of the kingdom at this early stage are all suggested to explain the 'yawning gap' in Ankole's remembered past. But an even simpler explanation is at hand. Perhaps nothing which the historians of Ankole consider important did happen?

Indeed, considering what is recorded it seems fairly certain that following Nkuba's consolidation of personal power over the Hima clans until the eventful reign of Ntare IV (1699–1727/26), the absence of historical information stems from the fact that few people in Ankole then or since would recognize the society of the first ten generations as either an historical or political unit much less as a state. Nkuba and his successors emerge dimly from the spare record as what Ruhinda himself was — a wandering herdsman and warrior. The *Mugabe* (king) of later years was at this stage merely the leading member of the central clan of a cluster of pastoral clans — the giver of gifts of cattle as his title literally implies rather than the monarch or ruler (*Mukama*) of a sovereign state. Thus, the suppression and reduction of 'clan rebellions' by Nkuba represents not the affirmation of state sovereignty but a successful attempt by the Hinda to retain their claim to be first among equals in pastoral society. The gift of honorific offices to particular clans first attributed to *Mugabe* Ntare I, Nyabugaro (1503–31±37), Nkuba's grandson, was not the consolidation of an established dynastic authority by binding the clans to the monarchy through the creation of reciprocal obligations. Rather, it was the use of patronage and personal obligation to bind the real sovereign units of the society — the pastoral clans — to the central clan. The Hinda were central but equivalent in political authority to the other pastoral clans who had migrated to Ankole with Ruhinda. Indeed, the system of gift exchange among the pastoralists called *okutoizha* which involved a gift of cattle in exchange for labor services or political support was probably a major adhesive element in pastoral society. Operating in the absence of any sovereign political authority, such personal contractual arrangements and marriage ties cemented the autonomous clans into kinship-based tribal society. The idea of the *Mugabe* as the titular owner of all cattle gave the system of exchange a central focus. Over time the *Mugabe* became the prime *giver* of cattle and 'liege lord' in the system of vassalage based on *okutoizha* contracts. The addition of honorifics and titles of office to the patronage pool by Nyabugaro and the extension of this system of clan office holders by Ntare IV could not in themselves create a state but merely generated something of a 'court life' (Karugire 1971: 161) around the peripatetic cattle kraal of the Hinda *Mugabe*, the leading descendant of the founding ancestor.

The other events recalled for this period of incubation (ca. 1500–1730) concern foreign and domestic wars and international affairs. The first recorded succession dispute between rival claimants to the title of *Mugabe* came around 1671. This dispute resulted in the death of the reigning *Mugabe* Kitera (1643–71) in battle against his half-brother, Rumongye, in a contest determined by the support of the maternal kinsmen of the rivals, while the Hinda themselves remained divided and aloof. This contest has been cited in support of the notion that by this time (the ninth generation from Ruhinda) Nkore's dynasty was sufficiently entrenched to afford a clash of arms without being unseated (Karugire 1971: 152). It might equally be used to support the contrary notion that succession to the *Mugabe's* position was still essentially a clan or family affair in which the other clans took little interest, only the Hinda and the maternal kin of the contestants being concerned in the outcome. It hardly constitutes firm proof of 'the success of the Bahinda clan in establishing itself as the dynasty of Nkore' (Karugire 1971: 152).

Two invasions by Bunyoro, the leading successor state to the Bacwezi Empire, are recorded by Ankole tradition and affirmed by Karugire. Ankole was overrun by the armies of *Mukama* Olimi I during the reign of Ntare I, Nyabugaro (1503–31 ± 37). The Ankole forces seem never to have opposed the invasion effectively and Ankole was saved from occupation and possible annexation to the Bito Kingdom of Bunyoro by a portentious natural event. A total eclipse of the sun (dated at 1520) appears to have persuaded Olimi I to abandon his successful conquests and return to Bunyoro.

Ankole's resistance to the second invasion[5] during the reign of Ntare IV two centuries later was hardly more respectable. Ankole was overrun by Banyoro armies and Ntare IV was forced to flee to the refuge of an island in the Kagera River. Cattle were confiscated and the Banyoro set up a capital in occupied Ankole territory. But for the success of Rwanda in repelling a Nyoro army and the Nyoro king's death during the campaign against Rwanda, Ankole might have remained occupied for some time. As it was, Ntare IV's forces, seizing the opportunity of the Rwandan victory, fell upon the Nyoro army returning through Ankole and inflicted a none too glorious defeat on the already defeated and leaderless Nyoro.

Both these military events occurring 200 years apart illustrate a curious anomaly. For a 'conquest state', Ankole was singularly lacking in even a defensive military capacity and clearly had never developed the organized force for carrying out any but the most casual of raiding operations. The absence of a military system for the defense of the territorial integrity of Ankole further attests to the nature of the society as a congeries of pastoral clans with only the most rudimentary institutions of chieftainship down through the reign of Ntare IV.

In the wake of the Banyoro invasions, Ntare IV began to experiment with political and military innovations which, after trial and error and under the impetus of new challenges and problems, would provide Ankole with the apparatus of a rudimentary state system. Indeed, even prior to the invasion, Ntare IV had begun to look to a wider field for the exercise of his limited authority. His first steps involved the neighboring pastoral kingdom of Mpororo where he contracted to marry two daughters of the royal house (Karugire 1971: 152–56), Mpororo appears to have been a monarchy welded together out of a similar congeries of pastoral clans, in this case collectively known as Shambo. The Mpororo state was closely linked to that of Rwanda, where a similar pastoral group was engaged in state-building activities (Vansina 1962: 10–16; Rennie 1972: 11–44). Ntare's matrimonial venture in this region, while greatly resented by the Hima clans of Ankole, seems to have strengthened his position at home by associating him with royalty from abroad and setting him a notch above the 'subject' Hima herdsmen who traditionally supplied wives for the Hinda. His refusal to marry more than these two Shambo royal women meant the exclusion of the Hima from the honored status of royal wives and the eventual passage of 'royal' authority to a son of the 'foreign' wives of Ntare IV. The Hinda ruling house was making of itself a dynasty, separated from its subjects by blood as well as honors.

Following the Nyoro invasion, Ntare also began to engage in military innovation, organizing the first regiments (*emitwe*) of trained warriors rather than relying upon a hasty call-up of able-bodied men. Trained in archery[6] as well as the traditional use of the long Hima spear, these young warriors were prepared to engage in offensive actions as well as the customary role of protecting cattle from predators and raiders. The system began with a disaster, when the first *emitwe* to try offensive action against the Lisa state of Buhweju on Ankole's northwestern marches was handed a resounding defeat by 'Buhweju's seasoned warriors'. (Karugire 1971: 162). The hastily built regimental system was abandoned at once. Nonetheless, the problem of effective military force for the creation and maintenance of state power was confronted for the first time by Ntare IV. Its solution would await more propitious times and more challenging circumstances.

One other innovation of Ntare's deserves some scrutiny. Tradition assigns to him the elaboration of the patronage system of clan offices and functions. From the beginning, the Yangwe clan had fulfilled certain important religious functions as well as some involving the 'royal' Hinda family. In time, a myth of common ancestry evolved to explain the special position of the non-Hima, agricultural Yangwe as 'half-brothers' to the Hinda. Karugire (1971: 96–97, 137–38) effectively explains the relationship as dating from the reign of Nkuba when the Yangwe were probably the most numerous and predominant of the farming clans and were treated in some ways as the original 'owners of the land'. Curiously, none of these functions performed by the Yangwe had anything to do with the royal drum, *Bagyendabwa*, the symbol of national unity and sovereignty. Yet Karugire, and Katate and Kamugungunu (1967: I, 23–24) assure us that the drum dates from the earliest times. Tradition speaks of it as the creation of Wamara, the last of the Bacwezi rulers. Although Karugire dismisses this as a legitimizing fiction invested by Ruhinda's successors, he believes that the drum's 'central role as the embodiment of the state . . . could hardly be of recent origin' (1971: 134). If the drum is central to the ideology of the state and its origins are in a later era, we have a further indication of a far later development of state institutions and ideology than tradition allows.

In this regard, the tradition that credits Ntare IV with appointing the Ruru clan as keepers of the royal drum may indicate the recent adoption of the symbolic royal drum. In addition, the tradition names a man from Mpororo, Kahurira, as having painted the Ankole drum to look like the royal drum of Mpororo (Karugire 1971: 160). Can this be taken to indicate that besides royal wives from Mpororo, Ntare IV also brought the Mpororo custom of a *royal* drum as opposed to a drum symbolizing only the unity of the clan?

Regardless of the validity of the details of the tradition, the reign of Ntare IV marks a transition from clan chieftaincy to incipient state institutions. In many ways, it was a period of experimentation and false starts. Only some dramatic new situation could provoke the successful creation of a state by the pastoral clansmen of Ankole. That situation was ripening.

3. THE TIME OF TROUBLES

Already in Ntare IV's reign indications of troubles ahead were becoming evident. Both foreign and domestic problems would increase to crisis proportions during the second half of the eighteenth century. External pressures in the period from the mid-eighteenth to the mid-nineteenth century began to shake and eventually destroy the less than splendid isolation of pastoral society in the dry, Isingiro hills. This was foreshadowed by the last Nyoro invasion which itself was probably triggered by what was a major source of disruption in lacustrine economy and society — droughts and the attendant famines. Moreover, the expansion of both Rwanda and Buganda made Ankole a marcher region subject to periodic raids, invasion and intervention by its powerful neighbors (Vansina 1962; Kiwanuka 1971).

Internal disruption, especially wars of succession which had been rare during the first two centuries of Ankole's history, also became a marked feature of the time of troubles following Ntare IV's memorable reign (Karugire 1972). The details of the succession wars which followed the death of *Mugabe* Rwabirere, the grandson of Ntare IV, need not concern us. Like the one previous disputed succession, the struggles following the deaths of Rwabirere, his brothers, Karara, Karaiga and Kahaya I as well as Rwebishenje has been attributed to the growing strength of the dynasty's grip on legitimacy (Karugire 1971: 167).

Two, and perhaps three, other explanations must be taken into consideration. First, the Ankole sovereign of 1750 and after ruled over a more extensive and wealthier society than the petty principality which Ntare IV received from his predecessors. Moreover, the personal power of the sovereign was increasing as he moved from primus inter pares to the undisputed ruler of an organized state apparatus. Thus, at around the mid-point of the eighteenth century, Ankole's succession became worth the fighting. Secondly, the increasing number of royal wives being taken from outside Ankole's pastoral clans and especially from Mpororo's ruling Shambo families may have led to situations in which widely separated maternal clans found themselves supporting their own favorite sons for the succession without the meliorating effect of any other cross-cutting linkages to temper their competition. Lastly, the general effect of the time of troubles which began near mid-century may have conduced to the spill over of violence from the expanding and aggressive pastoral economy into the arena of dynastic politics.

The sources on Ankole are silent on the precise sources of the internal troubles which befell the country at mid-century. But the responses of Ankole and of her neighbors in the marcher region between Bunyoro and Buganda to the north and east and Rwanda and Buhaya to the west and south are amply remembered. They testify to the dual process of militant pastoral expansion into new territories and of consolidation of a new political authority by the ruling herdsmen for a range of states running from Toro and the Salt Lakes region (Kamuhangire, n.d.) in the north to Kajara and Rwampara (Munyuzangabo, n.d.) and Ankole in the south. Principalities such as Kisaka, Kiyanja, Bugaya, Kitagwenda, Buzimba, Buhweju and Igara, Kajara and Rajumbura emerged as more hierarchical and more centralized than the previous societies in the area. It is argued (Steinhart, f.c.) that this widespread phenomenon can be attributed to a series of drought years and the resulting famine[7] which drove the pastoralists out in search of new pasturage in the better-water sections of country already inhabited by large numbers of agriculturalists living in settled villages (*ekyaro*). Persistent interregnum crises may have contributed to the famine conditions by prohibiting cultivation (cf. Katate and Kamugungunu 1967: I, 164) and increasing pastoral migrations out of the Ankole and Bashambo heartlands. Especially in the stretch of land running from Rwampara county of Ankole in the south through Shema, Igara, Buhweju, Bunyaruguru, Kitagwenda, Kibale, and north into Bunyoro west of Mubende and the Kafu River, pastoral and agricultural societies, both suffering from the effects of repeated crises came into an intimate, new relationship. The result was a transformation of the demographic, social and political features of the region, including the formation of a class system and the rudimentary state in Ankole later described in missionary and ethnographic literature.

4. THE EMERGENCE OF CLASS SOCIETY

The superimposition of a thin pastoral elite over an agricultural base comprising ninety to ninety-five per cent of the region's population is the distinguishing feature of the kingdoms of western Uganda. The stark contrasts in the economies, social systems and politics (Oberg 1943, 1938, 1940) of the two classes has led to undue simplification of the class structure of Ankole and to a distorted picture of the political system it supported. The first observers (Gorju 1920; Roscoe 1915 and 123; and Oberg 1940), marking the almost total exclusion of the agriculturalists from political power, described a system of class tyranny and pastoral hegemony of caste-like rigidity and confiscatory exploitation. Power over life and death and vast property rights in land and cattle were attributed to the ruling Hinda monarch which in fact he did not possess. Lesser powers of compulsion over Iru farmers and craftsmen were attributed to even commoner Hima which greatly exaggerated their real political and economic dominance. In short, the social and political system of Ankole was pictured as a rigid pyramid of power with an undifferentiated 'Bairu' farming class at base on which a Hima ruling class rested; all topped by the Hinda royal clan and its monarch, the *Mugabe*.

In contrast to this ethnographic picture, examining the events of the eighteenth century, particularly the expansion of herdsmen into new regions to the north and west of Isingiro, compels the conclusion that a caste-like hierarchy over the agricultural masses never existed in pre-colonial Ankole. Instead a dual pyramid with pastoral and agricultural legs was generated by Hima migration into agricultural areas. Both the herding and farming groups supported a very narrow apex of political leadership, the Hinda dynasty and court.[8] The pastoral pyramid placed the Hinda at top and below them a Hima aristocracy of owners of large herds of cattle. There were many such large herds which enabled the owners to enter into clientage contracts with poorer Hima who received the usufruct of a few head of his patron's cattle in exchange for his political loyalty and service in the menial tasks of the herdsmen. At the base of the pastoral leg of the pyramid stood those cattleless herdsmen, who without the title to ownership of cattle, herded the borrowed cattle of the wealthy rather than fall totally from the prestigious pastoral life into agricultural obscurity.

The agricultural pyramid was composed largely of semi-autonomous farming villages who accepted the nominal suzerainty of the better-organized herding community and their leading, and now, royal family. Often under the continued leadership of the lineage (*oruganda*) heads and big men of the farming community, the villages operated much as they had before the establishment of Ankole's dominance. Besides the ties of the new political claims to occasional tribute in beer and menial labor and the older connection of commerce in iron, agricultural and craft products and especially salt (Good 1972), a new instrument of subordination was forged. The clientage contract between free and independent herdsmen was amended to allow for a 'base vassalage' of farmers to the cattle-owning aristocracy and the pastoral ruling class. Ownership of cattle was still forbidden to the farming group with the important exception of special gifts for loyal service to the monarchy, especially in warfare (Karugire 1970). But the loan of non-reproductive cattle forged a reciprocal bond between the two classes to the clear advantage of the herdsman, who could breach the contract and recall his cattle at his pleasure. During the term of the contract the Hima received not only tribute in beer and agricultural products, but the labor power of those impoverished peasants who were without land or family and hence dependent on their patron's cattle and generosity for their support. It is probably through the extension of the term 'Bairu' or servant from these impoverished dependents of the herdsmen, made disparate and numerous by the impact of droughts and famine on agriculture, to the entire agricultural population that all farmers ultimately came to bear this approbrious name regardless of their status within agricultural society. By the late 1700s a parallel and a pyramidal structure of wealthy and prominent farmers, numerous smallholders and a base of propertyless agricultural workers stood next to the pastoral hierarchy, both supporting the Hinda dynasty and a new Ankole state (Steinhart 1973).

5. THE FORMATION OF AN EARLY STATE

The changes in social structure from the congeries of strictly pastoral clans and their direct dependants to a mixed pastoral–agricultural society under the hegemony of the pastoral groups led to the development of rudimentary state institutions of politics and administration, warfare and ideology over the century and a half left to the sovereign kingdom of Ankole. Certainly by 1850, the new state had developed a firm grip on the territory and populace of a wider Ankole society.

At the center of state power was the same Hinda group which had become central under Ruhinda and Nkuba. Now, instead of primus inter pares, the *Mugabe* was an autocratic ruler, 'whose rule was absolute and his decision on any matter final' (Roscoe 1923: 12). He presided over a court composed almost exclusively of Hima of means and some pretension, who sneered not only at the lowly 'Bairu' farmers, but at those Hima herdsmen whose pastoral activities kept them from the court and capital (Karugire 1970). While there were no official historians or court genealogists, men of good memory were present to advise on matters of precedent and propriety. Similarly, official poet laureates were unknown, but poetry composition and recitation was a major virtue of courtly life and manners (Morris 1964). The court gradually settled in one area somewhat to the north and west of the Isingiro heartland. Each new ruler was obliged to move to a new capital site on his accession and may have found it convenient to shift his capital to a more suitable grazing ground from time to time. Thus, while court attendance was encouraged, the capital did not emerge as an urban or administrative center, merely as the site of the large and prestigious royal kraal where other less imposing structures were erected.

The royal court served as a judicial and political center, but not as a bureaucratic focal point. The *Mugabe's* chief minister, the *Enganzi*, was not a prime minister in the usual sense of leader of government business. He was merely the King's favorite. Neither was there a cabinet nor governmental bureaux, although the colonial era saw the formation of a council of chiefs (*Eishengyero*) claiming traditional status. No distinction between the royal and state treasury was made and the heads of local administrative units were not required to attend court or reside at the capital as in Buganda, for instance. In fact, the only governmental business conducted at court was the hearing of cases, often involving the disputed possession of cattle or women by the Hima. The appointment and dismissal of military and administrative functionaries from among those aristocratic Hima and Hinda princes who regularly attended court was the *Mugabe's* sole administrative function.

Below the King and court was an irregular system of territorial authorities, chiefs in the common and colonial parlance, who administered the state in the name of the *Mugabe* (Richards 1960; Oberg 1940: 136–50). The most important pastoralist in a given area of the country was generally recognized by the herders as the local chief and confirmed in that post by the king. Often princes of the blood (*baginya*) were so recognized and hence made responsible for collection of tribute and taxation, especially in cattle which served as both a system of redistribution of pastoral wealth and a politically important addition to the system of cattle clientage practiced throughout pastoral society. One thing seems evident — little direct control over the *farming* community was exercised by this administrative hierarchy.

The military hierarchy seems to have had a more profound impact on the agricultural class. The system of standing regiments (*emitwe*) under the command of royal appointees begun by Ntare IV was revived by his successors and became fully operational under the command of royal appointees begun by Ntare IV was revived by his successors and became fully operational under *Mugabe* Mutambuka (1839–67) a century later. The intent was to establish both a defensive capacity in dealing with Ankole's expanding neighbors, specifically Buganda in the northeast and Rwanda in the southwest, and an offensive capacity in raiding the smaller marcher kingdoms for cattle and tribute. Thus, as the power of Bunyoro waned in the last half of the eighteenth century and the Mpororo kingdom disintegrated into a series of small Shambo statelets, Ankole was able to expand its frontiers among the petty principalities to the north and west. By establishing regiments and the herds of cattle to support them in the denser populated districts on the borders, Ankole not only secured and expanded its territory but continued the political transformations set in train by drought, famine and migration. Regimental command merged with the administrative hierarchy in the heavily farming districts as well as the pastoral frontier regions with Rwanda and Buganda. Hinda princes and royal appointees began to exercise direct hegemony over the loosely organized agriculturalists in these districts, collecting tribute and establishing new relationships of clientage. While territorial and military authority never became entirely synonymous, the fact that the Hima aristocrats held a nearly perfect monopoly of both ensured a close civil–military collaboration in the internal governance of the expanding state.

There is some evidence that recruitment of military leaders was open to a wider range of the population than merely the Hima herdsmen (Karugire 1970). A few notable 'Bairu' led regiments and became important military and court officials, presumably on the basis of service to the *Mugabe* in warfare. This must have been a very narrow avenue for social mobility among the Iru. Moreover, the achievement of high status generally meant the adoption of Hima clothing, customs and cattle (as the special gift of the *Mugabe*) leading to eventual inter-marriage and the obliteration of the Iru identification of the rising man of talents. Thus, military service, by operating as a safety valve of upward mobility, reinforced the hegemony of Hima values and the monopoly of state power by the pastoral class.

Only at the local level of village, or village cluster, was Iru political participation permitted. Here, as before the formation of state institutions, the daily life and communal decision-making remained largely in the hands of the leaders of agricultural society, unbothered and unconcerned with the larger affairs of state cherished by the Hima elite. The occasional tribute and taxation in beer, iron goods and other crafts must have been a small price to pay for the continued autonomy of the village communities in the heavily agricultural regions. The main burden of taxation, which was in cattle, must have fallen on the pastoral community, especially the poorer herdsmen whose cattle could be taken and who must have found themselves on the losing end when the herds were redistributed by the *Mugabe* to his courtiers, favorites and loyal supporters among the wealthy and prominent ('those who are known') of the Hima world. In any case, without a central bureaucracy or even an extensive dependent court to support, taxation in kine or in kind must have been well within tolerable limits for both the numerous farmers and the less numerous, but wealthy herders.

The emergence of a state was accompanied by the elaboration of a etatist ideology to support Hima dominance. In theory, the unity of the kingdom was symbolized by the *Mugabe* and the royal drum, Bagyendanwa, who stood in a mystical relationship of union with each other

(Oberg 1940: 156). The death of a *Mugabe* was symbolized by the overturning of the drum and marked by a period of interregnum chaos during which normal behavior was forbidden to even the lowliest of the realm. Planting and harvesting were interdicted and the herders often drove their herds from the kingdom until order was restored. The end of the interregnum was indicated by the successful claimant to the succession claiming, righting and beating Bagyendanwa; thus restoring the monarchy and its symbolic unity.

The veneration of the drum appears to have been the only state religion (Oberg 1940: 150–57). In the villages and kraals the veneration of clan ancestors and the various Bacwezi deities (*emandwa*) as well as the more recent and often anti-state 'Nyabingi' cult was practiced (Hopkins 1970). None of these beliefs or practices seem to support the state system and one must question the depth to which the etatist ideology of *Mugabe* and drum had penetrated Ankole society. While the Hima appear to have strongly supported the monarchy and those Iru who were personal dependants of the court or the Hima aristocracy seem to have shared their attitudes, there is some evidence that the vast majority of the agricultural community viewed the kingship and the drum as either irrelevant or inimical to their lives and interests.[9] By the late colonial era, the kingship did not possess the popular support of the majority of commoners — as was the case in Buganda or for that matter even in Bunyoro or Toro, the other pastoral kingdoms of western Uganda — to survive the colonial onslaught.

6. CONCLUSIONS

By the last half of the nineteenth century, Ankole had passed from being a collection of wandering herdsmen around a hero-chieftain to the stage of development of an early and very rudimentary state. The first European observers, coming from the developed industrializing states of Britain and France had no difficulty in recognizing in the *Mugabe's* court and regalia, the same general phenomena of kingship that they knew from their own not too distant histories. Occasionally, they even saw the territorial chiefs as earls and barons, the agriculturalists as serfs or peasants, the chiefly kraal as a kind of pastoral manor house in which the relations of European feudalism were reconstituted in an exotic and often barbarous cultural setting. Many of the analogs were more apparent than real. But at the basis of the perception of feudal and monarchical institutions was the fundamental fact that the people of Ankole and their neighbors had in isolation and by their own creative capacities solved many of the same problems of social and political organization in a manner similar to their European counterparts. Lacking in literacy and with a very rudimentary technology, the lacustrine people had created a hierarchical system based on a division of society into two classes. The dominant owning and ruling class preserved its position by monopolizing the scarce and strategic resources of cattle and controlling a political system which rewarded cattle ownership and pastoral values above all else. This 'cattle complex' often found in purely pastoral societies like the Masai or Nandi had produced first a proud and self-sufficient culture at a tribal level of development. In the confines of the lacustrine region, closely bounded by mountain and lake barriers and occupied by large numbers of cultivators, the resulting interaction of cattlemen and farmers — under pressure of drought and famine, which produced migration, expansion and resettlement — gave rise to a compound society with an ideology and institutions of monarchy and aristocracy, politics and warfare which we can classify as an early state.

Beyond this general conclusion, we can perhaps append a more specific statement on the nature of the Ankole state. Its compound nature, based on two originally autonomous economies and social groups, meant that the small pastoral ruling class, supported largely by the surplus produced by the herding economy, found it unnecessary to make heavy direct expropriations of labor or its product from the agricultural economy. The farming community, its village and lineage structure, continued largely undisturbed by high rents, taxation or tribute. The limited interpenetration and interdependence of the two economies and the overarching political authority of the pastoral ruling class supported by tribute from both economies gives rise to that sub-type of the tributary modes of production found in the lacustrine area and represented by such lacustrine states as the pre-colonial kingdom of Ankole and its neighbors.

FOOTNOTES

[1]   Neither the lacustrine nor other African modes of production constitute a separate or distinct type from the Asiatic or Tributary modes of production, itself understood as a variant of a more general primitive social formation. This is suggested on the basis of the absence of private property in land, the continuity of autonomous village communities and their systems of land tenure and the situation of these communities 'in the midst of the more elaborate social superstructure' (Hobsbawm 1964: 38) presented by the imposition of a state apparatus. The author understands these tributary modes to constitute a part of the primitive social formations between the patriarchal tribal societies and the full emergence of early class societies.

[2]   The original inhabitants probably practiced mixed farming, growing millet, sorghum and garden vegetables and keeping some cattle of the short horned (endora) variety, distinct from the Hima long-horned cattle (enshagara). Ultimately, under pastoral

pressure, all cattle came to be the possession of Hima. My thanks to M. T. Mushanga of University of Nairobi for this point.

[3] Cf. A. Munyuzangabo, *The early history of Kajara and Rwampara* on the dual status clan system of that region which he attributes similarly to 'eponymism'.

[4] At this stage it would be best to see Nkore as a chieftaincy of pastoral clans under the leadership of a central lineage figure. No standing army or administrative apparatus and irregular taxation appear to be in effect for the next 200 years during which time the centralizing role of the Hinda 'dynasty' over the pastoral population increased into what became, at most, a rudimentary early state (Cf. Karugire 1971: 135–37, 142–46).

[5] There is evidence for this being a third invasion following an invasion ca. 1627–35 during the reign of Ntare III Rugamba (or Kasasira), which was induced by cattle disease in Bunyoro and extensive raids of replenishment (Rennie 1973: 5–8).

[6] Karugire suggests emulation of Buhweju as the source for the use of archery in Nkore (1971: 162). I would suspect that the connection to Mpororo and through Mpororo to Rwanda is a more likely source. The use of Twa (Pygmy) archers especially by those states bordering the Congo basin like Rwanda, seems to be a much ignored feature of warfare among the herding societies of the lacustrine region.

[7] Two major droughts, the Nyamdere (1720–27) and the the Lamparanat (1785), are recorded for Northern Uganda (Webster, f.c.). Combined with the known tendency to use invasion and raiding to replace cattle lost to drought or disease, these droughts seem to have set in motion a major demographic and political process of concentration which accelerated during the eighteenth and early nineteenth century (Steinhart, f.c.).

[8] For a fuller description of the hierarchy, see Steinhart 1973. Contrast, Y. Elam 1974 and compare, M. Doornbos 1973. Graphically depicted, the Ankole hierarchy may be represented as follows:

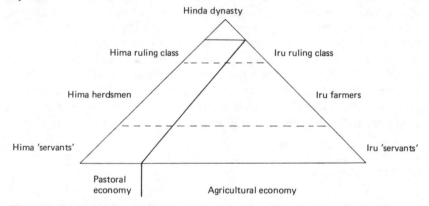

Figure 1. Social division of Ankole society.

[9] Personal interview with Rev. E. Kamujanduzi and Y. Katundu, leaders of the Kumanyana movement on 28 August 1968. Cf. Doornbos 1970 and Codere n.d. (1961?).

REFERENCES

Beattie, John (1971), *The Nyoro state*. Oxford: Clarendon Press.
Codere, Helen (1962?), 'Power in Rwanda', in: *Anthropologica* (series 2) 4: 45–83.

Cohen, D. W. (1968), 'The Cwezi Cult', in: *Journal of African History* 9: 651–57.

Coquery-Vidrovitch, Catherine (1966), 'Recherches sur un mode de production africain', in: *La Pensée* 144: 61–78.

Doornbos, Martin R. (1970), 'Kumanyana and Ruwenzururu', in: *Protest and power in black Africa*, ed. by R. Rotberg and A. Mazrui, New York: Oxford University Press.

— (1973), 'Images and realities of stratification in pre-colonial Nkore', in: *Canadian Journal of African Studies* 7: 477–95.

Dunbar, A. R. (1965), *A history of Bunyoro-Kitara*, Nairobi: East African Institute of Social Research.

Edel, May M. (1957), *The Chiga of western Uganda*. New York: Oxford University Press.

Elam, Yitzchak (1974), 'The relationships between Hima and Iru in Ankole', in: *African Studies* 33: 159–72.

Good, Charles (1972), 'Salt, trade and disease', in: *International Journal of African Historical Studies* 5: 543–86.

Gorju, Julien (1920), *Entre le Victoria, l'Albert et l'Edouard*. Rennes: Imprimeries Obarthur

Hobsbawm, Eric (1964), 'Introduction', in: Karl Marx, *Pre-capitalist economic formations*. New York: International Publishers.

Hopkins, Elizabeth (1970), 'The Nyabingi cult in southwestern Uganda', in: *Protest and power in black Africa*, ed. by R. Rotberg and A. Mazrui. New York: Oxford University Press.

Kamuhangire, Ephraim (1972), *Pre-colonial trade in southwestern Uganda*. Unpublished paper. Kampala. Uganda.

— (n.d.), *Migration, settlement and state formation in southwestern Uganda Salt Lake Region*. Unpublished paper. Kampala, Uganda.

Karugire, Samwiri R. (1970), 'Relations between Bairu and Bahima in nineteenth century Nkore', in: *Tarikh* 3: 22–33.

—(1971), *The history of the kingdom of Nkore*. Oxford: Clarendon Press.

— (1972), 'Succession wars in the pre-colonial kingdom of Nkore', in: *War and society in Africa*, ed. by B. Ogot. London: Frank Cass.

Katate, A. G. and Kamugungunu L. (1967), *Abagabe B'Ankole*. 2 Vols. Revised edn. Kampala: East African Literature Bureau.

Katoke, Israel (1971a), 'The history of the pre-colonial states of northwestern Tanzania: Introduction', in: *Journal of World History* 13: 512–14.

— (1971b), 'Karagwe: A pre-colonial state', in: *Journal of World History* 13: 515–41.

Kiwanuka, M. S. M. (1971), *A History of Buganda*. London: Longmans.

Krader, Lawrence (1968), *Formation of the state*. Englewood Cliffs: Prentice Hall.

Morris, H. F. (1962), *A History of Ankole*. Kampala: East African Literature Bureau.

— (1964), *The heroic recitations of the Bahima of Ankole*. Oxford: Clarendon Press.

Munyuzangabo, A. (n.d.), *The early history of Kajara and Rwampara*. Unpublished paper, Kampala, Uganda.

Oberg, Kalvero (1938), 'Kinship organization of the Banyankole', in: *Africa* 11: 129–59.

— (1940), 'The kingdom of Ankole in Uganda', in: *African political systems*, ed. by M. Fortes and E. E. Evans-Pritchard, London: Oxford University Press.

Oberg, Kalvero (1943), 'A comparison of three systems of primitive economic organization', in: *American Anthropologist* 45: 572–87.

Rennie, J. K. (1972), 'The pre-colonial kingdom of Rwanda; a reinterpretation', in: *Transafrican Journal of History* 2: 11–44.

— (1973) *The Banyoro invasions and interlacustrine chronology.* Unpublished paper, Kampala, Uganda.

Richards, Audrey, ed. (1960), *East African chiefs.* London: Faber and Faber.

Roscoe, John (1915), *The northern Bantu.* Cambridge: University Press.

— (1923), *The Banyankole.* Cambridge: University Press.

Steinhart, Edward I. (1973), *An outline of the political economy of Ankole.* Unpublished paper. Laramie, Wyoming.

— (f.c.), 'The kingdoms of the March', in: *Chronology in Africa*, ed. by J. B. Webster. Halifax: Longmans.

Taylor, Brian (1962), *The western lacustrine Bantu.* London: International African Institute.

Vansina, Jan (1962), *L'Evolution du royaume Rwanda des origines à 1900*, Bruxelles: Academie Royale des Sciences d'Outre Mer.

Webster, J. B. (f.c.), 'Noi-Noi, famines as an aid to interlacustrine chronology', in: *Chronology in Africa*, ed. by J. B. Webster, Halifax: Longmans.

Williams, F. Luckyn (1936), 'Sowing and harvesting in Ankole', in: *Uganda Journal* 3: 3.

Wrighley, C. C. (1958), 'Some thoughts on the Bacwezi', in: *Uganda Journal* 22: 11–17.

7 Axum

Axum was the second of the first three major states of intertropical Africa, and geographically the easternmost one. Complex ties of historical and cultural succession linked Axum with Meroe (and through the latter with Egypt and Sudan), the civilizations of South Arabia (and through them with the entire Semitic world) and the aboriginal cultures of the Kushites and other peoples inhabiting the Ethiopian highlands and the surrounding area.

1. GEOGRAPHICAL SITUATION

The administrative center of the Axumite kingdom and its surrounding territory embraces the Tigre plateau and the northern part of Ethiopia. This is a clearly defined area enjoying a mild, tropical and in places subtropical climate with regular monsoon rains. In the north, northeast and west it is bordered by desertlands, in the southwest by mountain forests and bush; its southern frontier is a high mountain range. In the central part of the plateau one comes across numerous sheer, flat-topped *amba* or 'table' mountains which once functioned as natural fortresses.

The isolated character of the Tigre plateau ensured protection from foreign invaders. Its geographical proximity to the centers of world civilization and sources of agricultural and natural products was an important advantage.

In the Arkiko–Zula district the plateau was separated from the Red Sea by only a narrow strip of land. The two major cross-roads of the ancient trade routes running through the Bab-el-Mandeb strait in the south and the Suez-Sinai isthmus in the north were only a few days' sea travel away. The Atbara-Taggaze and Gash river valleys connected the Tigre plateau with the fertile Nile valley and the civilizations of Nubia and Egypt. Immediately across the narrow Red Sea lay the fertile plateaux, valleys and oases of Arabia with its wealthy, ancient cities. Beyond the mountains in the south extended the vast and even more fertile plateaux of central, southern and eastern Ethiopia. Not far off, to the north and southwest of the Tigre (in the Nubian desert and Wollega), there were rich deposits of gold, platinum, silver and precious stones. Along the Red Sea coast lay coral reefs, pearl-oyster beds and turtle-hunting grounds. The area of the African Horn in the southeast was known for its incense- and myrrh-producing forests, and the central hinterland for its deposits of obsidian, antimony and mercury and its hunting-grounds abounding in elephants, hippopotamuses, giraffes, leopards and other valuable animals.

An important outcome of the pre-Axum period, embracing the third century B.C.—first century A.D., was the considerable level of development attained by petty, self-sufficient agriculture and craft production, thereby creating a sound base for the rise of a feudal-type economy on the Tigre plateau. At the close of the pre-Axum period another major socio-economic factor accelerating social progress emerged, viz. the sudden boom in trade in the Red Sea region and the northern part of the Indian Ocean as a result of the development of direct trade contacts between the Mediterranean countries and Egypt on the one hand, and India, Southeast Asia and East Africa along the trans-oceanic routes on the other. The heyday of this trade was from the first century B.C. to the early third century A.D. It is commented upon in the works of Strabo, Pliny, Claudius Ptolemaeus and Heliodorus, as well as in Pseudo-Arrianus' *Periplus of the Erythrean Sea*. These authors, together with the inscriptions discovered in Ethiopia and South Arabia, give the earliest information on the Axumites and on Adulis, the chief port of the emerging Axumite kingdom.

2. THE RISE OF AXUM

Adulis is first mentioned by Pliny somewhere around A.D. 60. One hundred years later by Claudius Ptolemaeus and in inscriptions from South Arabia the Axumites are mentioned. By that time Axum had brought under its sway all the *polices* and *demoses* on the Tigre plateau as well as on the coasts on either side of the southern part of the Red Sea.

The reasons for Axum's rise are not sufficiently clear. Apparently, Axum initially possessed the status of a ruling principality which in time developed into the metropolitan province of a feudal state. The principality attained its ascendant position owing to its location in the peripheral western areas of Tigre civilization, where it had relatively ample opportunity for expanding westward and southwestward with the aim of colonizing sparsely populated arable lands along the western edge of the plateau and seizing caravan routes running from the 'land of the Geez' and the seacoast to western Ethiopia and the 'island of Meroe'. The inhabitants of the Tigre plateau and of other areas belonging to Axum were divided into tribes. The structure of the latter is unknown. The stereotyped imprecatory formulas at the end of Axum inscriptions, telling of punishments of criminals and their families, perhaps refer to the 'extended family', about the structure of which, incidentally, nothing is known either.

One of the first tasks that history imposed on the Axumite rulers was the consolidation of their rule in the *polices* and principalities of northern Ethiopia, and the latters 'amalgamation' into a single kingdom. A guarantee of success was provided by the Axumite king's superiority in strength over the other rulers of ancient Ethiopia. Quite often the new king, upon his enthronement, assumed power through a campaign to subdue his vassals throughout his territory. This was definitely the case during the Axumite kingdom's golden age (third–sixth centuries), a time when its rulers began to subdue and subordinate the tribes inhabiting the Nubian and Danakil deserts and the territories of the Himyarite (Yemen) and Meroitic (Sudan) kingdoms. This led to the emergence of a huge empire which united under its rule the rich agricultural states of northern Ethiopia, Sudan and South Arabia, i.e., all the civilizations to the south of the Roman Empire between the Sahara in the west and the Rub'el-Khali desert in the east.

3. PRODUCTION

Most likely in this political system the highest level of production and culture was reached by the settled population of south Arabia, which had evolved a complex water-collecting and irrigation system, harvested two grain crops annually, built multi-storied houses and castles, and produced diverse handicraft wares that were famous throughout Arabia and were even exported to East Africa. In southern Nubia, the principal territory of the former Meroitic kingdom, which fell under Axumite rule in the fourth–sixth centuries, the level of economic and cultural development was much inferior. First priority here went to non-irrigated hoe farming (sorghum, millet), practised along with extensive cattle-breeding in the savannah lands; despite the downfall of the Meroitic civilization, iron-smelting and cotton-growing were not discarded, however. In central Nubia, which at times also fell under

Axumite rule, the level of development again was much higher, the plow being employed in farming, and in addition water-raising wheels; wheat, barley, grapes, various kinds of vegetables and date palms were cultivated here. During the first centuries A.D. the level of culture and production on the Tigre plateau fell below that in South Arabia and central Nubia, but in the fourth–sixth centuries the differences between their respective levels began to disappear. First, the rate of development in the territory of the Axumite kingdom proper was much higher. Secondly, in their military campaigns to Sudan and South Arabia the Axumites seized thousands of prisoners-of-war, as testified by inscriptions and certain narrative sources (Kobishchanov 1966. All other references in the present paper, unless otherwise stated, are also to this work). These prisoners-of-war were settled on the Tigre plateau. Most of them were peasants who brought with them valuable knowledge of irrigated farming, while craftsmen forcibly removed from other parts introduced into Axum proper as well as other Axumite cities the secrets of their trade, too. The population density on the Tigre plateau increased, not only as a result of the influx of prisoners-of-war from neighboring territories, but also due to the fact that the metropolitan province of the Axumite empire, being in its heyday, suffered fewer political catastrophes and hence escaped the inevitable resultant havoc. Thirdly, this latter factor (greater security) combined with the direct interference of the state power resulted in the diversion of trade routes of regional significance and the removal of stations located on the intercontinental trade routes within the boundaries of northern Ethiopia. This brought the country, and, in the first place, its principal cities, additional wealth which simultaneously stimulated the emergence of more sophisticated needs.

During the Axum period, particularly in the fourth–sixth centuries, remarkable social and cultural progress coupled with a vigorous development of production were to be observed in northern Ethiopia; a level of progress that was not to be rivalled until a thousand years hence. Dams and cisterns faced with polished stone, numerous terraced agricultural plots, and the remains of comparatively large and numerous settled areas all testify to the continual progress of agriculture. The Axumites grew wheat and most likely other grain crops as well, and also had a knowledge of viticulture. They reared huge herds of cattle and flocks of sheep and, like the Meroits, were skilled in catching and taming elephants, which were only used in the king's household, however. According to inscriptions, the people's daily fare consisted of wheat cakes, beer, wine, hydromel, honey, meat, butter and vegetable oils.

The history of Ethiopia displays an interesting feature, namely the development of cities on the eve of the Axum period, and more particularly during Axum's heyday (besides the capital, two other cities have been discovered: Adulis and Matara, and no less than three smaller towns).

In the cities whole quarters were covered with 'villas' of the local nobility. They were centers of large holdings, about which unfortunately too little is known. The Axumites had a fixed capital—the city of Axum, characterized by Byzantine travellers as 'a big city'. Its ruins now lie spread over several dozens of hectares. It included the royal palaces, royal necropolises and other cult structures, 'villas' of dignitaries, craftsmen's quarters, etc.

Considerable progress was observable in the sphere of the crafts. An important technological improvement was the more extensive use in comparison with the pre-Axumite period, of iron implements, which inevitably promoted agriculture, craft production and military science.

A number of crafts (casting, iron-working, pottery, weaving and others) in the cities of the Axum kingdom reached a high degree of technical and artistic perfection. However, we know nothing about the position of the craftsmen. In a later period, as also in neighboring southern and northern Arabia, Sudan and the Kushitic world, craftsmen formed closed castes, which were feared or held in contempt by agriculturists and husbandmen. Was the same true in Axum, however? However that may be, the entire range of crafts was quite probably separated from agriculture.

Another innovation was the introduction of clay mortar in building, leading to the construction of mixed stone and wooden structures. The new building technique was well adapted to the raw-material resources and climatic conditions in the Tigre plateau. It stimulated the development of urban house-building and led to the emergence of a new architectural style involving the use of a larger number of decorative elements and a greater variety of materials.

4. SOCIO-ECONOMIC RELATIONS

The little information that is available on the socio-economic and political structure of the Axumite kingdom allows us to characterize it as feudal, or rather early-feudal type of state.

According to our conception, the feudal economy, whose basic principle is the feudal rent in its most general form, is founded on the exploitation of the petty producer through 'extra-economic' coercion (Kobishchanov 1974: 233 ff.) The available data show that a primitive form of rent, or tribute produced through the labor efforts of farmers and cattle-breeders, who were personally free and united into communities, was the main source of income in the Axumite kingdom.

Non-free members of the population included palace slave-servants, slaves of foreign merchants and prisoners-of-war, but there is no information on their participation in production. In our opinion, slavery is an inevitable attribute of feudalism: the degrees of development of slave-owning and feudal systems are in many respects identical. For instance, patriarchal feudalism goes hand in hand with patriarchal slavery, while conversely 'penal' slavery in mines, galleys, etc., is usually accompanied by a high degree of feudalism, etc. (Kobishchanov: 202 ff.). Possibly the low level of development of the institution of slavery in Axum coincided with the low level of development of the system of feudal relations that is characteristic of the early-feudal stage in general.

The ruling stratum, headed by the king and his family, exploited the other community members not only by collecting tribute and employing them in large-scale building projects, but also by sending them off on military and trade expeditions. Aside from tribute, the Axumite king derived his income by appropriating the lion's share of the spoils of war. Cattle constituted a substantial portion of the latter. For instance, in the course of two particular campaigns, the one against the Nubians and the other against the tribes of Afan, the warriors of the Axumite king Ezana II (fifth century) seized on the whole over 32,500 head of cattle and over 51,000 head of sheep, to say nothing of the hundreds of camels. The recently discovered inscription of king Kaleb (sixth century) also dwells on the seizure of thousands of sheep, hundreds of cows and 200 camels from the rebelling Agwezats and Hasats (in the steppe lands south of the Nubian desert) (Schneider 1974: 775–776). It is not entirely clear whether these figures refer to the spoils taken by the entire army, or only to the king's share, though the latter is more likely. These animals were added to the huge existing royal herds. In an inscription telling of the migration of four Beja tribes, King Ezana I (fourth century) reports his gift of 25,000 head of cattle to these tribes. These figures enable one to form an idea of the vast numbers of cattle belonging to the king's household. The nature of the reports on the numbers of the king's beasts allow one to surmise that a strict record was kept of the size of his herds. We have no idea of the social status of the 'king's shepherds'.

In Axum, as in other states of pre-colonial Africa, cattle constituted a form of wealth that could only be converted into commodities with great difficulty. The systematic overseas export of cattle or sheep from Ethiopia was out of the question. It is true, however, that cattle could be driven to regions in the interior of Africa for sale to the local population there. Cosmas Indicopleustes, in his description of an Axumite trade caravan, mentions cattle being driven from Axum to Sasu. However, this cattle was taken along for the greater part as food for the members of the caravan.

5. TRADE

Although Axum's agriculture did not yield a notable surplus of produce for the market, the surplus from agriculture and stock-raising did
enable the Axumites to provide the needs of merchant vessels and
caravans and to engage in trade over great distances besides farming
and crafts. This trade was mainly channeled through socio-political
institutions, chiefly the state. In the world trade of the period, the
Axumite kingdom wielded considerable power. Evidence of this is
provided by the independent mintage of gold, silver and copper coins
between the late third and middle of the eighth centuries. The Axumites' monetary system was based on that of Byzantium. However, the
minting of coins, particularly gold, was both an economic and a
political act, and one that testified to the world at large the independence and flourishing state of the Axumite kingdom, while at the same
time acquainting it with the names and mottos of its kings. This
accounts for the frequent use of the Greek language—the most widespread international language between the fourth century B.C. and the
seventh century A.D. and the principal language of Byzantium—in
monetary inscriptions. The weight, metallic content and appearance of
Axumite coins, minted chiefly after the contemporary Byzantine
model, and the language of their inscriptions, as well as the objects of
foreign make discovered in the territory of Axumite Ethiopia, all
testify to the fact that Axum's chief foreign trade partner was the
Roman-Byzantine Empire. Of course, the situation was not entirely
the same throughout. For instance, the ban imposed by the Roman
emperors on the export of precious metals, iron and foodstuffs 'to the
Himyarites and Axumites' in the fifth to early sixth centuries must
have considerably affected the nature and volume of Roman imports
into Adulis. By the time of the Byzantine–Axumite alliance under
Iustinus and Iustinianus these restrictions, even if they had ever been
actually applied, had become quite insignificant. Commodities banned
for export outside the empire had to be procured from other sources
by the Axumites.

The trade carried on between the interior of Africa, the Roman
empire and the countries on the Indian Ocean through the intermediary of Axum and Adulis brought wealth first and foremost to the
Axumite nobility. In them foreign merchants found a group of consumers of luxury articles which enabled them to make the highest
profits. The prime consumers of foreign commodities were the king's
court and the courts of his vassal rulers. According to *Periplus* certain
goods, particularly gold and silver vessels and specific kinds of clothes,
were especially intended for the Axumite king. Most likely, foreign
merchants in the early third century were obliged to lavish gifts upon
the king in proportion to the extent of their wealth. The first reports of

trade duties in the Axumite kingdom, although not entirely reliable, date from the sixth century. The kings and their vassal rulers engaged in trade through agents. Cosmas Indicopleustes reported that a large trade caravan was regularly sent from Axum to Sasu, adding that 'The king of the Axumites sends his people for gold through the *arkhon* of Agaw'. The king's agents, who formed the nucleus of this caravan were usually joined by other persons (Axumites), most likely the agents of noblemen and other private traders. To all appearances the '*arkhon* of Agaw', who ruled a region in the neighborhood of Lake Tana, and whose territory the Axumite caravan always crossed en route to Sasu, was entirely responsible for its safety. An inscription by Ezana II specifies the punishment for assaulting Axumite caravans.

The population at large also derived certain advantages from trade. Many of the articles mentioned in *Periplus* were destined for the ordinary members of the population. Bracelets made out of imported bronze by local smiths, spears made of imported iron and clothes out of imported textiles virtually flooded the local markets and even reached the rural population. Yet there are no grounds for believing that the Axumite peasants paid for these goods with means procured through agricultural labor. War spoils, participation in caravans and gifts from the ruling classes, added to the privileged status of the peoples inhabiting the Tigre plateau and Adulis in northeast Africa and those living in South Arabia, as well as the residents of Axum proper—on the Tigre plateau—enabled them to buy and sell without having to produce any significant quantity of commodities themselves. In other words, the existing commodity–currency relations were not based on an adequate production of minor commodities.

It is only natural, however, that as far as monetary value is concerned the Axumites' trade should have been far below that carried on by the Roman–Byzantine Empire with the Asian states, or that of Sassanian Iran with its western and eastern neighbors, although in character it was identical. The political domination of the world trade routes gave the Axumite kingdom no less advantage than the direct participation in trade.

6. POLITICAL STRUCTURE

The structure of the Axumite kingdom was typical of the early-feudal, or, according to the terminology used by Skalník and Claessen, 'early' type of state. The kingdom fell into three zones girdling the capital in concentric circles. The immediate environs of the capital together with the city proper made up the Axumite kingdom in the narrowest sense of the word, where the king wielded power directly and his rule was the strongest. This was the part of the Axumite kingdom with the most privileges. The population of the city had, inter alia, the privilege of coming under the protection of the strong state power, while the agriculturists on the peripheries of the plateau were subject to the raids of nomadic tribes. The remaining part of the Tigre plateau together with the environs of Adulis made up the second zone, or the Axumite kingdom in the broader sense. It fell into several vassal territories whose rulers were subjects of the Axumite king and paid a more or less regular tribute to him. The third zone was made up first, of certain large kingdoms outside Ethiopia (Sudan and South Arabia), and secondly, of primitive states and tribes in mountain and desert regions where Axumite rule was the weakest. The full title of the Axumite king embraced the titles of his principal vassals and fell into three parts: as the ruler of the Axumite kingdom in the narrow sense of the word the head of the state bore the title 'King of the Axumites', or '*negus* of Axum'; as the ruler of the entire Tigre plateau he was called '*nagasi*'; and as head of the entire empire, king or *negus* of the principal territories of the 'third zone'. For instance, Ezana II called himself in written documents '*negus* of Axum and Himer [Himyar], and Saba, and Raydan [Dū-Raydān], and Salhen [the four latter in South Arabia], and Kasu [Meroitic kingdom], and Bega [of the Beja tribes], and Tsiyame [the latter in Africa]'; Kaleb Ella-Asbaha was known as '*negus* of Axum, and Himer, and Za-Raydān (Dū-Raydān), and Saba, and Salhen, and the Highlands, and Yamanat, and Tihamat [coastal plains of Arabia], and Hadhramawt and all the [nomadic] Arabs, and Beja, and Nuba, and Kasu, and Tsiyamo, and Darabat, and Atsfay' (the latter two being obviously also in Africa) (Schneider 1974: 771–773).

Moreover, the supreme ruler of the kingdom as a whole was called 'the king of kings'. There were also shortened titles, viz. 'king of the Axumites and Himyarites', or merely 'king of the Axumites' or 'king of Axum'. Each vassal area, both on the Tigre plateau and beyond had a ruler who was entitled to style himself '*negus*'. An inscription by Ezana II mentions '*neguses* of the armies', apparently referring not to special military leaders but to '*neguses*' of vassal regions at the head of military detachments from among their subjects. The number of the latter varied. The king of Himyar had hundreds of thousands of warriors, whereas '*neguses*' of the four Beja tribes during the rule of Ezana I had an average of 1100 subjects each, while the same holds true for *negus* Arabo on the Tigre plateau. Individual vassal kings (in South Arabia and Upper Nubia) in their turn also had vassals among the hereditary rulers of lower rank. Thus was formed a power hierarchy extending from the 'king of kings' down to the heads of individual communities.

The rules of succession in Axum are known to us only from the practice with regard to succession to the throne. The deceased ruler (king) was succeeded by his son, and more rarely his brother, that is all we know. Later traditions speak of a special kind of position of the ruler's mother and brothers. At any rate, the Roman emperor Constantine considered it necessary to address a specific message to two 'rulers of the Axumites' at the same time, viz. King Ezana and his brother Sheazana.

Nothing is known about the position of the elder sister of the king; she could hardly have reminded 'Lukokesha' of the empire of Lunda.

The Axum army was in all probability commanded by the king himself only, or by a person of virtually the same rank, namely a consanguineal or classificatory brother. Possibly, as in neighboring Meroe, perfect health and good looks according to a fixed concept were some of the requirements for candidates for the throne. The legends of northern Ethiopia (recorded in the fifteenth century) as well as southern Ethiopian traditions speak of the choice of the king by means of an animal oracle and of a ritual struggle of the candidates with a lion, bull or other strong and dangerous animal. However, in the actual documents from the Axum period, data on this are lacking (Kobishchanov 1963).

The death of almost every Axumite king led to a period of armed struggle for the throne and separatism in vassal principalities and kingdoms, although we know nothing of any sort of state of 'ritual anarchy' during the interregnum.

The king of Axum and his vassal kings took personal charge of building projects, and collected tribute from subordinate communities by touring around the country. This custom, observed in several early-feudal type of states in Europe, Africa and Oceania, involved the following: the king, accompanied by his numerous retinue, travelled through his lands personally collecting tribute from local rulers and heads of individual communities, who had to provide food for the entire party. In other cases vassal kings (like the King of Himyar, for instance) paid a yearly tribute to their suzerain.

The practice of these royal tours presupposes the existence of a certain surplus product under the conditions of an undeveloped state–political structure and undeveloped forms of appropriation and distribution, and furthermore a significant role on the part of the community and the prevalence of petty self-sufficient agriculture on the part of personally 'free' community peasants. However, we do not know anything for certain about the mutual duties and obligations of peasants and landlords, or about the influence of the state on the development of relations of ownership.

The sources give no information on the state apparatus of Axum, which to all appearances remained poorly developed. The king's nearest relatives (brothers, etc.,) played an important role in the country's administration and in the command of the armed forces. It may be supposed that the king's relatives formed a special ruling group in the state. The story of Frumentios, a prisoner from Axum who became treasurer and secretary to the king, and upon the latter's death—his infant son Ezana I succeeding to the throne under his mother's regency—the queen's most influential councillor, and later the first bishop of Axum, shows the significant role of the king's confidential slaves in the system of the state administration. It is further known that Abreha, also a former slave, became a vassal king of Himyar, which for some time was quite independent of Axum, coming to the throne here as a result of a military coup. Nevertheless, Abreha to all appearances held one of the key posts in the Ethiopian army which occupied South Arabia even before he became king. The army fell into a number of separate detachments, or 'armies' (probably numbering several hundred men apiece) bearing chiefly ethnic names. Among these latter one comes across ethnonyms of the Ethiopian tribes subjugated by the Axumites: Metin (in Ezana's inscriptions), Agaw (in the inscription of Wa'azeb, the son of Kaleb Ella-Asbaha), and several others which in the author's opinion were connected with the tribal organization of the Axumites proper (Schneider 1974: 784). Besides, there was the '*Hara* army', which under Ezana's rule formed a special detachment of the latter's troops and may have functioned as the king's guard. In Wa'azeb's inscriptions, however, one comes across the use of the expression '*ahzab* seemingly in opposition to *hara* (to the peoples) (Schneider 1974: 781). Meanwhile, in the inscriptions of Ezana and Kaleb the expression 'my peoples' ('*ahzabya*) served as a synonym for the term 'my army' (*sarawitya*). In the post-Axumite period the term *hara* was used to denote the entire royal army or armed retinue, guard and court at the same time. It was probably in the heyday of the Axumite kingdom that the term '*Hara* army' began to acquire this meaning in contra distinction to other 'armies', which were detachments of individual 'peoples' or large communities or tribes.

The Axumite kings used to settle, especially bellicose tribes, or parts of these tribes, along the state frontiers: 'Abyssinians' in South Arabia, and the four Beja tribes in the Matlia region, or 'BYRN region', and apparently also in Begemdyr. In their new areas these ethnosocial groups, having received land, cattle and certain privileges from the Axumite king, would enforce his rule over the aboriginal tribes and communities.

The only surviving record so far, of Axumite law is contained in the inscription from Sāfrā, concerning the ritual of the king's visit to that community and the agreement about this between the community and the king. The latter most probably was one of the vassal rulers or regional *neguses*.

The closing lines of all Axum inscriptions, containing a curse against offenders, speak of such penalties as ostracism of the entire extended family, together with confiscation (or dispersion) of its property. Other forms of punishment were shackling and the confiscation of clothes. There are no data on capital or corporal punishments or mutilation, etc., although the sources of the fourteenth–fifteenth centuries make only too much mention of this. In fact, we know almost nothing about the law and judicial processes in Axum.

Too little is known of the history of Axum as yet for us to be able to give a detailed picture of its political system. One can only surmise that at the height of its development the Axumite kingdom was concerned with the centralization of the state power. In the fourth century Ezana went no further than either subjugating recalcitrant vassals, the hereditary rulers of separate principalities, or taking them captive.

In the sixth century Kaleb found himself in a similar situation at the beginning of his rule: he had to cope with rebelling vassal states in both Africa, including the Tigre plateau, and South Arabia. But in Arabia, at least, he began appointing local rulers, both in the centre of the Himyarite kingdom and in the surrounding areas (Nagran) from among the members of the traditional dynasties.

Besides, Kaleb settled certain of his warriors in these regions, whose leaders were directly responsible to him and controlled the local kings and chiefs.

7. IDEOLOGY

An analogous evolution took place in the official ideology of the Axumite kingdom. Inscriptions (including legends on coins) dating from the middle of the third to the middle of the sixth centuries give some of the kings 'ethnic sobriquets'. An 'ethnic sobriquet' was a composite of the word *be'esi* ('man') with an ethnonym which in many cases is identical with the name of one of Axum's 'armies'. This particular element of the king's title (which in Ethiopia survived until the thirteenth century) was linked in one way or another with the tribal and military structure of the Axumite state, and may have been a survival of the ancient Ethiopians' form of military democracy. In the late fourth century one comes across the Greek moto: $Tοῦτο$ $'αφεσητη χώρα$ i.e., 'That is why the country is content', in legends on coins. This 'demagogic' motto is semantically congeneric with the concluding lines of several inscriptions of Ezana I and Ezana II (which are bilingual, containing three parallel texts, in standard Ethiopian, 'pseudo-Sabaean', Ethiopian and Greek), where the king expresses concern for the glory of his 'city' and states that his people bear no burden (Littmann 1913; Anfray et al., 1970; Schneider 1974: 768–770).

With the introduction of Christianity under Ezana II the ruling class of Axum acquired a well-developed ideological system, which is reflected in the recently discovered Greek inscription of Ezana II (Anfray et al., 1970), Kaleb's (Schneider 1974: 770–777) and Wa'azeb's (Schneider 1974: 777–786) inscriptions. Under subsequent Axumite kings coin legends revived former mottos, which then alternated with pious Christian formulas. This alternation of mottos in coin legends and partly also in longer inscriptions by kings reflects a struggle between two tendencies in official Axumite ideology, with the 'demagogic' tendency finding support in local traditions.

Axumite art at the height of the kingdom's development is distinguished for its gigantic dimensions: colossal monolithic stelae reaching a height of 33.5 m erected on more than 100 m² platforms made of huge stone slabs, colossal metal statues, and huge multi-storeyed palaces, unmatched in either ancient or medieval intertropical Africa. This passion for gigantic structures reflects the tastes of the Axumite monarchy, as well as fulfilling a definite socio-ideological role. There is also observable in the architectural style of Axum, and particularly Adulis, Matara and the Debre-Damo monastery a tendency towards ornamentation, likewise connected with the growing interest in interior decoration. This provides evidence of the developing need for comfort, which in the post-Axum period, with its general cultural decline and destruction of cities, was only dormant.

Apparently in Axum, as in other states of the same level of development, the right of the king's relatives to superior powers or feudal ownership of the country was based on tradition and mythology. Possibly, elements of the latter have been preserved in official Ethiopian legends of the nineteenth and twentieth centuries. They cover diverse stories, which may be lineally arranged into a single narrative (from the semiotic point of view). And although the chronological connections between the general narrative of these diverse stories are rather fantastic, in their succession they reflect actual events in antiquity. The earliest myth tells of the victory of the hero Be'ese-Agabo ('man of the Agabo tribe') over a mythical serpent or dragon that once ruled the Tigre plateau. The hero's progeny are alleged to have formed one of the most ancient dynasties in this part of Ethiopia. This myth in turn links up with the myth of the birth of Menelik, the first king of the subsequent 'Solomon' Dynasty, which in its turn is connected with the legend about the migration of 'Menelik's companions', the forbears of Axum's noble families, from Palestine (Bezold 1905; Conti-Rossini 1897). The fourth story lists the names of Axumite kings (Drouin 1882; Conti-Rossini 1909b), its first part having a purely legendary basis. The official legend was used on the whole to substantiate the 'historical right' of the Solomon Dynasty to power over Ethiopia, as well as the privileges of the noblest Axumite families. There are grounds for supposing that in one form or another this legend goes back to the Axumite period and is in fact a variety of a story of a 'mythical character' (Winans' term, 1962).

However, we do not know anything certain about the epic traditions of the Axumites, aside from the information provided by the inscription of hadānī Dān'ēl and a recently discovered inscription W'ZB (sixth century A.D.), which are in many respects reminiscent of the military epic 'narratives' of the fourteenth and fifteenth centuries (Kobishchanov 1962). In fact, we have no idea either who was or were the keeper(s) of these epic traditions. From the late Middle Ages down to the present day a caste of wandering singers and story-tellers, called *azmari*, have fulfilled this function. The *azmari* were not particularly attached to the official court traditions, the guardians of which in the fourteenth and fifteenth centuries were special high officials from among the clergy. We do not know what the situation was in the Axum period.

The Axumites did not write chronicles, but they did already have lists of rulers, providing an early Axum genealogical record, which has come down to us in a number of variants, all with great distortions. We do not know who was the keeper of these genealogies in the Axum period. In more modern times the *azmari* were. They were attached to certain lineages, the genealogies of which they knew narrated and praised.

It should be noted that Axumite inscriptions, though lacking all traces of even the general story mentioned above, do give some unique information on the Axumite's pre-Christian polytheistic religion. It had some features distinguishing it from the astral religion practised in pre-Axum Ethiopia. The general Semitic god Astar was common to both religions. Mahrem, the god of lightning, thunder, rain and war was at the same time the ethnic and dynastic god of the Axumites. The king was believed to be the son of Mahrem, 'invincible by the enemy', which ensured him victory over his enemies. King Ezana thus used to call himself the son of Mahrem. The two celestial deities had two terrestrial counterparts: Beher and Medr. Mahrem—the god of war and the monarchy respectively. The rule of the astral and chthonic deities was similar to that of the holy kingdom over the people. At the same time, in the person of Mahrem, war was predominant over peaceful labor. The religion of the early Axumite period displays features of an early-class ideology, i.e., the ideology of a burgeoning feudal society.

As the son of a god, the king was worshipped by his people; upon his death he ranked among the gods. A later tradition asserts that Axum possessed a 'sacral kingdom' type of rites, found also in other states of Northeast Africa and linking up with the 'mythical charter' to form a single text (as contained in the medieval Ethiopian book *Kebra Nagast*). The Sāfrā inscription permits us to suppose that the king was obliged to visit his possessions regularly at a certain time of the year in order to renew the fertility of the land.

We do not know anything about the ritual of 'sacral kingdom' in Axum. In the Middle Ages, the king ritually had to conceal himself from his people, also in the states of southern Ethiopia, speaking with the latter through the intermediary of a special title-holder (*afe-negus*, literally 'the king's mouth'), while another title-holder fed the king. It is our contention that one of the highest titles of medieval Ethiopia, *hadānī*, originally meant 'feeder' (of the king). At the end of the Axum period (eighth century?) the *hadānī* seized the power, turning the kings of Axum into their puppets, who were still highly revered but were stripped of all power.

The introduction of Christianity supplemented and reorganized rather than destroyed the traditional system of early Axum's state ideology, which accounts for the continuing flourishing of Axum in the fifth and sixth centuries. The new religion was ushered in peacefully and gradually (in the course of at least 150 years), thus producing syncretic forms. Ethiopian Christianity contains certain elements testifying to its descent from the cults of Mahrem, Astar, Beher, etc., as well as specific forms of social organizations resembling ancient Eastern temple communities. Unlike South Arabia, Axum escaped Christian persecutions and knew no acute antagonism between religious sects. From the time of Athanasius the Great (mid-fourth century) to that of the first Moslems (early seventh century) Axum often gave shelter to persecuted sectarians from other countries. At the same time the Axumites played an important role in the spread of Christianity in South Arabia and southern Nubia (Alwa).

As in other early-feudal states, the introduction of a monotheistic religion, especially one as highly developed as Christianity, provided the ruling social class with extremely effective means of social regulation which helped to preserve social peace under the conditions of a class society as well as the unitary character of the polyethnic empire. The wide distribution of Christianity promoted the cultural rapprochement of its peoples, as well as the ethnic integration of the population

groups of northern Ethiopia into a single nation. The high level of
Axumite culture became an example—long unrivalled—for Ethiopians
of the middle and late medieval period, as well as an authoritative
cultural frame of reference for the whole of northeastern Africa. For at
the end of the Axum period cities disappeared in Ethiopia, the capital
city being replaced by a temporary royal camp, scattered monasteries,
bazaars and thousand-year-old trade routes leading to the semi-Arabic
cities on the coast and the Nile. Only at the end of the Middle Ages
did cities and permanent capitals again appear in Ethiopia.

REFERENCES

Anfray, F. (1963), 'Une campagne de fouilles à Yeha (février-mars 1960)', in:
    Annales d'Ethiopie 5: 171–192.
— (1967), 'Matarā', in: *Annales d'Ethiopie* 7: 48–53.
— (1968), 'La poterie de Matarā: Esquisse typologique', in: *Rassegna di Studi
    Etiopici* 22: 5–74.
— (1974), 'Deux villes axoumite: Adoulis et Matarā', in: *IV Convegno
    Internazionale di Studi Etiopici* (Roma, 10–15 aprile 1972), 1: 745–765.
Anfray, F., Caquot, A. and Nautin, P. (1970), 'Une nouvelle inscription grecque
    d'Ezana, roi d'Axoum', in: *Le Journal des Savants*, 260–274.
Bezold, C. (1905), *Kebra Nagast: Die Herrlichkeit der Könige.* München.
Caquot, A. and Drewes, A. J. (1955), 'Les monuments recueillis à Maqallé
    (Tigré)', in: *Annales d'Ethiopie* 1: 17–41.
Contenson, H. de (1961), 'Les fouilles de Haoulti en 1959', in: *Annales
    d'Ethiopie* 4: 41–52.
Conti-Rossini, C. (1897), 'La leggenda etiopica di re Arwé', in: *Archivio per le
    Tradizioni Populari* 1.
— (1909a), 'Notes sur l'Abyssinie avant les sémites', in: *Florilegium Melchior
    de Vogue.* Paris, 148–151.
— (1909b), 'Les listes des rois d'Aksoum', in: *Journal Asiatique* 14: 259–320.
— (1928), *Storia d'Etiopia.* Milano, Bergamo.
Doresse, J. (1957), 'Découvertes en Ethiopie et découverte de l'Ethiopie', in:
    Bibliotheca Orientalis 14: 64–65.
Drewes, A. J. (1962), *Inscriptions de l'Ethiopie antique.* Leiden: Brill.
Drouin, M. E. (1882), 'Les listes royales éthiopiennes et leur autorité histori-
    que', in: *Revue archéologique*, août–octobre: 99–224.
John of Ephesus (1923), 'Lives of the Eastern Saints, 1' in: *Patrologia
    Orientalis* 17. Paris.
Kobishchanov, Iu. M. (1962), 'Skazanie o pokhode hadānī Dān'ēla. Epiches-
    kaya nadpis pozdnego Aksuma' [Story of an expedition of hadānī Dān'ēl.
    Epic inscription of late Axum], *Narody Azii i Afriki* 6.
— (1963), 'Izbranie tsaria v drevnem Aksume' [Election of the king in
    ancient Axum], in: *Vestnik drevnei istorii* 4: 140–144.
— (1966), *Aksum* (Axum). Moscow: Nauka.
— (1970), 'les données primordiales sur les chasseurs-cueilleurs de
    l'Ethiopie', in: *Actes du VIIe Congrès international des sciences an-
    thropologiques et ethnologiques*, vol. 9: 223–225. Moscow: Nauka.

—— (1974), 'Afrikanskie feodal'nye obshchestva: vosproizvodstvo i neravnomernost' razvitia' [African feudal societies: reproduction and irregularity of development], in: *Afrika: vozniknovenie otstalosti puti razvitia*, pp. 85–290. Moscow: Nauka.

Littman, E. (1913), *Deutsche Aksum-Expedition* 4. Griechische, Sabaische und altabessinische Inschriften. Berlin, No 4, 6, 7, 11.

Schneider, R. (1961), 'Inscriptions d'Enda-Čercos', in: *Annales d'Ethiopie* 4: 61–65.

—— (1974), 'Trois nouvelles inscriptions royales d'Axoum', in: *IV Congresso Internazionale di Studi Etiopici* (Roma, 10–15 aprile, 1972) 1: 767–786.

Simoons, F. (1965), 'Some questions on the economic prehistory of Ethiopia', in: *Journal of African History* 6, no 1: 1–12.

Winans, E. V. (1962), *Shambala: the constitution of the traditional state.* Berkeley: California University Press.

8 The Legitimation of the Aztec State[1]

DONALD V. KURTZ

A number of authors have put forth hypotheses which attempt to explain the emergence of early protohistoric states (Fried 1967; Wittfogel 1957; Oppenheimer 1975; Cohen 1969; Adams 1966; Carneiro 1970; Flannery 1972). However, a problem that has not been addressed is how early states survive once they have emerged. It is suggested here that their survival depends, in large measure, upon their ability to achieve legitimacy.

A state refers to a centrally controlled set of interlocking bureaucracies under the leadership of one man who is the central actor in the social and political affairs of a nation. A nation refers to the population and communities which reside within a more or less firmly demarcated territory over which a state extends control (Cohen 1969; Polanyi 1966; Sahagun 1954).

Cohen (1969) has suggested that most early states have been formed through a process of incorporation, and he has referred to these as 'incorporative states'. State formation in pre-Hispanic Mexico was based upon the process of incorporation. The Aztecs, the focus of this chapter, created the last incorporative state in central Mexico prior to the Spanish conquest.

An incorporative state is one which is still in the process of welding into a nation the peoples and communities which reside within a specified territory. An incorporative nation is one which has not crystallized into a sharply defined socio-political unit and whose territorial boundaries are somewhat indeterminate. Generally, the peoples which incorporative states attempted to unify lived relatively close together geographically. They were at approximately the same level of cultural development. Dominant and subordinate groups were culturally similar, spoke the same or similar language, and were

relatively ethnically homogeneous. Most commonly, early incorporative nations were established by conquest (Cohen 1969). This model
was approximated in the central highlands of pre-Hispanic Mexico.

Early incorporative states were also inchoate states; that is they had
not yet 'completely subverted local sources of solidarity, allegiance,
and authority' (Cohen 1969: 661). It was the existence of local sources
of autonomy which threatened the survival and persistence of early
incorporative states. In order to survive they had to rapidly acquire
legitimate status. The legitimacy of authority rests upon the support
which the polity provides the political system and the fulfilment of
mutual obligations between state and citizen (Swartz et al. 1966;
Weber 1947, 1962). Legitimacy is not given. States must actively
pursue it, and its accomplishment is the result of a protracted process.

A state which is engaged in the process of legitimation attempts to
shift the allegiance of the citizen from local centers of authority to the
state. In part the state accomplishes this by attempting to usurp the
functions of local groups, such as education of children, collection of
taxes, the right to punish criminals, regulation of marriage and divorce,
and conscription of military units. The state also attempts to reduce the
power of, if not supplant with state structures, local organizations
which the state perceives as a threat to its authority, such as lineages,
clans, age sets, secret societies, and the like.

Weber suggests (1954) that the transition from a social order whose
validation derives from mere tradition to the belief in legitimacy is
indeterminate. It will be argued here that the process by which the
early incorporative inchoate state attempts to achieve legitimacy is
highly predictable. However, particular aspects of the process may vary
depending upon specific circumstances which the state has to confront.
And different states may achieve comparable levels of legitimacy at
different rates. Broadly, the process entails three phases.

First, once the independent state is established it employs several
tactics designed to acquire power sufficient to promote its survival.
Secondly, the state will seek to validate its authority structure by
developing a legal basis for its actions. In large measure, the acquisition of legitimacy is based upon law. The state then imbues its
political–legal structure with divine sanctity derived from its religious
institutions. Finally, the state undertakes a broad program of political
socialization which involves benevolence, control of information, and
terror. The pursuit of legitimacy entails the mobilization of the state's
technology and institutions. It is a multi-pronged process, accomplished slowly, a step at a time, and it is rarely complete. This process
will be analyzed with specific reference to the Aztecs of central
Mexico. First, an overview of Aztec society and the state will be
presented. Then the process of legitimation will be discussed.

1. AZTEC SOCIETY: AN OVERVIEW[2]

After the decline of the influence of Tula in the central highlands in the twelfth century, Toltec peoples from Tula and Chichimec hunters and warriors from the north settled in the Valley of Mexico. They founded and lived in cities around the shores of the valley's lake system and fought with each other for political hegemony. One of the last waves of Chichimec nomads to enter the valley was the Aztecs.

According to legend, for over a century the Aztecs moved south from northwest Mexico. They were directed by their oracles through whom their tribal god, *Huitzilopochtli*, spoke. *Huitzilopochtli* promised to provide a sign for his chosen people informing them when their peregrination would end. Once in the valley the Aztecs acquired a reputation as fierce warriors. Around 1325 the long promised sign appeared. Under Tenoch, their paramount chief, they began to build the city of Tenochtitlan on the marshy islands of Lake Texcoco. Tenochtitlan grew and prospered. By 1520 it was the capital of the Aztec nation and the nerve center of a vast, but loosely-knit empire.

Around 1375 the Aztecs acquired their first king and entered a phase of incipient statehood. However, they were too weak to assert their independence and served for fifty years as vassals to the Tepanecs of Azcapotzalco. In 1428, led by their king Itzcoatl (1428–1440), the Aztecs defeated the Tepanecs in a war and their first step toward an independent nation was taken. Over the next ninety-two years the Aztecs vigorously pursued a career toward statehood and empire. That career had not run its full course when the state was truncated in 1521 by the Spaniards.

On the eve of the Spanish conquest of Mexico the Azetcs had hegemony over a vast region. Their technology and social organization were complex, differentiated, and specialized. Tenochtitlan was one of the largest cities in the world and, undoubtedly, one of the most splendid. Its population numbered around 200,000, and it was growing (Calnek 1972; Cortes 1928; Hardoy 1973). Aqueducts carried fresh water from the mainland to the city. Broad causeways connected the city to the mainland. Roads linked Tenochtitlan to other cities in the valley and beyond. Transportation on the lakes helped supply the city and was critical to its survival (Sahagun 1963; Motolinia 1950; Cortes 1928; Bray 1968; Brundage 1972).

Aztec society was socially stratified. Higher ranked social categories were the nobility, priests, military leaders, and the *pochteca*, traders for the state. In the cities commoners engaged in commercial and craft activities. An indeterminate urban population existed in poverty. Some rural commoners were peasants; others were serfs on the estates of nobles. Slaves occupied the lowest rung of the social hierarchy. Mobility across class lines was not common. Upward mobility for commoners came mainly through gifts of land with an attendant title from the emperor to brave warriors (Zorita 1963; Duran 1964; Caso 1963; Bray 1968; Carrasco 1971).

Subsistence was acquired through an intensive agricultural technology. Irrigation was widespread in the Valley of Mexico. Dikes separated saline from fresh waters in the lakes and helped control flooding. Hillsides were terraced. Human excrement was used as fertilizer (Bray 1968). *Chinampas* were worked year around.

Tenochtitlan was expanding through the on-going construction of *chinampas*, which also served as living sites (Calnek 1972). But only a small part of Tenochtitlan's population was engaged in agriculture as its primary occupation. Most urban occupations were specialized and diversified, consisting primarily of administrative, commercial, ecclesiastical, military and craft activities (Calnek 1972; Sahagun 1961).

Produce obtained by agriculture in the valley probably was insufficient to satisfy the daily requirements of the growing population. Produce had to be imported (Bray 1972; Molins Fabrega 1954–1955; Hardoy 1973). It was supplied in large measure by tribute exacted from conquered peoples and through trade (Duran 1964; Davies 1973; Zorita 1963). Aztec imperialism is explained best perhaps as a response to the press on resources in the central highlands and the inability of the population to produce sufficient food (Duran 1964; Brundage 1972; Calnek 1972; Kemp 1954; Hardoy 1973).

Trade on behalf of the state was conducted by the *pochteca*, a merchant category comprised of several specialized sub-categories, who forged to the frontiers of the empire. They traded in resources essential to the state, opened new markets, and often served as the vanguard for the conquest of new territories. They also represented a firmly bounded social category. They lived in separate neighborhoods with their own political organization, maintained separate shrines, worshipped their own deities through their own priesthood, and married endogamously (Bray 1968; Chapman 1957; Hardoy 1973).

Produce and goods were made available to the people through markets and by redistribution carried out through state bureaucracies and agencies. An extensive market system interlocked the cities of central Mexico and the diverse ecological regions beyond (Kurtz 1974). Redistribution by the state was based upon the collection of tribute from conquered peoples, taxes imposed upon Aztec citizens, and the trade in which the state engaged with other nations (Duran 1964; Sahagun 1959; Kurtz 1974). Although periodic doles of food, clothing, and other materials were made to the people, redistribution was most common in the periods of natural calamity which frequently hit Aztec society, such as famine due to drought or flooding (Duran 1964; Burland 1973).

The emperor, head of the state, was advised by a four-man council and a head minister, the *cihuacoatl.* Succession to the office of emperor was traced through the highest ranking 'clan' of Aztec society. Early in the state's history the ratification of the person who had been selected by the leaders (heads of the *calpulli* and possibly war chiefs) to be emperor was done popularly. By the sixteenth century the selection and ratification of the emperor was accomplished by a few high ranking individuals among whom were the *cihuacoatl* (Soustelle 1961; Duran 1964; Gómara 1877; Brundage 1972).

The emperor was commander-in-chief of the army, the central actor in the redistributive process, ultimate source of appeal in legal matters, and the central figure in many political and religious rituals (Sahagun 1954). He was also obliged to marry daughters of kings of other nations in order to establish and maintain alliances (Burland 1973; Duran 1971; Motolinia 1950; Caso 1963). The nobility occupied offices in the state bureaucracy. The bureaucracy extended over the empire and penetrated to the local level. It administered policy at home and abroad, collected taxes and tribute, and maintained social order in the empire (Cortes 1928; Zorita 1963).

Tenochtitlan was divided into four wards. Each was a political unit with leaders, tax-collectors, and police. Wards supplied corvee labor and military units to the state. Each had a men's house in which political activities transpired and schools in which the children were educated. Nobles and commoners lived interspersed in the wards (Carrasco 1971; Duran 1964; Hardoy 1973).

Each ward was made up of several *calpullis,* or administrative and territorial units. The primary function of the *calpullis,* the structure of which will be discussed subsequently, was to administer tenure over lands which some *calpullis* owned corporately. Each *calpulli* was governed by a council of elders with a head elder elected popularly. In addition, a head man of noble status was appointed by the state to oversee *calpulli* political affairs (Caso 1963; Hardoy 1973; Bray 1968; Carrasco 1971; Zorita 1963; Brundage 1972).

A complex legal system supported the state in directing civil affairs (Zorita 1963). Laws were codified and enforced by police. Jails existed to detain criminals until trial (Duran 1964; Bray 1968). Courts were established in a hierarchy, which also comprised a routed appeal. Punishment of convicted criminals was carried out by state-appointed personnel (George 1961; Sahagun 1951). 'Lawyers' may have represented individuals in some matters (Zorita 1963; Sahagun 1961;

George 1961). Ultimate appeal was to a high court over which the emperor presided (Duran 1964; George 1961).

Aztec religion was polytheistic. Its personnel and institutions complemented the support provided the state by the legal system (Matos 1975; Nicholson 1971; Caso 1937). The state religion was directed by a specialized priesthood which conducted rituals and ceremonies in the temple precinct of Tenochtitlan on behalf of the state (Duran 1964). At the local level each *calpulli* had its own temple, priesthood, and deities and a variety of household gods were propitiated (Caso 1958; Duran 1964; Carrasco 1971).

Calpullis may also have been significant as kinship structures, although, over time, administrative functions became increasingly important. When the Aztecs entered the Valley of Mexico, *calpulli* social structure may well have comprised some form of ramage, or conical clan. By the sixteenth century the *calpullis* were probably still ranked. Some were specialized in crafts; some were wealthier than others. One clan had the prerogative of supplying the emperors (Monzón 1949; Adams 1966; Carrasco 1971; Duran 1964; Bray n.d.; Sahagun 1952; Zorita 1963). However, *calpulli* kinship functions were probably a mere vestige of what had existed earlier.

Little is known of Aztec kinship rules. By the conquest it is likely that marriages between *calpulli* members were increasingly common and dominated by patrilineality and patriclocality (Zorita 1963; Carrasco 1971; Bray 1972; Hardoy 1973). Households were structured around single, extended, and bilateral joint families (Calnek 1972; Bray 1972). Marriages were often negotiated by matchmakers who served as intermediaries between families (Duran 1971; Sahagun 1951; Zorita 1963). Polygyny was permitted, although monogamy was the norm (Carrasco 1971). The decline of *calpulli* kinship functions is probably the result of the process of legitimation, for tightly knit kinship groups may pose a threat to the legitimacy of the state to the extent that they provide alternative sources of allegiance and loyalty for the citizenry (Fallers 1965; Engels 1942; Goode 1963).

Education in Aztec society was compulsory, but not equal (Bray 1968). Children of the nobility attended the *calmecac* school; commoners attended the *telpochalli*, or young mens' house in their ward (Carrasco 1971). Curriculum and education differed in each school, but both stressed the making of an Aztec citizen and conformity to state values and norms (Brundage 1972; Sahagun 1969; Bray 1968).

In the sixteenth century the Aztec state was still in the process of incorporating the disparate communities, groups, and populations which created its inchoatcy (Bray 1972; Hardoy 1973). The following sections explore the process outlined previously by which the state strove to reduce inchoatcy and thus achieve legitimacy.

2. LEGITIMATION OF THE AZTEC STATE

2.1. Imperatives at the Acquisition of Statehood

Upon achieving independence the Aztec state took several steps to ensure its survival. These included the expansion of social distance between the rulers and the ruled, specific moves to consolidate power, and alteration in the obligations between the state and citizen. Demands upon the citizens to which they undoubtedly had long been subject, such as taxation, corvee labor, and military service, became increasingly important to the survival of the state. Enforcement of these obligations by the state provided means by which allegiance of the citizen to the state could be obtained at the expense of that demanded by local authority structures, such as the *calpulli*.

2.1.1. Social Distance. In inchoate states a sharply delineated political structure above the local level seems essential to the survival of the state. Expanding social distance between the rulers and ruled advances the mystique of the rulers and enhances the respect which the state authority structure demands (Cohen 1969; Lenski 1966; Kuper 1972). In Aztec society the distance between social categories was stressed from the reign of Montezuma I (1440–1468) onward, and this was a critical period in the formation of an independent state. For example, the significance of this action is suggested by the first clause of Montezuma's law code which asserts that the emperor should not appear in public except on special occasions (Duran 1964).

At least from the reign of Montezuma I patterns of deference and demeanor were established by which commoners were obliged to relate to the nobility. By the sixteenth century commoners were forbidden to speak or look directly at the king, and they had to prostrate themselves before him (Duran 1964; Davies 1973). Sumptuary laws were enforced. Clothing styles, jewelry and other status symbols distinguished nobility from commoner (Duran 1964, 1971; Sahagun 1954; Brundage 1972). Differential education for nobles and commoners enforced the social distance. Validation for the subordinate status of the commoners was provided even by legend. At the time of the Tepanec war (1428) the nobles, anxious for a fight, made a pact with the commoners, who were less anxious to fight. If the war was lost the nobles agreed that the commoners could do with them as they wished, even kill them. But if the Aztecs were victorious the commoners forever after would serve the nobles.

Actions of Montezuma II (1502–1520) symbolized the role social distance plays in maintaining the mystique and power of authority. By the time of his reign the nobility had grown in size considerably, and internal and external problems were threatening the viability of the state and empire. Increased centralization of government was one way to respond to these problems. Montezuma II reduced the size of the nobility. Nobles of questionable birth were relieved of state posts and denied privileges; many were executed. The bureaucracy was restructured and access to state office was restricted to legitimate nobility (Duran 1964; Carrasco 1971). These actions had the effect of hardening the division between the classes.

2.1.2. *Consolidation of Power.* The consolidation of state power entails the imposition of state control over critical areas of the society and a neutralization of the power and influence of local groups. It is difficult to identify many specific social structures in Aztec society which opposed the state in demanding the allegiance of the individual. But, as noted, corporate kin and other groups are social entities which present alternatives to state authority and against which states react. In Aztec society, the *calpullis* and *pochteca* represent organizations which seemed to offer such an alternative. The Aztec state took measures to control these groups, and probably others.

Over time the *calpulli* was subjected increasingly to state controls and infiltration. As noted, headmen of noble descent and priests were appointed by the state over *calpulli* political and religious organization. *Calpullis* were ethnically mixed as a matter of state policy, presumably to reduce the possibility of rebellion (Brundage 1972). *Calpulli* members were expected to adhere first to state laws and, regardless of local deities, citizens were expected to venerate *Huitzilopochtli* (Brundage 1972). The individual's right to land was determined by his status within the *calpulli*, but status within the *calpulli* increasingly was determined by the state.

Upon marriage an individual was inscribed in the *calpulli* register for tax purposes (Zorita 1963; Carrasco 1971). If a male did not marry by a reasonable age he lost his rights to land (Zorita 1963). The state also may have been restricting polygynous unions (Duran 1964; Burland 1973; Carrasco 1971). And once married, divorces were granted reluctantly by the courts (Zorita 1963; Duran 1971).

The *pochtecas* were intimately involved with state economic, military and political affairs, and by the power they controlled and the firmness of their organization, it is likely that they posed a potential threat to the state. The state responded to this in two ways. It permitted, perhaps even promoted, the firmness of the social boundaries of the *pochteca* noted earlier and in this way functionally separated them from Aztec society at large. This permitted closer control over their activities. The state also restricted their activities. For example, certain categories of *pochteca* were not allowed to trade in local markets. Others were permitted to trade only in certain commodities, such as slaves. In general, the economic activities of the *pochteca* were restricted to international ports of trade (Sahagun 1959; Chapman 1957).

Conquered peoples and others in the nation and empire were controlled in part by changes imposed by the state in their political structure and the threat of military force. Officials at the local level, whose loyalty to the state was questionable, were either removed from office, or their authority was supplemented by the appointment of an Aztec official. As with the officials appointed over the wards and *calpullis* of Tenochtitlan, they were charged with the collection of taxes and maintenance of social order (Duran 1964). The Aztecs also dispersed peoples throughout the empire and nation so that each province was comprised of people from various ethnic affiliations. Peoples who were resettled had an Aztec noble appointed as ruler (Carrasco 1971).

The state ensured its power by controlling modes of production, especially those associated with agriculture. After the Tepanec war (1428) the state claimed most Tepanec lands. Thereafter the state continued to claim certain lands of the conquered peoples for itself. These lands provided a solid base for state power (Caso 1963; Brundage 1972). The state also promoted technological innovation, such as irrigation and flood control. It regulated markets, administered redistribution, imposed taxation, and fixed tribute schedules. Funds derived from taxation and tribute served to defray the expenses of government (Zorita 1963; Kurtz 1974; Sahagun 1954; Bray n.d.).

The basis of state redistribution was the tribute exacted from conquered peoples and levies imposed upon Aztec citizens. Tribute from conquered peoples probably provided the major source of income for the state (Zorita 1963). Since the tribute exacted from conquered peoples was often very heavy, it probably had a negative effect in terms of welding those populations into the nation. However, it provided a major source of goods by which the state could demonstrate its benevolence through periodic redistribution of food and clothing to the people.

The Aztec citizen was subject to heavy taxes and almost everyone paid taxes in one form or another (Zorita 1963). Payments were usually made in kind by the various social categories. Some nobles were exempt, although they were obliged to serve the state in military and political affairs. Commoners were also subject to communal corvee labor drafts by the *calpulli*, the priesthood, and the state in order to maintain and construct public works, such as dikes, fortifications, and temples (Bray 1968; Zorita 1963).

Finally, all Aztec males were subject to military service. There was a standing army; military training was a major part of the educational curriculum, and military service provided a route of upward mobility, at least until the reign of Montezuma II, for a brave warrior might be awarded lands and a title. For the nobility there existed the warrior orders: the Eagle and the Jaguar knights. The emphasis given to military training in the schools and rewards by the state for military service served as another means by which the allegiance of the people was shifted from local organizations to the state.

2.2. Validation of Office

Along with steps taken to consolidate power, the incorporative state mobilizes the society's religious and legal institutions. These institutions provide the initial legitimacy for the state, for they validate its subsequent actions to socialize the citizenry and alter the mutual obligations between state and citizen. Religion generates the ideology underlying state organization and behavior. The legal system, as suggested previously, is the fulcrum of the legitimation process, and gives the state the right to act in accord with the ideology and value structure it is trying to establish.

2.2.1. *Religion.* It may be hypothesized that the degree of social integration of a society will be reflected in the organization of its pantheon and religious structure (Cohen 1971; Durkheim 1954). Thus, an inchoate state, such as that represented by the Aztecs, will be marked by religious heterogeneity. It is difficult to assess the efficacy of Aztec religion in reducing state inchoatcy. Even though some steps were being taken toward this end, others seemed to promote inchoatcy.

As noted, the Aztec priesthood was differentiated and specialized. Aztec religion was polytheistic and bifurcated into state and local level systems (Duran 1964; Caso 1937). One means by which the Aztecs attempted to incorporate conquered peoples into the nation was by adopting their deities into the Aztec pantheon. However, this also served to promote state polytheism. In order to overcome the extensive state polytheism and reduce inchoatcy the Aztec priesthood was trying to reduce the several aspects held by many of the deities and to elevate *Huitzilopochtli* to a pre-eminent place in the pantheon, probably as a symbol of unity for the nation and empire as a whole (Caso 1937; Nicholson 1971; Bray 1968).

Religious support of the state is manifest in several ways. The Aztec state was a theocracy; emperors were deified and served as high priests (Bray n.d.; Sahagun 1969; Caso 1958, 1963). At the investiture of a new emperor, high priests admonished him regarding his obligation and duties. High priests could also invoke the wrath of the gods upon emperors who were evil or otherwise unfit for office (Sahagun 1969; Zorita 1963). Priests conducted the human sacrifices necessary for the state's welfare, and the emperor often participated in this. Religion was also a stimulus to Aztec warfare, for prisoners were the primary source of sacrifice on behalf of the state. The constant need for sacrificial victims by the state religion resulted in the establishment of a ritual war, the flower war, between peoples in the Valley of Mexico. The primary purpose of the flower war was to capture prisoners for sacrifice.

The religion penetrated the local level and infused almost all aspects of Aztec society. *Calpulli* religion was infiltrated by the state. Markets were subject to religious as well as state control. For example, persons who did not attend market on prescribed days or who transgressed market rules incurred the wrath both of the state and the gods (Duran 1971; Kurtz 1974). Priests attended court trials to make certain that religious observations concerned with the legal structure were carried out and that justice was dispensed with the approval of the gods (George 1961). In some instances, oaths to the gods were accepted as truth of the testimony being offered (Bray 1968). Priests also served in secular offices, such as military commands, and as teachers in the *calmecac* and *telpochalli* (Caso 1937, 1958; Bray 1968).

2.2.2. *Law.* Law provides one way that the legitimation of authority may be guaranteed, for law guarantees the probability that non-conformist, antisocial behavior will be met by sanctions aimed at compelling conformity or at punishing disobedience (Weber 1962). However, the argument that the means of law enforcement are quite irrelevant to the establishment and maintenance of legitimate authority (Weber 1962) does not appear to be true with reference to the legitimation of authority in incorporative states.

Legitimation of authority in incorporative states is in large measure a legal process. Codification of laws provides a critical mechanism by which incorporative states acquire the right to apply force in order to gain conformity with state goals and values. It also establishes a new set of social norms with reference not only to what most people will do, but what people think ought to be done. In incorporative states especially severe punishments are meted out for offenses which would seem trivial in contemporary Western states.

In Aztec society the death sentence was commonly invoked. However, punishment was not equal for the classes. Although Aztec law presumably was designed to apply to noble and commoner equally, penalties for the nobility for the same infraction committed by a commoner presumably were often more severe. The official state dogma regarding this matter held that greater responsibility went with greater privilege, and the nobility was expected to set an example for the commoners (George 1961; Zorita 1963).

The first legal code for Aztec society was established by Emperor Huitzilihuitl (1396–1415). It defined the relationship of persons to the deities (Duran 1964). Montezuma I, whose reign was important for the establishment of the independent Aztec state, was the law giver of Aztec society (Duran 1964). In fact, the relationship between the emergence of an autonomous state and the development of a legal code and formal legal institutions, such as courts, police, and jails, suggest that they are indispensable to the legitimation of state authority.

Aztec law was directed through a hierarchy of courts presided over by state appointed judges who were sometimes relatives of the emperor. The courts comprised a structured route of appeals. Local courts in outlying villages and towns and neighborhoods of cities comprised the lowest level courts. They were probably most commonly convened in the marketplace. Above the local level a court of appeals, a supreme court, and two special courts heard cases. Of the latter two courts, one handled matters important to the capital and met every ten days. The other met every eighty days for ten consecutive days in order to review local level court decisions. The emperor was the ultimate juridical authority. He rendered decisions when 'the court of eighty days' reached an impasse. He also approved all death sentences. In addition, military courts disposed of violations of the law by citizens and nobility committed in time of war (Zorita 1963; Duran 1964; Kurtz 1974; George 1961).

The legal system was also a mechanism of socialization. It provided a vehicle by which the state could intrude into the daily affairs of the citizenry and could convey its expectations regarding proper social behavior.

2.3. *Political Socialization*

With specific reference to inchoate incorporative states, political socialization is concerned with the means by which a state creates loyal citizens. In effecting socialization, as noted, the state attempts to transfer the allegiance of the citizen to the state and to neutralize local organizations which provide alternatives for the citizen's allegiance and loyalty. Socialization entails the complementary — and contra-dictory — practices of benevolence, information control, and terror. Through the socialization process the state demonstrates what it can do for the citizen (benevolence), what the citizen should do for the state (information), and what the state will do to the non-conformist (terror).

2.3.1. *Benevolence*. Wittfogel (1957) suggests that in despotic states, which approximate in form and function inchoate incorporative states, any benevolence by the state is designed explicitly to maintain in power the rulers and their prosperity. Thus state policies which outwardly appear to benefit the people really cannot be considered benevolent. Realizing that much of Aztec history was written to accomodate the image the state wished to present, considerable evidence still suggests that the state did engage in benevolent activities on behalf of the people, especially early in its career (Sahagun 1954). However, it is also clear that the motivation for state benevolence was not always altruistic. State-imparted benevolence functionally entails mutual obligations between state and citizen, and this reciprocity is a subtle aspect of the socialization process by which the allegiance of the citizen is shifted to the state.

'Welfare' programs represent one type of benevolence. In inchoate incorporative states the term welfare may be a misnomer, for state activities designed to materially benefit the population are not marked by the elaborate bureaucracy and funding policies of welfare programs in contemporary industrial nations. State benefits, such as food distribution during crisis periods, serve to demonstrate the power of the state and implant in the citizen a sense of dependence upon it (Sahagun 1954; Duran 1964). In this context, benevolence provides a subtle tactic by which the commitment of citizens to local level organizations is coopted.

Dispensation of such benefits requires the state to maintain sufficient wealth, and it must take measures to ensure this. Additional taxation is one means. This is couched in propaganda that such actions are for the good of the people and the nation. The state may also engage in conquest in order to acquire tributary states and empire to provide resources. In either case the state promotes its legitimacy by demonstrating its power and influence abroad and its wealth and indispensability to its citizens.

Rewards to commoners for service to the state may be considered another form of welfare. The Aztec state rewarded brave warriors with honorific titles and parcels of land. Such actions also served to remove persons from local centers of authority, such as the *calpulli*, and affiliate them with the state.

Construction and maintenance of public works, such as irrigation systems, roads, temples, and flood control systems are another form of state benevolence, for they are explained in terms of the services and goods they provide to citizens. The Aztec state was no different. Irrigation and *chinampas* were expanded to promote food production. Roads expedited the movement of goods, troops, and the *pochteca*. Dikes ensured fresh waters in the lakes and controlled flooding which periodically destroyed *chinampas* and sections of Tenochtitlan. Temples and other public buildings were constructed and maintained in order to please the gods and the state. The corvée labor upon which these programs depended is one example of the interplay of obligations between the state and its citizens.

2.3.2. *Information.* The control and dissemination of information is a critical political power resource. Control of information regarding such matters as state security, obligations of citizens to the state, tax policies, and so forth accrue to higher levels of administration in bureaucracies. Inchoate states selectively disseminate information among the citizenry. It is aimed at inculcating in the citizen the new ideology and the authoritarian values the state is trying to develop in order to supplant those of local organizations. Clearly in Aztec society the state maintained firm control of information (Bray n.d.), and it was disseminated in diverse ways.

Communication was an important function of markets in Aztec society, for only in markets could so many people be contacted at any one time. Announcements and edicts by the state were presented to the polity in marketplaces. Local courts convened there, and criminals were tried publicly. Punishments were also public and most frequently administered in marketplaces. Citizens often participated in dispensing justice to the condemned (Sahagun 1951; Kurtz 1974).

Schools were another institution by which information was conveyed in Aztec society. Mandatory public education was decreed by Montezuma I. His law code also outlined the curriculum. It stressed religious and military training, manners, morals, hard work, and discipline. The information that was disseminated served to educate the youth regarding state values. Intellectual curiosity was not stimulated. Rote learning was the norm, especially in the *telpochalli.* Conformity to state values was the goal (Duran 1964; Caso 1937; Sahagun 1969; Bray 1968).

As noted, the *calmecac* educated the children of the nobility; the *telpochalli*, the ward schools, served the commoners (Carrasco 1971; Bray 1968). Each school taught males and females. Sexes however were segregated, and separate schools for each sex may have existed (Sahagun 1969; Bray 1968). In the *calmecac* females were trained to become priestesses. The instruction of females in the *telpochalli* is not clear, but it is likely that it was extension of the training received in the home.

The *calmecac* was dedicated to training the elites of Aztec society — judges, priests, administrators, and military leaders. Its curriculum was broader and deeper than that provided by the *telpochalli* (Bray 1968). In addition to religious and military training which was stressed in both schools, reading and writing were taught exclusively in the *calmecac*. Still, crafts were taught to children of lower echelon nobles (Carrasco 1961; Duran 1971; Tezozomoc 1878). Since the number of nobility grew significantly over the years and state-level occupations were limited in number, training in crafts probably served as an alternative means of livelihood for the petty nobility. Students in the *telpochalli* also provided a major source of corvee labor for the Aztec state.

The Aztecs were attempting to establish the Nahuatl language as a *lingua franca* for the central highlands, and they may have been promoting it as a national language (Heath 1972). Certainly the imposition of a national language upon the polity facilitates dissemination of information and is a powerful way of creating unity. To what extent Aztec schools were engaged in support of this activity is not clear.

Communication of authoritarian values in the service of state legitimacy may come through other channels, such as public trials and executions. These phenomena seem best discussed in the context of the final mode of socialization by which legitimacy may be pursued — state terror.

2.3.3. *Terror.* State terror conveys a message to the citizenry regarding what may happen to the citizen who does not conform to authoritarian values and norms. Although terror may be an aspect of the politics of any state, it appears that it is most likely to exist either when the legitimacy of an established state is threatened or when a state is in a condition of extreme inchoatcy. In these situations the state demonstrates great concern with the behavior of its citizenry. Control and regulation of some areas of social activity which in stateless societies are the exclusive prerogative of kin groups, such as sexual activity and drunkenness, become of great concern, especially to the inchoate state.

Terror in Aztec society increased after the defeat of the Tepanecs, the early period of state incorporation. While it is difficult to ascertain a lull in the application of terror in Aztec society, it increased noticeably during the reign of Montezuma II. This was a period during which the state was reacting to unrest in the empire as a consequence of military defeats and poor administration of the two previous governments.

One characteristic of state terror is a severity of punishment exceeding what would seem to be reasonable retribution in more legitimate states. The severity of punishment demonstrated to the people the power of the state over the individual and local groups. As noted, executions in Aztec society were public, most frequently carried out in the marketplaces. Death was a common penalty for petty crimes, such as theft and drunkenness. Fornication and adultery were also punishable by death (Duran 1971; Motolinia 1950; Zorita 1963; Sahagun 1951, 1952, 1954).

Although theft is a serious offense in most societies and severe punishment, especially for recidivists, is somewhat understandable, the concern the inchoate state demonstrates over drunkenness and sexual activity is more difficult to explain. One possible explanation is that if a state can control fundamental areas of a citizen's affective behavior, it has made a giant stride toward control of other, less affective areas of his life.

Human sacrifice was made at almost all Aztec state and religious ceremonies and at the death of emperors and other important persons (Matos 1975). Human sacrifice was a state activity, conducted on its behalf by the priesthood. Frequently the emperor participated in the ritual which often involved hundreds — sometimes thousands — of victims (Duran 1964).

Aztec officials explained that the purpose of human sacrifice was to nourish the sun and appease the gods (Nicholson 1971; Bray 1968; Caso 1958). Human sacrifice was also an important aspect of the intimidation of Aztec citizens and neighboring peoples. On special occasions, such as the commemoration of a new temple, kings and officials from neighboring cities were invited to observe the festivities. They always included human sacrifice. The most common sacrificial victims were prisoners-of-war, and visiting dignitaries often had to watch the sacrifice of their own warriors (Duran 1964). Slaves, and on occasion criminals, were sacrificed (Sahagun 1952). However, Aztec citizens in good standing were rarely offered as victims. Certainly a message was conveyed regarding the ultimate power of the state over the life and death of its citizens (Bray n.d.). It was reinforced by the *tzompantli*, the skull rack upon which were impaled the heads of victims, which occupied a conspicuous place in the temple precinct of Tenochtitlan (Matos 1975).

The state enforced a kind of joint liability (Weber 1952; Cohen 1964) upon individuals whose behavior was sufficiently heinous to nullify their right to citizenship. Punishment for treason, aiding a traitor, drunkenness and a few other offenses was not confined to the treacherous individual. The offender's kin were also subject to punishment. For lesser offenses an individual's house might be destroyed (Sahagun 1954). For more serious offenses, an offender was executed and all his property was confiscated by the state (Sahagun 1954; George 1961).

Detaining at court persons who might threaten the state is another means of ensuring loyalty and conformity. Nobles and kinsmen of nobles were required to reside in Tenochtitlan part of the year, and from the reign of Montezuma I onward each emperor apparently required that a certain number of nobles or their children serve as courtiers (Cortes 1928; Zorita 1963). While the purpose of such service is not clear for Aztec society, one explanation that has precedence in other inchoate states, such as Tokugawa, Japan (Dore 1965; Befu 1965), is that the presence of nobility at court ensures the conformity, allegiance, and obedience of their kin and followers. The courtiers are, in a sense, a kind of hostage.

The inchoatcy of the Aztec nation was especially marked by the inability of the state to incorporate fully into the nation the hundreds of vassal societies within the empire (Hardoy 1973; Bray n.d.). It is predictable that especially severe methods would be employed to control subjugated peoples and break their ties with local traditions. As noted, ethnic groups were frequently dispersed throughout the empire. Enemy cities which resisted incorporation into the nation or empire, or that were rebellious, were frequently razed and entire populations exterminated. Sometimes the cities were rebuilt and those who escaped were granted immunity. Such magnanimity is probably better explained as a tactic to promote state legitimacy than as an act of altruism or benevolence.

3. CONCLUSIONS

The basic purpose of this chapter was to describe the Aztec state. As one means of accomplishing this goal a model was presented to explain the process by which the Aztec state sought legitimate status. It was suggested that the Aztec state represented an inchoate incorporative state (Cohen 1969), that is one which has not usurped the power of local centers of potential autonomy within its national territory and, thus, is not very legitimate. One way for a state to overcome inchoatcy is to acquire legitimacy, or the support of the polity, as quickly as possible.

Briefly, the acquisition of legitimacy by an inchoate incorporative state entails the mobilization by the state of the nation's institutions and technology for its own purposes. The ultimate goal of the state is to shift the allegiance and loyalty of the polity from local centers of authority to the state. At the core of this process is the establishment of authority based upon law, for the state requires and obtains validation to pursue legitimacy from legal institutions and codified laws. In addition, the state obtains religious justification for the social order, values, and ideology it is trying to develop from state affiliated religious institutions and personnel.

With the support of legal and religious institutions the state engages in a variety of specific activities designed to ensure its survival and promote its legitimacy. Social distance between the rulers and the ruled is expanded. The state infiltrates local centers of authority in order to weaken their influence and consolidate its own. It undertakes a broad program of political socialization conveyed through benevolent activities on behalf of the citizenry, control of information, and terror.

It also should be noted that many aspects of the legitimation process, such as state directed terror, are often more symbolic than real. Although the process of legitimation of the inchoate state is rooted in law, to what extent the more coercive and intrusive aspects of the law are enforced is not always important. For example, there is little evidence in the chronicles of Aztec society that suggest that the death penalty for adultery or prescriptions regarding joint liability were enforced frequently. It is more important that the laws by which the state attempts to regulate anti-social behavior are codified; they can be applied as the state deems necessary, as situations dictate.

Finally, although the inchoate incorporative state represented by the Aztecs of pre-Hispanic Mexico provides one example by which this model of legitimation may be explored, the model may well have broader application. It may be helpful in understanding the acquisition of legitimacy of emerging states in the contemporary world.

FOOTNOTES

[1] Thanks to Dr. Robert Harrison and Ms. Elizabeth Wright for their valuable comments on early drafts of this manuscript. Thanks also to Professor Y. A. Cohen who gave generously of his time in discussing some of the ideas presented in this paper both privately and in graduate seminars which he directed at the University of California, Davis. For especially seminal works regarding the theoretical foundation of this paper see especially Wittfogel (1957) and Cohen (1969). Obviously, any inadequacies or errors are my responsibility alone.

[2] For histories and ethnographic profiles of Aztec society which are easily available see Soustelle (1961), Bray (1968), Brundage (1972), Davies (1973), and Duran (1964).

REFERENCES

Adams, Robert McC. (1966), *The evolution of urban society*. Chicago: Aldine.
Befu, Harumi (1965), 'Village autonomy and articulation with the state', in: *Journal of Asian Studies* 25: 19–32.
Bray, Warwick (1968), *Everyday life of the Aztecs*. New York: G. P. Putnam and Sons.
—— (1972), 'The city state in central Mexico at the time of the Spanish Conquest', in: *Journal of Latin American Studies* 4(2): 161–185.

— (n.d.), 'Civilizing the Aztecs', due to appear in *The evolution of social studies*, ed. by J. Friedman and M. Rolands, London: Duckworth (mimeographed).

Brundage, Burr Cartwright (1972), *A rain of darts: The Mexican Aztecs.* Austin, Texas: University of Texas Press.

Burland, C. A. (1973), *Montezuma: Lord of the Aztecs.* New York: G. P. Putnam and Sons.

Calnek, Edward E. (1972), 'Settlement pattern and chinampa agriculture at Tenochtitlan', in: *American Antiquity* 37(1): 104–115.

Carneiro, Robert L. (1970), 'A theory of the origin of the state', *Science* 169: 733–738.

Carrasco, Pedro (1961), 'The civil–religious hierarchy in Mesoamerican communities: pre-Spanish background and colonial development', in: *American Anthropologist* 63(3): 483–497.

— (1971), 'Social organization of ancient Mexico', in: *Archeology of northern Mexico*, ed. by C. F. Ekholm and Ignacio Bernal, in: *Handbook of Middle American Indians*, Robert Wauchope, general editor, vol. 10. Austin, Texas: University of Texas Press.

Caso, Alfonso (1937), *The religion of the Aztecs.* Mexico City: Central News Co., Edificio 'La Nacional'.

— (1958), *The Aztecs: people of the sun.* Translated by Lowell Dunham. Norman, Oklahoma: University of Oklahoma Press.

— (1963), 'Land tenure among the ancient Mexicans', in: *American Anthropologist* 65(4): 863–878.

Chapman, Anne C. (1957), 'Port of trade enclaves in Aztec and Maya civilizations', in: *Trade and market in the early empires*, ed. by Karl Polanyi, Conrad Arensberg and Harry Pearson, pp. 114–153. Glencoe, Ill.: Free Press.

Cohen, Y. A. (1964), *The transition from childhood to adolescence: cross cultural studies, initiation ceremonies, legal systems, and incest taboos.* Chicago: Aldine.

— (1969), 'Ends and means in political control: state organization and the punishment for adultery, incest, and violation of celibacy', in: *American Anthropologist* 71(4): 658–687.

— (1971), 'Religion and magic', in: *Man in adaptation: the institutional framework*, ed. by Y. A. Cohen. Chicago: Aldine.

Cortes, Hernando (1928), *Five letters: 1519–1526.* Translated by J. Bayard Morris. Ed. by Sir E. Dennison Ross and Eileen Power. London: George Routledge and Sons, Ltd.

Davies, Nigel (1973), *The Aztecs: a history.* London: Macmillan Ltd.

Dore, R. P. (1965), *Education in Tokugawa Japan.* London: Routledge and Kegan Paul.

Duran, Fray Diego (1964), *The Aztecs: the history of the Indies of New Spain.* Translated, with notes, by Doris Heyden and Fernando Horcasitas. London: Cassell.

— (1971), *Book of the gods and rites* and *The ancient calender.* Translated and edited by Fernando Horcasitas and Doris Heyden. Norman, Oklahoma: University of Oklahoma Press.

Durkheim, Emile (1954), *The elementary forms of the religious life.* Translated from the french by J. W. Swain. Glencoe, Illinois: Free Press.

Engels, Frederick (1942), *The origin of the family, private property, and the state.* New York: International Publishers.

Fallers, Lloyd A. (1965), *Bantu bureaucracy*. Chicago: University of Chicago Press.
Flannery, Kent V. (1972), 'The cultural evolution of civilizations', in: *Annual review of ecology and systematics* 3: 399–426.
Fried, Morton H. (1967), *The evolution of political society: an essay in political anthropology*. New York: Random House.
George, Richard H. (1961), 'Crime and punishment in Aztec Society: An examination of the criminal law-ways of the Aztecs as a reflection of their dominant value orientations'. Unpublished M.A. Thesis, Mexico City College (currently University of the Americas), Mexico, D.F.: Mexico.
Goode, Wm. J. (1963), *World revolution and family patterns*. New York: Free Press of Glencoe.
Gómara, Francisco Lopez de (1877), *Conquista de Mexico*. Segunda Parte de *La cronica general de los Indies*, in: Biblioteca de Autores Espanoles, *Historiadores primitivos de Indias*. Madrid.
Hardoy, Jorge E. (1973), *Pre-Columbian cities*. New York: Walker.
Heath, Shirley B. (1972), *Telling tongues: language policy in Mexico, colony to nation*. New York: Teachers College Press.
Kemp, Fred E. III (1954), 'Warfare in pre-Columbian mexico'. Unpublished Masters Thesis, Mexico City College. Mexico D.F.: Mexico.
Kuper, Hilda (1972), 'The language of sites in the politics of space', in: *American Anthropologist* 74(3): 411–425.
Kurtz, Donald V. (1974), 'Peripheral and transitional markets: The Aztec case', in: *American Ethnologist* 1(4): 685–706.
Lenski, Gerhard E. (1966), *Power and privilege: a theory of social stratification*. New York: McGraw-Hill.
Matos Moctezuma, Eduardo (1975), *Muerte a filo de obsidiana: la nahuas frente a la muerte*. SEP/SETENTAS, Mexico, D.F.
Molins Fabrega, N. (1954–55), 'El Códice Mendocino y la Economiá de Tenochtitlán', in: *Revista Mexicana de Estudias Antropológicas* 14: 303–335.
Monzón, Arturo (1949), *El calpulli en la organizacion social de los Tenochca*. Publicaciones del Instituto de Historia, No. 14, Mexico, D.F.
Motolinia, Toribio (1950), *History of the Indians of New Spain*. Translated and edited by Elizabeth Andros Foster. Westport, Conn.: Greenwood Press.
Nicholson, Henry B. (1971), 'Religion in pre-Hispanic central Mexico', in: *Archeology of northern Mexico*, ed. by G. F. Ekholm and Ignacio Bernal, *Handbook of Middle American Indians*, Robert Wauchope, general editor, vol. 10. Austin, Texas: University of Texas Press.
Oppenheimer, Franz (1975), *The state*. New York: Free Life Editions.
Polanyi, Karl (1966), *Dahomey and the slave trade: an analysis of an archaic economy*. Seattle: University of Washington Press.
Sahagun, Fray Bernadino de (1951), 'The ceremonies', in: *Florentine Codex: general history of the things of New Spain. Book 2*. Translated from the Aztec into English by A. J. O. Anderson and C. E. Dibble. Published by the School of American Research and the University of Utah. Monographs of the School of American Research, No. 14, Pt. III. Santa Fe, New Mexico.
— (1952), 'The origin of the gods', in: *Florentine Codex: general history of the things of New Spain. Book 3*. Translated from the Aztec into English by A. J. O. Anderson and C. E. Dibble. Published by the School of American Research and the University of Utah. Monographs of the School of American Research, No. 14, Pt. IV. Santa Fe, New Mexico.

— (1954), 'Kings and lords', in: *Florentine Codex: general history of the things of New Spain. Book 8.* Translated by A. J. O. Anderson and C. E. Dibble. Published by the School of American Research and the University of Utah. Monographs of the School of American Research, No. 14, Pt. IX. Santa Fe, New Mexico.

— (1959), 'The merchants', in: *Florentine Codex: general history of the things of New Spain. Book 9.* Translated from the Aztec into English by A. J. O. Anderson and C. E. Dibble. Published by the School of American Research and the University of Utah. Monographs of the School of American Research and the Museum of New Mexico, No. 14, Pt. X. Santa Fe, New Mexico.

— (1961), 'The people', in: *Florentine Codex: general history of the things of New Spain. Book 10.* Translated by A. J. O. Anderson and C. E. Dibble. Published by the School of American Research and the University of Utah. Monographs of the School of American Research and the Museum of New Mexico, No. 14, Pt. XI. Santa Fe, New Mexico.

— (1963), 'Earthly things', in: *Florentine Codex: general history of the things of New Spain. Book 11.* Translated by A. J. O. Anderson and C. E. Dibble. Published by the School of American Research and the University of Utah. Monographs of the School of American Research and the Museum of New Mexico, No. 14, Pt. XII. Santa Fe, New Mexico

— (1969), 'Rhetoric and moral Philosophy', in: *Florentine Codex: History of the things of New Spain. Book 6.* Translated by A. J. O. Anderson and C. E. Dibble. Published by the School of American Research and the University of Utah. Monographs of the School of American Research, Vol. 14, Pt. VII. Santa Fe, New Mexico.

Soustelle, Jacques (1961), *Daily life of the Aztecs on the eve of the Spanish Conquest.* Stanford, California: Stanford University Press.

Swartz, M. J., Turner, V. W. and Tuden, A. (eds.) (1966), *Political anthropology.* Chicago: Aldine.

Tezozomoc, D. Hernando Alvara de (1878), *Crónica Mexicana,* ed. by Jose M. Vigil, Mexico: Imprenta y Litografia de I. Paz.

Weber, Max (1947), *The theory of social and economic organization.* Translated by A. M. Henderson and Talcott Parsons. Ed. by Talcott Parsons. New York: The Free Press.

— (1952), *Ancient Judaism.* Translated and edited by H. H. Gerth and D. Martindale. New York: Free Press.

— (1954), *Max Weber on law in economy and society.* Translated by S. Shils and M. Rheinstein. Ed. by M. Rheinstein. Twentieth Century Legal Series, vol. 6. Cambridge, Mass.: Harvard University Press.

— (1962), *Basic concepts in sociology.* Translated by H. P. Secher. New York: The Citadel Press.

Wittfogel, Karl (1957), *Oriental despotism: a comparative study of total power.* New Haven, Conn.: Yale University Press.

Zorita, Alonso de (1963), *Life and labor in ancient Mexico: the brief and summary relations of the Lords of New Spain.* Translated and with an introduction by Benjamin Keene. New Brunswick New Jersey: Rutgers University Press.

9 China

TIMOTEUS POKORA

1. HISTORICAL BACKGROUND

It is highly difficult to fix the chronological frame for the existence of
the early state or states in China, inter alia because the ancient sources
do not provide the necessary information, or their information is
ambivalent, allowing for different, even contradictory conclusions on
the basis of one and the same source. The same is true of the character
of this state.

Whatever the character of the ancient Chinese state may have been,
it was undoubtedly the earliest relatively centralized form of organization of a society possessing a certain ethnic, cultural and probably
economic unity in eastern Asia. From this point of view the Chinese
state as such, as well as in its perpetual dialectic relation to the
different 'barbarians' on its outskirts, played a major role over a very
large area, without regard for any sovereignty or suzerainty outside its
domain.

On the other hand, throughout the entire period understood by us as
that of the early state, China was almost totally independent of the
development of other ancient cultural centres like those of India, the
Near East or Greece. It follows from this that, while being independent and basing itself upon its own model, China at the same time
represented yet another kind of unity, which we may tentatively
designate as Chinese civilization. This civilization existed before the
Chinese state came into being and represented a certain unification of
all the Chu Hsia, or the many larger and smaller states of ancient
China. Chinese civilization also existed abroad, and it existed even
when part of China was ruled by foreigners.

The process of the unification of the different parts of the Chinese *oikumene* was continual, since the centrifugal forces were at work almost all the time. Unity, disunity and a unity at a new level — this was the general rule rather than a one-way movement towards a centralized state or empire. This tendency was due not only to inner contradictions — central authority versus the local centers of power, the ruler versus the aristocracy, etc., — but also to the fact that, owing to the gradual expansion of its territory, China became a subcontinent uniting certain very different traditions.

The recurrent emergence and collapse of unity makes it difficult for us to accept what is chronologically the earliest Chinese state as *the* early state we are interested in at present. We need to study several types of early Chinese state, each with its own particular characteristics. Although the points of view on this may differ, I would propose to regard as the period of the early state in China the entire long stretch of time between the beginnings of Chinese recorded, relatively reliable history on the one hand and the year 221 B.C.[1] on the other, when the foundations of an imperial Chinese state were laid in the form of the Ch'in unification of the Pan-Chinese states.

The relative length of this period covering some 1300 years will enable us better to analyse the main traits of the early, pre-imperial, more or less disunited state. Although the Ch'in dynasty did not rule for more than some fifteen years, it nevertheless created a prototype of a centralized, developed and efficiently ruled empire, as embodied in the subsequent rule of more than 400 years of the Han dynasty (206 B.C.–A.D. 220).

The geographical conditions played no positive role during the process of unification. Both of the big rivers, the Huang-ho (Yellow River) and the Yang-tzu-chiang, flowing mostly from east to west, constituted definite barriers for a north–south movement and, at the same time, endangered the broad, fertile lowlands, especially along their lower reaches. Another barrier for the maritime lowlands south of Peking was constituted by the rugged mountain areas in the west. More substantial problems were created by the difficulty of access of the southeastern regions of China, especially towards the southwest (the present-day Szechwan province), where access is far from easy even now. The region around present-day Canton and North Vietnam (The Hundred Yüeh, Pai Yüeh) formed a certain cultural unity, which was incorporated into the Chinese realm only after the creation of the Han empire.

Whereas the southern 'barbarians', as history had shown, were more submissive, and their territories might have been annexed without any notable difficulties, China always suffered at the hands of the northern barbarians. The defense–attack tactics of the Chinese became a constant factor in their history. This kind of experience was, of course, valid primarily in the military field. Later, in the fourth century, the Chinese adopted from these northern barbarians not only the crossbow and the cavalry, but also the breeches. It is clear also, that the frontier existing between the two ethnic groups did not exclusively give rise to mutual conflicts and skirmishes, but quite naturally also stimulated an exchange of those goods that either of the parties lacked. We may thus speak of some sort of dialectic of contacts and efforts, in which the Chinese civilization enriched itself without essentially deviating from its own set of values. The feeling of a certain superiority evidently resulted in some kind of sense for continuity and tradition which showed itself to be a very strong stabilizing factor.

Only the non-Chinese people of the northern regions were able several times in history to establish their rule over the whole of China. Already at the time of the late state, as defined by us, the Chinese had to construct large walls, which later became well-known as the Long Wall, in northern China as a defense against the nomads. The latter extended from the Liao-tung peninsula in the east into Kan-su province in the west. In addition there were, as there still are today, wide variations of climate in the different parts of China, beginning with the cold continental climate of northern China and ending with the tropical one in southern China.

All these factors made for a rather strong diversification of local centers, differing on the points of language (dialects), geography (maritime and mountain regions) and, what is more important in the given context, on that of the different experiences acquired through contacts with the barbarians.

This can be said notwithstanding the fact that the delimitation of the notions of civilization and barbarism is not altogether clear. They involved on the one hand the permanent aggressiveness of the nomads and the necessity to cope with this, even by military force, whereas on the other hand the Chinese felt the need for new places to settle in. They were sometimes also interested in subduing, perhaps through assimilation, some quite peaceful barbarian populations. This does not mean to say of course, that the Chinese never attacked the barbarians on their own initiative. The problem did not, from the Chinese viewpoint, involve the full assimilation of the non-Chinese, but rather the liquidation of existing barriers between the two groups, as a result of the barbarians accepting the Chinese way of life and Chinese civilization.

All the processes described above undoubtedly contributed to the formation of a variety of rather different models even inside the Chinese cultural realm. Whereas the center of Chinese culture was always in the east, in the present-day province of Shan-tung, important individual centers formed inter alia in the south already from the tenth century and in the west, namely those known as the states of Ch'u and Ch'in respectively, somewhat later. A certain 'barbarian' element has always been felt to be present in the two last-named states by other, more 'Chinese', more 'civilized' states.

Ch'u and Ch'in based their legal existence upon the authority of the central ruler from the beginning of the first millennium, and could not therefore be considered as wholly un-Chinese, but they represented, so to speak, a transition between genuine Chinese and barbarians. All the important Chinese states — not to mention the hundreds of smaller ones — under the sway of the Chou, showed a different degree of political, economic and social development. It follows that there did not, in fact, exist just a single early state but rather several such ones in China. We will therefore have to concentrate, when analysing the early state in China as such, upon certain common traits as well as on those which played an important role in the historical development.

Already Confucius (551–479) and numerous other thinkers following him, believed that there was a long past of cultural heroes and eminent rulers, fully Chinese, preceding them, a past inherited by the present generation of rulers and commoners. The trouble is that even the Chinese of antiquity always referred to already previously existing institutions, the origin of which was situated in some fabulous antiquity and could not always be precisely determined. There arises the question, therefore, if these institutions ever really existed or whether we have here the projection of certain wishful thinking into an almost sacred antiquity.

We shall therefore have to say something about the history of the period in which the early state evidently existed, though not, of course, in the same form throughout the entire period. We are not going to speak about the origin of the Chinese people or of its civilization, but will restrict ourselves to the period attested by written sources.

We should state, nevertheless, that in China the transition from prehistory to history coincides more or less with that from the neolithic to the bronze age, as also — and this is important — to sedentary agriculture with already fairly developed crafts. All this may be dated at around the turning-point between the third and the second millennium. It is in these centuries that the existence of the Hsia Dynasty is assumed by some records, though not yet proved by archaeological finds or other evidence.

The following dynasty, namely that of the Shang or, more correctly, the Shang-Yin (eighteenth–eleventh centuries) is the first dynasty in China to be partly attested by archaeological finds. We may already speak of a dynasty since the accession to the throne was regulated by certain rules (younger brother succeeds elder brother, and, later on, the son succeeds the father). The power of the Shang ruler was centered on the Shang capital, while relations with other centers of the Shang domain were rather of a political than compulsory nature; comparing them with mediaeval European feudal relations, we might characterize them as the relations of a ruler towards his feudatories. If we dare speak of a certain form of state already at this stage, this is because the Shang king represented all Shangs in contacts with all non-Shangs.

This kind of political unity, or possibly the idea of a certain solidarity, may have been of an earlier date. We now know that one of the names by which the Chinese of this period referred to themselves was Chu Hsia, 'all of the Hsia', i.e., all those subjected to the sway of the Hsia, an allusion to the previous dynasty. This was clearly something different from 'all Shang'. Besides such political 'inter-state' relations with other Chinese (= Hsia), there also already existed some commercial relations with certain other areas in southeastern and central Asia. The Shang used to import huge turtle-shells and the raw materials for the manufacture of large bronze vessels, beautifully worked by Shang craftsmen. There are also some correspondences between patterns on Chinese pottery and that of some other countries of Asia.

The initial period of the Shang Dynasty still reflects the transition to sedentary agriculture, as testified by the fact that the capital was shifted seven times. The first permanent capital, founded in 1401, was present-day An-yang, the dynasty being known as Yin from this time on. The general direction of the shifts was southwards, to both banks of the Yellow River and even further south into the valley of the Huai river in the maritime lowlands. The Shang-Yin Dynasty undoubtedly represented the climax of Chinese civilization up to that time.

There was another belt of neolithic sedentary agriculture, which was not subjected to the Shang-Yin, around the middle course of the Yellow River and its tributaries. The people concerned were undoubtedly Chinese belonging to the tribal federation of the Chou, which had also been in constant contact, most often military, with the northern barbarians. Small wonder that under these circumstances the cultural level of the Chou was lower, while conversely their fighting spirit and experience were more highly developed.

Headed by Wu wang (Warlike King), the Chou in a mighty attack along the Yellow River, from Shanhsi and Shenhsi provinces eastwards, uprooted the once mighty and currently still extremely cultured Shang, probably in the second half of the eleventh century.[2] The Chou, with a barbaric kind of efficiency, destroyed large areas of Yin territory, and founded one of their capitals, Hao (also known as Tsung-Chou, i.e., 'the honoured capital of the Chou') in present-day Hasian in Shensi province. In this way a rich and well-known maritime territory somehow became a peripheral area of the Chou domain, since the capital for some 2,000 years after that remained either in Hsi-an or in Lo-yang (on the Yellow River, some three hundred miles eastwards). This represented a unification, though only of northern China, while the large but relatively backward states of southern China (Wu, Yüeh and Ch'u) were not very much subject to the authority of the Shang-Yin or the Chou. Nevertheless, Ch'u always felt the need to be considered as a 'real' Chinese state.

The Chou inherited not only the glory of the Yin, but also their problems with the barbarians, while moreover they had their own internal dissensions. In the year 841, marking the beginning of a unitary chronology, King Li was deposed and exiled. This event did not bring any change in the principles of succession. The barbarians played an important role, as before, not only by attacking the Chou but also by encouraging certain centrifugal tendencies with their mere presence. The western state Ch'in, formally existing since the ninth century, came into being only thanks to the mighty attack of the Western barbarians, in fact. They eliminated King Yu in 771, and took possession of the Chou capital. The Chou, preferring to live at a longer distance from the barbarians, founded their new capital at Lo-yang, in the east, and the dynasty is known from then on as Eastern Chou. The lost territories in Shenhsi were magnanimously handed over to the Ch'in by the Chou, who had lost this western area anyway.

We may therefore speak of a certain unity in China, that is only northern China, for only some 250 years (or more, if we accept another chronology) during the eleventh–eighth centuries. Together with the weakening of the central power of the Chou we witness an increase in the relative independence of the peripheral states, also in southern China. The southern states formally acknowledged the authority of the powerless Chou, since this was one way of gaining equality with other Chinese states. Rather paradoxically, the disintegration of the central political power increased the need to acknowledge the existence of a Chinese 'commonwealth' presenting theoretically everybody with an opportunity to claim the leadership.

The period assigned to the Eastern Chou (770–454 or 256) comprises, inter alia, the Spring and Autumn period, so designated by the *Ch'un ch'iu* chronicle of the state of Lu, which describes the events of the years 722–481; a better term would be Spring and Autumn periods, because of course the chronicle is chronological, the events being recorded for each year. From the political point of view this is a period of mutually contending states, headed by mighty rulers known as *hegemons* (*pa*). The *hegemons* were not yet interested in the liquidation of the Chou king (*wang*) nor were they able to destroy some of the bigger states. Different states kept coming into foreground. The first of these was that of Ch'i, controlling the original

Shang territory, under the mighty Duke Huan; efforts in this direction were made also by the rulers of Ch'in, Ch'u, etc., however. It was a period of highly developed interstate diplomacy within the Chou realm, with the states checking each other at regular conferences and opposing the barbarians on the battlefield.

Neither diplomacy nor the frequent oaths of allegiance to the agreements concluded could prevent the inner and outer destruction of the state, however. The above-mentioned *Ch'un ch'iu* chronicle enumerates, mostly without any comment, thirty-six murders of rulers (though many more murders were committed) and the liquidation of fifty-two states. The general tendency involved not so much the liquidation of the tiny city-states as a radical reduction of the number of small states in the period of the strengthening of a few powerful states.

For instance, Yüeh destroyed Wu in 473. More important for the destruction of a certain balance was the inner disintegration of the mighty northern state of Chin in the year 453 and its division into three separate states, officially acknowledged by the Chou king only in 403. At one of the above two dates began the final period of a divided China, known by the telling name of Warring States.

The number of states decreased as the struggle became fiercer. A decisive role was played by three specific states, of which eastern Ch'i was the smallest, though it possessed a rather highly developed economy. In the west the large state of Ch'in gained in strength through the acquisition of the wealthy western province of Szechwan, while southern China came to be dominated by Ch'u from 446 onward, and more especially after 334, when it destroyed the state of Yüeh. Both of the 'big powers' were still partially barbarian, especially Ch'in, while Ch'u successfully penetrated the eastern, ideologically and culturally most important region with its armies.

The year 256 opened with a prelude to the last battle for supremacy. During that year Ch'u occupied the small state of Lu, the homeland of Confucius, while Ch'in, in its turn, deposed the last king of Chou. This was almost tantamount to a formal announcement that both Ch'u and Ch'in believed themselves to possess the right and had the intention to seize the power over the entire empire. What they still needed was the necessary power and strength to achieve their identical aims. It is important to know why these states on the periphery of Chinese civilization came into the foreground again, as the Chou had done some eight centuries before.

While there were substantial differences in the internal conditions of the two states, we can nevertheless observe in both the process of liquidation of the fiefs, and their limitation and replacement, especially in the frontier areas, by a certain form of direct administration by the state, or control from the center and administration by officials sent from the capital. At the frontiers, where a discontented vassal or an enfeoffed local ruler always has a better opportunity of opposing the central ruler by defecting to the other side, the districts *hsien* were instituted more or less resembling the German *marks*. These *hsien* were administered centrally, and not locally or privately. Clearly, not only the border areas but the entire country was thereby strengthened.

The disunity of China was finally ended by force of arms. Nevertheless, the ideas of the school of the *fa-chia* (legalists, administrators), embodying a martial ideology, were also instrumental here, being first applied in the state of Ch'in as early as the middle of the fourth century (there were several *fa-chia* schools, but we shall not explain their ideas and attitudes here). The legalist ideology demanded the abolition of all privileges bestowed by noble birth, and, theoretically, the submission of the entire population, without any exception, to the needs and will of the state. The legalists demanded a powerful state, and all means of achieving this goal were held to be correct. If the state of Ch'in and later the whole of China were to be centralized, the independent centers of power had to be annihilated. This necessity later, at the end of the third century, led to a partial liquidation of traditions stressing the necessity of following ancient examples of rulers and ruling methods, many of which of course reflected the conditions of the period of disunity.

The reduction of the influence of the aristocracy in administration and the institution of centrally appointed officials were not the only measures, devised for achieving unity. Also unified were the script (already existing in the fifteenth century, but showing a lot of local variants), measures, the gauge of carts, etc. The Ch'in empire founded in 221, had only a short life and none of the reforms introduced by its emperor Ch'in Shih-huang-ti can have had a very profound influence at the time. Nevertheless, the same type of reforms, together with the later experience of more than 400 years of the Han dynasty, showed that unification under one ruler, or the creation of a relatively centralized empire, was possible. This implied the creation of imperial (or traditional) China. During the Han period the state became fully developed.

2. THE EARLY STATE

In the first part of the present essay we have given an outline of the history of what we believe to have been the early state of China. Chronologically it extended from the Shang period, about which we do not possess much reliable information, until the year 221, when the unity of China was created, or restored, if we accept the view of H. G. Creel (and J. Gernet 1964: 13) that the Western Chou period may be designated as an imperial one, i.e., as one of a unified state.[3] We have fixed on this relatively long period because it may be viewed as a protracted prelude to the genuinely unitary empires of the Ch'in and Han, which we regard as examples of a developed and powerful state.

Referring again to Creel (1970) who entitled his book devoted to the Western Chou '*The origins of statecraft in China*', we may safely take mainly the indicated period as our basis. It is clear, however, that the early Chinese state already existed before that. From another point of view it was strictly the Western Chou period which represented the end of the first epoch of the early state, because not long after the establishment of the Eastern Chou, there occurred some quite substantial changes, beginning in the period known as Spring and Autumn. This is clearly expressed in the title of a book by Hsu Cho-yun, viz. '*Ancient China in transition: an analysis of social mobility*', devoted to the half-millennium between 722–222. Therefore we will try in the second part of our essay dealing with the characteristics of the early state to compare for the greater part the experiences of the Western Chou with those of the next five centuries. This comparison of two different stages will, we hope, contribute to a clearer understanding of the early state in China as such. The periodization of Chinese history into a pre-Ch'in and post-Ch'in period is not called into question by any historian or sinologist.

The origins of the Chinese state were not clear even to the Chinese. Early historians, misled by their regard for tradition, had to rely on myths and legends, and, what is more important, had to 'rationalize' these by reducing them to 'reasonable' proportions. After eliminating the most conspicuous chronological and logical discrepancies, the myths were woven into a systematic history. And this kind of history enjoyed a considerable authority in the Chinese mind.

More reliable for the contemporary historian is the epic tradition of the *Book of documents* or *Book of history* (*Shang shu*, later *Shu ching*), which represents, in the chapters which are held to be authentic, a series of documents originally preserved in the royal archives. We are informed in the great Announcement, part of the *Book of documents*, for instance of the difficult conditions prevailing after the death of the first Chou king Wu, when a section of the conquered Shang people revolted. The *Book* also includes proclamations and speeches of kings, and an account of the meeting of King Ch'eng with his ministers. We may say that the *Book* is a collection of historical documents, not written by a historian. It is relatively realistic and sober, while at the same time embodying a certain form of propaganda in support of the victorious Chou. Although it served as a source of inspiration for many generations of Chinese historians, it cannot be designated as a mythic charter of the state such as we find during the formation of certain other early states.

Each of the subject states of the Chou, at least the more important ones, had its own chronicle. In fact, the very existence of such a chronicle constituted proof, inter alia, of the legal existence of the state, or in other words, the unauthorized institution of an office for keeping an independent chronicle was liable to be interpreted as treason towards the central authority. The relevant entries were made by an astrologer–historian, or keeper of the archives. The earliest records are texts associated with divination, which, incidentally, corroborate the list of Yin rulers as given in much later written sources. Thus a historical sense seems to be innate in the Chinese. This sense manifested itself even in earliest times in the effort to note down and keep a record of events.

Local traditions may have been preserved and eventually brought into line with central traditions, inter alia, when laid down in the form of genealogies. These were very important because in their compilation, many rulers and aristocrats of the various relatively independent states tried to boost their own authority by establishing a link between themselves and some real or mythical ruler of antiquity. There also existed, of course, authentic genealogies, such as those of ruling families, which served as a relatively solid basis for writing up the history of a specific state. Such genealogies played a major role in the process of unification of the population of China, since they stressed the sense of solidarity brought about by the role of the family and long term associations. The genealogies were written only for rulers and aristocrats, i.e., those who had a name. No commoner would have thought of compiling a genealogy, because of the simple fact that he and his relatives did not possess a common surname.

The Chou originally comprised several tribes in western China which united themselves, mostly thanks to their conquest of the Shang-Yin. Certain traditions have survived, such as, for example, that whereby the Chou had two capitals at the same time. Under the Chou Dynasty, too, there existed barbarian tribes, which were mostly assimilated by the Chinese, or, much later, established their own states on Chinese territory completely after the Chinese pattern, which also resulted in assimilation. The Chou conquest did not play a principal role in the formation of the state as such, since the Chou in many respects followed the established patterns of the Shang-Yin; on the contrary, many different dynasties came into being thanks to the conquest.

From the Chinese or Confucian standpoint there existed only two social classes, viz. that of the lower ones who worked with their hands to support those above themselves and were, in their turn, ruled by those who 'worked' with their minds. As far as the ownership and cultivation of the land are concerned, there were, in point of fact, only two classes: the king and his feudatories on the one hand, and the peasants on the other. From this point of view the peasants also supported the craftsmen producing the magnificently worked vessels for the ruler, while it was also the peasants who maintained the army, etc. A proportion of the craftsmen of course produced pottery for general use. Theoretically, no land could be transferred without the sanction of the king. It should be noted that the peasants through their labor even supported the slaves used by the ruler and the aristocracy for domestic work. Slaves working directly in agricultural production are attested only from the fourth century on.

There was a certain aristocracy already under the Shang-Yin. It was recruited from among the royal family and the most prominent dignitaries. Fiefs were generally hereditary, but could be reclaimed by the lord in the case of treason, etc. The conquering Chou in the beginning had not much aristocracy worth speaking of, of their own, and therefore left some of the Yin aristocrats in their former positions. In general the aristocracy, as a powerful political group, came into being only in the Spring and Autumn period, hand in hand with the growing independence of the states.

The relation between aristocracy and the common people may also be considered in the context of two other notions, viz. *chün-tzu*, originally 'noble man', later 'noble' or 'aristocrat', and *hsiao jen*, 'small man', 'small people', meaning both a man of lesser quality and a commoner. The law was applied only to the latter, as a means of coercing those unable to reach the necessary moral standard. The social group of the *chün-tzu*, i.e., the upper class, was practically immune from the law because of its supposed high moral standards.

The interest of Chinese thinkers was concentrated not only on the notion of 'the people' but especially the family, the foundation of the state. In antiquity the family was large, consisting, in fact, of several 'actual' families as connected by kinship, preferably through a common ancestor. The extended family had its location in a fixed locality, irrespective of whether all its members were living there. People belonged to the locality of their family even if they were born in another place. Certain influential families directed, or at least controlled the life in the various localities. Rural communities with common ownership of land began disintegrating from the third–fourth centuries on. We do not know much about their previous history.

During the early period there was hardly any division of labor, although there did exist the craftsmen. Following a long period of a mere barter economy, trade developed later, after money began to be used some time in the sixth century. The division of labor increased greatly from the fifth century on, clearly due to the use of iron implements and the resultant increase in agricultural production. Already, under the Yin large bronze vessels were produced, which may have been made by full-time specialists, who, however, worked only for the king and less for other prominent figures. Inscriptions of a ritual and official nature are found on these vessels, many of them being of value for history on account of the facts recorded. The vessels were clearly produced in workshops, manufactories coming into being only much later, concurrently with the decline of the traditional natural economy. The division of labor between men and women was clear-cut and probably existed already under the Chou Dynasty, possibly even earlier.

At the apex of the state structure was the king, whose position was sacred since he was the son of Heaven, and as such might enjoy a connection with Heaven, being at the same time responsible to it. The ruler was revered and represented as both a secular and a ritual authority, always designated conjointly in the case of the earlier rulers. But it was not believed that the ruler was infallible. The official in charge of divining for the king was evidently of high rank — a 'grand invoker' or 'prayer master' — nevertheless divination was a form of general prophecy, and was not meant as demonstration that the ruler was divine. Most esteemed were the *sheng-jen*, or 'saints', the most highly accomplished men of antiquity and models for future ages and rulers. There were, of course, many kinds of rituals, especially offerings, to show the ruler's tie with Heaven, from which he received his 'mandate' to rule the country. This was demonstrated clearly during the inauguration. Strange animals were expected to appear, and unusual phenomena in nature were to occur. Under Confucianist influence elaborate rituals came into being to show Heaven's approval of the new ruler. From that moment on sacral and secular power became combined in his person. He was generally not concealed from the common people, but showed himself at the occasion of the performance of certain rites. No ritual anarchy occurred after his death and no human sacrifices were made, except at burials in the Shang period, when the ruler was accompanied by his servants (possibly slaves), horses, wives, etc.

There was also a 'negative' relation between the ruler and Heaven, which might punish him by sending down strange omens, like snow falling in summer, the appearance of unusual beasts, meteors, etc., and, of course, more clearly by causing a bad harvest. Where a low fertility was recognized as an expression of the will of Heaven, and not, let us say, as a result of natural aridity, the ruler was supposed to react by issuing a proclamation incorporating criticism of himself and proposing (more in theory than reality) his resignation of the throne, etc.

Much depended upon those who had to decide what a particular omen meant. The ruler constantly revered his divine ancestors, which gave some guarantee that he would not deviate from their ways.

The position of the royal family was central. The king, when choosing his feudatories, gave preference to members of his family, whom of course he believed to be reliable. He had his daughters marry feudatories with the same aim of strengthening his own power. The members of the royal family were often admitted to the government, but were always influential at any rate. The king's elder sisters did not play any role as such. The royal consorts influenced politics by securing official positions for their relatives, by intriguing against other wives of the ruler, by exercising an influence, later on, on the nomination of the crown prince, etc. Originally the succession to the throne was restricted, as already mentioned above, first to younger brothers and later to sons. At times when the original rules of succession were no longer followed, the spouses and not necessarily only the mothers of future crown princes, did not have much opportunity of influencing the nomination of the heir apparent directly, but only by means of some intrigue, such as by killing the infants of other wives of the ruler. The crown prince had a fair chance of becoming ruler unless he had been deposed due to some scandal or on account of his own behavior. Sometimes the new ruler was selected in practice by the ministers. The crown prince's health was not important, and sometimes even irrelevant, such as, for instance, when a specific child was especially selected in view of the actual political balance.

A somewhat broader center of power was represented by the court, though as a rule only during tranquil periods. Besides the royal offspring and other relatives, ministers and aristocrats, there lived at the court such different categories of people as scribes, keepers of records, archivists, diviners, scholars and even interpreters for the contacts with the barbarians. Some insignificant exceptions aside, such as by way of precaution or in the case of doubt as to somebody's loyalty, the aristocracy was not obliged to live at court, however, the feudatories had to come to court and present reports on the state of their territories on fixed occasions. The higher-ranking courtiers were members of the same social group as the feudal rulers, being relatives of these as well as of the ruler. Of course they also had to bring tribute. Occupation of an office at court or a ministerial post was originally incompatible with the holding of a fief, though later, due to the slackening of the king's power, it became possible to hold both kinds of position.

In the course of the evolution of the early state the relation between the king and his dignitaries underwent significant changes. During the Shang-Yin period the ruler's direct relationship to his people was stressed, implying that the ministers could not play an important role in their own right. The Yin ruler did not possess much authority outside of the capital, whereas the Chou *Ruler* had to try and maintain the precarious balance between the different holders of fiefs, i.e., the aristocrats. He was assisted by his brothers and sons, but not infrequently these were murdered by other members of the family. Therefore, no strictly adhered to rules of accession could maintain themselves.

Under the Eastern Chou certain powerful ministers, members of influential families, played an important, sometimes decisive role in the running of the state, although this was officially the exclusive prerogative of the ruler himself. During the Warring States period the role of ministers of an aristocratic background declined, and in many cases men of humble origin came to occupy their places. The higher offices were sometimes hereditary in certain influential families, but the actual ability of the prospective holder was also taken into account.

The ruler lived in the capital, which was mostly of fixed location; only the Shang Dynasty shifted its capital several times. At times the state had two capitals, as the Chou did immediately after their conquest. A proportion of the aristocracy resided at court, but most of them lived in the provinces, in their fiefs or on their estates. Towns were often established to serve as military strongholds or as sites of ancestral temples. The oldest ones may be designated as town palaces.

At the time when most of the production was concentrated in agriculture, prior to the development of a money economy, urbanization could not assume any significant proportions. A different type of town or city developed after the fall of the Western Chou, in the late Spring and Autumn period, when hundreds of city-states came into being. They may have shown a degree of democracy, of a specific kind, not unlike the Greek *polis*, but they were unable to resist the power of larger states and were liquidated. Cities as centers of economic life came into being only during the Warring States period, and never became centers of political power.

More or less the same can be said of the infrastructure, i.e., the system of roads and communications. The ruler of course undertook regular tours of inspection of his vassals, and not infrequently had to organize punitive expeditions, while there was further a regular traffic of goods and tributes if evidently stimulated by political and not economic factors. All this required a certain network of communications. Many roads were built during the Warring States period, while the first Emperor of the Ch'in Dynasty is credited with the construction of a whole system of strategic roads after 221. Nevertheless, the beginning of trade and commerce can be dated no further back than the sixth–fifth centuries. The Shang and Chou did not have much need for business or communications, and the traditional Chinese state despised trade and merchants, although it could not exist without them.

Confucian intellectuals were opposed to trade and, in fact, were against entrepreneurs of any kind, for the simple reason that for them agriculture represented the main source of the life of the state as well as of the livelihood of the people; consequently the people were to be prevented from engaging in any kinds of secondary professions. For the Confucians, commerce simply did not produce anything of value, but on the contrary, it depended on profits to the detriment of both the producer and the consumer. Needless to say, the great economic changes from the fifth–fourth centuries followed their own course.

Every Chinese state, even the early one, required a certain organization of the administration. Its system was continually elaborated. The principal departments were those of finance, ritual, the royal household, the army, the archives, and so on. A bureaucracy definitely existed, especially after the numerous states began to try to copy the administrative system of the Chou rulers. But there was no bureaucracy in the sense that the royal officials were paid for their administrative work in the center; they lived on the revenues from their fiefs.

The division of tasks is represented as quite clear-cut, at least theoretically. A very detailed picture of the Chou administrative system is given in the book 'Ritual of the Chou' (*Chou li*). If the system clearly cannot have existed in the elaborate form suggested here, it has even so been discovered that many of the officials and offices mentioned in the *Chou li* really existed. The Chinese system of administration was clearly very effective. This is demonstrated by the fact not only that it was adopted by all of the different rulers of imperial China and, moreover, some of other eastern Asian states, but that possibly it even penetrated into mediaeval Europe and the nineteenth century English civil service in the form of the examination of prospective officials.

We have already mentioned some particulars of the application of the law to nobles and to the 'small people'. The entire legal system was based upon the prevailing notions on morality, and was restricted largely to the penal law. It is characteristic for the whole period of the early state that we can say nothing definite about the existence of any code of law, i.e., some systematic exposition of the legal system. We are constantly confronted with a code of virtuous behavior which should not be violated. This is not surprising from the point of view of the subsequent historical evolution, since even in imperial China it took some 800 years before the great codification of the T'ang was proclaimed in the seventh century A.D.

New rules and laws were promulgated exclusively by the ruler.

Since, as was mentioned above, some of the laws and rules were of a declarative character, they were not always observed, especially in the distant provinces, although the emissaries of the ruler supervised their execution. In reality, local government, for a long time, was concentrated in the hands of feudatories, mainly the ruler's relatives, who were fairly independent. It was not always easy to obey the wishes of the central ruler. The influence of the people on the ruler's decision-making was many-sided, but mostly indirect. First, Heaven had appointed kings to take care of the people. Secondly, as the Confucian philosopher Mencius had postulated, the people had the right to revolt against a bad ruler. Thirdly, the people sometimes did revolt. All this may have influenced the ruler's decisions, though of course it was not his primary concern.

Laws and rules were issued by the ruler and made known to the limited number of dignitaries who were concerned with their execution and enforcement. For a very long time laws were not made known to the public. The reason for this was that supposedly the people would distort the law if they knew it, and might even use the law for their own ends by appealing to its wording. The promulgation of a law first took place only at the time of Confucius, when the first codification (of penal laws) is said to have been effected by the chancellor Tzu-ch'an in the state of Cheng in 536. Unfortunately, we know next to nothing about this particular law. There was not much need for the promulgation of the law as such, since it represented the ruler's will. Generally, there was no distinction between legislative and judicial executive powers, and the ruler was at the same time a legislator and judge and imposed penalties as he saw fit. He was restricted only by political and ideological considerations.

The pattern of the struggle for power during the Yin and Western Chou was primitive, being conducted mostly through force of arms, in the form of mutinies or punitive expeditions. But even at that time a certain striving for unification was to be observed. The picture became complex at the downfall of the central authority, when states began competing with each other, the same being true of influential clans within states. There were of course no political parties or secret societies, but there were certain factions based on different loyalties (e.g., courtiers, the members of a particular family, countrymen, the adherents of a certain philosophical school, members of particular military ranks, etc.). On the other hand, the ruler gained a following by virtue of his power and the careers of the individuals connected therewith. He was eager to attract scholars and other educated people who could take charge of the propaganda for him, appealing mostly to historical precedents, real or mythical.

A relative balance of power between competing groups existed of course only under 'normal' conditions, at the frequent times of crisis it had however to be established anew each time. We have already noted how the author of the Autumn and Spring annals quite laconically mentioned the liquidation of dozens of states as well as, with similar frequency, the murder of the rulers concerned. In general, the balance, if any, had to be maintained by the central power or by the most powerful of the *hegemons* (*pa*), or simply by whoever emerged victorious. Conflicts on the local and family level were not subject to the general power of the law but to the jurisdiction of a competent authority, i.e., the head of the village or family or clan. Local tradition also played its role in such cases. It is partly because of the local variations that a unified corpus of laws can hardly have come about.

The power of the ruler and of the state was based upon the exploitation of the people, i.e., mostly the peasants. Traditionally all the land was supposed to belong to the ruler, while the practical disposal of it was in the hands of the feudal lords who exploited the peasants working it. In this way the peasants were forced to contribute to the running of the administrative and military machine, while of course the economy was also based on agriculture.

Some economic changes came about slowly in the second half of the Spring and Autumn period when taxes based on the area of land held were instituted — concurrently with the beginning disintegration of the natural economy — in the state of Lu in 594. There may have already existed something similar in another part of the country around the year 800. There existed some form of taxation on trade at the same time. We may speak of the beginning of a tax system only in the sixth century, however, in connection with the slow development of private ownership of land. A regular tax system came into being only in the fifth-fourth centuries, while a money economy developed in the same way and at the same time. The taxes were levied by the State, i.e., by the ministers and other assistants of the ruler. The states paid tribute to the Chou. There was no immediate reciprocity on the parts of the central ruler, except that he offered his protection to the rulers of the states. The taxation system involved only a one-way traffic, and there was no redistribution. However, numerous lower court officials lived from the income given them by the ruler, whom they served.

We may note once again that we have a full description of the taxation and other administrative systems in the above-mentioned *Ritual of the Chou*. If any of the information contained in it is reliable, the question remains how to distinguish the notions it reflects from later ideas.

Throughout the history of China there has always existed the necessity of executing great public works. Already in remote antiquity the Chinese people had to take part in the construction of public works, organized by competent state or local authorities, in various localities and provinces. Major works, no longer at the local level, came to be organized only in the fifth century, and greatly increased thereafter. These were essentially the products of internal wars, requiring the construction of large walls and other defensive works; they were not, however, limited to the requirements of military exigencies. We have especially in mind here the great works in connection with the management of the water supply; not only the regulation of the water level of the big rivers but especially the irrigation of fields. It seems that there was no special remuneration for the people participating in these works, inter alia because this kind of work was supposed to be beneficial to the people itself.

We have no information on whether the army may have been used at times of natural disaster; it consisted mainly of common people, mostly peasants, however. During the Yin and Western Chou periods the soldiers of peasant origin were mostly foot-soldiers and were unarmed. They only performed auxiliary services while the nobles riding chariots and horses were fighting. The army was a standing one, organized and controlled personally by the ruler, and used as a tool of coercion by the rulers of states and districts alike. Later, under the Chou, the states organized their own armies. The army represented mostly an indirect form of exploitation, since it had to live off the work of the peasants. We know definitely of the use of the army for suppressing popular revolts from the period of traditional, imperial China, although this practice may of course have already existed before that. The army officers were originally recruited from among the feudatories and their offsprings, while later, with the decline of the feudal system of the old type and the inevitable downfall of hereditary aristocratic families, the more experienced members of the lesser aristocracy, the *shih* (= gentlemen), greatly improved the art of war. This was, however, mainly at the time when war chariots were used in military operations.

Another section of the social class of the *shih*, possibly more refined than the one mentioned above, devoted itself to thinking, and produced, from Confucius on, many fine philosophers, administrators, scholars, etc., thus definitely contributing to the flourishing of Chinese culture even during the period known by the invidious name of 'Warring States'. After all, Confucius' ancestors belonged to such a family under the Yin Dynasty.

All the relevant changes may have been brought about because of the advent, in the middle of the millennium, of the Iron Age.

We have already mentioned the traditional Chinese differentiation between those who rule and those who have to work. As far as the common people are concerned, they were for a long time bound to the land, though not in the same straightforward way as the *glaebae adscripti* of late fourth century (A.D.) Rome. There were no substantial differences within the peasant class, although there did exist certain possibilities, inside the different status groups, of changing profession. It was only after the break-down of the rigorous social system of the Chou, however, that political careers, even in the center, became open to the common people, from the Spring and Autumn period on. Many men of humble origin played an important political role during the Warring States, and on several occasions after the creation of imperial China peasants became emperors. It was also during the 'Warring States' that, due to increasing economic inequality a proportion of the peasants became impoverished and lost their land; only a fraction of them worked as slaves for the landowners. The same process resulted in the rise of rich merchants, wandering counsellors, etc., as well as great social mobility.

The basic duty of the common people was to maintain all the other groups and classes in several different ways, i.e., by paying taxes, performing corvée, doing military service and taking part in the execution of public works. The taxes consisted partly of produce, partly of labor on the fields of the king or the local ruler. On the other hand, it was the ruler's duty to arrange the corvée and military service in such a way that agriculture would not suffer. There were officially no sexual services, while human sacrifices were exceptional, as has already been mentioned.

The common people had in principle no right to a share in running the state, and could only influence its running indirectly. The population of Shang, Yin, Chou and even later China was not over-large, although we do not know the exact population figures, while some of the information concerning the size of the forces, for example, is clearly exaggerated. We may safely conclude, however, that there was no population pressure in ancient China, although the territory of the kingdom was expanding and the Chinese were looking for new places to settle. Partly owing to the unsatisfactory development of agricultural tools and techniques there was for a long time no significant eagerness for more land. In other words, within the above-defined narrow limits, the peasants worked their own fields in primitive village communities and were *relatively* free.

In some parts of the country, obviously in the vicinity of the capital, where the central administration could function more efficiently, and perhaps also on the borders, because of the proximity of the barbarians and the duties imposed upon the local people in states of emergency, the personal risks were somewhat higher. If the people had been able to read, they would surely have been surprised to discover that, according to the generally accepted political theory, it was the ruler who was responsible for their welfare.

Different periods in Chinese antiquity may be chosen for a description of the early state in China, but each choice has its own particular pitfalls. During the Shang-Yin period the state form had not yet been fully elaborated; but, if there is a certain amount of information available on the rulers, much of the more important information is totally lacking because of the nature of the sources, namely inscriptions on bones and bronze. The constitution of the Chou empire, provided it was an empire, may furnish much more information and provide better opportunities of study thanks to the texts written on silk. However, although Creel's penetrating study on this period is a must for everybody, some reviewers have pointed out that from Creel's numerous sources quite contradictory conclusion may be drawn, as Creel has in fact done himself. Therefore we have preferred to base ourselves on a longer period, for which there are richer and more reliable sources available, among them the texts written on bamboo tablets. We hope that this way both continuity and trends towards change may have been made clearer in the present article, written on paper.

OUTLINE OF A CHRONOLOGY OF ANCIENT CHINA
reliable from 841 B.C. only

3000–2205	legendary rulers
2205–1767	Hsia, not yet a historical dynasty
ca. 1800	beginning of the bronze period
1766–1022	Shang-Yin Dynasty
1401–1022	Yin Dynasty
1550	developed system of writing
1400	best bronzes
1022–256	Chou Dynasty
1021–771	Western Chou
897	the state of Ch'in founded
771–454 (or 256)	Eastern Chou
722–481	Spring and Autumn period
7th century	Book of Documents
594	land tax in Lu
551–479	Confucius
536	Tzu-ch'an's penal law
513	tripods with text of penal law in Chin
ca. 500	beginning of the iron period
453 (or 403)–222	Warring States period

453	disintegration of the state of Chin
ca. 300	the Korean state Choson accepts the Chinese administrative system
256	last ruler of the Chou deposed
221–207	Ch'in Dynasty
206 B.C.–A.D. 220	Han Dynasty

FOOTNOTES

[1] Unless otherwise stated, all the dates refer to the period B.C.

[2] The beginning of the Chou Dynasty, i.e., the Western Chou, is very variedly dated. The traditional date is 1122, and another one 1050, while many scholars accept 1027, or some even dates in the early tenth century. This is one of the few examples of the beginning of a dynasty varying by some 150 years, so that the chronology of events becomes rather uncertain. Cf. Creel 1970, Appendix B, Problems of Chronology, pp. 487–492.

[3] Cf. the title of his book. Creel does not give a definition of the notion 'empire', however.

REFERENCES

Bauer, Wolfgang (1961), 'Die Frühgeschichte des Eigentums in China', in: *Zeitschrift für Vergleichende Rechtswissenschaft* 63: 118–184.
Bodde, D. (1938), *China's first unifier. A study of the Ch'in dynasty as seen in the life of Li Ssu.* Leiden: Brill. Hong Kong 1967: U.R.I.
Chang Kwang-chih (1963/68), *The archaeology of ancient China.* New Haven: Yale University Press.
Cheng Te-k'un (1960/64), *Archaeology in China.* Vol. II: Shang China. Vol. III: Chou China. Cambridge.
Creel, H. G. (1964), 'The beginnings of bureaucracy in China: The origin of the hsien', in: *Journal of Asian Studies* 23: 155–184.
— (1970), *The origins of statecraft in China.* Vol. I: The Western Chou Empire. Chicago: Aldine.
Dewall, M. von (1964), *Pferd und Wagen im frühen China.* Bonn: Rudolf Habelt.
Erkes, E. (1954), *Neue Beiträge zur Geschichte des Choukönigs Yu.* Berlin: Akademie Verlag.
Felber, R. (1973), *Die Entwicklung der Austauschverhältnisse im alten China (Ende 8. Jh. bis Anfang 5. Jh v.u.Z.).* Berlin.
Fung Yu-lan (1937), *A history of Chinese philosophy.* Vol. I: The Period of Philosophers (from the beginning to circa 100 B.C.). Peiping. Translated by D. Bodde. Princeton, 1952.
Gernet, J. (1964), *La Chine ancienne des origines à l'empire.* Paris.
Ho Ping-ti, (1976), *The cradle of the East: An inquiry into the indigenous origins of techniques and ideas of neolithic and early historic China, 5,000–1,000 B.C.* Chicago and Hong Kong: Chicago University Press.
Hsu, Cho-yun (1964), *Ancient China in transition. An analysis of social mobility, 722–222 B.C.* Stanford: Stanford University Press.

Karlgren, B. (1946), 'Legends and cults in ancient China', in: Museum of Far Eastern Antiquities. Bulletin 18: 199–382.
Keightley, D. N. (1971), Review of H. C. Creel, etc., in: Journal of Asian Studies XXX: 655–658.
Kriukov, M. V. (1967), 'Formy social' noi organizatsii drevnikh Kitatsev. Moscow: Nauka.
Li Chien-nung, (1957), Hsien Ch'in liang Han ching-chi shih-kao [Outline of the economic history of the period of the pre-Ch'in and of both the Han Dynasties]. Peking: F.P.L.
Maspero, H. (1924), 'Les légendes mythologiques dans le Chou King', in: Journal Asiatique 204: 1–100.
— (1927), La Chine antique. Paris. Republished 1952, Paris: Presses Universitaires.
— (1952), Contribution à l'étude de la société chinoise à la fin des Chang et au début des Tcheou', in: Bulletin de l'École Française d'Extrême-Orient 46: 335–402.
Needham, J. (1958), The development of iron and steel technology in China. London: Newcome Society, The Science Museum.
Pokora, T. (1963), 'Existierte in China eine Sklavenhaltergesellschaft?', in: Archiv orientální 32: 353–363.
Průšek, J. (1971), Chinese statelets and the northern barbarians 1400–300 B.C. Prague: Academia.
Stumpfeld, H. (1970), Staatsverfassung und Territorium im antiken China. Ueber die Bildung einer territorialen Staatsverfassung. Düsseldorf: Fahle.
Teng Ssu-yü (1943), 'Chinese influence on the Western examination system', in: Harvard Journal of Asiatic Studies 7: 267–312.
Thilo, Thomas (1973), 'Die Entstehung des Staates in China', in: Beiträge zur Entstehung des Staates, ed. by J. Herrmann and I. Sellnow, pp. 56–72. Berlin: Akademie Verlag.
Vasil'ev, L. S. (1961), Agrarnye otnosheniia i obschchina v drevnem Kitae (XI–VII vv. do n.e.). Moscow: Nauka.
Walker, R. L. (1964), The multi-state system of ancient China. Hamden, Conn.: The Shoe String Press.
Wheatley, P. (1971), The pivot of the four quarters. A preliminary enquiry into the origins and character of the ancient Chinese city. Chicago: Chicago University Press.
Yang K'uan (1955), Chan-kuo shih [History of the warring states]. Shanghai: Rainbow Press.

10

The Early State in Ancient Egypt

JAC. J. JANSSEN

The present discussion will deal with the origin and structure of the state during the first period of Egyptian history,[1] which dates roughly from 3000 to 2150 B.C.[2] and is generally referred to as the Old Kingdom. Usually the first centuries of the foundation and consolidation of the state, the so-called Archaic Period (c. 3000–2650 B.C.), are considered as constituting a separate phase, being the transition from Prehistory to History. The era following this, the Pyramid Age, was the first period of florescence of Egyptian civilization, ending in a gradual decline and final dissolution of the state ca. 2150 B.C.

Following the Graeco-Egyptian Historian Manetho (third century B.C.), the period under discussion is divided into six 'dynasties'. Dynasties I and II constitute the Archaic Period, also called 'the Early Dynastic Age'. These are followed by the Third Dynasty, including, among others, King Djoser, the builder of the Step Pyramid at Saqqâra; the Fourth Dynasty, comprising the builders of the great pyramids of Gîza; and the Fifth Dynasty, with its sun temples at Abûsîr. Under the Sixth Dynasty the signs of decline became clearly perceptible, the disintegration of the state accelerating during the long reign of its last great ruler, Pepy II.

It should be stressed that in Egyptian history the word 'dynasty' is used in a strictly technical sense, merely to indicate a series of rulers with, though in some instances without, genealogical connections. In some cases an usurper might have ascended the throne in the middle of such a 'dynasty', while in others the first king of a new 'dynasty' might actually be a near relation of his predecessor.

The Old Kingdom represents certainly the least-known period of Egyptian history, not only since, being the oldest, most of its material achievements were destroyed in subsequent ages, but also because the documents that have been preserved, particularly those from the first dynasties, are written in a difficult script with many polyinterpretable signs and a rather elliptical expression of grammar. Moreover, the great majority of the texts preserved are in the form of inscriptions on vessels, seals and seal impressions, offering lists, and the like, more suitable material for our present purpose, such as administrative records, being hardly available at all. The implication of this is that we know a large number of titles, enabling us, by interpreting them either from their etymological meaning or from what we know about them from later periods, to suggest some basic principles of the structure of government; the actual functioning of the state remains absolutely unknown, however.

Apart from these titles, there is one other important source for the first dynasties, viz, the so-called Annals, also called the 'Stone of Palermo' after one of the larger fragments preserved at present. In this inscription, of which so far seven fragments, together comprising perhaps one tenth of the original text, have been discovered, the most important events as well as the height of the Nile inundation are recorded for each regnal year of each king, down to the Fifth Dynasty. It has been argued, however, that the inscription as it stands was only written in the seventh century B.C., although its contents are doubtless based on archive records (Helck 1970). If this is correct, we should be cautious in drawing conclusions from the Annals.

Even greater discretion is needed in the handling of data from the religious texts, since most of these exist only in later versions. For the *Sed* festival (see below) we have a series of reliefs from the Fifth Dynasty, which possibly represent the oldest rites in a fairly pure form. The oldest document concerning the coronation rites dates from the Middle Kingdom, and though it is clear from its contents that the original ritual was composed in the earliest period of history, it is equally obvious that these rites were greatly influenced by later religious and other developments (Altenmüller 1967; Barta 1975: 44 ff.). The important funerary texts from the Old Kingdom, namely the Pyramid Texts covering the walls of the royal burial chambers from the late fifth and sixth dynasties, are hardly relevant to our purpose. They deal with the deceased ruler, and contain religious conceptions from various periods, partly even from prehistoric times. Moreover, like all religious texts, they present an ideal situation, and not the actual practice; they reflect what the Egyptians conceived to be the eternal truth, and not the everyday reality of state and government.

One more preliminary remark should be made, particularly for those readers who are not familiar with the subject. In the older, and even in some recent handbooks on Egyptian history and civilization, one comes across a number of quite definite statements concerning the state and its origin, which on close scrutiny appear to be based on very scanty evidence. In general, the historian studying the present subject is struck by the great mass of purely speculative observations which are presented as 'history' for lack of actual data. Avoiding speculation as well as he could, the present author has tried to restrict himself in the following to mentioning only those facts which may be assumed to be reasonably certain. Many questions cannot be answered at all, to others the provisional answer is still most uncertain. That the result will appear disappointing, regrettable as this may be, is only in accordance with our present knowledge of these early ages.

1. THE ORIGIN

The birth of the Egyptian state is a subject that has been discussed in many studies, but about which the factual information is rather scanty. Without proceeding from any preconceived theory of the orgin of the state in general, we will mention the factors which may have had an influence on its formation in Egypt and see what proof we can find for their contribution to events.

One aspect, although rather a condition than a formative element, is the geographical seclusion of Egypt's territory. The country consists of two parts: the Nile Valley proper, nowhere more and mostly less than 25 km wide, extending over a length of ca. 950 km from Aswân to the area of Cairo; and, in the north, the Delta, a broad plain intersected by the branches of the Nile. The desert areas on either side, except for the Faîyum oasis, which more or less belongs to the valley itself, played hardly any part in most periods. Notwithstanding its curious shape, the country has actual political boundaries only in the south, where the first cataract constitutes a barrier against the Nubians, and the North-east, where the Sinai peninsula, thinly populated by nomads, forms another barrier, though well-organized states of the Near East have at times been able to break through it. Thus Egypt has by its geographical position always been fairly safe from attacks by foreign powers, so that the need for defence against them is not likely to have been the main reason for the birth of the state. Moreover, the problem of the gradual decline of power exercised by the central government as one proceeds from the center to the borders of a state in Egypt, notwithstanding the impressive distances, was far less significant than in other kingdoms because of the case of communication along the river.

In the opinion of later ages the first Egyptian state was a product of the wars of a king of Upper Egypt, known by the name of Menes, against the inhabitants of the Delta. With this pharaoh the history of the unitary state was supposed to have begun. Moreover, Menes was said to have founded the capital, Memphis, at a point where Upper and Lower Egypt adjoined each other. Modern research has shown this conception to be too simple.[3] The unification of the territory was a slow process drawn out over a number of generations and beginning long before the First Dynasty (Kaiser 1961; Kaplony 1970, col. 5). Whether it was, in fact, through a war between the South and the North that the unitary state was founded is uncertain. What is definite is that for millennia the Egyptians conceived of their kingdoms as consisting of two parts, Upper and Lower Egypt, and this dualism is reflected even by the royal titles and by the form of the administration. But whether this goes back to an actual political situation prevailing at the birth of the state, or whether it is due only to a characteristic trait of the Egyptian mentality, is a dubious question. That certain wars did play a role in the birth of the state is apparent from late prehistorical and early dynastic 'historical' records, such as the ceremonial slate palettes. These wars may equally well have been fought against the nomads along the borders of the Delta, however.

Some Egyptologists have suggested that the conquest of the Delta by Upper Egypt also involved the 'Ueberlagerung' of a sedentary agricultural population by pastoral nomads. Recent investigation has shown, however, that the way of life in the Nile Valley and in the center of the Delta in late prehistoric ages was the same, representing a mixed economy of agriculture, cattle-breeding, hunting and fishing (Atzler 1972; 234 ff.).The suggestion put forward by some scholars that cities were important in the Delta seems altogether improbable; ancient Egypt always lacked genuine urbanization (Wilson 1960).

Whatever the historical reality, conquest may quite well have been the process through which Egypt became unified at the beginning of history. The reasons for these wars are obscure. One might suggest that one of them was the desire to defend an agricultural community against the threat of nomad incursions, as mentioned above. The mention of Libyans on the early palettes might be cited as proof for this, were it not that evidence is insufficiently clear. The significance of the pressure resulting from increasing population density often suggested as one of the main factors in the formation of states is equally dubious. Even for later periods of Egyptian history population problems constitute one of the least-known subjects (O'Connor 1972). Any statement about their significance for the origin of the state would necessarily at the present juncture be tantamount to a sheer guess.

A factor mentioned by Wolf (1962: 104) is the rise of the level of technology, and more particularly the use of copper. Although copper implements were known in Egypt before the First Dynasty, there appears to have been a marked increase in their distribution during the Archaic Period. This may be partly explained by the incompleteness of our documentation with regard to earlier periods, however, while on the other hand it may have been rather the result than cause of the birth of Egyptian civilization, which occurred during the late Prehistoric and the Early Dynastic Periods, of which we further mention: the invention of writing and the calendar — both obviously due to the demands of a growing administration —, the awakening of a historical consciousness, the development of a specific style in art and architecture, and the origin of anthropomorphic conceptions in religion. They doubtless all contributed to the origin of the civilization, but can hardly be considered as formative elements of the state.

One factor usually mentioned as being decisive, namely irrigation, appears, in fact, to be highly dubious. The 'hydraulic hypothesis' of Steward, Wittfogel and others, no more than revivified a theory already found in early twentieth century textbooks, according to which Egypt owed its unity and specific form of government to the demands of irrigation and its administration. Once-yearly, from mid-July onwards, the Nile inundates the valley. In order to curb the turbulence of the flood-waters and to utilize them as well as the fertile silt deposited by them a complicated system of canals and ditches, dykes and dams, sluices and basins in said to have evolved, the construction and maintenance of which, together with the problems of a fair distribution of the limited volume of waters in years of low Nile level and of regulating the excess in years of high Nile level, allegedly required a strong centralized government. Unfortunately, at present we possess absolutely no knowledge of the actual irrigation system at the time of the Old Kingdom; even for the best-known period of Egyptian history, the New Kingdom (ca. 1550–1080 B.C.), the data on the subject are scarce. It has recently been suggested (Schenkel 1974) that the system or irrigation works was only evolved during the Middle Kingdom, while in the preceding periods the Nile regularly flooded the country without much human interference. Whether Schenkel's theory is correct is not quite clear; for this we must await his arguments in his forthcoming publication. One is inclined to ask where, then, the Egyptians can have learned how to organize large bodies of workmen, a technique they applied to the building of the pyramids. For the present we can only conclude that the extent of the possible influence of the irrigation system on the origin of a centralized political authority in Egypt is still a moot question.

One last factor to be mentioned here is the foreign influence suggested by some authors as having been of significance in the formation of the Egyptian state. Although much debated, and once called 'the catalyst producing civilized life in the Nile Valley' (Wilson 1951: 37), its existence has been denied by others (Kelley 1974). However that may be, the discussion concerned Mesopotamian influence on the civilization, of which the state is only a special aspect. Even if it was present, it seems improbable that the example of the

Near East was really important.[4] Egypt was certainly a 'pristine state' (Fried 1967: 231 ff.), and since such states are none too numerous, a study of its origin may help to solve this specific problem of political anthropology.

One more point may perhaps be mentioned in the present context, although once more through lack of evidence it will not help to broaden our insight into the matter under discussion. So far as we are aware there are no traces left of any kind of political organization preceding that of pharaonic times, in the form of either tribes, clans or lineage structures. In the texts of the Old Kingdom we come across a rather marked individualism as well as a rational structure of the state. It may be that the scantiness of the documentation is the cause of our lack of knowledge, but we have to admit in any case that the early Egyptian state is like a foundling without known parents.

Summing up, then, the factors contributing to the birth of the Egyptian state are still unknown. One may suggest that a growing population density played the decisive role, but all evidence in support of this suggestion is still lacking. We may be more or less able to trace the birth of Egyptian civilization, that is, of writing, architecture, art, and even of Egyptian religion, but the origin of the state remains obscure.

2.   KINGSHIP

During the Archaic Period there was a gradual development in the organization of the Egyptian state. Whether the same holds true for the position of its ruler is not certain, however (Wilson 1951: 44 ff.). Therefore, I will confine the following discussion to kingship in the Pyramid Age.

Pharaoh, the Egyptian king, is usually represented as a clear example of divine kingship. He was said to be Horus,[5] the falcon god who with his outstretched wings protects the country, and whose fierce eyes are sun and moon (Frankfort 1948: 37). He was the incarnation of a sacred power, the personification of an institution of divine origin (Posener 1960: 88).

It has been argued in a recent study (Barta 1975), however, that pharaoh's kingship was not so much divine as sacral. Through rites of birth and coronation he attained resemblance to the gods, without ever becoming their complete equal. He played the part of divinity and functioned as a god, but in essence remained a human being. Whether this is an appropriate formulation of Egyptian ideas seems to be doubtful. It is certain, however, that the usual conception of Pharaoh as a divine king is over-simplified. The so-called "complementary way of thinking' (Wilson 1949: 70 ff.; Hornung 1971, 237 ff.) enabled the Egyptians to conceive of kingship as at the same time human and divine.

It was the Pharaoh who guaranteed and maintained the cosmic order as well as its counterpart, law and order on earth, the two being to the Egyptian mind one and the same thing, called Ma'at. On the other hand, the king was also subordinate to Ma'at. His rule had to be, and according to the dogmatic texts always was, in accordance with the principle.[6] At the same time, the king exercised a mundane function, maintaining order in his realm through earthly means. The distinction between the divine ruler and the human head of the state possibly found expression in the use of two different words for 'king', namely *niswt* and *ḥm*, each indicating a specific aspect of kingship (Goedicke 1960). This calls to mind the distinction between 'the system of ideas' and 'the real political system', although this certainly does not correspond to the Egyptian view since to them both aspects were equally 'real'. To them — at least according to the dogma, though probably also in the view of the majority of the king's subjects — pharaoh was omnipotent. 'If anything comes forth from the mouth of His Majesty[7] it happens immediately' (Urkunden I, 39, 13–14). On the other hand, he was also dependent on the gods. 'We [the Enneade, a group of nine gods] are giving to him all life [that is] with us; we are giving to him all dominion [that is] with us; we are giving to him to celebrate Sed festivals' (Urkunden I, 154, 3–4).

Although a god, at least in his capacity of king, pharaoh was not a miracle-worker; miracles were wrought only by the gods. He was no rainmaker. He had not the power to cure the sick. So, for instance, we are told how once, when a certain Washptah suddenly fell ill during an inspection by the king and his courtiers of the royal tomb under construction, the king consulted the physicians and gave orders for a box with (medical) papyri to be brought. Although the text is damaged at this point it seems that he prayed for Washptah's health to the god Re. When the man died nevertheless, he ordered the necessary arrangements for his burial (Urkunden I, 42–43). Evidently pharaoh's power in matters of life and death was restricted. That the text is inscribed upon the wall of Washptah's tomb testifies that this was openly acknowledged by his servants.

The king's person was taboo, but the taboo could be overridden by him at will. There are two instances of high officials (one of them the above-mentioned Washptah) relating on their tomb walls how the king, on seeing that they were going to kiss the ground before his feet, ordered them to kiss the feet themselves (Urkunden I, 41, 12–15 and 53, 1–3). An especially illustrative incident is described in the autobiographical inscription in the tomb of one Rawer. Once, when in the presence of Pharaoh Neferirkare (Fifth Dynasty), the scepter in His Majesty's hand happened to strike Rawer's leg. Immediately the king uttered the words: 'Be uninjured', adding to the bystanders: 'My Majesty wishes him to be completely uninjured, for the blow was not intended for him' (Urkunden I, 232). Evidently the blight accumulated in the royal sceptre was deadly, but could be exorcized by the royal word.

Although the king did wear traditional state dress, he is also represented in ordinary garments and with an ordinary headdress. The royal garb consisted of a specific type of kilt called *šndyt*, with in front a central piece whose shape went back to the prehistoric penis-sheath (Staehelin 1966: 5).[8] In some earlier representations the king has a dog's tail hanging down from his waist. The full state dress also included a ceremonial beard, a crook and two crowns, the red one of Lower and the white one of Upper Egypt. During the Sed Festival his body was wrapped in a kind of short cloak, leaving only the hands holding the crook and 'flail' exposed.

There are no remains of any royal palaces from the Old Kingdom, since they were built of sun-dried bricks, wood and papyrus, all of them very perishable materials. Stylized representations of palace walls were incorporated in the writings of the Horus name (see note 5), while further the exterior of some tombs seems to imitate the outer appearance of the palace. Moreover, its constructional elements are repeated in stone and tiles in the pyramid complex of Djoser. Probably the complex in its entirety was designed on the model of the royal residence. From texts we know that it comprised, aside from the palace proper, temples of the crown goddesses (Kaplony 1962) as well as of other divinities, storerooms, bakeries and breweries, workshops of craftsmen and artists, etc. Whether high officials dwelt within the walls is uncertain. On the whole, the Egyptian royal residence may have resembled the usual African residency such as, for example, Jiren, the capital of the Galla Monarchy described by Lewis (1965: 68 ff.).

Whether each pharaoh built his own residence is not certain. From the Third Dynasty onwards, though possibly from the very beginning of history, the kings usually lived in the neighbourhood of Memphis, where most of them were also buried, although during the first dynasties most of them had a second tomb near Abydos. In this latter area there may have been located a lower-level administrative center, called This, but whether it incorporated a secondary royal residence is not certain.

An important feature of early Egyptian kingship may have been a biennial tour of the country by the pharaoh. Unfortunately, there is no direct evidence for this. Its occurrence is inferred from the expression *šmsi Ḥr*, 'the following of Horus', which in the Annals is determined with a boat (von Beckerath 1956). This tour had possibly some connection with the biennial census (see below). Whether it actually still took place after the First Dynasty is not clear.[9]

Probably the king did not have a harem proper during the Old Kingdom (Lorton 1976), although at least some pharaohs seem to have had more than one wife. One of these, the mother of the royal heir, was his official consort. It seems unlikely that they attained to this rank only after giving birth to the royal heir. Although most royal consorts were themselves also of royal blood, this does not seem to have been conditional during the Old Kingdom. We know, for instance, that Pepy I (Sixth Dynasty) married two daughters of a commoner from Abydos who either was, or afterwards became, a nomarch. Whether such a marriage would have been possible during the Archaic Period is doubtful. Evidently, the queen mother's descent was of significance for the legitimacy of the royal successor. In the Annals the king's name is followed by that of his mother, not by that of his father. Of course the ideal situation need not necessarily have reflected the actual state of affairs.

In view of the important role of women in Egyptian civilization it seems likely that the queen's influence on the government was not negligible. She had an estate of her own, and when a queen once became involved in a process, the case — possibly one of embezzlement (Lorton 1974) — was tried by a special court consisting of high officials, confidants of the king (Urkunden I, 100). The tombs of some of the early queens were not essentially different in size and construction from those of the kings themselves. One queen at least, Merneith, seems to have acted as regent for her son during his minority.

Usually the royal heir was the first-born son of the king by the principal queen. However, the first rulers of the Fifth Dynasty, two (or three?) brothers, seem to have based their claims to the throne on the descent of their mother, Khentkaus, who may have been a member of the royal family of the Fourth Dynasty (Altenmüller 1970). She had quite a conspicuous tomb in the area of the great pyramids at Giza. Possibly the first ruler of the Fourth Dynasty, Snofru, also derived his rights from his mother.

That some pharaohs actually were usurpers — though even in that case they may have been of royal blood — is evident from the available documentation, though nowhere officially admitted. The usurpers may have been ritually 'legitimized' as sons of their predecessors. In general, the right to the throne, even of the king's eldest son by his official consort, was never a natural fact; it had to be reinforced by rites. There is no proof that the crown-prince was sacral already before his ascent. Whether actual rights of birth were enacted, as Barta suggests (1975) — at the occasion of the name-giving?—seems to be doubtful; there is no testimony of the celebration of such rites on record.

The texts make no mention of any requirements as regards the physical condition of the crown-prince. The history of the period is not (yet?) transparent enough for us to be able to say whether in some instances a possible successor may have been passed over, and if so, for what reason. All we know is that in the Archaic Period the king's sons and other members of the royal family played a decisive part in the government, obviously since they alone were thought capable of bearing the mighty presence of the divine ruler and fit to transmit the power-charged royal words to the people. Nothing is known of any political parties formed by them, or by officials and notables in general. The documents may in some cases contain evidence of what seem to have been revolts — though not revolutions, that is, fundamental changes in the system of government — they present these events in the light of religion.[10] It is, in fact, dogmatic theory, not practical conditions that one finds recorded in the sources.

The new king usually ascended to the throne immediately after the death of his predecessor. Sometimes afterwards there followed the coronation ceremony, during which the pharaoh was ritually purified and crowned with the two crowns, whereupon he performed the rites of 'uniting the Two Lands' and the 'perambulation of the wall', a symbolic appropriation of the capital. It may be that the king also built a new residence (see above). He definitely ordered the renewal of the official seals and, in the earlier periods reorganized the government, introducing new titles. Dogmatically the beginning of each new rule represented a new creation of the world, a repetition of the original creation. No wonder the coronation day was anually commemorated.

As the king grew older, the coronation ritual was reenacted in the Sed festival. It is uncertain how many kings actually performed these rites, and after how many regnal years (Hornung and Staehelin 1974) — probably in most cases after some thirty years, the festivals being repeated at shorter intervals thereafter. The ceremonies involved roughly resembled the coronation rites and were aimed at renewing the physical and political powers of the pharaoh, closely connected as they were with the fertility of the land and people. The festival was preceded by the ritual burial of the 'old' king, represented by a statue for which the 'rites de passage' to the hereafter were celebrated. The dead king became Osiris, god of the netherworld. Hence the characteristic Sed festival garment (see above) resembled the familiar dress of this god. Whether originally, during the Early Dynastic Period, the king was ever actually killed is uncertain, though not altogether impossible (Barta 1975; 64; see also Jankuhn 1972 and Störk 1973).[11]

It may also be that a substitute was killed, however, which of course does not become apparent from the religious ceremonial texts and representations.

3. GOVERNMENT AND THE PEOPLE[12]

If we have devoted much attention to the king and his family, this is in accordance with pharaoh's central position in the state. Until the Sixth Dynasty this was not only a matter of dogmatic theory but also an actual fact. Although Egyptian scribes never give any information on the qualities of their rulers, so that we know very little about their individual capacities, it is clear that the early pharaohs indeed ruled the country themselves, a fact of which the huge pyramids of the Fourth Dynasty were meant to be an impressive symbol.

The pharaohs of the first dynasties ruled with the assistance of the royal princes and, as far as the less important functions are concerned, their private servants. The Egyptian governmental organization developed out of the royal household. In the beginning, its personnel was limited and, though it increased in the course of time, it remained so compared with that of more modern states.

The high officials of the early period were sons, brothers, uncles, nephews and cousins of the king's. This type of government is reflected by the lay-out of the cemeteries surrounding the pyramid of Cheops (Fourth Dynasty), where the tombs of the royal family are arranged in a regular pattern centred around those of the more important members. It was only in later ages that the pattern was destroyed by the construction of tombs in between the older ones (O'Connor 1974: 20 ff.).

One of the oldest of the high offices may have been that of the *sd3wty bity* — which should perhaps be translated as 'seal-keeper of the king' — the man who was in control of pharaoh's income in kind as well as of the storerooms and workshops of the royal residence (Edwards 1971). Another official, whose title has been translated as 'master of the largesses', was reponsible for the redistribution of food and other commodities among the members of the royal household and the royal servants in the widest sense. The Egyptian economy did not use money of any kind, although there may have existed already during the Old Kingdom a measure of value called *š(n)'ty* (Urkunden I, 157). Taxes were paid in kind and assembled in the storerooms of the royal residence (the 'Treasury') for later redistribution, in some instances after being converted into garments, etc., to a relatively large proportion of the population. Details of this system, which was still functioning at the time of the New Kingdom, and in which the temples played a special part, are virtually unknown.

Lower-level state offices developed out of the private service of king and palace. The later 'departments' in the state organization were indicated by a word which may have originally meant 'room' (in the palace buildings). The development is difficult to follow. The texts contain numerous titles, most of which were used to indicate rank towards the end of the Old Kingdom. It remains uncertain what exactly the functions they originally indicated may have been. A literal translation where at all possible, never explains anything very much. So the word for hairdresser was used with reference to the man who took care of the king's ornaments, and gradually became an honorary title standing for something like 'confidant' of the pharaoh (Junker 1959: 11 ff.). Whether this particular title was ever attached to a specific function in the state administration is uncertain; in other instances titles indicating rank are definitely survivals of actual offices in earlier periods. It is hardly possible, however, to reconstruct the functioning of the early state from this later material.

So much is clear that the state during the Archaic Period furnished a plain instance of what Max Weber (1972: 580 ff.) has called 'patrimonialism', though not quite 'patriarchalism' since non-royal servants also functioned as officials, although mostly, so far as we know, on the lower levels, From this first stage a permanent bureaucracy ruling to some extent in its own right developed, the first signs of which we come across during the Third Dynasty. An institution such as the treasury appears by that time to have become independent of the royal palace and permanently established in Memphis. The famous "sealkeeper' and architect Imhotep, the builder of the Step Pyramid complex — the earliest larger-scale stone construction in Egypt — was probably not of royal blood. In his time, under the reign of Djoser, the supreme office of vizier was created (Helck 1954: 134), although Imhotep as far as we know never held it. The viziers were general administrators of the country in its entirety, representatives of the pharaoh, controlling the economy, the jurisdiction and the provincial administration. Under the Third and Fourth Dynasties they were still all princes, but from the Fifth Dynasty onwards we find only commoners as viziers. It has been suggested that the viziers from the Fourth Dynasty and later were not so much bearers of the royal mandate as chiefs of independent government departments, the function itself constituting the source of their power (Helck 1954: 58),[13] but whether this is correct is still uncertain.

All state officials of the Old Kingdom were scribes, that is, they were able to read and write the fairly intricate hieroglypic script and were trained in the art of drawing up decrees and other documents. The forms of the decrees had already become fixed by the second half of the period (Helck 1974a: 10 ff.), which testifies to a regular bureaucratic practice of fairly long standing.

Military officers played no role in the state, the army being relatively insignificant. For the defence of the country some small garrisons at the southern and northern borders and in a few towns, where roads through the desert met the Nile Valley, probably sufficed. In the case of one of the rare regular campaigns conducted in a foreign country, either Nubia or Palestine, the leadership of the army was entrusted to a specialist in organization, not to a military expert, as the story of Uni proves (Urkunden I, 101 ff.). The army, consisting of conscripts and local militia units, was used mainly for expeditions to quarries and mines in the desert. The word usually rendered as 'army', *mš*', almost always indicates an expedition (Vandersleyen 1971: 178 note 7).

The conditions of the priesthood during the Old Kingdom are still obscure. It has been suggested that at least some of the priestly functions evolved from functions in the palace household (Helck 1954: 120), while early lower officials also acted as priests of the guardian divinities of their specific departments. Of an ancient priesthood attached to local sanctuaries we know as little as of the original social organization. Closely bound as they were to the pharaoh, who was god on earth, the priests will have had little if any independent political power. Until the end of the pharaonic times it was the king who was in theory the high priest in every temple. His authority over the priesthood may have been on a par with that over other state departments.

Above I pointed to the lay-out of the Gîza cemeteries as reflecting the organization of the state. One of the excavators of the area has noted, however, that tombs here are too few in number to have contained the mortal remains of even a substantial proportion of the state servants of the period (Junker 1955: 17 ff.). One should probably look for their tombs throughout the entire country; at present only little is known of them, however. This once more goes to show how scanty our knowledge of the actual situation during the first four dynasties is. It is only for the final period of the Old Kingdom that tombs of officials in areas other than that of the capital become more frequent. Whether central government functionaries were related in any way to local dignitaries, and if so, to what extent, is unknown. In general the local administration still constitutes a problem.

In later ages Egypt was divided into some forty provinces, called 'nomes' by us.[14] From what time this form of organization dates is not quite certain. Some nomes had more or less natural geographical boundaries, inasmuch as this was possible in a country like Egypt, covering a plain extending along one or both sides of the Nile, and centered around the main settlement. Helck suggested that most of the nomes already existed in the Archaic Period (Helck 1974b: 49 ff.), while he also argues that they were not, as is supposed by others, the successors of prehistorical political units, but rather the products of a general population resettlement during the first two dynasties. In my opinion this view is far from proven and not in itself very likely. We know that the later funerary domains still partly comprised villages with old names (Jacquet-Gordon 1961; 7), which does not seem to point to any wholesale resettlement. Moreover, I fail to see how such a massive population removal could have been organized by the small administrative body of the early state. If Helck's theory could be proved, however, the problem of why so few traces of an earlier social and political system have been preserved would be solved.[15]

Whatever its origin, the organization of the nomes had almost assumed its definite form by the beginning of the Third Dynasty. They did not yet at that time include the border regions of the Delta — which were inhabited by pastoral nomads — or the areas of the capital Memphis and the subcapital called This, which were evidently administered direct by the central government. These regions aside, they may have covered the entire country, including the southernmost area, which was probably the last to be incorporated into the state.

About the internal administration of the nomes very little is known. It seems that the titles of their functionaries changed in the course of the Old Kingdom (Helck 1974b: 51), while they were evidently different in Upper and Lower Egypt. Possibly, their administration was originally entrusted to representatives of the various departments of the central government, each of whom was responsible for his own particular field. This means that they were special functionaries. Later on the nomes were probably governed by general administrators (Baer 1960; 281 ff.). Helck believed that the administration developed out of that of the royal domains, though at present this seems hardly more than a possibility. Notwithstanding, and partly because of, the numerousness of the titles connected with the provincial administration we are still unable to distinguish its internal structure (Helck 1954: 78 ff.). One fact is clear, however: the nomarchs grew increasingly independent during the Fifth and Sixth Dynasties. At the time of the Fourth Dynasty high officials still customarily ruled over several provinces in turns and were still buried near Memphis. Under the later dynasties, however, they began building comparatively ostentatious tombs in their 'own' nomes. Below we will come back to this development.

In connection with the kingship I mentioned the two-yearly census. Whether it was, in fact, no more than a census proper, or also involved the collection of taxes does not become apparent from the sources. According to the Annals it covered cattle as well as (in some instances?) gold and fields. Probably grain taxes were collected yearly, as in later times; our present knowledge on the subject, even for the New Kingdom, is restricted, however. About the quantitative aspect in relation to the total production nothing is known, so that it is impossible to establish whether the burden of taxation was heavy or not, or how it was distributed over the population. All we know is that particular religious and other institutions were exempted from taxation and other obligations by royal decree, as will become apparent below.

The usual picture of Egyptian society during the Old Kingdom is that of a rather amorphous mass of peasants governed by a centralized state represented by a relatively small class of high officials, mostly of royal blood, and a slightly larger group of lower officials. On the whole this view seems correct. The suggestion that the Delta was an area of mercantile towns populated by free citizens should be rejected. Nonetheless, the actual conditions among the people may have varied more than is usually supposed. The obviously enormous amount of work involved in building the pyramids has led scholars from Herodotus onwards to assume that the workers lived under conditions not essentially different from those of slavery, or at least serfdom. There is no evidence to support this. The conception of the pharaoh as the absolute ruler (or despot), as the sole owner of all land, did belong to the dogmatic religious sphere, and this does not exclude actual freedom for his subjects. It is likely that *corvée* for the maintenance of what irrigation works existed at that time, together with the custom of conscripting men for expeditions to quarries and mines, constituted the legal basis for the right to summon laborers for public works, among which the construction of pyramids figured prominently; but this does not mean that the peasants and workmen were legally or socially slaves or serfs.

There are but few indications of the existence of class distinctions during the Old Kingdom. One high official from the end of the Third or the beginning of the Fourth Dynasty, called Metjen, states in his tomb inscription that he bought a substantial area of land from the *niswtyw*. Now, this word is usually connected with *niswt*, one of the terms for 'king'. It also occurs in other connections, e.g., in titles. Its exact meaning is uncertain. Some have explained it as being 'royal tenants' (Goedicke 1965), others as 'free peasants'. Helck has even suggested (1954: 81, note 26) that they were the remnant of the original free inhabitants of the country, who gradually lost their independence. That this latter was, in fact, the case with this group may be correct, but the legal or social status of these 'king's men' — if this is the correct translation — is quite obscure. Obviously, some of them were in a position to sell land.

In a later phase of the Old Kingdom we come across the so-called *ḫntyw-š*, the personnel of the pyramid towns, providing the necessary materials for and taking charge of the cult of the deceased rulers. They were headed by priests, and gradually attained a privileged status, entailing, among other things, the right to private property and exemption from taxes and forced labor. Their privileges induced high officials to try to secure the status of *ḫnty-š* for themselves. So one may conclude that other members of society were less protected against the demands of the state, which would then point to a really despotic power of the ruler over the population as a whole. Even for later periods in Egyptian history the evidence for the existence of 'free' landowning peasants is slight.

Other social differences, e.g., the frequently suggested one between Upper Egyptian pastoral nomads and Lower Egyptian agriculturists that dominates the picture of the Archaic Period in so many surveys of the age, are in my view still wholly unproved (cf. Atzler 1972). Of course Egyptian civilization did preserve certain vestiges of the Prehistoric Age in the rituals, the royal dress, and so on, while it is obvious that in that period hunting and nomadism were more important than later. If and how this should be connected with such old words for 'people' as *p't* and *rḫyt* is a matter for debate, however.

The existence of a class of free craftsmen producing articles for the market seems unlikely. Most specialists, such as leather-workers, sculptors, and even physicians were in all probability attached to the household of the pharaoh and the members of the upper class. On the whole the lack of evidence for any kind of class distinction or other forms of social differentiation suggests a picture of surprising individualism. No clans or lineages, and direct connections between the government through its local representatives and the individual members of society — it all sounds too modern to be true. Of course it may well be that our sources are inadequate, or have as yet been insufficiently studied on this point for them to provide an adequate picture of society during the Old Kingdom.

4. THE DECLINE

In the course of the Fourth Dynasty there began a religious development which exercized a deep influence on the dogmatic position of the king. Henceforth, he was conceived of as being not so much Horus as the son of the sun god Re. The social background of this religious movement is not at all clear. Whether a greater dependence of the pharaoh upon the power of the gods meant a loss of his central position in the state and should be connected with the evolution of the bureaucracy is uncertain, though plausible. Contemporaneously with, and most probably related to it, there occurred a gradual increase in the independence of the officials, based on and reflected in an increase in private property. Originally, the officials were fed and clad completely from the royal stores in the palace complex, though we see them being given fields already at the beginning of the Third Dynasty, partly in connection with their functions. These lands were more or less like fiefs, being partly grants from the king, intended as a provision for their funerary equipment and service (Menu and Harari 1974). The inheritance of the latter initially was subject to the royal consent, the king apparently remaining the exclusive landowner in theory. But as so often in history, landed property, both funerary domain and the estate attached to a given office, tended to become hereditary. It also appears to have increased in extent. This way an economically independent class of functionaries came into being, posing a danger to the centralization of the state. Its members tended to leave the capital and settle permanently on their estates. Its top layer was formed by the nomarchs, or provincial governors. The next step would be for this group to begin acting as de facto independent rulers of their nomes.

This development seems to have begun at the border of the state. Possibly the presence of a small garrison in the southernmost nome (Aswân) played a part, combined with the distance from the center. Gradually the growth of a local nobility spread to the north. Whether the development in the Delta was of a similar nature we do not know, owing to lack of relevant documents. A concomitant development was the concentration of the provincial administration in the hands of the nomarchs at the expense of the representatives of various departments of the central government, as mentioned above. The nomarchs seem also to have become the administrators of the temple domains of the local divinities. Thus a power in the nome that was similar to that which the pharaoh formerly possessed in the country as a whole became concentrated in the hands of the nomarchs.

Of course the kings did not fail to react to this fatal loss of power. One royal measure in this connection was the institution of a new central office for the supervision of a number of nomes and their governors. To this office were appointed personal confidants of the pharaohs. For several of them the office constituted a decisive step in their careers on their way to the top as viziers. In the long run the creation of the office of 'overseer of Upper Egypt' proved to be ineffectual, since it, too, fell into the hands of the ruling provincial nobility. This does not mean that the central government became completely dependent upon the new class. Until the end of the Old Kingdom it continued to be the supreme power in the state, not only in the dogmatic conception of kingship but also in actual practice. There seems to have existed some sort of balance of power, which does not in itself imply chaos, though it was rather far removed from the centralized state of the Third and Fourth Dynasties, vestiges of which may (for some time) have survived in Middle Egypt, which was still administered directly by the capital.

The rulers of the Sixth Dynasty accepted the new situation. Pepy I married two daughters of a nomarch whose relatives gained considerable influence in the central government; one of his brothers, in fact, became a vizier. But even this acceptance was not enough to check the development. Under the long reign of Pepy II, his second successor, who ascended the throne as a child and lived to be over ninety years old, the centrifugal forces definitely won the day, and shortly after his death the unity of the state in actual fact — though not in theory — disintegrated.

It is open to doubt whether the political development of decentralization described above was, in point of fact, an independent phenomenon. I pointed out above the economic evolution whereby an increasing proportion of land slipped out of the control of the central administration, which meant a loss of income for the state. As for a different cause of the decline, it has recently been argued that climatic changes at the end of the Old Kingdom resulted in lower Nile floods and, consequently, persistent famines (Bell 1970; O'Connor 1974). The occurrence of these phenomena is beyond doubt, but which of them acted as cause and which were only a result is a problem that will require further study. Historical events such as the decline of a state are usually too complex to be explained by one single cause.

Above I have attempted to sketch the essential characteristics of the early state in Egyptian history, through the stages of its birth, flowering and decline. Since it is one of the oldest larger states in history, possibly even the very earliest one, its study is certainly of interest for political anthropology. That our present knowledge of the facts is scanty provides all the more reason for continued research into the subject.

FOOTNOTES

[1]   For recent surveys see, e.g., Wolf (1962); Hallo and Simpson (1971); and the chapters by Edwards and Smith in the *Cambridge ancient history*, 3rd edn. (1971). Although much earlier, Wilson's book (1951) is also of importance for our present purposes, since the author was acquainted with the ethnological literature.

[2]   For the dating I have followed von Beckerath (1971). The reader not familiar with Egyptian history is hereby reminded of the uncertainty of the dates with regard to the Old Kingdom; the differences between the estimates of one scholar and another may be anything up to a hundred years or more for the early kings.

[3]   That a war between Upper and Lower Egypt may have been a historical fact may be inferred *inter alia* from the Narmer palette, which dates roughly from the birth of the Egyptian state. For its ritual meaning, which, however, does not altogether exclude an allusion to an actual historical event, see Barta (1975: 98).

[4]   The earlier hypothesis of the immigration of a 'dynastic race' is here left aside as being antiquated.

5 The oldest element of the royal title was the 'Horus name', frequently written within a rectangular frame symbolizing the palace facade, on top of which the Horus falcon was perched. This representation is found from the time of the earliest-known rulers onwards.

6 If, on the basis of the dogmatic texts, the Egyptian state is conceived of as an instance of 'Oriental Despotism', then this can only be so in the sense as circumscribed by Lewis (1965: 4), viz:
'Despotism does not mean illegitimate exercise of great power or brutality, but rather unlimited power . . . . . It is recognized, of course, that despotism is always a matter of degree, that complete arbitrariness on the part of the ruler is never institutionalized'.

7 Here, as in the following quotations, 'Majesty' is used as a rendering of *ḥm*, in accordance with the usual practice in Egyptological literature. If the suggestion put forward by Goedicke (1960) is correct, as I believe it is, this translation creates a false impression.

8 This kind of dress may be seen, for instance, on the famous diorite statue of Chephren (Cairo Cat. gén. 14), and on the representations of Mycerinus between two goddesses (Cairo J.E. 40078-'79 and 46499).

9 Goedicke (1967, 48 ff.) suggests that the *smsi Hr* was a 'Heerbann', but this seems to me less likely.

10 Even for the much later Amarna Period changes other than religious are hardly known. Egyptian scribes were not interested in political or economic affairs, regularly reducing them to mere religious motifs. What mattered was the eternal Ma'at, not incidental events. Hence all the evidence bearing upon the present subject aside from the dogmatic conceptions, is circumstantial.

11 Egyptian civilization during the dynastic Period showed a general tendency to discontinue earlier customs involving ceremonial killing. So, for instance, there are indications that burial around the royal tomb of royal retainers killed at the funeral of the ruler was still practiced during the First Dynasty (Kaplony 1963: 362 ff.; Emery 1961: 60, 62 and 72), but was abandoned at the end of it.

12 For the information in this section see particularly Helck (1954); cf. also the critical remarks in the review of this book by J. Vandier (*bibliotheca Orientalis*, Leiden 12, 1955: 171 ff.). Helck himself has given a summary of his views (1968, chapter 6) which, stimulating as it certainly is, seems to me far too positively formulated compared with the scantiness of the evidence.

13 Helck later repeated this (1968: 63) this time in connection with the rise of 'the kingship of Re'. See Goedicke's rejection of this idea in his review (*Bibliotheca Orientalis*, Leiden 27, 1970: 18).

14 The number of these was not constant, some nomes being joined together in certain periods, and others being split into two. In the Hellenistic Period, Upper Egypt consisted of twenty-two, Lower Egypt of twenty nomes.

15 Helck (1954: 18) suggests that perhaps a vestige of the old system was preserved in the function, or at least the title of 'the great ones of Upper and Lower Egypt', which he suggested was a survival of the tribal chiefs; the suggestion seems to me purely speculative, however.

REFERENCES

Altenmüller, Hartwig (1967), 'Zur Lesung und Deutung des dramatischen Ramesseumpapyrus', in: *Jaarbericht Ex Oriente Lux* VI, no. 19: 421–442.

Altenmüller, Hartwig (1970), 'Die Stellung der Königsmutter Chentkaus beim Uebergang von der 4. zur 5. Dynastie', in: *Chronique d'Egypte* XLV, no. 90: 223–235.

Atzler, M. (1972), 'Randglossen zur ägyptischen Vorgeschichte', in: *Jaarbericht Ex Oriente Lux* VII, no. 22; 228–246.

Baer, Klaus (1960), *Rank and title in the Old Kingdom. The structure of the Egyptian administration in the Fifth and sixth Dynasties*. Chicago III,: The University of Chicago Press.

Barta, Winfried (1975), 'Untersuchungen zur Göttlichkeit des regierenden Königs. Ritus und Sakralkönigtum in Altägypten nach Zeugnissen der Frühzeit und des Alten Reiches', in: *Münchner Aegyptologische Studien*, Heft 32. München-Berlin: Deutscher Kunstverlag.

Beckerath, Jürgen von (1956), 'Smsj -Hrw in der ägyptischen Vor- und Frühzeit', in: *Mitt. des Deutschen Archäologischen Instituts abt. Kairo* 14; 1–10.

— (1971), *Abriss der Geschichte des Alten Aegypten*. Darmstadt: Wissenschaftliche Buchgesellschaft.

Bell, Barbara (1970), 'The oldest records of the Nile Floods', in: *The Geographical Journal* 136: 569–573.

Edwards, I. E. S. (1971), 'The Early Dynastic Period in Egypt'. in: *The Cambridge Ancient History*, 3rd edn. Volume I, Part 2 (Chapter XI). Cambridge: The University Press.

Emery, Walter B. (1961), *Archaic Egypt*. Hammondsworth: Penguin Books. (Pelican Book No. A 462).

Frankfort, Henri (1948), *Kingship and the gods. A study of ancient Near Eastern religion as the integration of society and nature*. Chicago: The University of Chicago Press.

Fried, Morton H. (1967), *The evolution of political society. An essay in political anthropology*. New York: Random House.

Goedicke, Hans (1960), 'Die Stellung des Königs im Alten Reich', in: *Aegyptologische Abhandlungen*, Band 2. Wiesbaden: Otto Harrasowitz.

— (1965), 'Bemerkungen zum Siegelzylinder Berlin Inv. Nr. 20659', in: *Zeitschrift für ägyptische sprache und Altertumskunde* 92: 32–38.

— (1967), 'Königliche Dokumente aus dem Alten Reich', in: *Aegyptologische Abhandlungen*, Band 14. Wiesbaden: Otto Harrassowitz.

Hallo, Willem W. and Simpson, William Kelly, (1971), *The ancient Near East. A history*. New York: Harcourt Brace Jovanovich Inc.

Helck, Wolfgang (1954), 'Untersuchungen zu den Beamtentiteln des ägyptischen Alten Reiches', in: *Aegyptologische Forschungen*, Heft 18. Glückstadt: Verlag J. J. Augustin.

— (1968), 'Geschichte des Alten Aegypten', in: *Handbuch der Orientalistik* I, Abt., 1, Band 3. Abschnitt, Leiden: E. J. Brill.

— (1970), 'Zwei Einzelprobleme der thinitischen Chronologie', in: *Mitt. des Deutschen Archäologischen Instituts Abt. Kairo* 26: 83–85.

— (1974a), 'Altägyptische Aktenkunde des 3. und 2. Jahrtausends v. Chr.', in: *Münchner Aegyptologische Studien*, Heft 31. München-Berlin: Deutscher Kunstverlag.

— (1974b), 'Die altägyptische Gaue', in: *Beihefte zum Tübinger Atlas des Vordern Orients*, Reihe B, Nr. 5. Wiesbaden: Dr. Ludwig Reichert.

Hornung, Erik (1971), *Der Eine und die Vielen. Aegyptische Gottesvorstellungen*. Darmstadt: Wissenschaftliche Buchgesellschaft.

Hornung, Erik and Staehelin, Elisabeth (1974), 'Studien zum Sedfest', in: *Aegyptiaca Helvetica* 1, Aegyptologisches Seminar der Universität Basel et Centre d'études orientales de l'¡niversité de Genève.

Jacquet-Gordon, Helen K. (1961), 'Les noms des domaines funéraires sous l'Ancien Empire Egyptien', in: *Bibliothèque d'étude*, T. 34. Le Caire: Institut français d'Archéologie orientale.

Jankuhn, Dieter (1972), 'Steckt hinter dem Gott Rwtj eine Erinnerung an den rituellen Königsmort?', in: *Göttinger Miszellen* 1: 11–16.

Junker, Hermann (1955), *Gîza XII*, 'Bericht über die.... Grabungen auf dem Friedhof des Alten Reiches bei den Pyramiden von Gîza, Band XII: *Denkschriften Österr. Akad. der Wiss.*, Phil. -hist. Kl. 75, Wien: Rudolf M. Rohrer.

— (1959), 'Die gesellschaftliche Stellung der ägyptischen Künstler im Alten Reich', In: *Sitzungsb. Oestrerr. Akad. der Wissenschaften, Phil. -hist. Kl.* 233. en: Rudolf M. Rohrer.

Kaiser, Werner (1961), 'Einige Bemerkungen zur ägyptischen Frühzeit. II. Zur Frage einer über Menes hinausreichenden ägyptischen Geschichtsüberlieferung', in: *Zeitschrift für ägyptische Sprache und Altertumskunde* 86: 39–61.

Kaplony, Peter (1962), 'Gottespalast und Götterfestungen in der ägyptischen Frühzeit', in: *Zeitschrift für ägyptische Sprache und Altertumskunde* 88: 5–16.

— (1963), *Die inschriften der ägyptischen Frühzeit*, 2 *Bände*: *Aegyptologische Abhandlungen, Band 8. Wiesbaden: Otto Harrassowitz.*

— (1970), 'Das Wagnis der Darstellung ägyptischer Frühzeit', in: *Orientalistische Literaturzeitung* 65: 6–12.

Kelley, Allyn L. (1974), 'The evidence for Mesopotamian influence in predynastic Egypt', in: *Newsletter of the Society for the Study of Egyptian Antiquities* IV, no. 3; 2–11.

Lewis, Herbert S. (1965), *A Galla monarchy. Jimma Aba Jifar, Ethiopia 1830–1932.* Madison and Milwaukee: The University of Wisconsin Press.

Lorton, David (1974), 'Review of Elfriede Reiser, Der königliche Harim im alten Aegypten und seine Verwaltung', in: *Journal of the American Research Center in Egypt* 11: 98–101.

Menu, Bernadette et Harari, Ibram (1974), 'La notion de propriété privée dans l'Ancien Empire *Egyptien*', in: *Cahier de recherches de l'institut de papyrologie et d'égyptologie de Lille* 2: 125–154.

O'Connor, David (1972), 'A Regional population in Egypt to circa 600 B.C.', in: *Population growth. Anthropological implications*, ed. by Brian Spooner, pp. 78–100. Massachusetts and London: The MIT-Press.

— (1974), 'Political systems and archaeological data in Egypt: 2600–1780 B.C.', in: *World Archaeology* 6: 15–38.

Posener, Georges (1960), *De la divinité du pharaon.* Paris: Imprimerie nationale.

Schenkel, Wolfgang (1974), 'Die Einführung der künstlichen Felderbewässerung im alten Aegypten', *Göttinger Miszellen* 11: 41–46.

Smith, W. Stevenson (1971), 'The Old Kingdom in Egypt', in: *The Cambridge Ancient History.* 3rd edn. Volume I, Part 2 (Chapter XIV). Cambridge: At the University Press.

Staehelin, Elisabeth (1966), 'Untersuchungen zur ägyptischen Tracht im Alten Reich', in: *Münchner Aegyptologische Studien*, Heft 8. Berlin: Bruno Hessling.

Störk, Lothar (1973), 'Gab es in Aegypten den rituellen Königsmord?', in: *Göttinger Miszellen* 5: 31–32.

Urkunden I: *Urkunden des Alten Reiches* — Urkunden des ägyptischen Altertums. I. Abt., Band 1. Bearbeitet von Kurt Sethe. Leipzig: J. C. Hinrich'sche Buchhandlung (1933).

Vandersleyen, Claude (1971), *Les guerres d'Amosis.* Fondateur de la XVIIIe dynasti — *Monographies Reine Elisabeth* 1. Bruxelles: Fondation Egyptologique Reine Elisabeth.

Weber, Max (1972), *Wirtschaft und Gesellschaft.* Fünfte, revidierte Auflage. Tübingen: J.C.B. Mohr.

Wilson, John A. (1949), *Before philosophy. The intellectual adventure of ancient man* ed. by H. and H. A. Frankfort, J. A. Wilson and Th. Jacobson, Hammondsworth: Penguin Books (Pelican Books no. A 198).

— (1951), *the culture of ancient Egypt.* Chicago: The University of Chicago Press (first published as *The burden of Egypt*).

— (1960), 'Egypt through the New Kingdom. Civilization without cities', in: *City invincible.* Ed. by Carl H. Kraeling and Robert M. Adams, pp. 124–164. Chicago: The University of Chicago Press.

Wolf, Walther (1962), *Kulturgeschichte des Alten Aegypten.* Stuttgart: Alfred Kröner Verlag (Kröners Taschenausgabe, Band 321).

11   The Early State in France

HENRI B. TEUNIS

1. INTRODUCTION

When consulting literature of a more general nature on the history of Western Europe in the eleventh and twelfth centuries, we immediately come upon titles of books and chapters announcing that a really new development is going to be described. Halphen (1932) entitles his survey of the period 'l'essor de l'Europe'. Hollister (1969: 163) speaks of this era as an outstanding example of 'crucial epochs of transformation and transition'. Clagett (1961: 11) speaks of 'a great period of creative, even revolutionary, activity in all aspects of civilization'. Barraclough (1955: 78), finally, calls the twelfth century 'one of the great constructive ages in European history'.

When we look into the literature dealing with one specific aspect or another of this complex phenomenon, the same thing becomes evident. With regard to agriculture especially the term 'expansion' (Duby 1962: 131) sets the tone. Lopez (1971: 56) draws attention to 'the take-off of the commercial revolution'. Bosl (1972: 161) speaks of 'die Gesellschaftsstruktur der europäischen Aufbruchs-epoche'. One continually comes across 'the idea of a twelfth-century renaissance' (Holmes 1951). Furthermore, and this brings us to our present subject, one finds mention of 'a growth of government' (Southern 1967: 80). From the above survey of titles of books and chapters it is obvious that we are dealing here with a society that was changing from top to bottom.

Our present subject, then, as I have indicated, is the 'growth of government'. To make this growth understandable, it will be necessary to show in what ways the growth of the state in this period was connected with developments in other sectors of society. Indeed, one is invariably confronted with a set of 'mutually related principia media' (Mannheim 1940: 183). This interdependence makes it necessary for us to begin with an exposition of a general nature on changes in the demographic, economic, social and cultural spheres which may be discerned in the eleventh and twelfth centuries. The following will be an ideal reconstruction in the sense that the development, as outlined below, will not be found in the concrete stuff of history. But it is a necessary tool for an understanding of the growth of the more specific governmental systems which I shall describe in the other sections.

2. SOCIO-ECONOMIC DEVELOPMENTS

If one had looked around in Western Europe around the year 1000, one would have encountered an archaic type of society indeed. Nine out of ten people were peasants. Generally speaking they worked and lived in self-sufficient manors (Slicher van Bath 1963: 40); that is to say, they directly consumed what they produced. Whatever surplus they were able to grow went to their lords, the owners of the land, who exercised patriarchal powers over them and whose main business it was to fight, not to work. After their death they would go to heaven, or so they firmly believed, and generously endowed monasteries and bishops took care of that side of their lives.

Around the year 1200, in contrast, we see most of the great proprietors collecting rents on their lands — implying that there must have been money in circulation. There were towns, too; large areas had become full-blown states; universities were taking shape; and finally, there was a philosophy, theology, architecture and literature more sophisticated than could ever have been foreseen in the year 1000.

All this requires explanation. It may be stated with some caution that in the literature of the past decades some kind of consensus seems to have come about on the question of how such an explanation should be constructed. This is, of course, a gratifying state of affairs, since the same is not always true for all problems. Although a number of authors who have written on this subject might be mentioned, it should suffice here to draw attention to George Duby, who is an eminent authority in this field. In his argumentation priority is given to demographic and economic factors, and his reasoning is as follows.

Around the year 1000 (depending on the region) a certain degree of overpopulation became noticeable. Now, overpopulation is, as Slicher van Bath (1963: 12) points out, a relative concept. It is known for a fact, however, that the population had been growing for some time. In the year 700 the population of Western Europe stood at 27 million; in the year 1000 at 42 million (after a decline in the tenth century) (Slicher van Bath 1963: 78). For a period in which, for technical reasons, the possibilities of extending the area of agricultural exploitation were limited, this is a not inconsiderable increase. Considering the low level of development of agricultural techniques — with a seed/yield ratio of 1:3 or 1:4 — this was even a dangerous development. In this kind of situation, it is clear, the balance between the available land area and the amount of food consumed could very easily be upset. This may then lead to undernourishment or even starvation. Overpopulation, or *poussée demographique*, around and after the year 1000 at that time involved that the ratio between population and agricultural area was far from the optimum.

This particular problem — undernourishment and starvation aside — may be solved in three different ways: the agricultural area may be expanded, productivity may be raised, or a specialization of crops to meet the needs of international trade may be introduced. By these means an increase in the income of the total population may be achieved. Around the year 1000, however, Western Europe lacked economically significant intercontinental and international trade and constituted in this sense an insular community. The last solution was therefore not feasible.

The second possibility had been tried out to a certain extent (I shall return to this later), but the keynote was, unquestionably, expansion. For this the following was the most important reason, from which the interdependence of the various developments referred to in the first section of this paper becomes, moreover, evident. The landed proprietors were a privileged group, which did not have to work and could afford to have itself supported. They in fact prided themselves on this. The peasants, most of whom were unfree, lived constantly close to a subsistence level. The lords had their own storehouses — the fuller, the better — and their prestige increased in proportion to their ability to be generous: 'Idéal de consommation' (Duby 1973a: 61). The primary objective of the Germanic chieftains who had migrated to the Roman Empire had already been to take advantage of the great wealth existing there. Charlemagne's Frankish followers had been able to profit from his conquests and build up their own groups of retainers: 'Ravir, offrir' (Duby 1973a: 60).

When in the ninth century the Carolingian empire, due to its excessive dependence upon the personality of its ruler, fell apart, the officials had seized the opportunity to claim as much land as possible for themselves. When the Carolingian royal domains had almost all become alienated through gifts, which was already the case under Charles the Fat (876–888), the dozens of counts appointed by Charlemagne had gone at each other's throats. The cleverest and most powerful among them had managed, by blackmail, calculated marriage tactics and sheer force, to create their own lordships, known as the territorial principalities (Dhondt 1948). But they in turn fell victim to the same mechanism that had destroyed Charlemagne's empire: their officials, too, tended to become independent lords. These began to exercise, apart from their rights as owners of the land, the right called *bannum* i.e., to command and punish. They took over, more or less, what used once to be public authorities, and collected the revenues attached to these. This way they became at the same time, 'seigneur domanial' and 'seigneur banal' or in other words, territorial lords. Their control over the peasant population, together with the overpopulation to which we already alluded, was in the final analysis, responsible for an enormous expansion in agriculture in the eleventh and twelfth centuries. The lords exerted strong pressure on the productive forces. They furthermore increased in number, and were inclined to seize every opportunity to feed and clothe themselves and their families and followers better — if possible better than others could afford.

Whenever a second son was able to provide the necessary implements to cut down trees, together with provisions for the first year, and to arrange the division as well as, if necessary, the drainage of a particular tract of land, he might attract colonists. The extension of an existing manor in this way and/or the founding of totally new villages would raise the income of the aristocratic family concerned and created new opportunities for earning a living for the peasant population. And better opportunities, too, for the lords of the older manors began to treat their tenants in a less arbitrary way for fear of losing them. Whoever moved to new land there was bound to find more favorable conditions, for otherwise he would not have gone there to begin with, but would have looked for a better place. In most cases the colonists received the status of freemen though there were, of course, payments to be made. Arbitrary treatment here, too, was limited by the circumscription of the lord's rights — to which he was now more strictly bound than before. In the second half of the eleventh century land began to be cleared on a large scale, and this made possible a remarkable population explosion in the twelfth century.

In this way the income of the landed proprietors, and especially of the territorial lords who exercised the *bannum*, increased. Their bent for ostentation created a market for quality wines, fine clothes (a special cloth manufacturing process had been evolved in Flanders, which made this area wealthy at an early date), and spices (from Italy). Initially, the lords sent their servants for these, with precious objects to give in exchange. In this way they paved the way for the emergence of a class of middlemen, *mercatores*, who created a network of commercial centers throughout Europe. Nestling against castles and fortified abbeys, where merchants set up permanent shops or depots, towns sprang up.

The peasant too, could participate in this trade system. He could buy some clothes, iron for his plow, and salted food for the winter. He now had an incentive to produce more in order to be able to sell the surplus for cash, which was lacking in the period of direct agricultural consumption; and this, no doubt, helped to raise productivity.

Better techniques were increasingly adopted in turn, which again raised agricultural efficiency and yields. These included the use of horses, watermills and iron implements, especially the plow, and the rotation of crops. For this network of trading centers to be able to survive and expand, money was needed. The mints had plenty of work in the twelfth century. As the lords were able to buy more and more — services, weapons, horses, castles — they came to prefer to draw their income in cash rather than kind, and tended to become rentiers. Gradually they came to constitute a category with an ethos of its own, which accentuated the distinction between itself and the peasant group; this latter group had to abstain from the noble way of life, including politics.

Thus consumption by the lords increased, while the same is true of the towns (which were dependent on supplies of food from without) and the peasants. The population grew, prices kept rising, there was plenty of work for the artisans and trade was brisk: in short, there was a boom. This way the gears interlocked and it was possible for Europe to attain, economically, to a higher level. This was a process of development from a natural economy to an exchange economy, in which the role of money grew steadily more important.

3. THE POLITICAL SITUATION

These facts should be kept clearly in mind if one wishes to arrive at an understanding of the development of the state in Western Europe during this period. In point of fact, the state — one may speak of a state where the population of a particular territory shows obedience to a central government (Guénée: 1967: 17) — never disappeared in Western Europe in the Middle Ages. Undoubtedly, the Carolingian Empire was a state in the above-defined sense. It possessed an authority governing the entire network of its territories.

Charlemagne required all his officials to swear, besides the oath of allegiance he exacted from everyone, an oath of vassalage to him personally. They thereupon received a *beneficium*, mostly in the form of a tract of land to be held for life, and promised to support him whenever necessary with moral and material, i.e., military, aid — *consilium et auxilium*. This was clearly a relationship of subordination. Nonetheless, the vassals were and remained free persons, who had the definite right to cancel the contract if their free status was not respected. In this way Charlemagne augmented his officials' civil obligations with a personal bond (Ganshof 1965–6: 389). When, in the ninth century, the empire gradually crumbled as a consequence of too great a dependence on one person, family quarrels and Viking, Magyar and Saracen raids, there eventually remained only the personal, vassal relation, whereby the officials had factual possession (not ownership) of their source of livelihood. Some of them, namely the strongest and most capable, seized the lands belonging to the others — they could do so unpunished — and so the territorial principalities, such as, for instance, Burgundy, Flanders, Anjou, Aquitaine and Normandy, came into being (tenth century). The counts and dukes thus became sovereign lords in their own territories. No one, except the counts and dukes, had any direct connection with the king. As long as this pattern lasted, the state existed in the form of territorial principalities. Unless, that is, the counts and dukes were strictly subordinated, politically or ideologically, to the king (e.g., the Capetians in France, the successors of the Carolingians after 987). That such a bond existed in the political sense no one has ever contended. The existence and nature of the ideological bond, on the other hand, has been a subject of hot debate for a long time. Lot (1904: 254) asserted that the great counts and dukes retained a 'sentiment de leur dépendance légale'. Flach was willing to admit (1893: 524) that they continued to foster an 'affection réelle' for the successors of Charlemagne, but that concretely they were the equals of the king, who owned a (be it royal) principality just as they did. Before World War II, when the natural, 'pre-ordained' unity of France began to be called in question, there was much heated discussion on this issue among French historians, with most of the votes going to Lot's view. Today we are in a position to say that the decisive words were spoken by Lemarignier (1955): in the tenth century the *primores regni* still appeared as vassals in the royal charters, but not as regularly as might be expected from true vassals. They paid homage when this was politically opportune for them, e.g., when a pact was made with the king, or a quarrel with him settled. The feudal relationship became simply a form in which political ties were expressed, a set of terms the men in power used towards each other. Public authority having disappeared, indeed, nothing else remained. After the dukes and counts south of the Loire had severed their political tie with the king, their signatures no longer appeared in the charters, however much this may have been desired by the last Carolingians. After the accession to the throne of Hugo Capet (987), they disappeared totally from the king's field of vision.

Feudalism, by that time, had become a socio-political system in which all men in power, as far as the contemporary means (or lack of means) of communication permitted, participated; that is to say, it embraced all aristocrats who, in virtue of the possession of land, were able to dedicate themselves to the art of war and to join in the political game (Pacaut 1969: 146). The king, the lord of France (i.e., the area between Paris and Orléans and the region immediately north of Paris), was involved in continually changing alliances with the Count of Flanders, the Duke of Normandy, the Count of Anjou, the Count of Blois, the Count of Vermandois, and others. France, by then, was no longer a state. Nominally, the king was still suzerain (feudal overlord), and the counts and dukes allowed this situation, whereby they themselves were supreme feudal lords in their own territories and were able, in fact, to act as independent princes (viceroys, Werner 1968: 183), to continue.

In this way Anjou, under Fulco Nerra (987–1040) and Geoffrey Martel (1040–1060), was a state. Fulco Nerra united into a single entity all the lands his predecessors had accumulated in the course of four generations (Halphen 1906: 13–53). In these territories he had castles built, in which he appointed castle wardens, removable at will. Allied most of the time to the lord of the duchy of France, like a true vassal, he nevertheless harbored the intention to annex parts of the territory of the Count of Blois, which was situated in between them. In order to acquire Vendôme he married a daughter of the count of this region. He was a vassal of the duke of Aquitaine as well, and this secured him the castle of Loudun and other important strongholds. His successor, Geoffrey Martel, even allied himself to the emperor of the German Empire in order to be able to put pressure on the lord of the duchy of France, and temporarily succeeded in this.

The counts were in the process of gaining dominance. They set out to do so by trying to accumulate, by every possible means, as many possessions as they could. An important role was played in this by the church. In the first half of the eleventh century the count's gifts to the abbey of Saint-Aubin were extraordinarily large. This is quite understandable. Most probably the Counts of Anjou were first able to set themselves up as counts of the whole of Anjou by virtue of their claims as patrons of the abbey after the incursions of the Normans. They even acted as its lay abotts (929) (Werner 1958). Subsequently this central abbey remained firmly in the control of the counts, and provided a vital point of support for them. The same was true for the bishopric of Angers, the bishops of which were appointed by the count. Again, the counts' chief concern was to accumulate as much land as possible. With this aim in mind they declared themselves vassals of whoever promised them some right or some tract of land. Generally speaking, when a person became someone else's vassal, this meant that he received a piece of land with rights of possession to it. The nature and number of the services he had to perform in return was a matter of politics. In this way the Count of Anjou was a vassal of the King of France. Not because he exercised a particular office or certain rights which really belonged to the king, but because he and his heirs held a wide variety of concrete rights and possessions of his (Guillot 1972: 16). In his particular territory — comprising many different kinds of holding — he alone was supreme lord.

But while Fulco and Geoffrey were busy extending their power by means of this complex network of relations, certain local rulers were at the same time establishing themselves in the smaller territorial units which had, in turn, been entrusted to them.

Whenever a war of succession broke out, they had an opportunity of asserting their independence and extending their power. This is what happened in 1060, in fact. Geoffrey Martel had two sons, Geoffrey le Barbu and Fulco le Réchin, who disputed each others' right to rule. The local lords were able, under these circumstances, to play them off against one another. For the 'foreign powers' this was the opportunity par excellence to encroach upon the count's territory, which is exactly what did happen. And to make matters worse, the church, under the influence of a reform movement aimed at changing the relations between the church and the secular lords, took advantage of the situation. As a consequence Anjou, under Fulco le Réchin (1067– 1109), fell prey to anarchy, with the barons indulging in constant warfare against each other as well as against the count (Halphen 1906: 152–175). One can speak of a 'pulverisation' process here (Pacaut 1969: 143).

The count no longer had anything to offer, and was deprived of the means to exert his authority in cases of conflict. It is known of several local lords that they explicitly refused to acknowledge the count as their lord, and successfully so. Others did recognize him as such, but only by way of formality. How many lords each category numbered is not known (Guillot 1972: 346). The situation was, in fact, the same everywhere, there being a widespread 'dissociation territoriale' of the power of government. The castle warden and not the count was now considered the authorized holder of the right to command and punish (*bannum*). Fédou (1971: 59) speaks of 'Etats miniatures'.

In Anjou there were forty four such states. The area dominated by each was at most 25 km², which was most probably the area which one lord could then govern effectively. The reason for this was simple: the party of armed men setting out in the morning had to be able to return in order to find shelter for the night in the evening. Only in this way was a castle warden able to maintain effective control over the people coming under his *bannum* and his manorial rights (Boussard 1956: 46).

This is not to say that all these lords were equal in power and prestige. They were, however, all of them virtually independent. The smallest among them were the possessors of but a single castle. The barons, one level above them, possessed several castles, and moved about continually. The prince himself in turn owned more castles than a baron. The Count of Anjou possessed at least ten castles, which was more than anyone else in Anjou could claim. Everyone could be everyone's vassal. Except for Normandy, the situation was similar in most other parts of France (Boussard 1957: 45).

The count now constantly moved about visiting his castles with a personal retinue. He made sure, by solemnly presiding over his feudal courts everywhere, not to let people forget that there was a feudal overlord in the country. With regard to the 'ducatus Franciae' a similar development can be seen. Lemarignier (1965) has made a very thorough and accurate study of the signatories to the various royal charters. Up to 1025/8 the king, so it appeared, tried to uphold the fiction that he ruled with the assistance of the council of vassals, comprising bishops, abbots and counts, who regularly held the great *honores*. But in actual fact most of these attended only on exceptional occasions; the only ones who came at all, in fact, being mostly bishops. After 1025/8 the signatories were resident in the areas to which the charters applied. They signed not as faithful vassals but as the men in control of specific regions. They were the castle wardens or viscounts, who dominated these regions and possessed the land in them. This is what counted. It was the aristocracy of Ile-de-France which was actually in control. And, as in Anjou, after 1077 the king's personal servants formed the administrative core with whose assistance he pursued his goals and who signed his charters.[1] It was a government 'par conseil des grands officiers' (Lemarignier 1965: 191). Royal justice was administered mainly upon complaints being lodged by monks, while the king was utterly unable to make his decisions respected, moreover, even in Ile-de-France.

Nonetheless, these kings thought of themselves as annointed monarchs, and regarded themselves as the rightful heirs of the Carolingians. The replacement of the Carolingians had not been attended with any traces of revolution. No break had occurred, the crown having been conferred in 987 upon the person who by family connections and as *de facto* possessor of France (i.e., the principality) had seemed the most eligible candidate for the office of kingship by the barons and bishops.

Subsequently, the Capetians were fortunate enough to have a male heir all the time; he was designated, consecrated and crowned as king during the lifetime of his father (Dhondt 1939). This consecration consisted in, among other things, anointment with oil, which was believed to have been brought down from heaven by a dove at the baptism of Clovis (Schramm 1960: 145). This oil gave the king certain powers of healing (Bloch 1961), and brought him into the religious sphere. Almost equal to a priest, he had been entrusted with a special task by God, as the clergy already claimed with regard to kingship in late Carolingian times (Reviron 1930: 76–112). He had to be personally pious, and above all, just to his people. He was expected to provide peace, to honor the church, and to maintain the order instituted on earth by God, so that everyone might live in accordance with His will. If he did so God would bless him, the church would help him and all things would go well for him on earth. If he did not, God would punish him. In this way the church provided the king with a 'halo sacré' which tried to compensate for any real weakness (Lemarignier 1956: 13). It was effective only insofar as no count or duke ever claimed for himself a sacral character of this kind (acquired through consecration). There certainly was a need for the peace and order the king was supposed to bring about in the eleventh century. This constituted, in fact, the greatest and most urgent problem of the time (Pacaut 1969: 149). It was a turbulent world of mutually contending territorial lords. The wealth and power of each was manifest from lucrative clusters of rights. Their relationships vis-à-vis each other were expressed in feudal terms, in which the political theology of divine kingship played no part.

Whenever a solution to the problem of order had to be found, it had to be sought within the framework of feudal relationships. That this was not impossible is demonstrated by the contemporary situation in the duchy of Normandy. In a period when in most areas in France order was to be found only in the vicinity of castles, Normandy presented quite a different picture.

Here, too, we have a county dotted with castles. Here, too, this was essential for an effective exercise of government. And here, likewise, feudal relations were found; there being a supreme lord, barons and castle wardens. But the essential difference is that here we are dealing not with a type of feudalism that had developed from the bottom, but with a feudal system that had been imposed from above by the duke, and in which the latter, although with great difficulty, remained dominant (Boussard 1956: 235). How was this possible?

Douglas (1946) has clearly demonstrated that the counts found in Normandy around 1050, had all, from around 1000, owed their position to the duke. When after 1066 the duke was also king of England, understandably, the barons of Normandy were in no position to oppose his fiscal, military and jurisdictional rights in any fundamental way (Douglas 1969: 259–264). How he managed to give his position as feudal overlord real significance before 1066 is more difficult to explain, on account of the paucity of information on the situation in the tenth century.

In any case, he must have been able to put a halt to the disintegrative process taking place in other areas in sufficient time. One reason for this must be that the ducal position had not evolved from a Carolingian office. Rollo the Norman had been called in in 911, and so there had been no need for him to push his way to the top. He was immediately able to install various of his relatives in the *pagus*, the administrative unit he found there. None of the old Carolingian counts, on the other hand, were able to maintain their position in their respective territories (Yver 1969: 324). But even so, most probably their own men would have taken charge of the machinery of government in their territories in time if the duke had not possessed a source of power which the dukes and counts of the rest of France lacked: money.

Normandy had for a long time formed part of a trading community around the North Sea, and hence money had been circulating there since the end of the tenth century (Yver 1969: 341). There is proof that already at that time the viscounts were sending money to the duke's *Camera*. And, it should be noted at the outset, tolls and market dues were a much more profitable source of income for the ruler than any of his seigneurial rights.

Because of his wealth, he could afford to go on being generous, and thus install a group of great barons, composed of his relatives, as well as one of viscounts who could be removed from office, were subject to his juridiction, and could be called upon to answer for their management of affairs, in the border areas of Normandy. They formed a 'hand-picked group' (Brown 1969: 38), which included also the clergy. The duke's relatives held the offices of bishop and archbishop. There was a true religious revival, in which the duke himself and the entire aristocracy participated during the first half of the eleventh century. They founded abbeys, which they endowed richly. Fécamp was the ducal abbey par excellence. These abbeys were their 'depots of credit' (Douglas 1969: 114) on earth and in heaven.

The religious life of Normandy furnished the outstanding model of order for most of Europe. William of Normandy was 'the apex of a closely integrated social structure' in which laymen and clerics worked together. 'He was thereby enabled to claim a certain religious sanction for his administrative acts' (Douglas 1969: 154).

By about 1050 William of Normandy had found the solution for the problem of order within the framework of feudal relationships. It is highly probable that from 1050 onward (Haskins 1960: 8) every holder of a *feodum* was obliged to provide a number of knights. The duke had been able to formulate and impose this feudal duty as a result of his unequalled financial resources.

4.   GROWTH TO STATEHOOD

We lost sight of the Count of Anjou at the moment when there was nothing else left for him to do but to administer his territories and to assert himself as overlord where possible. Now, Fulco le Réchin had inherited a tiny court organization, consisting of a seneschal, a chamberlain and a cellarer, from Geoffrey Martel. They were, above all, trusted followers, often of unfree status. This staff he retained (Guillot 1972: 421). He also retained a number of officials (prévôts, vicarii) who exercised specific rights, in his name, in his scattered possessions. Furthermore, after 1080 he enlarged his retinue with trusted warriors.

The count's income must have been at least big enough for him to be able to support such a staff. It is even known for a fact that his income steadily rose during the last quarter of the eleventh century and the whole of the twelfth century. Here I must remind the reader of the exposition in Section 2 of this paper. The economic take-off which was to be observed in the first half of the eleventh century reached Anjou in the second half of that century: clearings were widespread, and there is evidence of a market economy (Boussard 1950). Here the economic development bore directly on the political one.

We see especially Fulco V and Geoffrey Plantagenet (1109–1151) restoring the authority of the counts all over the county (Chartrou 1928). They marched from one end to the other, though not in order to systematically enforce their judicial decisions — for this they were not able to do. Their jurisdiction, in fact, more or less took the form of arbitration. Moreover, their judgement was very often requested. The extent to which the count was able to impose his verdict depended largely on the situation. At any rate, he tried very hard to do so. He would fight against castle wardens and after their surrender give them their possessions back on condition that they pay him true homage, that is to say, that they acknowledge and accept the fact that the holding of a *feodum* implied the obligation to assist the lord under certain circumstances. Thus the bond of fealty came to assume real meaning again. Around 1150 there was no longer any lord in Anjou who denied the practical implications of his feudal submission to the count (Boussard 1957: 41). Without any doubt the latter could never have brought about this state of affairs if he had not had the proceeds from the unprecedented general economic growth at his disposal. These proceeds, we may remember, benefited him more than the lesser lords. The count owned more uncleared land and possessed more rights to tolls and market dues, and so became relatively richer than the barons and lesser lords. And the peace and order he slowly established in turn benefited the merchants. The development of the one is inconceivable without that of the other (Fourquin 1971: 135).

When the Plantagenets became Dukes of Normandy as well, they were able to rally the mutually warring lords and make them subject to their jurisdiction. Private warfare disappeared to a large extent; the count administering justice throughout the whole county. This was the work of Henry Plantagenet († 1189) (Boussard 1938). He established a personal but effective system of administration by becoming, as highest feudal lord, judge over all his vassals. He was the actual suzerain. A similar development may be observed in the royal principality of France. Lemarignier (1965: 141) has demonstrated how Philip I (1064–1109), too, created a permanent staff. With this he marched all over his possessions, where 'prévôts' enforced his rights. These officials he selected from the ranks of the castle wardens of Ile-de-France. They were able to build up a career in his service, whereas the other castle wardens were likely to become pauperized. Much of this development was made possible by the economic prosperity of the region (Duby 1968). Henry's successor Louis VI continued the attempts to subdue the castle wardens as effectively as possible.

Under the latter, the cooperation between the king and church first began. This eventually became of the utmost significance to the Capetians. It can be demonstrated that Louis VI's primary aim was the pacification of his principality. We are informed that he strove to make safe the roads between Paris and Orléans, and Paris and Rheims (Luchaire 1890: LXXVI; Bloch 1949: 112). Here it is clear from the outset how he took advantage of his pact with the church. Whenever he took action against anyone he would do so mostly in response to a complaint by a bishop or abbot against one of the lords. They would be first excommunicated, whereupon the king could then take up arms against them as protector of the clergy and with the aid of that same clergy. With their assistance he was frequently able to defeat such castle wardens and to destroy their castles if necessary. He would return their possessions to them only if they paid him true homage, i.e., acknowledged that they in fact owed him services, that this was his natural right.

The procedure by which the king managed greatly to enhance his power and authority in the first half of the twelfth century, namely, by combining feudal overlordship with religious prestige, becomes already manifest from these early actions. This is definitely true as regards the local level. When he combated the lord of le Puiset or of Marle, he did so as a faithful son of the Church and with the material (military) support of the churches.

But there was more to this relationship. Both Philip I and Louis VI had to deal with a church whose organization encompassed the whole of Europe, and whose head, the pope, saw himself as the sole authority, who held his position directly from God. He was the head of the most powerful organization known in Europe and pretended to be the moral leader of all, i.e., he felt entitled to pronounce a final judgment where anyone's behaviour was called into question. Kings and princes, as leaders of their people, were held responsible for the well-being of their subjects, and they were eagerly admonished in this by the pope. The power if necessary to condemn kings and relieve them of their office was initially disputed, understandably so, by the most powerful rulers of Western Europe, the kings of the German empire. At the time of Philip I and Louis VI the Pope was engaged in a bitter struggle with them, as was later to be the case also, though on different issues, under Louis VII (1137–1179). And more than once the pope was put to flight, viz. in 1107, 1119–1120, 1130 and 1139. Each time he sought refuge with the French kings. They received him cordially. As a result they could pose, for the first time, as leading actors on the European stage (Pacaut 1953: 22–24).

At the same time, the king earnt himself the support of the pope in this way, which meant that in the case of conflict all the bishops were his partisans. He even managed to have his own candidates — members of his own or other loyal families or clerics of his churches — appointed in twenty percent of the bishoprics. Most of these bishoprics were situated outside his principality. The situation was likewise with respect to about fifty abbeys. They could all invoke his help, which repeatedly provided Louis VII with a pretext to take action outside of France. He provided many churches in the south with documents aimed at protecting the bishops' rights. In this way he made his reappearance there as protector of the churches. He also went several times to Burgundy and Auvergne with an army to help certain oppressed bishops and abbots there, and concluded treaties with them which guaranteed him a part of their income (treaties of parage), gaining a substantial foothold there in so doing. This was not all, however. Since the pope was the representative of God, the sacral character of the king became automatically less accentuated. The fact that he turned this 'attack' into an advantage testifies to a considerable creative adaptability on his part.

The creator of the new ideology of kingship was Suger, abbot of St. Denis. If the pope had to watch over the well-being of all men, the king nevertheless also had a divine duty, viz. to maintain justice, so Suger stated. The king was the highest feudal lord, he alone owed homage to no one (Halphen 1950). He was thus obliged to see to it that all his vassals pay him due homage. The fact that he was the highest lord in this way appeared in a religious light. It was his duty to function in a hierarchy which put the pope above the king and the king above all others. The pope pronounced Louis VII the most trusted son of the Church, of which he gave evidence by protecting the Church everywhere, especially the abbey of St. Denis, the patron of the Capetians, whose protection they enjoyed always. This provided feudal kingship with a religious justification which none of the other princes could claim.

He, as paragon of piety, had to show his people that, with him, justice counted above all else. He was a *rex justus*. He had to exact fidelity. He was the head of a feudal corps of which the princes, who, far from being autonomous, had to recognize him as king and feudal overlord, were the members (Glaser 1960). 'Les diplomes royaux du XIe siècle ne revèlent ... aucune idée de hiérarchie' (Lemarignier 1965: 171). That Suger combined the developments which marked feudal society at that time (submission of the castle wardens) with the Carolingian tradition and the Gregorian church concept into a political doctrine whereby the king was able to realize his full potential, bears witness to the fact that feudal relations were becoming systematized into a whole in which a definite order could eventually be established.

This is not to say that this concept of kingship was accepted everywhere. At most, one can say that people everywhere were trying to conceive of larger and better-ordered units. Memories of the Roman Empire as well as of the Carolingian Empire in the person of Charlemagne were still very much alive.

But as yet, this ideological weapon, which enabled the king to pose as something more than a territorial prince, in fact, was only an ideal. In the west Henry II controlled a large expanse of territory, comprising Normandy, Anjou and Touraine, to which in 1152 he joined, through marriage, Aquitaine. The Counts of Toulouse and Barcelona were contending for the hegemony in the south. Who could have foretold at that moment that the house of Capet, blocked as it was by Flanders, Normandy, Anjou, Blois, Troyes, Chartres and Meaux, would once be the leader of the whole of France, in fact? 'Rien ne prédisposait à l'unification autour de rois de Paris' (Pacaut 1969: 201). Around 1150 a period of 'international' political rivalry seemed likely to begin, with a number of strong territorial princes, aiming at as much as possible personal power, at each other's throats.

All these political units were feudal states, however.

5. UNIFICATION

This was certainly true for Henry II and his territories. Henry II was a ruthless, ambitious man. He saw his way clear to becoming a super-prince, for since the principalities had all become more or less consolidated, only a few princes of the highest rank remained. When the heiress of Aquitaine again became marriageable, he came forward as the most promising candidate. He seized Normandy from his brother. But even then his ambition was not satisfied. In his early years he continually aimed at acquiring ever more territories, preferably the whole of France.

His financial resources made it possible for him to undertake large-scale military and diplomatic ventures. The disproportionate growth of income of the greater lords vis-à-vis the lesser ones was a phenomenon observable, as has been noted above, from the time of the emergence of a market economy. Especially so when this market economy stimulated the rise of more and more towns. This became apparent in the second half of the twelfth century. The income a lord was able to derive from towns was much larger than that from land. This was, politically, the main role of the towns, which had, as yet, no political objectives of their own. Whoever controlled the towns was the most powerful (Boussard 1956: 375); and Henry II held most of them.

As a result he was able to employ officials everywhere. He treated them as his personal servants in these years; they were not his plenipotentiaries, but they acted in accordance with his specific instructions in each individual case. In critical situations, such as in cases of a disputed succession, conflicts between barons, or refusals of help, he himself would come to their aid with his army in order to enforce his feudal rights. He drove home the notion everywhere that the holding of a fief involved the duty to fulfil certain obligations (which could be neglected only on penalty of forfeiture) and to recognize him as supreme judge.

Henry II himself, as did his sons in turn, regularly paid homage to their feudal lord, the king of France.

His expansionist policy also posed a threat, direct or indirect, to the king himself (Vexin, Auvergne and Toulouse). Louis VII thus felt obliged to form an alliance against his rival (Pacaut 1964: 179) in the usual way, viz. by strengthening and multiplying family ties with Champagne and Flanders. In Burgundy and Auvergne the king could pose as protector of important churches. The result was that by 1173 France had become divided into two parts. Hereby the organization into states as it had existed up to then was destroyed (Werner 1968: 209).

It is highly probable that Henry accepted the stalemate. As a consequence of his rigorous rule he had to cope with a series of revolts in his own territories. Here he experienced the impossibility of being personally present everywhere at critical moments. From this time on he appointed officials as his plenipotentiaries, whom he required to govern in his name. This was certainly necessary in a realm as large and complex as his. Clearly an impersonal, supra-territorial form of government was in the process of being created. The young king of France, Philip II (1180–1223), however, clearly realized that he had to make his feudal suzerainty respected. He was conscious of the fact (Teunis 1973: 76) that he would not be able to fulfil his task as king as long as a large part of his realm continued to be held by what might be said to be the most powerful vassal of the old school, or a de facto autonomous super-prince.

The French king's material resources increased, moreover. According to Duby (1962: 277) a 'mutation économique', a breakthrough in the market economy took place which provided the king with means to maintain a paid army and to employ paid knights, whose income had increased proportionally less and on whom the pressure to spend was heavy. In this way the conflict became not only very fierce in an ideological sense, but also exceptionally violent in terms of concrete action. The credit for first pointing out the true nature of the 'revolution' under Philip August goes to Petit-Dutaillis (1933). For the first time in history the king was able to uphold his rights not only against his lesser vassals, a common phenomenon since the late eleventh century, but also against his most powerful one. Had not John Lackland explicitly recognized him as his suzerain at the peace of Le Goulet in 1200? Subsequently, in 1202, when the lord of Lusignan (Aquitaine) submitted a conflict with John Lackland to Philip for arbitration, the king undertook to exercise his feudal judicial powers. At first he attempted to mediate a settlement, but when John proceeded to disregard his verdict, Philip went further: he declared all John's territories thereby confiscated. Of course this meant war, the ups and downs of which are not relevant here. What is important is that the decisive blow that struck John was the large-scale desertion of his vassals. In feudal terms this was quite justified. For he had for a long time been an unworthy feudal lord who had neglected their rights, and to such a lord no one owed loyalty any longer.

Philip now became Duke of Normandy, Count of Anjou, etc., and drew revenues from all of these territories. 'Mit einem Schlage wurden durch die Durchsetzung solcher Ansprüche der Krone aus Fürsten... blosse Barone' (Werner 1968: 222). The battle of Bouvines (1214) made his superiority manifest to the whole of Europe. Here Philip defeated the king of England, the emperor of the German Empire, and some of his own vassals who had allied themselves with his adversaries. Contemporaries regarded it as a judgment of God. The French king's invincibility was proven (Duby 1973b). Serious mistakes as a ruler from now on were held beyond him, and he was seen as the prince who would bring about the peace that once Charlemagne had achieved and which now had been hoped for so long and all.

The county of Toulouse, too, was brought into the family by the Capetians. Now they controlled a cluster of territories which had for a long time all had their own *consuetudines* (lord's rights). How to administer them all? The solution which Philip applied (and which had been already tried (by Henry II) was to send forth from Paris his plenipotentiaries (seneschals, bailiffs) to enforce his rights all over the territory[2]). These rights, like those of the respective regions, towns and abbeys, were codified in the thirteenth century. Lemarignier (1970: 228), on the basis of institutional considerations, uses the term 'royauté corporative'. Strayer (1970: 52) remarks that the result was a many-layered administration. The local leaders distrusted the strange officials who acted aggressively. Regional forces were difficult to mobilize. A very complex administrative system was necessary, which had to take into account numerous local and regional usages and institutions. On the other hand, this regional diversity gave the king an opportunity to monopolize the top leadership. So France would never unite in revolt against him as a whole. This complex system required competent administrators. The king's council, court of justice (Parliament of Paris) and audit office were manned by professionals (legists). These were produced by the (new) universities.

The king now represented the country as a totality. He had to see to its defense and to ensure peace for everyone in it. Not only his vassals, but everyone was subject to his jurisdiction in the last resort. He was now sovereign, as the lawyers put it. He stood above all. This was experienced immediately after the battle of Bouvines, but was formulated in a more sophisticated way later in the thirteenth century (Teunis 1973: 137). He came to be seen as the intermediary between God and the realm. The king, now also governor of many diverse units, was in a sense accorded the position which had hitherto always been claimed by the popes. He was the head of the body politic (Kantorowicz 1957: 207). He was God's viceregent and in this capacity had to guarantee the peace — he was *Rex pacificus*. In the years 1250–1260 the ideal of peace seemed indeed to have been achieved. With this, nevertheless, an era came to a close.

FOOTNOTES

[1] Together with the queen and the sons and daughters of the king, these servants formed what might be called a court. The most important of these functionaries were: the *sénéschal* who was the head of the royal household; the *connétable*, who originally was in charge of the king's horses and whose title in later times became an important military title; and the *bouteiller* who was in charge of the production and sale of wine. This latter function eventually developed into that of a kind of royal treasurer. With the exception of the *chapellain*, these functionaries were laymen, recruited from among loyal noble families. They were remunerated in kind. During the reign of Philip II this was changed to payment in cash. A small staff of secretaries, headed by a *chancellor*, was in charge of charters and documents.

[2] The most important of these plenipotentiaries were the *bailiffs*. They were envoys of the king and had considerable controlling and judicial powers. Control over taxation was also a part of their duties. As judges they formed a court of appeal against decisions by lower functionaries. Many of the *bailiffs* were of common origins.

As commoners, and as salaried functionaries, they were wholly dependent on the king, who could appoint as well as dismiss them.

Lower in rank were the *prévôts*. Like the *bailiffs*, they were general functionaries, with responsibilities for taxation and jurisdiction and certain military duties. To counter hereditary tendencies, this function used to be sold to the highest bidder. To a number of minor posts were appointed *vicarii*, who, on a lower level, had the same duties as the *prévôts*.

This system of appointed functionaries enabled the king to strengthen his position considerably.

REFERENCES

Barraclough, G. (1955), *History in a changing world*. Oxford: Blackwell.

Bloch, Marc (1949), *La société féodale* I. Paris: Albin Michel.

— (1961), *Les rois thaumaturges*. Paris: Colin.

Bosl, K. (1972), *Die Grundlagen der modernen Gesellschaft im Mittelalter* I. Stuttgart: Anton Hiersemann.

Boussard, J. (1938), *Le comté d'Anjou sous Henri Plantagenêt et ses fils (1151–1204)*. Paris: Champion.

— (1950), 'La vie en Anjou aux XIe et XIIe siècles', in: *Le Moyen Age* 56: 29–68.

— (1956), *Le gouvernement d'Henri II Plantagenêt*. Paris: Paillart.

— (1957), 'Les institutions de l'empire Plantagenêt', in: *Histoire des institutions francaises au moyen âge* I, ed. by F. Lot and R. Fawtier, pp. 35–69. Paris: Presses universitaires de France.

Brown, R. A. (1969), *The Normans and the Norman Conquest*. London: Constable.

Chartrou, J. (1928), *L'Anjou de 1109–1151. Paris: Presses universitaires de France.*

Clagett, M. (1961), 'The twelfth century', in: *Twelfth-century Europe and the foundations of modern society*, ed. by M. Clagett, G. Post and R. Reynolds, pp. 1–13. Madison: University of Wisconsin Press.

Dhondt, J. (1939), 'Election et hérédité sous les Carolingiens et les premier Capétiens', in: *Revue belge de philologie et d'histoire* 18: 913–953.

— (1948), *Etudes sur la naissance des principautés territoriales en France.* Brugge: De Tempel.

Douglas, D. C. (1946), 'The earliest Norman counts', in: *English Historical Review* 61: 129–156.

— (1969), *William the Conqueror.* London: Methuen and Eyre & Spottiswoode.

Duby, G. (1962), *L'économie rurale et la vie des campagnes dans l'Occident médiéval* I. Paris: Aubier.

— (1968), 'Problèmes d'économie seigneuriale dans la France du XIIe siècle', in: *Vorträge und Forschungen XII, Probleme des 12, Jahrhundert*, pp. 161–167. Konstanz-Stuttgart: Thorbecke.

— (1973a), *Guerriers et paysans.* Paris: Gallimard.

— (1973b), *Le dimanche de Bouvines.* Paris: Gallimard.

Fédou, R. (1971), *L'état au moyen âge.* Paris: Presses universitaires de France.

Flach, J. (1893), *Les origines de l'ancienne France* II. Paris: Larose et Forcel.

Fourquin, G. (1971), *Histoire économique de l'Occident médiéval.* Paris: Colin.

Ganshof, F. L. (1965–66), 'Charlemagne et les institutions de la monarchie franque', in: *Karl der Grosse, Lebenswerke und Nachleben* I, ed. by H. Beumann, pp. 349–393. Düsseldorf: Schwann.

Glaser, H. (1960), 'Sugers Vorstellung von der geordneten Welt', in: *Historisches Jahrbuch* 80: 93–125.

Guénée, B. (1967), 'Etat et nation en France au moyen âge', in: *Revue historique* 91: 17–30.

Guillot, O. (1972), *Le comte d'Anjou et son entourage au XIe siècle.* Paris: Picard.

Halphen, L. (1906), *Le comté d'Anjou au XIe siécle.* Paris: Picard.

— (1932), *L'essor de l'Europe* (XIe–XIIIe *siècles*). Paris: Alcan.

— (1950), La place de la royauté dans le système féodal. in: *A travers l'histoire du moyen âge*, pp. 265–274. Paris: Presses universitaires de France.

Haskins, C. H. (1960), *Norman institutions.* New York: Unger (1918).

Hollister, C. W. (1969), *The twelfth-century renaissance.* New York: Knopf.

Holmes, U. T. (1951), 'The idea of a twelfth-century renaissance', in: *Saeculum* 26: 643–657.

Kantorowicz, E. H. (1957), *The King's two bodies.* Princeton: Princeton University Press.

Lemarignier, J. F. (1955), 'Les fidèles du roi de France, 936–987', in: *Recueil de travaux offerts à Clovis Brunel* II, pp. 138–187. Paris: Société de l'Ecole det Chartes.

— (1956), 'Autour de la royauté francaise du IXe au XIIIe siècle', in: *Bibliothèque de l'Ecole de Chartes* 113: 5–36.

— (1965), *Le gouvernement royal aux premiers temps capétiens, 987–1108.* Paris: Picard.

— (1970), *La France médiévale. Institutions et société.* Paris: Colin.

Lopez, R. S. (1971), *The commercial revolution of the Middle Ages.* Englewood Cliffs: Prentice Hall.

Lot, F. (1904), *Fidèles ou vassaux?* Paris: Bouillon.

Luchaire, A. (1890), *Louis VI le Gros. Annales de sa vie et de son règne.* Paris: Bouillon.
Mannheim, K. (1940), *Man and society in an age of reconstruction.* London: K. Paul, Trench, Trubner & Co.
Pacaut, M. (1953), 'Louis VII et Alexandre III', in: *Revue d'histoire de l'Eglise de France* 39: 5–45.
— (1964), *Louis VII et son royaume.* Paris: S.E.V.P.E.N.
— (1969), *Les structures politiques de l'Occident médiéval.* Paris: Colin.
Petit-Dutaillis, Ch. (1933), *La monarchie féodale en France et en Angleterre.* Paris: Albin Michel.
Reviron, J. (1930), *Les idées politico-religieuses d'un évêque au IXe siècle et le 'De institutione regia'.* Paris: J. Vrin.
Schramm, P. E. (1960), *Der König von Frankreich I,* Darmstadt: Wissenschaftliche Buchgesellschaft.
Slicher van Bath, B. H. (1963), *The agrarian history of Western Europe.* London: Arnold.
Southern, R. W. (1967), *The making of the Middle Ages.* New Haven & London: Yale University Press.
Strayer, R. W. (1970), *On the medieval origins of the modern state.* Princeton: Princeton University Press.
Teunis, H. B. (1973), *Crisis. Studie over een structuur- en normverandering in het Frankrijk van 1150–1250.* Groningen: Tjeenk Willink.
Werner, K. F. (1958), 'Untersuchungen zur Frühzeit des Französischen Fürstentums', in: *Die Welt als Geschichte* 11: 256–289.
— (1968), 'Königtum und Fürstentum im Französischen 12. Jahrhundert', in: *Vorträge und Forschungen XII. Probleme des 12. Jahrhunderts,* pp. 177–225. Konstanz-Stuttgart: Thorbecke.
Yver, J. (1969), 'Les premières institutions du duché de Normandie', in: *I Normanni e la loro espansione in Europa nell' alto medioevo,* pp. 299–366. Spoleto: Presso la sede del centro.

12

Early States in Ancient Georgia

GURAM KORANASHVILI

1. METHODOLOGICAL PROBLEMS

Since the 1930s it has been held by some Marxist-oriented scholars that the development of a class society was conditioned by the appearance of cattle-breeding and agriculture as well as the spread of metallurgy. This way slavery became widespread and property came to be concentrated in the hands of a minority, while the majority became dispossessed. After the minority subjugated the majority, leading to the development of two mutually antagonistic classes, the state was formed. Its main function was the repression of the majority. These theorists went on the assumption that the fathers of historical materialism, Marx and Engels, had provided a universally valid picture of the origin of the class society and the state, as set out mainly in Engels' work, *The origin of the family, private property, and the state.* The problem is that Engels tried to explain the disintegration of the tribal system and the establishment of the class system on the basis of only three examples: Greece, Rome and Germany. And even in these the process in question was not the same.

Engels explained the origin of classes and the state in antiquity with the aid of the concept of 'civilization'. By this he meant, first and foremost, the increased production of commodities, the exchange of which involved not only the population of the capital and of a limited number of extrepot cities, together with a few neighboring villages, but also the bulk of the society. These included not luxury articles but also basic necessities. Civilization in this sense was the result of the widespread production and use of iron, while the development of society was due to favorable historical and natural conditions. This process also embraced the development of a money economy and the conversion of land into property and thus into an object of sale and purchase. Thus the concentration of property could take place. Only as a result of such drastic economic developments could a slave-holding society emerge and prosper.

Especially in Rome the socio-economic development was greatly stimulated by the formation of a *powerful state organization* and the conquest of vast territories and subjugation of many peoples.

All attempts at tracing analogous processes in regions other than the Mediterranean are bound to be vain. V. Struve and his followers have failed to find slavery as a characteristic feature of a number of ancient Oriental societies. By and large, the origin of slavery as an institution is associated by Engels with a civilization which was born only 2500 years ago. That is, at the time of Solon's, Cleisthenes' and Servius Tulius' reforms, which were the political expression of the triumph of private property. The state was formed in quite a different way among the Germans, Georgians and in oriental societies. Socio-political organization here became necessary not so much for the sake of the repression of the lower strata of the population (the economic differentiation within the society being insignificant, while the number of slaves was also small) as because of the necessity of organizing irrigation and/or defence. In the above mentioned countries the public power was vested mainly in the people and was directed against other societies.

Recent discussions have shown clearly that not everywhere did the formation of a class society and the state coincide with slavery or feudalism, or lead to the instant disappearance of communal ownership of land. Many societies displayed transitional types of structure, whereby the place of the former tribal communities was taken by rural communities and the collective ownership of land superseded by individual tenure. In this transitional type of society the state, as a substitute for the tribal form of organization, existed as a political organization fulfilling defence and irrigation functions. Societies of this type existed for quite a long time in many places. In Western Europe they were supplanted sooner or later by slave-holding, and later by feudal kinds of society or modes of production (for more details see Koranashvili 1976).

2. ORIGINS

According to the Georgian historical tradition, the campaign conducted by Alexander the Great prompted the transition from a stateless and classless phase to that of the state and classes, or, in Leonti

Mroveli's[1] words, the transition from *Mamasakhlisoba* (village community system) to *Mephoba* (monarchy). According to this same tradition, there already existed the kingdom of Arian-Kartli in the southwestern part of historical Georgia even before the campaign of Alexander the Great. But this particular state is given no further attention by the ancient Georgian historical tradition where it deals with the development of the state.

It was Pharnavaz who was the founder of the Georgian state, according to this tradition. It appears, by inference from the same historical tradition, that the formation of the state in Iberia was a precondition for the development of social classes there. After the political organization had been effected, legal and proprietary distinctions sprang up among the Iberians. To the upper population stratum belonged the *sephe-sakhli*, or king's relatives, the *eristavis*, or governors, and the *aznauris*, or nobility.

The bulk of the population was formed by the unpropertied and politically oppressed.

The formation of the Georgian state was a complex process. According to Javakhishvili[2] the tribal system and the state were not at all mutually incompatible phenomena. The phase of the tribal system was by no means a stateless one. Many researchers have considered this statement a-logical. However, in the light of recent developments in historical thinking, Javakhishvili's 'paradoxic' view appears to contain some quite important rational elements. Javakhishvili's viewpoint has recently been supported in essence by G. Melikishvili (1966, 1971).

Today it is evident that it was possible for the state to exist at the time of the definite disintegration of the tribal system.[3] We may find many an example of this in the history of Achaian Greece, ancient India, China, Germany, Scandinavia, Afghanistan and Russia.

A civilization including social classes and the state developed much later in Georgia than in the Middle and Far East. Geographical conditions put tremendous obstacles in the way of the development of civilization. Because of the comparative underdevelopment of agricultural implements and the absence of iron-working techniques it was impossible to overcome the natural obstacles. At the same time the territory was comparatively far removed from the ancient Oriental states (Hatti, Mithan, Assyria, Urartu). Assyrian and Urartian attacks on the ancient Georgian (proto-) states of Diaokhi, Colkha and Khalitu were not particularly destructive, nor did the foreign domination turn out to be firm or lasting. In the preservation of its independence the natural conditions of our country (high mountains separated by steep gorges) undoubtedly played an important part. What the sea, climate or isolation did for other states did the Caucasus mountain range, a natural defence against the northern nomads, for Georgia. All the Georgian states had to do was close the narrow, highly elevated Caucasian mountain passes to feel safe from the north. On the Black Sea side no serious danger threatened either, as for a long time no powerful state that might pose a threat to the safety of Georgia emerged here. Only the south of Georgia, and especially the southeast, was open to enemy invasions.

The essential complexity of the historical process in Georgia was connected with the following circumstance. At a certain stage of the economic development of the society some direct producers were able to produce more than they needed for their own subsistence, or in other words, a surplus product emerged. The preconditions for this arose with cattle-raising. Only southern Georgia possessed favorable conditions for this branch of economic activity (large summer pastures on plateaux, comparatively mild climate, winter pastures on plains). Under these circumstances slavery developed as the first form of exploitation of man by man. In Georgia this process took place in about a thousand years B.C.

The political basis of slavery as a social institution is as old as the neighborly coexistence of human settlements, together with internecine warfare between such communities. A society situated beyond the bounds of the unit made up by several communities already represented a hostile force. Previously, captives had been of no value. But at the stage of economic development mentioned above they did possess some value already and therefore were made slaves. But slaves represented only a small minority of the society as a whole, not only under the conditions of highly productive cattle-breeding, but also during the period of plow agriculture. Their labor was used, along with that of members of the family, only in families belonging to the tribal aristocracy. This was the so-called patriarchal stage, which was characterized by the small number of slaves in proportion to the total society, and their easy exploitability. To coerce them the formation of the state, with its special punitive apparatus, was not at all necessary, since the gentile or rural community and patriarchal family could easily fulfil this function.

The state in many places, among them Georgia, originated on quite a different basis, viz. the satisfaction of the common interests of a fairly developed community. For the purpose of defence against other units and the retention of the prime conditions of production (land, pastures) it became necessary to unite the population into political units. Thus the royal power and the stratum of organizers of military affairs arose. In some cases a coercive apparatus to repress invaded tribes (e.g., in the state of Colkha) emerged as well. The growing complexity of the religious cult led those in charge of this aspect of life to form a separate organization of their own. These bodies then formed the primitive state, whereby the broad strata of the population somehow lost their autonomy vis-à-vis the central power. Locally, however, they did retain their autonomy.

The organization of some thousands of people over a comparatively extensive area along the lines of *primitive democracy* became unfeasible, for under the new conditions it became impossible for the public assembly and the council of family heads to function any longer. Their role was taken over by a class of rulers.[4] They formed the privileged upper stratum of the society, enjoying higher incomes and greater political rights. The existence of a fairly developed degree of economic inequality is well attested by the archaeological remains from that time.

We have a picture of this kind of the social classes and the state from as early as the middle and end of the second millennium for early states of Thrialeti, Diaokhi, Colkha and, a little later, Khalibes.[5]

They did not represent a so-called military democracy, according to Melikishvili, but were early state forms. In the same historian's view these parts of Georgia were more advanced economically (the development of cattle-breeding and bronze-working), which was reflected by the above-mentioned social and political processes.

In this way classes and the state arose in ancient Georgia. The social and political processes mentioned before were connected with the exploitation of slaves as well as the local population by the upper population stratum. But this development took a long time. The coercive apparatus of the state was weak as yet. The basic military force was made up by the people itself. Thus the alienation of the political power from the people had not yet assumed significant proportions, nor had the division of the society into classes reached any complete form. The basic means of production (land, livestock, pastures, wood, the artificially created labor reservoir) were concentrated directly in the hands of small, independent producers. The slow pace at which the social and political processes took place is explained by the comparative underdevelopment of the economy in a rugged mountainous region, where agriculture was not nearly as productive as in the advanced centers of civilization in the Middle East and North Africa (Egypt).

The subsequent development did not take place in a straight line. All of the above-mentioned early states were destroyed by external enemies (Assyrians, Urartians, Cymerians, Scythians, Persians) or intestine wars. Endless migrations and intermixing took place, which definitely delayed society's progress.

The development of classes and the state began at the new stage after *iron-working* became widespread (during the first quarter of the first millennium B.C.). Owing to the new technological developments people began to be able to overcome the unfavorable natural conditions (in the form of hard soils, forests and the comparatively cold climate) and change these. Plow agriculture, advances in many spheres of handicraft production and the development of stone-, metal- and wood-working—the latter as a result of the new metal implements—greatly accelerated the economic and social evolution. Thus, iron was the first metal which, because of its cheapness and versatility, thoroughly changed the hitherto prevailing social and economic conditions. 'Progress was now irresistible, less fitful and more rapid' (Engels). In Georgia, the development took place in the plain, especially in the northeastern part of the country, the remoteness from a hostile sphere stimulated this process as well. Comparatively easy to overcome were the negative effects of invasions by Cymerian, Scythian and other peoples. After all this primitive communism based on common production and equal distribution was destroyed in agriculture as well (in cattle-breeding this had happened earlier). The rural communities with their extended and nuclear families became the basic economic and social units.[6]

Colkheti (not to be confused with Colkha) and Iberia in the sixth and at the end of the fourth centuries B.C. were comparatively developed states where the unification of agricultural communities in order to promote their common interests (e.g., defence, irrigation in the eastern part of the country) took place. This tendency was not at all a direct product of economic necessity (irrigation on a large scale, handicraft production, commerce).[7] Be that as it may, larger units, though they owed their formation to aggression rather than economic necessity, played a significant role in the subsequent progress of the society. As a result of them the defence against external enemies became easier and the population was able to grow used to social and political life.

We are best informed about the origin of the Iberian state and its social structure.

In early times the southeastern part of historical Georgia formed part of the Persian Empire, which had succeeded in subjugating this part of Georgia (as the eighteenth and nineteenth satrapies). The conquered part of ancient Georgia paid tribute to the conqueror; paid tribute and performed certain military services. Persia may possibly have allowed a measure of local autonomy to remain here.[8] Iberia, having taken advantage of the rivalry among the northeastern local centres of power, subordinated them all and made the naturally, politically and economically suitable area around Mtskheta the center of the centralized power. According to the Georgian historical tradition, these events must have taken place in the late thirties of the fourth century B.C. In this case the rise of the Iberian state was accelerated by external aggression, the examples of this being many in history. But all this is only hypothetical. So it is difficult to say anything about a supposed liberation movement on the part of the ancient Iberians against the immigrant Meskhs (one of the Georgian tribal branches).

3. STRUCTURE AND FUNCTIONING

At the end of the fourth century B.C., the state system was already established in Iberia. According to the historical tradition recorded by Leonti Mroveli, Pharnavaz was the first king of *Kartli* (Iberia) and the founder of the first royal dynasty (Pharnavaziani). Pharnavaz divided Iberia into seven *saeristavos* (*saeristavo* = district of an *eristavi*) and established a center in each of them. According to the same Mroveli, Pharnavaz converted the state of Egrisi (Colkheti), too, into a *saeristavo* or province, where his subordinate Kuji ruled. As for central Kartli (i.e., Iberia), it came under the rule of a *spaspeti* or general, thus forming a *saspaspeto* (district ruled by a *spaspeti*).[9] Sound political reasoning required that the *saeristavos* should not coincide with the former smaller political units. The archaeological and epigraphic evidence tends to confirm the Georgian historical tradition. It is also corroborated by some of the facts presented by Greek and Roman authors. Hence, there is quite rightly no hypercritical attitude to the historical tradition with respect to the origin of the state on the part of modern Georgian historians.

It is evident that the division of Iberia into *saeristavos* served first and foremost a military aim, namely, the organization of the population for the purpose of defence. This organization was not so much directed against other countries.

If we assume that the Iberian territory at the time comprised a minimum of $60,000 \text{ km}^2$ (i.e., little less than the present Georgian area), and the population density was at least 10 per km^2, then the total Iberian population, including foreign captives and the population of tributary areas would have come to 600,000.[10] From such a total, even excluding the above-mentioned population groups, it would have been possible to raise a fairly big army of not less than 100,000. But this total could have been reached only under conditions of a comparatively high standard of living among the free population (or of a lower degree of socio-economic development!), a fairly high level of development of communications and facilities for speedy mobilization. From what Strabo says in this respect we can conclude that the Iberian army numbered 70,000–80,000 so that it appears that each *saeristavo* contributed 10,000 soldiers. For purposes of comparison we may adduce

other information, provided in 'The Life of Kartli'. Under the eighteenth king, Amazasp, Iberia was attacked by the Alans from the
north. The fastest to come to Mtskheta to beat off the enemy were
spaspeti horsemen and three eristavis, in all 30,000 foot and 10,000
horse. An additional army was raised in other saeristavos. These data
agree with Strabo's above-said information. Thus it appears that each
saeristavo raised 10,000 soldiers.

The political organization of the saeristavo was as follows: at the
head was the eristavi, appointed by the king. He exercised the supreme
civil and public power on the local level. After him came the spasalari
(a military official of high rank, the exact determination of whose
functions is impossible), the atasistavi (headman of a thousand), and
perhaps also the asistavi (village chief). Military forts were governed
by tsikhistavi (head of a castle) and quite possibly atasistavis and
asistavis were such functionaries. It is evident that the asistavi might
have had a small coercive apparatus and body of officials at their
disposal. In order to maintain the saeristavo's political power, its
population was obliged to pay a special 'Saeristavo tax'. No other
officials are mentioned in the sources. They presumably did exist,
judging from the presence of the mamasakhlisi (head of a lineage)
institution in the villages. There were also other officials in charge of
irrigation, the religious cult, border defence, etc. There were more
officials in the towns, especially in the capital of Mtskheta, where a
complex pattern of economic, social and ethnic organization required
special functionaries. But we have no concrete information about
them. At any rate the towns did not play an important role in the
Iberian political organization (and correspondingly in the economy).

Finally, some state administrative functions (tax-collecting, army
recruiting) were also fulfilled in mountainous regions by Khevisberis
(valley priests).

At the head of the state organization stood the king, who is
sometimes referred to as 'great king'. A number of data and epigraphic
records show that in the king was vested the supreme power of the
state.[11] Perhaps the king was also the chief state priest (at that time
there already existed centralized cults in Iberia). At the top of the
military hierarchy stood the spaspeti, who in the king's absence commanded the army. The royal household was managed by the ezosmodzgvari or chief courtier (chamberlain), whose kheli or power was
greater than that of the msakhurtukhutsesi (head of the royal staff) of
the feudal period. For one thing, he exercised the command over a
royal guard of 1,000 men. Perhaps as far as his functions are concerned the ezosmodzgvari was equivalent to a vizir (he may have been
referred to by Strabo as 'the second personage after the king'). The
king's kin or sephe directly bolstered the royal power. From among

them the highest officials were appointed. This served to strengthen the central power. This stratum lived together with the king on the labor of the royal serfs (called by Strabo βασιλικοὶ δ0ῦλοί) and on the tax or tribute ('royal and *eristavian* levy') paid by the free population and the mountain folk.

Such was the structure of the Iberian state, which had assumed its completed form, i.e., was characterized by three principal traits, viz., the territorial division of the population into *saeristavos* in places where this may easily have happened earlier because of the clear abolition of the consanguineal principle in certain rural communities, the public exercise of power and the existence of taxation, by the beginning of the third century B.C. The principal function of the state organization comprised the national defence, which thus found expression in the specific form of organization of the population and the construction of forts. It manifested itself less in the organization of foreign campaigns.

The role of the Iberian state as a repressive apparatus was much less significant. The direct objects of oppression were the royal slaves of foreign origin and the mountain tribes (of the proportion they formed of the Iberian population Strabo had a most exaggerated idea). The oppression of the free population (through taxation, statute labor) by the upper stratum was connected with the functioning of the state apparatus. At any rate, there existed no stratum of impoverished freemen at that time. The slave force was small in number too. The army was made up of members of the free population (*Geography*, Lib. XI, cap. III–6, of Strabo), and its primary task was defence. The representatives of the state at the same time formed the dominant class. They were the royal kin, the high officials and the clergy. The latter possessed vast tracts of land, for the cultivation of which the labor of free men was mainly used.[12] The landowners themselves did not represent a very numerous social stratum either. The reason for this social phenomenon is quite obvious: the low level of development of commodity production and the relative insignificance of predatory wars (the Iberian Armasi (Mars) restricting itself mainly, as has already been mentioned, to defence) made the development of slavery on a large scale impossible. The upper stratum of the society lived on the labor, taxes and contributions exacted from the population. Thus the principal object of exploitation in ancient Iberia (Kartli) was the free population, in contrast to the manager stratum.

The origin of the Iberian state stimulated the subsequent development of justice. The regulation of social relations solely by ancient customary law or *adathi*[13] became unfeasible. Though no legal records from this period have come down to us, their existence at the time is beyond doubt. According to Strabo, jurisdiction had already been alienated from the broad masses of the population and was exercised by the clergy—(both state transactions and laws were recorded in the Aramaic script and language).

Finally some data on the political character of Iberia. As we have already mentioned above, the public power was vested principally in the free members of the population. In contrast to it, the central power was not strong. Accordingly, the state did not possess a despotic character. '*The life of Kartli*' provides some clear examples to illustrate this. When the fourth king, Pharnajom, became a fire-worshipper and began to condemn the indigenous Iberian gods, then the broad masses of the population rose against their own king. The revolt was headed by the majority of the *eristavis*. Having defeated him, they put the Armenian prince Arshak on the throne of Iberia (Kartli).

And when the eighteenth king, Amazasp, began to show signs of arbitrary behaviour and had many nobles of Kartli murdered, with Persian support, then five *eristavis* rose against him. They headed the people's revolt against the king (also driving the Alans out of the north). The despotic king Amazasp was killed in this struggle. In his place his nephew Rev was enthroned.

Almost the same picture of the origin of classes and the state emerges for Colkheti. There is very little information about the processes involved, however. We only know that after the state Colkha was destroyed, the northern part continued to exist in the form of the kingdom of Colkheti, even after the sixth century B.C. According to Strabo (*Geography*, Lib. XI, cap. II–18) the king of Colkheti divided the country into *skeptuxias* (a unit like the *saeristavos*) with *skeptouxos* at their head. They minted their own coins, they furthermore subjugated Greek colonists and ruled the country mildly or μέσως ἔπραπον (not at all despotically!).

The part played by the class society and state in Colkheti was not at all comparable to that of Iberia. For centuries the former failed to distinguish itself at all on the external political scene, was easily subdued by Iberia and then annexed by the kingdom of Ponto, and even after the disintegration of the latter again it was ruled by foreign governors, till eventually it found itself in the possession of the Romans.[14] In our opinion the weakness of Colkheti lay in the following: the country had poor soils and many swamps, and was covered with dense woods. A high precipitation stood in the way of agricultural development (especially in the absence of a high-yielding crop, such as maize, under these natural conditions). It was impossible to overcome these obstacles through an international division of labor. According to Strabo the country exported flax and ship-building timber. According to the same source neither export was significant, their use being restricted to luxury articles.

On this point Iberia was better off (fertile soils, better climate). Here the natural obstacle, namely the dry climate, was easier to overcome, through irrigation, than in Colkheti (swampy soil). As a result, Strabo noted that Iberia was wealthy, with a comparatively high standard of living, and well-populated. This natural basis found obvious expression after the society began exploiting the natural resources in the economic, social and political conditions, etc. In other words, Iberia later played a much greater role in the development of Georgian civilization than did Colkheti. The ancient Iberian and Colkhetian societies represented the type of the transitional phase or 'early class' stage. If the use of these terms with reference to ancient Eastern societies should make for misunderstanding, we should add that in the first case their use is quite justified. Tribal society here was not changed immediately by the feudal system and the state. Between these two stages other forms of social and political structure took shape here. The subsequent social evolution was directed not by patterns from antiquity (Greece, Rome), but by feudalism.

FOOTNOTES

[1] Georgian bishop, historiographer and chronicler, living in the eleventh century. He is the author of one part of the *Life of Kartli*, the most detailed chronicle of the ancient kingdom of Iberia.

[2] Ivane Javakhisivili (1876–1940) was a famous modern Georgian historiographer.

[3] This phenomenon was noted by Marx and Engels. See their *Sochineniia* (Works). Vol. 3: 32; Vol. 21: 169. Engels in particular pointed to the rise of the patrimonial order not only among the nobility and in patrician circles, but also among a proportion of the peasants.

[4] Lenin, like Engels, distinguished two social categories at the state level: the rulers and the ruled (cf. his *State and revolution* and *On the state*, in: Polnoe sobranie sochinenii. Vol. 33: 9, 77, 115; Vol. 39: 69, 72).

[5] In the second millennium B.C. there existed a large early state on the lower Alazani and Iori rivers. Only a few recent archaeological finds furnish some information on it.

[6] Strabo's information, that the Iberians shared property on the basis of the consanguineal principle is wrong. At most we can assume communal property by the extended family. The institution of communal property survived until much later times. For example, in the so-called 'Defence charter' of the Arabic period it is stated that the Arabs had no right to divide the family into smaller units. Survivals of this were still found in certain parts of Georgia as late as the late nineteenth century.

[7] The comparatively strong position of the Iberian kingdom was allegedly connected with irrigation. We consider this point of view incorrect. Irrigation systems in eastern Georgia were on a small-scale and served only vineyards, horticulture and vegetable farming.

[8] The Achaemenid kings did not abolish the local royal power everywhere in the remoter areas of the empire. So, for example, the Civician kings fulfilled the function of satraps till the fifth century B.C. The same thing happened in Syria, Phoenicia, Palestine, and a number of other kingdoms in the Middle East.

[9]   According to the ancient Georgian historical tradition the division of the country into *saeristavos* and *saspaspeto*, as well as the creation of the function of *eristavi* or governor by Pharnavaz, had their origin in the Persian political system. Perhaps Pharnavaz borrowed the idea from Persia, but its main cause, of course, was the internal development of the country.

[10]   There was almost the same population density among the German tribes of the first centuries A.D. Since the general level of development of Iberia was much higher than that of these Germans, the comparatively low population density has some connection with the mountainous conditions of Iberia.

[11]   According to Strabo's *Geography*, the power of the Iberian king was as weak as that of Mosinik (see *Anabasis* by Xenophon). It is precisely this piece of information a number of Georgian historians had in mind when describing Iberia in Strabo's time as a 'military democracy'. However, other data from the history of Iberia contradict this.

[12]   The Georgian ethnologist Vera Bardavelidze has drawn attention to the existence of the religious community of the Khevsurs in the mountains of northeastern Georgia, which likewise exploited church land.

[13]   The *adathi* or customary law regulated the life of the mountain people well until the late nineteenth century.

[14]   Iberia was quite capable of annexing Colkheti. But such powerful states as Ponto and Rome prevented it from doing so as a result of their strong influence and subsequent domination of Colkheti.

REFERENCES

Javakhishvili, I. (1928), *The history of Georgian justice.* (in Georgian). Tbilisi.
Koranashvili, G. (1976), *Problema dokapitalisticheskikh obshchestvenno-ekonomicheskikh formatsii v istoricheskom materializme* [Problems of pre-capitalist socio-economic formations in historical materialism]. Tbilisi: Tbilisi University Press.
—— (1976), *The development of thoughts of Marx and Engels on the pre-capitalist socio-economic formations* (in Georgian). Tbilisi: Ganatleba.
Marx, K. and Engels, F. (n.d.), *Sochineniia* [Works]. Moscow.
Melikishvili, G. (1966), 'Socio-economic problems of ancient Georgia' (in Georgian), in: *Matsne* 1.
—— (1971), *Essays on Georgian history.* Vol. 1, (in Georgian). Tbilisi: Mets-niereba.

13   The Early State in Hawaii

S. LEE SEATON

1. INTRODUCTION

The Hawaiian Islands were originally inhabited by Polynesians who most likely sailed from the Marquesas *c.* A.D. 750 (Finney 1967). Unlike their home islands, the islands of the Hawaiian archipelago provided a spacious land of plenty in which the old competition for survival paled. However, other Polynesian groups sought new lands and the fabled *Hawaiki*, the land of their ancestors. Tahitians from the Society Islands followed the earlier Marquesans and conquered the immigrants, imposing their own special version of the general Polynesian culture (Green 1967; Claessen, this volume). Yet under the influence of Hawaii's fertility, it appears these newcomers too fell into irreverence — intermarriage between the nobility and commoners occurred and the structures of the old Tahitian religion were abused. According to legend, about A.D. 1275, a travelling priest from Tahiti initiated a major revitalization movement among the noble class which featured the reimposition of the obdurate system of religious rules — the *kapu* system. Shortly after this, travel between Hawaii and the rest of Polynesia ceased. Just what role increasing population and the need for social control played in this sequence of events is a matter for prehistorians (for a report on the current status of prehistory in Oceania, cf. Bellwood 1975). However, the results were that Hawaii was to constitute a closed cultural system for the next 500 years, a system probably starting at the limits of its original ecology.

    The ecology of Hawaii is one of contrasts. The islands themselves are the products of volcanic eruptions and subsequent erosion. Volcanoes on at least two of the islands have remained active during the historical period. In fact, an eruption on the 'Big Island' of Hawaii killed a company of warriors opposing Kamehameha I during his wars of unification. (The event was regarded as further evidence of Kamehameha's spiritual power or *mana*.) The erosion of the volcanic mountains produced the key geo-political feature of the land, the valleys. In general, these valleys radiate from the center of the island and stretch from peak to sea. As each valley contained all the dimensions of the environment necessary to Hawaiian life (fresh water, the land, and the sea), each valley could serve as a basis for a reasonably self-sufficient population, a factor not without its political implications.

While we have no reliable estimates of the size of the Hawaiian population at the time of the Western contact, a figure of approximately 350,000 appears to be a compromise of high and low. By comparison, the 1970 population numbered just over 1,000,000. Of that total, approximately 12,000 are pure-blood Hawaiians. Postcontact war, disease, and out-marriage have obviously reduced the original population drastically. Today, Hawaiian culture survives in a primary form only on the privately owned island of Niihau. Yet the contemporary culture of modern Hawaii contains many elements of the traditional culture, both symbolically and functionally. Moreover, the State of Hawaii is integrated into the political processes of a major world power, the United States of America. In one sense, then, Hawaii represents the full record of political evolution. In this chapter we shall only deal with the period of independent evolution, the early state.

2. THE EARLY STATE IN HAWAII

The 'early state' in Hawaii may be said to have terminated with the removal of the Russian colony from the island of Kauai in 1818 for this event left the monarchy of Kamehameha I ('the Great') in unchallenged control of all the territory associated with the Hawaiian people. However, the *transitional* early state represented by the development of the Kamehameha kingdom was not purely indigenous. The arrival of the English explorer, Captain James Cook, in 1778 marked a sharp break in the relative isolation of the Hawaiian culture from exogenous forces of change. Hence, while the *early* state continues after Western contact, the *pristine* state prior to contact must be regarded as the unique product of indigenous political culture (cf. Fried 1967: 111). As the discussion of the *transitional* early state is available elsewhere (Seaton 1974), only the *pristine* (inchoate) early state will be discussed here.

Traditionally — from 1275 to 1738 — the Hawaiian archipelago was ruled as several competing polities. Certainly each of these political units qualified as *chiefdoms* per Service's definition as hierarchically centralized leadership (1975: 74). Moreover, each was characterized as a *rank stratified* society in which valued status differentials limited access to basic resources (Fried 1967: 109, 186). However, no polity could affect or guarantee that it maintained a reasonable monopoly of legitimate force over any stable territory. Inter-island warfare and rebellion were so much a part of everyday reality as to preclude any application of the classical Weberian requirement for *true* statehood.

However in 1738 the *ali'i nui* (paramount chiefs) of the five polities agreed to a treaty pledging inter-island peace. In a sense, this treaty prepared the way for *true* statehood by establishing an era of routinized political administration. Yet before the full impact of this insular détente could be realized, the tides of Western-influenced political unification pushed forward the Kamehameha kingdom.

Given the rapidity with which the Hawaiians moved toward political unification after Cook's intrusion, one may ask why they had failed previously. Similarly, given the fact that the back of traditional cultural system was broken shortly after Kamehameha's death in 1819, one may wonder what pre-contact unification would have produced. The suspicion, voiced by scholars such as Redfield, Linton, and Kroeber, is that there was something fundamentally defective in the Hawaiian culture. Of course, the same or similar concerns have been expressed for other Polynesian cultures (Hansen 1973). However, the Hawaiian case is so clear-cut, so dramatic, and by comparison, so well documented, that it stands out for anthropological analysis.

We shall begin with a review of traditional Hawaiian culture which was operative from approximately 1738 (date of the Treaty of Na-onealaa) to 1783 (start of the civil war which lead to unification). The final section will analyze the cultural and historical patterns in light of elements of a theory of state formation.

In order to examine the *pristine* state in Hawaii, we must reconstruct the ethno-history of the generation prior to culture contact. Inevitably, this requires more reliance on the early post-contact descriptions of the travelers, explorers, merchants and missionaries than we would wish. In the area of politics, this is particularly true as such early descriptions are likely to reflect ethnocentric treatments by casual observers. Hence, there is a tendency in these early accounts to regard the Hawaiian political culture as 'typically' feudal. Moreover, the influence of European and American agents may well have deliberately sought to instill distinctively Western elements of political organization precisely to render Hawaiian norms more analogous to the familiar Western models (Kelly 1967).

In order to off-set such interferences, an explicit model of political culture is required. However, this is not the place to present an abstract discussion of all the dimensions of a general theory of political culture. Rather, we shall sketch a political culture schematic for the Hawaiian data.

'Political culture' may be defined as the 'particular pattern of orientation to political actions' founded in every political system (Almond 1956: 396).

It is assumed that every system is embedded in and structured by a matrix of attitudes, sentiments, and cognitions which are coherent and mutually reinforcing. At the level of the individual, the concept assumes that 'each individual must, in his own historical context, learn, and incorporate into his own personality the knowledge and feelings about the politics of his people and his community' (Pye 1965: 7).

Of course, it must be recognized that not every member of a political system learns or practices the same orientations. Among the Hawaiian chiefdoms, there were even recognized distinctions in the basic patterns found on the several islands which make up the Hawaiian cultural area. Thus, Kauai was regarded as the most traditional. However, this distinction carried no particular honor or privilege. The *ali'i* of one island drew no apparent loss of status from mere territorial distinctions.

Using the political culture approach in ethnohistorical reconstructions does not permit sample surveys or even participant–observer fieldwork. In place of respondent data, we must turn to ethnographic descriptions (frequently written by amateurs) of behaviors closely associated with apparent basic value orientations. This is clearly second-hand, culture-at-a-distance analysis.

'But by focusing on basic value orientation — often implicit assumptions about the nature of man and the nature of physical reality — we may find a set of political attitudes that, though not structured as the political philosopher might structure them, nevertheless have a definite and significant structure' (Verba 1965: 523).

The raw data for the existence of basic value orientations is likely to be restricted to those items in the indigenous cultural repertoire which struck foreigners as unusual. Rituals, religions, beliefs, sumptuary laws, and the like are most likely to draw comment. From these, we must draw inferences about the pattern of orientations toward political action. Lucien Pye summarized the strategy as follows. 'The initial hypotheses about a political culture must thus take the form of statements which hold that the system behaves "as if" certain values, sentiments, and orientations were the most critical in giving the collectivity its distinctive character' (1973: 73).

Pye goes on to add a cautionary note to the effect that the political culture 'consists of those "orientations" that make the system distinctive among all the attitudes a population may hold' (1973: 73).

In Hawaii, the ease and frequency of interisland contact probably reduced or eliminated important regional differences. Thus in the following we speak of the 'Hawaiian political culture' as a general type of characteristic of all constituent chiefdoms in the pristine state era. To insure cross-cultural and intra-cultural validity, we require the identification of a set of 'cultural universals' for political systems. Of course, these key analytical points of reference will reflect our theoretical model of politics. A reasonably generic model of the political system identifies four analytical foci for comparative studies: inputs, outputs, conversion processes, and the political self (Easton 1965; Almond and Powell 1966). Table I suggests three presumably universal patterns of orientations toward these four political aspects (Rosenbaum, 1975: 61-62).

Table I. *Orientations toward political objects*

Pattern label	Inputs	Conversion	Outputs	Self
Citizen	Anticipatory	Partisan	Competitive	Participant
Subject	Obligatory	Observant	Reciprocal	Recipient
Parochial	Coerced	(Slavery)	Dependent	Inhabitant

The 'citizen' pattern of orientations implies the active involvement of the individual in all aspects of the political system as well as the self-assessment as a politically competent member of the community. The 'subject' pattern is typified by the allegiant who sees the political progress as positive and appropriate. However, the subject regards 'politics' as beyond himself both in terms of participation and personal competency. The 'parochial' is an individual who is either apathetic toward the entire political system or is alienated from it. Although he may be forced to work for the support of the system, he does so because of a lack of alternatives rather than from personal loyalties. While the citizen, subject and parochial patterns do not exhaust the possible permutations of orientations, there is reason to believe that at least these will be found in every political culture (cf. Almond and Verba 1965).

The three patterns identified in Table I had clearly defined social class referents in the traditional Hawaiian political culture. The *ali'i*, the nobility, were the only 'citizens'. Membership in this elite class was hereditary but progeny of relations between nobility and commoners could be incorporated into the *ali'i*. Differences in *ali'i* status was recognized in the basic ramage social structure found throughout Polynesia. However, the usual close association between a particular ramage or branch and a given territorial unit does not seem to have been as characteristic in Hawaii as elsewhere. It is possible that the frequency of warfare with its redistribution of land holdings had fundamentally disrupted the association. The commoner class, the *maka'āinana*, represented the 'subject' pattern making up the great majority of Hawaiians. The *kauwa* were Hawaii's 'parochials'. While the exact nature of the *kauwa* class is not known, there is some evidence to suggest that they represented individuals being punished for breaking not-too-serious taboos. It is clear that they were a relatively small group, despised and victimized.

The *maka'āinana* were the primary producers of both agricultural and marine foodstuffs. Indeed the stem *'āina* means 'land'. Working individual *mo'o* ('plots'), the subjects held their land at the will of the chiefs but were not bound to it in serf fashion. Commoners could leave and work land under another chief if they desired. Individual plots were aggregated into an administrative unit, an *'ili* ('plantation'), of the land tenure system. The production of each plantation was supervised by a *konohiki*. As an administrative group, the *konohiki* were not a hereditary social class, being composed of both able commoners and low *ali'i*. Several plantations were incorporated under the rule of an individual chief. A chief's territory ranged over a self-sufficient valley (*ahupua'a*). In general, several chiefs would be governed by a paramount chief, the *ali'i nui*. The *ali'i nui* would be further surrounded by a free floating set of armed retainers, the *kualana*. Sovereign chiefs laid claim to territory which comprised a *moku* ('chiefdom'), usually one of the eight major islands. Table II summarizes the land tenure system.

Table II. *Territorial basis of Hawaiian social structure**

Geographic division	Political division	Holder	Basis of tenure
1. Island	Moku	Ali'i Nui	Succession or conquest
2. Valley	Ahupua'a	Ali'i	Grant from Ali'i Nui
3. Plantation	'Ili	Konohiki	Ali'i grant
4. Farm	Mo'o	Maka'āinana	Tenant at will

* Adapted from Lind (1938: 33).

In order to examine how the *pristine* state actually operated in pre-contact Hawaii, we must refine the macro-foci identified in Table I. Again, we seek a generic model in developing the schematic representation of the traditional political culture. Table III displays a basically structural–functional variant of the general systems model presented in Table I. We shall term this the *political division of labor* (Easton 1965: 177–78).

Table III. *Schematic representation of traditional Hawaiian political division of labor*

Phase functions	Political objects
I. INPUT-DEMANDS FOR:	
1. Goods and services	
a. Land	'Cutting' and Ali'i land allotment
b. Produce	Makahiki (as national fertility ceremony)
c. Production skills	Kapu crafts (production specializations)
2. Regulation of behavior	Kapu (enforcement through sacrifices)
3. Participation	
a. Membership	Descent reckoning (genealogical respect)
b. Recruitment	Achievement recognition and apprenticeships
4. Display	Makahiki (as renewal ceremony)
II. INPUT-SUPPORTS OF:	
1. Goods and services	Makahiki (as tax-collection)
2. Obedience to regulations	Production, consumption, ceremony Kapus
3. Participation	Land tenure system
4. Deference to authority	Rank Kapus
III. CONVERSION	
1. Decision-making	Ali'i Nui, Kālaimoku, Kahuna Nui
2. Administration	Ali'i, Konohiki, Kahuna
IV. OUTPUTS	
1. Extractions of goods and services	Makahiki (as tax collection) and 'work days'
2. Regulation of behavior	Kapus and Kapu days
3. Distribution of:	
a. Land	'Cutting' and Ali'i land allotment
b. Produce	Production and consumption Kapus
c. Production skills	Ali'i employment
4. Communication	Makahiki and Luakini rituals

As is usually the case in non-bureaucratized states, rule in Hawaii was a combination of noble prerogatives and duties. While the ruling chief was described as the *ali'i 'ai moku* ('chiefdom eater') and had a formal absolutism, in practice the chiefs were bound by both social and religious obligations. The resultant political division of labor had two major analytic subdivision; the 'rank–mana–taboo' system (Webb 1965: 25) and the production–redistribution–consumption system.

The Hawaiians, of course, made no such conceptual distinction. The Hawaiian cosmology recognized a close interdependence between supernatural and natural affairs. The *ali'i* class held sway by virtue of being temporal descendants of gods and demi-gods. In turn the commoners held title from the *ali'i* in return for tribute and service. As the welfare of the land and people was perceived as dependent upon the approval of the gods, offerings to the principal deities were periodically required.

The Hawaiian pantheon was actually the local version of the general Polynesian cosmology. There were four main deities, each with numerous manifestations. The god of war and politics was *Ku*, particularly the manifestation as *Kūkā'ilimoku* ('Ku-the-island-snatcher'). *Kāne* and *Kanaloa* were responsible for the mystical life forces, especially sex. *Lono*, for whom Captain James Cook was mistaken, was the god of productivity from the land. Each was associated with a specialized priestcraft which maintained specific temples (*heiau*) for their patron deity and *ali'i*. Because of their centrality to political life, the priestcraft which maintained specific temples (*Heiau*) for their patron larly significant in legitimating the power of individual chiefs. A miserly chief was considered irreligious and unfit to rule, thus the generosity of the chief's offerings was an important component in maintenance of religious support.

Likewise, a chief who was not generous in the redistribution of goods among his followers and subjects was seen as forgetting that a 'chief is a chief because of his subjects'. As commoners could leave the land of a chief at will, a selfish ruler would soon find himself without workers or warriors. Such a singular ruler would soon be challenged by competing *ali'i*.

The distribution among his subordinates of lands held by a new ruling chief was accomplished by a 'cutting' of the *moku* at the time of succession. Indeed, the term for 'politics' is *kālai'āina* ('land carving'). In this division the *ali'i nui* was assisted by his *kālaimoku* ('island cutter') who functioned as the chief's principal advisor. In theory, land holdings tended to be divided on traditional bases. Hence political skill and genealogical knowledge were prerequisites for the *kālaimoku*. As was the case with the *konohiki*, where technical skill was thought critical the Hawaiians waived class status requirements, permitting commoners to serve as prime ministers. The *kālaimoku* also guided the distribution of conquered lands, for the lesser chiefs expected the ruling chief to attempt to increase his chiefdom through warfare.

While the advisor was directing the distribution of the new lands conquered in a successful war, the *Holoae* would prepare for the dedication of a new *luakini*. The *luakini*, the most sacred temple in the chiefdom, symbolized the supernatural mandate of the ruling chief to rule. After each conquest it was necessary for existing *luakini* to be rededicated by the conqueror. The principal component of the ritual was the 'binding up of the land', a ceremony in which the ruling chief acknowledged *Kū*'s ownership of both conquered and existing lands of the chiefdom (Davenport 1964: 24–25).

Succession to the office of *ali'i nui* at the natural death of the occupant was governed ideally by the distribution of *mana* among the existing *ali'i*. In Hawaii, *mana* was a kind of sacred power, one that could be inherited, acquired, or lost. *Mana* was inherited from both parents, passing in fact to the first-born (*hiapo*) child of equal-ranked parents. A child born *hiapo* of both parents would receive the *mana* of both, placing him at a higher rank than children born later to both parents or of a parent's later marriage. In fact, the *hiapo* child would be higher ranked than either parent (Handy and Pukui 1958: 58). If as in theory, the *ali'i nui* was in fact the highest ranked member of his chiefdom, the royal *hiapo* should be an automatic choice. However, at least two factors intervened in the operation of the natural rights of *mana*.

Because *mana* could be lost as well as acquired, it was possible to demonstrate empirically a shift in the affections of the deities. A rite (*ka-lii*) associated with the season of *Makahiki* required the ruling chief to renew his claim to rule. The paramount chief would come by canoe to an appointed place. The *maka'ainana* would mockingly attempt to prevent his landing. The ruling chief with his warriors would force his way to shore, thereby demonstrating his royal rights (Handy, 1931: 61–62). To what degree the mock defense was a sham battle is unknown. However, it is reasonable to suggest that the rite included elements of *ritual rebellion* (Gluckman, 1963). Conversely Kamehameha is said to have regularly demonstrated his *mana* by catching spears thrown at him during the *Makahiki* landings.

A second factor affecting the succession by *mana* was the division of the rule into two parts: possession of the land and possession of the war-god, *Kū*. Although this division was apparently rare, the legendary basis for it was firm and its historical operation critical during the post-contact period. The mythic charter for the division has its source in the legend of *'Umi*. As the tale reveals several of the principles noted about, we shall offer a synopsis of the legend.

The ruling chief of Hawaii, *Liloa*, met a woman bathing and was enamored with her. The woman, *Akahi*, was a commoner and yielded to *Liloa's* advances. 'If you have a child', *Liloa* said, 'and it is a girl, name her after your family. If it is a boy, name him for me'.

In fact a boy was born and was named *'Umi-a-Liloa*. Although *'Umi* was reared as part of the family, the father often beat him. Until *Akahi* finally stopped him by proving that *'Umi* was the son of a chief. The proof was a helmet, a *lei palaoa* (ivory neck pendant which symbolized *ali'i* birth) and a loin cloth given her by *Liloa*. *'Umi* was now about ten years old and decided to visit his royal father. After adventures which need not concern us here, *'Umi* arrives at the court of *Liloa* and shocked everyone by sitting on his lap. *Liloa* asked, 'Whose child are you?' 'Yours! I am *'Umi-a-Liloa*.'

The helmet, pendant and loin cloth were proof enough and *Liloa* declared *'Umi* his son.

Liloa also had a high rank son, *Hākau*, born of a high rank chieftess. *'Umi* and *Hākau* soon became rivals. Eventually *Liloa* named *Hākau* to be the heir to the chieftancy. However, at the same time he named *'Umi* to be the guardian of *Kū*.

After the death of *Liloa*, *Hakau's* jealously and irresponsible rule forced *'Umi* to flee, taking the idol of *Kū* with him. In turn, the *Holoae* came to *'Umi* to persuade him to mount rebellion, which through trickery, was successful. *'Umi* married the daughter of *Liloa* in order to maximize the rank of his children. In fact, *'Umi-a-Liloa* had so many wives and children that in later generations, any commoner could declare *'Umi* among his ancestors. (The legend usually contains a disclaimer: 'If a Hawaiian said such a foolish thing, it showed he was ignorant of his ancestry'.)

The importance of this mythic charter for rebellion by lesser-ranked *ali'i* cannot be fully assessed during the pre-contact period for lack of a recorded example. However, in the immediate post-contact era (and probably before significant culture change had occurred due to that contact), the ruling chief of Hawaii, *Kalani'op'u* had split the rule between his son, *Kiwaloa*, and his fraternal nephew, *Kamehameha*, who was given *Kū*. The entire mythic cycle repeated itself, only this time ending in the complete conquest of all the islands of Hawaii. *Kamehameha*, in turn, divided the land and god in his last will. However, the course of events was reversed by a number of new forces including the Western contact. *Kū's* guardian was defeated in rebellion and the whole superstructure of native deities was abolished in 1819.

Basically we must regard the loss of *mana* and the division of 'church and state' as exceptional cultural products. But, they demonstrate that the political culture provided the means to adjust to extreme malfeasance. However, direct conflict among the several ruling chiefs was usually sufficient to restructure power relations: in fact, was the norm rather than the exception. The only fixed period of peace was the four-month season of the *Makahiki*.

Makahiki was the season of *Lono* and was attended to by the *Kuali'i*. It was a time of tax-collecting, games, and renewal rites. The ruling chief, the ceremonial representative of *Lono*, received contributions of goods and food-stuffs, especially pork, as the *Kuali'i* went to each *ahupua'a* (named for the pig shrine located at each valley's border) to release the land from existing *kapus* (Yamamura 1949: 35). These *kapus* consisted of three basic types of regulations. First, production *kapus* regulated sacred crafts and professions. Secondly, consumption *kapus* governed patterns of harvesting and eating arrangements. The third set were based on dangerous *mana*, particularly that associated with high birth.

Production *kapus* regulated the major production specializations in the culture — canoe builder, fish master, house planner — as well as numerous ritual crafts such as the *hula*, priestcraft and the like. Both the practice and recruitment to these professions was controlled. In particular, sex discrimination was marked; each profession was restricted to a single sex. Male vocations were ranked higher than female ones which included the making of *kapa* cloth and baskets. The male vocations were rigidly controlled by either heredity or by a systematic apprenticeship (Handy 1931: 16). Once admitted and trained, a man's practice was dictated by conventionalized procedures and supported by the force of prospective *kapus*. To break a *kapu* frequently meant immediate execution.

In addition to production *kapus*, the harvesting and consumption of foodstuffs was regulated by *kapus*. Planting was controlled by the lunar calendar maintained by the *Kauli'i*. Similarly, harvesting of crops or marine products would be systematically determined by specific *kapus*. Thus, after Western contact had indicated the value of virgin sandalwood forests in Hawaii, *Kamehameha* placed areas of trees under *kapu*, as he said, 'for my grandchildren'.

Consumption patterns were also controlled by *kapu*. The basic trophic demands of the Hawaiian population were met by a diet of fish and *poi*. Although the basic diet of both sexes was the same, they could not share a dining place or common ground oven. The rule of *'ai kapu* ('eating taboo') extended from this prohibition of men and women eating together to specific items which were restricted for male consumption only. Foodstuffs prohibited for women ranged from pigs to bananas.

Birth *kapus* were associated with the *mana* received from the child's parents. The number of possible *kapu* ranks was enormous (Beckwith 1932) because all chiefs could claim descent from legendary gods. However, only members of the top three *kapu* ranks were regarded as eligible to become ruling chiefs. As we have seen in the story of *'Umi*, royal marriage was very much manipulated in order to maximize *kapu* ranks. Marriages between full brother and sister were not uncommon among the *ali'i*. Similarly, marriages of 'political convenience' were regularly arranged. These frequently resulted in a clear separation of a ruling chief's 'sacred wife' from his 'favorite wife'. The roles of *Kamehameha*'s two principal wives in the events of 1819 need not be told here, but they indicate the potential power of royal household working in concert (Seaton 1974).

The top *kapu* rank was the *kapu moe* ('prostrating kapu'). It was associated with the offspring of *nī'aupī'o* marriages, that is, marriages in which both partners were already of the *kapu moe*. If the parents were full brother and sister, the *nī'aupī'o* marriage produced an *akua* ('god') offspring. An *akua* child, in addition, to receiving *kapu moe*, would himself be restricted in various ways to prevent his exposing others to his *wela* ('burning'). The next ranked *kapu* was the *noho* which was the product of a *naha* marriage, a marriage of half-siblings or unrelated but equally ranked parents. Rather than fully prostrating themselves, lesser-ranked individuals needed only remain seated in the presence of a *kapu noho*. The lowest royal rank of *kapu* was the *wohi* ('sitting'). The *wohi* resulted from marriages of unequally ranked individuals who were, nevertheless, *ali'i*.

Other *kapus*, while not directly involved in governing access to rule, did influence the conduct of rulers. For example, *Kamehameha* was required to prostrate himself before his first-born son, *Liholiho*. *Liholiho* had been born to *Kamehameha's* sacred wife, *Keopuolani*, who herself possessed the *'uha kapu* ('sacred lap') which meant death to any child she tried to rear herself (Handy and Pukui 1958: 195–196). One significant consequence of *Kamehameha's* unification of Hawaii was that for the first time in history all the Hawaiian people would live under a single set of *kapus*. The fact that *Liholiho* who became *Kamehameha II* would impose a particularly high set of *kapus* (making him *kapukapu noho'i e* 'difficult to approach') must have influenced some of the participants in the abolition of 1819.

Another example further illustrates the limits which the *kapu* system placed on rulers. Because of the *mana* associated with certain sites, zones of safety in which revenge or apprehension was *kapu*ed existed throughout Hawaii. If a *kapu*-violator or defeated enemy could reach any one of these sites, their life was protected.

3. THE ECOLOGICAL EQUILIBRIUM

The foregoing consideration indicate that Kroeber, Redfield, and Linton may have been essentially correct in suggesting that there was something fundamentally flawed in the Hawaiian culture at least in so far as the formation of a full state was concerned. That is, in view of the presence of a number of prerequisites for the formation of true states, e.g., class structure, warfare, territoriality, one would normally expect 500 years of autonomy to produce a fully articulated state apparatus. Two explanations are possible. First, the system *could* produce a true state but the right combination of factors had not yet occurred. In Gluckman's terms, the structural time of the system had not been exhausted. In this view, if it had not been for the intrusion of Westerners, the Hawaiians would have sooner or later established a complete state. The second explanation suggests that Hawaii was suspended in structural time having reached the limits of cultural elaboration without achieving full statehood. In this view, the intrusion of Westerners was essential to breaking up the equilibrial condition of the system. While the actual course of events reflect the formation of a modern state after Western contact, it is not clear what precise role the contact played in the unification and formation of the Hawaiian state. Fortunately, we can address the question of the failure of Hawaiians to form a true state directly by analyzing the operation of the pre-contact political culture.

The dynamic operation of the Hawaiian political system depended upon the interaction of the two major political divisions of labor, the rank–mana–taboo sub-system and the production–redistribution–consumption sub-system. We have already indicated how the *Makihiki* season drew these two components together as a series of rites of renewal and fertility. We now wish to examine the systemic importance of the season to the overall operation of the political system. Our thesis will be that the *Makahiki* constituted a ritual instrument for the regulation of the Hawaiian ecological system. Further, the effect of such regulation was the maintenance of a political equilibrium which precluded the formation of a state. The model of ritual regulation which we shall adopt is based on the works of Roy A. Rappaport concerning the Tsembaga of New Guinea (1967 1968; also cf. Adams 1975: 130–37).

In order to evaluate the thesis proposed, we must demonstrate that: (1) the *Mahakiki* festival cycle did in fact regulate the material exchanges among members of the ecological system, and (2) that under conditions of equilibrium, no state was possible. The first demonstration must be the identification of the systemic *means* for ecological regulation. Our task will be to specify the ritual displays which could serve the requisite indicator function. In turn, we must show that these displays *actually influenced* ecologically relevant Hawaiian behavior.

The Tsembaga's ritual cycle centers on the pig festival (*kaiko*) which lifts certain sexual and consumptory taboos, and involves the slaughter of most of the pig population. During the period of the *kaiko* (about a year), peace prevails, trading flourishes, marriages are arranged, and kinship alliances extended. After the *kaiko*, fighting is permitted and would continue until either victory or truce. The formal marker of the terminatio of hostilities is the planting of a ritual plant, the *rumbim*. As long as the *rumbim* is rooted, no member of the group may attack another or kill a pig. Uprooting of the *rumbim* signals the beginning of a new *kaiko* season.

Rappaport's analysis of the *kaiko* cycle indicates that the pig population (which is restored to its maximal population in five to ten years) places increasing pressures on the carrying capacity of the Tsembaga territory while the *rumbim* is in the ground. Eventually, the pressures of the pig population force their ritual slaughter during a new *kaiko*.

Thus, the ritual cycle balances the pig and human populations in the ecological system by regulating the principal exchanges among member groups. The entire process is rationalized and protected by the sanctification imposed by the beliefs of the Tsembaga. Once established, the ecological system through its successful operation reinforces the supernatural ideology. The obvious implication is of socio-cultural equilibrium (cf. Rappaport 1971).

In order to evaluate the application of the ritual regulation thesis to pre-contact Hawaii, we must demonstrate that: (1) the *Makahiki* cycle did in fact regulate the material exchanges among members of the ecological system, (2) that the *Makahiki* was sanctified in such a manner as to integrate the political culture into maintenance of its political superstructure, and (3) the overall effect was political equilibrium.

The *Makahiki* season marked the beginning of a new lunar year for the Hawaiians. The season covered four months starting with the end of the growing period (*Kau*) and continuing into the *Hoo-ilo*, 'when the sun declined towards the south, when the nights lengthened, when days and nights were cool, when herbage died away' (Malo 1951: 141).

Games, sports and other forms of recreation were attended to by *ali'i* and *maka'ainana*. A series of renewal ceremonies were conducted through the *moku*. It is to these specific ceremonies which we shall turn.

The series of renewal ceremonies began with the first *kapu* days of *Ku* in the lunar month of *Ikuwa* with the suspension of services at the royal *heiau*. On the eighteenth day of the next month (*Weleehu*), the *ali'i nui* levied taxes on the districts in his *moku*. On the twenty-first, goods collected by the *konohiki* were distributed among the royal court. On the twenty-third, an image of *Lono-makau* ('father Lono') was constructed in a manner resembling a rigged sail (thereby the association of Cook with *Lono* according to Malo [1951: 145]). After a purification ceremony, the idol began a circuit of the *moku* accompanied by the royal tax-collectors. Once sufficient taxes had been collected, the *kahuna* would release the district from the *kapus* associated with the purification (no work, travel or bathing). Subsequently, the land itself was released from *kapu* and was permitted to be worked (Malo 1951: 47).

The circuit of *Lono-makua* was completed on the sixteenth of the next month, *Makalii*, with the return of the image to the *luakini*. With the return of the image came the ceremony *ka-lii* ('acting the king'). The *ka-lii*, as described earlier, has the elements of a rite of rebellion. The linking of this rite to the return of *Lono-makua* emphasizes the *mana*-based right to rule.

On the eighteenth, the *Makahiki* idols were dismantled and stored in the *luakini*. At the close of the day, the *kahuna* conducted a ceremony called 'the net of *Maoloha*' (*koko a Maoloha*). This ceremony consisted of the filling of a large mesh net with foodstuffs and then lifting and shaking it to make the food items fall through. If the food failed to fall, the *kahuna* declared that there would be a famine in the land; otherwise, the coming growing season would be fruitful (Malo 1951: 151).

During the next month until the *kapu* days of *Kaulua*, the eating *kapus* specifically associated with *Makahiki* (bans on pork, *aku* fish, etc.,) were incrementally lifted. The ordinary *kapus* returned in *Kaulua* along with the normal religious observances. After the return of the *kapus* and in declaration of his policy for the next eight months, the *ali'i nui* ordered the construction of a new *heiau*.

Five types of *heiaus* could be built, each reflecting a separate state policy. By ordering the construction of an ordinary *luakini*, the ruler indicated the renewed right to rule his territory per the status quo. Construction of a *luakini honolulu ai* signaled appreciation of an abundant harvest. A *luakini kaua* declared the ruler's intention to go to war. The selection of any one of the *luakini* types *heiau* thus reflected a satisfactory state of affairs within the *moku*. Of course without specific environmental data, we can only speculate as to the correlates of such decisions. However, from the fact that the total set of decision options includes two further types which reflect specific forms of dissatisfaction, it is reasonable to conclude that success was similarly differentiated. Therefore, let us suggest that the ordinary type indicated ecological balance within the *moku*. The second type would suggest the over-supply of food to population or simply a small population relative to carrying capacity. The *kaua*-type could likely be selected under conditions of population pressure for expansion. Of course, in view of the options reflecting inadequate production, we must assume that the *luakini kaua* was built at a perceived optimal point in the supply–demand curve.

The *ali'i nui* could select from two different types of *heiaus* if the *Makahiki* had indicated trouble with the basic fertility of his *moku*. As the sea and the land were the sources of Hawaiian foodstuffs, the *heiau loulu* directed prayers to the needs of fishermen, while the *heiau mao* addressed agriculture. The information necessary to determine which type of deficiency existed came, as for the successes, from the rituals and taxes evidence during *Makahiki*. Completion of the construction of the projected *heiau* placed the *moku* in a state ready for action, either expansion, defense or retreat.

In terms of political system, then, we may surely conclude that the *Makahiki displayed* the systemic status. The next question is whether it regulated that status or not. Without the precise measurement of the material exchanges which define the ecological system, we must rely on indirect measurement in order to approximate an answer to the question. Such indirect measurement will assess the material potentiality of the decision-making ritual apparatus evidenced in the Hawaiian political culture. Clearly we must separate the supernatural rationale from the actual achievements of the ritual cycle. However, it will be apparent that the Hawaiians possessed empirical referents for supernaturally sanctioned objectives of their rituals.

Let us begin this review of the ritual regulation of the political system of the *pristine* state in Hawaii by noting the points of similarity with the Tsembaga case described earlier. The ideological rationalization of the *kaiko* cycle is based on Tsembaga beliefs in ancestorial spirits, rejection of the ideology would affect the territorial claim. The ideological rationalization of the *Makahiki* cycle is based on beliefs in *mana* with all of its influence in war and fertility. As the rule of the *ali'i* is based on their claim to *mana*, the *Makahiki* is central to their legitimacy.

Whereas the *kaiko* is triggered by the growth in the pig population (which is subject to feral breeding), the *Makahiki* is a fixed calendar ritual. However, the epideictic function of communicating to participants information concerning the size or density of the group is similar (Wynne-Edwards 1962: 16). That is, given the annual production cycle of the Hawaiians, the *Makahiki* denotes at least a minimal harvest quota. As the Hawaiian trophic system was more complex than the Tsembaga's, we should expect a more highly differentiated epideictic function. Hence, we must examine the individual components of the *Makahiki* to detail the elements of regulation.

The test of productivity symbolized by the *koko a Maoloha* operationally measured the overall harvest as articulated through the *Lonomakua* taxation circuit. We should note that this is a second-order function which could be affected by popular resistance to paying taxes or corruption among the tax-collectors. Thus, while the *koko a Maoloha* parallels the *kaiko*, it is subject to more covert manipulation (cf. Rappaport 1971, on ritual sanctity). Nevertheless, the *koko a Maoloha* served to integrate the material exchange cycle with the ideological matrix.

The *ka-lii* rite of rebellion, like the *koko* ritual, has its cognitive origins in the conception of *mana* as a force or energy. That is, the *ali'i* was required to demonstrate his *mana* by forcing his re-entry into the *moku*. Successful re-entry then re-established the political superstructure upon the *moku*. Expressed through the rank subsystem, this superstructure determined the proper redistribution of exchange items. Particularly central to this ritual integration was the display of the rights to the land itself. As noted in Table II, the land tenure system articulated the entire rank-based political hierarchy.

The final phrase of the *Makahiki* season was the selection and construction of a suitable *heiau*. We have already reviewed the variety of models available. Common with the construction of any of the models was the reimposition of the ordinary *kapu* regime. Thus, the enforcement of the normal *kapus* associated with consumption returned with the new *heiau*. We should remark that it was these specific eating *kapus* which were the overt targets in the abolition movement in 1819.

In summarizing the ritual regulation of the *pristine* eco-system, Table IV is helpful. Each of the major sub-systems of the *pristine* state is arranged and distributed across the systemic elements of inputs, conversion, and outputs. That the system as a whole constitutes a regulatory mechanism is virtually inescapable. The ideological matrix provided a cognitive structure sanctifying the ritual displays which sanctioned the material exchange patterns in the state. Added to the conceptual closeness of this regulatory network, the geographical isolation of the Hawaiians guaranteed that the *pristine* system would be a closed system.

Table IV. *Ritual regulation in the pristine state*

	Input	Conversion	Output
Ideology	Mana	Rank	Kapu
Ritual	Koko *a* Maoloha	*Ka-lii*	*Heiau* construction
Exchange	Production	Redistribution	Consumption

Of course, not all closed systems are equilibrial systems. If the ecology had been subject to important climatic fluctuations or geomorphic changes, such stochastic factors might have prevented any significant degree of system building at all. On the other hand, the overall dynamic of the regulatory mechanism might have been governed by positive feedback. In this case, the eco-system would have either exhausted its carrying capacities or achieving a maximal sustained-yield level. Although there is not present means to testing the positive feedback hypothesis, two factors argue against it. First, the eco-system clearly had not been exhausted at the time of contact. Food and water were readily available to Western ships. It is unlikely that if the system were in a run-away loop that it wouldn't have consumed itself in 500 years of isolation. Second, the sustained-yield alternative is faulted by the fact that the abolition of 1819 while post-contact, the abolition seems to have represented the release of long-standing pressures. These pressures should not have been present if optimality had previously been achieved.

In short, the only supported conclusion is that the *pristine* state was in an ecological equilibrium maintained by the integrated ritual cycle centered around *Makihiki*. Each component of the political culture reinforced the next in systemic sequence. The sanctification of the tax-collection procedures insured the accuracy of the ritual redistribution and display. The utility of the conversion processes reinforced the *kapu* proscriptions over consumption which in turn supported the production schedule. Thus, the systemic integrity of the ritual/ideology was insolated from challenge. The failure of one *ali'i nui* was the success of another who honored the same religious matrix as those he dispossessed.

4. CONCLUSION

As our responsibility has been to report the characteristics and dynamics of the early Hawaiian state, and as it is others' duties to draw comparative generalizations from the totality of materials to be presented in this volume, we shall restrict our closing comments severely.

If there is a single most important feature to the Hawaiian case, it must be the failure of political development. Perhaps no place on Earth is as blessed in natural resources and beauty as the Hawaiian Islands. Few cultures have been permitted as much independence in their ethnic evolution as the early Hawaiians. Yet, the *pristine* state was not a tropical paradise. The lack of advanced political institutions did not guarantee equality or security. Rather the Hawaiian state, in each of its subdivisions, offered little more than Hobbes' 'state of general war' in which neither group or individual could pursue much beyond their means of existence. Of course, it would be difficult to say that the quality of life in Hawaii had been improved by Western contact and colonization. Even today, the handful of contemporary ethnic Hawaiians live on the margins of the society which has come to their islands. Yet revitalization of their indigenous culture would promise them little. Perhaps, they should remind us of the awful consequences entailed in the paradox of freedom and the state.

REFERENCES

Adams, Richard N. (1975), *Energy and structure: a theory of social power.* Austin: University of Texas Press.
Almond, Gabriel A. (1956), 'Comparative political systems', in: *Journal of Politics* 18: 391–409.
Almond, Gabriel A. and Powell, Jr., Bingham (1966), *Comparative politics: a developmental approach.* Boston: Little, Brown.
Almond, Gabriel A. and Verba, Sidney (1965), *The civic culture.* Boston: Little, Brown.

Beckwith, Martha W. (1932), *Kepelino's traditions of Hawaii: rank among the chiefs*. Honolulu: Bishop Museum Bulletin no. 95.

Bellwood, Peter (1975), 'The prehistory of Oceania', in: *Current Anthropology* 16: 9–28.

Davenport, W. (1964), 'Hawaiian feudalism', in: *Expedition* 6: 10–27.

Easton, David (1965), *A systems analysis of political life*. New York: Jolin Wiley.

Finney, Ben R. (1967), 'New perspectives on Polynesian voyaging, in: *Polynesian culture history*, ed. by G. A. Highland et al. Honolulu: Bishop Museum Special Publication 56: 141–66.

Fried, Morton H. (1967), *The evolution of political society*. New York: Random House.

Gluckman, Max (1963), *Order and rebellion in tribal Africa*. Glencoe: The Free Press.

Green, Roger (1967), 'The immediate origins of the Polynesians', in: *Polynesian culture history*, ed. by G. A. Highland et al., Honolulu: Bishop Museum Special Publication 56: 215–40.

Handy, E. S. Craighill (1931), *Cultural revolution in Hawaii*. Honolulu: Institute of Pacific Relations.

Handy, E. S. C. and Pukui, Mary Kawena (1958), *The Polynesian family system in Ka-u Hawaii*. Wellington, New Zealand: The Polynesian Society.

Hansen, F. Allan (1973), 'Political change in Tahiti and Samoa: an exercise in experimental anthropology', in: *Ethnology* XII: 1–13.

Kelly, Marion (1967), 'Some problems with early descriptions of Hawaiian culture', in: *Polynesian culture history*, ed. by G. A. Highland et al., Honolulu: Bishop Museum Special Publication 56: 399–410.

Lind, Andrew W. (1938), *An island community*. Chicago: University of Chicago Press.

Malo, David (1951), *Hawaiian antiquities*. Honolulu: Bishop Museum Press.

Pye, Lucien W. (1965), 'Political culture and political development', in: *Political culture and political development*, ed. by Lucien W. Pye and Sidney Verba, pp. 3–26. Princeton: Princeton University Press.

— (1973), 'Culture and political science: problems in the evaluation of the concept of political culture', in: *The idea of culture in the social sciences*, ed. by Louis Schneider and Charles Bonjean, pp. 65–76. Cambridge: Cambridge University Press.

Rappaport, Roy A. (1967), 'Ritual regulation of environmental relations among a New Guinea people', in: *Ethnology* 6: 17–30.

— (1968), *Pigs for the ancestors*. New Haven: Yale University Press.

— (1971), 'The sacred in human evolution', in: *Annual Review of ecology and systematics* 2: 23–44.

Rosenbaum, Walter A. (1975), *Comparative political culture*. New York: Praeger Publishers.

Seaton, S. Lee (1974), 'The Hawaiian *Kapu* abolition of 1819', in: *American Ethnologist* 1: 193–206.

Service, Elman R. (1975), *Origins of the state and civilization*. New York: Norton.

Verba, Sidney (1965), 'Comparative political culture', in: *Political culture and political development*, ed. by Lucien W. Pye and Sidney Verba. Princeton: Princeton University Press: 512–60.

Webb, M. C. (1965), 'The abolition of the taboo system in Hawaii', in: *Journal of the Polynesian Society* 74: 21–39.

Wynne-Edwards, V. C. (1962), *Animal dispersion in relation to social behavior.* London: Oliver and Boyd.

Yamamura, Douglas S. (1949), *A study of some factors contributing to the status of contemporary Hawaiians.* Doctoral dissertation, Seattle, University of Washington.

14 Early State of the Incas

RICHARD P. SCHAEDEL

1. FORMATION OF THE INCA STATE

There is general agreement among old standard sources and the new ethnohistorical studies on the tribal antecedents of the Inca state. Thus Means' summary (1931: 205–242) amended by Kauffmann (1973) which would have the probable formation of the dynasty and the hypothetical reign of the first chief of the Incas, Manco Capac, in the eleventh century is still accepted by most authorities. The likelihood that the legendary thirteen-king list has some rough correspondence to the fact has been questioned by Zuidema (1964) who considers the Inca kings to have always been paired according to moiety halves.

Sometime around the middle of the thirteenth century the Inca were a tribal group occupying a part of the Cuzco basin along with other tribal groups. The second Incas bear the title of *Sinchi* or chief and references to the first four Incas refer to marriages with local chiefdoms. In the course of the fourteenth century the Inca seem to have established a chiefdomship within the Cuzco basin, assuming a *primus inter pares* relationship with tribes at either end of the basin and in the pampa de Anta. Nothing in the archaeological record indicates manifestations of statehood until the fifteenth century.

The crucial period of transformation from chiefdom to state is almost surely related to events taking place in the early fifteenth century when the Inca chiefdom became engaged in warfare with chiefdoms to the south of the Cuzco basin.[1] We have no clear information on how the Inca assimilated the other tribes of the Cuzco basin into their chiefdomship, but it would appear to have been by a combination of alliances and warfare.

We have no reason to suppose there existed a specialized coercive institution in Inca society at the turn of the fifteenth century. The question of the initial dynamics that precipitated the Incas into a plan of expansion by conquest between 1400–1450 remains shrouded in mystery. It would appear that the environment of the south and central highlands of Peru from the late thirteenth century was one in which regional chiefdoms maintained an oscillatory pattern of encroachment and retrenchment with their contiguous neighbors, along with smaller polities which fissioned or aggregated to the regional chiefdoms according to their strategic position and capacity for enclavement.

Most chroniclers are in consensus in ascribing the initial expansion of the Incas to a defensive operation against the Chancas, who after having sustained a 'cold war' with the Incas for perhaps a decade or so, while 'colonizing' the Quechua chiefdom, invaded the pampa de Anta on the northern periphery of the Incas. The description of the battle and the ad-hoc recruitment of fighters on both sides certainly gives no indication that either had a very effective institutionalized mechanism of warfare. The famous battle of Xaquixahuana, won by Pachacutec, while his aging father, Viracocha, remained in retreat in Muyna at the southern extreme of the basin, marked the turning point in converting the Inca chiefdom into a predatory superchiefdom and, within the lifetime of Pachacutec, into a state.

Katz (1972: 270–272) has probably best analyzed and described the underlying dynamics of this paramount chiefdom, which seems to have encompassed the first twenty-five years after Pachacutec's victory. His analysis of a predatory chiefdom, based upon the rapid incorporation of the subdued peoples into a cumulative pattern of expansive aggression followed by rewarding with spoils, best accounts for the dynamics that enabled the Incas to expand the ecological base of a regional chiefdom into one that could support a state. The hypothesis that any change in the technical relations of production at this time was determinant so far lacks any ethnohistorical or archaeological confirmation. It is likely that a technical transformation in the productive relations took place as a response of the administrative elite of the chiefdom to the control and assimilation of conquered peoples during the comet-like expansion of Pachacutec's armies. This kind of conversion of the coordination of the redistributed surpluses of the subject chiefdoms through a network of roads, bridges and storehouses seems to have anteceded a later technical change, having to do with public works and the manipulation of *mit'a* labor on large irrigation, terracing and river channeling projects, which as nearly as we can infer from the archaeological record date to the last decades of the fifteenth century.

It would appear then that the Inca in the period 1425–50 represent an expanding chiefdom, presenting all the characteristics of an Oppenheimer 'Conquest state', and that the formation of the state took place somewhere after 1450 with the attempts of Pachacutec to consolidate the peoples that had been subdued by *Blitzkrieg* tactics into a system of permanent control. This involved a spatial and demographic widening of the capital to encompass and administer a massive storage and redistributional apparatus and the elaboration of a reticulated system of supply, defense and maintenance of roads for moving people and produce. In order to support the control between collecting points (provincial capitals) and the capital, Pachacutec had to consolidate their several surplus energies into a massive flow chart (looking much like the circulatory system of an octopus). The building of these systems (at the capital and at the provincial capital) constituted the change in the technical relations of production. It was not transformational in its initial phase, since technological productivity was not modified, but was in fact additive, in that the surplus energies were systematically channelled toward one central redistributive system instead of forty odd individual systems in the pre-existent states and chiefdoms.[2]

From 1450 to perhaps 1475 we may assume Pachacutec supervised the establishment of these systems and their integration constituted the first transformation in the technical relations of production.[3] The phase 1450–75 may also have been the period when the Inca state underwent a second change (in the technical relations of production). The change was predicated upon the widening of the Cuzco area to encompass an administrative sector that could plan and execute public works through the *mitayo* system of provincially allocated seasonal labor. This was essentially a method of centralizing 'dead season' agricultural labor between sowing and harvesting from most of the provinces in Cuzco, then reallocating the manpower to the projects, either in Cuzco itself, or the circum-Cuzco area. The massive corvée work force is alleged to have numbered in the tens of thousands; and these levies were utilized among other objectives in the channelling of the Ururbamba River, the building or extension of the longer irrigation systems (particularly in the highlands) and large-scale terracing projects.[4]

Probably related to this technical change in productive relations, guaranteeing the subsistence base of the state, was the incorporation of the 'socio-economic' *mitimae* into the empire-wide redistributive system. The *mitimae* probably owe their origin as an institution to the proto state phase of cumulative predatorism, when communities were removed wholesale from areas recently conquered where there was reason to expect insurgency, and sent to ecologically similar, but far distant zones. Together with this type of transplantation or forced emigration was the implantation of 'garrisons' in zones of probable insurgency of communities of Inca-by-privilege, communities which had been part either of the original Inca chiefdom or its immediate allies to the north or south. This kind of 'security' *mitimae* is contrasted by Espinoza (1969-70: 9–10) with the socio-economic *mitimaes*, which were communities, or segments of communities, moved from their original lands to either develop a resource not exploited in an ecologically similar zone (introduce llamas, grow coca) or develop a handicraft, the production of which was needed at a critical juncture in the processing of goods moving from the provinces to Cuzco. These *mitimae* 'colonies' or 'enclaves' were directly subject to the authority of the Inca political governor of the province and their production in goods or raw materials directly tied to the flow of products to Cuzco.[5]

It is clear that tribal structure persisted into the state, both at the provincial and capital level. The Inca used the kinship system to maintain their ethnic stratification at the top. At the lower levels, however, new classes were being formed by mobile groups, uprooted from their kin-groups; and marriage alliances among *yanaconas, acllas* and provincial nobility cross-cut old kin patterns. On these new bases for which no rules are extant, the middle strata of Inca society were largely structured.

2. SPATIAL, ECOLOGICAL AND DEMOGRAPHIC PARAMETERS

Despite considerable disagreement as to when various parts of the Inca state were penetrated, occupied and incorporated (Schaedel 1966: 339) there exists remarkable unanimity not only in the historical and ethnohistorical accounts, but also in the archaeological research done on the Incas on their maximum territorial extension. The Maule River in Chile forms the southern frontier, and the Ancasmayo River in what is now the border between Ecuador and Colombia forms the northern boundary. To the east the actual boundary lines are not as precise, although essentially the eastern border terminates as the eastern Andes grade off into the tropical rain forest at about the 1,000 m elevation. This holds as far south as Cochabamba, after which one can extend the line from Cochabamba to Tucumán to Mendoza, and to close in to the Pacific Ocean at Constitución in Chile.

This territory of some 984,000 km² was the largest territorial state in universal history to be united by non-quadrupedal locomotion. Its extent rather than sheer size emphasizes the point that the reticulated system of roads (supplied, maintained and defended) was the technological linch pin in the first major shift in the technical relations of production that brought the Inca state into being and allowed it to grow. The territory was divided only into two political levels of control, the capital and the provincial headquarters. The patterning shown by proximity and dispersal of provincial headquarters is a rough indication of the areas of high density and productivity and of the low. Of the eighty-odd provincial capitals, few can be denominated true cities, but most of those which we have been able to confirm archaeologically would be considered as either large towns, towns or nucleated villages (Schaedel 1969).

The ecological correlation with the territorial extent of Tawantinsuyu (Four Corners, or Sections) is deceptively close. This has lead some writers such as Manuel Valle (1964) to advance the argument that the ecological macro-niches into which the Incas divided the Andes determined not only the extent of the empire, but was the determinant in the division of the empire into four *suyus*. Antisuyu obviously corresponds to this explanation, since it is entirely on the eastern slopes of the Andes and is uniformly characterized by the closely juxtaposed cluster of niches from highland to tropical lowlands. By and large, Antisuyu bounds most of the eastern frontier, but it does not extend to the northernmost fringes, which are part of Chinchaysuyu nor to the southernmost, which pertain to Collasuyu. Collasuyu generally corresponds to the *puna* or altiplano macroniche, most of which in the central Andes is south of La Raya pass. But there are sections of *puna* in the central and of *paramos* in the northern Andes that fall within Condesuyu and Chinchaysuyu; and there are 'yunga' (lowland) areas, both dry and humid, encompassed within Collasuyu.

Chinchaysuyu covers most of the main concentrations of densely settled coastal kingdoms and chiefdoms, but there are important south coast centers and valleys that are in Condesuyu and a large sector of the central and northern highlands is in Chinchaysuyu. Condesuyu is also predominantly highland, but also includes zones of *puna* and coastal lowlands.

Thus, although one can perceive in Inca territorial divisions, an underlying principle of ethnoecology of dividing the Andes into four principal macro-niches that may well have been applicable to the original division of the state (at Pachacutec's organizational period 1450–1475), it did not correspond to the final extension of the state.[6]

The demographic parameters of the empire have been the most disputed. Estimates of Dobyns' 37,000,000, Means' maximum 32,000,000, and minimum 16,000,000, Smith's 12,139,498, Rowe's 6,000,000,

Steward's 3,500,000, Kroeber's 3,000,000, and Kubler's 3,000,000 all rest on some evidence, but the methods employed are all subject to serious errors in assumptions. Surprisingly enough, no authors (except for Kosok 1965: 35–36, in estimating coastal population) have used the carrying capacity of the present area encompassed as a check on maximum population.

Our calculations based in part upon Smith's interpretation of the data from the highlands, and part of which is based upon Kosok's estimates for the coast, yield a figure of ca. 8,000,000 for the Inca state. If one assumes the 'metropolitan area' or 'federal district' of Cuzco harbored 200,000, one gets an average of less than 100,000 per province. The larger ones such as Chuccuito probably had in excess of 150,000 (Smith: 7), while the smallest ones may not have exceeded 10,000. Probably few were much smaller, and there certainly were none in excess of 200,000.

While it is clear that the decimal system was not imposed rigorously over the provincial divisions of the empire as Means and Urteaga have suggested, there does seem to be growing archaeological and ethnohistorical confirmation for the existence of a principle of ordering the populations of provinces within decimal magnitudes which would account for disaggregation (as in the case of the Chimu state with 750,000 inhabitants) and the aggregation of the small chiefdoms into the Huanuco province. In a state of the magnitude of Tawantinsuyu without a writing system, one would suppose the existence of a number of ordering principles for reducing the complexity of census and tribute accounting.

The information on demographic trends in the last 1,000 years of Andean prehistory is simply not adequate to warrant any inferences as to whether demographic pressures played a role in the early formation of the Inca state. Later on, as Smith (1970: 8) points out, there are indications that non-expansionist warfare in Huayna Capac's reign and during the Huascar–Atahualpa struggle produced high casualties and would appear to have kept the growth rate low if not declining.

3. THE ECONOMY OF THE INCA STATE

We have seen how the Inca economy passed from a basically redistributive form to one of predatory surplus accumulation in which the newly conquered peoples were used as the new resource base for the expansion, and the peoples being long conquered were used to support them. Pachacutec then converted the several redistributive systems of the conquered chiefdoms into a centralized network with redistributive functions consolidated at provincial capitals and centralized in Cuzco.

This centralized redistribution was the first economic basis for the state. It was almost immediately followed by the formation of an independent state resource base in which the surplus energies of seasonal labor (*mitayo*), *yanacona* (or permanently allocated 'bondsmen'), and whole transplanted communities (*mitimaes*) were deployed to work two types of state land and exploit other resources exclusively for state consumption. Both systems depended upon the network of reticulated roads and waystations (*tambos*). The two systems coexisted for at least the last seventy-five years of the empire. For convenience of exposition, we shall refer to the first as the *redistributive system* (a label borrowed from Murra), and the second as the *state ownership system*.

3.1. The Redistributive System

Land tenure under this system was essentially based upon: (1) recognition of the prevailing system of land tenure and reapportionment in the conquered polity, and (2) separation of special arable lands and/or viable pastures to be farmed or herded for the Inca and the Sun (as well as other deities recognized by the Inca). In each province, at least ideally, there were three types of land.

(1) Land belonging essentially to the dominant ethnic group, which was to be exploited through the extant hierarchical arrangement for its own sustenance.

(2) Land dedicated to cultivation of crops necessary for the sustenance of the state religion (both at the provincial and partially at the national level).

(3) Land to be exploited for the maintenance of the secular state apparatus at the provincial and national level.

It is not yet clear whether these allocations of land for the state and state religion were effected at the sub-provincial level or were confined to the capital of the province. The administration of the exploitation seems to have been concentrated at the provincial level (fixing and maintaining of boundary markers, warehouses, determination of crop or herding patterns, allocation of surplus); while the labor seems to have been drawn from all the communities constituting the province.

Some writers assume that these allocated lands were created on the basis of outright expropriation, attributing to the Incas the articulation of the principle of eminent domain (and this probably can be documented for provinces where much resistance was encountered and the prevailing elite were either drastically reduced or eliminated). In other cases (and these seem to be in the majority) the Inca appear to have 'requisitioned' certain potentially cultivable areas (which may have been fallow or simply unused) to be set aside on a permanent basis for cultivation for one of the two state functions.

The labor relationships in this system would have been basically similar to the pre-existent ones in the conquered polity. As Murra (1966) has shown, even in the smaller polities, there were three kinds.

(1) The collective labor recruited at peak seasons for the working of lands of the chiefs (and administrative elite).

(2) Permanently, or semi-permanently 'loaned' individuals, or households, who were assigned to the chiefs largely on a consensus basis among the heads of lineages over which the chief presided, who represented a servile-retainer category, and whom the chief was obligated to feed, clothe and house (these later became recognized in the state as the *yanacona*).

(3) Those individuals (or more often households and segments of communities) who were assigned extra-territorial functions in niches different from their nuclear base, exploiting resources that were not available there.

For each of these three types of labor, as Murra points out, requests would have to be made, and in principle at least, the kin-group had to agree to their allocation and could withdraw its contribution.

It would also appear that in principle the Inca at the beginning of the centralization process attempted to preserve the implied reciprocity in 'requisitioning' sufficient labor to exploit the newly requisitioned land (witness the 'breaking of the earth' ceremony described by Cobo; Rowe 1946: 265). The numbers of *'yanacona'* retainers would also have had to be increased to man the storehouses, assume the permanent responsibilities for land management and in general contribute to the infrastructure of the metropolitan Cuzco area, where the provincial surpluses were being centralized and transformed into state-consumed and redistributed end-products. Until the second phase of the state economy, however, the drain of *yanaconas* would appear to have been slight from any one province. Emphasis in manpower demand in this phase of economic development was from the provincial capital, and one may infer that the flow of energies (to use Murra's term for what others refer to as tribute or taxation) was from community to provincial capital to enable the latter to act as a reliable collecting point for subsequently funnelling products and manpower into the main stream leading to Cuzco. Simultaneously, the emphasis in the Cuzco area seems to have been on providing the capital with the necessary infrastructure to coordinate the centripetal inflow of products and manpower from what probably at that point amounted to forty widely separated but still relatively adjacent provincial centers.

To this operation belonged the decree of Pachacutec, extending the ethnic label of Inca (by privilege) to the residents of the area adjacent to Cuzco, between Abancay and Quiquijana. By this device he widened the base of the ethnic elite from which the state could draw for staffing administrative and security functions which were interdigitated with those of the provincial elites. He thus articulated the body of the octopus with its forty tentacles. The labor of this group of Inca-by-privilege (which Murra appropriately calls the 'administrative Incas') seems to have been both servile and administrative. The personal attendants of the Inca were drawn on a seasonal and rotating basis from the adjacent communities (Murra 1956, says on a 'corvée' basis). This may well have been a device for binding this non-kin group to the Inca through intimacy and loyalty, which was constantly renewable. At any rate, the majority of the administrative Inca seem to have served as a pool from whence to draw middle-level functionaries for the state apparatus, who in turn had to be maintained either by the village of origin or by the allocation of *yanaconas* from the provinces. Here, as in the provinces, the drain of manpower was from the circum-Curzco region to the Ollantaytembo–Urcos axis, with Cuzco as center.[7]

The third labor category is the *mitimae*. Here again the likelihood is that the first *mitimae* were drawn from the circum-Cuzco area to insure a counter-insurgency force in rebellious provinces, and probably during the first redistributive phase of the Inca state, few *mitimaes* were drawn from the provinces. The first of which we have mentioned are from Nazca, who were settled (during the Pachacutec reign) in the valley floor of the Apurimac. Most of the references to *mitimaes* occur fairly late in the fifteenth century and on into the sixteenth.[8]

The actual increase in the productive forces that the centralization of the redistributive system should have produced was accomplished by diverting the manpower previously assigned to defensive and military activities to corvee labor of previously unworked lands.

3.2. *The State Ownership Phase of the Economy*

Hypothetically, the base for this new phase of the economy, which was linked to the redistributive one, was achieved by ca. 1475, shortly after the death of Pachacutec. The *hydrological* works, making the Cuzco basin, the upper Vilcañota and the Urubamba valley several times more productive than they had hitherto been, were well-advanced. These newly cultivable lands (properly speaking 'estates') were allocated to the Inca, the Sun, and the *panacas* (see below for *panacas*). Similar stretches of contiguous cultivable or pasturable land were allocated in other regions (Arapa). Cuzco itself had been remodelled to accomodate migrants from the four *suyus* and the major warehouses of the empire had been built. The road network and maintenance system had been the contribution of the provinces along with the provincial installations for provisioning and the movement of people and produce. While the state continued to derive revenue from the forty-odd 'and growing' tentacles of the octopus, the basis was now established for maintaining the Cuzco bureaucracy (secular and sacred) from resources in the circum-Cuzco area, providing that the labor supply for the new estates could be channelled into them. At this juncture the legitimization of *yanaconas* as a permanent labor force is clearly indicated. The tribute lists from the provinces that we possess record that large seasonal labor forces went to till fields and work on construction in Cuzco and a significant number of *yanaconas* was assigned to either Inca, Religion on *panaca* custodianship (Inigo Ortiz; Garci Diez).[9]

Neither the *yanaconas* nor the *mitimaes* were part of the redistributive economy. They formed the permanent work force of the state. The rest of the work force consisted of the seasonal labor draft or the administrative, technical, and professional categories of the bureaucracy.

Land tenure under this state ownership system can only be partially reconstructed. The lands of the sun present no real problem as they were administered by the state religion in corporate fashion. The state lands, or lands of the Inca, however, were, in part at least, divided into lands of the *panaca*, the descendants of the dead Incas. It is not clear whether all new lands developed by the reigning Inca passed into the custodianship of his *panaca* at his death.[10]

At the provincial level, the two types of state lands were administered, or at least supervised, by state delegated officials, and the *mitimae* enclaves constituted a specialized version of state tenure. Other lands in the provinces, however, were allocated by the Inca (or confirmed if the newly incorporated province already had such a system) for support of provincial and regional shrines. Otherwise the land tenure system seems to have followed the pre-Incaic pattern.

3.3. *Technology, Specialization, Organization of Production*

While the level of technology varied throughout the Tawantinsuyu, generally speaking, by the early fifteenth century, it was at a fairly uniform level from Tomebamba to Cochabamba. Whether in weaving, agriculture, wood-carving or masonry, the crafts had reached their peak prior to the Incas, and few technological increases occurred in Inca times (except via diffusion). The significant changes in technology came about in output. This occurred by two methods of organizing production. Large supra-community work forces were concentrated for major engineering projects (stream canalization, large-scale irrigation canals, large-scale terracing) on work that could only be accomplished between rainy seasons by a huge work force. Quarrying of huge blocks of stone for public buildings, many of which required special access roads, temporary retaining walls, etc.; stretches of highway that again needed to be completed or sufficiently well-buttressed between rainy seasons to avoid repetitive washouts and hence a massive labor force for from three to six months. These tasks fall into the construction–engineering category.

The second organization of production had to do with manufacture and transformational activities. Here the effort was placed on organizing the concentration of raw materials at some central point where the artisans could concentrate on elaborating a standard product. This applies to the weaving establishments of the *Acclacuna*, other weaving colonies (*mitimae*), provincial weaving establishments. Pottery was similarly processed by specially designated villages in this case (to the best of our knowledge) near to the raw material base; metallurgists were concentrated in Cuzco, where all metals (particularly gold and silver) were brought. It is clear that the higher grade textile workshops were in Cuzco, where a series of raw materials (not used in the others) were channelled exclusively, e.g., feathers, special dye-stuffs, possibly mordants, and probably the 'bangles' of metal, shell, etc., that were attached.

While both technological advances can be detected in the redistributive phase of the state economy, the heavy emphasis was on the engineering — construction technology — which laid the basis for the second phase. There is less evidence of late hydrological projects than there is for 'prestige' architecture. The product-transformation changes in production were characteristic of the state ownership economy and seem to be correlated with the expansion of the *mitimae* system.

4. THE POLITICAL, SOCIAL, AND RELIGIOUS ORGANIZATION

In the foregoing diachronic analysis of the economy, from the one based on the cumulative predatory distribution of spoils through one based upon the redistribution of surplus and corvee labor (Murra's 1956 model) to a state ownership ('*feudal–despotic*') phase, we have focused on shifts in the technical relations of production, which seemed to have been crucial. The corresponding changes in the social relations of production have been introduced in the new property relationship of state-owned resources, both natural and human. In explicating how these new property relationships affected the restructuring of the social relationships into the macro-group components of the 1530 Inca state, it will not be feasible to continue with the diachronic approach. We will have to 'freeze' the analysis at the demise of Huayna Capac, when the evidence is most abundant and consistent, rather than trace the growth of the institutions that accompanied the economic changes

4.1. *The Political Organization*

The government of Tawantinsuyu consisted of what we may term the federal bureaucracy, based in Cuzco and the circum-Cuzco area, and the eighty- provincial bureaucracies. Recruitment for the central bureaucracy at the decision-making level was (1) from the Incas-by-blood and (2) the Incas-by-privilege of the ethnic groups in the circum-Cuzco area. The provincial bureaucracies were drawn from the ruling lineages in the conquered polities. Middle and lower level posts in both bureaucracies were staffed mostly by *yanaconas*. The federal bureaucracy, at least in theory, included appointed governors (*tocricoc*) for each province, security enclaves (garrison *mitimaes*) in frontier and rebellious provinces as well as socio-economic *mitimae* enclaves.

The central bureaucracy is distinguished from the provincial bureaucracies in the civil administration to make clear the fact: (a) that with few exceptions the central bureaucracy was exclusively staffed by ethnic Incas (either by blood or privilege), and (b) that they were sustained for the most part by either outright income from state property or by exclusive access rights to specific surplus in goods or services (usually rights to retainers—*yanaconas*). In other words, members of the central bureaucracy could have been distinguished from the provincial bureaucracies by two criteria: ethnicity and source of income. The provincial elites were largely sustained by partial surplus of their own constituents and were non-Incas. That the total empire-wide redistributive economy allowed for numerous cases of central surpluses being funnelled back to provincial elites and (in times of prosperity or crisis) to grass-roots villagers, should not obscure the fact that the late Inca state operated on the basis of a central bureaucracy that was differentiated ethnically, economically and politically from its provincial underpinnings.

The central bureaucracy encompassed a series of functions that were performed at the provincial level as well as those that were specific to itself. Some of the economic functions (collection of tribute in the form of provision of raw and preliminarily processed materials and man and womanpower), certain of the religious (legitimizing) functions, the military function of the draft, and some jural functions (most of which had to be ratified by the central bureaucracy) were performed by the provincial elites in coordination with the central state apparatus. Exclusively administered by the central bureaucracy, however, was the production of high-status ritual and luxury goods; 'higher education'; census and cadastral compilation; transportation and communications;

'supreme court' sanctions; and, most important, the operation of the regal court. There is no clear-cut synthesis of how this central bureaucracy functioned, or how the discrete administrative units were hierarchized or interdigitated. There does not appear to exist any linguistic terminology that would indicate this 'bureaucracy' was so considered, either as a whole or from the component sub-divisions that we, using admittedly modern Western labels, have delineated.

There is every indication in the sources that the posts of highest responsibility were filled by a principle of kin-closeness. Nepotism certainly was a reigning principle in Inca 'public administration'. There are data on appointments and replacements in high office which indicate that certain lineages as well as moieties were specifically considered appropriate for certain categories of responsibility, but at this stage of research it is not possible to indicate in any detail how these kin statuses were correlated with the highest administrative statuses. One principle seems to be clear, that the Inca, *qua* absolute monarch, at any point in time could occupy the role of the chief of any division of government.

4.1.1. *The Central Bureaucracy.* Most of these institutions were rapidly destroyed by the Spanish conquest, so that it is possible to reconstruct only a shadow of them. There is enough evidence to show that institutions did exist which discharged the functions which are normally associated with a central bureaucracy.

4.1.2. *The Royal Court.* The matrix out of which the legitimacy of succession was guaranteed consisted of the institutions of the *panacas*, a device apparently created by Pachacutec to both honor the previous reigning Incas and to eliminate the threat of pretensions by their kinsmen. The *panacas* consisted of the family of the dead monarch and their descendants.

There were eleven *panacas*, each with a palace where the mummy of the principal Inca and his Coya (queen) were kept, as well as 'estates' which were allocated upon the death of the Inca and became a kind of corporate property, administered by the *panaca* heads. The property consisted not only of elite residences in the environs of Cuzco, but included shrines and lands for crop cultivation and pasturage. The evidence indicates that the stewards of *panaca* estates as well as the menials and some of the field and flock foremen, were drawn from the *yanaconas*, while the bulk of the unskilled labor was drawn annually from the corvee labor assignments.

The eleven *panacas* formed the basis of what might be termed the royal court, and their activities and personnel had much to do with maintaining the ritual calendar of the Inca state. The major secular center and focus of the court was the palace of the reigning Inca, but the focus for the *panaca* ritual activity was the principal plaza (Huacaypata). Most of the functions of the court were ritual. It is rather likely that *panaca* members provided a source for recruiting administrative chiefs and perhaps even military chiefs (captains general, as they are referred to by the Spanish chroniclers). Nevertheless, most references to the *panacas* have to do with their role as perpetuating the memory of their ex-Inca creator through daily and seasonal rites which seemed to have consumed much of the produce of their estates via sacrificial offerings. One can only speculate as to how the *panaca* members obtained the luxury goods (raiment, gold, and silver vessels, litters, etc.,) with which they were to perform their public acts. Since there is no reference to them having special artisan *yanaconas*, it would appear that the Inca and his stewards arranged a redistributional mechanism that took care of their provisioning. We only know that the Incas of Cuzco were given food every four days from the imperial storehouses (Rowe 1967: 62).

Outside the *panaca* corporations were the ten royal *ayllus* of upper and lower Cuzco from which the 'bailiffs' of the court were presumably appointed. They seem to represent kin groups without corporate property but from which the next potential *panaca* might be formed. It would appear that together, the corporate and non-corporate *ayllus* amounted to about twenty-five units of varying size. The royal *allyus* apparently maintained their residences in Cuzco, while the *panacas* seemed to have had their main residences in the principal 'estate' of the founder in the Cuzco or circum-Cuzco area and another in Cuzco (if their principal nucleus was elsewhere). Rostworowski (1960) summarizes the complexities of the operation (and intrigues) of the *panacas* in arranging for the succession of the Inca. It seems clear from her account and the references to the activities of the *panacas* and the royal *ayllus* that they behaved like most regal courts in Europe in the seventeenth century, i.e., they were responsible for the 'pomp and circumstance' of empire and 'in-house' intrigues.

4.1.3. *Administrative Offices and their Institutional Support.* There exists no single attempt to coordinate all the scattered and contradictory evidence on the central bureaucracy, so the material is presented in summary form, arbitrarily establishing six functional clusterings of administrative officials with presumed institutional bases.

4.1.3.1. *The royal council.* ('The council of twelve), for which a building in Cuzco has been identified by Chavez (1970), seems to have been a supra-provincial consultative body, composed both of Incas (one or more representatives of each Cuzco moiety) and one or two representatives from each of the four *suyus*. Their functions seem to have been to: (1) effect liaison between the central government and the provinces in their respective *suyus*, affecting levies of manpower and products, and (2) in marshalling special troop levies for campaigns. They also presumably related to their respective 'wards' in Cuzco where representatives from each of the provinces were supposed to maintain a residence (Rowe 1967: 62). They were probably assisted by *quipu*-readers and a secretariat, the status of whom may have been noble, *yanacona*, or both.

4.1.3.2. *The jural–political cluster.* Sources are totally contradictory on the question of whether the juridical and political officials were united or formed distinct administrative entities with separate jurisdictions and ranking. At the top of this cluster there seem to have been, in addition to the monarch, one or more 'viceroys' who were of the nobility (although these officials might have been simultaneously members of the royal council) and who had total administrative responsibility for the empire when the Inca was absent from Cuzco.

The political officials were appointed by the Incas as governors, usually or ideally one to a province. They represented the interests of the federal government at the provincial level and supervised or corrected the highest echelon of provincial officials. In the major provinces, and those that received *mitimae*, we are given to understand that the office of governor (*tocricoc*) had jurisdiction over the *mitimae* and *acllas* as well as whatever *yanacona* might be in residence, while the rest of the population was under the jurisdiction of the *curaca* hierarchy from the province. Despite the concern of the chroniclers to equate the *tocricocs* with the Latin position of prefect, it would appear that *tocricocs* were part of the Inca state political structure. Their principal function was to look out for the central bureaucracy's holdings (whether in buildings, fields, flocks or manpower) in the provinces, and not to form an additional and ranking echelon in the hierarchy. It would appear that they were more often travelling representatives than permanent residents in any one province.

The juridical officials were the *tocoyricoc* (inspectors) who were less numerous and who were specifically assigned the role of informing on the administration of justice. These inspectorships seem to have been assigned to members of the royal *ayllus*. They reported on, but did not administer, justice.

Another juridical term, *michoc*, is used to describe judges, but it is not clear whether this term refers to the juridical functions of the *tocricoc* or may be a subaltern to the latter.

In Cuzco itself, two bailiffs are designated as those who could 'arrest' one of the nobility. The apprehension of criminals below provincial nobility status was the pregerogative of the *tocricoc*, but for the nobility a special procedure was necessary. There were two prisons in Cuzco, one with wild beasts where condemned prisoners were sent and another, which was for detention. In judging these cases, the court may have consisted of the Inca or his surrogate, (possibly members of the royal council).

4.1.3.3. *The treasury cluster.* There is a hierarchy of officials in charge of *quipus* related to storehouses, the chief of which may have been the secretary of the Inca (*Incap Cimin Quipococ*) or the secretary of the general council (*Tauantinsuyo Capac Apocona Incaconap Cimin Camachicuyin Quipococ*). An accountant general (*Tauantinsuyo Runa Quipoc*) seems to have been the next in line, who knew both the census and revenue totals, and under him are two categories of major and minor accountants, which seem to have had the same range of responsibilities as the accountants in the provincial capitals. The first three officials were apparently of the nobility, the accountants at the lower levels appear to have been drawn either from the youths of the nobility or possibly *yanaconas.*

As in the case of the administrative officials in the jural–political cluster, there seems to have been a differentiation of treasury officials between those responsible for the central state census and revenue and those who were responsible at the provincial level. Ethnohistoric sources (principally the *visitas*) indicate that the provincial officials knew the customary allocations to the central state as well as those destined to their own provisioning. Somewhere in the central bureaucracy these individual provincial totals were aggregated, probably through secretaries in the royal council; but in addition, the treasury functionaries would have to account for the elaborated goods consumed by the Inca nobility that were exclusively a product of state-owned workshops. It is not clear, but fairly likely that the treasury cluster of officials fiscalized the *acllahuasi* workshops and storehouses of religion, which in other respects seem to have had their own administration.

Rowe (1967: 60) has identified some of the Cuzco areas where the central storehouses were located, but no one has as yet established the area of what might be the central treasury where the accountants correlated their *quipus* or where the elaborated items of gold, silver, lacquered wooden cups, litters, stools and fine cloth (which were not supposed to leave Cuzco) were housed.

4.1.3.4. *Yachahuasi: boy's school.* This is the only formal institution of higher learning in the Inca state. It amounts to a school for training adolescents of the nobility, and it was presumably run by the nobility, although it may have included *amautas* (wise men) drawn from the *yanacona* category or provincial nobility. In the time of Pachacutec it was expanded to provide instruction for selected sons of provincial nobility as well as the nobility. It appears to have existed only in Cuzco, and Chavez (1970) has identified an extant structure in Cuzco where it stood. The training consisted of four years (one in language, one in ritual and religion, one in *quipu*-reading and one in government and oral traditions), after which the graduates took minor administrative posts (probably as clerks to the *tocricoc*) in Cuzco or the provinces. Although not stated, it is rather likely that military training was part of the education, as about the time the students would leave, they were expected to participate in the breech-clout ceremony, which involved rigorous tests of endurance.

4.1.3.5. *The military cluster.* The likelihood that the royal council provided the 'general staff' of the military establishment is high. Each Inca seems to have had his own procedure for selecting, promoting and demoting or executing his 'generals' most of whom we hear about only in their field campaigns or as partisans in military coups and palace revolts. The drafting of the armies for campaigns seems to have devolved upon the representatives of the four *suyus*, presumably one of their functions in the royal council. For the actual field generals, however, there were both Incas, including the sons of the reigning Inca, and there were appointed provincial generals, some of whom were the highest ranking *curacas*. In any one operation, they both seem to have acted as part of a staff. The troops of the *suyus* fought mostly under their own leaders, and the Inca nobility seem to have had their own elite troops with *yanacona* camp-followers. In addition the Inca himself had a kind of mercenary bodyguard, made up of Canari or Chachapoyas warriors. They were a kind of *mitimae* group, transferred to Cuzco with this specific function.

The Incas by privilege staffed the outlying garrisons, and they were transferred as whole segments of communities from the circum-Cuzco area either to secure a particularly difficult frontier or to act as a counter-insurgency force in potentially rebellious provinces. They were provided their needs by the province to which they were sent, at least until as long as they needed such assistance. One assumes that in these provinces the *tocricoc* mediated between them and the provincial hierarchy in a fashion similar to his role with the socio-economic *mitimae*.

In the Cuzco area itself, there was the large fortress of Sacsahuaman and a Pucara somewhat further out, which were presumably staffed by garrison troops of the Inca nobility. There is, however, no evidence for the residence of a standing army or even an officer corps. For a -centralized government, it is strange that the military manifested such little specialization. It would appear that the military role was considered to be an alternative one for any member of the administrative hierarchy. As such, all members of the nobility might be expected to perform in a military capacity as the need arose, after which they would resume their civilian roles. In this connection, it is worth noting that Poma de Ayala said that the posts of *tocricoc* were given to members of the nobility who had some physical defects and would not make good warriors. By implication the more important administrative posts would be given to more combat-worthy nobility.

4.1.3.6. *Transportation, communication, and cadastre, the security cluster.* The central bureaucracy included, in addition to the clusters of administrative officials already alluded to, an indeterminate number of functionaries who: (1) supervised the bridge and road maintenance throughout the empire, (2) supervised the system of *chasquis* (or messengers) and (3) supervised the division of boundary markers for distinct types of property. This cadastral function was delegated to two chiefs, one from the Upper and one from the Lower Cuzco moieties. The first was to make the divisions, while the second placed the boundary markers. They also defined the water rights to all properties in the empire as well as access to pasture and firewood. No clue is given as to how many assistants might be involved in this most important activity. We have only some references in the 'laws' that moving a boundary marker was a punishable offense. The chief of bridges was selected from the Inca *ayllus* of the circum-Cuzco community of Acos, while the chief of roads was selected from those of Anta.

4.2. *Religious Bureaucracy*

The state religion is considered here as part of the bureaucracy, although at the federal and provincial level it had a parallel administration and economic base to that of the state *per se*. It is suggestive but certainly not demonstrable that the *Villac Umu*, or head of the state religion corresponded to one of the hypothesized 'two kings' that Murra and Zuidema suppose to have constituted the kingship. Consensus among sources exists that the high priest was a close relative of the Inca. He was also seconded by a council of nine or ten *hatun huilca* (higher priests) which had regional jurisdiction (analogous to a diocese one assumes), and then there is a category of *yanahuilca* (lower priests). The derivation of the *hatun huilca* is also noble, although we are not sure whether they were drawn exclusively from the Inca-by-blood category (Means 1931: 407). There are references to the 'clergy of the temples other than in Cuzco' as being drawn from the *curaca* class of provincial nobility.

Also parallel to the civil bureaucracy, the religious bureaucracy (the first two categories) had a 'staff of inspectors' who could punish the *yanahuilca*, and, presumably, the priests of the provincial level. All of the foregoing references (sketchy though they are) indicate a roughly parallel system of civil and religious administration.[11]

Since the activities of the religious personnel were intimately interlocked with the governance and economy of the state, it seems appropriate to consider the entire system within the bureaucracy.

4.3. The Provincial Political System

All of the provinces, despite their wide socio-cultural and economic differences were subjected to a standardization, once the Inca state took its territorial format under Pachacutec (ca. 1450). This standardization consisted, among other things, in the delimitation of the encompassed peoples according to a combination of demographic, ecological and ethnic factors. Generally speaking, the ethnic integrity of the conquered group was respected, providing its demographic mass was not excessive or too small. The minimal critical mass appears to have been 1,000 households. The maximum seems to have been 20,000 households.

The Inca articulated a well known theory of public administration in which, at the provincial level, authority was granted to chiefs on a decimal basis. Thus the highest chief of a province called a *hunu curaca* had authority over 10,000 households. This actually meant authority over 100 *curaca pacha*, each of whom had authority over 100 households. At this point, those who were accorded or confirmed (in cases where systems of retainer privileges antedated Inca governance) in the category of the provincial nobility (*curaca status*) stopped. Below them, but following the decimal classification were headmen in charge of household units of ten. Within these latter categories there was room for splitting degrees of responsibility into units of five. These sub-divisions were presumably devised to cover cases in which the settlement pattern was dispersed and clusters of ten residences were not common.[12]

Most *curacas* shared the commonalities of not being Inca and being supported by the surplus of their own provinces. They had rights and obligations both to their constitutents and to the central state. To the former they could assess retainers and products, and they administered the redistribution of surplus and reallocated lands and flocks of the non-state lands in their jurisdiction. They administered justice in matters not involving the central state or its minions. To the state the *curacas* owed the administration of the products of the state lands and rendering of the produce and manpower levies to Cuzco (oftentimes fiscalized by a 'federal' accountant or *tocricoc* — 'governor'). The *curacas* also furnished their daughters to the provincial and royal *aclla huasi*, their sons were either appointed to middle-level administrative posts, or designated as *yana* in such capacities as messengers (*chas-quis*). Offspring of either sex were requisitioned on special occasions as human sacrifices.

From the state the *curacas* received the privileges of luxury (reserved for the Inca nobility) gifts and the privilege of a wife from the *curaca* category of *acllas* on his trips to Cuzco. Occasionally he was granted the right to be carried in a kind of hammock (the more elaborate litter being reserved for the Inca and the most favored *apus*).

4.4. *Intersection of the Inca and Provincial Nobility*

From the foregoing some general observations on the degree of integration of the Inca state can be made:

(1) The guiding principle was one of central state control over individual provinces with no horizontal bonds between provinces. Only in a very inchoate form was a regional (supra-provincial) echelon recognized in the dubious position of a 'viceroy' for each *suyu* or in the twelve-man royal council.

(2) The bonds of ethnicity clearly separated provincial nobility from the state nobility.

(3) The exclusively state-owned resources were administered, even at the provincial level, by echelons of the Inca nobility.

All of these factors would tend towards a weak integration of the state with its provincial underpinnings. There were, however, mechanisms which held it together, albeit in a multi-stranded, octopus-like format. They were predicated upon the redistributive system of manpower and goods providing a constant circulation of population, both seasonally and on a permanent allocative (*mitimae* or *yanacona* or *acllacona*) basis. This economic system was administered and legitimized through the interlocking jural–administrative bureaucracy of the central state (with its tentacle-like appendages in the provinces) with the eighty-odd elite constellations (tiny micro-bureaucracies).

As Katz pointed out, the Inca state was both a giver and receiver as contrasted with the Aztec. Even though the drain on the provinces in terms of corvée was perhaps excessive, and the imposition of *mitimae* was intrusive and in some cases onerous, other aspects of Inca administration can be argued for as input to the provinces. Such would be the maintenance of warehouses, resource conservation and maintenance, and internal security. The myth of 'reciprocity writ large' that the Inca propagated as official doctrine may have had its ideological repercussions at some grass-roots levels, however hollow it may ring through the corridors of time.

The principal integrative factors seem to be located at the juncture points between the Inca and the provincial nobility. Both in Cuzco and in the provinces there seems to have been structured, if asymmetrical, exchange relationships in the interaction of Incas with the *curaca* officialdom. Basically, these exchanges were economic, took place when tribute was rendered from the provinces, and implied some token response, embodied in produce drawn from the Inca storehouses of limited but high quality goods or even services. Other occasions for exchange were: celebrations of the major holidays, the accession of an Inca or his triumphant return from an extended campaign. The forced 'hospitality' of the Inca to the principal *curaca* and his retinue in Cuzco kept a certain quota of inhabitants from all the provinces in the capital and certainly provided the opportunities for the more intensified exchanges, as did the famous ceremony of *Situa* when the provincials were ritually removed *en masse* from the city, only to return after they had been purified. The idols of the provinces were also brought to Cuzco as one-year 'hostages' to symbolize the encompassment of the subject polities through that of their projected protectors. Finally, although the information is most contradictory, the institution of the *acllas* seemed to provide a mechanism for training, segregating, and exchanging nubile members of the nobility: and at least in some of the *acllahuasi* the daughters of the Inca nobility and provincial nobility were confined together. The Inca himself and many of the ranking Inca nobility took *curaca* women as secondary wives and concubines. It is not as clear that *curaca* men could be allocated women of Inca status, since the *pacoaclla* are not very presisely defined (the name suggests they would be at least Inca-by-privilege).

Therefore, although the boundaries of ethnicity clearly separated the two categories of nobility, there were mechanisms for upgrading the favored *curacas* in their lifetime. *Curaca* women bred substantial numbers of Inca nobility, and even the male *curacas* might conceivably have Inca sons through marriage with Inca *aclla*. Hence, despite the rigid rules separating the two nobilities, there were means of passage and means by which the provincial elite could acquire almost equivalent status to the Incas.

If one considers the lower ranking Incas who were sent as garrison *mitimaes* to the provinces, their life-style was certainly more austere than that of the *apus* and *hunus* of the provinces.

4.5. *Social Differentiation Below the Elites*

The Yanaconas represent an interesting transitional group, that in theory should have bolstered the central state, as they were 'selected' or recruited from the provinces to serve one or another dependency of the state. While in a sense they were 'uprooted' individuals, in another sense they were considered in the Andean value system as kinds of liegemen or women, and hence ultra-loyal. Stripped of their regional ethnicity, they were supposed to consider themselves bound to, though not participant, in 'Incaness'. They went as individuals, (as distinct from the *mitimae*) and Murra (1956: 288) makes a good case for the argument that they were supposed to be considered in a kind of relationship as a captured prisoner to his deliverer to whom he was in perpetual bondage. The term was used for a title of chief priest, *Intip yana* (servant of the Sun); and *Intip huarmin* were women of the Sun in Cuzco, indicating that the term was not necessarily derogatory or pejorative.

They were exempt from the corvée, which one might consider a privilege, they were provided for by whatever institution or individual to whom they were assigned, and they could only be punished by an Inca or his surrogate. The relationship fostered was clearly of the patron–clientage type between the state and the *yana*. *Yana* seems to have been clearly severed from their ethnic identity base, where relationships had elements of reciprocity.

In a similar vein, but now with collective and ambi-sexual membership, the socio-economic *mitimae* became collective 'clients' of the central state. In both of these new institutions of the state, the transfer of lines of political authority from provincial (and in most cases extended kin) hierarchies to the national hierarchical system ran into the problem, if not the contradiction, of substituting a system based essentially on feudal principles of allegiance or patron–clientage for a kin-based system. This seems to have been the principal reason why the *yanaconas* and *mitimaes*, on balance, represented elements of disintegration in the empire (considering the federal- and state-level entities as a whole) rather than supportive. Certainly, these two components of the Inca society represent the most interesting aspects of Inca ethnopolitics, and as such they have lent themselves to the most varied interpretations by commentators from the sixteenth century onwards.

Today, we are far from understanding how they are to be evaluated within an integrative frame of reference, and the case histories of *mitimaes* and *yanacona* so far adduced from recent ethnohistoric research provide ambiguous evidence. As in most patron–clientage relationships, the effectiveness of the bond depends upon the degree to which certain myths of symmetry, if not reciprocity, are built into them. Examples of behavioral cases where the *yanaconas* were presumably treated as transferable 'chattel' have been adduced by some (Choy) to argue that they represented a class of slaves. Jural evidence tends to support Murra's judgement that they enjoyed a 'liege-type' protection and immunity not usually attributed to slaves. It is supported by other behavioral evidence that certain *yanacona* achieved high status in accord with responsibilities that were delegated to them. The evidence on their loyalty is decidedly the most ambiguous, since the many cases of *yanacona* switching allegiance to the Spanish can be interpreted as an extension of the allegiance principle being rooted in the patron *qua* conqueror (or captor).

The most that can be concluded at this juncture of available research is that most evidence supports the disjunctive character of the *mitimaes* and the *yanaconas*, but that in certain regions and under certain conditions they were integrative (supportive to the state). One can only surmise that the institution of a patron–clientage system, which would have had to be based upon a commonly shared coding of rights and privileges similar to the feudal liege–lord arrangements, did not have a long enough time to become established in Andean tradition.

4.6. *Structural Differentiation v. Cognitive Integration: State Religion*

Enough has been said in the sections on economic and political systems to indicate that the Inca state developed socio-political differentiation as a means of guaranteeing the economic integration of an everwidening and varied resource base. The contradictory tendencies were in many ways resolved at the cognitive level through the state religion, whose administrative apparatus as we have mentioned, was structured to parallel the political system and penetrate all regions and every socio-economic unit from hamlet to metropolis.[13]

Through ritual involvement, at least ideally, almost everyone in the empire was made cognizant of the Inca cosmogony. The state religion as expressed on the Coricancha, presumably represented not only primordial Inca deities, but could, and presumably did, allow for the incorporation of new deities from conquered provinces, such as Viracocha, the Pleiades or Pachamama. In addition, minor provincial deities were brought annually to Cuzco as guests from the provinces, so that local and provincial or regional deities were 'legitimized' by their year's pilgrimage to the 'navel of the Universe'.

In terms of lands, flocks and manpower something like one third of the GNP was invested in what Eric Wolf calls the *ceremonial fund*. Just as the state, in order to guarantee its resource base, developed the system of state ownership of flocks and lands and permanent retainership to husband them, it developed parallel mechanisms to guarantee the functioning of the state religion, even extending this principle to important regional shrines. Thus the guarantors of the principal resources of the state were propitiated by servants who were supplied by the resources being guaranteed, and the guarantors of the secondary resources were cyclically attended to. The orientation of the religion was clearly economic (in the sense of renewability of ecological potential and economic security) and only anti-economic (in the modern capitalist sense) since it involved excessive manpower in 'wasted' ritual behavior and 'extravagant consumption' (e.g., mass sacrifices of animals, food and other products).[14]

A point worth stressing in this connection is the regulation that seemingly pervaded the empire that the *curacas* were to eat in public (at least on certain occasions) with the 'commoners'. The Cuzco daily ceremonies involved sacrifices of llamas, which were presumably consumed by the participants and perhaps the privileged audience. Could this have been an imperial example of yet another case of the myth of reciprocity?[15]

Thus the ecologically sophisticated cognitive scheme of the state religion, which would have reinforced the redistributive economic system and to some extent legitimized hierarchical levels of differentiation within the redistributive format, was differentially implemented to the advantage of the central bureaucracy. Instead of a uniform penetration of all provinces, the state religion appropriated large blocks of land and allocated large groups of *yanacona* to Cuzco and certain regional areas, or key provinces, leaving the majority of provinces with token custodianship of perfunctorally allocated *acllas* and lands.

We have tried to show how the interdigitation of the two economic systems (the redistributive one and the state ownership one) was implemented on the political level. The Inca nobility reacted to the role implicit in their responsibility for implementing the changes in the technical relations of production by augmenting and defining the state-ownership principle. Incas-by-blood, and then Incas-by-privilege assumed dominant roles in administering the permanent state partrimony. Maintenance of the former resource base of the redistributive economy was left to the provincial nobility, who, however, were also expected to contribute cyclically to the growing state apparatus in goods and manpower. The strain of integrating the two economic systems into an overarching political administrative system was felt at this level. The *curacas*, dependent upon the *ayllu*-shared property principle, were administering essentially a peasant mode of production from which the corvée surplus could be extracted on a seasonal basis and a limited number of retainerships for their own sustenance. With the new technical change in production of the central state, the *curacas* were placed in the position of what were unabashedly coercive seasonal levies and even more coercive retainerships. Those *curacas* at the upper level of the hierarchy, especially those who had been drawn into the central or federal state for military or administrative purposes, were already participating in the new property relationships, receiving land grants and other privileges, and were assuming the liege-type relationships with the Incas that has already been elaborated between members of the Inca nobility through the extension of kin and ethnic ties.

The lower rungs of curacadom and the masses, however, retained their former social relationships in the redistributive process that maintained the self-sufficiency of the provinces or were selected out to accomodate to new roles in the productive process of the state.

The two 'new groups' which were uprooted from the peasant infrastructure to support the state-ownership apparatus were the *mitimaes* and *yanacona*. The ideological suprastructure, which would have encompassed and legitimized these contradictory role changes and stresses on the total polity, was the state religion. That it was to a degree successful can be deduced from the lack of any institutionalized coercive force (police, militia) to maintain internal security in the sense of compliance with the unwritten laws of Inca governance regarding the masses. Its weakness derives less from the sophistication of its dogma than from the fact that its implementation was from the outset structurally wedded to the central hierarchy.

FOOTNOTES

[1]   This domain of warfare extended as far as Chucuito; and the Incas felt pressures from the Chancas, a chiefdom in the Andahuaylas region to the north, who were protected from the Incas by the 'buffer' chiefdom of the Quechua. Some time prior to the confrontation with the Chancas, the Incas made an alliance with the Lupacas (about which some reasonably reliable ethnohistoric information exists) against the Collas, both chiefdoms on the western shores of Titicaca. If we can assume that the ethnohistoric reconstruction of the Lupaca 'Kingdom' (Murra 1968) corresponds to the type of polity that their alliance partners had, then we can presume the Lupaca chiefdom at the beginning of the fifteenth century was a basically kin-oriented society, probably hierarchically structured by several segmentary or conical lineages or ramages. The dual chiefdomship of the Cari (reconstructed by Murra) may (as Zuidema suggests) have also characterized the early proto-Inca state. If so we still know too little to indicate how it might have functioned, and whether it or a single chieftain would have favored the subsequent expansion to statehood. From Murra's careful reconstruction of the Lupaca chiefdom, we may also deduce a degree of specialization and differentiation within a contemporaneous Inca society that corresponds to the 'generals' who were kin and who seemed to have special rank in the reign of Viracocha Inca, which enabled them to lead campaigns or war-parties (Rowe 1946: 203). The Lupaca chiefs of the moieties and the sub-chiefs of what the Spanish called *cabeceras* were provided with retainers, which were allocated by the subject communities and had to be requested. They performed tasks of herding, weaving, cooking and farming the chief's fields. Although the ecology and economy of the Cuzco basin was characteristically highland and lacked the lacustrine and altiplano environment of Chucuito, it is a reasonable inference to suppose the Inca chiefdom had by this time a similar kind of retainership, attending a similar elite for tending the fields and more limited pastures of the administrators as well as providing them with the cloth and foodstuffs that the administrators redistributed along essentially reciprocal lines.

There existed among the Lupaca an 'ethnic minority' of Urus who seemed to be remnants of an earlier population, highly specialized in a lacrustine adaptation, and who appear to have been encompassed by the Lupaca and to be subordinated to the several Lupaca sub-chiefdoms (cabeceras). We have no clear information on how the Inca assimilated the other tribes of the Cuzco basin into their chiefdomship, but it would appear to have been by a combination of alliances and warfare.

² The added energy in manpower and goods derived from the Inca state system of surplus centralization hypothetically was derived from what would have been expended previously in maintaining separate defensive mechanisms, since under the pax Incaica this function was removed from the subject provinces and became a state monopoly as did much of the inter-provincial trade.

³ These dates coincide more or less with his delegation of authority for military action to other generals, and Rowe (1946: 207) refers to Pachacutec devoting his time 'to organization and to the elaborate program for rebuilding Cuzco which he had undertaken'. Topa Inca, the principal campaigner (whose conquests compare to those of Kublai Khan after Genghis) from 1471 on, spent his time between campaigning and administering, but it would seem he already took over a well-established system if he could afford to devote so much time to the field. From a number of references regarding 'captains' and 'generals' (capitanes) from provinces that occur in the chroniclers (especially Poma de Ayala), one can infer that the predatory system, described by Katz, in which large contingents of men from recently conquered provinces were immediately drawn into campaigns of expansion, was continued in Topa's military campaigns. The 'apus' were ex-provincial war leaders who were rewarded with booty (see Cabello, 1951: 368 and Garci Diez: 107, for reference to presumably the same person) and retainers. But sometime after the end of Topa Inca's reign, a more controlled 'draft' form of recruitment must have been instituted. This is described by Cieza de Leon and explicated by Wedin (1965), and indicates that from about 1490 on the cumulative predatory system was substantially modified. On the one hand, the boundaries of the state had been virtually fixed by Topa Inca, and there was not enough bounty from the conquests of his successor, Huayna Capac, to reward the troops who campaigned under him in what is now Ecuador or in all the other campaigns between 1493–1527 when he died. Hence it is reasonable to suppose that the octopus-like redistribution system of goods and manpower was the mechanism of staffing and supplying the military as well as forming the circulatory system of the state economy that continued to function on various provincial levels well into the colonial period.

⁴ This kind of regional-development planning (as we might call it nowadays) resulted in opening up significant tracts of land for cultivation, and although it cannot yet be absolutely documented, we presume most of them were allocated as state lands (lands of the state, state religion and panaca 'estates' for which the work force came from a combination of *yanacona* and *mitayos*). With the production from these new lands, the state not only had a wider base for the sustenance of the incipient bureaucracy but a *guaranteed* base. Previously, the volume of both sustenance and special state products would have fluctuated from year to year according to the potentialities of the provincial zones of production.

⁵ Thus by these two changes in the technical relations of production (development of new productive properties and specialized colonies of producers of special goods) the state guaranteed a steady flow of goods for the maintenance and functioning of the bureaucracy. These innovations were related to the earlier centralization process, but were less dependent upon it, at least in terms of production. Within this vast network of redistribution of products and manpower, the component ex-polities, now converted into provinces, were maintained or rather maintained themselves to a large extent at their former level of subsistence generally with their own hierarchical arrangements only slightly modified by their obligations to the state. Thus, the larger chiefdoms continued to function on a chiefdom basis, the tribe-like smaller chiefdoms continued as subdivisions of provinces, the kingdom of Chincha seems to have been maintained intact, and only the large kingdom of Chimor seems to have been 'balkanized' into what were probably pre-Chimu chiefdoms.

The Incas themselves maintained their ethnic unity as a kind of ethnic 'bureaucracy'. The complex rules of Inca kinship have not yet been satisfactorily deciphered, although Zuidema (1969) has shown (utilizing Lounsbury's unpublished analysis of Inca kinship) how the system was adapted to keep the noble lineages from increasing. We cannot improve on Kirchhoff's summation (1949: 296) of how kinship and hierarchy were interlocked:

'While it is nowhere definitely stated that noblemen and commoners were members of the same clans, circumstantial evidence makes it likely that this was the case; in other words, there were no clans composed exclusively of one or the other, except for the royal clans and possibly all the (noble) Inca clans of Cuzco. Shortly after the foundation of a new clan, it may have consisted mainly or even exclusively noblemen, but this must have constituted only a transitional situation. With the growth of the clan an ever larger number of its members became so far removed from the direct line of its founder that they were no longer considered noble. Not only was each clan internally stratified, but the various clans and the two moieties has different standings, resulting in a rather complex structure. Clans and members of clans had different ranks, and these ranks were based on descent. It was a social stratification based on kinship. Throughout the Andean area noblemen and commoners, even though belonging to the same clan, married only within their own rank. In the Inca empire, such marriage was required'.

6   Without discussing in detail the many micro-niches within the four major macro-niches (for which see Tosi 1957) we can indicate that operationally the ethnoecological principle already functioned as an organizing idea in the Lupaca chiefdom (see Murra: 1972). In areas of close juxtaposition of three of the four niches (ceja de la montaña), communities still exploit all on an annual basis (Schaedel 1959; Nuñez del Prado 1958), and in many of those where this is not so, the use of Murra's (1975: 59–116) concept of the archipelago was in practise. The Incas seem to have clearly built on this organizing principle in their utilization of the *mitimae* for socio-economic purposes. But in this sense one must consider these 'islands' (e.g., coca plantation settlements, mining settlements) as part of the verticality–archipelago system of the state, whose center or nucleus was Cuzco. Thus, one whole region like Arapa belonged to the lands of the Sun (and probably functioned exclusively as the island for provisioning the specifically state religion with wool and textiles). Mining settlements in Chile and Argentina seem to have been similar islands for the state monopoly of extraction of metals; and the several coca *mitimae* colonies seem to be so many scattered islands dedicated to the state consumption of this important ritual leaf.

This system was part of the second change in the transformation of the technical relations of production and is not to be confused with the first centralization phase which as a general rule preserved the verticality and archipelago systems of the several polities which already had them, simply redirecting and intensifying the flow of surplus. On occasions, of course, the Incas did disrupt the earlier systems (e.g., see Rostworowski 1967–8); and whenever the two macro-systems came into contradiction, the Incas seem to have opted for the latter.

7   Before discussing the third type of labor in the early Inca state, we should refer to Murra's (1956) dilemma regarding the socio-economic definition of the *yana*. He summarized every piece of evidence in a masterful attempt to define the group, but was unable to disentangle them from the *mitimaes* (or the colonist category of labor). What seems probable, if we accept the hypothesis of two phases of transformation in the elaboration of the state economy, is that the *yana* and *mitimae* both antedated the Inca state as forms of labor that the chiefs could 'request', more or less on a 'permanent loan' basis. When the Inca extended the 'citizenship' of the state to the nearby ethnic groups, it may well be that, in return for the privileges of being fictive kin and being free of the state-wide seasonal labor recruitment (corvée in Murra's terms), they were obligated to enter into the chief–retainer relationship with the Inca by supplying the transplanted labor force the chiefs formerly required of their subject ayllus; and this subsequently became known as the *mitimae* system. (Some of the circum-Cuzco tribes were sent to the earliest conquered polities — now provinces.) They were also apparently obligated to the cyclical 'retainership' of personally serving the Inca, and (as Murra has indicated) fulfilling middle-level administrative assignments. Probably, at the outset, they did not enjoy the services of their own *yanacona* recruited from the provinces. The fact that the

alleged origin of the *yana* category is during Topa Inca's reign, *after* our proposed initial phase in the formation of the redistributive system, lends support to this conjecture.

Further support for this hypothesis would be that we have little evidence, until the end of Pachacutec's reign, that the large public works and demarcation of estates of the *panacas* were completed. The labor force employed in the Cuzco area during this period seems to have been largely corvée, probably being supplied with their own 'foremen' by the provincial chiefs (*curacas*), and not until the vast new cultivable areas were ready for cultivation for the benefit of the state, religion or *panacas* was there a sharp demand for a core of permanent farmers and herdsmen of the *yanacona* category. Finally, the implied contradictions in the status of potential '*yanaconas*' from the surrounding area (on the one hand, 'privileged', on the other 'obligated and servile') would have required some *de facto* clarification of the Inca-by-privilege category. This ambiguous situation seems to be the basis for the origin 'myth' of the *Yanacona*, told to Cabello de Valboa (Murra 1960: 36). After the institutionalization of this category by Topa Inca, it is clear that the *yana* are derived almost exclusively from the provinces and that their status is below that of the Incas by privilege to whom they were indeed assigned.

[8]   Clearly there were transfers of recently captured populations since the early cumulative expansion to the homelands of the provincial military contingents and to Cuzco, but we have no indication of how the status of these 'booty' groups was determined (the only example of these early orphans of conquest so far known may be the Uru). It is conceivable that they had a kind of subservient 'ethnic minority' status (as opposed to a more privileged ethnic minority status when they were imposed on a province by the Inca) if we can infer this from oblique references to the Canas and Chinchaysuyu *mitimaes* in Juli (Chucuito province).

Hence we would separate the first phase of the economic transformation of the state from the second by emphasizing the nature of the labor force as: (1) most heavily dependent upon corvée labor from the provinces; (2) an incipient development of the *yanacona*–retainer category, largely confined to the circum-Cuzco area, and (3) the *mitimae* 'security' colonies. All these supported the central state apparatus, but they depended upon each province developing its own traditional labor supply of corvée and retainer labor along with the maintenance of its own 'colonies'.

[9]   In a similar fashion the 'islands' of resources which were not in the circum-Cuzco area were systematically delimited and exploited by *mitimaes*, specifically affiliated with the Inca (not the regional ethnic) governor. Their produce was funnelled to Cuzco or to the provincial capital, and they were expected to sustain themselves after an initial period of assistance from state supplies in regional depots and exactions of supplies and labor from the adjacent province. These enclaves were basically concerned with exploitation of coca plantations, herding areas, mines, fishing zones and forests; but some concentrated on transformational activities (e.g., potters for bulking and 'packaging'), weavers (possibly to decongest camellid traffic to Cuzco) dye-stuffs, etc.

[10]   There are references to other favored members of the nobility in the echelons below the Incas-by-blood, such as administrative and military beneficiaries of the Inca (whether originally Incas-by-privilege or *curcacas* delegated to Cuzco from the provinces) who were also awarded pasturelands and fields, but we do not know: (1) whether these were portions of newly developed land in the circum-Cuzco area or in the provinces, and (2) the proportion of these holdings compared to the others. It is only known that these grants were given to the kin head, presumably to be administered by his descendants according to the prevailing inheritance code of his province. There is no indication (in the tribute lists) that these grants included a fixed allocation of *yanacona* or would fall in the category of corvée-supplied labor, both of which are confirmed for the other three types of property.

[11]   The system of *mama-cona* ('mothers') was somehow integrally incorporated into the religious bureaucracy at the federal level, since these women formed the supervisory group of graded *aclla* (chosen women). The 'high priestess' was of noblest birth, being referred to as *Coya pacsa* (Queen-moon-like). Three classes of *aclla* follow in hierarchical and functional order: *yurac aclla* (consecrated to the Sun like the *coya-pacsa*); *vayru*

aclla (potential concubines or wives of nobles), both categories apparently stemming from Inca nobility (whether by blood or privilege or both is not clear); and *pacoaclla*, who were to be allocated as wives to *curaças* of the provinces, and whence they were presumably recruited (although they may also have been drawn from the nobility). Below them, came the category of *yana-aclla* who served temporarily in the *aclla-huasi* (houses of the chosen women) and were subsequently allocated to 'commoners' (in this case it is not clear whether these commoners included *yanaconas*).

[12] In the earlier provinces to be incorporated in the Inca state and in those which already had a well-defined hierarchy (such as Chincha, and Chucuito) the ranking below the chief authority was honored, and there seems to have been no superimposition of Inca titles, 'Curaca' seems to have been the generic name for nobility from the province. At the upper end of the ranking one frequently finds '*apu*' added. This seems to have been a designation that the Inca bestowed on high-ranking *curacas* who either formed part of his royal council (and had some kind of jurisdiction over the *suyu* of which their province was a part), or were outstanding 'captains' in the campaigns. These *apus* represented a kind of provincial elite, who were honored in all ways except by extension of the Inca ethnicity. They were the only *curacas* who seem to have been awarded grants of land in perpetuity, of the type allocated to the *panacas*. It is conceivable (but not demonstrated or denied by the sources) that the Inca bestowed upon them women of Inca nobility so that their children might inherit the ultimate prerogative of the central bureaucracy, Inca ethnicity.

[13] The cognitive scheme is schematically best represented in the sketch of the images and their placement on the Coricancha (Sun temple) wall in Cuzco. It has been interpreted with minor variations by Lehmann–Nitsche, Means (1931) and Zuidema to represent a symmetrical combination of cosmic, social organizational, ecological and ethnic principles that characterize Inca society and even to represent a kind of cognitive consensus of central Andean society.

This interpretation rests upon the intimate relationship between astral (cosmic), ecological (with a heavy emphasis on telluric) and human factors, seen basically as resources which have to be renewed through the interaction of male and female at all levels.

The Andean calendar, which represents an integration of the solar and lunar calendar as well as the probable intercalation of other astral–calendrical divisions, was largely correlated with the cosmology of Coricancha, and we have numerous indications that divinities having to do with the propagation of all the resources of Andean society were attended to by designated kin groups on a daily, seasonal and annual cyclical basis.

[14] By supporting the work ethic through the sanctification of pastoral/agricultural activities for men and weaving/food preparation for women, and separating large domains as 'sacred', the Inca also induced a focus on both productivity and conservation. The emphasis in Cuzco on ritual activity led Rowe to call the 'entire puma-shaped capital' a ceremonial center of the empire. This observation emphasized the fact that the cognitive scheme which was viewed as *the* integrative and legitimizing underpinning of the Inca state has become as bureaucratized by the time of Huascar and Atahualpa as the non-religious institutions of the state with which it was structurally parallel.

[15] One observation which seems to emerge from this very poorly documented realm of Inca society is that the *panacas* were considered even by Huascar as 'inflated' corporations who were more parasitic than functional. They apparently exploited the patron-clientage system to maintain or augment their ranks. If the same was true of the state religion in general is less certain. There seem to have been only a few important regional or provincial-level centers and there are no certain references that corresponding Inca nobility (to the *tocricoc*) were in control of the provincial state religion apparatus. This would argue for a concentration of the state religious apparatus at Cuzco and certain focal points such as the Titicaca shrine region (Isla del Sol — Copacabana) and Pachacamac on the central coast. Hence despite the application of the redistributive circulatory system to the provinces (in which *acllas* were selected out, lands of the Sun specially cultivated, and products specially deposited by community levies) the ritual

benefits seem to have been 'clotted' at several large regional shrines, above all at Cuzco, with much smaller apparatus at the provincial capitals. There is no indication that anything, except mandates on calendrical ordering of market days and the like, trickled down from the state religion to the sub-provincial villages.

The archaeological evidence for the provincial capitals so far reconnoitered or excavated, backs up the ethnohistorical and scant specific historical references as to the shabby nature of the religious installations, which tends to refute the claims of some chroniclers that the state religion was uniformly established in each province with temples of the Sun, *acllahuasi* and sizable warehouses.

REFERENCES

Brundage, Burr Cartwright (1967), *Lords of Cuzco*. Norman: University of Oklahoma Press.

Cabello Valboa, Miguel (1951), *Miscelanea antartica* (1586). Lima Instituto de Etnología. Universidad Nacional Mayor de San Marcos.

Chavez Ballon, Manuel (1970), 'Ciudades Incas: Cuzco capital del imperio', in: *Wayka* 3: 1–15.

Choy, Emilio (1960), 'Sistema social incaico', in: *Idea*, 10–12.

Diez de San Miguel, Garci (1964), *Visita hecha a la provincia de Chuciuto* (1567). Lima: Instituto de Etnología. Universidad Nactional Mayor de San Marcos.

Dobyns, H. F. (1963), 'Estimating aboriginal American population: an appraisal of techniques with a new hemisphere estimate', in: *Current Anthropology* 7: 395–449.

Espinoza Soriano, Waldemar (1969–79), 'Los mitmas yungas de Collique en Cajamarca, Siglos XV, XVI, XVII', in: *Revista del Museo Nacional Lima* 36: 9–57.

Guaman Poma de Ayala, Felipe (1936), *Nueva Coronica y buen gobierno* (codex peruvien illustré) (1615). Travaux et mémoires de L'Institut d'Ethnologie, XXIII. Paris.

Katz, Friedrich (1972), *The ancient American civilizations*. New York: Praeger.

Kauffmann Doig, Federico (1973), *Manual de arqueologia peruana*. Lima: Ed. Peisa.

Kirchhoff, Paul (1949), 'The social and political organization of the Andean peoples', in: *Handbook of South American Indians*, vol. 5: 293–312.

Kosok, Paul (1965), *Life, land and water in ancient Peru*. New York: Long Island University Press.

Kroeber, A. L. (1963), *Cultural and natural areas of native North America*. Berkeley: University of California Press.

Kubler, George (1946), 'The Quechua in the colonial world', in: *Handbook of South American Indians*, vol. 2: 331–410.

Lehmann-Nitsche, Robert (1928), 'Coricancha, el Templo del Sol en el Cuzco y las imagenes de su altar mayor', in: *Revista del Museo de la Plata* 31: 1–260.

Means, Phillip Ainsworth (1931), *Ancient civilizations of the Andes*. New York: Columbia University Press.

Morua, Martin de (1962–4), '*Historia general del Peru, origen y descendencia de los Incas*', Ed. by Manuel Ballesteros-Galbrois, in: Colección joyas bibliograficas, Bibliotheca americana vetus, II vols., Madrid.

Murra, John V. (1956), *The economic organization of the Inca state*. Ph.D. dissertation, The University of Chicago
— (1966), 'New data on retainer and servile populations in Tawantinsuyuy', in: *Actas del XXXVI Congreso Internacional de Americanistas* 2: 36–45.
— (1968), 'An Aymara kingdom in 1567', in: *Ethnohistory* 15: 115–51.
— (1972), *'El 'control vertical' de un maximo de pisos ecologicos en la economia de las sociedades andinas'*. Ensayo publicado en el tomo II de la Visita de la Provincia de Leon de Huanuco (1562), Inigo Ortiz de Zuniga, visitador. Huanuco: Universidad Hermilio Valdizan.
— (1975), *Formaciones economicas y politicas del mundo andino*. Lima: Instituto de Estudios Peruanos.
— (1975), 'Dynastic oral tradition, administrative records and archeology in the Andes', in: *World Archaeology* 7 (3): 268–279.
Nunez del Prado, Oscar (1958), 'El hombre y la familia: su matrimonio y organización politico social en Qiero', in: *Revista universitaria. Universidad Nacional del Cuzco* 47: 114: 9–31.
Ortiz de Zuniga, Inigo (1967), *Visita de la provincia de Leon de Huanuco*. Tomo 1, Visita de las quatro waranqa de los chupachu (1562). Huanuco: Universidad Hermilio Valdizan.
Rostworowski de Diez Canseco, Maria (1960), 'Succession, cooption to kingship and royal incest among the Inca', in: *Southwestern Journal of Anthropology* 16 (4): 417–427.
— (1967-8), 'Ethnohistoria de un valle costeno durante el Tahuantinsuyu', in: *Revista del Museo Nacional* 35: 7–61.
— (1970), 'Mercaderes del valle de Chincha en la epoca prehispanica: un documento y unos comentarios', in: *Revista espanola de antropología americana* 5: 135–78.
Rowe, John Howland (1946), 'Inca culture at the time of the Spanish Conquest', in: *Handbook of South American Indians*, vol. 2., 'The Andean civilizations': 183–330.
— (1967), 'What kind of settlement was Inca Cuzco?', in: *Nawpa pacha* 5: 59–77.
Santa Cruz Pachacuti Yamqui Salcamayhua, Juan de (1927), *'Relacion de las antiquedades deste reyno del Piru*, ed. by Horacio H. Urteaga in Coleccion de libros y documentos referentes a la historia del Peru, vol. IX. Lima.
Schaedel, Richard P. (1959), *Los recursos humanos del departamento de Puno*. Plan regional para el desarrollo del Sur del Peru. vol. 5. Lima.
— (1966), 'Incipient urbanization and secularization in Tiahuanacoid Peru', in: *American Antiquity* 31 (3): 338–344.
Smith, C. T. (1970), 'The depopulation of the Central Andes in the 16th Century: the Province of Chucuito', in: *Current Anthropology* XI (4–5): 1–8.
Steward, Julian H. (1949), 'The native population of South America', in *Handbook of South American Indians* 5: 655–668.
Tosi, J. A. Jr. (1957), *Mapa ecologica del Peru*. Lima: Instituto Interamericano de Ciencias Agricolas de la Organizacion de los Estados Americanos.
Urteaga, Horacio (1938), *La organización juridical en el imperio de los Incas y en la Colonia*. Lima: Libreria e Imp. Gil, S.A.
Valle, M. M. (1964), 'Bases biologicas del mundo andino: la errada interpretación europea frente a la autentica concepción indigena', *36 Congreso Internacional de Americanistas*. Madrid.

Wedin, Ake (1965), *El sistema decimal en el imperio incaico.* Instituto Ibero-Americano. Gotemburgo, Madrid.

Wolfe, Marshall (1966), 'Rural settlement patterns and social change in Latin America: notes for a strategy of rural development', in: *Latin American Research Review* 1(2): 5–50.

Zuidema, R. Tom (1964), 'The Ceque system of Cuzco: the social organization of the capital of the Inca', in: *International Archives of Ethnography.* Leiden: Brill.

— (1969), 'Hierarchy in symmetric alliance systems', in: *Bijdragen tot de Taal-, Land- en Volkenkunde* 125: 134–139.

15   The Galla State of Jimma Abba Jifar

HERBERT S. LEWIS

The Galla state known as Jimma (sometimes called Jimma Abba Jifar) arose in southwestern Ethiopia in the nineteenth century and endured as an entity for about 100 years, until 1932. Although surrounded by several other earlier non-Galla states it rapidly developed its own distinctive characteristics in terms of political structure and culture. Almost from the beginning, a set of features appeared which the editors of this volume would consider more typical of the 'transitional' early state than the 'inchoate' form.

Whereas in their early formulation (at least) the editors of this volume envisaged a developmental sequence from an 'inchoate' early state marked by vital kinship, family and community ties, with few full-time political specialists and irregularly vague systems of taxation, Jimma seems, from its early days, to have featured appointed rather than hereditary officials, a simple form of bureaucratic apparatus, highly organized taxation and conscription, free market in land, and hardly any political role for kinship or descent. The fact that this Galla state could have these characteristics so early in its history — while even its powerful, much larger and much older neighbor, the Abyssinian state (Ethiopia) did not—suggests that the variations in early state organization delineated by the editors should not be arranged in a developmental sequence but may rather be part of the range of variation among state societies in general, without necessary evolutionary implications.

1. THE ORIGINS OF THE GALLA STATES

Jimma and four neighboring Galla states[1] (Limmu, Gomma, Guma, Gera) arose in southwestern Ethiopia in the early to mid-1800s in an atmosphere of economic change, political and military ferment and general ethnic complexity (Lewis 1965; Abir 1967). Central and northern Ethiopia had long known state organization. The dominant political force in the whole region today called Ethiopia was the Abyssinian (or Ethiopian) state, associated with the Amhara and Tigre of the center and north. But there were numerous other smaller states in the south and southwest, some Muslim and some 'pagan', about whose history very little is known.

In the seventeenth and eighteenth centuries many areas of southern, southwestern and southeastern Ethiopia were invaded from further south by the people known today as the Galla or Oromo. This people, never politically united but sharing (at least, at first) a common language and customs, moved in among and between the inhabitants and states of the north and center of Ethiopia and began to settle on the land in a series of local groups, each with its own leaders and regional and personal loyalties (Lewis 1964, 1965). There was a great proliferation of these on the landscape of Ethiopia, and we begin to read, in the accounts of travellers, as early as the seventeenth century, of many named local groups and of local Galla 'lords' or 'chiefs'.

These local groups and their leaders competed with each other and with neighboring peoples and states for land, livestock, and the control of markets and trade routes. It was apparently in the interplay of economic and political ambitions and rivalries, and the fortunes of war, that the five states arose. While in some cases they replaced earlier states in the area, they cannot be considered mere 'successor states' to the older, non-Galla, ones. While they evolved partly in interaction with the older states, and certainly borrowed some aspects of political organization and certain traits from the previous states, Jimma, at least, seems to have arisen more as a new state born out of the defeat and submission of a number of Galla groups to one dominant Galla leader and faction. (Hence, while the state arose from conquest it cannot be considered a 'conquest state' in the sense of Oppenheimer or Oliver and Fage—that is, as a result of the conquest of herders over farmers or of one culturally superior group over another (cf. Lewis 1966]. Its political culture was in many respects *sui generis*, and distinctly 'Galla' in contrast to that of the Amhara state to the north, and in contrast also to the political system of the Kafa and Janjero states to the south and northeast respectively.

2. ORIGINS OF JIMMA ABBA JIFAR

It is uncertain just when the Galla entered the area north of the Gojeb River and west of the Gibe River which came to be called Jimma, but it must have been in the seventeenth or eighteenth centuries. The previous inhabitants of the area may have fled or been absorbed but, in any case, there remained hardly a trace of them when fieldwork was conducted in 1958-60; nor is there any good evidence of an earlier population from the accounts of travellers. Only in the most recently conquered area of the state, Garo, was there evidence of an earlier population.

There was no state at first, but rather a series of competing local Galla groups, each under its own leaders. According to both oral traditions and the evidence of G. Massaja, who was in Jimma in 1854, a series of war leaders ruled their own territories and fought with neighboring groups (Lewis 1964; Abir 1967). In time, one group, the Diggo, conquered an important market center on the trade route from Kaffa to the north and under two successive leaders, Abba Magal and his son, who took the throne name of Abba Jifar, went on to force numerous neighboring Galla groups to submit to their control. Abba Jifar further expanded his domain at the expense of neighboring states. By 1830 Abba Jifar was sufficiently powerful to be considered the ruler of a state. It was also in this year that Abba Jifar became a Muslim and declared Islam to be the state religion.

In the period of a few years Jimma was apparently transformed from a congeries of small warring factions to a centralized state of growing economic and political power. Abba Jifar and his successors built a distinctive political structure which held together firmly until the coming of the Amhara and the direct rule of Hailè Selassie in 1932. There were *models* of the state for Abba Jifar *to draw upon*, and he and his successors were influenced and aided by outsiders from the north, especially Muslims who acted as religious experts, as an armed bodyguard, and as technical experts, helping with record-keeping, trade, and building. But the structure of the political system was distinctive in many respects; above all, it differed from non-Galla states in precisely the ways that the non-monarchical Galla differed from the Amhara and the Kafa peoples.

3. PRE-MONARCHICAL GALLA SOCIAL ORGANIZATION

The socio-political background of non-monarchical Galla is relevant to the discussion of the state structure. To begin with, Galla social organization, as that of many groups in Ethiopia and East Africa (Lewis 1974) was *not* kin-based. In contrast to common stereotypes of African 'segmentary' or 'acephalous' societies, even among the non-monarchical Galla, kinship and descent is not, and was not, a basis for social and political organization. Rather, territoriality, neighborhood, friendship, and voluntary association are and were the key to group activity. Thus, at its very beginnings, the state of Jimma Abba Jifar was not 'encumbered' by lineages or other descent groups involved in political affairs. Neither the monarch nor the governors had powerful lineages of their own to satisfy, nor were commoners arranged in politicized descent groups. The land was *not* owned by descent groups. Even among non-monarchical sedentary Galla land was, and still is, owned by individuals or small families. Hence land could be allotted and alienated without consideration of the impact on descent groups.

Secondly, leadership among the Galla was not based on kinship or descent. It was, instead, achieved either through election (in the *gada* system) or through building a following through leadership and success in war or in the control of markets and trade routes (Lewis 1964). Thus, the kings, both in the early stages of the monarchy and throughout its 100 year lifetime, were not constrained to appoint 'traditional' leaders but could choose from among those they deemed useful for their administration, whether local or foreign. In the characteristics of the pre-state social system of the Galla we find predisposing factors which enabled able monarchs to obtain and maintain despotic control, and which imparted to the state features which the editors would consider more typical of 'transitional' rather than 'inchoate' early states.

4. SOCIAL AND ECONOMIC SETTING OF THE JIMMA STATES

At its height the kingdom of Jimma Abba Jifar covered an area of about 13,000 square kilometers) and its population must have ranged somewhere between 150,000 and 300,000. It was located in a region of rolling and hilly land, 4,000 to 6,500 feet (1,220 to 2,000 metres) in altitude, which is for Ethiopia the temperate middle highlands. With about 65 inches (165 cm) of rainfall per year and warm temperatures, cultivation was possible all year round.

The basis of the economy in Jimma and the neighboring states was mixed agriculture, with the use of the oxen-drawn plough, concentrating upon grains such as *t'ef*, barley, sorghum and maize. Root crops were, and are, also important in the household economy, and coffee has been, since the middle of the nineteenth century, an important cash crop. Livestock are appreciated and kept, but the cattle holdings of most families range between two and eight in number. The very rich, of course, had huge herds.

Settlement in Jimma is in open-country neighborhoods, with homesteads dotted about the landscape amidst the grain fields and gardens.

The homes and fields of farmers are located upon either their own property, that belonging to others (who range from the wealthy and powerful to smallholders with only a marginal advantage over the able-bodied landless), or *wakf* lands (land granted in return for religious services). Land can be freely bought and sold, and a family may work both land they own themselves and land rented from others in return for a share of the crop or currency.

There is also an extensive system of marketing, organized through a host of cyclical markets which operate one day per week, on alternating days. These markets dot the countryside, giving everyone access to at least one market almost every day of the week but Friday. Women and men attend the markets, buying and selling (often very small items and amounts), while professional traders visit the larger markets, with their trains of donkeys, along the caravan routes. Hirmata, the trade center of Jimma's capital, was the greatest market of southwestern Ethiopia, attracting tens of thousands of people to it from all directions. In this way produce from Jimma and all the other districts in southern Ethiopia make their way from the countryside to the north of Ethiopia and even to the sea, and imported items reach the people of Jimma.

4.1. Occupational Specialization

Most of the people of Jimma are farmers. Theirs is an agrarian society, and even the wealthy live mainly from the production of food on the land and the product of the labor of their tenants. As in most of Ethiopia and the Horn of Africa there are artisans, organized in hereditary endogamous castes. The potters, blacksmiths, silversmiths, woodworkers, weavers, tanners, hunters–foragers belong to separate endogamous groups, and each was organized, under the monarchy, with its own leadership, accountable to the king and his representatives. They manufacture items on a small scale, for sale on commission or in the market, or for the king. (For more on this topic see Lewis 1962, 1965). There were few other specialists except for the professional traders and those involved in the service of the palace and the state machinery.

4.2. Slavery

Slave-holding was very common in Jimma and the slave trade passed through Jimma in the nineteenth century, making Jimma an important center of the trade. Some Jimma Galla participated as traders themselves.

Abba Jifar II, who reigned from 1878 to 1932, is said to have had as many as 10,000 slaves in his service, and according to informants, it was not rare for a powerful man to have as many as 1000 slaves. But even simple farmers might own one or two slaves, to work by their sides in the fields, or to relieve them from farmwork so they could go on trading trips. On the other hand, slaves in the service of the king or the great men could be placed in high and responsible positions and rise to considerable power and prominence. The term *soresa*, 'notable', 'man of wealth and power', could be applied to a slave as well as a free man. This, of course, is a well-known phenomenon in monarchical systems, and Jimma was no exception.

4.3. *Social Stratification*

Except for the artisans and slaves, who occupied special positions within the social system, it is difficult to isolate 'strata' in the population. There were the rich and powerful (*soresa*) and the weak and poor, but these can perhaps best be seen as a continuous series of distinctions among people rather than in terms of relatively fixed strata. There were no 'estates' or 'classes', but a range of freeborn people, from top to bottom. Nor was a freeborn person's status fixed from birth. The Galla in general are highly universalistic and recognize personal achievement and the right of an individual to advance. Notables could fall from favor and wealth and even be enslaved, especially if caught in a serious crime or captured in war, and the previously poor could rise rapidly, especially through good fortune in war and politics, but also through success in trade and the accumulation of land and slaves. Even slaves, as noted above, could rise in wealth and power and esteem—and become slave-owners themselves.

In summary, great inequalities of wealth, power and prestige existed in Jimma and were accepted as the normal state of things. But it does not seem that one can speak of fixed strata except for those in the hereditary statuses of 'artisan' and 'slave'.

5. THE MONARCHY

5.1. *The King*

The kings were figures of great power and wealth, far overshadowing any others within the realm. They owned vast lands, thousands of slaves and great herds of cattle. Their palaces were staffed with huge corps of servants and artisans, theirs to command. But this power was not enhanced with an air of sacredness, at least not as far as one can gather from either informants' recollections or travellers' accounts. The king was treated with deference, but was not hedged about with the taboos so common in most African monarchies, including those neighbors of Jimma: Kaffa, Janjero, and Abyssinia itself. The kings were not veiled or hidden from view and there are no legends connecting them with supernatural powers or events. The king was a secular ruler, not a sacral one. This may, perhaps, be explained with reference to two factors.

(1) Jimma was a Muslim state, and the kings were the 'protectors of the faith'. They supported Islam and propagated the faith but had no pretention to sacredness themselves.

(2) The Galla generally do not treat mortals as sacred. Even the *k'allu*, spirit mediums of great power among the Shoa Galla, are treated as representatives of the spirits rather than as sacred figures themselves (cf. Lewis 1970).

The Jimma kings were not considered to be high priests, the 'fathers of their people' nor representatives of the ancestors (communication with ancestors is not known in Galla religion). They were merely the most powerful mortals in the land. Only one case came to light in the oral traditions which shows Abba Jifar I acting as a spiritual leader outside the context of Islam. It is said that, in a time of intense hardship, many people begged Abba Jifar to sacrifice a bull on a mountain associated with the pre-Muslim spirits. He is said to have done so, reluctantly, and as this involved the old 'pagan' religion, informants were not anxious to speak of it.

5.2. *The Royal Family*

Close kin of the king, especially those in his immediate family, naturally shared in the monarch's glory and wealth. If they were loyal and capable they might hold high office, but members of the royal family did *not* have automatic rights to claim any particular offices. The king was under no traditional constraint to appoint his kinsmen to office. Normally the kings were strong enough to utilize those brothers and sons and in-laws who were loyal to them and capable of holding office—and to exile those who threatened them and demote those unworthy or incapable of high office. Royalty were, therefore, neither excluded from high office nor automatically entitled to it.

The women of the family might have their own lands, slaves and cattleherds, but there is no record of their holding office. There was no institutionalized position for the queen mother or the king's sister. Political marriages were arranged by the king for his sisters and daughters, as well as for his sons, in attempts to contract alliances with other ruling houses. The kings would attempt to attract their new in-laws to the kingdom, often offering them administrative positions.

5.3. *Palace and Court*

The palace compound of the kings of Jimma, located on a hill near the modern town of Jimma, was the heart of the kingdom. It was the center of power and wealth and also the largest settlement in the land. The Galla do not normally live in towns, and large settlements arise only around the habitations of great men. As lesser lords gathered followers and servants around them, so the kings of Jimma attracted thousands of people to their homestead. The palaces at Jiren and elsewhere were the homes of the king, to which were attracted (freely or by compulsion) slaves, servants, artisans, merchants, travellers, the ambitious and the powerful, those who would make their way by serving the king and his court and those desirous of favors and opportunities. At its height the palace area of Jiren had a population of thousands. In 1960, however, virtually nothing remained but a tiny settlement with a couple of shops and a minor market one day a week. Several palace buildings still stood, but the palace was no longer the seat of wealth and power and as it never served as more than the camp of the king there was nothing to hold people there once the monarchy ended.

The palace was a compound at least a kilometer in diameter, surrounded by a high fence of woven split bamboo, breached by gates guarded by armed soldiers. There were inner fences as well, guarded by eunuchs in guardhouses. Within these fences lived soldiers, composing the king's bodyguard, guests of the king; the king and the royal family; and some of the servants of the king and the court. Around the palace of Abba Jifar II there were more than 2,000 armed men, hundreds of servants, slaves and concubines; artisans of all kinds, jailers and overseers. Near the palace lived court officials, such as the prime minister, war minister, chief judge; and scribes, court interpreters, lawyers, musicians and other entertainers. There were granaries, stables, storehouses, treasuries, workshops, reception halls, houses for the royal family and for visitors, servants, soldiers; and jailhouses and a mosque.

Although Jimma had a fixed capital, the kings maintained other palaces elsewhere throughout the kingdom. At least four others were kept in readiness for the monarchs' visits should political or other reasons lead them to move the court to one of them temporarily.

Although notables were not required to be at court for any part of the year, as far as is known, it was clearly in their interest to spend time there, and many maintained second residences in Jiren, near the palace, in order to attend the king and the court.

6. ORGANIZATION OF ADMINISTRATION

Jimma was governed by appointed officials, not chiefs or hereditary leaders of descent groups. With the exception of the royal office itself, there were no hereditary positions in the state at all. Administrative positions were generally not the 'all-purpose' ones of chiefs or feudal lords, but were functionally specific ones such as those of: tax-collector, market judge, courier, border guard, jailer, military officer, and so on.

The king maintained a high degree of control over appointments, though lower-ranking officials were appointed by his lieutenants, often with his agreement. In addition, the kings were able not only to appoint, transfer, promote and demote officials, but to create new positions and even to change the boundaries of provinces and other administrative districts. This seems to be an ideal which was generally conformed to.

Officials were drawn from several different categories: members of the king's family and his in-laws; wealthy men who pleased the king or whose families had good relations with the royal family; the king's slaves; foreigners with special skills, including armed mercenaries, merchants, and learned Muslims; and men who distinguished themselves in war. While it was not uncommon for a son to inherit his father's position, this was by no means an automatic occurrence.

6.1. *Remuneration of Officials*

As a general rule officials in Jimma were *not* permitted to live from direct taxation. In contrast to the practice in Abyssinia, officials could not collect taxes, keep a portion and send the rest on to the king. They were rewarded in a variety of other ways. Palace officials were supported directly from the king's storehouses, and might have their own lands which yielded revenue. Foreign mercenaries, chiefs of the toll-gates, and certain other officials were paid salaries. But most of the governors were wealthy men, with their own lands and cattle, who could afford to serve without special recompense, and for whom the opportunity to receive bribes and some free labor on their lands, and to collect occasional fees and tribute were an added material consideration. If the king wanted to raise a slave to an important rank he would simply give that man a grant of land—and thus crate a new 'notable'.

(In Weber's terms, a 'notable' is a man of means who can 'live *for* politics without living *from* politics' [Weber 1947: 413–414]. 'Notables' is Bendix's term for Weber's *honoratioren*, rendered as 'amateurs' by Gerth and Mills [Bendix 1960: 348]. To some extent the *soresa* of Jimma approximate this concept). In addition, late in the regime of Abba Jifar II, governors were given a percentage of the tax collected from their districts. But it is important to note that the taxes were collected by others and the governors' portions sent to them subsequently from the palace. (See below.)

7. THE ADMINISTRATION OF THE STATE

7.1. *Boundary Maintenance, Control and Communications*

Jimma, like the other states in southwestern Ethiopia, was marked by definite and maintained boundaries. In some cases rivers and thick forest served as the boundary, but in the absence of such natural barriers deep ditches and earthworks were dug and maintained by corvée labor. These borders were policed by special forces of border guards under the leadership of trusted warriors. (In return for this service the soldiers received grants of land from the king). Watchmen were posted to guard against surprise attacks, and manned signal drums which were beaten to warn of impending attacks. Beyond the borders, between Jimma and the borders of the neighboring states, lay areas of no-man's land which often served as the sites of prearranged battles.

At various points along the borders, at the major caravan crossings, there were tollgates. These were manned by special officers with troops or armed men who served to control movement in and out of the state as well as acting as toll-collectors. Emissaries of the king travelled to and from these posts, bearing double-bladed spears as symbols of their authority and authenticity, carrying information to and from the palace and relaying the orders of the king regarding strangers travelling through the kingdom. Thus the king and his immediate lieutenants kept very close watch on the comings and goings of their own subjects as well as strangers. (Cf. Abir 1967: 81ff. on the organization in neighboring Limmu.)

7.2. *Provincial and District Organization*

Jimma was divided into sixty provinces, called *k'oro*, each under the jurisdiction of a governor, called an *abba k'oro*. These provinces were not necessarily based on earlier political or descent group areas but were created for administrative purposes and could be changed in size, subdivided, or merged with others, at the will of the ruler.

The governors were not looked upon as representatives of the people who lived in their provinces but as appointees of the king who served at his sufferance, at least theoretically. Frequently they did not come from the provinces they ruled, nor did they necessarily have their primary landholdings there, although they might. In no case were these provinces to be considered fiefs which the governors were *free* to exploit to their own benefit.

Regardless of the wealth they might extract from their own private lands, and despite the opportunities for the gaining of wealth through fees and bribes, the *abba k'oro* were not given free rein to exploit their provinces for their own purposes. For this reason they were forbidden to collect taxation in their provinces and to maintain more than token forces of armed men.

Each province was further divided into five to ten districts known as *ganda*, each under a district head known as the *abba ganda*. To enable the governor to communicate with the *abba ganda* and for these district heads to communicate with the people, use was made of the services of heralds or couriers. Each community had one of these couriers.

The governors were the links between the king and the countryside. While there were other officials in each province responsible for certain specific tasks, the provincial governors were responsible for seeing that the king's general commands were carried out and that there was order and peace in the land under their jurisdiction. But they were kept on short leashes by the king, and their powers and ability to develop independent action were quite limited.

Governors could hold court and serve as judges over certain types of disputes, but they could not try murder cases or other major cases involving violence. They could deal with cases of thievery, land disputes, and quarrels between people within their districts, if these could not be solved at lower levels. But when disputes arose in markets these were dealt with by special judges in the markets, and murder cases went to the judges at the palace, as did appeals over the heads of the governors.

Governors could maintain small troops of armed men to help them maintain order, pursue minor law-breakers and implement punishment, but they could not keep so large a group of armed retainers that they could become a danger to the central authority. According to informants, a governor could not even send a large group of armed men in pursuit of bandits preying on caravans in his districts. He had to send word to the palace and request that troops be sent to deal with the problem.

In time of war the governors had to supply men from their provinces prepared for battle. While some governors were warriors who would participate with their men in the fighting, many were not, and their task was to send messages and mobilize men for war. The exceptions to this were the governors in the border districts who had to be prepared to react swiftly in the event of incursions from across the borders. They might command their own men, and were chosen for their military skill as well as loyalty to the king.

The governors were also responsible for the mobilization of manpower for public works, especially for corvée labor on the lands of the kings and for work on the defensive fortifications that surrounded the state. They had to see to it that the roads in their areas were kept in good repair and that bridges over rivers and streams were maintained.

Although the governors could not themselves take taxes they did extract wealth in several ways. They had the right to demand some corvée labor in their own lands and they received gifts of goods and services from some of the artisans. And they managed to extract bribes for favors, such as granting exemption from military service or corvée labor and taxation.

8. ECONOMIC ORGANIZATION OF THE STATE

Aside from the wealth derived from the king's own vast lands, which was available as an instrument of royal power and control, revenues and goods flowed to the palace as a result of the king's control of trade and markets and from the general taxation of all subjects.

8.1. *Taxation*

Taxes were collected yearly, except from those exempted on other grounds. Those exempted included men performing regular military service, border guards, artisans who supplied goods or work-service. Taxation was based at first on property holdings in land and cattle, but shifted, late in the nineteenth century, to a household tax. Taxes were payable in Maria-Teresa thalers, which became a common form of currency late in the nineteenth century; earlier, bars of salt, which were standard currency throughout much of Ethiopia, were used.

Taxation was organized directly from the palace. Officers from the palace guard were sent to the provinces to oversee both the census and the actual tax-collection. (Census-takers used knotted cords for recording.) In the provinces they were joined by representatives of the governor, and when the collection had been completed they and the governors went together with the taxes to the palace, where the revenues were counted and placed in the treasury. Late in the monarchy governors were given ten per cent of the tax revenues for their own use, in an attempt to try to discourage the governors' extra-legal exaction from their subjects.

8.2. *Control of Trade and Markets*

By late in the nineteenth century Jimma's market at Hirmata had become the greatest in the southwest. Abba Jifar II, the ruler for all of this period, was able to tap this flourishing trade in ivory, hides, cotton, grain, coffee, civet musk, gold, and many other items. By the mid-1880s, however, a heavy percentage had to be passed on to Menelik II, emperor of Ethiopia, as the price of internal autonomy.

Tolls were levied on caravans passing through the tollgates of the kingdom. Some of the revenue from this went to pay the gatekeeper and his men, but most went to the palace to be used for various palace expenses and to help pay for the upkeep of the king's bodyguard. In addition, the monarch was considered the patron of all the foreign traders in the land, and he maintained direct control over those who stayed for any length of time near the palace and the Hirmata market. He was thereby able to extract favors and gifts from the merchants and make use of their services in many ways.

The king also maintained direct control over the artisan castes, acting as their protector. In return for his protection (which partly removed them from the control of the provincial governors) the artisans owed either service to the king or an annual payment of their products. These products were used to outfit the king's troops and palace, to reward followers, or to be sent as presents to other monarchs. Each artisan group was organized with its own officers, appointed by the king, who acted as their chiefs and organized the collection of their contributions.

The overall control of trade and marketing was in the hands of a palace official called the *nagadras* ('chief of trade'). He was a high palace official who served as a treasurer, high judge, and overall coordinator of toll-collection and markets. The post was usually filled by former traders whom the kings would raise to high office.

All the markets in the land were under royal control. Each had its own law enforcement and judicial authorities stationed in it, to maintain order, deal with disputes and legal cases arising there, and to organize the market and its sections. Any fees paid in market dispute cases went to the *nagadras*' treasury in the palace. It was also in the market that heralds might proclaim new rules and messages from the king and governors.

The king was also in charge of the annual collection of grain and livestock for charity, used to support the poor and the religious teachers and leaders. The *k'adi*, the religious judge, was in charge of this collection and together with local governors, was supposed to decide on distribution among the needy. According to one nineteenth century traveller, Abba Jifar II sent salt each month to the governors to be distributed among the poor, through the district heads. In general, however, it could not be said that the taxation system was a redistributive one. Its prime function was to support the monarchy and the system of political control.

9. MILITARY ORGANIZATION

The core of the military organization of Jimma was the king's own forces, composed partly of regular corps of volunteers, who served on a rotating basis, and partly of paid merchants, often from other countries. Two groups of volunteers, each about four hundred in number, and each with its own commander, served at the palace each week. They were replaced by another eight hundred men the next week, and so on, each group serving one week in four. Aside from serving as palace guards they might also be sent on tax-collecting missions, or in pursuit of bandits, or might work around the palace, keeping the grounds and buildings and fences in good repair. The third group, about fifteen hundred strong, was composed of mercenaries, mainly from such northern Ethiopian regions as Shoa, Wollo, Gojjam and Gondar. This force comprised the permanent bodyguard. Its members were paid salaries, whereas the members of the other units served in return for exemption from taxation and corvée labor. Each group had its own commanders.

The king thus always had at least 2,000 soldiers, some armed with guns, at his immediate command. There was no other force in the land that could challenge such a group.

In addition to these palace troops any able-bodied freeman was liable to military service. In practice, however, during the reign of Abba Jifar II, in each province there were men prepared to serve if the king so ordered, and directed the governor to call them for service. They were to go to the palace, or the site of a battle, and serve there under the leadership of the king and/or his war minister and other military commanders. Forces of considerable size might be assembled rapidly, numbering 20,000 and more. Governors, except for those on the borders, could not mobilize troops themselves. And the overall direction of the military was the business of the king and his close advisor, the war minister.

10. CONFLICT RESOLUTION AND JUSTICE

There were many agencies for resolving conflict in Jimma. Disputes might be settled by arbitration and discussion on the local level, in hamlets; or the district heads and governors might become involved at their courts. At the highest level there were judges at the palace charged with dealing with serious cases and acting as courts of appeals. And the king might become involved as the highest judge in the land, especially in cases involving murder, armed robbery, and other serious crimes. Only the king could sentence a person to death.

In addition, there were special courts for particular types of disputes: the *k'adi*'s court for problems of marriage, divorce and inheritance, for which Muslim *shari'a* law was recognized; and the market judges and *nagadras* for cases involving disputes arising in the marketplaces or centering about debt, property, ownership, theft, and rights to market privileges.

11. THE OBLIGATION OF SUBJECTS

The major obligations of subjects were to pay taxes, perform corvée labor, and to perform some military tasks if the need should arise. However, exemption from taxation and corvée service was available for those who served in other ways: for the members of the rotating military corps and the border guards; for the artisans who gave time or goods; and for all those who acted as administrators, couriers, heralds, etc.

12. CONCLUSIONS

The Jimma monarchy exhibits both a high degree of central control ('despotism') and a rudimentary 'bureaucratic' administrative organization in an agrarian, non-urban, and largely non-literate context. In its governmental structure it contains many of the features Weber (1947: 329-41; Bendix 1960: 418–25) considers typical of bureaucracy: government was a continuously functioning structure with permanent and institutionalized positions; government was by officials and ministries, not by chiefs; officials had definite duties inherent in their offices; offices were ranked and there was a system of supervision and appeal, and there was a relatively high degree of role differentiation between various spheres of activity. The military and economic resources necessary for the fulfilment of duties and positions were not the property of the incumbents of those offices. These and other characteristics (see Lewis 1965: 125–26) give Jimma's government a highly sophisticated appearance. And yet they do not seem to be the product of a long development from simpler to more complex, but rather to have been instituted early in the history of the monarchy. It seems most likely that this is due in good measure to the nature of the pre-state organization of the Jimma Galla people. That organization was not based on descent but featured community leadership by achievement (either through election or the rise of war leaders) and, to some extent, task-oriented leadership. (See Lewis 1965: 29–30; 127–28). In this and other ways we suggest the final form of the Jimma state owed much to the underlying social system.

Finally, Jimma was a state in which the king ruled supreme throughout the period of the monarchy. As far as we know there were no effective 'counterweights' (Claessen 1973b) to the king's power. This was *not* a matter of ideology, of a theory of an all-powerful monarch, but seems simply to have been the reality of power in Jimma. Neither the governors nor the military leaders nor any group in society, including the 'nobles', ever effectively checked the ruler's power. If the state had lasted longer we may assume that forces would have arisen eventually to weaken the king's control, but this did not happen in the period under consideration. That this was so seems to be due to several factors.

(1) The inheritance of the pre-state socio-political system, which left the rulers of the new state with few competitors: no hereditary leaders, and no powerful descent groups to deal with.

(2) The compactness of the kingdom and the ease of communications, which meant that the king could have his troops at trouble spots on short notice, and that governors and even border guards could be kept under close control.

(3) Eternal vigilence, which is the price of despotism, on the part of the monarch. The kings applied the tricks of the ruler's trade, using bodyguards (both mercenaries and presumably loyal subjects); keeping regional governors from gaining entrenched strength in local areas and limiting their powers; maintaining control over all aspects of administration—which is both a definition of and a technique of despotism.[2]

Jimma Abba Jifar seems to have gone directly from its non-monarchical beginnings to a centralized and bureaucratized monarchy without passing through any intervening 'stages'. This suggests that the specific forms that states take depend upon the multiple factors of geography, culture, underlying social structure, demography, technology, and that these forms are too various, and their interactions and permutations too multifarious, to be codified in a relatively small set of 'types'. While there are certainly parallel processes and homologous and analogous structures in monarchical systems (early states) all over the world, the variations in socio–cultural-political systems may be sufficiently numerous and permit so much independent variation among their aspects as to render futile efforts at typology building and sequence discovery in any but the crudest form (cf. Lewis 1968).

FOOTNOTES

[1] A fuller account of Jimma, its history and political system can be found in Lewis 1965. That volume contains supporting evidence, full references, and an expanded discussion of monarchical rule in African states. This reconstruction of Jimma's political system is based on fieldwork in Jimma in 1958–60 (supported by the Ford Foundation) and is supplemented by travellers' accounts from the nineteenth and early twentieth centuries. The other Galla monarchies in the area have not been studied in the same manner, but Mordechai Abir's *Ethiopia: The Era of the Princes* (1967: 73–94) contains a chapter on the Galla states, with a reconstruction of the Limmu Kingdom based on close inspection of published and unpublished nineteenth century accounts. From his description it is clear that Limmu and Jimma shared many aspects of their political systems and administration.

[2] It should be noted at this point that there was virtually no irrigation practiced in Jimma, certainly none involving extensive cooperation or supervision. Nor were there other vital waterworks. Despotism was an autochthonous development in Jimma and occurred in an area of rainfall agriculture. Cf. Claessen 1973a.

REFERENCES

Abir, Mordechai (1967), *Ethiopia: the era of the princes*. London: Arnold.
Bendix, Reinhard (1960), *Max Weber: an intellectual portrait*. 'New York: Doubleday.
Claessen, Henri J. M. (1973a), 'Despotism and irrigation', in: *Bijdragen tot de Taal-, Land- en Volkenkunde* 129: 70–85.
— (1973b), 'The balance of power in primitive states'. Paper presented at the *IXth International Congress of Anthropological and Ethnological Sciences*. Forthcoming in: *Political Anthropology and the State of the Art.* ed. by S. Lee Seaton and Henri J. M. Claessen, The Hague: Mouton.
Lewis, Herbert S. (1962), 'Historical problems in Ethiopia and the Horn of Africa', in: *Annals of the New York Academy of Sciences* 96: 504–511.
— (1964), 'A reconsideration of the socio-political system of the western Galla', in: *Journal of Semitic Studies* 9: 139–43.
— (1965), *A Galla monarchy: Jimma Abba Jifar, Ethiopia, 1830–1932*. Madison, Wisconsin: University of Wisconsin Press.
— (1966), 'The origins of African kingdoms', in: *Cahiers d'Etudes Africaines* 6: 402–407.
— (1968), 'Typology and process in political evolution', in: *Essays in the problem of tribe*, ed. by J. Helm.

Lewis, Herbert S. (1970), 'Wealth, influence and prestige among the Shoa Galla',
    in: *Social stratification in Africa*, ed. by A. Tuden and L. Plotnicov. New York:
    The Free Press.
— (1974), 'Neighbors, friends and kinsmen: principles of social organ-
    ization among the Cushitic-speaking peoples of Ethiopia', in: *Ethnology*
    13: 145–157.
Weber, Max (1947), *From Max Weber: essays in sociology*. Trans. by H. Gerth
    and C. W. Mills. London: Routledge and Kegan Paul.

16 The Kachari State: The Character of Early State-like Formations in the Hill Districts of Northeast India

SOFIA A. MARETINA

Ancient states with large populations in India from the middle of the first millennium A.D. have for a long time attracted the attention of historians. This is not the case with early state-like unions which emerged periodically in the outlying areas of the developed class societies of the Indian subcontinent. This is due to a virtually complete lack of historical evidence, compensated partly by the possibility of observing certain stages in the process of the emergence of state systems on the basis of live ethnographic material, however. It is noteworthy that, although chronologically the peripheral state-like formations, as, for example, those of East India, date from a relatively late period (early second millennium A.D.), they, even so, represent the earliest forms of the state system, since they were evolved by peoples who were just reaching the class society stage. The specific nature of the evolution of the outlying areas is conditioned by a complex of both historical and ecological reasons.

The present paper deals with the early state-like formations of the hill peoples of Northeast India. Geographically, Northeast India is a combination of two landscape types, namely plains and hills. The former embrace the fertile valleys of the Brahmaputra and its numerous tributaries; the latter the slopes of the Assam plateau, extending along the southern bank of the Brahmaputra, the Assamo-Burmese Hills in the east and northeast and the Assam Himalayas in the north. On the whole, mountains and hills here occupy up to two thirds of the entire area. The geographical contrast is emphasized by the ethnic and socio-economic dissimilarity of the populations of the two main landscape types: that of the plains is made up of agriculturists using the plough, speaking languages of the Indo-European family and living under advanced class society conditions, while that of the hills comprises minor Mongoloid peoples and tribes speaking the Tibeto-Burman and Mon-Khmer languages; hoe farmers who have not up until now cut the navel-string connecting them to the communal tribal system. The specific ethnic composition of the hill districts has something to do with their borderline position between South and Southeast Asia: politically they belong to India, with which their political history is connected, while genetically their roots extend a vast distance back to the areas south of the Yangtze River.

The Assam Hills region now is one of the main areas of habitation of the *Adivasis* ('first settlers', tribal minorities), whose village communities lie scattered throughout the dense jungle covering the hillsides and are loosely interlinked. This was not always so, however. For instance, in the densest part of Nambhor Forest, near the ancient town of Dimapur in the Naga Hills, some majestic ruins — the remains of an old fort, brick walls and temples — and the traces of irrigation canals and roadways were discovered at the end of the last century. Some of the structures, namely the huge carved stone monoliths with incised representations of birds and other animals as well as other figures, go so far back that the name of the people who created them has fallen into oblivion (Shakespear 1914). The origin of the fort ruins is traceable, however: the structures belonged to the Kacharis, a people who have contributed some vivid chapters to the history of ancient and mediaeval Assam. Traces of their dominion have also been found in several other areas of Northeast India.

The Kacharis are a Tibeto-Burmese people, belonging to the Bodo ethnic group. It is interesting to note that of the several dozens of ethnic groups represented in the Assam Hills, the Bodo were the only one with state-like unions. Besides the Kacharis, a number of peoples belonging to the same group can be mentioned, viz. the Chutiya, who dominated a number of areas of East Assam in the thirteenth–fifteenth centuries, the Koch, who created a prospering state and were once the main rivals of the Kacharis on the political scene, and the Tipperah, who succeeded the latter as the dominant power in Lower and Middle Assam (*Encyclopaedia of religion and ethics* 1909: 754–755). All these peoples in the thirteenth to seventeenth centuries (no reliable data are available with respect to earlier times) had primitive state-like formations that replaced the former Hindu dynasties of the Guptas and Palas, the evidence of which is very scanty. These formations covered one or another part of Assam (in both the hills and plains) for longer or shorter periods, and, like all states of this type, were fairly unstable (they emerged swiftly and, even more rapidly, disintegrated), hence the extreme instability of political frontiers in mediaeval Assam.

Of all the unions formed by the various Bodo peoples, we shall dwell only on the 'Kachari Raj', the Kachari state, on the structure of which interesting, though far from exhaustive information is available. It permits one in particular to stress the spontaneous nature of the development of social institutions over several centuries.

To begin with, we shall briefly discuss the principal stages of the development of the Kachari state. The first sufficiently reliable references to the early history of Assam date from the thirteenth century A.D. and relate to the Ahoms, the militant Burmese Shans, who first appeared in Northeast India in 1228 and have left behind historical chronicles in the Pali-Buranji language and inscriptions on brass plates (Assam District Gazetteer 1905, 17: 18). These records indicate that in the period under consideration (the thirteenth century) a large portion of Assam was dominated by the various above-mentioned Bodo peoples, the strongest among whom was the union of the Kacharis, which occupied all of the valleys of the rivers Dhansiri and Kopili (southern tributaries of the Brahmaputra), and had its center in Dimapur on the Dhansiri River. Probably the Kacharis came here from the northern bank of the Brahmaputra, the site of their first known capital, Gauhati. L. Shakespear, a specialist on the Kacharis, characterizes them as a 'peace-loving, prospering people' and states them to have possessed an advanced culture (Shakespear 1914). The area around Dimapur, now covered with dense forest, was once cultivated and built up by them. The Kacharis maintained active trade relations in particular with Bengal, whence they borrowed techniques for building brick structures (Gait 1926). The ruins of the aforementioned towns testify to the Kacharis' highly developed skill and to the enormous scale of their constructions, which would have been impossible without the employment of vast multitudes of laborers. The organization of manpower is likely to have been one of the main functions of the state.

The Kachari state existed under conditions of incessant warfare, which led to frequent changes of habitation area. From the fifteenth century on, the gradual ascendancy of the Ahoms, who ousted the Kacharis from their fertile river valleys and by the middle of the sixteenth century had forced the Kacharis to retreat southwards to Maibong, situated in the North Cachar Hills, can be observed. Independent local tribes, i.e., the Nagas and the Kukis, became subjected to the *raja*, taxes in whose favor were levied upon their households. As a result of numerous changes of habitation area due to their pursuit by the Ahoms, the Kacharis split up into a number of separate groups, which later on came to be considered as independent tribes. Thus some of the Kacharis became alienated from the *raja* and settled in the plains, so that, gradually, differences in language and customs sprang up between them and the Kacharis of the hills. Moreover, the plain

Kacharis became the vassals of subsequent conquerors and were absorbed by them.

Massive walls, carved rocks and the remains of water reservoirs are still to be found on the site of Maibong, the new place of residence of the Kacharis. Relations, both political and cultural, with adjacent states, particularly the Hindu states of North India, were increasingly strengthened by the Kacharis, which was an important factor in the establishment of the Kachari state structure. However, the destruction of Dimapur was a fatal blow for the Kacharis, from which they never recovered completely. The continual struggle against the Ahoms and hostile hill tribes eventually resulted in their complete collapse. In 1696 one of the Ahom armies destroyed Maibong. Half a century later, in 1750, the *raja* had to retreat to the Cachar plains with his court and a small number of followers, while the majority of the Kacharis remained in the North Cachar Hills, where they retained some degree of independence, though they continued paying tribute to the *raja*.

It is at precisely that same period, namely in 1790, that *raja* Krishna Chandra and his brother adopted Brahmanism. In actual fact this was only the official admission of a long-established fact. The influence of Hinduism and Hindu-dominated states on the unification of the Kacharis is testified by such telling facts as, for example, the *rajas'* names, sounding wholly Sanskrit, the terms for official titles, the wide use of Sanskrit by courtiers, etc. After their official conversion to Hinduism, the Kacharis were recognized as worshippers of the goddess Kali. To account for this conversion to Hinduism, the Brahmans had to invent a special legend according to which the race was descended from Bhim, a hero of the Mahabharata (Soppitt 1885: 8).

The Kachari state as a whole comprised a conglomeration of various territories with different levels of socio-economic development, which becomes especially apparent from a comparison of the plain and hill districts coming under the Kachari *raj's* rule. The difference between the *raja's* immediate environment and the remote hill communities was particularly great. The hill communities were linked to the *raja's* residence only by tax and labor relations. There was as yet no economic basis for the unification and consolidation of the complex of separate territories, war and the proximity of developed class-type societies being the most important factors in the establishment of the state. In all early class states war was a vehicle 'by means of which inequality was maintained' (Danilova 1968, I: 60) since it led to the rise of certain individuals and groups and to their domination of others. As for the proximity of advanced Hindu states, their influence provided such necessary attributes of the state as an ideology, a system of power organization, a language for decrees and other forms of official communication, etc., essential for shaping tribal unions into states. Examples of all state-type formations of this kind at this particular level of development prove the significance of contacts with fuller developed state systems for the development of their own state structure (Kozlova et al. 1968: 521; Maretin 1967: 131 ff.).

Socially, the Kachari state constituted a system of individual village communities, relations within which still corresponded to the pattern of the distintegrating clan system. The formation of a state accelerated the process of disintegration of the Kacharis' clan structure. The community remained their basic social and economic unit, while other institutions, pre-eminently that of slavery, were subordinate to it. Hence it is in the community that one should look for the social prerequisites for the formation of the state, such as the emergence of socially unequal groups, or 'pre-classes', whose status was further consolidated by wars, but which had their origins precisely in the core of the community in the course of its social stratification. These kinds of processes are of particular interest for our study.

The available facts regarding the beginning of the stratification process in the Kachari community allow us to trace the main trends of this process. By the beginning of the Dimapur period, i.e., by the thirteenth century, the earliest period for which information is available, the Kacharis had seven clans, called *semfongs* (*senfongs*). This was probably the stage at which the *semfong* began to develop from a purely genealogical group into a group of the socio-professional type, which amounted in fact to the rise of certain individual clans acquiring a privileged social status. Therefore social differentiation took place not so much within as among clans. It should be noted that the term 'social group' (stratum), which is widely used in the ethnographical literature with reference to groups of the kind in question, applies to social units which each possess their own specific rights and duties and their own status (Soviet Hist. Enc. 1971: 347). Social groups emerged in pre-class societies and when classes began to form they entered these as social subdivisions (cf. the position of the ancient Indian *varnas* Bongard -Levin and Il'in 1969: 170).

Those Kachari clans which were most closely connected with the *raja* and his entourage were the first to rise to dominant positions. They were the Bodosa, the most senior, known as the former ruling clan; the Thaosengsa, the clan to which the ruling dynasty belonged in the period for which data are available; the Hasyungsa, the clan of the king's relatives (Crace 1930). The further progress of social stratification resulted in an increase in the number of socially differentiated groups which developed on the basis of existing clans (and possessed the same names) and acquired a definite social status, as well as in the emergence of totally new social groups, which eventually led to the formation of a complete hierarchy. With the migration of the Kacharis to the North Cachar Hills, the number of the *semfongs* increased to twelve, while at the time of their shift to Khaspur in the plains the names of forty-two *semfongs* are mentioned; the latter number corresponds to that of the present-day Kachari groups.

The term *semfong* refers to the 'male', i.e., patrilineal clan, the only type known in the period of the rule of the Dimapur. However, from as early as the end of this period there are references to *jaddi*, or female clans, then thirteen in number. Later, their number equalled that of the 'male' clans, at present also coming to forty two (Ghosh 1965: 190). According to the Kachari legend, the origin of the 'female' clans is to be explained as follows. After the Kacharis lived close to a number of alien tribes (Nagas, Kukis, etc.,), they could marry the latter's women and admit these to their communities. Striving to confine marriage within the tribe in order to subject it to some sort of control, the Kachari *raja* brought together all his female subjects and formed the *jaddi*, or 'female' clans, linked by a complex system of marriage relations to the *semfongs* (Soppitt 1885: 36). Unfortunately aside from the legend mentioned above, there are no other data available as regards the appearance of the *jaddi*, so that we are unable to ascertain how exactly this original clan system emerged. Moreover, the historical material fails to explain the background of the rise of 'male' and 'female' clans, so that one has to resort to contemporary data in order to grasp the difference between them.

The Kacharis have preserved both *semfongs* and *jaddi* to this day, though they have completely lost their specific social features and have retained only marriage-regulating functions. The linear principle in the present-day Kachari clans works as follows. All males trace their descent along the male line and hence belong to the father's *semfong* ('male' clan), while all females belong to the *jaddi* clan of their mother, i.e., they keep to the matrilineal principle. At the same time, sons are aware of their blood relationship with members of their mother's clan, and refrain from marrying these, while daughters likewise do not marry members of the father's clan. After marriage a woman is officially adopted into her husband's clan (Ghosh 1965: 187).

But let us now return to the epoch of the Kachari *raj*. The first stage in the social stratification process was thus marked by the rise of noble clans, the most eminent of which were those related to the king. This development is characteristic of the beginning of social differentiation in the majority of societies. The further advancement of the noble clans was largely stimulated by the continual warfare the Kacharis were engaged in — it is no mere chance that the headman of any hill tribe invariably possessed the greatest power as commander of the military forces, his rise to supremacy being primarily due to his accomplishments as a military leader. The further process of social stratification involved the formation of 'ignoble' or commoner clans of agriculturists.

As a result of this process, by the sixteenth century the Kacharis had evolved their complete hierarchy of social–professional groups, whose stratification followed along two main lines. On the one hand, the emergence of new, and the division of existing noble clans (both with the genetic clans as point of departure) continued, this applying to 'male' and 'female' clans alike. The *jaddi* of the *raja's* mother may serve as an example. On the other hand, however, new social groups arose, among the common clans, such as the Songyabsa, or 'clan of the king's cooks', the Nyablaisa, or 'clan of the king's hereditary fishermen', the Nobidasa, or 'clan of professional hunters' and the altogether 'ignoble' Bengyasa, or 'clan of servants, slaves and other outcasts', this constituting the main trend of the process at this period (Crace 1930). On the whole, the process of the formation of socially mutually unequal groups on the basis of existing clans is clearly reminiscent of the process of caste formation, which found its culmination among the Hindus of India. There is a like correspondence in the very order of the advancement of the various social groups (among the Hindus the process also began with the rise of higher or pure *varnas*) in the course of development of the process, i.e., the separation of constantly more new groups, and with such characteristic features of the caste as the professional principle and the mutual social inequality of the emerging groups. The stability of the original clan organization was largely responsible for the fact that the process of social stratification was often similar to that of caste formation. It was likewise this stability that provided the basis for the development of a social hierarchy.

The rise of caste-type groups is a process characteristic of a transition from a tribal, socially homogeneous situation to the system of stratified social groups. It is important to note, however, that the Kachari social groups cannot yet be regarded as classes, since membership of a more or less high social stratum is determined by birth (as in the case of castes) rather than by relation to means of production as in typical class societies. That is why the higher social groups ('strata' in the above indicated sense) here are not pre-dominant economically (cf. Danilova 1968: 62). Social stratification within the elementary cells or communities of the society resulted in the emergence of a state structure as well as being the social basis for it. The Kachari state thus was not an early-class type of society, but rather a pre-class one, in which the further evolution of social groups and their development into classes was arrested by the destruction of the Kachari state and its disintegration into a number of separate territories, since the latter were united not by organic economic ties but only by the force of military power.

What remained, then, after the fall of the state? The respective fates of the plain and the hill areas were quite different. The former were overrun by continually changing waves of conquerors, which resulted in the assimilation of the remaining plain population by the conquerors, so that they practically ceased to exist as a distinct ethnic group. As for the hill communities, they retained their specific ethnic features and traditional institutions to a greater extent; the hill people never attained the level of a class society, moreover, their institutions having lost the traces of social stratification manifest at the time of the Kachari raj. The latter circumstance needs some comment.

The fact is that stratified social groups did not embrace the whole of the society of the Kacharis. There were two types of clan with different functions in the period of the Kachari state, viz. as blood relationship categories regulating marriage, exogamic in essence (this was their primary function), and as social groups which had lost their original function with regard to exogamy (and moreover, had often become endogamous) and occupied different ranks on the social scale. The transformation of clans into social groups took place mainly in the raja's immediate surroundings, in areas with the closest connections with the court. The fact that the more advanced social strata were linked with the upper sections of the noble clans and were attended on by subordinate professional groups is illustrated by the very names of the various groups. Notably the occurrence of the term 'king's' before the names of the majority of the professional clans — e.g., the king's fishermen, the king's laundresses, etc., — indicates that these refer not to the usual trade groups which had become separated as a result of the natural division of labor in a given community, but to professional groups intended to supply mainly the needs of the court. It is only natural that the designations for precisely these groups should have come down to us since the historical evidence concerns mainly the raja's activities, the royal court and those institutions which were most closely connected with both of these. After the fall of the Kachari state, new conquerors assimilated the most highly developed and cultured upper groups — politically the most active population strata with their socially stratified clans. As for the outlying and particularly the hill districts, the clans here are more likely to have retained their primary functions; the need for the division of laborers into professional castes, or for the professional differentiation of the mass of agriculturists living and practising a natural economy in the communities scattered all over the hills having not yet arisen. Whereas the *raja*'s immediate entourage — who were all members of some noble clan — his closest associates and his officials originated from communities and now secured a superordinate position over these, the hill communities retained their social integrity, and the clans within them preserved their exogamic principles and social homogeneity.

This is, as far as the available material allows us to judge, what the social structure or, to be more exact, the social basis of the Kachari state looked like. As for its administrative and political systems, the scantiness of the available data permits us to consider only a comparatively late phase of the Kachari *raj* (i.e., from the beginning of the sixteenth century). These data moreover refer mainly to the structure of the administration and to the organization of the state in the North Kachar Hills, which formed the center and the core of the Kachari *rajas* domain in that period. As we said above, the Kachari state comprised both the plains and the hill areas. The latter, owing to their ecological peculiarities, always enjoyed greater autonomy. The hill territories (both in the Maibong period and later, when the *raja* retreated to Khaspur in the plains) were governed by the *Bara Bhandari*, chief judge, assisted by an extensive bureaucratic apparatus. All serious offences were adjudicated by the *raja* of Maibong. Minor cases such as conflicts over inheritance were solved by the village representatives, the *kunangs*.

The raja performed his judicial activities together with the *bara bhandari*. The *kunang* of a village in which an offence had occurred appeared before the court of the *raja*, together with both parties involved in the conflict. The *kunang* was responsible for the security of the accused during the judicial procedure. There were no barristers, and the accused defended himself.

Among the Kacharis of the Maibong period there existed a complex system in which punishment was relative to the seriousness of the offence. For a wilful murder, the death penalty was prescribed, and the sentence was characterized by elaborate cruelty. The offender's hands and legs were bound and he was placed in the square. Each day he was given smaller portions of rice. The offender died slowly of hunger; (the graver his offence the longer his period of suffering). For a wilful murder by brawling, the sentence was long-term imprisonment. Prison was also the punishment for theft. Incest was punished by an announcement in public and by the cutting off the tips of the nose and ears, followed by ostracism from the village. Bribery among simple people was punished by placement in the stocks; but if a courtier in an official post was found guilty of bribery, the death penalty awaited him — in this case, however, it was carried out secretly. Conflicts over land between villages were solved by the *raja* and the *bara bhandari;* those between individuals by the *kunangs*. In the judicial process, especially in serious cases, oaths, which were characterized by an elaborated ritual, were common practice.

In this way, the Kachari developed a complex system in which each offence was punished according to its graveness. There was, however, no written code of justice.

The second most important figure was the *senapati,* commander of the military (it should be noted that all the relevant titles are Sanskrit). Their power extended not only over all the hill Kacharis, but also to those inhabiting the foothills: excluded were only the *raja*'s court and those Kacharis (comparatively few already at this period) dwelling among the Bengalis in the plains. There is mention also of the existence of a large number of officials who supervised the *raja*'s subjects in the plains (Soppitt 1885: 5). However, with the ousting of the Kacharis from the plains by the Ahoms the plain Kacharis gradually decreased in number so that many posts turned into mere sinecures. Unfortunately, we do not know the names of these posts. Obviously, however, the system, as was rather common, was an imitation of the bureaucratic system of some more advanced people (in this case the Bengalis), although the level of development of the primitive state-like union was not always adequate to this system. As for the Bengali farmers inhabiting the Kachar plains, who were subjects of the Kachari *raja*, they obtained some sort of a constitution of their own. They were to a large extent autonomous, following their own system of government; their elected representatives of the individual *khels* (basic administrative units) had to be approved by the *raja*, however. They were put in charge of tax-collecting and were made responsible for the fulfilment of the labor obligations to the *raja* by his Bengali subjects. All officials here, of course, had titles of Bengali origin (e.g., *chaudhuri, mozumdar, lashkar, bara-bhuiya,* etc.,) (Soppitt 1885: 6).

The mountain Kacharis, as well as other mountain peoples, practiced slash-and-burn agriculture. This technique, which was called *jhum* in Assam, required the alternation of a short tilling period with a long fallow period. This type of agriculture did not by any means facilitate the establishment of distinct patterns of land tenure, particularly since forest areas were plentiful at that time. The village community retained common control and management of the agricultural process. However, each individual family cultivated on its own plot sufficient quantities of rice, cotton and other crops for its own subsistence, plus additional amounts to be exchanged at the local market for salt and other indispensable goods. This exchange was predominantly carried on by bartering. There are data to be found which prove the existence of private *jhum* fields belonging to the court of the *raja* (Soppitt 1885: 27). The Bengali settlers, who lived in the Khaspur and eastern Kachari areas and formed a part of Kachari Raj, fixed their rules of land tenure. In the final analysis it was the *raja* who allocated it to collectivities of community members. Collective possession, *khel*, functioned as a voluntary kith association of agriculturists. Within a *khel*, land was divided among the members who ran their individual plots independently. However, the partners remained bound by certain obligations, both one member to another and each member to the *raja*. If one of the owners neglected his plot and this fact negatively affected other plots (e.g., wild animals multiplying and thus endangering neighboring plots), the members of a *khel* could appeal to the *raja* who could then compel the guilty party to cease neglecting his land, by threatening to deprive him of it. If the occupant of a plot did not pay his part of the tax on the land, he could also lose his rights to the land, which would then be allocated to those members of the *khel* who could make the necessary payments. If anyone member did not pay the tax, the *khel* was collectively held responsible for this, and the *raja* confiscated all its land. Even when there had not been a breach of the rules, the *raja* could deprive a *khel* of its land; if this was determined to be in the interest of the state.

Let us now return to the administration of the hill areas. Each community had its own autonomous administration. Each village was headed by a *kunang*, a village head who represented his community in all state matters. This post was hereditary and descended from father to son, though always subject to the sanction of the *senapati*. The duties towards the *raja* and his government included the payment of taxes as well as several kinds of labor obligation. The collection of taxes was the responsibility of special officials, usually four in number. The latter were accompanied by the *kunang* of the village in question. Taxes were payable per household. Villages had to perform a certain amount of work for the state (e.g., the construction of public buildings and roads, etc.). In addition some villages and individual families had certain special duties towards the *raja*. So the gurubarisa were people who tilled the private *jhums* of the *raja* and his entourage; the sergasa (blacksmiths) met the needs of the court in forged articles, etc. (Soppitt 1885: 27). Moreover, each village supplied a certain number of coolies to meet various other needs of the court.

In a state which was to a considerable degree based upon armed strength, the army played an important part. There existed a special method of collecting recruits for the *raja*'s army. The *senapati* would order each village to supply a certain number of men who were

provided with arms but did not undergo special training. A small
detachment remained permanently in Maibong as the *raja*'s guard. At
the threat of foreign aggression or at the beginning of an offensive
campaign all able-bodied men were put under arms. There existed
unwritten laws governing the conduct of war. Before launching an
attack, messengers were sent to declare war on the enemy. Villages
supplying soldiers were exempt from taxation.

The Kachari state was familiar with the institution of slavery. Slave
trading was widely practised. The Kacharis purchased slaves from the
hill tribes, who took numerous captives in the course of their incessant
inter-tribal wars, and paid for them in cowries, salt and dogs. Slaves
were treated tolerably well; they were well looked after and all their
vital needs were met. A slave could marry only with his owner's
consent, but this consent practically amounted to release of the slave:
the couple could acquire a separate house of their own and became
practically free. Nominally, domestic slaves remained their owner's
property, but their dependence was henceforth restricted to minor
services in favor of the owner's family. Children of slaves were
considered to be free, though it was difficult for them to marry
Kacharis. Ethnically, the bulk of the slaves were related to various
Kukis tribes and the Manipuris. The latter in most cases were ran-
somed by their relatives and returned home.

The principal duties of slaves consisted in clearing hillsides for
agriculture, collecting firewood and cooking food for their owners. The
Kacharis were allowed to eat food cooked by slaves, but the latter
usually had their meals separately. Slaves wore the same kind of
clothing as the Kacharis; they were not allowed to retain their own
tribal costume. Dead slaves, according to the law, had to be buried,
though a favorite slave might be cremated, in keeping with the Kachari
custom (Soppitt 1885: 48). On the whole, slavery was of a typically
domestic kind, whereby slaves lived and worked together with their
owners and were gradually admitted to the latter's communities.

It is worthy of note that there were no purchased slaves at the *raja*'s
court. All the necessary work, as has been mentioned above, was
carried out by the Kacheri themselves. It should be stated that the
position of court servants was much the same as that of slaves: they
were taken away from their villages against their will and were not
paid for their work. To the forced nature of their labor testify the
stories relating that, on the arrival of the *raja*'s representative at a
village, young boys and girls would flee to the jungle, the former to
escape being forced to work at court, the latter to avoid being put into
the *raja*'s harem.

Another category of dependent laborers was formed by debt slaves,
who included not only those who were kept in servitude to redeem

their own debts, but also the descendants of debtors who had been unable to repay their creditors in their lifetime. There was a special scale of redemption of debts in the period concerned, which has come down to us: a debt of fifteen rupees was repaid by a year's work, a debt of thirty rupees by two years, etc. During the period of debt servitude the creditor had to provide the debtor with food, clothing and shelter.

Lastly, there is some scanty evidence of the religious organization at court before the Kacharis' conversion to Hinduism. To the *raja*'s court were attached eight families from among which priests were appointed. Each family provided one priest, who sacrificed only to one particular deity. The high priest — *alu raja* — was regarded as chief spiritual adviser to the *raja*. Only the *raja* and the persons closest to him could offer sacrifices to the main gods such as Alow, Mali and Wa. Once a year human sacrifices were made at Maibong; these were usually war captives from foreign tribes; if, however, there were no captives two fellow tribesmen were sacrificed instead. The victims had their throats cut and priest received the heart and liver (Soppitt 1885: 31). The functions of the other priests were hereditary within their respective families. Priests (except for the high priest) could dwell in their own villages, though sometimes the *raja* would summon them to Maibong. They were not entitled to any reward but were allowed to keep the heads of sacrificial animals for their own use. As was mentioned above, even prior to the Kacharis' formal conversion to Hinduism the latter's influence was manifest as reflected by, for instance, the names of deities: the Kacharis' principal deity being named Bangla raja (King of Bengal).

The above is a general outline of the Kachari state. This was based, in social terms, on inter-communal stratification, which with the stabilization of the state structure, stretched beyond the community. Social stratification and social inequality are pre-conditions for the establishment of the state. However, the examples of other peoples, in particular the peoples of the hill territories of Northeast India neighboring upon the Kachari area, show that social stratification by no means always results in state formation.

Let us now compare the Kacharis' position with that of some of these peoples whose forms of stratification it has been possible to trace on the basis of contemporary (very recent) ethnographic material.

Thus a number of peoples inhabiting the hill areas of Northeast India (though not all of them) possessed certain patterns of stratification; patterns which have survived to this day. These patterns are comparable to those of the Kacharis in the distant past, which later disappeared together with their state. The peoples concerned belong to the different Tibeto-Burmese groups (i.e., the Kuki-chins and various groups of Nagas). Their various social forms are extremely diverse, but

characteristic of them all, as also of the Kacharis, is the advancement
of particular social strata based on clans, whose evolution followed
along the lines of transformation from blood-relationship categories
into social groups. The emergence of social groups on the basis of clans
is linked directly with the problem of senior and junior clans and
branches of clans, from which, under certain specific circumstances,
social inequality may have arisen: the senior branch clan or group of
clans, depending on the concrete circumstances, gradually came to be
regarded as a superior 'aristocratic' one. Among some peoples the
process takes place along the lines of the steady rise of a single noble
stratum, among others it is accompanied by the gradual formation of a
whole hierarchy of socially stratified clan groups, etc. Let us now look
at some concrete examples (Maretina 1972: 130–147).

The Lakhers (a Kuki-chin group) have the most highly stratified
social structure; but below their primitive class forms one can clearly
trace the clan background of these. The several dozen Lakher clans
belong to different social stages; each of these stages corresponding to
a particular social stratum. (Again, a parallel with the Indian castes,
which, in all their variety, still belong to definite social strata, suggests
itself; these strata were already present in outline in the ancient Indian
social groups, the *varnas*.) The Lakhers possess three such strata. The
highest of these is *abei* (including six clans), the second 'aristocratic'
one, *phansang* (seventeen clans), and the lowest *macchi*, an undifferentiated social conglomeration of productive clans (Parry 1932:
229). This social structure is topped by the head, while its lowest
positions are occupied by slaves. Yet this social differentiation does not
encompass the people as a whole, but takes place within each individual community: the dominant clans have not overstepped its
bounds, and each community has its own head.

Another people belonging to the Kuki-chin group, the Mizos
(Lushai), exemplify a different type of social stratification. Here the
situation, rather typical of this particular stage of development, is as
follows. The place of a ruling social stratum has been taken up by one
specific clan, the Sailo (Shakespear 1912: 43–46). Each community,
usually coinciding with a village (and only sometimes also including a
related village ruled by the head's son), had its own head, but all heads
belong to the ruling clan Sailo. The solidarity between kindred heads
has promoted the consolidation of the dominant clan.

Another type of differentiation is represented by the Konyak Nagas;
one of the most inaccessible and rarely studied groups of Nagas. Their
topmost clan, the Ang, had gone through a process of fission, as a
result of which a particularly privileged sub-clan, the so-called 'clan of
the great Ang', emerged. This former sub-clan developed into a
self-contained endogamous groups. (Von Fürer-Haimendorf 1939, pt.

III). This gradual diminution of the leading group is characteristic of many peoples in the East at similar stages of development. Among the Konyaks the sacralization of the head and hence a particular concern with the purity of his descent and the gradual narrowing of the bounds of the endogamous group can be observed. This gradual splitting up of self-contained groups which themselves came about as a result of the fission of some larger group, and the fixed position of these in the social scale once again, is reminiscent of certain stages in the development of the caste system. In the case of both the Konyaks and the Kacharis, this process had not reached completion — the slow rate of evolution under conditions of isolation from external contacts in these cases resulted in a rather indefinite character of the social forms concerned. On a mutual comparison of the evolution of the Kacharis and the Konyaks, it becomes apparent that only some elements of the caste structure were developed by each: the Konyaks stressed the need for protection against contamination by alien blood and the self-sufficiency of the rising group, while the Kachari groups may be characterized as socio-professional. At the same time the main trait of both, is obviously, the social inequality of the splitting groups, as in the case of all caste-like groups.

We could well continue this enumeration of peoples who in one way or another underwent the process of social stratification. The above will, however, be enough to convince one of the similarity between the course of development of the Kacharis in the Kachari Raj period and that of a number of hill peoples lacking a state organization. The distinctive feature of all is that at the establishment of the state system, certain privileged groups rose above the community structure and emerged as ruling group of the entire political union. But where the community remained the basic political unit, social stratification took place within each individual community (though affecting the entire society), which was an independent, self-governing entity not linked to others by an overarching supreme power. In the latter case the social strata appeared to be organically linked to the community to a greater degree than in the former, where stratification was conditioned by requirements with respect to state employees and disappeared together with the fall of the state.

We would like to stress the feature, common to all forms of stratification (both among the Kacharis and among contemporary hill peoples) of the pre-eminence of purely social factors. The division into social strata need not necessarily lead to economic stratification. Economic superiority is merely one of a number of factors promoting the rise of a man on the social scale; the social factor being the essential one. It is not material wealth but one's affiliation to a certain social group that determines one's social position. One should reflect that this phenomenon — the emergence of social inequality prior to economic differentiation — is testified by ample ethnographic and historical evidence (Danilova 1968: 60 ff, 346, 434 ff.).

Taking into consideration all that has been discussed above, one will naturally ask why, in spite of the similarity in character of the social stratification process among a number of hill peoples of Northeast India, only one group, namely the Bodo peoples, were able on the basis of this process to evolve a primitive class state. It is hardly possible to give a definite answer to this at present, due to the scantiness of the available material. We would, however, like to put forward some considerations which are the result of a comparative analysis of the available data.

We believe that it is a precondition to the solution of the question raised above that the specific environmental factors in each of the districts concerned should be taken into account. The ecological peculiarities that determine many aspects of the economy and culture of the peoples in question are far from irrelevant to the latter's history, both ethnic and political. Characteristic of Assam is the distinct topographical contrast between hill country and valleys. The hills, though not excessively high, are nevertheless steep and almost inaccessible; the plains, on the other hand, are low, and dissected by a close network of rivers, which provide excellent conditions for agriculture. The plains of Assam are able to sustain a large population, and it is this factor that attracted numerous immigrants, who created more or less stable political unions here. The hills, divided into a number of separate massifs and covered with dense forests, provide habitation for only a limited number of people due to the ecological conditions. Therefore conquerors could neither become firmly established nor accommodate large garrisons: neither could they settle their people, nor found new settlements in the hills. The hills protected the autochtonous people against all kinds of unfriendly intrusions, but at the same time prevented them from establishing useful contacts, thus inevitably delaying their cultural development.

This great difference between living conditions in the hills and on the plains prevented the unification of their respective populations within one state: the entire economic system and mode of life of the two differed so greatly that the state power could extend to the hills only nominally. As we saw above, in the example of the government of the hills in the Maibong period, this power was made manifest here through the levying of taxes, troops, etc., but did not affect the fundamental essence of the mountain peoples' life. In short, any kind of hill country, owing to its ecological peculiarities, is ill-adapted to the formation of state-like unions, which requires the unification of a wide range of different territories, indispensable contacts with more advanced neighbors and the large scale organization of manpower. (We are not maintaining that there can be no state in hill areas — here only those early 'empires' which emerged as a result of the unification of a wide variety of different ethnic groups are considered). In hilly country communications, both between individual communities and between the hill communities as a whole and the outside world, are hampered, so that there is no opportunity for the penetration here of a new ideology, religion, language, etc — i.e., those attributes of the state which we already mentioned above when stressing the importance of the contacts with the Hindu states of North India for the Assam state-like unions — whereas these attributes were easily able to penetrate the Brahmaputra Valley, which is open to the west.

To return to history, all dramatic conflicts and all significant events in the political life of Assam took place (or were resolved) in the plains. It was here that all the various states emerged, rose to eminence and were destroyed, and it was here that the assimilation of all the heterogeneous ethnic elements and the synthesis of the integral nation took place. In short, under the conditions prevailing in mediaeval Assam, for a territory to become a state-like union it had to include the plains: this statement has been corroborated by the entire history of the region. This circumstance sheds some light on the question of why the early states of Assam were associated exclusively (of all the hill peoples) with the Bodo peoples.

The ethnic history of Assam may be outlined as a succession of waves of settlement of various ethnic groups. Traces of the earliest (probably negroid) of these waves are manifest with a number of anthropological variations, only among a few peoples. The next one was represented by the Mon-Khmers, who were assimilated by subsequent immigrants; (and partly driven into the hills, because all new immigrants strove to settle in the rich valleys of the Brahmaputra and its tributaries, but later had to retreat to the hills, when pushed back by a stronger rival than themselves). The same applies to the Tibeto-Burmese, who followed the Mon-Khmers and also first spread across the plains.

The Tibeto-Burmese penetrated into Northeast India in several, chronologically divided streams. The Bodo made up the first of these streams. Thus, unlike other Tibeto-Burmese tribes who immediately settled in the hill districts of Assam, the Bodo people first occupied vast parts of the plains. There is a record testifying that already 'two thousand years ago, if not earlier, the Bodo are likely to have occupied the whole of the Assam Valley, the major part of North Bengal and the Surma Valley' (*Encyclopaedia of religion and ethics* 1909: 753). This statement is corroborated by a number of historical indications. Among the most convincing of these is the evidence provided by toponymy, which reflects the influence of Bodo languages on the place names of Assam. For example, the majority of the names of rivers in Assam are prefixed by '*di*' or '*ti*', meaning 'water' in Bodo (e.g., Dibang, Dihong, Dibru, Dikho, Tista, Tilao — the former of which is the local name for the Brahmaputra) (Gait 1926). These traces of the linguistic influence of the Bodo witness to the long period of their rule in Assam, particularly in the valleys. Further evidence is furnished by such linguistic facts as the presence of a number of verbal roots as well as words derived from Bodo in the Assami language; e.g., *agach* — 'to prevent', *chelak* — 'to lick', *Haphala* — 'embankment', *bonda* — 'cat', etc. [Cf. Gait 1926; *Encyclopaedia of religion and ethics* 1909: 753 ff.]. Lastly, the famous Chinese traveller Hsuang-ch'uang, who visited Assam in A.D. 640, directly mentioned the Bodo as constituting the main population group of Kamarupa, or ancient Assam. It was, incidentally, precisely against different tribes of the Bodo group, which at that time occupied the Brahmaputra Valley (i.e., not only the Kacharis, but all the Bodo peoples), that the Ahoms invading Assam in the thirteenth century had to fight.

Thus, at the period of the emergence of the Kachari state the Bodo were settled in the plains of Assam. It is probably due to this fact that they were able, unlike other tribes which had long been confined within an enclosed space of hilly terrain, to enter the stage of state formation. This idea is supported by Gait, a scholar of Assam history, when he says: 'Life under conditions of the Valleys helps to consolidate power. In the hills these processes are less intensive. Several, now hill, tribes previously occupied the plains. These are the Kacharis pushed by the Ahoms into the North Kachar Hills' (Gait 1926).

The rise of another Bodo state-like union — the Koch state — also dates from the period when the Koch occupied Lower and Middle Assam (fifteenth century). There are records of wealthy towns and temples built by Koch rulers, of a regular system of state government with periodical population censuses and of a powerful Koch army. The high level of development of the Koch state can be judged from the following utterance — even if exaggerated — of Nagandra Natha Vasu, a scholar engaged in the study of the ethnic history of Northeast India: 'What a terrible catastrophe was to befall upon the people who evoked admiration of the whole western world by raising a shining light of culture and civilization' (Vasu, p. 83). Their end was similar to that of the Kacharis: the bulk of the Koch and Chutiya were so strongly influenced by Hinduism that they now call themselves '*rajbansi*' and '*bhanga kshatriya*', thus tracing their descent from a side branch of the *kshatriyas* who, according to the Hindu tradition, while escaping from the range of Parasurama took refuge in Northeast Bengal (Risley 1915: 74); but unlike the Kacharis, who in their hill domain — the *dimasa* — preserved their ethnic identity on a low tribal level, the Koch and the Chutiya had no separate hill settlements, and they have completely lost their specific ethnic features.

Let us briefly summarize the basic points of our conclusions concerning the specific characteristics of the formation of primitive state-like unions in outlying districts as exemplified by the region discussed.

(1) The slow rate and, due to the short period of the existence of state-like unions of this type, the incompleteness of the process of class formation in early states. Hence the pre-class (or early class) character of these states.

(2) The basic preservation of traces of the clan structure in the hierarchy of the social strata.

(3) The importance of the role played by war in the stabilization of states and in the strengthening of the dominant position of privileged social strata.

(4) The indispensability of contacts with advanced state systems to provide the required attributes of a state structure.

(5) The greater role played by the ecological factor than in the case of more advanced stages of development, as reflected in the difference in evolution between the hill areas and the plains.

(6) The transfer to the plains as an indispensable factor in the formation of the early state.

REFERENCES

Assam District Gazetteer. (1905), Vol. 17. Allahabad.
Bongard-Levin, G. M. and Il'in, G. F. (1969), *Drevniaia Indiia* [Ancient India]. Moscow: Nauka.
Crace, J. H. (1930), 'The Hill Cacharis'. *Census of India* I, part 8.
Danilova, Ludmila V. (1968), Diskussionnye problemy teorii dokapitalisticheskikh obshchestv [Problems under discussion in the theory of precapitalist societies,], in: *Problemy istorii dokapitalisticheskikh obshchestv*, ed. by L. V. Danilova. Vol. I. Moscow: Nauka. This article was also published as: 'Controversial problems of the theory of precapitalist societies', in: *Soviet Anthropology and Archaeology* 9: 269–328 (1972).
Encyclopaedia of religion and ethics. (1909), Volume 2. Edinburgh.
Fürer-Haimendorf, Ch. von (1939), *The naked Nagas.* London: Macmillan.
Gait, E. (1926), *A history of Assam.* Calcutta and Simla: Partridge.
Ghosh Dipali (1965), Descent and clan among the Dimasa. *Man in India* 45: 3.
Kozlova, M. G., Sedov, L. A., and Tiurin, V. A. (1968), Tipy ranneklassovykh gosudarstv v Iugo-Vostochnoi Azii [Types of early class societies in Southeast Asia], in: *Problemy istorii dokapitalisticheskikh obshchestv*, ed. by L. V. Danilova. Vol. I. Moscow: Nauka.
Maretin, Y. V. (1967), 'Obshchestvennye otnosheniia u batakov' [Social relations among the Bataks], in: *Obshchina i sotsial'naia organizatsia u narodov vostochnoii iugovostochnoi Azii*, pp. 146–167, ed. by R. F. Its. Leningrad: Nauka.

Maretin, Y. V. (1974), Indian influences on Bali culture, in: *The countries and peoples of the East. Selected articles*. Moscow: Nauka.

Maretina, Sofia A. (1972), Obrazovanie soslovii i klassov u gornykh narodov Severo-Vostochnoi Indii (k probleme klassoobrazovaniia) [Formation of estates and classes among the mountain peoples of northeastern India (on the problem of class formation)], in: *Strany i narody Vostoka* 14, Indiia— strana i narod. Book 3. Moscow: Nauka.

Parry, N. E. (1932), *The Lakhers*. London: Allen and Unwin.

Risley, R. H. (1915), *The people of India*. Calcutta and Simla: Partridge.

Shakespear, L. W. (1912), *The Lushai-Kuki clans*. London: Macmillan.

— (1914), *History of Upper-Assam, Upper-Burmah, and the Northeast frontier*. London: Macmillan.

Soppitt, S. A. (1885), *An historical and descriptive account of the Kachari tribes in the North Cachar Hills*. Shillong.

Sovetskaia Istoricheskaia Encyclopedia. (1971), [Soviet Historical Encyclopaedia]. Vol. 13. Moscow: Nauka.

Vasu, N. N. (n.d.) *The social history of Kamarupa*. Calcutta: Thacker.

17   The Kuba State

JAN VANSINA

Kuba is the name given to a state now in Zaïre, which occupied the territory between the Kasi, Lulua and Sankuru rivers and covered an area at least the size of Belgium. The period considered here in the latter part of the nineteenth century ends in 1885/6 with the foundation of a Congo Independent State post nearby on the Lulua at Luebo and is most valid for 1875–1885 beginning with the full expansion of Luso-African (Vellut 1972) trade. European attempts to dominate the country began by 1897 culminating with the capture of the capital in 1900. The population was from 100 to 150,000 persons, the population density being perhaps 6 km² but variable from one part of the country to the other. An absolute low existed in the 'empty' quarter of the east roamed only by Cwa (pygmoid) hunters. By ethnic self-identification eighteen groups lived in the state (Vansina 1964: 8, map I). The ethnographer recognizes major differences between the pygmoids, aboriginal Kete, late Coofa immigrants, the Ripuarians of the northwest and the northeast, the central Kuba who dominated the state and the peripheral Kuba similar to the previous group in many respects. From the point of view of language such differences are upheld. The first three groups spoke languages related to Luba, the next two had their own, either southern Mongo or belonging clearly in that orbit, whilst the last two have a distinctive form of speech of which the form spoken at the capital, Bushoong, was the official language. Outside of the state a small militant Kuba group related to the peripheral people lived far up the Sankuru near Lusambo and another, closely tied to the central Kuba lived south of the junction of Kasai and Lulua near the former river. The kingdom itself had no name. Kuba is the name given by its southern neighbors who also called it Lukengu after the name they had given to the king.

The inhabitants used their ethnic names or stated that they were people of the 'king' *nyim*, one term being used for kingship in general and for the Kuba king. After all, there was no other kingdom anywhere nearby.

The political situation was simpler than the ethnic picture. Essentially the state consisted of a core with about forty-three per cent of the population and perhaps forty per cent of the land in the center, with satellite chiefdoms east and west. The core consisted of the single Bushoong chiefdom of which the king was chief. It was by far the largest in the country and the Bushoong dominated the state. The core further incorporated a large number of Kete villages and a few one to three village-sized chiefdoms located as enclaves on its Kasai border. Within the core ten per cent of the population lived at the capital, a real city even though it did move at least once each reign, but moved only in a radius of 20 km by 25. Its plan was unchanged from one site to another, its buildings 'prefabricated'. It was the center for manufacturing luxury goods and the center of trade. No one was supposed to cultivate there (Vansina 1976). Its military potential exceeded anything that could be fielded by any other chiefdom or by any group of villages in the core itself. It dominated the state.

Most Kuba (the exceptions are the pygmoïd Cwa and patrilineal Coofa) were organized in matrilineages belonging to matrilineal clans. In every one lineage, excepting for the dynastic one, genealogical memory did not extend beyond the generation of the grandparents of adults and all lineages were equal in the clan: even the lineages were fragmented as marriage was virilocal and children stayed with their fathers until the latter died. After that the sons could, if they wished to, rejoin the seat of their lineage to join a few other oldsters there (Vansina 1964: 58–73). In practice the corporate expression of the lineage was a residential group: the clan section. It made up a ward in a village and included spouses and children of the members there. By 1954 such sections counted, on the average, eighteen members (Vansina 1964: 59). Functions were limited to representation of the ward in the village council. Lineage functions proper concerned the inheritance of movable goods (the most precious of which went to the son of a male deceased person) and management of a small common fund kept in cowries or perhaps blocks of redwood. Neither clans nor lineages held rights over land nor could they indulge in feuds. Membership to a clan could be acquired only by birth. To belong to a clan was important as a proof of free status (slaves have no clans) and for potential rights to political office that might be hereditary in that clan (but such offices were very rare; perhaps five per cent in the central adminstration and none in local administration at the village level). The kinship structure was completely dominated by the political structures except among the Coofa, where segmentary patrilineages governed sizeable settlements, and among the Cwa whose fluid bilateral groups were their only form of social organization. Proof of the dominant position of political institutions is seen by the fact that by 1954 fully thirty-three per cent of all lineage scissions were attributed to the influence of a political authority; and such authority had actually diminished during the colonial period (Vansina 1964: 71, table). Kings at least told their friends where to live and a few traditions from Mbop Mabiinc *ma*Mbul who ruled from ca. 1935 to 1885/6 and his predecessor bear this out.

Marriage was monogamous. Bridewealth was relatively moderate (Sheppard 1917: 124, 1893: 187b), and men married very young, perhaps before they were twenty (Sheppard 1893: 187b). Bridewealth was paid by the father of the groom to the father of the bride, not by members of the clans involved (Vansina 1964: 28–44). In this way bilateral kinship was stressed and the elementary family enjoyed real autonomy (Vansina 1964: 45–57). It was also the household. This unit also often comprised one or more slaves and *ngady* or female pawns. These bore children for their masters. They were common and acquired as security against a debt that could not be met by the treasury of a lineage or clan. Such heavy debts were most often incurred as fines in court; usually when someone was convicted of having killed a person by witchcraft.

But even commercial loans could lead to such a result. Pawns were rarely redeemed. At the time of handing her over, agreement was reached over the number of children to be born, which would belong to the master's clan and which would be retained by the original clan. Quite a number of variations in custom occurred here from one country to another, so that some households could boast of four producers, the man, a wife, a pawn and a slave; richer ones had more and the 'average' in the village somewhat less, the poorer ones consisting of just the man and wife, or a widowed person with children, who did not want to be integrated into another household.

Several neighboring households formed a clan section if their heads were kinsmen, and wards made up villages. Each village was ruled by elected officials, if it was a free village. It held its own domain, a territory including a spring or portion of river and usually some forest and some grasslands i.e., the types of land required for its economic well-being. Title was with the village but backed up by chiefs or kings (Vansina 1956). Most villages were smaller then than the average of the 1950s, when they averaged 175 or 200 (Vansina 1964: 96, fn. 3, 85). Some were certainly as large then though (Sheppard 1917: 88, 89, 140, 144, 146; Lapsley 1893: 94: Kete town 1000 or more).

The household was the domestic unit of production. Its output

exceeded its needs, including natural surplus (Allan 1965: 38), because
of the demands imposed by the tribute system. The staples planted
were maïze–beans–cassava for one rotation and maïze–groundnuts–
cassava for the other type of field; the first being 'forest' and the
second 'savanna' fields. Fallows lasted for perhaps seven to ten years.
Two crops of maïze were harvested a year, which was then unique in
this part of central Africa (Sheppard 1917: 97. 141). This means that
other crops were also doubled. Some farmers, moreover, planted yet
another type of field near the springs of streams where maïze ripens a
few weeks before the second main harvest of the agricultural year.
Besides this, orchards of palmgroves (usually raffia) and bananas, as
well as dawn-gardens were cultivated all around the village site (Vansina 1964: 13–17).

Compared to their neighbors the Kuba used a labor-intensive system
in that both men and women performed all farming tasks save only
weeding, which was women's work. Unmarried men did not farm, but
because of the low age of marriage the labor force here, compared
with other areas, was swollen by strong young men as well as by the
additional input of the men in general. Still the bottleneck for output
remained labor, as land was relatively plentiful (there is no evidence
for overly short fallow periods and soil degradation); every known
advantage had been pursued with the existing technology and the
capital investment in tools (axes and hoes) was limited. Control over
production, therefore, had to be limited to control over the producers,
and this is what happened (Douglas 1962).

Some Kuba, along the main rivers, were professional fishermen.
Their wives cared for the cassava gardens and helped repair the nets.
This way of life required sizeable capital tool input (for canoes and
gear) and more collaboration (crews) than agriculture (Verner 1903:
403–405). Its effects can be seen, in that part of the catch went to the
owner of a boat whether he was part of the crew or not and that the
crew were 'paid' in fish. Collaborative work also was common in other
villages for maintaining fish ponds and complex hunting traps. Because
of the difference in capital input there should be found greater differences in wealth between households of fishermen than between households of farmers. But there are no data (even for a later period) to test
this proposition.

Division of labor by craft was developed. Besides the fishing, professional fishermen were also potters along the Sankuru and the Lulua.
Pygmies were professional hunters and each chief seems to have had
some Cwa at his court. Such specialization was in part imputable to the
environment — good clay was found on the banks of the Lulua and
Sankuru, hence the fishermen were potters — in part it was a matter of

choice. Cwa adamantly refused to cultivate and still do. So by their own volition they were specialized hunters. Most specialties were a combination of both types of factors, and most villages had part time specialists of which the most important one was the smith (Sheppard 1917: 96–97; Wharton 1927: 52–53); since no other persons knew how to smelt or even forge metal. Specialized woodcarvers for drums and fancy articles could be replaced by unskilled persons for most purposes. Still their skills were high enough to make them specialists. And so it goes for many crafts, but not weaving. Weaving was mens' work assisted by children for making the thread, and women to render the cloth supple, and eventually to embroider it (Lapsley 1893: 81–82). Except for salt makers who cultivated the salt-bearing grasses in marshes and the iron-ore foundries, most other specialties were found at the capital, where specialists were full-time. They included smiths, carvers, hat makers; probably basket weavers as well; leatherworkers, jewellers, carvers by sub specialty such as pipe bowls, who left the carving of pipe-stems to others. Most people there were engaged in part-time crafts, such as the women's task of embroidering cloth and mens' of carving or sewing. If political and ritual tasks were included, every one in the capital was a specialist in some sense and no one was supposed to be farming (Vansina 1964: 17–21).

Specialization by area was also well developed. Besides fishermen and potters the eastern Kete were salt makers, other Kete and a Kuba group were renowned smiths, the Coofa basket weavers, the north-western people hunters, especially of guinea fowl, and specialized elephant hunters formed an association known as *Itwiimy* (Sheppard 1893: 187a). They furnished some of the ivory which was essential to the long-distance trade. In fact each part of the realm had its specialties (Vansina 1964: 19–20).

Given this specialization it is not surprising that trade within the kingdom flourished and markets existed everywhere. The four-day-week was based on them and central place theory seems to have applied to them since markets being held on the same day were spaced about two days walk apart (Sheppard 1893: 184 a–c, 1917: 88–96). The most central one was at the capital which also had daily food markets. The traders in this network were regular villagers (Sheppard 1893: 185c).

Professional traders lived in the capital and went for long-distance trading to the country north of the Sankuru, to the southernmost market in the country (Kabao before 1885), and further along Kasai to the nearest connection with Luso-African traders (Sheppard 1893: 186a for a caravan; Von Wissman 1890: 77). In this way the state was connected with the Luso-African trading system which reached from

Luanda and Benguela to this area and beyond (Vellut 1972). Foreign
caravans composed of Imbangala from the Kwango River near Cas-
sange, Ambaquistas from the hinterland of Luanda and Ovimbundu,
frequented Kabao from at least 1875–1880 bringing with them sea salt
(Verner 1903: 287), beads, cowrie-shells, brass from the coast as well
as copper from Shaba and slaves bought among the Luba further
south. They bought ivory above all and rubber as well for export on
the world market. They also bought raffia cloth and red camwood for
resale further south. The ivory and redwood came to a large extent
from the country north of the Sankuru where it was bought by the
caravans for luxury products of Kuba manufacture fashioned at the
capital. Such was the importance of trade, that by 1892 the villages did
not only all pay their taxes in cowries but bridewealth also, was at least
expressed, and often paid, in cowries, which found their way into the
regional trading system from the markets at the capital and at Kabao
(Sheppard 1917: 132, 124). Thus, every household was affected by it.

The material organization of markets was well-developed. A representative of the king or chief saw to law and order, a royal tax-
collector took in sales taxes, and disputes could be settled by a court
on the spot. Common commercial usages existed, such as lending on
credit, pawning, prescription, sale before witnesses and prescribed
gestures to close a deal legally (Sheppard 1893: 183a; De Macar 1893:
110; Vansina 1964: 22–27).

1. THE KINGDOM

The kingdom consisted of chiefdoms ruled over by hereditary 'eagle
feather chiefs'. The central and biggest chiefdom, that of the
Bushoong, was ruled by the king. All others were so much smaller
(Vansina 1964: 166) — by a factor of ten at least — that even the
capital alone could dominate any of them. Some chiefdoms, but not
the Bushoong, formed clusters when they belonged to the same ethnic
group, shared the same dynastic and the same electoral (aristocratic)
clans but as clusters did not act together. Even if they had, the
Bushoong chiefdom would have still outclassed them. The aristocratic
clans held their status from the conviction that they had been the first
immigrants after the Kete and Cwa autochtones, coming with or even
before the dynastic clans. This may have been true only for some of
them though. Others attained the status centuries ago, when the first
chiefs had to rely heavily on their support.

The king was supposed to be the matrilineal descendant of the first
man, the lineal descendant of the man who was chosen by the nature

spirits (with a bit of deception) to be 'chief of chiefs' whence his mythical charter to rule over all others, and the lineal descendant of the great culture hero Shyaam, who had shaped Kuba culture. His life was surrounded by reverential protocol — including a special court vocabulary — and replete with layer upon layer of symbols which 'explained' kingship. Quasi-ritual prohibitions were mostly related to his unique status and his life-giving status. The king was the deputy of the creator on Earth which is reflected in his title, 'God of the hills' (the Earth) (Vansina 1964: 98–99). His office was more than 'by divine right'. Many of his people held him to be responsible for life itself. As one once said, 'If I sleep it is the king, if I eat it is the king, if I drink it is the king' (Vansina 1964: 101) and he attributed this only to the fact that without kings there would be anarchy; the statements of true believers were much stronger (Torday 1925: 117–119; Torday and Joyce 1910: 59–61). Everyone accepted that after his death the king became a nature spirit, that was the strongest of sorcerers as well and responsible for all fertility. The Kuba who believe in metempsychosis do not have any ancestor cult, but a cult of the nature spirits of the deceased kings exists. So, in ritual, the kingship is certainly sacred, whatever the convictions of individuals were, and these differed. For some the supernatural powers stemmed from the fact that kings possessed the strongest charms available in the realm. For others they were innate in the office. Others derived them from the socio-political structure. Both Frazer and Evans Pritchard, at least in the 1950s, found local followers here who had never heard of their controversy.

Once a month, at the new moon, the king performed an important ritual sacrifice and was assisted by his (eldest?) sister in this, by his wives (through songs) and by the members of the council of the realm 'the diviners of the basket (charm) *ncyaam*' who are representatives of each of the eighteen aristocratic clans of the Bushoong. The link between the moon and the king was so strong that he should not show himself during the new moon when all life stops, when a woman cannot bear a child nor a man die' (Vansina 1964: 99). He had power (*paam*) over rain which he sent or withheld, over the yield of the fields, the success of the hunt and the fertility of women. Rituals for all of these contingencies existed in which his blessing was essential. The king possessed a carved double, the *ndop* which his wives put beside them when they delivered a child, or when the king was away and which the next king was supposed to put beside him for one night so that the 'power' of the deceased could flow into the new incumbent. In 1892 four such statues of previous kings were set up in the royal reception hall (Sheppard 1917: 112). They were then 'highly prized and regarded as sacred'. This was the equivalent of a royal ancestral cult.

The great rituals of kingship, when its full meaning and pageantry unfolded, were royal funerals and installations. By 1885 none of these had taken place since ca. 1835. The descriptions we have (Torday and Joyce 1910: 63–65; Vansina 1964: 111–117) are based on later practices. The details may not correspond to the earlier practice but the main discourse and the sequence of rituals was certainly similar. And as for funerals there were those of the queen mothers which came close to the royal rites. The splendor and wealth of kingship was emphasized by the funeral gifts — including many human sacrifices of slaves, criminals, women and free men. The political key role of the institution was underscored by a patterned anarchy that followed the announcement of death. If the funeral rites were awesome, the installation rituals which lasted a full year were even more so. This action included the cooperation of all the segments of the population, and the building of a new capital. It began with a formal recognition — and a real choice — by the title-holders of the successor as king. It included such rituals as incest (the king no longer has a clan: the incest is not incest), a ritual instruction by the council of the realm, another secret ritual instruction by the major titleholders and a ritual voyage to the residence of *muyum*, the keeper of the national charms and the most official keeper of dynastic tradition (others were the *mwaaddy* and the king himself). This was the highlight. By night, in the forest, the king and *muyum* met alone. The king said, 'I am looking for life' and was shown the sacred relics, especially the skullcap of a former monarch. After this he could never again set eyes on *muyum*. The ritual was so important because *muyum's* national charms included the magical kaolin egg which rolling by itself could go out of hiding to destroy any unjust rulers or tyrants. It was the ultimate control on kingship (Vansina 1964: 111–117).

In theory the succession was adelphic and matrilineal, and the successor should also be the oldest in age in the dynastic lineage: the two conditions of seniority by line and by age are not always present in one person. In practice there had been competition in every single generation. Indeed when the king died in 1885 or in 1886 his brother and his nephew competed for several years. The royal succession was the focal point for the organization of the two main political parties or factions. The ruling king was supported by his sons and gave them command over all delicate operations and lucrative posts in so far as he could. His daughters and grandchildren also were behind him. The tie to kingship for them was through one *person*. He was opposed by his closest successor, acknowledged as such by the title *bweemy*, and the sons and   descendants of the latter.

The successor to the successor, however, the *ncwaal* and his children, backed the king again, since he was the enemy of the enemy. For the same reason, the descendants of the previous ruler sided with the *bweemy* and those of the ruler before with the incumbent. One party was in power during a reign, the other in opposition. During the next reign the roles were reversed. In the 1870s the king was old and one of his sons was taking over. His sons and those of the *bweemy* had already fought, especially those who had been invested with a title and an office. But an overthrow of the ruler was out of the question as an unwritten rule of the political game. The dignitaries and the public at the capital would have thwarted it, and their support was vital to all camps. Otherwise, these men were divided between the factions as friends, protégés or hangers-on, hoping for some spoils (Vansina 1964: 153–155).

Besides the parties, and within the arena of the Bushoong chiefdom, the institutions maintained a fine balance between the authority and power of the king and that of the 'Bushoong', i.e., the officials. The structure of the councils was such that a king could not legally unilaterally become too autocratic with regard to war or tribute. A formal way of rebuking him was provided by the council of the realm and the rallying of opinion against the ruler, even though such meetings were secret, and even though the council had no force at its disposal to enforce its wishes. The other councils could block any royal action, or rather rob it of its legitimacy. The only sanction was the supernatural one of *muyum*, and the awareness of it, as well as the awareness that if villagers were too oppressed they would flee and weaken the state. For Kuba kings have always been fully aware of the need to attract people (and labor!) and of the dangers involved in losing them.

The king's power was not merely supernatural or granted by council action, nor did it stem from his command only, for fines he alone could inflict. Such orders and such fines were known and accepted but limited to one individual or one village at the time. Much of the king's real power came from his wealth. His palace contained several filled treasure houses and he could reward friends, followers, emissaries and his children. He owned some 500 fighting slaves, forty of which — under the command of one of his sons — formed the only constabulary in the land. Moreover, every Bushoong clan and every chiefly clan outside of the chiefdom gave him women. His harem of over 600 persons worked for him, mostly making the velvet-pile cloth which wound up in his treasury or with his traders abroad. The whole palace organization was cared for by special menial villages called Matoon, after the royal clan name. For all daily matters, services and commodities these villagers had to be responsible. The establishment of the monarch was autonomous. In this at least he was independent of the 'Bushoong' — the councils. In the last resort, it was the police, and

even more his treasure house, which backed his authority; and the
conviction of his supernatural powers rationalized the situation (Vansina 1964: 102–107).

2. ORGANIZATION OF GOVERNMENT

Government consisted further of a bureaucracy of title-holders: the
kolm. Their praise names, protocol, etiquette, insignia, and symbols
made it immediately clear that (1) they were part of an organization,
(2) the king stood at its apex and (3) indicated everyone's precise rank
in the organization. Over 120 titles existed and all *kolm* of the central
government lived in the capital. Their positions were not hereditary.
They were appointed on the authority of the king for some posts but for
most were selected from candidates, elected by the senior *kolm* in
rank. No one could hold two offices or abandon one for a more lucrative
or prestigious one after appointment. Achievement was primary, even
for some of the senior titles where some hereditary rules were added to
ascriptive rules. Here the balance of power between the king and the
'Bushoong' — represented by the aristrocrats — was evidenced by rules
holding that the nominee should belong to one of the eighteen aristocratic clans[2] or in some cases to one of two such clans and be at the
same time a king's son or grandson: or the balance was obtained in
other situations by opposing royal children to aristocrats. Succession
was never automatic, not even to the seat each aristrocratic clan held
in the council of the realm: the peers chose the person, whether he was
senior in the lineage involved or not. The resources of all these *kolm*
came from payments as judges, part of the taxes they collected and
occasional gifts from the treasury (Vansina 1964: 126–133; Torday
and Joyce 1910: p. 62 [which is incorrect *re* income]).

Collectively then, the council of the realm was the highest authority
and the king only sat as one of its members. But it only met during
crises such as succession rituals or to rebuke a king when something
clearly extraordinary had happened which went far beyond the rules of
the political game. For instance they did not meet for every small war.
They met in secret and we do not know whether they ever met
between 1835 and 1886.

Beyond this outward organization the whole population was divided into fairly clear social classes. The stratification was based not on unequal
access to resources or even labor, but on the differential controls over
the output of production. The highest class consisted of the king and
the successors, the members of the council of the realm and the highest
kolm, as well as the king's most favored sons. Truly, they were the
patricians, the *kolm* par excellence. Their houses were larger, their

finery more splendid, their domestic staffs larger, their comforts greater, their company more refined, their leisure more elegant and their tasks less physically demanding than any others (Wharton 1927: 26). They were also a tiny minority to be emulated.

The next class comprised most of the population of the capital as well as the courts in the small chiefdoms. Its members were lower officials, specialized craftsmen and traders none of whose households — in the capital at least — was concerned with agriculture and whose education also was deemed a cut above the common people. In the chiefdoms all officials besides chiefs themselves worked at least part-time in agriculture but otherwise they resemble the second stratum of the capital in many particulars especially as both were the main group eager to emulate the top people. This class can be roughly estimated at ten per cent of the population.

Then followed the *bakon* 'the villagers' or common people, the free village farmers. These constituted the bulk of the Kuba, or at least half of them. Their villages were led by their elected officials; they paid taxes and did corvée labor but they could also get ahead. They were much better off than the inhabitants of the Matoon villages, considered as menials. Such villages began as settlements of prisoners-of-war, or had been reduced to the status by a fine or simply by force. Most Kete villages were not Matoon; yet if they were small enough they were treated as such. People here could not easily get away from their condition. They were free, yes, but not free to move as they wished — at least in Matoon settlements. As for the Kete they could do so but usually only to find themselves in other Kete villages. The main distinction between the fifteen–twenty-five per cent of the population in this group and the higher stratum was that local self government was either non-existent (Matoon) or not efficient (Kete), and that impositions took up a considerable amount (no estimate can be made) of the people's time.

The bottom layer was made up of those who were tied to foreign households — the equivalent of proletariat. They were female pawns and slaves. The latter were not really represented at the political level and yet they made up a not inconsiderable proportion of the total, probably over ten per cent (*at least* six per cent slaves, [Vansina 1964: 20]; six per cent, fifty years *after* imports ceased, were slaves or descendants of slaves as remembered), or even fifteen per cent counting over five per cent *ngady*. Children of slaves were free and slaves could buy their freedom by paying the going price to their masters from funds gained by doing extra work beyond their duties. Slaves could also be reduced to slavery by some court decisions (De Jonghe 1949: 74, 79, 83, 84, 97, [an error] 103, 104, 139, 158, 161–162). The pawns and slaves were servants, working like every one else but having more than their fair share of the more arduous or boring tasks. Moreover, these persons ran the risk of being sacrificed when, among the Bushoong (Sheppard 1917: 129–131), their master or mistress died. And they suffered from public opprobrium.

One outcast stratum were the Cwa hunters. Their self-consciousness and separate ways of living certainly qualify them as a social class and one into which other people did not marry easily. But they considered themselves superior to the farmers whom they disdained as much as they themselves were disdained. They too came close to a ten per cent total of the population, at least by 1950 (Vansina 1964: 8, Table I).

Except for the Cwa, upward mobility existed in all the strata except for the top stratum which was only partially open for achievers. A quarter of the Bushoong men succeeded in becoming title holders during their lives. No estimate can be made as to the number of slaves who bought their freedom. The number must have been small and even less *ngady* women were ever redeemed by their kin. But their children were free. Downward mobility for men was much less frequent. Very few were condemned to slavery. But pawning occurred often, and prisoners-of-war were taken, while once in a while whole villages fell to Matoon status among the Bushoong. That class was recognized, can be documented not only by the use of names such as *kolm, bakon, ngady, nsho* (slave), but by the sumptuary laws which reserved special items of dress or finery to specific sub ranks in the two upper classes (Vansina 1964: 118–122). On the whole, Kuba society was agonistic and social stratification rather supports this contention here.

The territorial administration had each chief linked to the capital by an official, the *ibwoon*, who resided there and saw to it that tribute was paid. The *paangl* fulfilled the same role vis à vis Kete villages and the *meshoosh* was responsible for several groups of Cwa. Within the Bushoong chiefdom nine provinces were governed by six provincial chiefs: the king, the *bweemy* and four others. Provinces consisted of counties and those grouped villages. Village headmen were held responsible for their communities (Sheppard 1917: 97–100; Wharton 1927: 113). Within free villages elected officials and a council managed the administration (Sheppard 1917: 72, 96). The county headman was usually elected by the inhabitants of his seat and the office could become semi-hereditary (Vansina 1964: 94). Matoon villages had headmen appointed by the court and were not under county supervision.

The main task of county headman was to transmit orders from the capital. Provincial chiefs did the same and also collected tribute when it was not forthcoming by the regular (and different) channels and they

also called the men of specified villages for corvée labor when required
or for military duty in time of general war. Their major responsibility
towards their constituents though, was to represent them in court cases
at the central tribunal. Once a year, towards the end of the dry season,
all the village headmen came with some villagers to the capital for a
fortnight. They brought tribute, gave a report on the state of their
village and a census (with pebbles) was kept. The occasion was quite
festive. It kindled the villager's feeling of admiration for their capital
with its fine denizens and they renewed their acquaintance with main
representatives there, a royal wife who had come from the village
perhaps and certainly a royal son or grandson whose mother or
grandparent came from the village and to whom the annual tribute was
given (Sheppard 1917: 133–134).

In other chiefdoms the chief usually relied directly on the village
authorities, since they were so small. In a few cases only, did provinces
or counties exist. Kete and Coofa, who had no chiefdoms at all, were
treated rather like Matoon villages.

The central organization of the Bushoong chiefdom served for the
whole kingdom, just as the king was chief of the Bushoong. Laws,
regulations and day to day administration were carried out by councils.
The council of the realm has already been mentioned. It met most
infrequently. Its members were called diviners and also had ritual
concerns (Vansina 1964: 147–153). Two other councils took care of
everyday matters. The *ishyaaml* consisted of the most senior *kolm:* the
'prime minister', four provincial chiefs and *kolm* representing the kings'
children, the royal lineage (perhaps an appointment made after 1885),
the senior ritual officer of the king and a few others. Neither the king,
nor military title-holders nor those who commanded the capital could
be there, let alone speak. Seven less exalted *kolm* could be present but
not speak; among them subordinates of the first group and the men in
charge of the royal harem, the royal slaves (a military title), the royal
charms and the official responsible for administering the poison ordeal
to suspected witches (Vansina 1964: 148–150). The council's delibera-
tions were secret. Any of its members or the king could call it together.
Its decisions were taken to the king. If the latter disavowed them a
complex procedure was put in motion to present him again and yet
again with the decision. For *ishyaaml* was the voice of 'the Bushoong'
as opposed to the king.

The king called the *mbok ilaam* council together in his palace. It
consisted of all the members of *ishyaaml* with the *kolm* in command
over the capital, some of the senior military and the highest representatives for women. The king presided. Procedures were so tailored that
the decision he wanted would be passed; if any was passed at all since

filibustering was used in case of real disagreement. Then the senior *kolm* would go at night to tell the king to abandon his attempt. If not decisions reached here could be taken up once again at *ishyaaml* where a king never came. Decisions of councils were proclaimed by towncriers and if need be messengers were sent out to counties or villages. The *mbok ilaam* was presumably the council which allowed Sheppard to proceed to the capital in 1892 (1917: 101; 1893: 185a, 187b).

Sometimes the king merely wished to report or to communicate a wish. The same persons then met at another square in the palace, the king dressed up differently — more in military garb — made the address and was ceremonially approved by the *kolm* heading the capital (Vansina 1964: 151).

Business concerning other chiefdoms came to the *mbok ilaam* in the presence of the eagle feather chief(s) involved. Matters concerning two chiefdoms were settled among the contestants, the king being called in as arbitrator if they wished; which did not happen often since the king had to be paid dearly for such services (Vansina 1964: 168).

The biggest council at the capital was called 'the court' after the plaza where it was held. Absolutely all the title holders spoke here and the meeting was open to the public which vented its feelings. It was called together almost as seldom as the council of the realm, mainly in matters of peace and war (Vansina 1964: 152–153). The decisions of such meetings were at least heavily influenced by popular desire.

The balance between *ishyaaml* and *mbok ilaam* reflects the balance of authority between 'king' and 'Bushoong'. Within each of these the even more delicate balance between parties was maintained while all power groups were represented and equalized, including the interests of the capital (*mbok ilaam*) versus those of the whole chiefdom (*ishyaaml*). The councils were thus an incredibly delicate mechanism of representation and balanced legislature.

Two councils existed in all other chiefdoms: one involving chief and senior *kolm* and one involving all title holders and open to the public. A council of electors met to name or depose a chief. Deposition of a king was impossible: deposition of chiefs by their aristocrat electoral council was common (Vansina 1964: 161–162; Torday and Joyce 1910: 72–74).

The judicial system comprised moots at the village level and tribunals at the capital or the capital of a chiefdom. The Kuba system was rather unique in Africa. The tribunal was presided over not by one judge but by a panel or jury made up of those *kolm* who were connected with the case. There were status representatives for the parties. The dignitaries representing their territorial origin (provinces or parts of capital) were seated and if the party was a Cwa, a Kete, a royal slave, a royal child, a successor, a twin, appropriate representatives for those conditions sat. The type of crime dictated the seating of others. Theft was one speciality; adultery went to the *baang*, debts to the prime minister etc. When the case involved any specialist or specialty the *kolm* for that specialty was seated: a matter concerning salt saw the salt expert on the bench (Vansina 1971).

Appeal could be lodged first with *baang*, then with the prime minister and finally with the council of the realm whose senior half sat with the king as a tribunal. At each step, though, the fines increased; and at the highest level the loser forfeited the freedom of his whole lineage (Vansina 1964: 143–147). Procedural law was detailed and rules of evidence were strict. Court messengers saw to convocations and if necessary the royal constabulary saw to it that sentence was carried out. Penalties were: well-defined fines according to the type of offence, enslavement or death (the latter only for murder). The existing jail was in use only for detention before sentencing. Cases involving bloodshed or death were handled by special tribunals — military courts and death sentences had to be approved by the king.

The system reveals how much the courts were designed to protect the privileged! Debt was immediately handled at the prime minister level and adultery (interference with property) was for the *baang*. The power of the political system compared to social organization is gauged from the fact that no compensation was given to the kin groups of a murdered person. Murder was a crime against the state and the slave given as compensation went to the state. A portion of all the fines went to the state because all court cases had disturbed the peace. Moreover the parties paid the judges a flat rate. Lastly, the importance not only of territorial origin but of social stratification and status is evident. Not only are there the special 'status' judges but slave, pawn, women and children were never jailed since they were wards of their masters, husbands and fathers. The whole bottom stratum of society was considered as permanently beyond the pale of responsibility.

Only the king stood above the courts. He could order fines as he pleased (Wharton 1927: 71–72) and even order the maiming or killing of lower-level administrators whom he judged not to have carried out orders properly, whether the orders came from a council or from him. Rulers were felt to be harsh (cf. Sheppard 1893: 184a, where a royal son was killed in Bieeng country on orders of his father, probably before 1885), but effective. But the king was effectively restrained, not only by his own conviction in the killing power of *muyum's* national charm but also by the need for cooperation from his *kolm*, and less so, but still effectively, by the rebukes of his council of the realm. With regard to the other chiefdoms the king only possessed the power of arbitration when invited. Within the chiefdoms chiefs and their notables were the highest courts, although these held no rights over life and death. That was reserved for the king — in theory at least, since actual cases are unknown (Vansina 1964: 143–147, 161).

Coercion lay first in the constabulary — some forty royal slaves led by a trusted son of the king (Sheppard 1893: 184a, 184c; 1917: 99, 101). It could deal with any matter up to the rebellion of a whole village. This force was clearly at the king's beck and call and it ensured that, within the central core, the king's and the central administration's commands were really heeded. The Kuba state was not a 'loose confederacy'. Beyond this level a king could and did order one village to attack another one if that had rebelled by refusing tribute or some such similar offence. In such a case, the king could also request volunteers from the capital led by one or more of his sons; although this was already an escalation. Such forces attacked the offending village and occupied it until the villagers sued for peace. Both these techniques were used against chiefdoms and succeeded in solving all the problems that came up from 1835 to 1886. Lesser used but still real was the inspection trip led by the king, accompanied by many of his soldiers and courtiers, to live of the land in chiefdoms which were in arrears of tribute or were rebellious (Vansina 1964: 140, 151, 169). Beyond this a formal army organization existed with marching formation and battle formation and all the officers. The royal slaves furnished some 500 men with their own officers. This was complemented and offset by the contingent of the capital led by the generals and the combined force of over 2,000 would be sufficient for any emergency inside or out of the realm[3]. If that was not deemed enough, villagers on the line of march were drafted as troops and in extreme cases the provincial governors called up all able-bodied Bushoong. No such mobilization occurred in the nineteenth and twentieth century and none may ever have occurred.

The first type of coercion sufficed even to bring so-called independent groups such as the Bieeng chiefdom or Luba to pay occasional tribute, to avenge wrongs done to Kuba traders or to fetch any criminal who had fled the kingdom. Within the core of the state the military were used sparingly. Peace was a king's strongest weapon. It drew people. Personal safety was remarkable here, and over the decades and centuries had thus led to a sizeable emigration from the peripheral chiefdoms, which were always warring, to the peaceful core, and this despite the burden of taxation which may have been just a bit higher there.

The central administration was well informed by (1) provincial and county governors, (2) permanent representatives at the capital, (3) the king's traders (Sheppard 1893: 187a; 1917: 94–99), (4) special tribute-collectors and (5) special police. These were present in every county and in most villages of the Bushoong. One was also responsible for each province but reports could be made directly to the king. Anything untoward was to be passed on at once and the king could send secret orders to arrest or kill persons who rebelled (they had usually interfered with tribute). This was not a secret police in that all knew who those men were. Moreover, information to the villages could also be carried by official messengers carrying the king's knife or 'mace' (Sheppard 1919: 139; 1893: 185a; Torday and Joyce 1910: 61). Towncriers were used and messages were sent by signal drum from capital to village or village to village although this last technique was not used systematically (Sheppard 1917: 142). It was more normal to have the provincial governors send officers around their provinces.

Taxation and corvée labor made the political bureaucracy possible. Every village paid an annual tax in cowries, in goods and in food from a special field for the king. Subordinate chiefdoms sent tribute in specified commodities. Matoon villages provided for the palace and the successors. Special tribute was levied when required and the great bulk of offices were assigned such a task. Almost every *kolm* was responsible for a product: iron, salt, ivory, mats, hats, even shrimps. Whenever a commodity was required the *kolm* in charge went off to fetch the requested amount and his own commission from the villages which specialized in them. These *kolm* were those which Torday dubs the representatives of the different 'guilds' (Torday and Joyce 1910: 55–56). The representation came about historically first, as a by-product of the system of taxation and later, taxation became the income attached to newly created titles invented to reward faithful supporters of the king. The jury system of the tribunals evolved, partly at least, from this development as well.

In case of pressing need for general produce the provincial governors went out but this seems to have been rare. *Ibwoon, meshoosh* and *paangl* brought the tribute in from the chiefdoms and the Cwa and the Kete (Sheppard 1917: 87; Verner 1903: 288–289). Chiefdoms did not pay much and special tribute here came only when a new chief was installed and when a successor or king died (Vansina 1964: 167). The *paangl* — often king's sons — in Kete villages imposed as much as they dared to increase their own income.

Corvée labor saw to the building and maintenance of every public building in the capital, including the whole palace quarter minus the harem. Every house or wall was assigned once and for all to a village. When repairs or reconstruction was needed the provincial governor called its men out. The same held for bridges (there were few) and paths. When special services were needed such as those of singers or drummers, special *kolm* of the tax-collector corps gathered them. They could also bring smiths or carvers in when their special talents were needed.

It would be wrong to think that tax and corvée burdens were intolerable. They were not more so than in the satellite chiefdoms which were less peaceful. Only among the Matoon villages and to a lesser extent among the Kete was a goodly portion of produce, and, often, time, taken up by these duties. Only in Matoon villages was it necessary to watch that the villagers would not emigrate elsewhere. Despite taxes and stratification the bulk of the population supported the regime enthusiastically not only because it was there and traditional, because no alternative came to mind ('without kingship anarchy would prevail'), because of the supernatural powers of the king, because of the reflected glory that stemmed from belonging to the only kingdom in the area ('we have a king and a city; we are civilized', etc.), but also, and perhaps most, because so many participated in the system. By 1953–1956 twenty-seven per cent of the free men were *kolm* of some sort, and the proportion was even higher in the satellite chiefdoms although the titles meant less and potential income was lower. The percentages of the 1870s stood not much lower perhaps. They mean, in effect, that every man had one chance out of two to acquire some title, however unimportant, by the time he was forty. By accepting it he became part of the establishment. The Kuba participated in their political structure to an unusual degree. It was their grandiose collective endeavor.

3. SHORT HISTORY

The Kuba kingdom (Vansina 1963) really took shape in the seventeenth century. Before that time only chiefdoms existed, of which the Bushoong were only one. These had formed after the arrival of immigrants from north of the Sankuru who mixed with the Kete and Cwa autochtones. Chieftainship as a role had existed among the immigrants but the title did not correspond to an elaborate structure. South of the Sankuru, though, some chiefdoms acquired 'subjects'. Especially the Bushoong, who overcame Kete villages and developed a charter. Their king — they claimed later — had been chosen as overlord at the 'throwing of anvils and hammers' by the nature spirits over all the other chiefs. But the creation of new institutions and the system of *kolm* as well as the first conquest from the Bushoong chiefdom outwards began with Shyaam aMbul aNgoong, a foreigner from a country in the west that was already then (ca. 1620) in a loose trading contact with the kingdom of Kongo and the Atlantic coast. He is said to have brought the plan (and the model?) of a strong capital from his home area as well as most of the American cultigens which became the Kuba staples. The completion of both the internal organization and the conquest of other chiefdoms was mostly left to his successors but already by 1700 the state had acquired both its historic boundaries and its basic organization. After that it did not expand significantly anymore but its internal development with regard to political parties and the creation of new titles continued into the period described. Shyaam is also acclaimed as the first king to be a nature spirit and a much more intensive sacred king than any previous chief. A further shift came by the last quarter of the eighteenth century with the abolition of 'ethnic' spirits — competitors with the royal spirits and promotors of separatism. The growth of a collective representation and a cult for Ncyeem, an imported deity but a single Creator and First Cause who replaced previous gods, can be associated perhaps with the growing unity of the state and its links with the outside. It can certainly be tied to the trade route with the west, just like the American crops.

The trading connection brought by Shyaam was never lost. It gradually increased and perhaps by the mid-eighteenth century the Kuba were already linked to the Luso-African sphere of trade (rather than the earlier Kongo state one). After 1870 the volume of trade greatly increased and a few years later foreign caravans and guns made their first appearance on the southern border. There too Luebo, the first Independent Congo State post was founded in 1885 and through it huge masses of cheap goods flowed in.

The Kuba kingdom shows a genuine economic development between its creation and 1892 (Vansina 1976). The kings forced American crops with their higher yields. Agricultural output per farming household doubled over the period. This was not due primarily to technological change although this played a role, but mostly through an increase in the labor supply by a shift in the division of labor by sex, the lowering of the age of marriage and imports of slaves. Hence the surplus, which made the bureaucracy and the grand style of life in the big capital possible.

The surplus was not just natural. It was coerced from the farmer by the political authorities. They wanted it not only to feed the bureaucracy and the traders and artisans of the capital but also so that the traders and artisans could bring in or manufacture prestige goods, either rare foreign items, or luxury goods. Some of the latter went for exports to sustain the trade. Prestige goods implied first, a control over resources in a manner visible to all (they required a high input of labor) and secondly, they allowed the king to build up a treasure in commodities that would not perish to be used at his discretion as spoils for his supporters, when he wanted to reward them. This is very different from food which *must* be distributed before it spoils. Finally the economic development had brought more well-being to even the farmers by allowing them to market excess commodities and buy slaves and luxury goods with some of the proceeds.

The development of the political organization was a dialectic between the development of the bureaucracy and the growth of agricultural output with the diversification of the task of other producers. Surplus did not make the state. Rather the reverse. But once the process was launched it would not stop. The ideology kept a pace both by justifying the existent political organization and by providing initial and new models for society. Without the ideology — at least the 'idea of a kingdom' — no kingdom was possible. Nor was it without the presence of surplus. Without the kingdom none of the other two spheres would have acquired the rich development that they in fact showed. And the same even holds for Kuba art which produced luxury objects for the patricians and later even for the common people.

The Kuba case is unique. Not merely because every case is unique, nor only because this polity survived the socio-economic upheaval which toppled the other states in Central Africa even *before* the colonial period, leaving the Kuba state as a unique witness to the splendors of old, but because of its very complexity and the clarity of the documentation about it which allows us to see how a state developed. It did so in such a way as to become at least a typical if not perhaps a transitional early state.

There is logic to this history. One sub-system became dominant giving direction to other sub-systems to what otherwise would have been but stochastic backfeeding between the different parts of this social universe. Even so, the political sector was not *always* the dynamo of the system. The dynamic effect stemmed from the interplay of the political, economic, technological and ideological sectors, probably because it mediated between all of these. In the process it reduced the kinship system to a modest subordinate position. If colonization had not interrupted development, drastic change might have been on the cards. Increased trade was bringing fire-arms and large foreign caravans equipped with them. The kingdom could have faced this by furthering this import but centralizing the weapons at the court. Given the degree of centralization this was possible. Even so, it might not have survived. Not only would it depend for its strength on imports which could be witheld, but the opportunities for a redistribution of wealth were too tempting. Challenges to the crown could have become severe and the kingdom could have disintegrated from within by the destruction of its social stratification. As it was, and despite the presence of the Congo Independent State, it managed to survive essentially unchanged from 1885 to 1900.

Its actual history confirms that society is at best a 'part system' because its institutions are 'open-ended' and especially because its ecological and human environmental parameters alter independently. Despite its relatively high internal cohesion the kingdom was absorbed into a colony by 1900.

FOOTNOTES

[1] The body of data for this essay stems from Sheppard 1917, Torday and Joyce 1910 and Vansina 1964 which gives a virtually complete bibliography to 1963. Vansina, 1978, was also extensively used.

[2] A member of each of the eighteen clans (*mbaangt*) was counted as high aristocracy and member of the council of the realm, because it was claimed the clan 'came' with the king. In fact these clans were early supporters. All other statuses were achieved.

[3] In theory, the king was the supreme commander of the army, but, as there had not been large scale wars for most of the nineteenth century, he seldom acted as such.

REFERENCES

Allan, W. (1965), *The African husbandsman*, Edinburgh: Boyd.
Douglas, M. (1962), 'Lele economy compared with the Bushong' in: *Trade and markets in Africa*, ed. by P. Bohannan and G. Dalton, Evanston: Northwestern University Press.
Jonghe, E. de (1949), 'Les formes d'asservissement dans les sociétés indigènes du Congo belge', in: *Mémoire 19*, Brussels: Section des Sciences Morales et Politiques de l'Institut Royal Colonial Belge.
Lapsley, S. N. (1893), *Life and letters of Samuel Norvell Lapsley*, Richmond: Whittet and Shepperson.
Macar, G. de (1893), 'La tribu des Bakuba', in: *Le mouvement géographique*, pp. 103–119.
Sheppard, W. H. (1893), 'Into the heart of Africa', in: *The southern workman*, pp. 182–187.
— (1917), *Presbyterian pioneers in Congo*, Richmond: Presbyterian Committee of Publication.
Torday, E. (1925), *On the trail of the Bushongo*, London: Seeley Service.
Torday, E. and Joyce, T. A. (1910), 'Notes ethnographiques sur les peuples communément appelés Bakuba', in: *Ethnographie–Anthropologie*: 3, 2, 1. Brussels: Musée royal du Congo Belge.
Vansina, J. (1956), 'Le régime foncier dans la société kuba', in: *Zaïre*, X: 899–926.
— (1963), 'Geschiedenis van de Kuba', in: *Sciences humaines. Annales du Musée royal de l'Afrique Centrale*. No. 44, Tervuren: Musée royal de l'Afrique Centrale.
— (1964), 'Le royaume kuba', in: *Sciences humaines. Annales du Musée royal de l'Afrique Centrale*, no. 49. Tervuren: Musée royale de l'Afrique Centrale.
— (1971), 'A traditional legal system: the Kuba', in: *Man in adaptation: the institutional framework*, ed. by Y. Cohen, pp. 135–148. Chicago: Aldine.

380   *Jan Vansina*

— (1976), 'La houe et la hache' in: *Mélanges en l'honneur de G. Malengreau,*
   ed. by R. Yakemtchouk. Brussels.
— (1978), *The children of Woot, a general Kuba history.* Madison: University
   of Wisconsin Press.
Vellut, J. L. (1972), 'Notes sur le Lunda et la frontière luso-africaine (1700–
   1900)', in: *Etudes d'histoire africaine* 3: 61–166.
Verner, S. (1903), *Pioneering in central Africa.* Richmond: Presbyterian Committee of Publications.
Wissmann, H. von (1890), *Unter deutsche Flagge quer durch Afrika.* Berlin:
   Walther und Apolant.
Wharton, C. T. (1927), *The leopard hunts alone,* New York: Wiley.

18   The Mauryan State[1]

SUDARSAN SENEVIRATNE

The Mauryan state developed from the nucleus of Magadha (South Bihar), which had acquired power and territory from the time of the reign of Bimbisara in the fifth century B.C. Further expansion under the Nandas was indicative of a more systematic and intensive state organization. Their successors, the Mauryas, accelerated the pace of expansion by conquering a number of kingdoms and tribal oligarchies, and during this period the crystallization of the agrarian empire took place. The imperial system set up by Chandragupta Maurya was continued by his son Bindusāra and grandson Aśoka. The empire began to crumble under the successors of Aśoka. Finally, the last of the Mauryas, Bṛhadratha, was assassinated by his commander-in-chief. Thus the total time span of the Mauryan state extended roughly from 321 B.C. to 185 B.C.

The amount of source material for this period is quite extensive as compared with the preceding one, thus giving us fuller access to the nature of the Mauryan state. The most significant among the sources are the edicts of Aśoka. *Kauṭilīya Arthaśāstra* (whose date remains controversial) is the most authoritative work on ancient Indian political economy, though the text should be used with caution, as it refers to an ideal rather than an actual state. The archaeological finds are mainly useful for a reconstruction of the extent to which Mauryan culture spread and its qualitative development. Unquestionably, the archaeological evidence is restricted to the urban areas, but at least it provides a picture of the prevalent material culture. Some data may also be gleaned from the punch-marked coins which circulated at this time. Sections of Buddhist literature, such as the *Aśokavadana*, the *Divyāvadāna*, the *Mahāvaṃsa*, and the *Jātaka* stories may also be used, although again with the necessary caution insofar as they are not always contemporary sources, but are often reflections of a later period; even where they refer to events which took place in the Mauryan period. Among the non-Indian literary sources Megasthenes' *Indica* remains the most authoritative, in spite of the fact that it has come to us in the form of a collection of lengthy quotations by Greek authors subsequent to Megasthenes, being as a result a collation of his observations during his visit to the Mauryan court as ambassador of Selucas Nicator.

The main conditions which made the establishment of the Mauryan imperial state possible in the fourth century B.C. were connected with the expansion of the agrarian economy. An increase in cultivation with the use of the plow made for a widening of the agricultural basis. This implied that by this time agriculture constituted the chief means of subsistence, the fertile areas in the Indus and Ganges River systems and in parts of the peninsula becoming the natural foci of agricultural production. This considerable growth and form of specialization, in combination with the ability to manufacture iron, resulted in a greater surplus production. It is this development of the agrarian-based economy which became the major factor in state formation. It made possible the support of a large standing army necessary for expanding the state frontiers as well as, to some extent, for maintaining law and order. The resultant surplus also encouraged the formation of a well-paid bureaucracy which is indispensable to any imperial system.

The gradual spread of iron technology which encouraged the intensification of agriculture also made possible the necessary surplus for the production of commodities for exchange and the emergence of social groups possessing the opportunity to enjoy the luxuries of an exchange economy. The concentration of the population in urban centers gathered momentum when the necessary conditions for a money economy came into existence. The expanding state — which provided incentives for greater agricultural production, and in turn appropriated existing trade routes connecting the markets, and annexed areas producing raw materials, at the same time establishing safer and more efficient communications and finally law and order for the sake of free movement within the empire — was furnished with an additional social basis for empire as a result of the close association of commercial groups in addition to that of the peasants.

The Mauryan state can thus be characterized as 'a typical early state'. The imperial system of the Mauryas was in a sense a culmination of a socio-economic process which began roughly around the sixth century B.C., when a pastoral-cum-agricultural economy with a tribal social organization was transformed into an agrarian-based economy with urban centers. The agrarian character of the empire of the Mauryas thus became rather unique where the state spread horizontally and maintained its unitary character through its bureaucracy and armed force; a feature which did not mark the post-Mauryan state, based on a land grant economy which underwent a more vertical development.

The Mauryan state was an expression of the concept of the state as emerging from earlier sources. This concept of the state is apparent from a number of myths, the foremost among which attribute the rise of the state to social inequality, the existence of private property and the need to maintain law and order. The latter then becomes the prime responsibility of the ruler, whose remuneration for this is a percentage of the revenue. Thus the collection of taxes also becomes a major function of the state.

The mythical charter of the state is found in variant forms in literary sources such as the *Mahābhārata* and the *Dīgha Nikāya*. In the epic tradition of the former text it is discussed in the context of kingship and political spheres of activity. The epic tradition originally preserved by bards and chroniclers, in the post-Mauryan period was committed to the keeping of *brahmans*. The gradual growth of a sense of history is apparent from the fact that the *Mahābhārata* was eventually classed as *itihāsa*, a term used with reference to historical literature. The influence of the epic spread gradually to many parts of the subcontinent, while it acted as the vehicle of both the propagation of the Great Tradition and the assimilation of the Little Tradition.

Part of the *itihāsa* literature comprised genealogical material. These genealogies included those of land owning *kṣatriya* families in the earlier parts and those of the dynasties of northern India in later parts. The Mauryas are included among these dynasties, but are listed as being of lowly origin (although the reference to their origin is ambiguous). The emergence of dynasties of low social origin is interpreted as a sign of a general trend towards moral decay in the declining cycle of time.

From the second millennium B.C. there is evidence of the existence of settlements which can be described by inference as being of a tribal nature. The earliest literature, as represented by the *Ṛg Veda*, refers to tribal groups with a predominantly pastoral economy in the Punjab, Haryana, and northern Rajasthan. Gradually a transition to greater dependence on agriculture occurred, together with an increase in the movement and migration of the original tribes, until by the middle of the first millennium B.C. the population distribution covered virtually the whole of northern India. Areas along the main river valleys tended gradually to turn into monarchical states, whereas those in higher areas and particularly in the Himalayan foothills, retained oligarchical systems until much later. The dominant group in each case was that of the land-owning *kṣatriyas*, whose lands were worked by the *dāsa-bhṛtaka* (slaves and hired laborers). There was a close affinity between the tribal elite and agriculture. The patriarchal family unit became increasingly the norm, even in areas in which there are at least hints of a non-patriarchal tradition.

The capitals of the new states often coincided with the main commercial centers as trade along the river routes and certain land routes gradually increased. The slow but perceptible spread of iron technology resulted in far-reaching changes, particularly in urban centers. The use of money in commerce radically changed the nature of trade and commerce, stimulating manufacturing to a higher degree than before, as well as encouraging a more complex social stratification. Tribal states as political entities held their own for a while, but gradually the centralized state began to undermine tribal organizations.

From the sixth century B.C. onward, aggression in northern India was spearheaded by the monarchical states, particularly the ones located in the Ganges Valley. Reputedly Chandragupta overthrew the Nanda Dynasty and took over their kingdom, which covered the Ganges Valley. The annexation of the Punjab and the Indus region, which was among the conquests of Chandragupta Maurya, was facilitated by the breaking up of the tribal states by Alexander, followed by the gradual weakening of the Greek hold in this region after the latter's death. At least one Greek source (Appian) speaks of clashes preceding the treaty between Chandragupta and Selucus, whereby the Mauryan dynasty extended its territory up to modern Afganistan, the Mauryan occupation of this area being confirmed by inscriptions. During the reign of either Chandragupta or Biṅdusāra, the southern frontier was extended as far as (if not beyond) the Mysore region. The last major conquest of the Mauryans was that of Kalinga by Aśoka.[2]

Conquest was essential in the process of territorial expansion because by the sixth–fifth century B.C. not only where there mutual relations between states and geographical regions, but other factors besides, such as the emergence of an agrarian economy, private ownership of land, and lucrative trade routes, coming into being. Conquest was necessary in order to establish political control over these. The sequence of conquests until the time of the Nandas corresponds closely to a particular geographical pattern. While, on the one hand, the conquests spread along the fertile Ganges plain with its important urban sites, on the other hand, they also began to follow important trade routes. It was inevitable for the Nandas to subjugate the states between the Ganges valley and the eastern Punjab region, thus extending their control towards the adjoining fertile plain, the area which had direct contact with the west. By the third century commercial activity had also penetrated well into the Deccan, and the potential of its resources was known in the north. Thus it was not surprising that the empire should extend as far as Mysore in the south.

Ancient theoreticians regarded a state guided by a king as an essential instrument by which the weak were protected against the strong, and as a means of averting anarchy (*Arthaśāstra* I, 13; *Manu* VII, 20–24). The paternalism implicit in this, stressed in the *Arthaśāstra* (II, 1; IV, 3) finds a parallel in the Aśokan edicts (*First Separate Rock Edict*, located at Tosali). It ushered in a new kind of relationship between the state, the king and the community. The main interest of the state was in the rural areas, which not only yielded the bulk of the revenues but also supported the majority of the population. The socio-economic unit of the rural areas was the village, which was a settlement of groups of close kin. Several such villages (five–ten), which formed an administrative unit under a *gōpa* (accountant) and *sthānika* (tax-collector) (*Arthaśāstra* II, 35), may have comprised extended family groups in most cases marked by common customs and other forms of social behavior, which conferred cultural as well as kinship identity. Aśoka explicitly stresses the importance of the family (*Yerragudi Minor Rock Edict*) which may also be interpreted as a characteristic feature of the paternal attitude (*Rock Edict* XIII).

Social stratification in northern India by around the sixth century B.C. had become more complex, though complexity did not imply rigidity of stratification without social mobility (Rhys-Davids 1959: 27–32). The Buddhist sources (Vinaya IV) mention the *Brahmīns*, *Kṣatriyas* and the *Gahapatis* as forming the upper social class (*Ukkaṭṭajāti*). Megasthenes, though aware of the theoretical divisions of the caste system, describes a seven-class system based rather more on occupation. Interestingly enough he mentions a prohibition on every caste, other than that of the philosophers, against marriage outside the caste and the pursuit of occupations not prescribed to the caste group in question (Diodorus II, 40; Strabo XV, i, 48). The *Brahmanas* were a small but privileged group, who were exempt from taxes and not subject to forced labor. Aśoka in his edicts exhorts his subjects to respect the *Śramanas* and the *Brahmanas*.

The fact that early Buddhist sources (Morris and Hardy 1885 III: 362 ff.; *Jātaka* III, 19; IV, 205) place the *Kṣatriyas* in the topmost class in the social scale may be a reflection of the latter's political dominance, especially in the oligarchies, augmented by economic power as big landowners. However, after the fifth century B.C., with the rapid rise of Magadha as a centralized kingdom with expansionist policies, both the oligarchic republican states and the political power of the *Kṣatriyas* seem to have rapidly declined, at least in the Ganges plain. The epithet 'the destroyer of the *Kṣatriyas*' (*Visnu Purana* IV, 24) attributed to Mahapadma Nanda, may not have been so mythical after all. If the Puranic, Jain and Greek sources are to be believed the Nandas were of low origin, perhaps even *Śūdra*. The Mauryas also had obscure origins and were either *Vaiśyas* or *Śūdras*, although the Buddhist sources refer to them as *Kṣatriyas*. The Mauryas saw no need to seek legitimacy by establishing a *Kṣatriya* origin through lineage connections. The need to trace *Kṣatriya* origins of ruling families in a later period stemmed from another combination of historical factors.

The *Khattiyagahapati*, which is so frequently mentioned in connection with the sixth century B.C., is not found anywhere in the course of the period of the empire. Even the Aśokan inscriptions do not mention the term. The *Arthaśāstra* (I, 3) mentions a military occupation and the protection of life as the duties of the *Kṣatriya*. But it never refers to any right to rule over others, which the *Kṣatriyas* may have possessed. In fact, along with the *Kṣatriyas* the *Arthaśāstra* (IX, 2) mentions the *Vaiśyas* and *Śūdras*, as well as guilds and forest tribes as a source of recruitment for the army. Even the important function of provincial governor in Saurāṣṭra (western India) was held by (probably) a *Vaiśya*, followed by a Greek, clearly neither of them belonging to the traditional ruling class of the *Kṣatriyas*.

The *Gahapatis* referred to in the Aśokan inscriptions may possibly have been of *Vaiśya* origin and have resided in urban centers, although literally the term refers to heads of households of no specific caste. It is perhaps the small landed proprietors, who worked their land with slaves, or hired laborers (*Jātaka* IV, 281; III, 162; IV, 276) and the numerous peasants who worked their lands themselves (probably *Śūdras*), who formed the second class listed by Megasthenes, namely, that of cultivators (Diodorus II, 40). They constituted the largest occupational, as well as the most vital economic group in the empire. The *Arthaśāstra* (II), speaking of the *Śūdras*, stresses their role as cultivators and their part in an elaborate procedure with regard to the establishment of villages on either waste or reclaimed land in new areas. Although the *Arthaśāstra* does recommend the recruitment of *Śūdras* to the army, the cultivator was nevertheless to be kept unarmed. The continuance of pastoralism, though undoubtedly on a lesser scale, is testified by Megasthenes (Diodorus II, 40) listing shepherds and herdsmen as forming the third class.

The artisans and craftsmen forming the fourth caste in Megasthenes' list (Diodorus II, 41; Strabo XI, i, 46) emerged with urbanization and the growth of manufacturing; they were organized into guilds. Again, the lower stratum of the guilds was formed by *Śūdra* elements, namely the *Karmakārakas* (artisans) and *Antevāsikas* (apprentices), the slaves and hired laborers (*Arthaśāstra* III, 13, 14). The two latter are known from the Aśokan inscriptions as the *Bhataka* and *Dāsa* (*Rock Edict* IX at Girnar).

Though Megasthenes states that India had no slaves (Diodorus II, 39), the Indian sources indicate that slaves were used along with hired laborers for domestic work, by the guilds, in mines and in agricultural work. However, while the social status of the wage laborer was superior to that of the slave, the services of the former were in turn differentiated from the forced labor (*viṣṭi*) which was exacted of everyone, whether free persons or slaves. As a social group the wage laborers occupied a very low position in the social structure. The Buddhist sources (*Vinaya, Bhikkunīvibhaṅga Sanghādisesa* I, 2, 1) state that a person might be a slave by birth, through purchase or as a result of a gift. The *Jātakas* (*Kulavāha* I, p. 200, III, 13) suggest that someone might be made a slave as a form of punishment by the law. Prisoners taken in war, as in the case of Kalinga, were in all probability employed as slave labor in the mines and in agriculture. According to *Arthaśāstra* the Aryas (*Brahmanas, Kṣatriyas, Vaiśyas*) could not, under normal circumstances, be sold as slaves. The *Śūdras* and the *Mlechhas* were not, however, included in this category (III, 13). The fact that slaves were commonly associated with daily household chores indicates, that they were not considered impure, as were the members of the lowest social category of untouchables.

Unlike the slaves, those below them, the untouchables, were outcasts, who were considered impure; They lived in isolated parts of the inhabited areas (*Arthaśāstra* II, 4). The *Chandalas*, as also the *Pukkusas* (*Anguttara Nikaya* 1. 162; Jacobi, Jaina Sutra II. 301), for example, were described as the products of mixed unions between the castes of the *Brahmanas* and the *Śūdras* (*Manu* X, 12). They were employed in professions which were considered unclean, including that of executioner, cemetery attendant, hunter, acrobat and juggler, leather worker, scavenger, basket maker, potter, weaver, barber, snake charmer etc. Being socially ostracized, they were not permitted any form of social organization other than that of caste, and access to education was denied them.

The relative progress in the use of metals suggests that the need for these was becoming quite great, especially where the emphasis was on military power and on agricultural and commercial expansion. The increased use of coinage is also indicative of a more general use of metal.[3] Commercial expansion can also be traced by the spread over a large area of Mauryan terracottas and related kinds of pottery such as the famous Northern Black Polished Ware.

Aside from the development of urban centers that had been going on mainly in the Ganges valley from the sixth century B.C., that of similar such centers was given an added boost by political and commercial expansion. It is during the Mauryan period that urbanization spread effectively beyond the Ganges Valley into areas such as Bengal, Mysore and Kalinga. Northwestern and western India saw the emergence of urban centers just before the rise of the Mauryas. In each of these regions, though the degree of urbanization varied, the development of urban nuclei was significant. Although a more systematic and regular form of city planning was evolved in the post-Mauryan period, nevertheless, the Mauryan period is characterized by well-constructed houses and an efficient drainage system. The Mauryan settlements had carefully constructed cess pits and ring wells, indicative of a concern with civic planning.

In the urban centers, the main building material gradually changed from wood to brick and stone. The Aśokan pillars and capitals testify to an undeniable expertise in stone-working. It has been argued that this expertise developed from long familiarity with construction in wood. The wooden prototype is evident also from the cave architecture of the period. Constructional skill will moreover have gone not only into the erection of monuments, palaces, etc., but also into the construction of canals and dams. Canals built by the Nandas and a dam constructed by the Mauryas are known from the inscriptions.

A great number of artisans and craftsmen were organized under the aegis of the state and in guilds. Those employed by the state were called *rājaśilpīn* and *rāja-kumbhakāra* (*Panini* VI 2. 63; *Jātaka* V, 290). According to Greek sources, armorers implement makers and shipbuilders were paid by the royal treasury and were exempt from taxes (Diodorus II, 41; Strabo XV, i, 46; Arrian, *Indica* XII). The *Arthaśāstra* also speaks of the employment of skilled workmen at the armorer's workshop.

The hereditary nature of occupations pursued by full-time specialists who had organized themselves into guilds increased specialization. The localization of industries in special areas was also significant for the development of guilds. The sources speak of streets (*Jātakas*), or specific quarters of towns (*Arthaśāstra* II, 4), or villages occupied by the artisans of one particular craft. Apart from the proximity of a market or trade route, ready access to the necessary raw materials was an important factor in the localization of a given craft (*Jātaka* II, 18). One locality might, however, contain more than one organization of craftsmen of the same category (*Samudda Vāṇija* (*Jātaka*)). At times a guild might shift its center of production (ibid). The *Jātakas*, furthermore, mention large guilds with up to a 1000 members.

The emergence and establishment of the empire stimulated the development of trade and commerce. The wide network of diplomatic relations which the Mauryas established with countries beyond the northwestern borders (such as Syria, Egypt, Macedonia, Cyrene, Conith/Epirus) and in the south with Tambapaṇṇi (Ceylon), opened up new prospects for commerce.[4] The location of Aśokan edicts and other archaeological evidence shows that newly settled areas beyond the Ganges Valley also evolved urban nuclei. Many of the administrative changes introduced by Aśoka were aimed at improving rural administration, and doubtless also, at linking up rural areas in question with urban centers.

In the urban centers the evidence as to state control of production varies. Doubtless shipbuilding and probably also the manufacture of arms were a state monopoly (Strabo XV, i, 46; *Arthaśāstra* II, 28), though the state may not have exercised rigid control over artisans and traders. The evidence from *Taxila* (the reference to the *negama*) may indicate that the city guilds possessed a degree of autonomy, at least in commercial matters. In all likelihood the issue of coins, for example, was controlled by the commercial guilds.

The *Arthaśāstra* seems to suggest a fairly strict state control over guilds, however, particularly with respect to prices and profits. According to the same source (II, 1) guilds encroaching on the territory of villages in which there were already corporations in existence were prohibited. Possibly this represented an attempt by the state to ensure a smooth functioning of production and commerce, so that maximum benefit might be derived therefrom; by the public in the form of goods and by the state in the form of taxes.

The state pursued a policy of vigilance in the cities in order to prevent fraudulent practices, to make sure that traders paid their taxes, and to facilitate a smooth flow of goods into and out of the city (Strabo XV, ix, 50; *Arthaśāstra* IV, 20). Popular discontent in the capital or in other urban centers was not politically healthy and appears to have always been quickly repressed. Regular reminders in the form of edicts that slaves and wage laborers should receive proper treatment (*Rock Edicts* IX, XI) point to a desire to avoid social tension.

As regards land ownership, the difference between ownership and tenure appears to have been recognized early in the historical period. The *Arthaśāstra* (III, 10) distinguishes between the owner (*kṣetrika*) and the tenant (*upavāsa*) of a field. Another early source, although dating from the post-Mauryan period, states that ownership of property might be acquired through inheritance, purchase, distribution, seizure or discovery (*Gautama-Dharmaśāstra* X, 39). According to *Manu*, ownership was vested in him who cleared the land (IX, 44). *Manu* further recommends large fines for illegal appropriation of land (VIII, 264). Other sources considered land, including all movable and immovable items upon it, as the property of the householder occupying it (*Suttanipāta* X, 11; *Mahāvagga:* III, ii, 4).

Private landowners were referred to as '*khettāpati/khettasāmika*' (*Jātaka* IV, 281; III, 301). The *Jātakas* also refer to *gahapatis* and *gāmabhojakas*. Generally speaking landowners belonged to the *Brahmin*, *Kṣatriya* and *Vaiśya* castes. Large landholders worked their land with the aid of wage laborers and slaves (*Jātaka* III, 293; IV,

276; *Suttanipāta* I, 4; *Samyutta Nikaya* I, 172). There were also smaller landholders (*Jātaka* IV, 281) who worked the land themselves (*Jātaka* II, 162; IV, 276) or occasionally used slaves (*Jātaka* III, 162).

By the Mauryan period the position of the *Kṣatriya* landholders may have deteriorated. In all likelihood large landholdings during the third century B.C. were smaller than those in the Gupta or post-Gupta period (from the fourth century A.D. onwards). Thus, if landholdings were relatively small they may have been of a manageable enough size to obviate the necessity of the distribution of land among tenant farmers. The position of the slaves and hired labor on these agricultural holdings should not be equated with that of the later serfs either.

This very feature of private ownership of lands is in flat contradiction with the statement by some Greek authors (i.e., Diodorus and Strabo quoting Megasthenes) that all land in India was owned by the king. It is quite likely, however, that this refers to crown-lands (*sīta*) (*Arthaśāstra* II, 24). Alternatively, with the rise of the empire and the increasing emphasis on the central position of the king as the focal point of the state structure, the concepts of state and king may have coalesced. Thus a statement that the king owned all the land might imply that it was owned by the state and not by the king personally. Judging from the pattern of expansion along the Ganges River, it would not have been impossible for the more fertile areas in the central Ganges plain to have been worked in the form of state farms. The Greek author possibly mistook these for lands owned by the king.[5] If the *Arthaśāstra* is to be believed, full-time state officers were remunerated with grants of state lands (II, 1). This only gave them a right to the produce and not the ownership of such lands. Possibly this circumstance in combination with payments in cash (*Arthaśāstra* V, 2) prevented the development of a class of landlords from out of the bureaucracy.

The *Arthaśāstra* gives a detailed list of the various sources of state revenue (II, 6). These included land (agricultural, pastoral, mining), trade, commerce and related industries. The *bali* and the *bhāga* mentioned in the Indian sources were viewed by the Greek historians (Diodorus II, 40) as a land tax and a tax on produce. The *bhāga* varied according to the region. Megasthenes records a rate of one quarter, possibly only with reference to the Ganges region, because Indian sources put the figure at one sixth. The fertility of the soil may have been a consideration in the variation of the amount, as was the method of irrigation (*Arthaśāstra* II, 24). Increased taxes on produce were permitted during an emergency or in fertile areas (*Arthaśāstra* V, 2). The range of taxes extended from the *hiranya* on special categories of crops, to the exemption of some villages from taxes in return for supplying soldiers (*Arthaśāstra* II, 35).

Land taxes seem to have been assessed on the basis of the size and quality of the land. The assessment was not made on the combined lands of the village, but on that of each individual cultivator (*Arthaśāstra* II, 35). At Rumindai, Aśoka himself changed the tax on the village, indicating the absence of intermediaries (*Rumindai Pillar Edict*). According to Strabo (XV, i, 40) cultivators received one quarter of the produce as payment. This may have been the rate paid to cultivators on crown lands, or a misquotation for the quarter portion payable to the state by the cultivator. The state, furthermore, took the initiative in expanding agriculture by instituting *Śūdra* villages. The prisoners taken in the Kalinga war may possibly have provided a labor force for some state-sponsored scheme for the settlement of waste land (*Arthaśāstra* II, 1). Theoretically the king also had the right to remove defaulting or lazy cultivators and install more industrious ones in their place (*ibid.*).

In the rural areas and the provinces, revenue administration was handled by the *prādeśika*, *rājuka* and *yūkta* (*Rock Edict* III at Girnar). The *prādeśika* (*pradṣṭr* in the *Arthaśāstra*) supervised the district officials and made reports on this to the *samāhartṛ* (chief collector) (*Arthaśāstra* II, 35). His main concerns were supervising the collection of taxes and maintaining law and order. Below the *prādeśika* was the *rājuka*, who had direct contact with the rural areas (IV *Pillar Edict*) and combined fiscal (assessing) with juridical functions. The assessment of land naturally implied surveying it, which is referred to in the title of the *rajjugāhaka* (*Jātakas*) and the *cora rajjuka* (*Arthaśāstra* II, 6; IV, 13), the rope-holding officer, measuring the lands of tax-paying cultivators. Megasthenes' *agoranomoi* or market officers were possibly these *rājukas* (Strabo XV, i, 50). The *yūktas* carried out secretarial and accounting duties (*Rock Edict* III; *Arthaśāstra* II, 9).

On the level between the district and the village, the *gōpa* and the *sthānika* were in charge of groups of villages (*Arthaśāstra* II, 35). In this unit the *gōpa* acted as accountant which involved the registration of various kinds of lands, buildings and gifts, and the remission of agricultural taxes. He kept records of the population, listing people according to their tax-paying ability, profession and age. Apparently, records were kept of the income and expenditure, population and livestock of each village. The taxes were collected by the *sthānika*, who functioned directly under the *prādeśika*. The officials of the individual villages may have been directly responsible to the *gōpas*.

In the city, the *nāgarika* (Municipal Superintendent) was also assisted by a *gōpa* and *sthānika* (*Arthaśāstra* II, 36). While the *gōpa* kept accounts of the income and expenditure of various households, the *sthānika* kept a record of the various sections of the city and of the taxes collected. The city administration as seen by Megasthenes comprised six different committees (Strabo XV, i, 50). Of these the third kept a record of births and deaths for census and taxation purposes.

These officers were possibly the *gōpas*. The fourth of these committees was in charge of trade and commerce. The fifth committee supervised the public sale of manufactured goods, while the sixth collected the sales tax on these. The *sthānikas* mentioned in the *Arthaśāstra* probably formed Megasthenes' sixth committee.

Thus the first, fourth and sixth committees of Megasthenes' above classification were directly linked with manufacture, trade, commerce and taxation. The superintendent of commerce valued all articles for sale, taking into consideration price fluctuations and transport costs. A tax remission was granted to people importing foreign goods (*Arthaśāstra* II, 16). The rate of the customs dues was the same as that of the excise. This was one fifth of the toll dues. The rate of the general tax levied on merchandise was one tenth, though it may have varied for certain commodities (*Arthaśāstra* I, 13; II, 22). These dues were paid in cash and not in kind.

The payment of commercial taxes in cash promoted the circulation of coins. The majority of Punch-marked coins occur in strata related to the Mauryan period. This is especially evident in urban centers, however, indicating perhaps that the use of cash was more widespread in the urban areas. We are ignorant of the degree to which the money economy had penetrated into the rural areas. It would seem that most of the products required by the village were manufactured locally. Goods coming from urban areas may have been obtained through barter. Even the salaries listed in the *Arthaśāstra* (V, 3) are stated in monetary terms (thus the *purōhita* received a salary of 48,000 *paṇas*, the *mantri* 24,000, the soldier 500 *paṇas*). It is unlikely that the extremely high salaries of the upper levels of the bureaucracy were paid completely in money.

The *Arthaśāstra* prescribes that one quarter of the state revenues be set apart for salaries for the king's officials (V, 3). Another portion was to be stored away in the treasury store-house as a capital reserve for use in emergencies. In reciprocating its subjects, gifts and services, the state also diverted a substantial proportion of its revenues to public works. Although the *Arthaśāstra* (III, 9) speaks of irrigation as a state concern, it nonetheless also mentions the private ownership of ranks and the right to transfer their ownership or to mortgage them. It also refers to cooperative efforts in connection with the construction of watertanks on the founding of new settlements. The buildings at Pāṭalīputra were the products of state-sponsored projects falling within the category of public works.

The frequency of construction of public works increased during the reign of Aśoka. His inscriptions speak of the building of roads and rest houses, the planting of trees along roads, the digging of wells, and the creation of medical facilities for men and beasts. The Aśokan pillars and caves made during the Mauryan period might also be classified as state-sponsored works. While such activities were part of a prestige economy, state investments were also drawn on for agricultural expansion. State-sponsored works were financed by the treasury, the craftsmen also being paid by it. But these works were also to some extent the result of forced labor (*viṣṭi*) whereby craftsmen were compelled to contribute one day's labor per month to the state.

Primogeniture was the accepted rule for the royal succession (*Arthaśāstra* I, 17, *Mahāvamsa* IV, 1–4). Aśoka, however, not being an eldest son, secured the throne through sheer efficiency as an administrator, ruthlessness and palace intrigue (*Divyāvadāna* XXVI, pp. 372–373; *Mahāvaṃsa* V, 39–40; *Dīpavaṃsa* VI, 21–22). It then took him several years to consolidate his position. In 265 B.C. he was consecrated (Thapar 1961: 25). After Aśoka his grandson, and not his son Kunāla seems to have come to the throne, though the order of succession remains unclear in the sources.

The *Arthaśāstra* places the crown prince (*Yuvarāja*) in the highest income group (48,000 *paṇas*) in the state administration (V, 3). The king's first choice for dealing with delicate administrative situations seems to have fallen upon the crown prince. Thus Biṅdusāra sent Susīma to settle the Taxila revolt, and Aśoka sent Kunāla to the same place for the same purpose.

There is a possibility that Aśoka's grandmother or mother was of Greek origin. But her foreign origin (though rendering her impure according to orthodox views) did not disqualify Aśoka from the throne. During the latter stages of Aśoka's reign, Tissarakkā (*Mahāvaṃsa* XX, 2–3) who had been given the status of chief queen after the death of Asandhimittā, attempted to secure the crown for her son. Thus, at least in the latter stages of the empire, the mother of the crown prince actually attempted to influence the succession. A king had to be in good health to be accepted as such. The plot to blind Kunāla, the legitimate successor of Aśoka, according to one source (*Aśokavadana*), may have been aimed at disqualifying him as king owing to a physical defect.

In the competition for power, open warfare and intrigues were quite common. So Chandragupta sought an alliance with the Greek invader to oust the Nandas (Plutarch, *Life of Alexander* LXII, p. 403). Further, his mentor Chānakya intrigued to undermine the power of the Nandas. The struggle for power was, however, conclusively decided on the battle field. Biṅdusāra recommended his son Susīma as his successor, but the chief minister, Rādhagupta, successfully championed the cause of Aśoka (*Divyāvadāna*). Internal palace intrigues were perhaps followed by a civil war in which Aśoka eliminated the other claimants to the throne (*Mahāvaṃsa* V, 40; *Dīpavaṃsa* VI, 21–22). The prohibition on social gatherings, '*samājas*' (*Rock Edict* I) as part of Aśoka's policy of *dhamma*, may have been aimed at undermining political conspiracies directed against the regime by discontented groups. Even the death of Bṛhadratha seems to have been the outcome of a conspiracy.

The emergence of the aristocracy and the nobility should be considered as taking place from the ranks of royalty, the bureaucracy and the senior ranks of the armed forces. The latter two were particularly essential to the new monarchy in establishing and consolidating its power, the real basis of the strength of the state.

There is little information on the methods of recruitment under the Mauryas, however. In a centralized type of state personal loyalty to the ruler rather than to the state became the dominant factor. This was a result of appointments to the upper levels of the bureaucracy and senior ranks of the armed forces coming under the king's direct control, there being no non-personal recruitment system. These officials in turn are likely to have appointed junior officers who were either relatives or associates, a process which probably continued all the way down the structure, thus making for a vast network of personal connections.

The *Arthaśāstra* (I, 9) lists certain general qualities as necessary qualifications for a minister, such as birth, integrity, intelligence, etc. Megasthenes states (Diodorus II, 41) that advisers to the king were selected from the caste of councillors and assessors, a highly privileged body. If we accept Rādhagupta's involvement in the succession of Aśoka, the ministers seem to have had very close links with the royal power.

The *kumāras* (possibly sons of the ruler) and the *āryaputras* mentioned in the inscriptions were in charge of provincial administration, and formed the upper crust of the aristocracy. A matrimonial alliance between a provincial ruler and a local family obviously raised the social standing of the latter as they automatically entered into the aristocratic fold. The *Vaiśya*-merchant family to which Vidisa devi belonged may have experienced such mobility (*Mahāvaṃsa* XIII, 6–9; *Dīpavaṃsa* IV, 15–16). Tuṣāspa was appointed during the reign of Aśoka to the governorship of the province of Saurāṣṭra and his name suggests a Hellenised West Asian. Considering the location of this region, he may have represented the local community with strong commercial interests.

The *mahāmattas*, whose precise designation is uncertain, appear to have acted as a ministerial or advisory council as well (*Rock Edict* VI at Girnar). Not only were they a highly responsible group of officials but were also respected. They were entrusted with senior positions and controlled various aspects of the administration. This group, it has been suggested, represented the seventh class listed by Megasthenes from whom selections were made to the ministerial council (*Mantrīpariṣad*).

It is uncertain whether the *dhamma-mahāmattas* who were appointed in the fourteenth regnal year of Aśoka (*Rock Edict* V, XII; *Pillar Edict* VII) were created by entirely new selections or from the existing upper bureaucracy. With time they seem to have developed into a separate category within the bureaucracy with extensive powers granted by the king (*Pillar Edict* I and II). Their duties included welfare activities, teaching of the *dhamma*, obstructing unprofitable social functions etc. They had under their care not only *Brahmīns*, members of the royal family and the harem, but also other social groups such as peasants and perhaps untouchables and tribal people. The traditional upper caste groups i.e., *Brahmīn* and *Kṣatriyas*, may have had some reservations about working among the so-called lower social groups. The *dhamma-mahāmattas* therefore may have been chosen from recently elevated social groups (having less prejudice against lower social groups and little regard for orthodox observance) and possessing high status under the new regime, which perhaps gave them the power to interfere even in the royal household.

The salary scale as given in the *Arthaśāstra* (V, 3) indicates large outlays on the upper levels of the bureaucracy. While all posts in the bureaucracy seem to have been institutionalized, there was no clear-cut division of responsibilities. At one level, there was no distinction between the executive and judiciary powers, at another, certain officials combined juridical, fiscal and military functions and even propagated the *dhamma* to the people. Furthermore, the very position of the bureaucracy with regard to the palace and the provinces made it, intentionally or unintentionally, a channel of information to the center.

Of the few actual known officials in the upper layers of the bureaucracy of the Mauryan empire, two, Chānakya and Pusyamitra, were unquestionably *Brahmīn* by caste. The other two mentioned by name, Puṣyagupta and Rādhagupta, may have belonged to the *Vaiśya* caste, but there is some uncertainty about this. Tuṣāspa is definitely a Persian name, and its bearer may not have fallen within any caste category. This would suggest either that the name ending Gupta was not indicative of *Vaiśya* caste and that the ministers concerned were of high caste, or, if they were of *Vaiśya* origin, that the theoretical rules were not observed in practice.

Aśoka's notions of paternal rule included the conception of the king not only as protector but also as the controller of all spheres of life. This attitude is expressed in Aśoka's own dictum 'all men are my children' (*1st Sept. Rock Edict*). This was to determine the nature of the new relationship between the king and his subjects, marked by the king's concern for the welfare of his subjects. Interestingly enough, the same word, *prajā*, was used for both subjects and children.

Traditionally the king was also expected to maintain the existing social order (*varna*) (*Arthaśāstra* I, 4). The divine sanction which the king needed for the performance of these tasks, was transmitted through the *purōhit* (the *Brahmīn* adviser), who guided the king in spiritual matters and at times also in political matters (*Arthaśāstra* I, 10). Aśoka seems to have eliminated the *purōhit* since there is no reference to any such functionary in the contemporary documents. He perhaps wished to emphasize his direct links with the divine powers in exercising his rule. His royal title/name Devānaṁpiya (beloved of the gods) suggests that he sought the support of the sacerdotal power. The statement that his policy of *dhamma* made Jaṁbudvīpa a place fit for the gods again indicates a connection between kingship and the divine power. Yet his active support went to Buddhism, a religion which excluded notions of divinity.

The Mauryan rulers at any rate were not concealed from the eyes of the people. Although the *Arthaśāstra* cautions the king on the dangers of too great an accessibility to his officials and subjects at all times (I, 19), the Mauryan rulers acted contrary to this. They were accessible to their officials at all times (Strabo XV, i, 53–56; *Rock Edict* VI at Girnar) and Aśoka at least initiated the extensive royal tours to various parts of the empire. To protect themselves the Mauryan kings were surrounded by a bodyguard of armed women (*Arthaśāstra* I, 21; McCrindle 1877: 70 ff.).

Although the figures regarding the standing army of the Nandas quoted by Diodorus and Plutarch seem to be exaggerated, it must nevertheless have been a considerable force. This army would have served Chandragupta after he seized power. Considering the size of the empire, the Mauryan army must also have been a substantial one. The Kalinga war seems to bear this out. Even though advocating a policy of non-violence, Aśoka never demobilized his armed forces. In fact, he did not disdain to threaten the unruly forest tribes with punishment and total annihilation (*Rock Edict* XIII). The tragedy of Bṛhadratha indicates that the Mauryas maintained a standing army throughout the period they were in power. The threat of Greek invasions on the northwestern frontier must have kept the regular troops mobilized during the final phase of the empire also.

The *Arthaśāstra* divides the troops into three main categories, viz. hereditary troops (or the standing army), hired soldiers and corporation soldiers (II, 33). Megasthenes lists the standing army as the fifth class in his classification of Indian society, although stating at the same time that numerically it was the second largest group (Diodorus II, 41). According to him the standing army was well-paid. This is confirmed by the scale of wages for the army outlined in the *Arthaśāstra* (V, 3). The wage of 500 *paṇas* for a trained soldier was the same as that received by staff accountants and clerks. The lowest wage for officers in the royal service was as low as 60 *paṇas*. The rates of payment furthermore rose in accordance with ascending rank.[6]

The civil administration entertained close links with the armed forces and was dependent upon the latter for protection. This provides a basis for the efficient functioning of the bureaucracy. The prompt action taken by Bindusāra during the Taxila revolt and the duties of *Amta-Mahāmatta*[7] (*Second Separate Rock Edict; Pillar Edict* I) testify armed forces and the administration.

With the establishment of the empire, better and speedier communications were needed for political, administrative and economic reasons. The Royal Highway connecting Taxila and Pāṭalīputra extended up to Tamluk in the east. The capital of Kalinga, Tosali, could be reached either by sea from Tamluk or by land from the Ganges plain. This overland route then continued further south as far as the Kṛṣṇa valley and further on to the Mysore region. The sea route linked Tamluk to the South Indian trade centers, northern Tambapaṇṇi (Ceylon) and Swarṇabhūmi (Burma) as well. The northwestern and western routes extended beyond Taxila, one via Kandahar, another via Kabul and yet another one along the Arabian gulf to the Greek kingdoms of the eastern Mediterranean. The imperial administration included special officers entrusted with the construction and maintenance of roads (Strabo XV, i, 50). These officers are called *agoranomoi* in the Greek sources.

Aśoka's officials were required to tour the country at regular intervals of three to five years. Aside from tours, the ruler had a number of other means of keeping himself informed on public opinion. The *Arthaśāstra* deals at length with espionage, instructing the king to be accessible to messengers and spies at any time of the day (I, 12). The sixth class mentioned by Megasthenes, the *episcopoi* of Diodorus (II, 41), were not a class of spies in the strict sense, but acted rather in the capacity of superintendents who made secret reports to the king (Strabo XV, i, 48). This practice was not abandoned during Aśoka's reign. In fact, it may have intensified, since the administrative officers, and later the *dhamma-mahāmattas* were expected to make regular tours and report to the king wherever he was. The *pulisāni, yūktas* and *pativedakas* acted as informers during Aśoka's reign.

The *yūktas* mentioned in the *Rock Edicts* were employed in secretarial work and accounting, which is confirmed by the *Arthaśāstra* (II, 9). According to the *Aśokavadāna* legend, Tissarakkā sent Aśoka's orders to Taxila endorsed with the king's seal. This would suggest that the orders were written. The inscription of edicts on stone and other materials in various parts of the empire also testifies to considerable familiarity with writing, which was originally a pre-Mauryan development. The fact that Aśoka ordered his edicts to be read to the public on prescribed days may indicate either that the level of literacy was low, or that an attempt to propagate a uniform language throughout the empire was being made through the inscription of the edicts. Although quite familiar in some parts of the empire, the Aśokan *prākrit* and *brahmī* scripts would have been relatively new to other parts. However, concessions were made to local scripts and languages wherever these were in regular use, as is evident from the use of the *kharosthi* script and of Greek and Aramaic for the edicts issued in the northwest.

Pātalīputra, the erstwhile strategic fortress of Pātalīgrama, founded by Ajātaśatru in the fifth century B.C., was converted into the capital of Magadha by his son Udayabhadra. It remained the capital of the Sisunāgas, the Nandas and the Mauryas. The classical accounts mention Palibotra as the royal capital, and so does the *Mahāvamsa* (V, 22). *Patañjali* (I, i, IX) recalls the Chandragupta Sabha as the center of the king's royal activities.

The Greek accounts also provide details on city administration (Strabo XV, i, 50), which broadly tally with the data on urban administration in the *Arthaśāstra*. Archaeological excavations have brought to light fortifications and the remains of royal buildings at Pātalīputra (*Ancient India* 9: 146–147). The provincial capitals of the empire, namely Taxila, Ujjain, Tosali and Swarnagiri, were also the residencies of the viceroys, who were either princes or other members of the royal family. The provincial nobility would also have been concentrated in these capitals.

The most powerful political institution apart from the king appears to have been the ministerial council (*Mantrīparisad*). The council's control over the king depended on its power vis-à-vis that of the king. Ministerial power was probably quite considerable when Aśoka ascended the throne. Aśoka refers to the council twice in his edicts. In *Rock Edict* III it is clearly stated that the council was expected to communicate all new administrative measures adopted by the king to the *Yūktas*. In *Rock Edict* VI at Girnar, this institution is mentioned as possessing greater authority with regard to matters left to the council by the king. It is said that the council could discuss his policies in his absence and suggest improvements. But the ultimate sanction for all decisions had to be given by the king. The legend of Kunāla shows that the king's orders might be passed on direct to the provincial ministerial council and that this institution could oppose the viceroy. In all probability the provincial administration did, as a rule, roughly follow the lines laid down by the center, allowing for local variations.

The *mahāmattas* were sent (by the center and the viceroys alike) on periodic tours of inspection. Aśoka even drew up a code of conduct for these officers (*First Separate Edict*). The king's proclamations were made known to the public through the medium of the royal edicts. Public readings of these were ordered on prescribed days (*First Sepa-*

rate Edict). In addition all officials, especially the *dhamma-mahāmattas*, were required to tour around to propagate the *dhamma*, thereby ensuring that the king's words reached the public at large. Perhaps the *dhamma-mahāmattas* became the king's actual agents spreading all over the empire and infiltrating all socio-economic groups in order to enforce the law of the *dhamma* (*Rock Edict* V).

The texts seem to express the view that the king's orders had to be enforced by a court of law (*Manu* II, 186). For the administration of justice were two sets of courts, namely the *dharmasthīya* and *kaṇṭakaśōdhana* (*Arthaśāstra* II, 6). The former were each presided over by three *dharmasthas* and three *amātyas;* they were found in every city and in other important centers. The latter type was presided over by three *pradṣtrs* (*Arthaśāstra* IV, 1). The towns as well as the rural areas were under the supervision of legal officers. There was a special category of *mahāmattas* who were sent on tours of inspection of the work of magistrates and legal officials. Legal matters arising in the rural areas came under the authority of the *rājukas*. Like those in the city, legal officials in rural areas might sometimes be contacted directly by the king (*Pillar Edict* IV). In his twenty seventh regnal year Aśoka extended the powers of the *rājukas* in legal matters, which suggests a certain decentralization of the administration at this level.

The king personally concerned himself with legal procedures and punishments, which he attempted to make uniform throughout the empire (*Pillar Edict* IV). The Greek sources indicate that punishments in Mauryan India were severe (Strabo XV, i, 50). The *Arthaśāstra* approves of torture (V, 8) and such punishments as the death penalty without torture (IV, 9, 10, 11, 12, 13). Aśoka never abolished the death penalty, but granted the right of appeal or a three days stay of execution (*Pillar Edict* IV). The notion of appeal is also known in the *Arthaśāstra* (II, 36). Popular reaction seems to have constituted the sole check on the king's actions. Thus the entire concept of the welfare of the people was aimed at keeping the people contented. The people did sometimes revolt out of discontent, as in Taxila. The degree of social development of the different regions had to be taken into consideration in the formulation of any policy by the central authority.

The main theories on the decline of the Mauryas attribute this on the one hand to a *Brahmanic* revolt directed against the low-born Mauryas, who professed a heterodox social ideology while they neglected and oppressed the *Brahmanas;* and on the other hand to Aśoka's pacifistic policies undermining the strength of the political power and thus cutting short the existence of the empire. It would be more appropriate, however, to view the decline of the Mauryan empire within the context of the dynamism of the total structure, with particular reference to the agrarian nature of the empire.

Obviously the greatest empire-building impulse initially came mainly from the Ganges Valley, which at that time was the most highly developed area, from a socio-economic point of view. It was due to this that the initial spread of the empire was so dramatic. The crucial question is whether this dynamism continued to prevail. It would seem that this was not the case due to certain contradictions within the imperial structure. Firstly the very unevenness of the socio-economic development of the sub-continent deprived the Mauryan empire of additional bases similar to the Ganges Valley. Rapid expansion stimulated by the search for additional producing areas entailed simultaneous extension of the bureaucracy and the army. If the Kalinga war provides even an approximate indication, every effort towards political expansion necessitated a gigantic investment of resources. These factors combined with the geographical limitations on expansion put a virtual halt to territorial annexations after Aśoka's Kalinga campaign. Thus the need to expand in order to obtain a greater surplus to maintain the establishment versus the inability to expand, developed into a basic and major contradiction of the Mauryan empire.

Secondly, the rise of the agrarian empire naturally coincided with the expansion of the economy. With territorial expansion, the number of subjects under its rule increased. In proportion to the vast territory of the Mauryan empire, its developed areas were relatively few. Thus the empire may have been faced with the problem of meeting increased demand for services, while the economy was unable to cater to an expanding population. As long as a strong central authority existed it could control the empire's resources. Thus it was possible during the early phases of the existence of the empire to divert the resources of the economically more developed areas to the less developed ones. But at the first signs of weakness in the central hold, the more developed areas began to turn their spheres of interest inwards, thus making for a regional concentration of resources. The rapid decline soon after Aśoka's death, leading to the fragmentation of the empire and the rise of regional kingdoms, should be seen in this light.

Thirdly, the structure of the empire was essentially pyramidal comprising a network of relations based ultimately on personal relationships. Thus on the one hand the personal ability of the ruler at the apex was of crucial importance. On the other hand loyalty, by implication, was commanded by the individual ruler instead of the system. This internal contradiction naturally affected the cohesion of the structure, with every political change at the top touching off a chain of changes. This became most evident after Aśoka, due to the relative lack of ability and weakness of character of his successors and to the mounting tension between the Mauryan empire and the Greek kingdoms in the northwest.

FOOTNOTES

[1] A draft of this chapter was read critically by Professor Romila Thapar of the Jahawarlal Nehru University, New Delhi, India.

[2] The conclusion of royal marriages from political motives, the exchanging of envoys, use of spies, erection of strategic forts (*durga*) and maintenance of a standing army (*daṇḍa*) were some of the features adopted by the Magadhan rulers and are in conformity with the policy laid down by the *Arthaśāstra*.

[3] Even literary sources such as the *Arthaśāstra* furnish details on metallurgy (II, 12). The weapons locally produced, which are listed in the above source (II, 18) correspond with some of the weapons described in Greek sources (Arrian, *Indica* XVI). The *Jātakas* mention various metals as well as agricultural and domestic implements, ornaments, etc., (I, 351; IV 60; 85, 296). Many of these descriptions are corroborated by the archaeological evidence (*Hastinapur*, A.I.X; *Taxila*, Marshall Vol. I, pp. 103–107).

[4] The availability of loans (to furnish capital) from the state treasury for commercial ventures (*Arthaśāstra* III, 2) and the reduction or remission of duties on goods arriving on damaged ships (*ibid.* II, 28) is clearly indicative of a policy of providing incentives for commercial activities.

[5] There were also state lands which would not be cultivated directly by the state and were thus given on lease to share-croppers (*Arthaśāstra* II, 24).

[6] Physicians, chariot drivers, and horse trainers were paid 2000 *paṇas;* infantry and cavalry leaders, and superintendents of chariots and elephants received 4000 *paṇas*, the heads of military corporations and commissions received 8000 *paṇas*, commanders 24,000 *paṇas;* and finally the commander-in-chief, along with the other highest ranks in the state, 48,000 *paṇas* (*Arthaśāstra* V, 3).

[7] These were the superintendents of the tolls. Tollhouses were located on the borders of the state. According to the edicts of Aśoka these officials were directly responsible to the king. They were expected to extend goodwill and confidence in the Mauryan state toward the peoples living outside of the realm.

REFERENCES

Ancient India (1953), vol. IX; (1954), vol. X (New Delhi).

Anderson, D. and Smith, H., ed. (1965), *Suttannipāta* (1913). London: Pali Text Society.

Bloch, J. (1950), *Les Inscriptions d'Asoka*. Paris: Maspéro.

Böhtlinck, H., ed. (1887), *Panini Astadhyayi*. Leipzig: Brockhaus.

Cowell, J. and Neill, R., ed. (1886), *Divyāvadāna*. Cambridge: Cambridge University Press.

Epigraphia Indica, (1927–28), vol. XIX, (New Delhi).

Fausbøll, V., ed. (1877–97), *Jātakas*. Vols. I–VII. London: Pali Text Society.

Geiger, W., ed. (1950), *Mahāvaṃsa*. (1908). Colombo: Oriental Publishers.

Gupta, R. C., ed. (1952), *Visnu Purana*. Gorakhpur: Asian Pub. House.

Hultzch, E., ed. (1888), *Corpus Inscriptionum Indicarum*. Vol. I. London: Routledge.

Jacobi, H., ed. (1884–95), *Jaina Sutras*. 2 vols. London: Sacred Books of the East.

Jolly, J., ed. (1887), *Manu Dharmaśāstra*. London: Pali Text Society.

Kangle, R. P., ed. (1972), *Kauṭilīya Arthaśāstra*. 3 vols. Bombay: Orient Longmans.

Kosambi, D. D. (1975), *An introduction to the study of Indian history*. (1956). Bombay: Popular Book Depot.

Majumdar, R. C. (1969), *Corporate life in ancient India*. (1918). Calcutta: Punti Pushtak.

Marshall, J. (1951), *Taxila*. 3 vols. Cambridge: Cambridge University Press.

McCrindle, J. W. (1877), *Ancient India as described by Megasthenes and Arrian*. Calcutta: Privately printed.

— (1896), *The invasion of India by Alexander the Great* (as described by Arrian, Curtius, Diodorus, Plutarchus and Justin). Westminster: Rider.

— (1901), *Ancient India as described in classical literature*. Westminster: Rider.

Morris, R. and Hardy, E., ed. (1885–1900), *Anguttara Nikaya*. 5 vols. London: Pali Text Society.

Narayan, A. K. and Gopal, L., ed. (1969), *The chronology of the Punch-marked coins*. Varanasi: Chowkhamba.

Oldenberg, H., ed. (1864), *Vinayapitaka*. 5 vols. London: Pali Text Society.

— (1879), *Dipavamsa*. London: Pali Text Society.

Przyluski, J. (1923), *La légende de l'empereur Açoka*. Paris: Maspéro.

Ray, N. (1945), *Maurya and Sunga art*. Calcutta: C.O.B.A.

Rhys-Davids, T. W. (1959), *Buddhist India*. (1903). Calcutta: C.O.B.A.

Sastri, K. A. N. (1967), *The age of the Nandas and Mauryas*. Delhi: English Book Store.

Thapar, Romila (1961), *Aśoka and the decline of the Mauryas*. London: Oxford University Press.

19   The Early State in Norway

ARON IA. GUREVICH

The process of the rise and formation of the early state in Norway coincides with the final stage of the decline of tribal society and the first stage of transition to a socially differentiated order. This order has some features in common with pre-feudal and early-feudal societies of other European countries in the early Middle Ages. Nevertheless, being proto-feudal from the typological point of view, this social order can be designated as such only with major qualifications, that is if it is studied in connection with its subsequent history. As a matter of fact, Norway never became a feudal state *sans phrase*, and the prerequisites of feudalism never developed fully. The Norwegian state assumed the outward appearance of a feudal monarchy during the High Middle Ages under the influence of more developed European states and of the Church. But it is hardly possible to speak of an organic growth of feudalism as a socio-juridical system permeating the whole of society.[1] The most characteristic feature of the early Norwegian state, in contradistinction to the early European kingdoms, was that the main bulk of the peasantry was not wholly excluded from local government or national defense; the ruling strata had no power to deprive the *bönder*, i.e., the rural population, of their personal freedom or consequently to develop themselves into a group, severing all direct connections between the king and his ordinary subjects. The exploitation of the peasants' resources was to a considerable degree carried out by the state. Consequently the underdevelopment of feudalism in Norway manifested itself, in particular, in the preponderance of public (state) functions over private ones, while the latter predominated in feudal European states (Schwerin 1943).

For an investigation of the early state in Norway we have a fairly wide range of historical sources at our disposal, including laws, sagas, poetical texts and, to a lesser extent, title-deeds. However, these sources were compiled chiefly in the twelfth and thirteenth centuries only for the appearance of writing in Scandinavia was connected with the late introduction of Christianity. Therefore, the historian is confronted with all the usual difficulties arising from a necessarily retrospective examination of sources. There is a tendency in contemporary Scandinavian studies to reject the bulk of the evidence relating to the epoch preceding the time of recorded history. This is quite a sound approach as far as the sagas are concerned, but as regards the juridical sources there seems to exist a possibility of distinguishing the archaic strata by virtue of the strongly traditional character of legal norms and customs. There is, moreover, the important evidence of archaeology, numismatics and toponymy, which provides even more adequate information.

The conditions of the early Norwegian state are very imperfectly known because of the above-mentioned peculiarity of the historical sources. Up to the ninth century Norway was a conglomeration of separate regions. This disunity was determined by a variety of factors, such as Norway's peculiar geographical features (its mountainous landscape and extended North Sea coastline), the scantiness of its population, settled wide-apart in scattered farmsteads, and the dominance of farming (a sporadic trade was carried on with other countries rather than internally in Norway itself, with its homogeneous population engaged in cattle-breeding and, to a much lesser extent, agriculture[2] and domestic crafts). One may speak of a relative unity only in language and religious rites and customs (Andersen 1972: 52). Each region had its own military leaders, *konungar, hersir* or *jarlar,* but the local administration was a concern of the people's assemblies, or *things.* Here legal cases were tried and general matters discussed. These *things* had strong connections with the heathen religious life.

The barbarian kingdoms in Western Europe came about as a result of Germanic conquests of Roman provinces. Here the royal power had to be strengthened in order to assert the dominance of the conquering minority over the native population, and here elements of the old Roman state machinery were adopted. The early states in Scandinavia came into being under very different conditions however. These political bodies were ethnically homogeneous. Most of the Northmen were not involved in the Great Migrations of the fourth-sixth centuries. They were romanized to a much lesser extent than other Germanic tribes, and before the beginning of the Viking expansion their contacts with the outer world remained rather sporadic and superficial. Longer than any other elsewhere, the Scandinavian social order remained akin to that under the old Germanic system (Wührer 1959).

The Vikings Age began at the turn of the ninth century. The Northmen then took part in raids of plundering and conquest of other countries and colonized the islands of the North Atlantic; their trade went hand in hand with piracy. The causes of the widespread and multifarious Scandinavian expansion are far from clear, but there is good reason to suppose that the shortage of resources in the north constituted an important motive for the participation of a section of the rural population in this migration. At the same time the disintegration of large patriarchal families into individual 'limited' families had begun.

The first emergence of a form of political unity in Norway, i.e., the establishment of the power of one monarch over the majority of the population, was an outcome of Viking expansion, or at least was connected with it. The power of more minor kings strengthened in a period of mounting aggression, this aggression being directed not only abroad, but partly also against other sections of the Norwegian population. One of the rulers of eastern Norway, Harald Fairhair, from the line of Ynglings, ruling both Norwegian and Swedish regions undertook the conquest of other parts of Norway in the second half of the ninth century.[3] Ship-burials in eastern Norway of representatives of Ynglings (?), which date back to the ninth century, testify to both their widespread contacts with other countries and to their increasing power. It seems plausible, that the latter had some connection with military expansion. Thus, the beginning of the unification of Norway constituted a stage in the process of Viking expansion and took the form of the conquest of the western and northern areas of the country by a king already established in the eastern region. This connection of Norway's initial political unification with Viking raids is suggested also by the fact, that the majority of the Norwegian kings of the tenth and the first half of the eleventh centuries began their career as Vikings: they were either mercenaries in the service of the English, Byzantine or Kiev rulers, or members of expeditions conducting raids of conquests and plunder abroad, who upon their return to Norway claimed its throne.

This does not mean to say that the war leader who succeeded in securing the Norwegian throne continued to behave as a conqueror. As it was necessary for many kings to crush the resistance of the local nobility[4] they had to try and win the *bönder's* support. As a rule a pretender would go to the provincial assemblies and ask the members to acclaim him as king in return for giving them certain concessions. Only a king proclaimed as such at the *things* possessed authority and could feel relatively secure. Only scions of the house of Harald Fairhair had any claim to the Norwegian throne. It is significant that not even such a popular and powerful country regent as *jarl* Hakon (at the end of the tenth century) ever dreamt of getting himself crowned, not only because he was a subject of the Danish king and ruled Norway in his name, but also owing to the firm conviction that all claims to the Norwegian throne had to be restricted solely to the members of one particular family.

There were, nevertheless, local rulers in different parts of the country throughout the entire tenth century, some of them also styling themselves king. But these petty kings, not belonging to Harald Fairhair's line, had no rights to the Norwegian throne.[5] Though resisting the Norwegian king's attempts to deprive them of their power and influence, these petty kings did not display any ambitions to subject the entire country to their own rule. These local potentates were bulwarks of particularism.

There arises in this connection the complicated question of the sacral nature of kingship in Norway in the pre-Christian epoch. Many historians believe that the Norwegian kings were, in fact, considered as bearers of sacral powers by their people. The sagas and scaldic poems speak of the kings' descent from heathen gods. It is not clear, however, when these royal genealogies were made up. There are some traditions about Ynglings being sacrificed by their people in olden times in order to ensure the fertility of the land; the body of one of these kings was dismembered and its various members buried in different areas in order that the entire population might benefit by the prosperity magically associated with his person. People believed in the king's special luck increasing as a result of ritual sacrifices and libations drunk during feasts 'for the king' and 'for peace and a good harvest'.[6] Some scholars, adhering to the hypercritical attitude towards the truthfulness of the historical records, reject the above ideas, considering them as products of the projection of Christian notions into heathen times (Baetke 1951, 1964, 1973). It seems to me that conceptions of the sacral nature of royal power in pre-Christian Norway might be seen in their proper perspective if we compared them with the interpretation of kingship made by other peoples in analogous phases of development (see Hocart 1927).

Strictly speaking, Harald Fairhair did not unite the country; he only subjected some of its regions to his personal rule and here established strong points. The fragility of the edifice he constructed was revealed after his death, when discords between his sons intensified in the struggle over their inheritance. There was no law governing the succession, the royal power being evidently hereditary in the king's family, like the farmstead in the *bóndi's* family. The local nobility was not eliminated by Harald or his successors. Nor was the *bönder's* right to self-government essentially limited.[7]

The first Norwegian kings had very restricted material resources at their disposal. Taxes were exacted only from their Ugro-Finnish neighbors living in the north. Nevertheless, even these contributions were collected originally by powerful local rulers, as is attested by Ottar the Norwegian, whose report was accordingly noted down by Alfred, Anglo-Saxon king, at the end of the ninth century. The *bönder* did not pay the king any taxes and the very idea of compulsory taxation ,provoked the most energetic resistance among them, even in later times. The concept of freedom presupposed the absence of any form of dependence, and the *bönder* would have considered the payment of taxes as an encroachment upon their proprietary rights (see below). The only form of material assistance to the ruler under these circumstances might be an entertainment or gift, which was meant to symbolize the reciprocity and equality in the relations between the king and the *bönder*.[8] Travelling from one region to another, the king would be treated to entertainments by the local population. The feast which the *bönder* gave the king and his bodyguard in the heathen era bore a definite religio-magical character. The ruler's direct contact with his people was a necessary condition for the country's well-being, as also for the king's exercise of authority. In conformity with the cultural conditions of the epoch, not so much the abstract idea of kingship, as the person of a specific monarch was of importance. It was necessary to pour libations to both the heathen gods and the king. The king guaranteed the peace and prosperity of the country, and the *bönder*, for their part, supplied him with the necessary provisions, which were consumed by the ruler and his subjects together at these special banquets; these festive meals being one of the principal institutions of that particular society.[9] The term *veizla* (feast) acquired in time the status of a technical term. We shall see how the *veizla* might develop into a kind of fief with which the king endowed certain of his subjects. This development began not much earlier than the eleventh century. For the time being, the chief source of the royal income, besides military loot and provisions supplied by the *bönder*, were the revenues from the king's private estates. Like other landowners, the kings had slaves and tenants raising livestock and tilling small parcels of land on their estates and paying them in kind.

The Norwegian kings had no judicial powers either. Side by side with the local *things* there were established, in the ninth and the beginning of the tenth centuries, the provincial assemblies. The kings, who favored their institution, regularly attended them; but the jurisdiction remained in the hands of the *bönder*. A powerful king might be able to exert pressure on the members of such an assembly and so obtain the decision he desired, but the norm, as before, was self-government for the *bönder*. Naturally, the most prosperous and powerful *bönder*, as well as the local nobility, exercised a decisive influence on jurisdiction and government in general.

The king's military power seemed to be more pronounced; it should be stated, however, that the functions and powers of commander-in-chief of the country's armed forces were not concentrated in his hands. There existed in each separate province an independent military force, of which all males possessing the right to bear arms were members (every *bóndi* possessed arms, this being an inalienable mark of his freedom). In maritime Norway the fleet played the principal part in defense, and the population of coastal regions regularly equipped warships to defend themselves against the raids of Vikings and other aggressive neighbors. These units were led by the local nobility. In the course of the tenth century the military leadership gradually passed to the Norwegian king, and the population of coastal regions was organized into 'ship districts', each of which had to provide one warship together with its crew. Nevertheless, the king did not possess unlimited power as a war leader, and occasionally the soldiery might refuse to follow him or even rebel against him.

The one military body on which the king could depend unconditionally was his bodyguard. Naturally its number gradually grew as young men eager for glory, loot and high positions joined his troops. The king's power at this stage depended first and foremost on the number of his followers.

Thus, the king became, to some extent, a focus of social interest, and proximity to him provided a sure way to promotion and favored the strengthening of social prestige (Piekarczyk 1968). But this royal influence was not yet institutionalized; it depended to a high degree on the king's personality. The king with a reputation for luck was willingly followed. However, when the country was ravaged by famine—a frequent phenomenon in Norway, with its undeveloped productive forces and limited natural resources—or by other disasters, the blame invariably fell on the king, for it was then believed that his mystical good fortune had abandoned him.

It is evident that the royal power in Norway during the ninth and tenth centuries was relatively ineffectual and hardly capable of strongly influencing the internal situation. The king had so far no administration at his disposal. All special tasks were carried out by his retainers or the stewards of his estates. The king was not yet able to organize his own power machine, and all mentions in sagas of such a bureaucracy are anachronistic.

The early Norwegian state at that initial stage was characterized by the lack of any social 'division of labor'. Public, military, religious and administrative functions were undifferentiated. The *bönder* were not only husbandmen, but at the same time also members of military forces and local assemblies. The heathen cult was practised in temples belonging to the nobility or powerful *bönder*; the Norwegians had no priesthood. The *bóndi's* freedom consisted in the unrestricted exercise of his full rights with regard to his personal and proprietary relations. It is important to stress that landed property was neither at that time nor later, subject to arbitrary alienation. Landownership consisted in the family right to inherit land and possess it (Gurevich 1956). The farm was considered not only as an object but also as a kind of extension of the owner's personality, and organically and inseparably one with it. The term *óðal* meant not only 'family estate' (*patrimonium*) but also 'fatherland' (*patria*), the term having the same origin as the terms *eðli*, *aðal* (birth, nobility). Personal and proprietary rights formed an indissoluble unity and were considered inalienable properties of the members of society. This kind of social order, characterized by a strong resistance to every kind of change, and traditionalistic to its very foundations, constituted a serious obstacle in the process of the strengthening of the state.[10]

The subsequent development of the early state in Norway can be understood only provided we bear in mind the reality of external aggression. So the first Norwegian king, Harald Fairhair, had to organize an expedition against the Vikings. Throughout the ninth century Norway was continually in danger from Danish and Viking invasions. For a time, it was even dependent on Danish kings. The need for national defence was urgent. Despite its rudimentary character, the monarchy was considered by the Norwegian population as a power opposing similar powers in other countries. There already existed the idea that only the king was able to represent the common interests of Norsemen vis-à-vis the world. It is significant that *Noregr* is first mentioned as the name of the country as a whole in records of the end of the ninth century, and that side by side with the tribal names for the different regions of Norway the name 'Norsemen', 'Northmen' appeared as a common denominator for the entire population of the Norwegian kingdom in skaldic poetry from that time on. It would be erroneous to attach too much importance to these facts, since the internal division remained extremely marked even after that time, but it is nonetheless hardly possible to ignore them. Some elements of a collective Norse consciousness already existed and became manifest at moments of danger from without. The royal power was able to utilize these.

Although Norway was situated on the periphery of the mediaeval world, it was nevertheless penetrated by influences from politically and socially more advanced European countries. The bearers of these influences were, first and foremost, the Norwegian kings. Coming to the Norwegian throne after passing their youth in more civilized and feudalized states, the kings strove to strengthen their power using experience accumulated abroad. Kings Olav Tryggvason and Olaf Haraldsson (the Saint), at the end of the tenth and for the first three decades of the eleventh century, consistently fought independent local princes through a policy of Christianization. Not to mention the part played by the Christian Church in the triumph of the monarchical principle in Norway as everywhere in Europe; conversion to the new faith additionally undermined the basis of the power of the old nobility, which controlled the heathen cult. Destroying pagan temples and forbidding the offering of sacrifices, both Olafs deliberately liquidated the trinity of 'cult–thing–ruler' which encouraged local self-government. The people were also aware of the connection between their independence and the old cult, as the records testify. Christianization carried out resolutely and ruthlessly by the Norwegian kings, led to the annihilation of part of the old nobility. Those who were not done away with in this bloody struggle were compelled to submit to the king's authority and become his servants.

The replacement of the old cult by the new one was accompanied by changes in the institution of the *veizla*. Formerly, as we have seen, the *veizla* was a sacred feast attended by the king and the *bönder*, in whose eyes it ensured the peace and well-being of the country; now there was no longer any obligation for the monarch to attend. The material basis of the *veizla* was revealed, and, henceforth, the *veizla* was no more than a means of supplying the king and his men with necessary material resources. If the king's travels all over the country continued, it was only because he had to administer it and because the transportation of foodstuffs over long distances was impossible. However, instead of attending feasts in a specific region, the king could delegate the right to collect victuals to some of his retainers. These were feudal grants of sorts but they involved the endowment of a vassal not with land, but with the right to collect provisions from the regional population which, as before, retained the proprietary rights over their lands. Another important difference between these grants and fiefs in more feudalized European countries was that in Norway (as in all the Scandinavian countries in general) these were not made hereditary (Lie 1907; Christensen 1968). The person who, with the king's permission, received authority to collect foodstuffs from the population of a certain district enjoyed this privilege only for the term of his service, or for life, but had no right to hand it on to his heirs. Eventually the distribution of food for the *veizlas* developed into a system of 'feeding' the king's men, the amounts varying according to the rank of the person concerned.

The absence of heredity with respect to the Scandinavian *veizla* 'fief' was connected directly with the structure of the ruling stratum and its relations with the central authority. The nucleus of this stratum was formed by the king's retainers. The word for bodyguard, *hirð*, was later used to refer to the king's entire court. The impossibility for the *veizla* man or feofee, to convert his *veizla* into absolute property and secure it for his family perforce bound the *veizla*man to the throne.

The old Norse *veizla* had its parallels in other countries, e.g., in Kievan Rus. The Anglo-Saxon system of book-land is also reminiscent of the Scandinavian *veizla*; English social development followed a different course, however, and book-land developed from the royally granted right to collect victuals and legal fines into that to hold land in fee. Meanwhile, the Norse *veizla* for a long time retained pristine traits distinguishing it from the Frankish-type fief.

The introduction of this system did not go smoothly. With the cult changed and the regular relations between the king and the *bönder* broken off the *veizla* ceased to be reciprocal; the ceremonial feast demonstrating the unity of the ruler and his people made way for the practice of a unilateral duty enforced by the king's officers. This change in the *bönder's* attitude became fused with the destruction of temples and idols, and was conceived of as the violation and profanation of the entire body of customs.

Some sagas, committed to writing in the thirteenth century, tell of 'the usurpation of the *óðal*' of the population of the entire country by king Harald Fairhair: as a result of this total confiscation the *bönder* supposedly became the king's tenants, liable to payment to him for the use of their land. Norwegian historiography has proved the unauthenticity of this story (Sars 1872; Hertzberg 1893; Nielsen 1907; Taranger 1907; Bull 1920). But was it in any way based on facts? To my mind it seems useful to compare this saga report with other evidence, especially that contained in the scaldic poems. Here Norway is called the king's '*óðal*' or 'hereditary estate'. The notion of the kingdom as the private estate of its ruler came into existence at about the time of king Olaf Haraldsson. The idea of the king's sovereignty over the entire population and its possessions in land seems to stem from the strengthening of the royal power and the above-mentioned change in the system of *veizla*. This idea nevertheless failed to find adequate juridical and terminological expression, since Roman law remained alien to mediaeval Norsemen. Consequently, this idea was interpreted in the most natural, only possible way, namely in terms of a 'memory' of the alleged confiscation of the *bönder's* *óðal* by the first king. The development of the *veizla*, the feast voluntarily offered the king by the *bönder*, into a rudimentary system of taxation was interpreted by the population as a violation and a usurpation. In reality, the landed property of the majority of the rural population, not to mention the estates of potentates fallen into disgrace, remained in their hands. But the obligation to support the king and his men was, in actual fact, imposed on the *bönder* and aroused their dissatisfaction and opposition (Gurevich 1967: 93 ff.).

The strengthening of the royal power, the acquisition by the king of additional authority, the suppression of heathenism and its adherents, in fact, the whole policy of open rejection of the traditional order resolutely carried through by Olaf Haraldsson engendered bitter conflict between the king and the majority of the old nobility, which latter met with the *bönder's* support. The king was forced to leave Norway, and his attempt to re-establish his authority resulted in his complete downfall (in the battle of Stiklastaðir, 1030). But it is highly significant that the king's defeat turned out in the end to be a major victory of the monarchy over the traditional peasant society. For the rebellion and the king's assassination were followed by the establishment of Danish rule over Norway, whereupon the advantages of the native monarchy became apparent. Not long afterwards, the late king Olaf's prestige rose to such a degree that the Church was able to proclaim him a saint, the divine champion of Norwegian kingship and even *perpetuus rex Norvegiae*. The sacral conception of kingship gained a new basis. At the same time, Olaf's canonization demonstrated the influence of the Church and the new, strong support of the royal power.

Catholic priests in Norway were mainly English. In religious matters Norway came under the control of the archbishop of North Germany (till 1152/53, when an archbishopric was established in Nidaros-Trondheim). But the policy of the clergy furthered the consolidation of the Norwegian monarchy.[11] The Church, in its turn, gained the king's support, political as well as material. Unlike in other European countries, the Church in Norway was not able to rely upon the flow of private donations. The alienation of family estates was hampered by *óðal* rights and the clergy's attempts to have these rights abrogated were unsuccessful (Bull 1912: 60 ff.). The estates of the Church, which soon began to grow, were mainly the result of gifts by the king. Later on were added to these the gifts of the nobility, as well as the plots of poorer peasants who found themselves unable to redeem the mortgages on their properties, and in addition to these, asserted lands. The Church succeeded in introducing the tithe only in the first half of the twelfth century.

The introduction of Christianity marked a new stage of the development of the early Norwegian state. A new ideology emerged, with the clergy representing the force struggling against the old heathendom that permeated traditional social order from top to bottom. Formerly, the social and juridical unit, namely the *thing*-community, had been at the same time the cult community. From now on, however, this unity was destroyed since the parishes were organized according to a new scheme not coincidental with the organization of public assemblies.

Side by side with a clergy that was intimately connected with the monarchy, the king's officials, or *lendir menn* ('landed men'), began to play a considerable role in the state machinery. The *lendr maðr's* functions consisted mainly in summoning the *bönder* to military service, which circumstance gave them the opportunity to interfere in independent local government, although the customary law forbade this. Whereas the stewards of the king's estates, being men of low rank or slaves or their offspring, were completely dependent on their lord, the *lendir menn* occupied a much more independent position, as the majority of them possessed fairly large properties of their own. As it happens, the *lendir menn* were recruited from the ranks of the old nobility, provided they expressed their willingness to serve the king.

Thus the institution of the *lendir menn* was the outcome of a compromise between the sovereign and a small proportion of the old nobility. In the opinion of some scholars the old aristocracy adapted themselves to the new state order more or less automatically, without any special difficulties, so that consequently it is possible to speak of a certain continuity between the upper stratum of Scandinavian society in the period preceding the emergence of the state and the ruling class of later times (Mitteis 1959: 410). However, the study of the relevant records gives rise to a more complicated picture. The power of the Vikings was based on warfare, loot, trade and the exploitation of slaves, whereas the eleventh and twelfth century Norwegian aristocracy was composed of men serving the king, to whom they were indebted for their high position, and deriving their income from the *veizlas* and their own tenants; slavery having already disappeared by that time. There may have been continuity between the old and the new aristocracy in principle, but they represented, on the whole, two distinct social groups. A considerable proportion of the old nobility perished in the struggle against the rising royal power; the sagas containing many stories of dramatic conflicts between the king and certain magnates trying to maintain their independence.

The *lendir menn* included not a few men of high birth, who were relatively independent, both materially and socially, this circumstance being characteristic of a special stage in the history of the Norwegian monarchy, though at the same time partly explaining its instability (Seip 1940–42). The old nobility, deeply rooted in the traditional social order, remained strong, for the old pre-class relations were converted very slowly and with great difficulty into a new, more highly differentiated social system. The radical change in proprietary and productive relations which had taken place in the Frankish kingdom was impossible in Norway, where the forces of social inertia showed strong resistance to all change. A substantial proportion of the *bönder* never became dependent peasants at all, but continued their independent farming activities. Although the essence of their freedom began to change (see below), the Norwegian *bönder* differed greatly from the dependent villeins and serfs in other European countries of that time.

It seems necessary to establish a link between this essential feature of the Norwegian social structure and the specific character of its political order in the eleventh and twelfth centuries. The Norwegian monarchy possessed certain advantages over the royal power in Western European countries, weakened and without a broad social basis as they were. The Norwegian kings did not lose their direct connections with the mass of the people, for there did not come between them a powerful class of grands seigneurs, who might subject the majority of the peasants to their own rule and usurp political power. The Norwegian kings, unlike many other Western rulers, were not wholly dependent on the military support of their noble vassals, and themselves controlled the army (see Seip 1940–42: 100 ff., 109 ff. on the functional relation between the royal power and the *bönder*). The old nobility maintained their traditional ties with the *bönder*, partly also because it was not feudalized and, consequently, did not exploit them. Therefore the nobility was able to involve the *bönder* in its own struggle against the king, who, in its eyes, was gaining excessive power. As we have seen above, the majority of the *bönder* fought a decisive battle against their king, in which king Olaf the Saint perished. This is easy to explain. The king was the principal innovator, who destroyed the heathen cult and infringed on the custom of the blood feud, reformed the *veizla* and granted it to his retainers. Traditional peasant society responded negatively to these innovations.

Not long after Olaf's death, however, the national monarchy was restored, and his son Magnus returned from Kiev and was crowned. He, nevertheless, had to promise to take the country's customs and the liberties of the *bönder* and nobles into consideration. All these conditions were provisions, however, of the status of the monarchy, depending on the king's personality and on vagueness with regard to the succession to the throne. Throughout the twelfth century the institutional instability of the monarchy manifested itself in feuds between various pretenders and their respective factions. The uncertainty of the succession was not, of course, the cause of the conflicts (Bjørgo 1970; Blom 1972) but was a symptom of the weakness of the monarchy, a certain proportion of the old nobility having interests at stake in this weakness. In the second half of the twelfth century this internal strife spread beyond the ruling clique and ended up being an internal struggle in which wide strata of the population were involved. This struggle is known as the Norwegian Civil War, or the War of the Birchlegs and was directly connected with the genesis of the early state. However, it is necessary first of all to dwell on the change in the *bönder's* status, since this change left its mark on the course and the outcome of the Civil War.

As we know, the Norwegian *bóndi* retained his personal freedom. The actual essence of his freedom changed slowly but surely, however, and grew more restricted. The basis for this development was provided by the break-up of the large family, which had already begun on the eve of the Viking Age and which was to continue for centuries. The large family, which had never existed as an actual social and economic unit, now made way for the limited family. Whereas the large family, embracing as it did three generations of close relatives, as well as dependants, used to include enough men for both farming and other forms of communal activity, for the husbandman of the limited family it became increasingly difficult to combine productive with political activities. As a result the *bönder*, full and equal members of society and of the people's assemblies and military levics as they were, now changed, by force of circumstances, into a peasantry fully engaged in agricultural work. It was possible for them to fulfil unproductive public functions only at the expense of their farming activities.

It is evident from the historical records, that many *bönder* tried to evade their public responsibilities (a trip to a *thing* and back home under Norwegian conditions took up a considerable amount of time). Ultimately, the royal power reorganized the provincial *things*, transforming them from meetings attended by all adult males into assemblies of representatives nominated by the *bönder*, together with the clergy and the king's officials. At the same time the military focus shifted from the people's militia to a professional mounted army of knights, an identical process to that which had taken place, though on a much fuller scale, two or three centuries earlier in the Frankish kingdom, and subsequently in other feudal states of the West. Although the Norwegian *bönder* were not completely released from the obligation of military service, they might pay a tax instead of enrolling for such service, this marking the appearance of the first secular tax in Norway[12] (Johnsen 1938).

It being beyond the scope of the present article to dwell in detail on the essence of this process, I should merely like to emphasize its grave consequences both for the *bönder* and for the early Norwegian state (see Gurevich 1967). To begin with, the *bóndi's* right to bear arms as well as to take part in public assemblies was at the same time his duty, since he was obliged to be a member of the militia and of the *thing*. Rights and duties were not mutually distinguished or opposed, but formed in such a primitive society, a close and indissoluble unity as marks of the freedom of every full and equal member of society (Neussychin 1961). But not long after, as we have seen, the negative aspect of these rights began to emerge on account of their onerousness: the obligations to the state connected with the exercise of these rights became more real and perceptible than the rights as such. Attempts to obtain a release from these obligations in point of fact deprived the peasants of their rights. The very substance of the *bönder's* traditional liberty changed in such a way that unlimited freedom degenerated into a partially restricted one. It was not, of course, a dependence of the seignioral type, which was widespread in contemporary Europe, but a type of freedom, an integral feature of which was state exploitation of the peasantry.

This change was far from complete. One may, nevertheless, regard it as reflecting to some extent the progressive social 'division of labor' between a peasantry on the one hand, and a military and governing elite on the other.[13] It would be erroneous to underestimate the significance of this process by viewing it merely as a social differentiation into peasants and lords, since it was much more complicated than that. The same kind of social differentiation took place among the *bönder* also. Side by side with, and above the ordinary freemen, there emerged, precisely in the twelfth and thirteenth centuries, a new social category of *höldar*. They were well-to-do husbandmen, who differed from the mass of the *bönder* on the point of their public activities and the preservation of their full freedom. The *höldar* were not so very much above the rest of the *bönder* in the absolute sense (Maurer 1890), but rather remained on the former high legal level, while the other *bönder* degraded socially, juridically and, to some extent, materially. As a result of this erosion of the mass of the *bönder*, the *höldar* became privileged, whereas ordinary freedom deteriorated and more or less acquired the character of 'state dependence' (Gurevich 1964).

Accordingly, the social basis of the monarchy changed. The king now had to rely, first and foremost, upon a professional knighthood instead of the people's militia with its rather primitive weapons. In jurisdiction and administration he had to deal with the elite and the *höldar* or 'powerful *bönder*', but not, as before, with the mass of the *bönder*. The aristocratization of the state was making visible progress.

But, although on the one hand some of the *bönder* tried to evade their public responsibilities, on the other hand they could not avoid the suffering caused by the infringement on their liberties, and this bred discontent. The center of gravity in public affairs shifted upwards, so that the leading role in goverment henceforth belonged to the powerful men of the king's entourage. Consequently, the pressure exercised by them on the peasantry intensified, the taxes rose and the arbitrariness of government increased.

During the second half of the twelfth century the proportion of peasants who were not owners increased noticeably. They comprised ruined farmers, tenants of lands belonging either to the Church or to secular lords, and settlers of newly reclaimed areas to which the king claimed a proprietary right. The class of tenants or *leiglendingar* developed into an essential component of Norwegian society. Though *leiglendingar* were not the same as dependent tenants in feudal European states, inevitably some traits of personal juridical inferiority accompanied their material dependence at that time.

Thus, in the course of the twelfth century there was an accumulation of factors which finally engendered a complicated social and political crisis in Norwegian society.[14] The public protest of the lower strata, the dissatisfaction of the *bönder*, the conflict between the old nobility, led by *lendir menn*, and the 'new men', brought into prominence by the royal power, the friction between the different provinces striving to maintain their traditions and independence and the opposition between the urban and rural population,[15] all this was further complicated by the struggle for power between the Norwegian monarchy and the church, which was striving for independence from the state everywhere in twelfth century Western Europe (the Scandinavian North became involved in the conflict between the Empire and the Papacy at the end of that century). Thus the strife between the various pretenders developed into a civil war. Leaving aside the peripheral facts relating to it, I should like to concentrate on the main events, which have a direct bearing on the problem of the early state (for a review of historical theories cf. Helle 1964: 21 ff.).

During the first stage of the civil war the royal impostor Sverrir and his followers, the Birchlegs—comprising déclassés and members of the lower strata of society—fought against the group of *lendir menn* led by King Magnus Erlingsson and his father, together with the high clergy.[16] Owing to the support of a proportion of the *bönder*, Sverrir succeeded in winning the crown and establishing his rule.[17] It is highly significant, however, that his followers, the Birchlegs, seizing state offices and landed estates confiscated from the nobles, whom they eliminated, ennobled themselves and refused to have anything more to do with the peasants' revolt. This is the first time we are able to observe a high degree of solidarity amongst the ruling strata surrounding the throne. Parvenus who owed their career to the king saw a guarantee for their dominance in a strong monarchy.[18] The change of ruler did not bring the peasants any advantage and, disappointed in the Birchlegs, they continued to rebel. They were subdued by the united forces of the Birchlegs[19] and their former antagonists, the Baglar, the adherents of the Church party.[20] By the middle of the thirteenth century the royal power had become completely consolidated, the opposing factions of the nobility had been reconciled, and the privileged, aristocratic upper class made its effective appearance. It consisted of secular and ecclesiastical landowners, the king's retainers and military men, the tenants of royal estates and the *höldar* (significantly, the *höldar* in thirteenth century records are called *riddarar*, or 'knights'. The main body of the peasantry now definitively forfeited any influence on public life that it had formerly had, and was degraded to the condition of producers, at whose expense the new aristocracy supported itself.

On the whole, Norwegian society was divided into a ruling class, which rallied round the king, and a peasantry. The juridical records on the thirteenth century, while treating of agrarian conditions, take the basic division of the society into landowners and tenants for granted. It seems that this division was considered more essential than the old division of society into a nobility, a class of freemen and a class of slaves. Nevertheless, the institution of large landownership was less developed in Norway than in other countries of northern Europe, and it seems plausible that this lack of independence on the part of the nobility was the main cause of its attachment to the royal power. Never before had the Norwegian state so resembled any of the feudal European monarchies, in structure as well as in form. The civil war saw the emergence of the state as a culmination of the early stages of its development.[21]

CONCLUDING REMARKS

I have tried to give a brief outline of the genesis of the early Norwegian state, and to characterize it by means of a model which takes into account, as much as possible, the economic, political and legal structure as well as the kinship relations, religious ideology, warfare and the ecological and geopolitical factors. Under due recognition of the prime importance of the relations of production, it is necessary at the same time to stress that an analysis of historical processes in the early Middle Ages must presuppose all the other aspects of a society functioning. The model under discussion is dynamic, for, in spite of its traditional character and the strong tendency towards the self-perpetuation of its archaic structure, Norwegian society was not altogether static and stationary.

Accordingly, the early state in Norway developed from the 'inchoate' to the 'typical' stage, and, partially, to the 'transitional' stage (using the terminology proposed by the editors of the present volume). These stages, or types, cannot be clearly distinguished in Norway, however, for the traits of earlier types never completely disappeared in subsequent stages. An explanation for this is provided by the fact that the social history of Norway is different from that of other European states in the early Middle Ages.

Leaving this period aside for a moment, and looking at the stage of the early state in Norway in a wider historical perspective, we shall see that the underdevelopment of feudalism, and especially the absence of personal serfdom of the peasants were the causes of the early liquidation of large landownership in Norway (earlier than in the majority of European countries). There was no need for a bourgeois revolution in order for a transition to a state and social system of the modern type to take place. This problem does not lie within the scope of our essay, of course, but seems to me nevertheless worth mentioning by way of demonstration of the far-reaching consequences of the nature of the early state in Norway. Though having much in common with early states all over the world, the early Norwegian state at the same time differed considerably from the typical forms of political organization of mediaeval Europe.

In conclusion, I should like to stress once more that it is hardly proper to study the history of the early Norwegian state in isolation. It can only be understood if one also takes into consideration the broader European development, whence issued strong and multifarious stimuli. The very institution of the monarchy here was set up under western influence. The principal buttress of the royal power was the Church, the source of certain organizational patterns and of the ideological sanction (Johnsen 1948), but this fact could not prevent the outbreak of fairly severe conflicts between the clergy and the king. The northern Germanic tradition, going back to an archaic period of barbarism, and the feudal political tradition of Catholic Europe—these were the two poles of the magnetic field within which the early Norwegian state took shape.

FOOTNOTES

[1] The view expressed here differs to some extent from that put forward in my earlier works (Gurevich 1967).

[2] Even today only about three per cent of the country's surface area is cultivated.

[3] At one time historians attached some importance to the interest shown by this king and the rulers of the northern part of the country in taking control of the trade route along the Norwegian coast (Schreiner 1928; 1929; Koht 1955: 16 ff.). Though this is not perhaps unjustified, it is hardly plausible to view trade as a decisive factor in the process of the formation of the early Norwegian state.

[4] A certain faction of the nobility seemed to support Harald Fairhair, who was able to turn its disunity and internal division to his own advantage.

[5] The most recent saga represents one of the East Norwegian kings as a husbandman who personally supervised the agricultural work performed by his men and ruled his region, but who absolutely lacked both the wide vision and the political aspirations characterizing the kings of the whole of Norway (*Heimskringla: Óláfs saga helga*, 1, 33).

[6] There existed a belief that the king had the ability to transfer his personal luck to his men, in particular by giving them weapons, rings and other precious things, this being connected with the belief in the magic association between people and their belongings.

[7]   Significantly, when Harald's younger son Hakon the Good, reared at the court of the Anglo-Saxon King Ethelstan, became king of Norway, the *bönder* resisted his attempts to introduce Christianity, and he was compelled to yield to them immediately.

[8]   Social relations in that particular society were based, in general, on the principle of reciprocity. In particular, every gift had to be countered with an equivalent gift, at least in the case of relations between equals, for otherwise the recipient would feel under an obligation to the giver, not merely a material obligation but also a moral one, since a man was as a rule injured to the very core by such a one-sided relationship (Gurevich 1968).

[9]   In different parts of Norway, as well as in other Scandinavian countries, *Huseby* was a frequent toponym. As A. Steinnes (1953; 1955) has demonstrated, these were the bases frequently visited by the kings during their seasonal tours of the country. Here the *bönder* brought food and prepared feasts for the king and his retinue.

[10]   It seems instructive here to compare Norway with Iceland, occupied by emigrants from Norway as well as from the Scandinavian colonies in the British Isles at the end of the ninth and the beginning of the tenth centuries. Iceland's isolation from the rest of the world made the danger of invasion unreal and therefore the emergence of a military authority unnecessary. As a result of the natural conditions and the paucity of resources the economy was mainly dependent on cattle breeding. The scattered population lived on isolated farms. The Norse emigrants, who left Norway in an attempt to escape from King Harald's despotic rule, strove to maintain their traditional social order in Iceland. Their social and economic differentiation, during the first two or three centuries after colonization of the island, was not marked enough to provoke serious internal conflicts. Until modern times there were no towns in Iceland. The Icelandic *bönder* were able under these conditions to develop a form of self-government, which excluded the emergence of any kind of central power, aside from the *Althing* (general assembly), where the common law was laid down and legal cases were tried. The Icelandic 'democracy' of the tenth and eleventh centuries was analogous, in the main, to the Norwegian social order during the period preceding the establishment of the royal power. But the differences began to become evident after that.

[11]   The creation of the archbishopric (1152/53) was connected with the activities of an assembly of the high clergy, the nobility and representatives of the *bönder*, twelve 'wise men' from each bishopric, who seem to have been appointed by the bishops. Norwegian historians have called this meeting the first state assembly (*riksmøte*) in Norwegian history (Holmsen 1971: 201 ff.).

[12]   *Leiðangr* was the name for both the people's militia and the military tax which substituted the levy.

[13]   This process went slightly further in Sweden, where the principal lines of development were, in the main, the same as in Norway. Swedish society was differentiated, during the twelfth and thirteenth centuries, into two major groups, namely one of *frälse*, or privileged knights, exempt from taxation, and one of *skattebönder*, or tax-paying peasants exempt from military duty. Nevertheless, these groups were not closed, after the model of feudal states in Sweden either, for any peasant who was able to perform knightly services had the right to be exempted from taxes and pass into the class of *frälse*.

[14]   Some Norwegian historians regard as the main cause of the civil war the country's economic development during the twelfth century, and more especially the transformation of the growing number of *bönder* into tenants (Holmsen 1971: 220 ff., 257; cf. Helle 1964: 21 ff, 113).

[15]   The towns, which had sporadically played a part in the economic life of Norway during the Viking Age, started to develop from the end of the eleventh century onward and soon became points of Hanseatic penetration. The royal power, controlling foreign trade and being in need of money, which was more easily obtainable from the rich

German entrepreneurs than from the rather more modest Norwegian merchants, felt compelled to make considerable concessions to foreigners. Bergen and other towns became satellites of the Hanseatic league for a long time after that.

[16] There was promulgated, with the energetic cooperation of the high clergy, a law of succession (1163) which subjected the king to the control of the Church. This law was never carried into effect, and its importance consisted only in the fact that it served as model for later legislation regulating the status of royalty. At the same time the first Church coronation took place in Norway, and in Scandinavia in general; it was conducted after the western European fashion, with Magnus Erlingsson being annointed by the papal nuncio and proclaiming himself 'Saint Olaf's vassal'.

[17] An interesting polemical document, *The Oration against the Bishops*, was put out at the height of the war, by the circles surrounding Sverrir. The document abrogated all secular pretensions of the clergy, to which it opposed the king's superiority (Gunnes 1974: 98 f.).

[18] During the Norwegian civil war the *syselmen*, or representatives of the king, made their first appearance. These might be qualified as royal functionaries. All local government was concentrated in their hands.

[19] 'Birchleg' eventually ceased to be a nickname and became an honarary title.

[20] 'Baglar' from *bagall*, a Bishop's crozier.

[21] After the civil war such central state organs as the King's chancellery and the state council made their appearance in Norway; the assemblies of nobles and *bönder* representatives were sporadically convened, but these assemblies never developed into a 'parliament'.

REFERENCES

Andersen, P. S. (1972), *Samlingen av Norge og kristningen av landet 800-1130*. Oslo: Universitets Font.

Baetke, W. (1951), 'Christliches Lehngut in der Sagareligion', in: *Berichte über die Verhandlungen der Sächs. Akademie der Wiss. zu Leipzig, Philol.-hist. Kl.* 98:6.

— (1964), 'Yngvi und die Ynglinger. Eine quellenkritische Untersuchung über das nordische 'Sakralkönigtum', in: *Sitzungsberichte der Sächs. Akademie der Wissenschaften zu Leipzig, Philol.-hist. Kl.* 169:3.

— (1973), *Kleine Schriften*. Weimar: Herman Böhlaus.

Bjørgo, N. (1970), 'Samkongedøme kontra einekongedøme', in: *Historisk tidsskrift* 49:1.

Blom, G. A. (1972), 'Samkongedømme-Enekongedømme-Håkon Magnussons hertugdømme', in: *Det kongelige norske videnskabers selskab, Skrifter* no. 18.

Bull, Edv. (1912), *Folk og kirke i middelalderen*. Kristiania and København: Gyldendal.

— (1920), 'Sagaenes beretning om Harald Hårfagres tilegnelse av odelen', in: *Historisk tidsskrift* 5:4.

Christensen, A. E. (1968), *Kongemagt og aristokrati*. København: Munksgaard.

Gunnes, E. (1974), 'Tale mot biskopene', in: *Kulturhistorisk leksikon for nordisk middelalder* 18.

Gurevich, A. Ia. (1956), Bolshaia sem'iaa v Severozapadnoi Norvegii v rannee srednevekov'e (The large family in northwestern Norway in the Early Middle Ages), in: *Srednie veka* 8.

Gurevich, A. Ia. (1964), Norvezhskie bondy v XI–XII vv. [Norvegian bönder in the 11th–12th centuries], in: Srednie veka 26, II.

— (1967), Svobodnoe krest'ianstvo feodal 'noi Norvegii [The free peasantry of feudal Norway]. Moscow: Nauka.

— (1968), 'Wealth and gift-bestowal among the ancient Scandinavians', in: Scandinavica 7, II.

— (1970), Problemy genezisa feodalizma v Zapadnoi I evrope [Problems of the genesis of feudalism in Western Europe]. Moscow: Nauka.

Hasund, S. (1924), Bønder og stat under naturalsystemet. Kristiania: Nikoa Olsen.

Helle, K. (1964), 'Norge blir en stat, 1130–1319', in: Handbok i Norges Historie, Vol. I, part 3. Kristiansand: Scandinavian University Books.

Hertzberg, E. (1893), 'Lén og veizla i Norges sagatid', in: Germanistische Abhandlungen zum LXX. Geburtstag Konrad von Maurers. Göttingen: Akademische Druck und Verlagsanstalt.

— (1907), 'Harald Haarfagres skattepaalaeg og saakaldte Odelstilegnelse', in: Historisk tidsskrift 4.

Hocart, A. H. (1927), Kingship. London: Oxford University Press.

Holmsen, A. (1971) Norges historie fra de eldste tider til 1660. Oslo–Bergen–Tromsø: Universitets Font.

Imsen, S. (1974), 'Tronfølge', in: Kulturhistorisk leksikon for nordisk middelalder 18.

Johnsen, A. O. (1948), Fra aettesamfunn til statssamfunn. Tromskø: Fylkes.

Johnsen, O. A. (1938), 'Die wirtschaftlichen Grundlagen des ältesten norwegischen Staates', in: Wirtschaft und Kultur, Festschrift zum 70. Geburtstag von A. Dopsch. Leipzig: Brockhaus.

Koht, H. (1921), Innhogg og utsyn i norsk historie. Kristiania: Det Mallingske.

— (1955), Harald Hårfagre og rikssamlinga. Oslo: Lindkvist.

Lie, M. H. (1907), Lensprincipet i Norden. Kristiania: Det Mallingske.

Löfqvist, K. E. (1935), Om riddarväsen och frälse i nordisk medeltid. Lund: Universitets Vorlaget.

Maurer, K. (1890), 'Die norwegischen höldar', in: Sitzungsberichte der königlich. bayer. Akademie der Wissenschaften, Philosophisch-philologische Cl. (1889), Bd. 2, H. 2.

Mitteis, H. (1959), Der Staat des hohen Mittelalters. Weimar: Böhlaus.

Neussychin, A. I. (1961), Vozniknovenie zavisimogo krest'ianstva kak klassa rannefeodal'nogo obshchestva v Zapadnoi Yevrope VII–VIII vv. [Origin of the dependent peasantry as a class in the early feudal society in Western Europe in the 6th–8th centuries]. Moscow: Nauka.

Nielsen, Y. (1907), 'Studier over Harald Haarfagres Historie', in: Historisk tiddsskrift 4.

Ordres et classes (1973), Colloque d'histoire sociale Saint-Cloud 24–25 mai 1967, Paris-La Haye: Mouton.

Piekarczyk, St. (1968), Barbaryñcy i chrzešcijañstwo. Warszawa: Wroclawska Druk. Naukowa.

Sars, J. E. (1872), 'Om Harald Haarfagres Samling af de norske Fylker og hand Tilegnelse af Odelen', in: Historisk tidsskrift 1, 2.

Schreiner, J. (1928), 'Trøndelag og rikssamlingen', in: Vid.-Akad. Avh. 2, no. 3.

— (1929), Olav den hellige og Norges samling. Oslo: Centraltrat.

Schwerin, C. (1943), 'Der Bauer in den Skandinavischen Staaten des Mittelalters', in: Adel und Bauern im deutschen Staat des Mittelalters. Leipzig: Universitäts Verlag.

Seip, J. A. (1940–42), 'Problemer og metode i norsk middelalderforskning', in: *Historisk tidsskrift* 32.
Steinnes, A. (1953), 'Utskyld', in: *Historisk tidsskrift* 36.
— (1955), *Husebyar*, Oslo: Lindkvist.
Taranger, A. (1904), *Udsigt over den norske rets historie* 2, 1, Kristiania: Gyldendal.
— (1907), 'Harald Haarfagres tilegnelse af odelen', in: *Historisk tidsskrift* 4, 4.
Wührer, K. (1959), 'Die schwedischen Landschaftsrechte und Tacitus' Germania', in: *Zeitschrift der Savigny-Stiftung für Rechtsgeschichte, Germanistische Abteilung* 76.

20 The Early State Among the Scythians[1]

ANATOLII M. KHAZANOV

The early state is the product of an early class society, i.e., a society which has just left the primitive level and is still connected to the latter by many surviving threads of continuity. This type of society is represented by various concrete cases, whose typology is a task for the future, however. Nevertheless, they display a series of common characteristics, among them the existence of a large group of free (at least formally so) producers, a diversity of forms of exploitation, a relatively undeveloped character, incomplete stabilization of the composition of the ruling class and the mutual relations between its different strata, etc. Accordingly, early states are elementary political forms with various, though insufficiently developed, systems of administration and coercion.

The actual formation of early states also occurred in different ways. Among these, conquest was fairly widespread as a temporary means of solving internal conflicts; thus carrying the solution beyond the framework of the society proper. In the course of subsequent development, interethnic conflicts, or relations of dependence and exploitation emerging as a result of conquest, may have become transformed into class ones. However, at the early state stage these processes usually had not yet reached completion.

1. HISTORY

Early states of the conquest type are particularly characteristic of nomadic peoples. They developed among them in antiquity, during the Middle Ages, and even in modern times. Perhaps the first such state

[1] Translated from Russian by Peter Skalník

was evolved by the Scythians. Therefore it offers the purest model of the kind of state we are interested in, so that its study is of considerable importance in spite of the limited number and poor quality of the sources on the social and political history of Scythia.

Ancient authors, as well as a number of contemporary scholars following them, have used the name 'Scythians' in two different senses:

(1) as a name for all or almost all of the nomadic peoples inhabiting the Eurasian steppes, semi-deserts and deserts in antiquity;

(2) to designate one particular ethnic group appearing on the historical scene in the eight century B.C. and living in the south of eastern Europe for many centuries. To the latter the present essay is devoted.

Greek authors have preserved vestiges of several Scythian epic traditions dealing with the origin of Scythian society and the state. In one of these traditions the emphasis is placed on a conquest leading to the formation of the Scythian kingdom. In another one, conversely, the emphasis falls on the legitimacy of its character, on divine sanction and voluntary agreement as the main factors responsible for the formation of the kingdom. Possibly, the difference between the various traditions may be explained not so much by a difference in socio-ethnic roots as by a chronological difference reflecting different stages of the development of Scythian society and its character as a state. All of the traditions are at any rate connected with the 'Royal Scythians', that is the ruling tribe in the Scythian kingdom, and the latter's royal dynasty.

According to one of these traditions, recorded by Herodotus (IV, 5–7), which also offers the best opportunities of analysis (Christensen 1918: 130–139; Dumézil 1962; Grantovskií 1960; Khazanov 1975b), the first man in Scythia, Targitaus, was of divine origin. He had three sons, Leipoxais, Arpoxais and Coloxais, the youngest. In their time the sacred golden treasure descended from heaven to the land of the Scythians. The two elder brothers were unable to seize it, and after they grasped the meaning of this miracle, they offered the whole of the kingdom to the youngest brother. The three brothers became the ancestors of specific ethnic or social divisions with unequal rights, while the descent of the ruling tribe and dynasty in Scythia was traced from the youngest brother. Genealogies apparently played an important part in the ideology of the Scythian state, for they sanctified the existing social and ethnic inequality.

An analysis of the above tradition (Khazanov 1975b) led me to the conclusion that it is heterogeneous and includes certain epico-mythological motifs of the various local tribes conquered by the Scythians. Evidently, the final redaction of the legend came about after the formation of the Scythian kingdom, in circles of the 'Royal Scythians'. Its main aim was to underline the identity of origin of all Scythians, to confirm the divine sanction of the existing social relations in Scythia, more especially the subordination of all of its tribes to the 'Royal Scythians' and their ruling dynasty, and to strengthen the idea that the Scythian kingdom came about as a result of the voluntary recognition of the supremacy of the descendants of Coloxais.

Such, in brief, is the social history of Scythia according to the official version. There are signs in the sources which may point to the existence of local traditions side by side with the official one, but it is difficult to say anything definite about them. The epic *Coloxais*, known also from other sources, to some extent connects the epic account to actual Scythian history, which may be briefly summarized as follows (cf. Minns 1913; Rostovtsev 1922; Grakov 1971; Khazanov 1975a): The Scythians appeared in the area north of the Black Sea in the eight century B.C., having first expelled their predecessors — the Cymerians — from here and incorporated half of them into the Scythian polity. Not later than the 70s of the seventh century B.C. the most energetic of the Scythians spread to the Near East and began to play an important role in the political life of this region. It is here that the First Scythian Kingdom emerged, with its centre in the territory of contemporary Azerbaijan and adjacent areas. It was a primitive state of the conquest type, in which externally interethnic dependence predominated. The latter was a result of: (1) the comparatively strict subordination of the local agricultural population of the conquered territories, especially in eastern Transcaucasia; (2) military exploitation through raiding and looting (at times as far a field as Syria and Egypt); (3) the levying of tribute and contributions in the form of gifts (Egypt); (4) the levying of regular tribute from other states (Midia). Eventually, their defeat by Midia compelled the Scythians to return to the area north of the Black Sea. There they suppressed an uprising of the previously subdued population and conquered vast new territories in the forest–steppe belt of eastern Europe, inhabited by agriculturists. As a result, some time in the first half of the sixth century B.C. a new Scythian state emerged — the Second Scythian Kingdom — which existed for more than three centuries. It was composed of both the Scythian tribes proper and the assimilated Cymmerian tribes as well as non-Scythian peoples belonging to other ethnic groups. As a result, tribal conflicts in Scythia were not always separable from ethnic ones.

The Second Scythian Kingdom successfully survived the war with Darius (ca. 514–512 B.C.) and from the fourth century B.C. pursued a policy of systematic pressure on the Greek *poleis* of the northern Black Sea area, while at the same time penetrating into the Balkans. However, around the second half of the third century B.C. the Second Scythian Kingdom fell under pressure from the Celts and the Thracians in the west and the Sarmatians in the east.

We know very little about the internal conflicts in Scythia of the sixth–third centuries B.C. It is known, however, that among the Scythian aristocracy there were conflicts with regard to the relations with the Greeks and Greek culture. In the sixth century B.C. prince Anarcharsis, brother of the Scythian king, was assassinated on the pretext that he had adopted Greek customs. In the fifth century B.C., following an uprising of the opponents of friendly relations with the Greeks forming a kind of 'Old Scythian Guard', king Scylas paid with his head for his Hellenophilism. But in the fourth century B.C. the ascendancy was on the side of the 'Young Scythians' interested in maintaining economic relations with the Greeks and allured by the charms of Hellenic culture. There are no more detailed facts on any 'parties' or 'factions' existing in Scythian society. There is also no mention of the existence of fraternities or secret societies.

In the last few centuries B.C. the Scythian state revived in the limited region of the Crimea and the Lower Dnepr area. I have designated it the Third Scythian Kingdom. In ethnic composition it was considerably less complex than its predecessor. The Scythians here formed an overwhelming majority, at least until the first centuries A.D., when the process of miscegenation accelerated in the Crimea. The Third Scythian Kingdom continued the struggle over agricultural areas, ports and markets with the Greeks, but, all in all, without much success. Within its framework mass sedentarization of the nomads occurred. In the third century A.D. it ceased to exist altogether as a result of the beginning of the Great Migration. Yet another small Scythian state emerged in Dobrudja in the final centuries B.C., but it turned out to be short-lived.

Evidently all three of the Scythian states can be related to the type of the early states. Some differences can be discerned between them, nonetheless. The First Scythian Kingdom resembles the inchoate sort of early state of the conquest type, based on the most primitive form of interethnic dependence. The Second Scythian Kingdom seems to have been more developed. But it is also a typical early state, whose development was largely conditioned by conquest and its consequences. The Third Scythian Kingdom probably also belonged to the early state type, though it already represented the final phase of the early state. A series of facts point to the possibility of its having reached the stage of transition to a higher level of state organization. At any rate, conquest and interethnic dependence did not play an essential role in either its origin or its later development.

Thus the most typical kind of early state among the Scythians was formed by the Second Scythian Kingdom. What is of the utmost importance is that the greater part of the data at our disposal relate to this second kingdom. Hence the present essay mainly concerns the Second Scythian Kingdom.

2. ECONOMIC STRUCTURE

Scythia of the sixth–third centuries B.C. was a state with a mixed nomadic and agricultural population. The politically dominant nomads roamed the steppes to the north of the Black Sea along comparatively fixed routes. Their economy, as is usual among nomads, was predominantly of the natural type. A large part of the surplus produce was evidently absorbed in the trade with the Greeks (Strabo XI, ii, 3; Polybius IV, 38, 5). The agriculturists inhabited the forest–steppe zone also north of the Black Sea, as well as the steppes immediately bordering on the Greek *poleis*. Agriculture utilized the plow (Shramko 1961), eastern Europe having entered the Iron Age already at the beginning of the first millennium B.C. Agriculture on the chernozem soils yielded a comparatively large surplus. According to Herodotus (IV, 17), 'the Scythian cultivators' — forming one of the ethnic subdivisions in Scythia — grew cereals especially for sale.

The same Herodotus (II, 167) mentions the Scythians as one of those peoples who had no regard for the art of the craftsman. In this particular case the Father of History is referring to the nomads. Until the end of the fifth century B.C. most of the weapons and other metal objects of common occurrence in the steppes of Scythia were fashioned by craftsmen of the forest-steppe settlements, where the main iron-mining and -processing were located (Shramko 1971: 95). However, a number of indirect references allow us to assume that a complete separation of crafts from agriculture had by this time, not yet taken place with the possible exception of metallurgy.

At the end of the fifth century B.C. urbanization began in Steppe-Scythia. Until then the royal headquarters had always moved from place to place. The kings wandered freely not only about their domains but also over the whole of the territory of the kingdom in times of both war and peace. The most well-known urban site is that of Kamenskoie on the Dnepr, which was probably the capital of king Ateas, who reigned in the fourth century B.C. It was the main administrative, commercial and industrial center of the whole of Scythia, the metallurgists here being full-time or virtually full-time specialists. Probably certain taxes in kind, in the form of products of their respective crafts, which were presented to the state or its ruling stratum, were imposed on these craftsmen. Recently, excavations were carried out on an acropolis on a site where members of the aristocaracy or certain official personages lived (Grakov 1954).

I would like to remark for the sake of comparison that in the Third Scythian Kingdom agriculture and urbanization predominated over nomadic husbandry, which continued to exist only as a secondary sector at the time. The crafts here attained a higher level of development. The kings, the aristocracy and persons forming part of the administrative apparatus all lived in urban centers (Shul'tz 1971). The economic conditions in Scythia of the sixth-third centuries B.C. favored the development of trade, though mainly foreign trade. Inside the state itself, part of the produce of the agriculturists was requisitioned in favor of the politically dominant nomads. From that same time (as early as the fifth century B.C.) date the reports of the long caravan trek of Scythian traders to the Volga and Ural areas (Herodotus IV, 24). However, most important of all was the trade with the Greeks, which was functioning well, served as it was by permanent trade routes, partly along rivers, and by special trade centers.

The matter moves into clearer perspective when one bears in mind that owing to the state of the Mediterranean market following the Peloponnesian war, Athens became dependent for its grain on supplies from the area north of the Black Sea. As a result the Pontic Greeks increased their purchases from the local population. The control of trade with the Greeks remained in the hands of the nomads, however (Artamonov 1974: 113–114). As regards Greek exports to Scythia, luxury articles and wine were the chief commodities here. The Scythian aristocracy and the king derived the greatest benefit from this trade. The policy pursued by the Scythian kings for over a century testifies that the state was greatly interested in foreign trade. From the fourth century B.C. onward this was aimed at securing control of important ports, as well as the elimination of unnecessary intermediaries, notably the Greek *poleis* in the area north of the Black Sea. The kings of the Third Scythian Kingdom even introduced a number of measures against piracy on the Black Sea.

In accordance with the economic conditions prevailing in Scythia and the characteristic division of labor between nomads and agriculturists, there was practically no money in circulation at any period of its history. It is true that some kings of the Second and Third Kingdoms had coins minted at Greek mints, but this was due solely to prestige considerations or the requirements of foreign trade. In the interior of the country only primitive equivalents of money in the form of bronze arrow-heads were more or less widely used.

There are no indications, or almost none, that an indigenous literature existed in Scythia. The extremely limited demands in this respect were met by the use of the Greek language and script.

Such was the economic basis of the Scythian state to the description of the social structure of which I am now coming. The social and political history of the Scythians is described in greater detail in my recently published monograph (Khazanov 1975a). In the present essay I shall be repeating some of the conclusions arrived at in this book, though I am prevented by lack of space from repeating the relevant detailed argumentation.

3. SOCIO-POLITICAL STRUCTURE

The forms of social organization existing in Scythia were characterized by the considerable complexity that is so typical of all early states. The basic unit of social organization was the family, which was also the basic economic unit. Among the nomadic Scythians the nuclear, or partly extended family, which possessed cattle and moveable property, was most prevalent. The extended family was probably most common among the agricultural peoples of Scythia.

Groups of kin related by consanguinity represented the next unit up among the nomadic Scythians. Individual families belonging to these groups usually travelled together, or at any rate not far away from one another, giving each other mutual help and support. Among the agriculturalists analogous kinship groups were found as the archaeological material shows.

Among the nomads these kinship groups formed part of subdivisions of a higher order, which in their turn formed part of other structures, formally also constructed on the basis of consanguinity, and so on. As a result, a multi-level structure came about, which is usually referred to by ethnologists as the 'genealogical clan' (Abramzon 1951; Krader 1963: 10), or '*obok*' (Bacon 1958). One of the levels of this structure as a rule corresponded to the nomadic community, which has the usufruct of a specified tract of grazing land. The existence of the territorial community among both the nomadic and the sedentary Scythians is testified only by indirect data; we are unable to trace its structure in detail.

Higher units of the Scythian social organization were formed along the lines of actually existing ethnic divisions. The next level up was represented by the tribe, a unit of the politico-administrative state structure called *nome* (νομόσ) by Herodotus (IV, 62, 66). Each tribe had its own specific territory in which to live its nomadic or sedentary life. It apparently had an administrative apparatus of its own, headed by the tribal chief, who was subordinate to the central authority. The tribal military unit was a subdivision of the all-Scythian military organization. This was assembled by the tribal chief, who was at the same time military chief, not less than once a year.

Very little is known about the fiscal and tributary obligations of the tribe towards the central authority. However, the term '*nome*' was always used by Herodotus in his '*History*' to denote not only the politico-administrative but also the tributary unit. Evidently most of the financial burdens fell on the agricultural tribes, which were subordinate to the nomads. Finally, it should be observed that the tribes themselves recognized their own unity. Each possessed its own tribal shrine. At least among the nomads, probably also the idea of the genealogical kinship tie uniting all tribal members was preserved.

The next level of the Scythian social organization was formed by the *regions* or provinces (αρχαί), about which also very little is known. Most probably they originally constituted some form of tribal grouping or union, integrated into the Scythian kingdom, but also as individual tribes, preserving to some extent their autonomous organizational structure. Probably the agricultural provinces of the Scythian kingdom were incorporated into the kingdom in some kind of relation of vassalage, though preserving considerable internal autonomy, around the middle of the fifth century B.C. The social organization did not essentially change, except that their higher levels were incorporated into the politico-administrative organization of the state.

The next level of this organization was composed of three 'kingdoms' (βασιλειαι), into which triune Scythia as a whole was divided. One of these kingdoms was directly headed by the sovereign king of the whole of Scythia; it more or less provided his personal domain. Obviously, it was here that the 'Royal Scythians' were found.

The Scythian epic dates the said division of Scythia into three 'kingdoms' back to the time of the first Scythian king — the legendary Colaxais. 'As the extent of Scythia is very great, Colaxais gave each of his three sons a separate kingdom, one of which was of ampler size than the other two, (Herodotus IV, 7). On this point the legend touches directly on reality.

The three 'kingdoms' formed not only the politico-administrative but also the military organizational units of the Scythian state. They acted as such in, for example, the war against Darius. Each of the 'kingdoms' was headed by members of the Scythian royal clan. It is possible that groups of the dominant tribe moved about and ruled not only in the main 'kingdom' but also in the others.

Thus the basis of the Scythian social organization was provided by a multi-level clan–tribe structure, which only in the lower levels rested on actual kinship ties. The higher levels of the structure under study, beginning with the tribal one, constituted in fact varied forms of political organization. At this level the formal kinship ties (which were, in fact, only fictive ones) were supplemented by territorial ones. The development of the latter was to a large extent determined by the administrative needs stemming from the extension of the central rule over a large area embracing agricultural regions as well.

The same clan–tribe structure at the same time provided the basis of the military organization. Every free Scythian (particularly if he were a nomad) was a warrior and his clan or tribal chief a military leader. The sovereign king of Scythia was also its paramount military chief. There was no standing army, but the king, and possibly also wider groups of the aristocracy had their own bodyguards.

Not less complex and varied were the social stratification and relations of dependence and exploitation existing in the Scythian state. The traditional three strata model which, according to Dumézil, the ancestors of the Scythians shared with other Iranian and, in a wider perspective, Indo-European peoples at the time of their original unity (Dumézil 1958) was no longer in conformity with reality.

The lowest rung of the Scythian social ladder was occupied by the slaves. They played an insignificant role among both the nomads and agriculturalists, and were employed chiefly in domestic work. The practice of purchasing slaves did not develop in Scythia. They were originally prisoners-of-war, the majority of whom were sold to the Greeks, however. Often slaves were offered as sacrifices to the gods, and were put to death at the funeral of their masters (Khazanov 1972). The view that slavery in Scythia must have been a prevalent form of social relation (Smirnov 1966; Terenoshkin 1966; Grakov 1971) is based on the confusion of slavery with vassalage.

There were various categories of dependent populations subject to exploitation, who were somewhat higher upon the scale than slaves. They included the stratum of pauperized nomads who had been deprived of the possibility of living an independent economic life and, as a result, were compelled either to serve their richer kinsfolk by working in their households, or grazing their cattle in the position of servants, clients and tenants, or to settle on the land.

Well-known also are the *therapontes* ($\vartheta\epsilon\rho\alpha\pi o\upsilon\tau\epsilon\sigma$), or servants of the Scythian king (Herodotus IV, 71–72) who usually accompanied him to the other world. The king's guard was probably also composed of *therapontes*. It is not impossible that such guards were at the disposal not only of the king, but also of broader groups of the aristocracy (Lucianus' *Toxaris:* 48, 54).

The main category of dependants however, was formed by the tributaries, who likewise did not constitute a homogeneous stratum (Khazanov f.c.). Those in positions of tributary dependence were mostly members of Scythian agricultural tribes subdued by the nomads. This particular tie varied from a rather loose to a very burdensome one depending on the circumstances. Besides paying tribute the agriculturalists had to fulfil a number of other duties. Various kinds of tribute were levied on them to feed the king or representatives of the nomadic aristocracy whenever these visited their territory, while they also had to contribute to royal funerals and make auxiliary military contingents available. The construction of labor-consuming fortifications around the main settlements in forest–steppe Scythia and later also in Steppe-Scythia required incidental though large-scale concentrations of human resources. However, it is unknown who organized such schemes and how, and who took part in them.

Tributary relations formed the main type of relation of dependence in Scythia in the sixth–third centuries B.C. It has sometimes been identified, though without reason, with feudal dependence. Hence the conception of Scythia as a feudal state (Rostovtsev 1922: 8 ff.; Ebert 1921: 102, 341). In the Third Scythian Kingdom, where the possibilities of interethnic dependence were lacking, the tributary type of relations had to give way to other forms of exploitation.

There was yet another type of relation of dependence, namely that which periodically involved some of the Greek *poleis* of the area north of the Black Sea. Sometimes these were obliged to pay a kind of redemption to the Scythians in the form of tribute or gifts which were in fact tantamount to tribute, though less regular and not quite as painful to Greek pride. However, in all other respects the *poleis* were fully independent.

Besides the dependent population estates there were in Scythia several estates possessing full rights. According to Lucianus (*Scythia* 1) these were the ordinary non-noble Scythians, the aristocracy and the royal lineage or clan. A special estate was apparently formed by the priesthood.

Lucianus designated the common, free Scythians as 'those with eight legs' (οκτάποδεσ), i.e., owners of a couple of oxen plus one carriage and most probably a tent. It is interesting to note that the nickname 'octapodes', hardly Greek in origin, has a somewhat derogatory connotation as it points to a limited number of belongings. There are grounds for assuming that a certain differentiation also existed, however, within the estate of the 'octapodes'. Apparently in Scythia status on the basis of wealth was not always identical with social status.

It was the right and duty of ordinary Scythian nomads belonging to the estate of the 'octapodes' to participate in military activities. They formed the bulk of the army, so that the words of Herodotus are most applicable to them. For Herodotus says (IV, 46):

> Having neither cities nor forts, and carrying their dwellings with them wherever they go, accustomed, moreover, one and all to shoot from horseback and living not by husbandry but on their cattle, their waggons the only houses that they possess, how can they fail to be invincible and even unassailable?

At the same time, in all of the external and internal political events known to us from Scythian history, the role of the Scythian commoners was a purely passive one. There is not even one example to show that they took part in the administration of the state or the solution of important problems.

The available sources do not give us any clues as to the imposition of any taxes on the ordinary nomads, or other duties fulfilled by them. At any rate, it is certain that such taxes and duties were far from severe. As long as external forms of exploitation prevailed — which circumstance changed only in the Third Scythian Kingdom — there were certain limitations on the exploitation of certain categories within the society itself, because the latter had to be consolidated vis-à-vis the outer world. Most of the king's revenues and those of the state were drawn from tribute, contributions and gifts from conquered and dependent tribes. The exploitation of slaves and dependants and more especially of free tribesmen, apparently assumed lesser proportions.

Probably there were some differences between the position of the common members of the tribe of the 'Royal Scythians', who considered all other Scythians their slaves (Herodotus IV, 20), and the ordinary free members of the other nomadic and the agricultural Scythian tribes. But there are no reflections of this in the sources.

The priests, the secular aristocracy and the royal clan constituted privileged estates in Scythia. The data on the Scythian priesthood are very fragmentary. However, its existence as such does not raise any doubts (Grantovskii 1960; Khazanov 1973). It is known, for example, that a special corporation of professional and hereditary diviners, called *enarei*, who were drawn from the aristocratic strata and possibly even from circles near to the royal dynasty, existed in Scythia. They enjoyed considerable influence and prestige. Judging from isolated allusions, the interrelationship between the priesthood and the state power in the person of the king was quite complicated. Besides sanctioning of the royal power, the priesthood took part in the propagation of concrete measures for its consolidation and initiated reprisals against anyone no longer loyal to the king. At the same time conflicts between the king and the priests are alluded to in the records. These were evidently connected with the struggle for power and influence in the society. However, the advantage was always on the side of the royal power.

The secular aristocracy was another privileged estate in Scythia. It regularly appealed to its noble origin and its wealth and stood in contrast to the free commoners. Its predominantly military character is clearly apparent from both written and archaeological sources. Probably there exists such special terms as '$\pi\iota\lambda o\phi\acute{o}\rho\iota\kappa o\iota$', '$\sigma\kappa\eta\pi\tau\acute{o}\upsilon\chi o\iota$', and possibly also others, for designating the aristocracy as a whole or its component parts.

The Scythian aristocracy formed no homogeneous stratum either. Besides the clan–tribal one, a sort of 'blood aristocracy', an administrative aristocracy composed of members of the servant nobility, existed. The social status of the latter was dependent on proximity to the king, position in the administrative apparatus, etc. But even the leaders of the clan–tribal aristocracy were mutually differentiated, depending on their degree of nobility as well as on the size of the subdivisions of the Scythian society which came under their administration.

The lowest level of the aristocracy was probably formed by the elders and heads of lineages or clans, or other subdivisions taxonomically similar to these. In wartime they led the lineage and clan military unit, in times of peace they exercised certain juridical functions. However, their burial places are among those of the common people and do not in any way distinguish themselves from the latter, being at best slightly more elaborate.

Above the elders were placed the tribal chiefs and chiefs of the ethno-tribal groupings, i.e., the '*nomes*' and '*regions*'. Archaeological finds testify to striking differences in lifestyle between this particular group of chiefs and the rest of the population.

The written sources allows us to determine the rights and duties of the tribal chiefs quite fully. They administered their tribes and probably possessed certain juridical powers. They had control of the cult practices and organization, and most probably also supervised the payment of tributes and other compulsory services in favor of the central power. Most prominent is the tribal chiefs' role as military leaders, or heads of tribal armies. They were, moreover, under an obligation of reciprocity vis-à-vis their tribesmen. Herodotus (IV, 64) observed that the *nomarch* regularly organized a feast for his warriors once a year.

The administrative nobility and other officials were apparently less respected and less influential than the clan–tribal aristocracy. They were concentrated around the king and his rather primitive administrative apparatus, of which they were the direct products. There was evidently not yet a sharp distinction between the royal guard and the administrative apparatus at the time. The guardsmen might act as king's messengers and execute his commands of an administrative nature. Sometimes Greeks, who were more educated and experienced than the Scythians, were attracted into the administration as agents for special purposes. The administrative nobility was sometimes integrated into the retinue which followed the king as he travelled over the state territory. For example, in the fifth century B.C. king Scylas several times came in the vicinity of Olvia with such a suite, which included unidentified 'chiefs' or 'leaders'.

Finally, we should mention the aristocracy of the dependent agricultural tribes in Scythia, the existence of which is attested by archaeological data. Its existence alone was wholly compatible with the widespread existence of tributary relations in Scythia, which were characterized by the incomplete integration of the socio-economic structure of the conquered into that of the conquerors.

At the apex of the social pyramid of Scythia was located the royal clan or lineage. It originated from the tribe of the 'Royal Scythians', but pretended to the rule of the whole of Scythia. Most probably the same dynasty reigned over Scythia throughout the greater part of its history. The ideological background of this was provided by the notion of the divine origin of the royal power and the royal clan itself. The Scythian king was not a deity in the Frazerian sense of the term, but rather a divine king, a direct descendant of the gods who received his power from their hands (Rostovtzev 1913). A false oath to the deities of the royal hearth (i.e., lineage) was punishable by death. Herodotus (IV, 71, 72) has left us a detailed description of the funerals of Scythian kings, in which he emphasizes their spectacular character, the offering of human sacrifices, and the practice of placing precious articles into the tombs of deceased royalty. His account is supported by archaeological data. The entire population of Scythia, both free and dependent, had to participate in the king's funeral and express their grief at his death. Moreover, the construction of a grand *kurgan* barrow over his grave required the large-scale concentration of human resources. At the same time, the king was comparatively accessible to his subjects.

Judging from the available sources, in Scythia the throne as a rule passed from father to son, a practice observed since time immemorial. The Scythian kings were polygynous. The rules governing the selection of the successor to the throne (if any rules existed at all) are unknown, however. It may be supposed, on the basis of certain indirect indications, that the selection of the successor took place during the lifetime of his father.

However, we know of several conflicts in connection with the succession to the throne between the various children of the deceased king. This kind of struggle might to some extent also reflect certain conflict situations existing in Scythian society as a whole.

The sovereign king of Scythia was its supreme ruler and military chief, while he probably also participated in the cult practices and had juridical authority. However, very little is known about the concrete mechanisms of decision-making and the implementation of decisions. It is interesting to note that in the sixth century B.C. there existed in Scythia a certain council composed of the kings of each of the three 'kingdoms', and possibly also other persons. This council functioned at the time of the war with Darius, though it possibly also met in less extreme circumstances.

At the same time a number of data allow us to suppose that there prevailed in Scythia the *ulus* principle of the distribution of power (to use the Turkish–Mongolian term) so characteristic of the nomads of the Eurasian steppes throughout their history. This principle involved that every member of the ruling lineage had the right to rule over a specific group of nomads together with a particular tract of grazing land, as well as the right to some conquered agricultural territory. So my view of the Scythians from the sixth to third centuries B.C. is, of course, limited to what the available sources tell us. It was a state based on interethnic and intertribal dependence, which in its turn was based on the dominance of the nomads over the agriculturists. A state in which various though still mostly primitive forms of exploitation were widespread. A state with a complex system of social stratification, to which material position did not always entirely correspond. A state, finally, in which blood ties were still very strong. It was literally, in every respect, a typical early state, Scythian society itself being a characteristic example of an early type of class society. I assume a similar development for the other state forms evolved by the nomads of the Eurasian steppes in the course of their centuries-long history (Khazanov 1975a: 251 ff.). Scythia in this connection is only a typical example.

REFERENCES

Abramzon, S. M. (1951), 'Formy rodoplemennoi organizatsii u kochevnikov Sredney Azii'. [Forms of clan–tribal organization among the nomads of central Asia], in: *Trudy Instituta etnografii AN SSSR*. Novaia seria. Tom XIX. Moscow.

Artamonov, M. I. (1974), *Kimmeriytsy i skify* [Cymmerians and Scythians]. Leningrad: Nauka.

Bacon, E. E. (1958), *Obok. A study of social structure in Eurasia*. New York: Viking Fund Publication 25.

Christensen, A. (1918), 'Le premier homme et le premier roi dans l'histoire légendaire des Iraniens', in: *Archives d'Etudes Orientales* 14. Leipzig: Harrasowitz.

Dumézil, G. (1958), *L'idéologie tripartite des Indo-Européens*. Bruxelles: Musée Royale.

— (1962), 'La société scythique avait-elle des classes fonctionelles?' in: *Indo-Iranian Journal*, vol 5, no. 3.

Ebert, M. (1921), *Südrussland im Altertum*. Bonn-Leipzig: Themig.

Grakov, B. N. (1954), *Kamenskoie gorodishche na Dnepre* [Site of the town of Kamenskoie on the Dnepr]. Moscow: Nauka.

— (1968), 'Legenda o skifskom tsare Ariante' [A legend about the Scythian king Ariantes] (Herodotus IV, chapter 81), in: *Istoriya, archeologiya i etnografiya Sredney Azii*. Moscow: Nauka.

— (1971), *Skify* [The Scythians]. Moscow.

Grantovskii, E. A. (1960), *Indo-iranskie kasty u skifov* [Indo-Iranian castes among the Scythians]. Moscow: Nauka.

Khazanov, Anatolii M. (1972), 'O kharaktere rablovladeniia u skifov' [On the character of slave-holding among the Scythians], in: *Vestnik drevnie istorii*, no. I.

— (1973), 'Skifskoe zhrechestvo' [Scythian priesthood], in: *Sovetskaia etnografiia*, no. 6.

— (1975a), *Sotsial'naia istoriia skifov. Osnovnye problemy razvitiya drevnikh kochevnikov evraziiskikh stepei* [Social history of the Scythians. Main problems of the development of ancient nomads of the Eurasian steppes]. Moscow: Nauka.

— (1975b), 'Legenda o proiskhozhdenii skifov' [A legend about the origin of the Scythians] (Herodotus IV, 5–7), in: *Skifskiy mir.* Kiev: Academy of Sciences.

— (f.c.), 'Les formes de dépendance des agriculteurs par rapport aux nomades antiques des steppes eurasiennes', in: *Oeuvres de l'Université de Bésancon.*

Krader, Lawrence (1963), *Social organization of the Mongol-Turkish pastoral nomads.* The Hague: Mouton.

Minns, E. H. (1913), *Scythians and Greeks.* Cambridge: Cambridge University Press.

Rostovtsev, M. I. (1913), 'Predstavlenie o monarkhicheskoy vlasti v Skifii i na Bospore' [Knowledge about the monarchic power in Scythia and Bosphorus], in: *Izvestiia arkheologicheskoi komissii* 49. Saint-Petersburg.

— (1922), *Iranians and Greeks in south Russia.* Oxford: Oxford University Press.

Schul'tz, P. N. (1971), 'Pozdneskifskaia kul'tura i ee varianty na Dnepre i v Krymu' [Late Scythian culture and its variants along the Dnepr and in the Crimea], in: *Problemy skifskoi arkheologii.* Moscow.

Shramko, B. A. (1961), 'K voprosu o tekhnike zemledeliya u plemen skifskogo vremeni v Vostochnoy Evrope' [On the question of agricultural technique among the tribes of the Scythian period in eastern Europe], in: *Sovetskaia arkheologiia* 1.

— (1971), 'K voprosu o znachenii kul'turno khoziaistvennykh osobennostei stepnoi i lesostepnoi Skifii' [On the question of the significance of cultural–economic specificities of the Steppe and Forest-steppe Scythia], in: *Problemy skifskoy arkheologii.* Moscow.

Smirnov, A. P. (1966), *Skify* [The Scythians]. Moscow: Nauka.

Terenoshkin, A. I. (1966), 'Ob oshchestvennom stroe skifov' [On the social system of the Scythians], in: *Sovetskaia arkheologiia* 2.

21 Early State in Tahiti[1]

HENRI J. M. CLAESSEN

1. EVOLUTION

On June 19th of the year 1767 Captain Samuel Wallis of the Royal Navy, sailing in the Pacific Ocean on His Majesty's Ship, Dolphin, discovered the island of Tahiti. After some fierce fighting with the inhabitants, the English succeeded in establishing friendly relations. Once landed, they soon found out that they had come upon a people possessing a relatively highly developed culture. Shortly after their departure Tahiti was discovered for a second time, now by the French explorer Louis de Bougainville. With the publication of the journals of these captains the extensive literature on Tahiti began.

Who were these Tahitians? From where did they come, and how did they come by the fascinating culture that attracted the attention of so many voyagers and anthropologists? In a recent article the prehistorian Bellwood (1975) summarizes the present state of knowledge of Oceanic prehistory. From this survey it appears that already several millennia ago Tonga and Samoa, islands in the western part of the Pacific Ocean, were inhabited. From one of these islands, probably Samoa, once a group of people, for reasons unknown, sailed out into the vast Pacific, and somehow reached the Marquesas Islands — 2,000 miles (3,200 kilometres) away to the east. This voyage must have taken place about A.D. 300. From the Marquesas Islands a group of settlers shortly afterwards reached the Society Islands, of which Tahiti is the main island.

The western (Tonga, Samoa) as well as the eastern Polynesians (Marquesas Islands, Tahiti) developed their respective cultures in relative isolation; winds and currents making contact between the two centers virtually impossible (Claessen 1964; Lewis 1972). Before the end of the first millennium A.D. settlers from Tahiti, in their turn, reached the Hawaii Islands (cf. Seaton in the present volume) as well as New Zealand. Though voyages between Tahiti and these islands were at least possible, they were never frequent (cf. Finney 1967).

Now, what was the culture of the first settlers of the Society Islands? Nothing is known with certainty, but some guesses may be hazarded. As they came by canoe, it is not probable that they brought a great quantity of objects with them. Some utensils and weapons, as well as some food and food plants, and some animals such as pigs and dogs, will have been among their belongings (Suggs 1960: 137). More important in this context, however, are the ideas they imported. Especially the ideas on social organization and ideology, for from these germs developed the entire fabric of intergroup relations and rules as described by the eighteenth century visitors. It is reasonable to suppose that in a general way these ideas resembled those found everywhere in Polynesia, even in the smallest and remotest islands.[2] The general pattern of the social organization can be described by means of the following model, called *ramage* by anthropologists (for a detailed description cf. Sahlins 1958: 140–151). A ramage is a non-exogamous, internally stratified, unilineal — in Polynesia patrilineal — descent group. Distance from the senior line of descent from the common ancestor is the criterion of stratification. This common ancestor is usually a mythical figure, a descendant of the gods. This descent invests the senior line of the ramage with sacral powers (*mana*). The mode of succession in the system is by *primogeniture*, whereby the eldest son succeeds to the position of his father. A major consequence of this is that the eldest brother in a family is differentiated from the younger brothers — a situation permeating the entire life of these people. Further, every brother is ranked according to the principle of *seniority*, and sisters may also be integrated into this hierarchy. This system of ranking extends to embrace the whole of society; descendants of elder brothers ranking higher than descendants of younger brothers. In fact, each individual within these groups occupies a different status, in accordance with his distance from the senior line of descent in the group.

An entire society can be analysed as being composed of component sections of a single genealogical system at the apex of which stands the *paramount chief* (the direct descendant, in the senior line, of the reputed founder of the society). His position is reinforced by the deification of the founding father, and a certain sacredness and power (*mana*) is believed to be inherent in chieftainship.

Where an entire society is seen as one all-embracing ramage, the different sections (sub-ramages) will not appear to be completely superstratified the one above the other. Although one specific large sub-ramage may be said to 'outrank' all the others and supply the paramount chief, it does not follow that all the members of this particular sub-ramage will outrank all the members of the other sub-ramages. In most societies the chiefs of the group are drawn from among those senior in descent in the various (sub-) ramages, while the lower-ranking members of all of the various sections are roughly equivalent to each other in status. The chiefs, however, are ranked according to their distance from the senior descent line of the society — at least as long as this hierarchy is not disturbed by political developments.

At this point it may not be irrelevant to repeat that there is no proof that this model conforms exactly to the Tahitian situation of long ago. However, the model does appear to be in conformity with the facts of historically known Tahitian society.

Goldman (1970), who thoroughly studied the evolution of Polynesian cultures, considers the basic ramage structure of the utmost importance, especially where it came to be combined with a *non-unilineal* principle. According to Goldman this principle involved that people could reckon their descent either along father's or mother's line. This view has been criticized by Elman Service (1971: 154) as follows.

> The child's mother provides by her marriage, a linkage of sorts to her own line while the child's father's line may be ignored in favour of it, but this is a linkage to her *patrilineal* line — that is, succession and/or inheritance, not descent, is involved and descent lines of the child's father and mother both remain patrilineal or cognatic or whatever they were.

In this way ambitious Polynesians, by making use of father's or mother's patri-line, could build up solid claims to the inheritance of certain property and/or titles. Usually more than one person would try to establish a claim to these limited goods. Rivalry between claimants was then the result. This type of rivalry — *status rivalry* as Goldman calls it — acts as a counterweight against the seemingly rigid Polynesian status structure. In his opinion it is the motor behind the evolution of Polynesian cultures.

Though Goldman's arguments are quite cogent, a weak point in his theory is that he does not explain how and when this rivalry became characteristic of such evolution. It is even possible that the principle only developed after a relatively long period, as the prizes in the game became more and more attractive.

To summarize our arguments — hypothetical thus far — the first settlers in Tahiti were rather limited in number. They had a kinship system dominated by seniority and primogeniture, while by a non-unilineal principle they could claim positions outside their patrilineal descent group.

The fertile volcanic island of Tahiti made possible a tremendous population growth. As Sahlins (1958) convincingly shows, good ecological conditions are a necessary condition for social and political development (cf. Claessen 1974: 97 ff.). The number of inhabitants at the moment of discovery is not known. The estimates vary between 200,000 by Cook — a number also adopted by queen Marau — and about 35,000 as the result of careful calculations by McArthur (1968: 240) and Oliver (1974: 34). However, this latter number may be too modest.

It is not impossible that growth was boosted by the advent of new settlers. In the first centuries these new immigrants may have exercised some influence on the development of Tahitian culture. However, as the size of the settled population increased the size of the groups of newcomers relative to the number of inhabitants of Tahiti decreased, and consequently their impact on the existing social structure weakened. Thus, further development came to depend predominantly on internal factors (cf. Oliver 1974: 1122).

The first consequence of a population growth is the spread of human settlement over a larger area (cf. Sorenson 1972). In this way the fertile coastal plains and valleys gradually became inhabited. The mountainous interior, however, did not attract people. Most probably it was junior sons of the senior line who, with their descendants and followers, left to settle somewhere else. This way the social structure of the new settlements became a replica of the original one: a kingroup organized along the principles of the ramage system. The original ramage broke up into a number of sub-ramages which in their turn became more or less independent. Between the leaders of the several settlements some kind of hierarchical kinship relation remained, whereby the senior line in the Vaiari polity was considered the eldest and therefore the most prestigious. The sense of kinship and hierarchy was still alive when the eighteenth century voyagers arrived in Tahiti (cf. Taimai 1901; Marau 1971).

The growth of the population must have had other consequences besides. As the (sub-) ramages grew bigger and bigger, though all the people belonging to a particular ramage still looked upon each other as kin, the social distance between the descendants of the senior and the junior lines grew bigger also (cf. Oliver 1974: 782, 1098, 1130 ff.).

This development had two consequences. First, in the course of time the more attractive parts of the islands were gradually occupied, so that only the less desirable parts remained. In the Tahitian case this implied land at some distance from the sea. This land thus fell to those with the weakest claims — in the ramage system, the juniors of junior lines. This hypothesis finds some confirmation in queen Marau's description of the position of the lowest group in Tahitian society, the *vao,* a term under which she classes the *manahune* as well as the *titi* ([1971: 85 ff.] For an explanation of these terms see below). These people were obliged to live in the hills and mountains, and had only limited access to the sea. Though there was no absolute shortage of land, the fact that land of an inferior quality had to be used led to a sense of population pressure — a psychological pressure, in point of fact (Van Bakel 1976). In this kind of situation developments may have followed along the lines indicated by Carneiro in his subscription theory (1970; cf. Introduction to the present volume), viz. a lessening of the influence of kinship in favor of political (non-kinship) loyalties as a consequence of tensions arising from differential access to resources. Secondly, social stratification attained a fuller development in the local ramages (i.e., sub-ramages). To this development much attention is paid by Oliver (1974: 1126, 1130 ff.). He suggests that the social distance between the senior and junior branches grew so great that in the end marriages between members of these groups were no longer considered possible. So groups belonging to the same ramage became endogamous. In the course of time the following social strata developed this way in Tahitian society,

— an upper group, or the *arii,*
— a middle group, or *raatira,*
— a lower group, or *manahune.*

Political divisions developed along the same lines. There is no reason to suppose that this development took place without any struggle or tension. On the contrary. Goldman (1970: 20 ff., 186 ff.) thinks that many times contentions occurred between people with the ascribed status of *arii* and people from other strata with an achieved status based on individual capacities and qualities. Though Oliver points to the possibility of people of outstanding ability being somehow raised in status, the sources are rather confused on this subject. Better known is the fact that families originally of high status might in the course of several generations gradually become so far removed from the senior line that they were no longer considered as *arii,* but as *raatira* (cf. Claessen 1975: 72 ff.). The traditional history of Tahiti, as related by Arii Taimai and queen Marau, does not contain much information on this point. On the other hand, since their historical interest is restricted to the history of the *arii* families only, the occurrence of these kinds of struggles and changes of status must not be ruled out. Be that as it may, by the time Tahitian society became the object of anthropological interest, the system of stratification had become fairly rigid.

Between the *arii* of the different ramages there has always existed frequent contact. Marriages between members of this exclusive group reinforced their lofty position with regard to the other strata. As a consequence of this, rights to titles, succession and inheritances often became the object of such marriages. This was the field where status rivalry and the application of non-unilineal principles assumed the greatest importance. This field was not restricted to Tahiti. Several times marriages with high-ranking male or female chiefs from other islands, especially Moorea and Raiatea, considerably complicated the situation (cf. Marau 1971; Arii Taimai 1901; Gunson 1975).

Thus far, little or no attention has been paid to the political implications of this evolution. Though hesitantly, some conjectures will be made in the following passages. The data advanced make it possible to ascribe to the local ramages the status of chiefdoms, defined by Service (1975: 74) as polities where 'leadership is centralized, statuses are arranged hierarchically, and where is to some degree a hereditary ethos'.

In accordance with Fried's view (1967: 109, 186) the earlier period would have to be described as having a rank society, 'in which positions of valued status are somehow limited so that not all those of sufficient talent to occupy such statuses actually achieve them', while the later stage of development, when some form of social stratification became visible, might be characterized as a *stratified* society 'in which members of the same sex and equivalent age status do not have equal access to the basic resources that sustain life'.

The increasing growth in prestige of Tahitian chiefs is parallelled by the growth in importance of the *marae*, or temples, of which Suggs (1960: 138 ff.) gives many details. Queen Marau — like others as well — stresses the fact that the sacral base of the chief, by which he legitimized his position, lay in his relation with certain *marae*. The Farepura *marae* of Vaiari was the oldest and therefore the most venerable of these *marae*. As mentioned before, the *arii* of Vaiari were considered the most prestigious line of all.

There are reasons to suppose, however, that the development of Tahitian polities went further, and that at least some of them reached the level of statehood. This view is in contradiction with Oliver (1974) and Service (1975), who recognize only chiefdoms in the traditional Tahitian political organization. However, Oliver's analysis of the Tahitian polities at the time of the discovery by Wallis (Oliver 1974: 1173–1202) makes it clear that there were considerable differences between them. For instance, Hitiaa in the northwest of the island showed the characteristics of a chiefdom (cf. the description by De Bougainville (1772) of his negotiations with the *arii* Reti). Papara in the south, as well as several other polities, on the other hand give a definite impression of an *inchoate early state*. Before giving a structural analysis of these early states, the question of how these polities evolved to statehood will have to be considered.

The most probable explanation is that a number of factors were responsible (cf. Cohen in the present volume, Polgar 1975: 16 ff.). To begin with, the increasing population density gave rise to the necessity of defending the territory of the respective groups against neighboring groups. Furthermore, the many quarrels in the upper *arii* stratum, mostly arising from status rivalry, gave cause for attack and defense. In a number of cases this may have led to a strengthening of the position of the ruling group. Another outcome of the population growth was the need for widening the range of the ruler's governing activities. Thus the need for full-time functionaries made itself felt. The development of a governmental organization, including an armed force, was then only a matter of time. Where the number of officials increased, there arose a need for increased taxation. This in its turn led to a greater control of production and labor. Moreover, the growing influence of priests and religion, as reflected in the growth in size and number of the *marae*, necessitated a greater degree of organization and interference in the life of the population. A deliberate marriage policy may also have exercized an influence. Corvée labor became an important aspect of everyday life. Especially the introduction of the Oro cult at the beginning of the eighteenth century had a great impact on this development (Oliver 1974: 1213 ff.; Newbury 1961: xxxvi). Not only did more and greater *marae* have to be built, but also the competition of the *arii* for the possession of the image of the god Oro led to a series of wars. Escape from these burdens became impossible because of 'social circumscription' (Carneiro 1970), and people just had to accept them. So in the end, there developed, in at least some of the Tahitian polities, a political organization characterized by a central government with specialized functionaries which enabled the people to differentiate themselves into a number of relatively stable groups with unequal access to basic resources, whereby the authority of the ruler was based on legitimacy and backed by force, and whereby fission was out of the question: the early state. As the structural analysis following below will demonstrate, all the features of this characterization were actually found in the polities under consideration.

2. STRUCTURE OF THE EARLY STATE[3]

Soon after the establishment of friendly relations with the Tahitians, the European visitors found out that the island was divided into a number of polities. Though the sources are rather confused on this point, the following reconstruction of the political map of Tahiti can be presented with some confidence.[4] The south was dominated by the

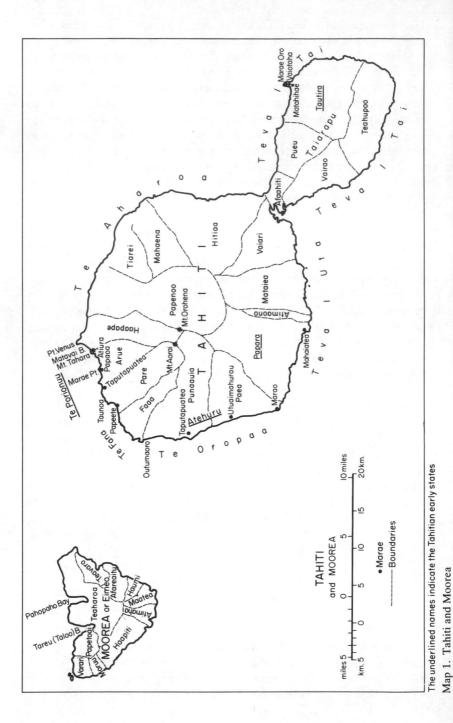

The underlined names indicate the Tahitian early states

Map 1. Tahiti and Moorea

important state of Papara. To the east of this were situated Atimaono, Mataiea and Vaiari. Together the four polities formed the *Teva-i-uta*, or Landward Teva. The political hegemony fell to the ruler of Papara. However, the *arii rahi* of Vaiari, being a descendant of the oldest *arii* line in Tahiti, enjoyed a higher social prestige. Also in Vaiari the famous Farepura *marae* was located. The peninsula of Taiarapu, to the east of Vaiari was dominated by the *arii* of Tautira. They were the leaders of the *Teva-i-tai* or Seaward Teva, comprising the polities of Vairao, Teahupoo, Tautira, Pueu and Afaahiti (going counter-clockwise). The *arii* of Tautira bore the title of *Vehiatua*, a title associated with the Matahihae *marae* in Teahupoo. In Tautira was found the important Vaiotaha *marae*, dedicated to Oro. Going from the peninsula in a northwesterly direction, one reached Hitiaa, where De Bougainville once landed. From there, following the north coast in a westerly direction, one came to Mahaena, Tiarei, Papenoo, and the well known Haapape with its Matavai Bay, which Cook and his associates visited so many times. Between these five polities there seems to have existed some kind of bond. Some of the older sources mention as the name of this confederacy Te Aharoa. The exact nature of the relationship is not clear.

West of Haapape was Te Porionuu, the product of an alliance between Pare and Arue. Here lived the *arii* of the Pomare family (the name under which its rulers are usually mentioned in the literature). South of this area was the small but important Tefana. The *arii* of this chiefdom were connected by marriage with nearly all the important families of the island. Between Tefana and Papara, finally, lay the powerful Atehuru, consisting of Panaauia and Paea.

Of these polities most probably Papara, Tautira, Te Porionuu and Atehuru had attained the level of early states. From here on, they will therefore be called 'states' in this chapter. As, on the one hand, the political structures of these states greatly resembled each other, and, on the other hand, there does not exist a complete description of any one of these princedoms, in the following analysis data from all of them will be used to *construct a model* of the political structure which may be applied to each one of these states individually (cf. Claessen 1970: 5).

2.1. *The Ruler*

As was mentioned before, the ruler of the state was the *arii rahi*, the eldest descendant of the senior line of the territorial ramage. As primogeniture was one of the key principles here, the question arises, what happened if the first-born was a girl. As far as the sources contain information on this subject at all, the prevailing custom seems to have been that succession passed only through the male line. This means that women, no matter how high their status as first-born might be, did not succeed. Usually they married an important chief somewhere else and in this way created a strong link between the two polities concerned, or caused a great many status rivalry problems (Claessen 1970: 6; Oliver 1974: 1184, 1200; Taimai, passim). This is not to say that women did not play an active role in Tahitian political life. On the contrary, Tahitian history contains many instances of high-born women who actively and radically influenced events in the island. However, in all these cases the women concerned were not themselves ruling *arii*, but consorts of rulers. In this position they evidently deeply influenced their husbands' policies and tried to promote the future interests of their sons (Claessen 1970: 14 ff.).

In consequence of his above-mentioned divine descent, the *arii rahi* was believed to be invested with a certain sacredness and special power, called *mana*. The *arii rahi* was not the only bearer of this *mana* in his society, but he possessed it in the strongest measure. To protect the people surrounding him against the alleged dangers of this power, there were numerous rules and regulations guiding his conduct as well as that of the people (Claessen 1962). These rules included the often mentioned prohibition against the *arii rahi*'s touching the earth.[5] For this reason he was, outside his own domain, carried on the shoulders of special servants (cf. the famous picture by R. A. Smirke, 'The cession of the district of Matavai to the missionaries 16 March 1797', reproduced in Oliver 1974: 1289). Furthermore, *arii* were not allowed to enter houses or canoes belonging to other people, for, once this had happened, they could no longer be used by their owners. In general, any objects touched by the *arii rahi* became *tapu* to everyone else. Another custom connected with his sacred position was that it was forbidden to use the name of the *arii rahi* for any other purposes. A consequence was that when he changed his name (which happened frequently), the word chosen and even its individual syllables, must be confined only to this goal. As a result people then had to invent new words to replace the tabooed ones.

In the presence of the *arii rahi* every person was obliged to uncover the upper part of the body. Though it was believed that supernatural sanctions would be applied to anyone breaking these rules, the armed servants of the *arii* never waited for this punishment to take place, but would immediately give the wrongdoer a beating.

Some of the data in the sources give us reason to believe that the *arii rahi*, after reaching a certain age and after passing through a number of specific ceremonies (most probably puberty rites, including circumcision) was less strictly surrounded by *tapus* (Claessen 1962; 1970: 7 ff.).

On certain ceremonial occasions in the *marae* the *arii rahi* would wear a feather girdle, or a *maro*. Such a girdle, in the words of Oliver (1974: 1214),

> served to symbolize and legitimize certain of the very highest-ranking kin-Titles of Tahiti-Moorea. One of these was the red-feathered girdle (*maro ura*) reportedly introduced in Papara (along with the Papara image of "Oro") as the result Te'eva's marriage to Ari'imao (i.e., the marriage of a girl of Papara to a high-born man of Raiatea, C.). Another was the fabled yellow-feathered girdle (*maro tea*) allegedly bestowed upon the first Te'eva by his genitor, Hotutu's shark-god lover from overseas. Henceforth, after Te'eva moved from Vaiari and settled down at Papara, entitlement to this girdle was identified with the dynastic line holding the chieftainship of Papara's principal kin-congregation, and it was the only such yellow-feathered girdle recorded for Tahiti-Moorea.

However, not only the *arii* of Papara could boast a *maro*. In Pare there also existed a *maro*. With this particular one Pomare was invested in the *marae* of Tarahoi of Pare in 1791, as witnessed by James Morisson, one of the mutineers of the Bounty (Morisson 1966: 91). Most probably this *maro* also originally came from Raiatea, as a result of the marriage of Teu, the grandfather of Pomare II, to the daughter of Tamatoa III, the ruler of Raiatea.

The investiture of an *arii rahi* with one of these *maro*'s represented the formal recognition of his right to the highest-ranking titles of the island. The building up of a sufficient claim to such a title was one of the most contested pursuits in the rivalry-ridden Tahitian polity. So a number of wars in which both the Oro image and the *maro*'s were hotly contested ravaged Tahiti in the years between 1760 and 1780. In the end, the Pomares of Te Porionuu, with the aid of English guns, succeeded in getting the upper hand. With that same aid they were gradually to succeed in establishing their sovereign rule over the entire island (Newbury 1961: xxxvii ff.).

The investiture of an *arii rahi* with a *maro* must have been a most solemn ceremony. Unfortunately, the data in the sources regarding such occasions are rather scant and are for the greater part based on hearsay. In fact, only James Morisson was an eye witness to an inauguration ceremony once, though it is not impossible that some protestant missionaries also attended such ceremonies (Davies 1961: 44 ff.). Their accounts show that a number of high-ranking people, among them related *arii* of other polities, attended such occasions. Oro priests made long harangues to the young chief and in conclusion presented the bodies of a number of human sacrifices, who were slain especially for the occasion. Of these human sacrifices the priests would offer one eye to the young *arii*; this was afterwards placed on a kind of altar, together with offerings of plantains and pigs. Probably after that the young *arii* was bathed in the sea, whereupon the Oro-priest wrapped the *maro* around his loins. Then a ceremony — not mentioned by Morisson — took place, in which a number of people were 'exposing themselves in a most shameful manner', as Davies puts it (1961: 45). Probably this was a fertility rite.

This was not the only occasion on which the ruler was associated with fertility. He demonstrated a connection of this kind also during the offering of the first fruits (cf. Morisson 1966: 151, 179).

Not only the investiture with the *maro* was accompanied with large-scale ceremonies. In point of fact, every occurrence of importance in the life of an *arii rahi* was surrounded with ceremony, starting with his birth. Numerous *tapus* would then be imposed on the population of the territory in question, and all had to be silent. After his birth the child was presented to the gods by the high priest, his umbilical cord was placed in the *marae*, and official messengers everywhere proclaimed that an *arii rahi* had been born. Also some human sacrifices were made. With the exception of his marriage, all his *rites de passage* were accompanied with such sacrifices.

The marriage of an *arii* was an event preceded by prolonged negotiations with the family of the bride-to-be. In view of the importance of descent lines and hereditary claims, the choice of a wife was a very serious matter and only after lengthy consideration was the final decision made. Then the numerous gifts involved would become the subject of lengthy negotiations. In the mean time *rahuis* (see below) were issued on a large scale to ensure that, once the day of the marriage arrived, enormous quantities of food would await the guests.

The death of an *arii rahi* was accompanied with many rites too. The information on the subject in the sources is rather divergent (Claessen 1970: 12). Probably the differences in the descriptions should be related to the question of whether the deceased had still been ruling or had already retired. This can be inferred from the extensive rites surrounding the death and burial of the young *arii rahi* Vehiatua of Tautira, as witnessed by Spanish missionaries in 1774. Here even traces of a 'ritual anarchy' were found. However, neither the death of Teu, the father of Pomare I, in 1802, nor that of Pomare I himself in 1803, occasioned much ritual. In this case the young Pomare II had already been ruling for several years (Claessen 1970: 13; Davies 1961: 59, 64).

The preceding paragraph has already hinted at the fact that though the father — and even the grandfather — might still be living, the son might already bear the title of *arii rahi*. This was a result of the custom whereby once a son had been born, the father would immediately abdicate in his favor. The title and the sacral obligations then passed to the infant son, who thus became the new *arii rahi* — 'at least to the name, for it is most likely that the latter must have the power during his Son or Daughters minority' (Cook 1968: 134).[6] What happened in fact, was that the father, and in a few cases someone else, acted as regent for the child.

This custom is sometimes 'explained' by saying that it was a consequence of the ramage system, together with the idea that the combination of the status of the father with that of the mother raised the child to a status higher than that of his parents. Though this might be true, it does not explain why the father had to abdicate and act as regent for his son. Everywhere in Polynesia the concepts of ramage and status played a definite role, but nowhere did this lead to abdication of the father. Hence another explanation may be suggested. As was mentioned before, the *arii rahi* was hedged in with numerous *tapus*. His freedom of action as a ruler in this way was seriously hampered. In this kind of situation a ruler was obliged to find a way to escape from the sacral burdens imposed by his position, or else to accept the impossibility of ruling. The institution of a regency was one such method. Once he had abdicated, the former *arii rahi* had an opportunity of governing without being restricted by the inconveniences of his divine descent. (For other instances of the separation of sacral and secular duties cf. Claessen 1970: 222 ff.).

The young *arii rahi*, together with his brothers and sisters usually grew up in some remote place, far away from the turmoil of political life.

From here on the more general word *ruler* will be used to indicate the man who actually governed. This may therefore be a ruling *arii rahi* as well as a regent.

Sometimes the marriage of an *arii rahi* might remain without issue for a long time. This was a result of the fact that as a rule the *arii* and his wife were members of the Arioi Society. Membership of this Society demanded childlessness. To fulfil this condition, infanticide was practiced (Claessen 1970: 14, 23; Oliver 1974: 939 ff.). The need for a successor, however, would in most cases put a stop to the effective membership of the Arioi Society after some years. As the successor could be borne only by the official wife of the *arii rahi*, she was accepted as such only after careful selection. This situation did not prevent him — or her — from having lovers, however. The wife of the *arii rahi* was, nonetheless, not supposed to have children by any other man (cf. Marau 1971: 77). Notwithstanding this, the ruler and his wife often worked closely together in the political arena. The best example of such cooperation is perhaps provided by Pomare I and his wife Itia. She was said to be his councillor in all matters, and more than once succeeded in finding solutions to difficult problems. The ruler relied not only upon his wife for help. His brothers, sisters, uncles and children were also counted upon to look after his political interests.

Sisters and daughters were married off to influential men in order to make new allies or to ensure the cooperation of other rulers. Sons and brothers were appointed to government posts.

2.2. The Organization

The administration of the state was not confined to members of the ruler's family only.

> By the time under study, tribal units had reached sizes and orders of complexity that permitted or required a number of officials to perform these various offices (Oliver 1974: 1027).

The reconstruction of the bureaucratic apparatus of the early states in Tahiti is no simple task. The letters and journals of early visitors, as well as the lengthy descriptions of missionaries, mention numerous personages, titles, functions and ranks, often in the most exotic orthographies. To complicate matters, a considerable overlap in functions was usual. The following summary, therefore, can represent no more than a rough outline, only too often based on arbitrary conclusions (Claessen 1970: 15 ff.; Oliver 1974: 1027–1037).

High among the various functionaries ranked the high priest, or *tahua rahi*. He was usually a near relative of the ruler. His position seems to have been rather ambiguous. On the one hand, his principal duties were religious. In this capacity he conducted the ceremonies in the state *marae*, and was the head of a priestly hierarchy. He furthermore inaugurated the *arii rahi*, eventually presenting him with the *maro*. Moreover, he decided on the necessity of human sacrifices (Claessen 1970: 22). On the other hand, well-versed as he was in religious traditions, he might easily influence the ruler's political actions by declaring them in accordance with — or contrary to — the wish of the gods. Marau (1971: 82) points to the fact that the high priest was a member of the highest state council. There are instances known of high priests deeply influencing the political actions of rulers (e.g. Tupia or Haamanemane, cf. Claessen 1970: 21).

The *tau mi hau* was the principal administrator after the ruler. In some of the minor polities the chief himself fulfilled this function, but in the early states under discussion these administrators actually existed as separate functionaries. Possibly, this title was used on different levels, but in this chapter only the *tau mi hau* at the state level will be considered. The busy Tii described by Cook during his second voyage (1969: 384 ff.; 410) most probably was such a *tau mi hau*.

Less clear is the position of the district chiefs. Oliver gives much attention to this problem, ending with the somewhat vague conclusion that in a number of polities at least there existed territorial subdivisions, 'second order tribes', as he calls them (1974: 976). The chiefs of these districts may have had the title of *toofa*, though the title of *papa-i-raro* has also once been mentioned (Claessen 1970: 19). The administrative tasks of the *toofa* were probably of a *general* nature, like those of the ruler at the higher level. As far as the evidence goes, the ruler did not always possess sufficient power to impose his will on the district chiefs. However, this conclusion may be influenced by the circumstance that most of the early visitors were in Tahiti at a time of unrest and war.

As *special* functionaries, must be considered the *orero*, the *vea* and possibly also the *hiva*.

The *orero* was the ruler's official speaker. He delivered most of the formal speeches and had to be a man of great eloquence. He often acted as the ruler's official negotiator. In view of the nature of these duties, the *orero* must have been a man of high rank.

The *vea* was the official messenger of the ruler, the 'herald of the nation', in the words of Ellis (1831 III: 99, 122). He was the man who announced the birth or death of the *arii rahi*. The *vea* also summoned the councillors to council meetings. He went forth to mobilize the warriors when war was at hand. In all these cases he acted not only as messenger, but often also as official ambassador to the ruler. Probably the ruler had in his service, besides the principal *vea*, a number of messengers of lesser rank.

With the *hiva* again a title is introduced, the connotations of which are none too clear (cf. Oliver 1974: 1037). Probably the *hiva* was in the first place a kind of military leader. There were several *hiva* in each state, and together they formed a group or council, also called *hiva*. According to queen Marau (1971: 83) the *hiva* formed a kind of bodyguard of the ruler's which is not in contradiction with the fact that they were military leaders. A *hiva* had to be a man of high rank, and there are indications that they sometimes used their power to enforce the ruler's wishes. Some *hiva* at least belonged to the highest state council.

To complicate matters, a number of prominent Tahitians are referred to in the source as *hoa*, or *taua*, a title that should be translated as 'friend' in a more or less formal sense, or 'blood brother' of the ruler. Though this title points to a personal relation with the ruler, it does *not* refer to any function or office. Unfortunately, however, the exact positions of several influential persons have been obscured by the use of only these titles. It is also possible that at the ruler's court lived some *hoa* without any formal government position, who, nonetheless, sometimes acted on behalf of the ruler. There is no reason to suppose that these functionaries had full-time jobs.

Beneath these high-ranking functionaries there were officials of a lesser rank (agents) performing various tasks in the governmental organization. Some of them have been rescued from obscurity. The most important of these probably were the *aito*, or distinguished soldiers. Together with the *hiva* they formed a small but powerful force behind the ruler. Backed by this group, the ruler, but also his lowest servants, could permit themselves liberties of all kinds with regard to the *raatira* or *manahune*. These unfortunate people had no means of defence and could only complain. The writings of early visitors contain many examples of the way in which they were mistreated (cf. Claessen 1962: 443; Jongmans 1955).

The *taata ere* was the navigator of the royal canoe. He had to be an expert at this craft.

Sometimes there is mentioned an *arata-i-rahui*, the officer who had to supervise the execution of the *rahui* (see below).

The lowest level of functionaries was formed by the numerous servants, domestic and otherwise, cooks and carriers. Among them were found a number of 'strangers', i.e., people from other ramages, or even from other islands. Especially these strangers were charged with the task of carrying the *arii rahi* and his consort. It is possible that this was an outcome of the idea that they, not belonging to the same ramage as the *arii rahi*, could not be harmed by contact with his sacred body (Claessen 1962: 443 ff.).

2.3. Social Stratification

After the foregoing discussion it will now be possible to go further into the social stratification, as already outlined in the section on evolution.

2.3.1. *The Arii.* The composition of this group was rather complex. To it belonged all the *arii* families of Tahiti, arranged according to an internal hierarchy, in which the *arii rahi* of Vaiari enjoyed the highest social status. Via the patrilines of high-born women — often from *arii* families in the nearby island of Raiatea — lower-ranking *arii* might establish claims to high-ranking titles. This way the formerly comparatively straightforward picture became distorted, and the highest status and the greatest political influence were no longer identical by the middle of the eighteenth century.

Each of the individual *arii* lineages possessed in its turn an internal hierarchy. The most important member, of course, was the *arii rahi*, followed at not too great a distance by his immediate kin. The further the genealogical distance from him, the lesser the status as *arii*. The least significant members of the *arii* group were probably the *iatoai*, comprising mainly members of junior branches. This group being the most numerous, many of the government functions were fulfilled by *iatoai*. It is not clear whether they inherited these positions, or were somehow selected but, given the fact that only *arii* were supposed to possess the necessary qualities to be able to govern, the difference is but of academic interest. Most probably the *toofa*, the alleged district chiefs, were *iatoai*, too (Claessen 1970: 19; Oliver 1974: 761 ff.).

Though, in theory, an unbridgeable social gap separated the *arii* from the other levels in the hierarchy, the question arises whether this theory was in conformity with reality. As mentioned above, the actual difference between junior descendants of junior *arii* lines and the senior members of senior *raatira* lines was not great. More than once in the course of time the lowest-ranking *arii* lost their status as such and came to be regarded as *raatira* (Oliver 1974: 775). However, as long as one was regarded as an *arii*, one's social behavior showed marked differences from that of the other groups. The *arii* formed a nobility, privileged, exalted and status-conscious. The clearest manifestation of these ideas was probably the fact that marriages between *arii* and members of the other social groups were forbidden (Oliver 1974: 759). Moreover the *arii* possessed the strongest claims to the land of the ramage, and as a result appropriated the best areas (cf. Panoff 1970: 251 ff.).

2.3.2. *The Raatira*. The *raatira* are usually described as landowners, a kind of landed gentry, or 'barons' (Ellis 1831 III: 121), or 'une bourgeoisie terrienne' (Marau 1971: 85). They were entitled to land, and, according to the information contained in the sources, their rights as landed proprietors were the same as those of the *arii*. Their land was inherited and no *arii* had the right to expropriate it (Claessen 1970: 20, 26). Of course, it was possible for the ruler to banish a proprietor, but in that case a successor from his family would replace him. This creates the impression that the land was, in fact owned by family groups, consisting of ramage members of roughly the same status, whose claims were inviolable and inalienable, and that the 'proprietor' was the person who actually had the usufruct of the land. So the only legal solution for the ruler in such cases would have been to banish the entire family; but there are no instances of such behavior on record.

Like the *arii*, the *raatira* had the right to transfer the usufruct of parts of his land to other people, or tenants, most often members of the *manahune* group. He further had the right to impose a *rahui*, that is, a *tapu* forbidding anyone to harvest any crops yielded by or drawing any other advantages from the land in question for a given period, on his land.

Apart from the marriage prescriptions there were no clear and precise criteria for distinguishing the *arii* from the *raatira*.

Especially the protestant missionaries draw a very favorable picture of the *raatira*, whom they describe as pleasant, diligent and trustworthy people. This favorable opinion seems to have been influenced by the fact that the *raatira* appear to be more interested in the Christian faith than the *arii*. Most probably, major differences in status, rank and wealth existed among the *raatira* internally — as among the *arii*. Differences that were connected with descent from senior or junior lines, better and poorer quality of land, and more or less fortunate marriages. Aside from a possible prohibition on intermarriage, most probably the transition to the next level below, namely that of the *manahune*, was gradual. Perhaps in the border area between these two levels were found the skilled craftsmen.

Several times the sources mention specialists, among them the highly respected boat builders, *marae* builders and wood carvers (cf. Oliver 1974: 855 ff.). Their exact position in the status system is not known. Some of them would have belonged to the *raatira*, while others would have been *manahune*. At least some of these people must have been full-time specialists.

2.3.3. *The Manahune*. As in the differentiation between *arii* and *raatira*, rather vague criteria were used for the distinction between *raatira* and *manahune*. There are reasons to associate *manahune* with poor people, or people of low descent. This does not mean to say that they were unfree, or without rights. Like all Tahitians, the *manahune* too, had claims to land. However, their place in the ramage system was so distant from the senior lines, that usually — though not always — their claims were overridden by those of other people. In the words of Oliver (1974: 766): 'They were, so to speak, relegated to a 'waiting list''; but to call such persons landless is, I believe, a misnomer'. This view finds confirmation in the classification of the rights to land by queen Marau (1971: 85), in which the rights of the *manahune* are included, but rank very low. She also points to the fact that *manahune* sometimes only possessed land in the interior of the island, far from the sea. These lands were, in the eyes of the Tahitians, unfavorably situated (cf. Panoff 1970: 251 ff.).

In a number of cases *manahune* are mentioned as tenants of the land of *arii* or *raatira*. Here they tilled the soil and enjoyed the usufruct of it. In exchange they paid their landlord in several different ways, namely by contributing food for his household, producing objects he needed, and, when necessary, working as domestics or other kinds of servant. Moreover they had to meet the obligations involved in the special labor levies or general corvée (Oliver 1974: 767). The common sense consideration that *manahune* were free to leave and look for land in the domains of other ramages probably kept these impositions within reasonable bounds.

If the position of a *manahune* improved, that is to say when his claims to land were no longer overridden by the claims of other people (who might have been killed in war or died without offspring), he could easily attain the status of *raatira*.

2.3.4. *The Titi and Teuteu.* It seems useful to describe the bearers of these designations as separate categories, though it is also quite possible to term most of them *manahune*, as is done by Oliver (1974: 750, 768).

Teuteu were servants, domestic or otherwise, *arii* as well as *raatira* usually employing various *teuteu*, male and female. Sometimes the positions they fulfilled were hereditary. Though most of the *teuteu*, in terms of marriageability, might be classified as *manahune*, some of them belonged to higher social levels (Oliver 1974: 768).

In contrast to the *teuteu* the *titi* seem to have been unfree people. The sources refer to them as prisoners-of-war. In the majority of cases human sacrifices were selected from among this group. Presumably they were obliged to work for their masters on the same terms as the *teuteu*. The designation 'slaves' with reference to them seems not unwarranted (cf. Nieboer 1910).

The foregoing analysis shows that differences in economic position followed along the lines of social stratification, which in turn were a result of the relative genealogical position of individuals. Though all members of a ramage alike had certain claims to land, the claims of the *arii* were stronger and more extensive than those of the *raatira*. The claims of the *manahune* were so weak that only by way of exception was land allotted to them. Moreover, this land was sometimes located in the more unfavorable areas. Considerable numbers of *manahune* therefore worked the land of *arii* and *raatira* as tenants, while some of them were servants in the households of such notables.

Intensive horticulture produced plantains, breadfruit, taro, sweet potatoes, yams etc., in large quantities. This way a large population could be fed, and the existence of a number of specialists was possible. Not only the gardens yielded abundant produce. There were also numerous pigs and other small animals to satisfy the appetite of the Tahitians—though it appears that some foodstuffs were reserved for *arii* only, or for men only.

Thus far only the relations of the population to the land were considered. But what were their relations to other basic resources, such as the products of the sea? From the lengthy analyses by Oliver (1974: 281 ff., esp. 309 ff.) it seems probable that every man possessed canoes, hooks, lines and small nets.

'Only with respect to the large nets and the right to command the services required to man these and other large-scale fishing enterprises ... individual differences became important' (Oliver 1974: 309).

Thus nobody seems to have been excluded from fishing, not even the lowest of the *teuteu* (cf. Marau 1971: 85). Only the right to command men to assist with the large fishing nets etc., was restricted to certain notables. So leaving causes and evolution out of consideration can Tahitian society on the eve of its discovery be described as being 'differentiated into relatively stable groups with unequal access to basic resources'? (cf. Introduction to this volume). As far as access to the sea is concerned, there are no reasons for assuming so. As regards access to the other principal resource, land, the definition should be applied with some qualifications. For, as stated above, everybody possessed claims to land, which, however, were not in all cases fulfilled. As there were ample opportunities for securing land on lease, nobody was excluded from access to means of subsistence. However that may be, it is clear that persons of about the same age and sex did not have equal access to land (cf. Fried 1967: 186). In the eyes of Western observers this was an important fact. To Tahitians probably the only thing that mattered were the rules of marriage, by which *arii, raatira* and *manahune* were distinguished.[7] With all this in mind it is no longer easy to apply to this society such labels as 'caste' or 'class'. In fact, only specific aspects of these broad characterizations were to be observed here. Therefore, the ultimate choice of the relevant epithet will depend on the conceptions of the investigator and the definitions he uses.

2.4. *The Functioning of the State*

In analysing a state organization it is insufficient to describe only its functionaries and institutions. More important still is the way in which the machine works: what was the interaction of the functionaries and institutions, how was the course of state policy determined?

To begin with, the ruler, according to all the sources, had the right and power to command. This power he used extensively, and in Western eyes, sometimes abused. People, again according to the sources, seem to have accepted this state of affairs as being in conformity with the rules and traditions, and to have obeyed his commands and wishes. The ruler's orders varied greatly: He could impose on his subjects a *rahui* as a consequence whereof no pigs might be killed, no fish speared, all fires had to be extinguished and trade with foreigners stopped. The complaints of Cook and many other voyagers provide sufficient indication that people took these *rahuis* very seriously. It is not clear whether the *rahui* were obeyed unsupervised, or whether the *arata-i-rahui* saw to it that the *rahui* were not violated. Aside from the formal revocation of a *rahui* by the ruler, there was only one other way of ending it, namely when a visitor of sufficiently high rank entered the territory concerned, the ruler being obliged by the rules of etiquette to receive him (or her, as was sometimes the case) hospitably. Challenges of this kind only occurred, however, if the proclaimer of a *rahui* had exceeded his powers, or extended his *rahui* beyond the borders of his territory. Usually, the *rahui* was extended over a limited part of the island, and only for specific periods. Though its proclamation was surrounded with supernatural occurrences, at the root of every *rahui* lay the rational wish to accumulate food or pigs for certain ceremonies or festivities to be held in the future, or, as was sometimes necessary, to allow the land a much needed rest and let it recover from the heavy demands made on it. Therefore, everyone, the *arii* included, had to fulfil the conditions of a *rahui* (cf. Marau 1971: 60, 62).

The ruler could order the construction of a new *marae*. This was a tremendous undertaking, for which corvée labor was needed, and skilled craftsmen had to be brought together. The numerous ruins of *marae*, scattered all over the island, testify that people were often summoned for the construction of such buildings. Prolonged *rahui* made it possible to build up considerable reserves of food, for during the work on a *marae* there was no time for much work in the gardens. About the organization of the work, but little is known. Oliver (1974: 858) supposes that the master builders may have been priests. This could point in the direction of priestly influence on the decision to build a new temple. In view of the close relations between the ruler and the high priest this would be hardly surprising. It was, however, the *arii rahi*, and not a priest, who consecrated the *marae* (Claessen 1970: 21). Not only major decisions, but also numerous minor ones were made by the ruler. One of them even once went so far as to personally get a European visitor some planks (Wilson 1799: 158).[8]

In all these cases, whether important or trivial, the question is whether the decisions ascribed to the ruler were really his, or whether he was only the man proclaiming the decisions of other people. Were there extraneous influences acting upon his decision-making, or was he alone responsible? As far as the information goes, important decisions were mostly influenced to a high degree by the advisers of the ruler. Among these his wife, the high priest and some of the court notables formed a kind of inner circle, or privy council. Other people of high rank outside this inner circle occasionally gave their advice. There was yet another council, namely the tribal council, as Oliver calls it. Here the ruler, the *arii* and the *raatira* (and possibly some *manahune* too) occasionally met to discuss matters of major importance, among which war seems to have been preeminent. Only in this council could the ruler enlist the necessary manpower to wage war. Probably corvée labor for important buildings was enlisted in the same way. At these meetings the *oreros* usually conducted negotiations on behalf of the ruler, who at the end would try to formulate the relevant decisions. That the influence of the *raatira* in this council was not imaginary is illustrated by some of Davies' descriptions of such meetings (Davies 1961: 45 ff., 65 ff.). In the first of these Pomare I and his son, assisted by their *oreros*, tried, in vain, to persuade the assembled *raatira* of Paea (part of Atehuru) to give them the Oro image. In the second Pomare II tried, also in vain, to persuade a council of *raatira* of Pare, Matavai and Tefana to transfer his dead father's body to a certain *marae* in Atehuru.

Aside from his formal influence, the ruler often tried informally to gauge the opinions of the *raatira* before taking some decision (Claessen 1970: 25).

Once a decision was made, the *vea* informed the district chiefs accordingly and they in their turn set messengers to the respective heads of families. There were a number of people who saw to the execution of the ruler's commands. The *arata-i-rahui* has already been mentioned in this connection, as have those of the servants of the *arii rahi* who immediately punished anyone who failed to show sufficient homage. Add to these the many *arii*, *iatoai*, priests, *toofa* etc., acting as the 'eyes of the ruler', in each of the tiny states, and it will become clear that, all in all, a fairly efficient control apparatus existed (Claessen 1970: 26).

There is sufficient reason to believe that people generally obeyed the orders of the ruler. For, in their eyes, he was entitled to give these. Because of his descent he was a near relative of the gods. His position was legitimized by religion. Perhaps the most effective guardians of his power, therefore, were not the armed retainers, but the priests. This is not to say that the ruler could do without an armed force to back his rule. There were a number of high-born men in his state whose relations to the gods were only slightly less close than his, and who by fortunate marriage policy could build up strong claims to high positions. Such persons could be held in check by the existence of an armed group of *hiva* and *aito*. In this way some kind of a 'balance of power' was maintained (Claessen 1978). Besides, the ruler's or his servants' neglect of the interests of the people sometimes also necessitated the existence of an armed force to protect the ruler (Rodriguez 1774: 27 ff.).

Though he regularly travelled all over the island, the ruler usually lived in his own territory. There he possessed a few large houses. He would keep some sort of a court in the shade of a few big trees. Here great quantities of food and objects were accumulated. These came partly from the ruler's domains, being produced here by his tenants. The district chiefs and the *raatira* also contributed largely to this stream flowing to the court — though in their case, too, tenants would have been the actual producers. This may well be considered as a form of taxation (Oliver 1974: 1001 ff.). The ruler, in his turn, distributed great quantities of food and objects to his councillors, friends, district chiefs, warriors and servants. Also when visiting related rulers, canoe-loads of food were, as a rule, presented to the host (Gayangos 1775: 133; Rodriguez 1774: 24 ff.). Occasionally, enormous feasts, attended by large numbers of people, were held. At these feasts, those who had actually produced the food and wealth received some of it back. If *redistribution* is defined as a system whereby large quantities of food and goods are first brought together by a ruler, who then distributes the greater part of it to others, the system under discussion was redistribution. If, however, the term redistribution involves that at least reasonable shares of the amassed wealth are returned to the actual producers, then the Tahitian system falls wide of the requirements (Claessen 1970: 28; cf. Sahlins 1958: 39, 110, 149). There is no reason to suppose that the rulers were interested in trade or commerce.

Taxation in produce and goods was not the only burden imposed on the common people. Corvée labor also absorbed much of their time and energy. Not only *marae* but also the houses and canoes of the *arii* were built in this way. The data in the sources on commoners are few and confused. Some visitors considered their life burdensome and poor. Others however, portray that life, even that of tenants, as peaceful and happy, and one of relative luxury. In comparison with the life of the poor in eighteenth-century France or England this may have been true. Possibly the contradictoriness of the information is a function of the different moments of observation, namely, of whether it took place at a period of war or peace, while the question of who did the observing is also important for an evaluation of the sources (cf. Claessen 1970: 1–3).

Up to now we have only mentioned that a ruler made decisions and that he punished those who disobeyed his will. Should this be interpreted as a form of arbitration? Was there some sort of law and order in Tahiti? In some cases the ruler did in fact act as judge. This was only when crimes such as lese-majesty or crimes committed directly against the ruler or his family were involved, however. In addition, certain cases concerning landrights seem to have been put before the ruler. To interpret this as a sort of juridical system, or to regard the ruler as a kind of lord high justice would be incorrect. Only incidentally did the ruler act as judge. In most cases it was left up to the wronged party to mete out punishment or take revenge (Claessen 1970: 26 ff). Sometimes, criminals were appointed as human sacrifice by the ruler. It is not clear, however, whether this should be viewed as a form of justice.

More prominent was the ruler's function as war leader. Several rulers were redoutable warriors, and more than one ruler lost his life on the battlefield. Others kept away from the often bloody battles and left the fighting to experienced *hiva* and *aito*. Extensive rites accompanied the preparations for war. Human sacrifices were made to win the favor of the gods and priests prophesied success. There are no references in the sources to the mustering of food or weapons. The combatants, apparently, were supposed to look after themselves. Once the tribal council agreed to war, the ruler could make an assessment of the number of armed men he could expect to have at his disposal. Then the *vea* would go around to summon the district chiefs to assemble their men. Also a number of members of the Arioi Society seem to have reinforced the ruler's army (cf. Claessen 1970: 23).[9] After all these preparations the war would finally begin. A fierce scrimmage in which no quarter was given. Slaughter, rape, arson and looting marked its final phases. It is not clear whether a victory led to the actual conquest of the territory of the vanquished party. This seems to have occasionally been the case, but it certainly was not the rule (Oliver 1974: 987 ff.). The arrival of the Europeans and the subsequent ascendancy of the Pomare Dynasty was to change this picture drastically.

The general picture presented by the Tahitian states is thus one of societies centered around an *arii* group, of which the highest ranking member was the ruler. These societies were stratified, and the impression is given that the lowest stratum bore the greater part of the burdens of the state, the members of the higher strata enjoying the more pleasant sides of life. Yet this situation seems to have been accepted by everyone. This raises the question of reciprocity. Did the ruling group somehow return something to the common people? The principle of redistribution has already been alluded to. It appears that in Tahiti the balance between taxes and benefits was quite uneven. The ruler's role as maintainer of law and order seems to have been but poorly fulfilled. As a rallying point in the never-ending wars he may have been of definite importance. Of the greatest importance, however, was his relation to the gods it seems. For it was he who ensured fertility and prosperity, he who conducted the principal rites such as the consecration of *maraes*, the offering of the first fruits and the making of human sacrifices. In this way, by meeting the religious and social expectations of his society, the ruler legitimized his position and reciprocated his people's services (cf. Robineau 1973: 8).

FOOTNOTES

[1] I am indebted to Simon Kooijman, Piet van de Velde and Martin van Bakel, who kindly read and commented on an earlier draft of this paper.

[2] Such as, for example, Tikopia (Firth 1963), Rangiroa (Ottino 1972), Raroia (Danielsson 1956), Marquesas Islands (Suggs 1965), Tonga Islands (Gifford 1929) and Hawaii Islands (Davenport 1969). For a general survey cf. Sahlins 1958, Goldman 1970.

[3] This structural analysis of the early states is based mainly on Chapter I of Claessen (1970), which covers virtually all the source material. The monumental volumes recently published by Oliver (1974) have been used as a check on our own findings. In several cases his opinion has been deferred to. Some attention will be given also to the recently published memoirs of queen Marau (1971), which work neither Claessen (1970) nor Oliver consulted.

The spelling of the Tahitian names and words has no scientific pretensions whatever.

[4] This reconstruction, which follows Claessen (1970: 3 ff.), is based mainly on Wilson (1799: 185 ff.), Bligh (1794: 117 ff.), Morisson (1792 [ed. of 1966]: 67, 137 ff.) and Taimai (1901). Oliver's reconstruction of the political map (1974: 1173 ff.), though more detailed, is in essence the same.

[5] Panoff (1970: 258) connects this with the *arii rahi's* right to all the land of the ramage. Wherever he touched the earth, this claim would be demonstrated and he might appropriate the land.

[6] As was mentioned above, there are no clearly recorded cases of the existence of female *arii rahi*. It is not clear either whether the custom of abdication was observed if the first-born was a girl, as the comment by Cook seems to suggest.

[7] In fact, these two points of view represent two divergent ways of looking at ethnographical facts, viz. the *etic* and the *emic* approach. (Cf. Harris 1968: 568 ff.)

[8] Some authors, among them Jongmans (1955), accuse the rulers of abuse of power and despotism on account of this behavior.

[9] Notwithstanding the lengthy discussions of the Areoi Society by Mühlmann (1955) and Oliver (1974: 913–964), the character of this society and its impact on administration is still obscure.

REFERENCES

Bakel, Martin van (1976), *Bevolkingsdruk en culturele evolutie [Population pressure and cultural evolution]*. ms. Leiden.

Bellwood, Peter (1975), The prehistory of Oceania, in: *Current Anthropology* 16: 9–28.

Bligh, William (1794), *Captain Bligh's second voyage to the South Sea*. Ed. by Ida Lee. London (1920).

Bougainville, Louis de (1772), *Voyage autour du monde par la frégate du roi la Boudeuse et la flûte l'Etoile*. Paris: Le Monde en 10/18 (1966).

Carneiro, Robert L. (1970), A theory of the origin of the state, in: *Science* 169: 733–738.

Claessen, H. J. M. (1962), Enige gegevens over taboes en voorschriften rond Tahitische vorsten [Some data on taboos and prescriptions around Tahitian kings], in: *Bijdragen tot de Taal-, Land- en Volkenkunde* 118: 433–453.

— (1964). Een vergelijking van de theorieën van Sharp en Suggs over de lange afstandsreizen van de Polynesiërs [A comparison of the theories of

Sharp and Suggs on Polynesian long distance voyages], in: *Bijdragen tot de Taal-, Land- en Volkenkunde* 120: 140–162.

Claessen, H. J. M. (1970), *Van vorsten en volken* [Of princes and peoples]. Amsterdam: Joko.

— (1974), *Politieke antropologie* [*Political anthropology*.] Assen: Van Gorcum.

— (1975), 'From rags to riches and the reverse', in: *Rule and reality*, ed. by Peter Kloos and Klaas W. van der Veen. Amsterdam: University of Amsterdam, A.S.C.

— (1978), 'The balance of power in primitive states', Paper presented at the IXth ICAES, Chicago. Forthcoming in *Political anthropology and the state of the art*. ed. by S. Lee Seaton and Henri J. M. Claessen. The Hague: Mouton.

Cook, James (1968), *The voyage of the Endeavour, 1768–1771*. Ed. by J. C. Beaglehole, 2nd print. Hakluyt Society Extra Series 34. Cambridge: Cambridge University Press.

— (1969), *The voyage of the Resolution and Adventure, 1772–1775*. Ed. by J. C. Beaglehole. 2nd print. Hakluyt Society Extra Series 35. Cambridge: Cambridge University Press.

Danielsson, Bengt (1956), *Work and life on Raroia*. London: Allen and Unwin.

Davenport, William (1969), The 'Hawaiian cultural revolution', in: *American Anthropologist* 71: 1–20.

Davies, John (1961), *The history of the Tahitian mission, 1799–1830*. Ed. by C. W. Newbury. Hakluyt Society 2nd series 116. Cambridge: Cambridge University Press.

Ellis, William (1831), *Polynesian researches, during a residence of nearly six years in the South Sea islands*. 4 vols. London: Fisher, Son & Jackson.

Finney, Ben (1967), 'New perspectives on Polynesian voyaging', in: *Polynesian culture history*, ed. by Genevieve Highland, pp. 141–166. P. B. Bishop Museum Special Publications 56. Honolulu: Bishop Museum Press.

Firth, Raymond (1963), *We, the Tikopia*. Boston: Beacon Press.

Fried, Morton H. (1967), *The evolution of political society*. New York: Random House.

Gayangos, Thomas (1775), 'The official journal of the second voyage of the frigate Aguila from El Callao to Tahiti and the islands near-by and back to El Callo', in: *The quest and occupation of Tahiti by emissaries of Spain during the years 1772–1776*, ed. by B. G. Corney. Vol. II, pp. 103–199. Hakluyt Society, 2nd series 36. Cambridge: Cambridge University Press. (1915).

Gifford, E. W. (1929), *Tongan society*. B.P. Bishop Museum Bulletin 61. Honolulu: published by the Museum.

Goldman, Irving (1970), *Ancient Polynesian society*. Chicago: University of Chicago Press.

Gunson, Niels (1975), Tahiti's traditional history—without Adams? in: *The Journal of Pacific History* 10: 112–117.

Harris, Marvin (1968), *The rise of anthropological theory*. London: Routledge & Kegan Paul.

Jongmans, D. G. (1955), *Politiek in Polynesië*. [*Politics in Polynesia*]. Thesis, Amsterdam.

Lewis, David (1972), *We, the Navigators*. Canberra: Australian National University Press.

Marau Taaroa (1971), *Mémoires de* ———— *dernière reine de Tahiti.* Traduits par sa fille la princesse Ariimanihinihi Takau Pomare. Publications de la Société des Océanistes 27. Paris: Musée de l'Homme.

McArthur, Norma (1968), *Islands populations of the Pacific.* Canberra: Australian National University Press.

Morisson, James (1966), *Journal de* ————, *second maître à bord de la 'Bounty'.* Traduit par B. Jaunez. Publications de la Société des Océanistes 16. Paris: Musée de l'Homme.

Mühlmann, W. E. (1955), *Arioi und Mamaia.* Studien zur Kulturkunde 14. Wiesbaden: Steiner.

Newbury, C. W., ed. (1961), See Davies.

Nieboer, H. J. (1910), *Slavery as an industrial system.* 2nd Print. The Hague: Nijhoff.

Oliver, Douglas L. (1974), *Ancient Tahitian society.* 3 *vols.* Honolulu: University of Hawaii Press.

Ottino, Paul, (1972), *Rangiroa, parenté étendue, résidence et terres dans un atol polynésien.* Paris: Cujas.

Panoff, Michel (1970), *La terre et l'organisation sociale en Polynésie.* Paris: Payot.

Polgar, Steve (ed.) (1975), *Population, écology and social evolution.* The Hague: Mouton.

Robineau, Claude (1973), Réciprocité, rédistribution et prestige chez les Polynésiens des Iles de la Société. Paper, presented at the IXth ICAES, Chicago.

Robineau, Claude (1973), Réciprocité, rédistribution et prestige chez les Polynésiens des Iles de la Société. Paper, presented at the IXth ICAES, Chicago.

Rodriguez, Maximo (1774), 'Daily narrative kept by the interpreter ———— at the Island of Amat, otherwise called Otahiti, in the year 1774', in: *The quest and occupation of Tahiti by emissaries of Spain during the years 1772–1776,* ed. by B. G. Corney. Vol. III, pp. 1–210. Hakluyt Society, 2nd Series 43. Cambridge: Cambridge University Press (1919).

Sahlins, Marshall D. (1958), *Social stratification in Polynesia.* Seattle: University of Washington Press.

Service, Elman R. (1971), *Primitive social organization.* 2nd print. New York: Random House.

—— (1975), *Origins of the state and civilization.* New York: Norton.

Sorenson, E. R. (1972), Socio-ecological change among the Fore of New Guinea, in: *Current Anthropology* 13: 349–383.

Suggs, Robert C. (1960), *Islands civilizations of Polynesia.* New York: Mentor Books.

—— (1965), *The hidden worlds of Polynesia.* New York: Cresset Press.

Taimai, Arii (1901), *The memoirs of* ————. Edited by Henry Adams. Paris: Privately printed.

Wilson, James (1799), *A missionary voyage to the Southern Pacific Ocean, performed in the ship Duff.* London: Chapman.

22

Early States in the Voltaic Basin[1]

PETER SKALNÍK

The Voltaic states are one of the most interesting manifestations of the early civilized society in pre-colonial Africa. Their evolution was uninterrupted until the end of the pre-colonial period. As a matter of fact, this cluster of states displayed both internal and external stability, which perhaps helped them to survive formally until the present day and even to try and play a role in the political systems of the contemporary republican regimes of Ghana and Upper Volta (cf. Skalník 1975).

My task here is to characterize briefly, though in as much detail as possible, the origins and structural development of several of the larger, probably fairly typical, but, at any rate, so far the best-described early Voltaic states; namely those of Moogo, Yatēnga, Mamprugu, Dagbong and partly also Tēngkudugo. We will thus attempt to cover, in fact, the entire pre-colonial situation, placing more complex structures of the nineteenth century.

The literature drawn on for the writing of this essay is of three types: (1) the largely biased colonial accounts by administrators and military personnel; (2) critical modern analyses by trained anthropologists and historians; (3) romanticized or subjective works by authors who do not have scholarly training.

Critical analysis of these library sources had to be completed before the present synthetical discussion could be undertaken. Unfortunately, no unpublished written or oral sources of local origin could be used. No fieldwork was done due to causes beyond my control.

1. ORIGINS

As several comparative critical studies of oral sources have shown recently (Izard 1970; Iliasu 1971; Benzing 1971), the state formation process first began in the Voltaic basin in the fifteenth century (cf. Fage 1964). The impulse to this process was provided by a migration(s) of warriors from the northeastern part of West Africa, crossing the Niger to the area close to present-day Gambaga and Nalerigu in Mamprugu, northern Ghana. The immigrants most probably rode horses but were of the same racial subtype, namely that of the Sudanese Negroes, as the autochthonous peoples living in the Voltaic Basin at the time of the immigration.

The myth of origin of the Voltaic states has not yet been comprehensively analyzed, and there are too many questions still to be answered before a general interpretation can be attempted. Nevertheless, a provisional critical summary of this myth, which has a number of local variants, can be attempted. The interethnic political and cultural confrontation between the autochthonous, sedentary, agricultural peoples and the warrior immigrants inevitably created the necessity of evolving some kinds of situations for the regulation of the relations between these two basically antagonistic groups now occupying a common territory. These institutions became systematized over the years into the specific organization of the rule of one social stratum (or emerging social class) over another, or in other words, the early state.

The rather small and inchoate state of Mamprugu around Pusiga, where the first ruler settled according to the legends, was, without any doubt, the first to be developed. A set of similar, but often subjectively interpreted or totally adapted legends and other traditions informs us that the institution of kingship and, in fact, the entire system of the monarchic state, spread in almost all directions throughout the entire Voltaic area. To the north there formed the cluster of no less than about twenty Moose kingdoms, to the south the early states of Dagbong and Nanumba, and to the west the Wa kingdom.

While the genetic relationships between these kingdoms were generally recognized by all of the ruling dynasties in the Voltaic basin, the affinity between them and the remoter states of Grumah, Sansanne-Mango (the Chakossi tribe) and Bariba is doubtful, though by some scholars and contemporary incumbents of the traditional royal offices[2]) (see map of the Voltaic states, p. 478) is still considered true.

Lambert (1907) and, following him, Izard (1975b: 219), and especially Iliasu (1971: 96), mention that the immigrants, after crossing the Niger, came to an halt in the Grumah area (on the Grumah origin of the immigrants see Benzing 1971: 41). Iliasu quotes a Mamprusi tradition according to which Kpogonumbo, a son of Tohazie, the 'red hunter' and leader of the immigrants, married the Grumah princess Sohiyini. This would provide the basis of the claims of the existence of genetic ties between the Voltaic states and of the Grumah state. Benzing (1971: 45), when discussing various historical traditions of the

Dagbamba, also mentions that 'Kpoghnimbu' originated from the Grumah area. According to her records, however, this son of 'Tohazhie' married Sinsabga, the eldest daughter of the earthpriest (*tindana*) of Sogpolse, i.e., that part of the territory which later became part of the state Dagbong.

Prior to the formation of the early states, the Voltaic basin was inhabited by several autochthonous groups, such as the Kurumba or Fulse and the Dogon or Kibse in the north, the Samo or Ninise in the west, and the Gurunse,[3] Konkomba and Gurensi, as well as the Mande tribe of Bisa, in the northern part of the area. All these ethnic groups, except for the Bisa and Samo, spoke related Voltaic or Gur languages. These peoples lived in savanna conditions with a low precipitation and poor soils, on millet and other agricultural products supplemented by the yields of incidental hunting, fishing and animal husbandry. Land was tilled by hoe and manuring was rarely used.

The autochthons of the Voltaic basin, though perhaps not so productive economically (although Yatēnga, for example, produced much of West Africa's iron, thanks to its native blacksmiths), evolved an extremely complex system of world views in their cosmology and religion (cf. Zwernemann 1968, Griaule and Dieterlen 1954), which was in turn reflected in their social organization. As a result, the institution of *sacred chieftainship* emerged among the Kurumba, the southern Gurunse and the Bisa well before the advent of the immigrants. As Schweeger-Hefel and Staude (1972) have shown, the *ayo* of Mengao was a veritable, dynastically vested, religio-political authority whose office possessed some elements of effective executive power and who was surrounded by a simple court structure.

The Kurumba of Lurum had their own mythical charter explaining how the chief's clan of Konfé had managed to reorganize the 'world', so that it was entitled to rule over the native clan of Sawadugu. This made for religio-political dualism (male having the ascendancy over female; heaven over earth; and the Konfé, descending from heaven, over the Sawadugu, who are the earthpriests or *asendesa*). The Konfé were, in fact, usurpers of the political power (Schweeger-Hefel and Staude 1972: 21–127). In this account one finds an analogy to the later social dualism between autochthons and immigrants in the early Voltaic states.

Moreover, among the Gurunse (Nuna, Kasena) in the southernmost part of modern Upper Volta, the chiefs, called *peo* or *pyo* here and who were surrounded by more or less elaborate courts, were guardians of the *kwara* fetish, a symbol of power. The *peo* again stood in a complementary kind of opposition to the *tega-tu*, or earthpriests (Dittmer 1961). Benzing (1971: 46) suggests that the existence of a hierarchy of earthpriests was preconditioned for the establishment of the kingdom of Dagbong. Kurumba autochthonous chiefs were, in fact, later integrated into the structures of the nearest Voltaic states. All this suggests a comparatively high degree of political complexity and of social organization that is characteristic of the chiefdom which is so typical for incipient state development.

Looking at the economic basis of both the segmentary tribal units and the small religio-political chiefdoms, we see the prerequisites for the emergence of the state organization to be present, without any doubt, in both of them. The autochthons produced enough grain to have a surplus, theoretically and also practically capable of expropriation by a ruling stratum. In fact, the religio-political chiefs of the Kurumba and Gurunse, as well as the earthpriests in all of the autochthonous communities received a portion of this objectively existing surplus either in the form of gifts or as remuneration for their services.

It seems justified to characterize the autochthonous societies of the Voltaic Basin prior to the coming of the immigrants as *rank* type of societies with locally restricted offshoots of the *stratified* type of society (Fried 1967). This has one extremely important implication, it being hardly possible for our purposes to conceive of the original state in the Voltaic area as a conquest state of the classical 'armchair' model (cf. Gumplowicz 1899, Oppenheimer 1909). The immigrants, though mounted and militarily well-equipped, were not numerous at the beginning and did not subdue population groups lacking an adequate degree or readiness for state formation. These invaders constituted only a final catalyst in a process already underway in slow motion. The same view was already held, perhaps less consciously, by Rattray (1932).

2. FORMATIVE PERIOD

The very process of state formation, sometimes rather neutrally called 'political incorporation' (cf. Skinner 1970), in the Voltaic area covered no less than three centuries. The original dichotomic opposition between the immigrant concept of *naam* (power, office) and the autochthonous concept of *tĕnga* (earth, land) most probably reflecting original violent conflicts between the two groups, became transformed with time into a *dual unity*, bolstered by the interconnected ideology and political system (cf. Wilks 1971: 350).

Especially through religious conceptual interpenetration, the two groups merged into one whole, overarched by the common institution of the state, subsequently supported by *post quem* mythical charters relating to the origin of each state in particular and Voltaic statehood in general. The relation between the two groups mutually, and later also between them and other groups (captives, strangers) integrated into the various Voltaic states, gradually became ritualized and thus 'etatized' (cf. Bloch 1974). The actual relation of inequality between the rulers and the ruled was masked by the 'convenient' organization of the state.

A similar process of assimilation took place in the kinship sphere. Generally speaking, consanguineal kinship units (and their genealogies) developed separately in each group. However, more and more matrimonial alliances were formed between immigrants on the one side and autochthons, as well as strangers and even captives on the other. This led to an expansion of the immigrant group, as it was mostly immigrant men who were able to marry girls from other, socially subordinated groups. One legendary tradition held that such alliances between immigrants and autochthons were sanctioned by marriages between immigrant chiefs, or *naam* holders, and daughters of earthpriests. According to some traditions (cf. Tiendrebeogo 1964), the Moogo kingdom was founded subsequent to a request for protection by Guilungu *tēngsoba* (earthpriest) to Naaba Zūngrana. This protectorate was buttressed by a matrimonial union between Zūngrana and the daughter of a local earthpriest, of which the first ruler of Moogo, Naaba Wubri, was born.

It is not always certain, however, whether this opposition immigrants–autochthons, though complementary, was as explicit in all the other Voltaic states. But little is known about this. Only a few legends tell us about the reign of the first Mamprugu ruler Gbewa, who allegedly migrated with his followers from the Grumah area to Pusiga in Mamprugu, where he supposedly settled and from where the expansion of the state began (Iliasu 1971: 96; Tamakloe 1931; Cardinall 1920, 1931; Benzing 1971).

The continuous processes of expansion and fission constitute two sides of the one coin. Those among the immigrants who were unsuccessful in the struggle for power, or who were sent to conquer new territories, might try to establish themselves at a safe distance from the original center of power. They would found their own ruling clans. Those who were definitely unsuccessful in the struggle for *naam* were also no longer recognized as members of the politically relevant kinship groups. The process I call 'commonerization' then began. Thus were founded Dagbong and Tēngkudugo, and later also the Moose states.

As Benzing has shown (cf. also Tamakloe), the initial rise of Dagbong was marked by the violent act of killing the highest earthpriest (priest–chief) in the area, together with a number of other priests of the cult in question, as well as by the introduction of new customs

(1971: 78; Tamakloe 1931: 8, 15–17). In Těngkudugo, according to Kawada, the autochthons played a fairly important role from the beginning of this early state. The ruling Moose and the autochthonous Bisa frequently intermarried and even Těngkudugo chiefs married Bisa women (1970: 39; 1971).

Těngkudugo, founded perhaps by Naaba Wedraogo, the common ancestor of all Moose dynasties, was the source from which sprang the proto-states of the Moose, from which in turn the majority of the early Moose states developed as a result of a process of extinction, fission and division as well as of direct intervention by the central state of Moogo. This took place some five generations after Wedraogo, namely towards the end of the sixteenth century.

Prost (1953), and after him Izard (1970: 217–227), the latter using the results of Kawada's research, have pointed out that the polity from which the Moose (or *Nakombse*) states evolved was not Těngkudugo proper, but more likely the tiny chiefdoms of Zambalga and/or Kinzem. They were to give birth to the small kingdoms of Lalgay and Wargay alongside the larger kingdom of Těngkudugo. The process of state formation is not clear even from the strictly formal viewpoint; in the latter three states there could even have been two or more levels of statehood. The total number of Moose states ever existing exceeds the number as stated for these, by Izard century (1975b: 217).

The agricultural communities, originally composed mostly of autochthonous inhabitants, but gradually acquiring a multi-ethnic and socially stratified character, during the formative period, became 'peasantized', i.e., they became involved in a complicated relationship of dependence on the emerging state organization, in which the immigrants played the dominant role. These communities, developing within such varied types of settlement structures as compounds, quarters and villages, comprised the majority of the population of each respective Voltaic state. All groups, whether autochthons, immigrants, captives or strangers, depended on agriculture as the source of their livelihood, irrespective of the specialization of the individual groups in politics, handicrafts, trade or religion. Most settlements became mixed, containing inhabitants from at least two different Voltaic population groups. Only a few communities remained ethnically and socially homogeneous.

As shown in detail by Kawada, the village of Yargo in the Moogo kingdom was composed of both *těngbiise* (autochthons) and *yarse* (Mande traders) compounds, though Yargo men were provided with women by different social groups, such as the *nakombse* (nobility), *nyonyose* (autochthons of Samo origin), *silmimoose* (descendants of Moose–Fulbe unions), *nayiridamba* (court servants of either commoner or captive origin), *bendre* (court drummers, chroniclers or keepers of genealogies, of captive origin) and *saaba* (autochthonous blacksmiths). The same sort of situation prevailed in the predominantly *nakombse* village of Tanlili, which also comprised three *zaka* (compounds) of *tēngbiise*, the two social groups practicing intermarriage (1967: 38, 56, 65). Although Kawada's data are recent, they still reflect the confrontation between different ethnic, professional and other groups within the developing state society in the Voltaic basin.

A typical political process during the formative period was, besides separation, the delegation of power within more or less established states. The latter reflected the endeavor of the ruling group to extend its power all over the territory of the new state. For example, members of immigrant clans, or *buudu*, in the Moose kingdoms were often sent from the center of power to the outlying districts to govern particular villages, or *tense*. On the one hand, this process made it possible for the power to remain within the ruling group, while, on the other, it was responsible for the crystallization of the division between the *nakombse* or Moose nobility and the *talse* or Moose commoners.

As Benzing (1971: 246–247) has explained very clearly with regard to Dagbong, only sons of chiefs could attain to political offices. Those who were unsuccessful in the competition for higher political office inevitably sank to the social substratum of commoners, who could only aspire to court offices or some offices connected with the military chiefs. This process of 'commonerization' was most intensive during the formative period, though it could occur later, too.

The noble clan of each state gradually split up into various subclans, each of which evolved its own claims to particular village chieftainships. Only the members of one of these subclans, namely the royal lineage, retained the right to select the ruler from among themselves. Even so, only comparatively few members of the nobility were able to secure political offices. Those who failed to do so or lost the patience to await their opportunity attempted to set themselves up as chiefs without the consent of the rulers. However, the majority of the nominal nobles 'waited'.

It was a typical phenomenon of the centuries immediately following the emergence of the Voltaic kingdoms that the nobles without office lived by constant raiding and pillaging. They were poor warriors, with their horses (their status symbol *par excellence*) and spears as sole possessions. Their interest was focused exclusively on organizing successful raids on autochthonous villages or stateless peoples outside in order to amass enough wealth for distribution among potential followers, which could then help them to attain their ultimate goal — acquisition of the office of village chief. Yatēnga Moose maxims say aptly: *nakombse* renounced their claims to the *naam* only seven days after their death; a *nakombga* who did not give could not become chief.

It is extremely likely that only few coercive means of economic exploitation were evolved during the formative period. The rulers had first and foremost to strengthen their position *vis-à-vis* other members (potential pretenders to the *naam*, including the highest office) of the royal lineage. Most probably in the remoter past the competition for and the potential rights and claims to high office on the part of different groups of the nobility were broader and more open than later.

For the sake of balance of power they would surround themselves with courtiers and servants of both commoner and captive origin. These specialists saw to the collection of revenues for the rulers in the form of either informal gifts as a token of allegiance or quasi-tribute from nearby communities. However, these revenues were not so much utilized for consumption as towards the political end of gaining a following. The daily material needs of the ruler and the officials of his court, none of whom, as a rule, participated in the productive process, could be easily met through the labor of their numerous wives and children living in their respective compounds in the principal village. These women, who were often of autochthonous origin, tilled the private lands of their title-holding husbands and, together with their children, were usually able to produce a sufficient quantity of millet and vegetables for the needs of the entire court population.

There were, in fact, no true capitals in this formative period. The ruler and his court had to be almost constantly on the move in order to be able to keep a check on the village chiefs and the officeless nobility. Practically every ruler chose a different site for his more or less permanent residence. The graves of all of the early rulers are scattered throughout the territories of the Voltaic states.

This was also one of the reasons why the economic system could not be effectively based on the exploitation of agricultural communities in this period. The latter still remained fairly independent economically, perhaps the only effective means of exploitation being 'booty production' (Goody 1971) on the part of the officeless nobility. It is likewise hardly possible that a universal state-wide judicial system evolved in this formative period. It was mainly in the *ideological* sphere (religion) that a really functioning supra-local unity evolved. Of course it was among other things the noble immigrants' *ad hoc* military system that stimulated the relatively rapid integration of different population groups into a particular social unit which was kept together by the institution of the state.

3. VOLTAIC STATES IN THE NINETEENTH CENTURY

Around the middle of the eighteenth century certain new developments began to influence the development of almost all the larger

Voltaic states. The change in question was due to a considerable strengthening of the royal power under the Moogo Naaba Warga, the Yatēnga Naaba Kāngo, and Ya Naa Zanguina in Dagbong and Na Yiri Atabia in Mamprugu.[4] Thus in Moogo and Yatēnga the 'dark age' of intestine strife between various pretenders to high office, supported by different groupings of nobles, came to an end, and new, more bureaucratic, structures began to come into operation. Warga and Kāngo made Wogodogo (Ouagadougou) and Waiguyo (Ouahigouya) more or less stable capitals of Moogo and Yatēnga respectively.

Dagbong happened at that time to come under pressure from the expanding Gonja state and the powerful Asante kingdom. Dagbong's subsequent dependence on Asante gave rise to the internal reorganization of this kingdom, which in fact strengthened centralist tendencies.

Least affected appeared to be Mamprugu, which was rather small and thus easier to govern. Mamprugu was not very vulnerable to external dangers, as it was surrounded on all sides by either affiliated Voltaic states or stateless other peoples. Mamprugu state therefore constituted perhaps, along with Tēngkudugo, the most inchoate example among the five larger Voltaic states.[5]

The reasons for these profound changes were various. Internal political stabilization on the one hand and the necessity to effectively face up to external political threats on the other were certainly not the only essential factors. The slow penetration of Islam might play also a role (Skinner 1966; Levtzion 1968). However, we know more about the *effects* than the causes of this most important transformation, which marked the beginning of a qualitatively new, much more developed phase of West African statehood. Future research may broaden the interpretative framework considerably.

The population of each Voltaic state in this period may be classified into four basic groups, viz.: (1) autochthonous agriculturalists and blacksmiths; (2) immigrants; (3) captives; (4) strangers. Not universally present was the category of offspring of mixed marriages between immigrants and the Fulbe. The Fulbe themselves, though engaged in cattle-grazing in the territories of the northernmost Voltaic states and involved in a symbiotic economic relationship with the sedentary population, did not come under the sovereignty of these states. The exact ratio between these four groups is not known for the pre-colonial period. It is certain, however, that by the nineteenth century the number of descendants of immigrants had risen so steeply (through marriages) that the autochthons had become a minority. For Yatēnga, for example, Izard states that 'the Mossi are more numerous than the *tēngbiisi*, contrary to the expected tendency, whereby the descendants of the conquerors would form a minority dominating over a majority of the autochthons' (1975b: 221). Captives and strangers were numerically much weaker than the former two groups, but their importance

Map 1. The early states in the Voltaic basin. After Izard (1970) and Benzing (1971)

for the state system was enormous as will be shown below. In Waiguyo, the capital of Yatēnga, captives formed the numerically strongest population group (Izard 1975b: 222).

All four groups alike were formally subjects of the state. However, their relation to the *naam* or political power and/or office varied quite widely; some having access to it, either *de jure* or *de facto*, and others lacking such access. Consequently, the disposal of economic resources and the eligibility for religious functions were also differential. The ever-growing group of original immigrants, which identified itself with the respective states of the point of name, (e.g., Moose, Mamprusi, Dagbamba), split into two rather antagonistic social groups, viz.:

(1) Noble clans which were *de jure* holders of, or pretenders to, the *naam* (*nakombse* in the Moose kingdoms, *nabiisi* in Mamprugu, and *yan'naa bihe* in Dagbong).

(2) Commoners, i.e., those who were unsuccessful in the struggle for the *naam* (*zemba* or *talse* in the Moose states, *tarima* in Mamprugu and *dagban daba* in Dagbong).

Commoners, like the captives, had access to few of the lowest political offices, such as that of village chief, who had the title of 'war chief'. But they fulfilled mostly administrative functions at the royal courts or courts of village chiefs. Some of these functions, especially those of the more important war chiefs and higher royal servants, were quite crucial as far as the state as a whole was concerned and as such incorporated much of the *de facto* or achieved *naam*.

The autochthons also sometimes had access to the lowest offices. *De jure*, however, they could only be *kasemdamba* or administrators of villages. In Mamprugu, according to Drucker-Brown (1975: 88), there were four crucial appointed from among the earthpriests. Such *priest-chiefs*, called *buguba*, existed also in Yatēnga, alongside the abovementioned pre-state chiefs of the Kurumba (Izard 1975b: 224). Though the earthpriests were occupied mainly with their religious cult, without their blessing no *naam*-holder could rule. According to Izard: personal communication, a considerable portion of the earthpriests in Yatēnga at least was of Moose, i.e. immigrant, origin, This so far unknown fact broadens dramatically immigrants' social field. It is, unfortunately, not clear in which period of the Yatēnga statehood this transformation of certain Moose immigrant kin groups into earthpriests occured.

The strangers were of a different stock being of Mande, Ashanti, Songai or Hausa origin, and were mostly specialized in crafts or other professions. Besides various types of craftsmen, they included traders, armorers, warriors, and Muslim councillors at chiefs' courts (cf. Levtzion 1968). Most strangers were subordinated to the royal councillors or other senior state administrative officials.

Now, this brings us to a more dynamic picture of the structure and functioning of the nineteenth-century Voltaic states, Our special attention should go to the mechanism of the state, which was so syncretic, and the political, economic, ideological and kinship spheres so interwoven, that none of these can be treated as a separate entity.

By the nineteenth century the early states in the Voltaic basin had developed into rather elaborate organizations for the regulation of complicated and syncretic relations between population groups, social substrata, as well as larger social strata or emergent social classes. The division into emergent classes, in fact, cut across all four population groups. If we look at the relative statuses of specific social groups within a particular state in broader *politico-economic terms*, and not only from the point of view of eligibility for political offices and functions, we are able to distinguish two basic social strata or emergent social classes.[6]

Thus we may differentiate between the emergent social class of the rulers or *tribute recipients* and that of the *ruled* or *tribute producers*. These two emergent classes stood in complementary opposition to each other, marked by economic exploitation elaborately disguised by religious integration and political protection.

Within the emergent class of the rulers we may distinguish about seven substrata roughly graded here on the following hierarchical scale: (1) royalty; (2) nobility (both with offices and without them): (3) administrative functionaries; (4) non-noble village chiefs; (5) priest–chiefs, autochthonous chiefs and earthpriests; (6) administrators of servant villages; (7) representatives of strangers. The members of the emergent social class of tribute recipients did not participate in productive activities. All of them were occupied in the exercise of their state functions. However, sometimes their wives, children and perhaps their closest client-servants worked their fields or in their households, thus sharing some of the privileges of their 'masters'.

The first four substrata were the actual holders of *naam* or political power in each kingdom. They held it either legitimately, or *de jure* (first and second substrata), or *de facto* (third and fourth substrata). All of these substrata, though mutually differentiated, of course stood in the most advantageous and independent relation to all the other social groups within the state. The members of the emergent class of the rulers (tribute recipients) as a whole stood in *objective* opposition to the subordinated and dependent emergent class of the ruled (tribute producers) although this opposition was often disguised by mutual interdependence in ritual or political activities. The eligibility for political and administrative functions, supported by the religious ideology further served as a permanent basis of economic inequality.

Subjectively the people in early Voltaic states did not find anything unnormal in their social order, and, of course, they were but little or not at all aware of their class appurtenance (class consciousness).

The emergent class of the ruled or tribute producers comprised the following substrata: (1) officeless autochthons; (2) officeless immigrants; (3) officeless captives and servants; (4) most strangers. The first two groups represented the bulk of the population in the Voltaic

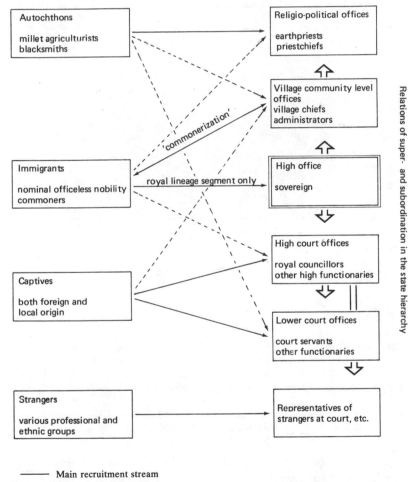

POPULATION GROUPS   OFFICES *

Autochthons / millet agriculturists / blacksmiths

Religio-political offices / earthpriests / priestchiefs

Village community level offices / village chiefs / administrators

'commonerization'

Immigrants / nominal officeless nobility / commoners

royal lineage segment only

High office / sovereign

Captives / both foreign and local origin

High court offices / royal councillors / other high functionaries

Lower court offices / court servants / other functionaries

Strangers / various professional and ethnic groups

Representatives of strangers at court, etc.

Relations of super- and subordination in the state hierarchy

———— Main recruitment stream
----- Side recruitment stream

* no distinction is made between offices of *de jure* and *de facto* power holders

Figure 1. Recruitment of the office in the early states of the Voltaic basin.

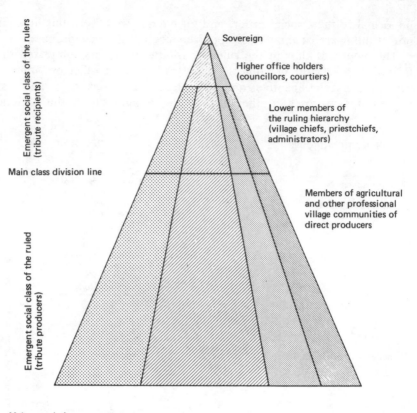

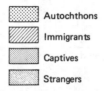

Main population groups

- Autochthons
- Immigrants
- Captives
- Strangers

Figure 2. Social division in the early states of the Voltaic basin (basis scheme)

Note: Due to schematic representation of the social division in the Voltaic states in this table, the proportions of the graph reflect only very approximatively the quantitative sizes of the division.

kingdoms. There was practically very little social mobility possible between the two emergent classes. Nor was mobility between the different categories (substrata) within one class conceivable. By the nineteenth century the relations between all the substrata, as also between the two emergent classes, had become so stabilized that only a few shifts could occur.

The foregoing figures schematically represent the population structure and eligibility for various kinds of office in the early Voltaic states.
Recruitment should not be considered as being synonymous with social
mobility, but should be viewed as a process whereby a particular
population group supplies recruits for a specific kind of office. An
attempt is made at the same time to delineate the division into
emergent social classes graphically seen as a pyramidal hierarchy.

Although there was cetainly *no private ownership of land* as the basic
means of production in the early Voltaic states, it is possible to speak
of exclusive *private appropriation rights of the sovereigns and chiefs to
the products of the land,* including minerals or any lost property. The
officeless nobility, as only potential members of the ruling class,
however, had to maintain itself not with regular tribute but mainly with
booty 'products'. It should be emphasized once again that in the
nineteenth century as well, all, or virtually all, economic wealth,
especially that appropriated via redistributive (exploitation) from direct
producers, was utilized by the title-holders or potential title-holders,
either for gaining or for retaining a political following and thus the
office in question itself. The way to *naam* was paved with gift-giving of
all kinds as also with services and with other forms of reciprocation
between candidates mutually and between them and their followers
and electors, phenomena which in the eyes of a modern lay observer
are not very different from bribery. Politics (together with ideology)
serves as both infrastructure and superstructure; it has the function of
relations of production (cf. Godelier 1976).

Another source of revenue in the Voltaic states (in fact, for their
emergent ruling class), was provided by trade and markets. The Yarse,
a Mande ethnic group settled among the Moose, and the Hausa, living
as subjects in Dagbong and Mamprusi, were able traders throughout
the whole of western Africa. They, for the greater part, linked up the
north, the Inland Niger Delta, with the forested south. They imported
kola nuts from the south and horses and salt from the north. Yatēnga
exported iron, Wogodogo eunuchs and domestic slaves. The Yarse also
traded in cotton (which they themselves cultivated and processed) and
various foodstuffs and spices. Every caravan passing through the
Voltaic states had to pay a toll in the form of gifts to both local chiefs
and rulers. Each chief had special court officials engaged in tax and
tribute collecting. There are unfortunately no statistics available concerning the volume of trade passing through the Voltaic basin, nor
concerning the share of the proceeds from trade in the total state
income. It is not possible to think about the early Voltaic states as
organizers of the interregional trade as was the case with some larger
Sudanese kingdoms. Markets held in larger localities were a regular
event for both local agricultural surplus producers (mostly women) and

specialized wholesale merchants. In market transactions cowries were used as currency, besides livestock or other forms of payment in kind. Each merchant had to pay market dues to a state tax official (Skinner 1962; Zahan 1954; Izard 1971).

With regard to the political system in the early Voltaic states of the nineteenth century, it is apparent even from the data given above that there was a clear-cut difference between hereditary offices belonging to particular families and those which could be secured through competition between members of certain lineages only. It seems reasonable and useful, therefore, to distinguish between the 'party-political' and the administrative sectors (cf. Smith 1956, 1960) of the political system in different Voltaic states.

The *naam* or political power was the *Alpha and Omega* of all public life in the early Voltaic states. Here, in the *'party-political'* struggle for *naam*, more than in the economic sphere, should we look for the basis of civilized social forms in the Voltaic basin, i.e., early states. The pursuit of *naam* was *de jure* the exclusive privilege of the immigrant nobility. But *de facto* also immigrant commoners, captives, and perhaps in rare cases priest–chiefs could attain to power as holders of the lower office or administrative function on village level. The administrative officials (servants, councillors) who also wielded *de facto* power, will be discussed below.

Every *de jure* political office was sought for amid tough competition and even armed conflict between the various pretenders and their followers. The higher the office, the stiffer the competition. Those who were unsuccessful in the competition for *naam* sank to the commoner substratum. If meta-economic prestations ('bribery') were insufficient to bring about success in the political competition, then physical force was the only alternative. Though it was against the norms to use *pãnga* or force for other purposes within the polity, it was permitted in the struggle for *naam*.

Succession was never restricted to only one person. Usually the right to a specific title or office was vested in a particular consanguineal kinship group, and not in some limited family. The right of primogeniture did not necessarily apply. None of the candidates was supposed to aspire to a rank higher than that of his 'father', i.e., head of his kinship group. Attempts to restrict the competition for high office to a limited number of lineages (or only a single lineage) — 'parties' of descendants of certain sovereigns — succeeded only in Yatênga, and then not until the end of the nineteenth century, but never in Moogo or Dagbong (cf. Skalník 1975; Staniland 1975). In broad terms, adelphic succession alternated with filial in the concrete cases of competition for high office. No strict rule of succession was ever evolved in any of the early Voltaic states. If a rotational system was agreed upon, as in the case of the 'gate' chieftainship in Dagbong, this rarely worked smoothly. An important role was played in connection with the succession by the royal court officials, royal women and war chiefs. All these people were excluded from high office by custom. Therefore they had a major say in the selection and ritual appointment and installation of a new sovereign.

After a sovereign died only the highest official, the deceased's closest relatives, and the principal war chief were notified. Only after an army had been raised for keeping order was the death announced, and the whole country

> was plunged into an interregnum, which was characterized by ritual and often by actual anarchy. The people in the towns immediately looted the markets and stole their neighbour's goods; the prisoners and captives in stocks were released by their guards; the nakomce in all the territories, district, and villages subjected the local populations to robbery and pillage; and the members of the monarch's babissi began their intrigues for power (Skinner 1964: 50).

The sovereign's eldest daughter would put on the deceased sovereign's garments, formally assuming his power until a new sovereign had been elected. This was also aimed at preventing a usurpation of power. The new sovereign was appointed (formally elected) by a closed college composed of some of the most prominent officials of the state administration, after all pretenders to power had presented their respective gifts. The successful candidate was summoned in secret and announced only after preparations for the installation ceremony had begun. The entire procedure lasted several days. After the new sovereign had been installed in a complicated ceremony in the royal courtyard during which he donned new raiment, pronounced his three main guiding principles, imbibed a sacred potion ('eating the *naam*'), etc., he would visit several quarters of the capital in order to receive the homage of the earthpriests and village chiefs gathered together here especially for the installation. In Mamprugu and Dagbong the new ruler was 'enskinned', i.e., made to sit on a skin as a symbol of royal power (inthronization) (Skinner 1964: 36–40; Drucker-Brown 1975).

The royal office was without any doubt an expression of the supreme sovereign power within each early Voltaic state. This office as a rule combined several sources of power, which in the concrete case of Yatênga (as in other Voltaic states) were reflected in the three titles: *naaba*, 'chief', *rima* 'king', and *pângasoba*, 'master of force'. The first and third of these titles refer to the relations of power and coercive force respectively. The second title was the most important, however, for it referred to the interdependence between immigrants and autochthons, thus symbolizing a sort of *politico-ritual pact* between the two groups. This pact was renewed each time a new sovereign went on his official installation tour, called *ringu*, during which he visited the most important places of the earth cult and asked the principal earthpriests for formal recognition and their official blessing. After his recognition has been confirmed by a series of rites, such an elected Yatēnga *naaba* would then become a *rima* or true king. As a *rima* he had a right to a king's burial, and his sons could become *rimbilo* or effective, *de jure*, pretenders to high office (cf. Izard 1975b: 231–232, 234). The sovereign himself thus became a sacred personage, isolated from the masses and believed to act with the cooperation of the deities either via the earthpriests or directly. In this sense the king's office was a syncretic political and religious function. As such, the sovereign also stood at the top of the pyramid of economic tributary relations. Through the village chiefs and courtiers he received his share of the tributary gifts.

The royal capitals were more permanent in the nineteenth century Voltaic states. Although there were in most kingdoms at least several residencies and old (sacred) capitals, the population of the current capital generally rose, thanks to the presence of captives and other dependent (client) groups here. The capital did not include many craftsmen or other specialists. In the case of Mamprugu, there was an official capital at Nalerigu and a commercial and craft center at nearby Gambaga, where Muslims also resided. In Yatēnga, the capital of Waiguyo comprised only the court, divided into several sections according to the number of top courtiers. Waiguyo consisted of two halves: Moose and Bīngo. Moose, inhabited by immigrants only, was further divided into Toogē, Balongo and Werāse, in accordance with the number of the councillors of the Yatēnga Naaba. Bīngo, the quarter of the captives, was administered by a Rasamba Naaba, a special captive chief (Izard 1971: 234).

In the villages, the courts of village chiefs were smaller replicas of the ruler's court. Likewise all ceremonies, including the appointment and installation of the village chief's successor, were conducted in the same manner as in the center of state power. However, the actual decision as to who was going to assume the village chief's office was taken in the capital, by the ruler and his closest councillors (cf. Skinner 1964: 52–59).

Foreign policy was not very important in the Voltaic states. The army, mobilized in only rare exceptions by the war chiefs (recruited from among commoner or captive families), rarely had to take action in conflicts with non-Voltaic states or stateless peoples. Though relations between the four larger of the culturally related Voltaic states might sometimes be frequent, it was rather uncommon that an armed force should be used in likely conflicts between them. Ruling hierarchies in these states believed in a common royal ancestry, and this very 'fact' prevented them from waging wars against one another. Armed conflicts were common only in areas of disputed sovereignty, as was the case between some of the Moose states. There the larger states never recognized the independence of some smaller ones.

The only real danger threatened from the south and southwest, where the kingdoms of Gonja and Asante emerged as major powers. Dagbong happened to be in a relationship of vassalage to Asante, but did not very much influence its internal order. The army of Dagbong even became more efficient and better-organized as a result of Ashanti aid. The obligation to pay an annual tax in slaves to Asante compelled Dagbong to improve its state organization, which resulted in a more radical social stratification.

Armies in the Voltaic states might much more often be used as a potential or real means of coercion in internal political struggles. The state, represented by the courtiers and war chief(s), would keep the society in a state of equilibrium in times of uncertainty, including interregnal periods by exerting its privilege of using force simply through threats of army intervention. The army was not a standing one, although, especially the cavalry, the famous striking force of the Moose kingdoms, could very easily be put in readiness. It was composed exclusively of members of the nobility, which possessed the exclusive right to own horses. Commoners and captives could only be infantrymen. The army was maintained with the aid of the tributary gifts received by the ruler and other chiefs from the peasant majority of the population in each early Voltaic state.

The structure of the state administration in the Voltaic kingdoms comprised only two levels. In this sense the territorial division was simple. The kingdom was divided only into villages and not, as some authors, including Skinner (1964) and Hammond (1966), have asserted into districts and provinces as well. Benzing (1971: 234) speaks of four provinces of Dagbong, each comprising a certain number of districts. However, this may be correct for Dagbong, but it is hardly so for the other Voltaic states. Izard remarks that the division into cantons (districts) and provinces was introduced only during the colonial period (1975b: 229).

Each village — in point of fact a community of lineage segments under the authority of a chief and an earthpriest (cf. Izard 1975b: 224–225) — was an autonomous unit, subordinated to a higher official of the royal court or directly to the ruler. The latter directly controlled the servant villages located around the *natênse* or royal residences on so-called royal lands. Their products were distributed to servants and visitors in order to secure a political following. The ruler did not need the products of these lands for his own maintenance, as he had his own personal compound.

Wealth constituted for the ruler no more than a sort of status symbol. Whatever he received was in the form of gifts or customary tribute in kind. As Izard has put it for Yatēnga:

As the king possesses everything, he need not possess anything, and his palace is only a ritual place through which compulsorily pass women, services, goods [1975b: 236, my translation — P.S.].

In Yatēnga, and perhaps also in the other Voltaic kingdoms, the king's wealth further consisted of a herd of cattle and horses which was by far the largest in the kingdom. A special group of captives was in charge of this herd, which was constantly augmented through raids by officeless nobles or vassal Fulbe, who had to present the ruler with gifts of cattle or horses (Izard 1975b: 237).

By the nineteenth century the process of bureaucratization of the early Voltaic states had advanced considerably. The ruler's court was quite elaborate and almost every official had several tasks. There was a certain hierarchy among the courtiers and servants. At each court there were special courtiers whose task it was to record the royal genealogies. Interestingly enough, no ruler in the history of the Voltaic states was omitted from the genealogies as a member of the royal lineage. Even if a usurper seized the power, as was the case in Dagbong during the formative period, he was subsequently tacitly incorporated into the royal genealogy (cf. Benzing 1971: 109–113).

The office-holders at both royal and village courts, like all the servants subordinated to them, had no genetic relationship, real or fictious, with the ruler or the nobility. The office-holders, i.e., the higher courtiers or councillors, occupied a key position in the power structure, as they surrounded the ruler or chief, exerted influence upon him, and protected him against other pretenders to power. They were, as was said above, the holders of *de facto* power.

Although there are indications that centralization was considerable in the early Voltaic states, the effectiveness of this centralization is doubtful. Though the population density here was higher than among the neighboring stateless peoples, there are no apparent signs of any real population pressure that would have influenced the functioning of the state organization. Nor was agricultural land scarce.

Communications were slow and poor. The greater the distance from the center of power, the greater the chance of success of any likely separatist movements. There was no maintenance of paths, roads or bridges, and no central organization by the state of major works. No system of messengers existed.

The legal process was only formally centralized. So the people of, e.g., Moogo believed that 'the truth is at Ouagadougou' (Skinner 1964: 90). The law in the Voltaic states was a customary and unwritten one. No laws were ever formulated or promulgated. Village communities themselves dealt with most minor cases through their elders. Hammond (1966: 144–146) argues that even cases of murder, provided it had been committed within a particular kin group, were tried by the latter's council of elders. He concludes that 'most problems related to the maintenance of social cohesion among the Mossi can be dealt with without recourse to the political system' (1966: 144). Skinner, on the other hand, has demonstrated that most local (in his phrasing, village and district) chiefs adjudicated various cases in the name of the state. These lower chiefs even used to sentence criminals to death, in spite of the fact that it was the ruler's prerogative to pronounce death sentences. This was, nonetheless, tolerated, unless the lower chiefs were challenging the power of the center of the kingdom.

Appeal to the ruler was possible, although this was not common, and village chiefs usually put pressure on the litigants to forgo appeal. Among the most heinous crimes were murder, arson, abduction, witchcraft and, more particularly, lese majesty (especially adultery with a chief's wife). Even a thief or rapist if detected on the spot, might be put to death; but usually no action on the part of the state system followed here (Skinner 1964: 79–81; Hammond 1966: 144–146).

Cases of treason and lese-majesty were uncommon, but if committed at all they were all the more severely punished. A special form of punishment for crimes of this type was compulsory suicide by a poisoned arrow. Nobles were adjudicated differently from commoners or other categories. If a noble committed a major crime, such as treason (e.g., rebellion) or lese majesty, he was usually executed by strangulation — noble blood was not supposed to be shed — and only on the verdict of the ruler himself. If he wished to avoid execution or suicide by poison, there was only one possibility — to flee from the center of power and try to set himself up independently in an area far enough from the capital. Nobles guilty of pillage within the territory of which they were residents were not considered criminals, and their actions were not qualified as crimes (Skinner 1964: 86–91).

There were some differences in administrative structure and functioning between such larger states as Yatēnga or Moogo, and the smaller Moose states or Mamprugu. The latter were much easier to govern. It seems reasonable to suppose that the type of administration evolved in the states of the Voltaic basin was much more 'suited' to the medium-sized states, such as Mamprugu or Tēngkudugo, than to the larger structures of Moogo, Yatēnga or Dagbong. In Mamprugu, contacts between important villages posed no problems. At the same time, as far as we know, separatist tendencies were rare or nonexistent there. The ritual aspect of kingship was perhaps more developed in Mamprugu than in the larger kingdoms. It likewise seems to have been more original and more efficient (cf. Drucker-Brown 1975). In the larger kingdoms religious beliefs and rites were overtly abused to suit the ends of the emergent ruling class, and they thus helped to unbalance the entire state organization.

4. CONCLUSIONS

The larger Voltaic states of Dagbong, Moogo and Yatěnga represented the climax of the development of the early state in the Voltaic basin. They can be compared to other larger early African states which strove for power over large areas and population groups. The problem lies in the discrepancy between the formal elaborateness (cf. Kabore's idealization of the Moose political system, 1962, 1966) and the actual functioning of these states. The considerable general neglect of technology and the economic system, together with the emphasis on internal political competition and prestige considerations, caused these states to be quite unprepared to deal with disintegrative forces from outside, either from African neighbors such as the Asante or from overseas.

Moreover, the method of administration and the way of regulating the succession prevented a smooth functioning of the state mechanism in the larger states. They were comparatively weak, while the medium-sized states, as indicated above, seem to have been more stable, at least internally. All early Voltaic states constituted closed systems: all turned in on themselves.

However that may be, the political and ideological (ritual) powers were inextricably intertwined in these states. The economic life, though essential for the material existence of every state, played only a secondary role here: it was realized through politics and ideology which played the role of relations of production.

The well-known adaptability and elasticity of the early Voltaic states was an outcome of their weakness. It was quite easy for the ruling political elite to give up both economic and administrative activities in favour of a foreign power in order to keep intact the 'party-political', ritual and kinship systems as aspects of the functioning of the state. These aspects, though objectively seeming more formal and less essential for the survival of the state, were subjectively considered, by those who identified themselves with the state organization and ruled in the early state, prerequisite for the preservation of the identity of their traditional polity. What was most highly valued by the emergent ruling class of the early Voltaic state seemed less important in the eyes of the Asante and European colonialists.

In conclusion, it may be suggested that the early states in the Voltaic basin were characterized predominantly by their politico-religious profile. Their structure was segmentary, both within each state individually and from the point of view of the supra-state 'cultural' unity of the Moose states and, finally, the Voltaic states collectively. The claims of an imperial type of sovereignty of the larger Voltaic states are not justified. The character of these states, both as regards the internal and the external balance of power, prevented them from overcoming the tendencies towards pluralism.

In reality, the entire cluster of the early Voltaic states displayed a variety of relations, ranging from the complete independence to the semi-independence of each individual state and principality. This pattern of multiple forms of early statehood continued endogenously in greater or lesser isolation from the outer world for centuries.

FOOTNOTES

[1] This essay could not have been written without the help of my friends in different countries who sent me most of the literature unavailable in Czechoslovak libraries. My most sincere thanks are due to Michel Izard of the Laboratoire d'anthropologie sociale du Collège de France et l'Ecole des Hautes Etudes en Sciences Sociales, in Paris, who willingly read all the drafts and commented on them in detail. The responsibility for the views expressed in this essay is, of course, entirely mine.

[2] The idea of a common Voltaic ecological and historico-cultural background (cf. Colloque 1967) is supported by the belief in the common origin of the ruling dynasties of all of the monarchies. This belief is also reflected in the use of kinship terms with reference to the different sovereigns and states; e.g., the Mamprusi people and their sovereign, when referring to the other Voltaic states, considered themselves as grandparents in relation to these, and called them 'grandchildren'. Again, between other Voltaic states a parent–child relation existed, the relevant terms being used by them, and especially the sovereigns, with reference to each other here, too.

[3] Gurunse (Gurunsi) is a relative term, used by the Yatênga Moose to refer to the Moogo Moose, who in turn applied the name Gurunse to the Lela, Kasena and Nuna of the southwest of the Voltaic basin. We use the term Gurunse to refer to the latter.

[4] Though the Voltaic or Gur languages are mutually very closely related, there are of course some differences in their respective vocabularies. So if we are mentioning all four variants of the word for 'sovereign' here, it is impossible for us to do so by means of all the relevant Voltaic terms introduced in the present essay. Therefore general sociological terms are preferred, local terms being used only where this seems apt.

[5] Unfortunately, Kawada's work on Têngkudugo has not yet been published, which makes it difficult to form a more reliable judgement on the character of this early state. I had only a limited opportunity to consult his manuscript.

[6] I have seen fit to introduce the term *social class* here with the reservation that it is not dogmatically defined and understood solely in terms of property relations (private ownership of the means of production). With reference to a situation in pre-capitalist Africa where there was no private ownership of the means of production (namely land), a 'capitalistically' biased definition of class is inappropriate. Due to the fact that class formation was far from being completed in the Voltaic states, I utilize the adjective 'emergent' in usage of the term 'social class'.

[7] In introducing the term 'tributary gift' I wish to underline the semi-voluntary character of tribute payment in the early Voltaic states. The tributary nature of the economic relations seems to be one of the most common features of early states in general.

REFERENCES

Benzing, Brigitta (1971), *Die Geschichte und das Herrschaftssystem der Dagomba*. Meisenheim: Anton Heim.

Bloch, Maurice (1974), 'Symbols, song, dance, and features of articulation: is religion an extreme form of traditional authority', in: *European Journal of Sociology*, XV: 55–81.

Cardinall, A. W. (1920), *The natives of the Northern Territories of the Gold Coast*. London: Routledge.

— (1931), *Tales told in Togoland*. London: International Institute of African Cultures.

Colloque (1967), *Colloque sur les cultures voltaïques*. Recherches Voltaïques 8. Paris–Ouagadougou: CNRS–CVRS.

Delafosse, Maurice (1912), *Haut-Sénégal–Niger*. Paris: Larose.

Delobsom, Dim (1928), Le Morho Naba et sa cour. *Bulletin du CEHS*, 11: 386–421.

— (1932), *L'empire du Mogho-Naba. Coutumes des Mossi de la Haute-Volta*. Paris: Domat-Montchrestien.

Dittmer, Kunz (1961), *Die sakrale Häuptlinge der Gurunsi im Obervoltagebiet*. Hamburg: De Gruyter.

Drucker-Brown, Susan (1975), *Ritual aspects of the Mamprusi kingship*. Leiden–Cambridge: Afrika-Studiecentrum–African Studies Centre.

Fage, John D. (1964), 'Reflections on the early history of the Mossi-Dagomba group of states', in: *The historian in tropical Africa*, ed. by J. Vansina, L. V. Thomas and R. Mauny, pp. 177–192. London: Oxford University Press.

Fried, Morton (1967), *The evolution of political society*. New York: Random House.

Godelier, Maurice (1976), 'Le marxisme dans les sciences humaines', in: *Raison présente* 37: 65–77.

Goody, Jack (1971), *Technology, tradition, and the state in Africa*. London: Oxford University Press.

Griaule, M. and Dieterlen, G. (1954), 'The Dogon', in: *African worlds*, ed. by Daryll Forde, pp. 83–110. London: International African Institute.

Gumplowicz, Ludwig (1899), *The outlines of sociology*. Philadelphia: American Academy of Political and Social Science.

Hammond, Peter B. (1966), *Yatenga. Technology in the culture of a West African kingdom*. New York: The Free Press. London: Collier–Macmillan.

Iliasu, A. A. (1971), The origins of the Mossi-Dagomba states, in: *Research Review*: 95–113.

Izard, Michel (1970), *Introduction à l'histoire des royaumes mossi*, Recherches voltaïques 12, 13. Paris–Ouagadougou: CNRS–CVRS.

— (1971), 'Les Yarsé et le commerce dans le Yatenga pré-colonial', in: *The development of indigenous trade and markets in West Africa*, ed. by Claude Meillassoux, pp. 214–227. London: Oxford University Press.

— (1973a), 'Remarques sur le vocabulaire politique mossi', in: *L'Homme* 13(1-2): 193–206.

— (1973b), 'La lance et les guénilles', in: *L'Homme* 13(3): 139–149.

— (1975a), 'Les captives royaux dans l'ancien Yatenga', in: *L'esclavage en Afrique noire*, ed. by Claude Meillassoux, pp. 281–296. Paris: Maspero.

— (1975b), 'Le royaume du Yatenga', in: *Elements d'ethnologie*, ed. by Robert Cresswell, vol. I: 216–248. Paris: Armand Colin.

Kabore, Gomkoudougou V. (1962), 'Caractère féodal' du système politique mossi', in: *Cahiers d'Etudes Africaines*, 8; 609–623.

— (1966), *Organisation politique traditionnelle et évolution politique des Mossi de Ouagadougou.* Recherches voltaïques 5. Paris–Ouagadougou: CNRS–CVRS.

Kawada, Junzo (1967), *Le Zitenga — rapport de mission dans le cercle de Zinaire.* Recherches voltaïques 6. Paris–Ouagadougou: CNRS–CVRS.

— (1970), 'The basis of chieftainship among the southern Mossi and the Yansi (Upper Volta)', in: *Proceedings VIIIth ICAES,* vol. 3: 38–40. Tokyo: Science Council of Japan.

— (1971), Genèse et évolution du système politique des Mossi méridionaux. (Haute-Volta). Unpublished thesis. Paris.

Lambert, Capt. (1907), *Le pays mossi et sa population. Etude historique, économomique et géographique suivie d'un essai d'ethnographie comparée.* Unpublished manuscript. Paris.

Levtzion, Nehemia (1968), *Muslims and chiefs in West Africa.* London: Oxford University Press.

Mangin, Eugène (1914–16), 'Les Mossi: essai sur les moeurs et coutumes des Mossi au Soudan occidental', in: *Anthropos* 9: 98–124, 477–493, 705–736; 10-11: 187–217, 323-331.

Marc, Lucien (1909), *Le pays mossi.* Paris: Larose.

Oppenheimer, Franz (1909), *Der Staat.* English edn. (1975), *The state,* New York: Free Life Editions.

Pageard, Robert (1962), 'Réflexions sur l'histoire des Mossi, in: *L'Homme* 2(1): 111–115.

— (1963), 'Recherches sur les Nioniossé', in: *Etudes voltaïques* 4: 5–71.

Prost, André (1953), 'Notes sur l'origine des Mossi', in: *Bulletin d'IFAN,* B, 15: 1933–1938.

Rattray, R. S. (1932), *The tribes of the Ashanti Hinterland.* London: Oxford University Press.

Schweeger-Hefel, Annemarie and Staude, Wilhelm (1972), *Die Kurumba von Lurum.* Wien: A. Schendl.

Skalník, Peter (1966), Review of Skinner, E. P.: The Mossi of the Upper Volta. Stanford 1964, in: *Archiv orientální* 34: 475–478.

— (1971), Review of Hammond, P. B.: Yatênga. New York 1966, in: *Ceský lid* 58(3): 180–182.

— (1973), '*The dynamics of early state development in the Voltaic area (West Africa)*'. Unpublished CSc. dissertation, Charles University, Prague. For abstract of it see *Political anthropology and the state of the art,* S. Lee Seaton and H. J. M. Claessen (eds.). The Hague: Mouton (1978).

— (1975), 'Monarchies within republics: early Voltaic states in the twentieth century', in: *Asian and African Studies* 11: 177–193.

Skinner, Elliott P. (1959–60), 'Succession to political office among the Mossi of the Voltaic republic', in: *Journal of Human Relations* 8: 394–406.

— (1962), 'Trade and markets among the Mossi people', in: *Markets in Africa,* ed. by Paul Bohannan and George Dalton, pp. 237–278. Evanston: Northwestern University Press.

— (1964), *The Mossi of the Upper Volta. The political development of a Sudanese people.* Stanford: Stanford University Press.

— (1966), 'Islam in Mossi society', in: *Islam in tropical Africa,* ed. by I. M. Lewis, pp. 350–370. London: Oxford University Press.

— (1970), 'Processes of political incorporation in Mossi society', in: *From tribe to nation in Africa,* ed. by Ronald Cohen and John Middleton, pp. 175–200. Scranton: Chandler.

Smith, M. G. (1956), 'On segmentary social systems', in: *Journal of the Royal Anthropological Institute* 86: 39–80.
— (1960), *Government in Zazzau*. London: Oxford University Press.
Staniland, Martin (1975), *The lions of Dagbon*. London: Cambridge University Press.
Tamakloe, E. F. (1931), *A brief history of the Dagbamba people*. Accra: Govt. Printer.
Tauxier, Louis (1912), *Le noir du Soudan*. Paris: Larose.
— (1917), *Le noir du Yatēnga*. Paris: Larose.
— (1924), *Nouvelles notes sur le Mossi et le Gourounsi*. Paris: Larose.
Tiendrebeogo, Yamba (1964), *Histoire et coutumes royales des Mossi de Ouagadougou*. ed. by Robert Pageard. Ouagadougou: Larhallé Naba.
Wilks, Ivor (1971), 'The Mossi and Akan states 1500–1800', in: *History of West Africa*, J. F. A. Ajayi and M. Crowder, eds., vol. I: 344–86. London: Longmans.
Zahan, Dominique (1954), Notes sur les marches Mossi du Yatēnga, in: *Africa* 24: 370–377.
— (1961), Pour une histoire des Mossi du Yatēnga, in: *L'Homme* 1(2): 5–22.
— (1967), 'The Mossi kingdoms', in: *West African kingdoms in the nineteenth century*, ed. by Daryll Forde and Phylis Kaberry, pp. 152–178. London: Oxford University Press.
Zaongo, B. J. (1973), 'Le pouvoir traditionnel des nanamse de Haute-Volta' (paper presented at the IXth ICAES, Chicago), to be published by Mouton, The Hague in *West African Culture Dynamics*, ed. by B. Swartz (forthcoming).
Zwernemann, Jürgen (1968), *Die Erde in Vorstellungswelt und Kultpraktiken der sudanischen Völker*. Berlin: Reimer.

23   Yoruba City-States (at the Turn of the Nineteenth Century)

NATALIA B. KOCHAKOVA

The Yoruba city-states took shape in the tropical forests and wooded savannahs stretching south and west of the Niger River, or, to use present-day geographical concepts, in the territories covered by the states of Kwara, Lagos and western Nigeria in the Federation of Nigeria, and, in addition, partly by the republics of Benin and Togo.

Politically, pre-colonial Yorubaland (prior to the second half of the nineteenth century) comprised a complex system of larger and smaller city-states in varying states of dependence on one another.

The state, as a rule, comprised a capital, one or more dependent cities, and the surrounding villages, which absorbed much of the urban population at peak periods of field work. All settlements were connected by a network of well kept roads. In the seventeenth–eighteenth centuries the city of Ọyọ united under its sway the majority of the Yoruba cities as well as several neighboring peoples, thus giving rise to the Ọyọ Empire. As one of the most powerful politico-military leagues in tropical West Africa, which experienced the peak of development of Yoruban statehood, it held its ground until the turn of the nineteenth century.

The Yoruba cities were veritable fortresses, surrounded by walls, ramparts and moats or protective forest belts encircling the city walls. By the middle of the nineteenth century the population of the biggest among them stood at twenty, twenty-five or seventy thousand (Bowen 1857: 35). H. Clapperton's figures for the 20s of the same century are far more modest, viz approximately eight–ten thousand. Archaeological finds, however, allow us to assume that those figures are considerably underestimated.[1]

The emergence of these cities had no connection whatever with the separation of crafts from agriculture. The Yoruba cities took shape in the course of the transition from a primitive communal to a class society as a specific form of organization aimed at the protection of property belonging to territorial–genealogical farming communities in their respective territories.

To all appearances the process of state formation in the tenth–twelfth centuries encompassed the entire Yoruba region and was uneven in character. According to oral traditions, most Yoruba cities trace their origin to the Ile-Ifẹ city-state. This is confirmed by the installation ceremonies of traditional rulers and by several other rites. Archaeological finds testify that the site of this city was settled not later than the ninth century, or even as early as the sixth century A.D. (Biobaku 1973: 137), and that it reached its golden age, generally attested by the development attained by sculptured, terra-cotta and bronze images of kings and tiled pavements, in the tenth–fourteenth centuries (Biobaku 1973: 128). The foundation of other city-states is placed (through an analysis of oral traditions) in the thirteenth–fourteenth centuries (Smith 1969: 100–106).

Until recently, the autochthonous origin of Yoruban statehood was doubted and even denied. Reference was made to oral traditions mentioning migrations of the first Yoruba kings from lands in the northeast. Most likely these were ancient local migrations within the areas concerned. There are no reliable grounds for assuming borrowed statehood. Hypotheses concerning the foreign origin of state organization here as a rule stem from the supposition that the uncivilized state of the people in question would have made them incapable of independent political and cultural development, and hence forced them to borrow social and political institutions elsewhere. However, even what little is known of the Yorubas' ancient cultural achievements allows us to refute these suppositions. The borrowing, if it did take place, was done by a society whose economic and social development was sufficient to enable it to proceed towards state formation. A slash-and-burn type of shifting cultivation, involving the use of the hoe, formed the economic basis upon which the Yoruba state took shape.[2]

The transition of the area as a whole to a productive economy took place in the first centuries A.D., prior to the large-scale use of iron implements,[3] although in several parts of the Guinea forest area iron smelting may have been first practised in A.D. 500 at the latest. Owing to imperfect smelting techniques this metal was long used only in small quantities in Yorubaland (Biobaku 1973: 148, 149). The shortage of iron at the beginning of Yoruban state formation is confirmed by the ritual incorporation of iron in ancient Ile-Ifẹ stone statues. It is assumed that, from the sixteenth century, deficiency was made up chiefly through imports of iron from Europe (Biobaku 1973: 148, 149), although pre-colonial sources do not mention iron or ironware among the principal European export items in Yoruba, but do draw attention to local iron production (Lander 1832: 179–180; Clapperton 1966: 39; Johnson 1921: 121).

1. SOCIO-ECONOMIC BACKGROUND

At the turn of the nineteenth century an advanced type of hoe farming formed the economic backbone of the Yoruba city-states. Contemporary European sources dwell on the flourishing state of agriculture, mentioning vast areas under crops, well-cultivated fields, a diversity of crops (yams, millet, maize, cotton, bananas and other fruits, indigo and vegetables), and an abundance of foodstuffs sold in the local markets (Clapperton 1966: 6, 12, 59; Lander 1832: 59, 165, 179–186, 202; Curtin 1967: 232, 239). These agricultural economies boasted horses, sheep, goats and fowls. The tsetse fly, however, made for undersized cattle and high prices of meat. The shortage of animal foods was made up by hunting and gathering (e.g., frogs, lizards, caterpillars, etc.) (Lander 1966: 323; 1832: 179–180).

The crafts failed to develop into an independent productive branch. Households, as a rule, functioned along lines of self-sufficiency. This did not prevent the development of crafts calling for specialist skills. Products of weaving, pottery (without the use of the potter's wheel), blacksmith's, woodcarving and several other crafts were sold at local markets at the beginning of the nineteenth century (Clapperton 1966: 14, 16, 59; Lander 1832: 90–91, 165, 179–180; Curtin 1967: 232).

Craft products were usually made to order; the more skilled craftsmen being invited to work for the king and nobility and enjoying their protection (Johnson 1921: 123; Ojo 1966: 73). According to European sources of the eighteenth and early nineteenth centuries, local textiles were a major item of Yoruba's exports to other African countries and even to Brazil (through European intermediaries) (Norris 1968: 125, 138; Clapperton 1966: 57; Lander 1832: 112–113, 139; Curtin 1967: 263, 269–170). In the bigger cities in the early nineteenth century one might find households working eight–ten weaving-looms and engaged in the regular production of textiles (Clapperton 1966: 14, 16). Foreign trade was monopolized by the king. Local handicraft wares reached the foreign market chiefly through acquisition of surplus products direct from the producers outside the market.

The community formed the basis of social organization in the Yoruba city-states. Surplus production and the development of an economic basis for the emergence of a special ruling stratum began at a time when tribal relations had not yet reached a stage of disintegration.

Land and titles did not descend along individual lines, but were hereditary within kin-groups or *idile* ('root of the house'), i.e., patrilineal groups descended from a single ancestor, having a common family name, common taboos with regard to certain foods and a common tutelary spirit, and practising exogamy. The predominance of the communal principle over the individual one is also testified by the system of inheritance of movable property, this passing not from father to son but from a deceased person to his mother's children (Fadipẹ 1970: 140). W. B. Schwab's remark that membership in the *idile* was 'among the major factors determining the individual's social, economic and political role' is quite applicable to pre-colonial Yorubaland as well (Schwab 1955: 301). Each city was a conglomeration of such kin groups. Members of one specific *idile* (or often one of its segments) formed the nucleus of the residents of the traditional Yoruba dwelling, called *agbole* or compound.[4] They were regarded as its owners, 'the masters of the house'. This privilege did not accrue to their wives, known as 'the wives of the house' (who, upon their husbands' death were inherited by the latter's brothers or by the children of their husbands' brothers and sisters). The *agbole* residents nearly always included a number of 'strangers', i.e., persons who for one reason or another had broken with their own *idile*, and slaves.

The word *agbole* (lit. 'group of houses') covers something more than just a single dwelling. This traditional group was the basic social and political unit of Yoruban society. The rights, privileges and duties of each individual member were exercised indirectly by him, through the head of the *agbole* — the *bale* ('father of the house'). It was his duty, inter alia, to look after the *agbole*'s common property, i.e., the houses, land and farm buildings, to see to the distribution and redistribution of the group's landed property and supervise its cultivation and to organize mutual assistance inside the compound and ensure that each member of the group had the necessary means of subsistence.

The *bale* further adjudicated minor disputes between members of his group, organized the sale of the marketable part of the aggregate products, took charge of household religious ceremonies and played the role of intermediary between his group and the outside world (procuring brides and bridegrooms for members of his group, arranging funerals, defending the group's interests in land disputes, supervising the collection of taxes and dues and the fulfilment of other obligations towards the major chief, etc.).

He at all times represented the interests of the individual members of his group outside the *agbole*, and conversely was responsible to the urban authorities for the conduct of each member (Ajisafe 1924: 3).

The *bale* was elected from among the senior male members of the *idile* with preference usually being given to those having a relatively high economic status (Fadipẹ 1970: 110). The right to stand for election was enjoyed by all 'masters of the house', i.e., all *idile* members, whose canditature has to be approved by the chief or the city council.

Economically, the *agbole* (which was often inhabited by segments of several *idile*) could not as a rule be identified with the primary unit. The inhabitants of an *agbole* were divided into families — *ile te mi* ('the house which is mine'). Each *ile te mi* occupied a special allotted part of the *agbole* and worked a separate plot of land allocated from the *idile*'s total landholding. Each man could claim as much land as could be tilled by his family. Even so the *ile te mi*'s economic independence was only partial, its main property, the land, remaining in the collective ownership of the *idile*, which was free to redistribute it at any time and reserved (through the *bale*) the right of control over its use.[5] The rights of the community prevailed over those of the individual in all spheres of life.

Several *agbole* (often genealogically related) formed a quarter — *adugbo* — with a chief at its head. He ruled it through the *bale* or *agbole* elders, and represented its interests in the city council. Thus compounds and quarters were the units in which the entire population of the city without exception was organized on the basis of both territorial and kinship relations. Wherever guilds of craftsmen and traders formed, their structure was identical to the structure of the kinship groups. Where all the members of particular *idile* were specialized in the same craft, the *bale* combined his functions as such with those of a guild chief, and general patrilineal group affairs were discussed jointly with guild problems. In this specific case the two forms of organizations coincided completely.

2. THE CITY-STATE

The social structure of the Yoruba city-states reflected a transitional type of society where tribal relations were already in a state of disintegration and the process of class formation was far from completed.[6] Its character was dualistic, since one might find here elements of both a pre-class and a class society in all spheres of life. The overwhelming majority of the population of the city states, namely the community members, preserved their economic and personal independence as *idile* members. They controlled the principal sources and means of production and were personally free. One of the basic productive resources — the land — which was regarded as an indispensable prerequisite of production, was the collective property of the town community. All members of the town community, regardless of status, wealth or function, received land on an equal basis: the working capacity of each individual family. Each patrilineal *idile* group had full control of its particular landholding. According to tradition, neither the king nor any of his subordinate chiefs could alienate the land or dispose of it without the consent of its owner. Although an individual community member could be banished from the state for committing a grave offence, his landholding was retained by his family.

There also existed a privileged type of landholding known as the 'palace lands', comprising the king's residence and farmlands. The latter could be extended by the king through the escheatment of community lands and wastelands. Common law regarded these lands as a kind of public property. Upon the king's death they passed to his successor. Income from such lands was also considered public property, and was used to cover the expenses of running the state. The use of these lands for other purposes could result in the king's deposition (Lloyd 1962: 47).

Nevertheless, the king was entitled to the lion's share for the maintenance of the royal property (Ajisafe 1924: 87) and could demand the community's assistance at sowing time. The community members performed this work gratis but were provided with free meals at the king's expense, the community bore the expense of all repairs to the royal quarters and all damages caused by natural calamities. This was regarded as the public duty of all members of the population, the shirking of which was punishable.

In pre-colonial Yoruba society, social and property differentiation had reached a high level. A man's social status was determined by his function. *Ijoye* ('title-holder') was a special term used to specify a person's position in the administrative hierarchy. Outwardly the social differentiation was reflected in the pattern of subordination and superordination, the rules regarding costume and ornaments, and public behavior. Subordination and superordination permeated all spheres of life

The *iwofa* system of debt bondage was a characteristic symptom of growing material inequality. Its only difference from slavery was that the pawn retained his personal freedom and the right to landowner-ship.

The society was divided into freemen and slaves, the latter of whom were usually war captives. In contrast to the free members of the community, slaves were stripped of all rights and, together with their belongings, were the property of their masters. The main legal distinc-tion between the slave and his master lay in their relation to the land. Slaves only had the use of land allotted to them by their owners. Moreover, a slave-owner could easily deprive his slave of any land the latter might have managed to buy or received as a gift. A fellow tribe member could be made a slave only as punishment for a grave offense. Slave labor was employed chiefly in agriculture. Slavery, in general, had a patriarchal character. Slaves would join the basic social units, or *agboles*, as unequal partners of freemen. They would be given the use of implements as well as a plot of land, which they could spend part of their time tilling and where they could build a dwelling and set up a household.

There was also a small group of privileged slaves who, together with the tribal nobility, made up the developing military bureaucratic apparatus of the state. They could appropriate part of the surplus produced by the regular freemen, *iwofa* bondsmen and slaves, and enjoyed a higher social and economic status than their fellows.

Differentiation in the ruling stratum of Yoruban society was based on an extensive scale of ranks by which the different categories of 'title-holders' were graded. Each category was entitled to a specific share of the surplus produced by the efforts of the working strata.

The lowest rank in the *ijoye* system was that of *bale*, or head of the *agbole*. He often (but not always) took a direct part in production but his main concern was the management of affairs of his unit. His services were remunerated by the members of his *agbole*, to a share of whose property, including slaves procured by them in raids on other tribes, he was entitled. The younger members of the *agbole* were obliged to till his land and perform other services for him. This gave the *bale* considerable economic advantages over the other members of the community. His living-quarters in the compound were bigger and better-furnished, and he had a harem and personal slaves. In matters concerning the entire community the *bale* took counsel with its elders, who played a certain part in organizing production and the community's social life. For instance, for any measures involving the alienation of the community's joint property, the *bale* needed its approval. All the same, the *bale* wielded considerable personal power. His word was law for the community, which viewed him as the master of the *agbole*, and likewise his principal wife as mistress over all its female members (Johnson 1921: 99–100). The *bale* had extensive opportunities of profiting by the misfortunes of his fellow members. He could increase and appropriate fines imposed on offenders, and usually also appropriated part of the taxes collected from members of the community. When new slaves were captured by community members a few inevitably passed to him (Fadipe 1970: 111). The city authorities normally supported the *bale* in the exercise of his function. The *agboles*, while retaining the features of communal collectivism, gradually developed into exploitation units, into a means of increasing the joint responsibility of the community members for their labor duties in favor of the ruling stratum.

Second on the scale of ranks was the quarter chief. With regard to his own *idile* his function was that of a regular *bale*. Yet, as chief, thousands of people could come under his jurisdiction. He did not play a direct part in production but dealt with its organizational aspects, settling land disputes between *agboles*, taking charge of the distribution and redistribution of community lands, fixing the appropriate dates for the commencement of agricultural work, organizing raids to procure slaves (a regular feature of the community's everyday life), and so on. The public functions of the common people within the bounds of the quarter (or village) were restricted to a minimum: the chief held counsel only with the *bales*, while the others were forced to accept their decisions. The chief's income was provided by the produce derived by the efforts of his slaves and relatives from the land belonging to his family unit, and by shares of the yields from other compounds in this quarter (or village). These might come to him in the form of taxes and duties, repairs on his dwelling following natural calamities, special levies imposed upon the community whenever the chief offered sacrifices on its behalf, shares in booty, etc.

At the top of the scale of ranks figured the crowned ruler of the Yoruba city-state — the *ǫba*. The king was the richest person in the state and derived his income from the following sources.

(1) Regular tribute in the form of produce and handicraft goods which he received in the form of yearly presents from dependent cities and territories (e.g., on the occasion of harvest celebrations).

(2) Statute labor on public works (building and repairing the royal palace and cultivating the palace lands) imposed on the entire population of the state.

(3) Special levies for sacrifices to the gods on behalf of the state.

(4) Irregular additional levies (on the occasion of a fire or other natural disaster).

(5) Duties on goods coming in through the city gate.

(6) The royal monopoly on foreign trade, including the slave trade.[7]

(7) Confiscation of the property of offenders, alienated on behalf of the state by the *ǫba*, and shares in other special court fines.[8]

(8) Inheritance of the property of deceased subordinate chiefs.

(9) Presentations to the king of the best handicraft products.

(10) War spoils.

(11) Exploitation of slaves.

All this wealth was to a large extent redistributed among the chiefs and members of the royal court both during the king's lifetime (sacrifices, distribution of gifts on annual religious holidays, etc.), and after his demise, in accordance with the customary laws of inheritance of royal property, which was regarded as a kind of public property (Fadipę 1970: 143). In conformity with these rules the lion's share of the king's possessions in the form of widows, slaves, pawns, horses and clothes went to his successor, the remainder being distributed among his numerous children and subordinate chiefs.

Only the king's regalia and royal servants from among the slaves were unaffected by this procedure and were automatically handed over to the new king (Fadipẹ 1970: 144).

The characteristic features of the *bale*–chief–king structure show that the diversion of a portion of the surplus product in favor of the nobility stemmed from its monopolization by holders of economic-organizing (and military-organizing) functions, a process that was not completed in the pre-colonial period.

According to Yoruba oral traditions the institution of the monarchy took shape simultaneously with the cities themselves: the first city (Ile-Ifẹ) and the first king were creations of the gods, setting the stage for the emergence of the entire human race. The genealogies of Yoruban kings (*ọbas*) all go back to Oranyan, the first king of Ile-Ifẹ.

According to these Yoruban traditions the *ọba* was endowed with special supernatural powers, which enabled him to exercise his functions as patron of the town community and intermediary between his people and the gods. This power passed to each new ruler from his predecessor, the deceased *ọba*. A system of ritual taboos served to ensure his sanctity. Divine homage was rendered to deceased kings. Human sacrifices formed an integral part of every royal burial ceremony. The cult of the sacred king was inseparably linked to agriculture, the economic basis of the Yoruban states. However, the control of natural forces through magic did not form part of his duties.

Succession to the throne was restricted to members of the royal *idile*. The new *ọba* was selected by the titled members of the royal lineage and had to be approved by the most influential representatives of the nobility (in Oyo the *Ọyọmesi* or Council of Seven), who had the deciding vote. Preference was given to a candidate born of a free woman; good health and the absence of physical deformities were believed to be auspicious signs for the future *ọba*'s supernatural power. The candidate's age and proximity to the throne were next taken into account, as was also the opinion of the king's harem (Johnson 1921: 41).

3. THE OYO STATE

Although the basic features of the political and social systems in different parts of Yorubaland had much in common, there was a difference in their respective levels of development. The best study so far has been made of Ọyọ, the biggest of the Yoruba states. Its ruler possessed the title of *Alafin,* i.e., 'master of the palace'. The palace, i.e., the king's official residence (*'afin'*) was located in the center of the city. It was encircled by a *pisé* wall, and towered above the other buildings in the city. It was the center of the state's political and religious life. In its precincts were found the principal sanctuaries, and the execution of the gravest offenders took place here. Furthermore, the state council held its meetings in the royal palace, while the palace square was also the main marketplace.

The title *Alafin* had three different meanings, all of which testify to the king's exceptional powers, viz. 'lord of the universe and of life', 'master of the land' and 'companion of the gods' (Morton-Williams 1960: 363). According to tradition he was authorized to depose the ruler of any subordinate city and to declare war. He wielded the highest judicial powers and was also chief priest, in this capacity taking part in all the principal religious ceremonies. Finally, he was superintendent of markets and foreign trade.

The king's decisions were indisputable, but could be enforced only with the approval of the *Oyomesi,* membership of which was restricted to several specific *idiles.*

The *Oyomesi* served as a link between king and commoners via a chain of subordinate chiefs. At the same time its members formed a close association of nobles constructed on the basis of a secret society known as the *Ogboni.* All the *Oyomesi* were at the same time members of the *Ogboni* leadership. Like other secret societies, the *Ogboni* had its roots in the tribal system. The priesthood sanctioned the powers of the *Ogboni* by asserting the latter's direct link with the spirit of the earth, the object of their worship. In the Yoruba states, particularly in Oyo, this alliance developed into an organization that was to ensure the political dominance of the nobility over the commoners at a stage of social development when, owing to the weakness of the state, the burgeoning exploiter nobility took recourse to pre-class institutions which it adapted to suit its interests. According to custom, the *Ogboni* had the right to select and enthrone the king (or chief), take part in the running of the state and administer justice in cases involving bloodshed (Ajisafe 1924: 90). In Oyo these functions of the *Ogboni* were eventually usurped by the leaders of an alliance comprising representatives of the highest nobility, including the *Oyomesi* and the priesthood. Through special rites its members were bound to a system of mutual aid and protection.

The *Oyomesi* was headed by the *Basorun,* one of the most influential members of the *Ogboni.* He deputized for the king in the three-month period between the death of the old king and the enthronement of the new one. During the annual celebrations in honor of Ogun, the war god, the *Basorun* would seek the opinion of the gods on the ruling *Alafin.* If the oracle's reply was negative the *Alafin* was faced with the necessity of taking his own life. This custom was genetically connected with the once widespread practice of doing away with decrepit chiefs, since according to ancient beliefs their enfeeblement sapped the fruits of the land, the livestock and the people of their vital force (Frazer 1928, II). Yorubaland retained but a relic of this custom, which was resorted to as an instrument in political struggles. During the period, of which memories have been preserved in oral traditions, there was a growing tendency towards strengthening of the royal power. However, in times of especially devastating wars or popular unrest kings were apt to be replaced through the use of violence; the *Oyomesi* resorting to an ancient custom in order to settle internal conflicts.

At the same time the *Oyomesi* tried in every way to promote the dogma of the king's divine character and showed outward submission to his person. With the strengthening and alienation of the king's power his court also increased. Its basis was constituted by the slaves, who lacked roots in the tribal institutions. The apparatus of government, headed by the king, which formed a kind of super-structure superimposed on the urban community, was exploited by the nobility — a burgeoning exploiter ruling clique — to bend the community to its will.

The king's court comprised two diametrically opposed groups of people as regards their origin: (1) the king's wives and relatives, and (2) slaves of the most diverse ranks — from sweepers and menial servants to high court officials.

The king's *idile* was usually the biggest. Its most influential members resided in dependent cities and villages as local rulers or other high authorities (Johnson 1921: 67). The royal *idile* fulfilled an important role in the choice of a new king. Its representatives (usually the uncles or cousins of the future *oba*), all of whom possessed the hereditary title of 'king's father', gave the future ruler the necessary instruction in the course of the three-month installation ceremony. Upon the *oba's* enthronement his actual kinship relations were converted into official ones: to replace his deceased father he received two official 'fathers', who were in effect his uncles or brothers; his own mother was obliged to depart from this world, and was replaced by an official 'mother' in the person of the priestess of the god Orun and the keeper of the royal tomb, who held the highest office in the court's scale of ranks. The king's sons, except for the eldest, who was his co-ruler, were removed from court upon reaching a marriageable age. When the king of Oyo died, the co-ruler (one of his sons) had to follow suit.

Women (whose number in the Oyo *afin* exceeded 500) played an important role at court. They included members of the royal harem, the priestesses of the numerous religious cults, who were simultaneously the 'mothers' of the city's religious organizations, and slaves, who waited on the divine *oba* and performed services in connection with the organizational side of the state's religious life, which had the royal palace as its center.

The actual governmental functions were fulfilled by the second category of members of the royal court, made up of slaves of various ranks. The most numerous and influential of these were the eunuchs, three of whom were the king's closest assistants and in effect exercised his authority on his behalf. The first eunuch discharged the highest judicial functions, his decisions being considered just as valid as those of the king himself, from which there was no appeal. The second eunuch was the high priest of the god Shango, the embodiment of the royal power in Qyǫ, and performed rites in Shango's honor on behalf of the people. He was also responsible for the education of the king's children. The third eunuch was authorized to speak on the *Alafin*'s behalf in all civil and military affairs, displaying the *ǫba*'s regalia and being entitled to all the honors due to the king on these occasions. His main task however, was superintending the royal market and administering the royal revenues deriving from duties and tribute.

Second in rank after the eunuchs were the *ilari*. Their original duty — keeping the royal palace in good repair — gradually degenerated into a secondary function. The *ilari* were mainly bodyguards or 'keepers of the king's head', messengers, privileged servants and collectors of tribute from subjugated peoples. The *ilari* were recruited from among the palace slaves and prisoners-of-war. In the course of the inauguration ceremony each *ilari* was given an official name by the king, which at the same time served as a particular political slogan, which the *ilari* propagated among the people as the king's representative. The most characteristic of these were names such as *Ilu gbohun* ('the town obeyed him'), *ǫba gbe nle* ('the *ǫba* promoted me'), *Maa gbori imi pete* ('do not flout my authority in order to plot'), etc. (Abraham 1958: 19).

For their services the *ilari* received a share of the tribute from subject cities and villages. The king would reward particularly trustworthy *ilari* by bestowing cities or quarters upon them, from which they might draw an income. They were often placed in charge of big compounds in different parts of the city whose inhabitants were chiefly royal slaves who would then attend on the *ilari* in times of both war and peace (Johnson 1921: 62).

The court police force, comprising the royal executioners and guards (*tǫtu*), were also recruited from among the slaves and their progeny. The number of *tǫtu* and their assistants often reached 150.

Slaves also held the posts of collectors of trade duties in the royal markets and at the city gates. The granting of extensive powers to privileged slaves constituted a step towards the creation of an administrative apparatus superimposed upon the city community and did much to destroy the tradition of tribal democracy. The slaves, who came from alien tribes, were regarded by the freemen as foreigners and were wholly dependent on the king.

With this large body of servants the king was able to concentrate in his hands all external judicial and punitive powers as well as to control the collection of duties and tribute and put ideological pressure on the population through his devoted eunuch, the high priest of the god Shango. However, the process of the alienation of public powers and the institution of coercive bodies standing in opposition to the people was still in progress.

In the Yoruba states each community member had the right to carry arms and be a warrior. The troops were made up of citizen volunteer corps.

The structure of the latter was determined by the division of the city into compounds and quarters along the above discussed territorial and genealogical lines. Positions of subordination in the army corresponded to subordinate positions in urban life. Usually a state of war was declared and the people were called to arms on behalf of the king, while in the more backward districts of Yorubaland decisions were accordingly taken by popular assemblies (Jones 1964: 132–133). In the state of Ọyọ military expeditions were sent out on plundering raids and to instill awe in tributaries by the king every few years. Compulsory military service was necessary only in the event of a defensive war (Johnson 1921: 131). However, if able-bodied men refused to go to war at a time when the king was badly in need of soldiers, the king might send a punitive expedition to destroy the homes and crops of the evaders (Ajisafe 1924: 20). The warriors had to provide their own food and arms.

Alongside the citizen volunteer corps there existed certain privileged military units. In Ọyọ there was a special category of noble warriors called *bada*. Each *bada* had to have at least two horses and several bodyguards whom he maintained at his own expense. The *bada* was expected to be skilled in the military art, to fight only on horseback and to be ready to plunge into the thick of the battle at crucial moments. All high commanders had at least one *bada* warrior at their disposal.

Another category of privileged soldiers was that of the *esho* or commanders of the palace guard. The title of *esho* was not hereditary, but was conferred on warriors in the king's service who were renowned for their prowess and bravery. The *esho* were second after the *Ọyọmesi* in the scale of administrative ranks.

The formation of hand-picked detachments from among slaves and poor freemen as another means of building up a military organization to coerce the people was more typical of the nineteenth century. The custom whereby the king or chief was obliged to equip his soldiers with arms and ammunition (since otherwise they had the right to enter the service of some other ruler) which was observed in the twentieth century, evidently applied only to these personal detachments (Ajisafe 1924: 19).

The indivisibility of the politico-administrative and the juridical and police powers was characteristic of the Yoruba city-states. The judicial and police functions were discharged by various functionaries beginning with the *bale*, i.e., the *agbole* elder. Traditionally the *bale* had extensive disciplinary powers. Under his jurisdiction came all crimes and offences committed by members of the *agbole*, with the exception of manslaughter, sorcery, incest and initiation of women into secret societies (Fadipẹ 1970: 108). He had the right to pass sentences of various kinds: the accused could be put in chains or in the stocks, flogged, forced to pay damages or a fine, or thrown into a dungeon, if there was one available in the compound in question (Ajisafe 1924: 3).

The higher juridical authorities were represented by the quarter chiefs followed by the city council (in Ọyọ this body was the *Ọyọmesi*). They constituted a court of first instance, where the gravest crimes were tried, among them manslaughter, high treason, burglary, arson and incest. Sentences passed by the city council only came into force after approval by the king, the supreme judge of the people.

All legal procedure was based on the rules and norms of customary law. The king was regarded not as a law giver, but as an interpreter of ancient customs and a spokesman of the gods. The king's interpretation could not be called in question. Even in cases where his tyranny became unbearable there was nowhere else to go in search of justice. The only way out then was outright rebellion against the king. Proceeds from fines and legal fees were among the major sources of income for the administrative stratum. By custom, each crime was punishable by a specific punishment; regardless of the types of punishment, every accused had to pay a fine in clothes, money, cattle, etc. (Ajisafe 1924: 38).

It has already been mentioned that most of the Yoruba city-states were incorporated into the Ọyọ empire. Many of Yoruba's neighbors (Bariba, Ga, Fon) were debtors of the *Alafins*. By the second half of the eighteenth century the *Alafins* were in control of the entire vast area between the Niger River in the north and northeast and the frontiers of present-day Ghana in the west. At the turn of the nineteenth century, when the Ọyọ imperial system was falling into decay, H. Clapperton noted 'a high degree of subordination' and 'skilled administration' in the peripheral areas of the empire (Clapperton 1966: 13). The relationship between the subordinate cities and the capitals of Yoruba was strictly regulated by customary law. The subordinate cities were ruled either by representatives of the local dynasty or by the *bale*s, uncrowned viceregents of the king. All local affairs of the city community were settled autonomously (Ajisafe 1924: 17). The supreme ruler (in the capital) was in charge of the state's foreign policy. He also inquired into cases of high treason and disputes between the rulers of subordinate cities. In the Oyọ empire the subordinate *ọba* and *bale* received their power from the *Alafin* and their inauguration took place in the capital. Besides, they had to leave representatives behind in Oyọ, as hostages (Johnson 1921: 26). The subordinate cities had to pay the *Alafin* tribute in the form of gifts on the occasion of important holidays and help to pay any damages resulting from natural calamities in the capital. Moreover, the local rulers were obliged to make a journey to Oyọ once-yearly during the harvest celebrations to pay their personal respects as vassals of the *Alafin* (Johnson 1921: 41).

The rulers of provincial cities were often appointed by the *Alafin* from among his slaves instead of the local nobility. It was felt that devoted slaves were more capable of maintaining order and security in remote but nevertheless strategically important parts of the country.

FOOTNOTES

[1] For instance according to archaeological data from the fourteenth–sixteenth century the city of Ile-Ifẹ extended far beyond the borders of the contemporary city, whose population in 1953 fell short of 150 000 (Willet 1960: 144).

[2] On slash-and-burn cultivation as a primary stage in growing crops serving as basis for the emergence of more highly developed types of human society than those given birth to by certain intensive forms of cultivation see Semenov 1974: 311).

[3] The possibility of the existence of slash cultivation in the Neolithic age has been demonstrated experimentally (Semenov 1974: 121).

[4] The remains of such an *agbole* have been uncovered by excavations at Ile-Ifẹ and Old Oyọ. Hence, this type of dwelling had come into being long before the turn of the nineteenth century (Fagg and Willet 1960: 358; Willet 1960: 66).

[5] Even in the middle of the twentieth century the *idile*'s collective rights to both the land and dwellings prevailed over individual rights (Lloyd 1962: 78; Elias 1951: 91–92).

[6] For a more detailed account of the social structure of the Yoruba city-states in the pre-colonial period see Kochakova 1968: 109–134, 182–185; Kochakova 1970: 17–67.

[7] An example of the king's monopoly of trade was observed by the Landers. In Yadoo they came across at least 100 of the king's wives functioning as his trade agents. To distinguish them from other tradeswomen their goods were wrapped in special cloth; encroachment on this privilege by a 'commoner' was punishable by enslavement. The king's wives were exempted from all duties and enjoyed the protection of the chiefs of all the cities through which they travelled (Lander 1832, I: 110).

[8] Almost throughout the whole of Yorubaland the *ọba*'s servants had the right to confiscate the property of any inhabitant at any time in his name. This could never be recovered once it was brought into the palace precincts (Ojo 1966: 22).

REFERENCES

Abraham, R. C. (1958), *Dictionary of modern Yoruba.* London: University of London Press.

Ajisafe, A. K. (1924), *The laws and customs of Yoruba peoples.* London: Routledge.

Biobaku, S. O., ed. (1973), *Sources of Yoruba history.* Oxford: Clarendon Press.

Bowen, T. J. (1857), *Adventures and missionary labors in several countries in the interior of Africa from 1849 to 1856.* Charleston.

Clapperton, H. (1966), *Journal of a second expedition into the interior of Africa.* (2nd edn.). London: Frank Cass and Co Ltd.

Curtin, Ph. D. ed. (1967), *Africa remembered. Narratives by West Africans from the era of the Slave Trade.* Madison: The University of Wisconsin Press.

Elias, T. O. (1951), *Nigerian land law and customs.* London: Routledge and Kegan Paul.

Fadipẹ, N. A. (1970), *The sociology of the Yoruba.* Ibadan University Press.

Fagg, W. and Willet, F. (1960), Ancient Ife: an ethnographical summary, in: *Odù, a Journal of Yoruba and related studies* 8: 21–35.

Frazer, James (1928), *Zolotaia vetv'* [The golden bough]. Leningrad: Ateist.

Johnson, S. (1921), *The history of the Yorubas.* (Reprinted 1966). London: Routledge and Kegan Paul.

Jones, A. (1964), Report on the Egba Army in 1861, in: *Yoruba warfare in 19th century*, ed. by G. F. A. Ajayi and R. S. Smith, Supplement, pp. 129–140. Cambridge: The University Press in Association with the Institute of African Studies, University of Ibadan.

Kochakova, N. B. (1968), *Goroda-gosudarstva iorubov* [City-states of the Yoruba]. Moscow: Nauka.

— (1970), 'Proizvodstvo i prisvoenie pribavochnogo produkta v stranakh Beninskogo zaliva (traditsionnye formy)' [Production and appropriation of the surplus product in the countries of the Bight of Benin], in: *Sotsial'nye struktury dokolonia'noi Afriki*, pp. 17–67. Moscow: Nauka.

Lander, R. (1832), *Journal of an expedition to explore the course and termination of the Niger.* Vol. I–III. London: John Murray.

— (1966), Journal of Richard Lander, servant to the late Captain Clapperton, in: *Journal.....* pp. 257–327. (see Clapperton H.).

Lloyd, P. C. (1962), *Yoruba land law.* London: Oxford University Press.

Morton-Williams, P. (1960), 'The Yoruba Ogboni cult in Oyo', in *Africa* 30: 362–374. (New impression). London: Frank Cass.

Norris, R. (1968), *Memoirs of the reign of Bossa Ahadee, king of Dahomy.* (New impression). London: Frank Cass.

Ojo, G. J. A. (1966), *Yoruba palaces.* London: University of London Press.

Schwab, W. B. (1955), 'Kinship and lineage among the Yorubas', in: *Africa:* 352–374. Leningrad: Nauka.

Semyonov, S. A. (1974), *Proiskthozhdenie zemledeliia* [The origin of Agriculture]. Leningrad: Nauka.

Smith, R. (1969), *Kingdoms of the Yoruba.* London: Methuen.

Willet, F. (1960), 'Investigation at Old Oyo, 1956–1957 — an interim report — in: *The Journal of the Historical Society of Nigeria*, 2: 59–77.

24   Zande

JOSEF KANDERT

1. HISTORY

The region of East Sudan was, apparently from the end of the sixteenth century, settled by three waves of immigrants speaking central Sudanic languages. The third and last of these waves comprised a people known as the Mbomu. They conquered many smaller ethnic groups in later times, the resultant conglomerate gradually giving rise to the Zande ethnic community. It would seem that the invasion lacked central organization, simply taking the form of a number of independent warrior groups gradually penetrating further and further. In the middle of the eighteenth century the Mbomu apparently settled in the area bounded by the Mbomu and Shinko Rivers in the north and west, the Uere River in the east, and the river Uele in the south. Their migration was not confined to just one direction, they spread northwards, southeastwards, and southwards. The Mbomu territorial expansion stopped in the second half of the nineteenth century. The Mbomu migrated mostly under the leadership of chiefs from the privileged and ruling Vongara clan, who later controlled practically the whole of the territory inhabited by the Zande[1] (Baxter and Butt 1953: 20–22; Evans-Pritchard 1958: 3–4).

The Mbomu had no knowledge of their own history, and the historical traditions of the various Mbomu clans are incomplete and fragmentary. The Mbomu traced their name to the River Mbomu near which the first Zande state in the area was established. According to some histories, the chiefs of the Abakundo lineage — probably of the lion totem — formerly ruled over the Mbomu. Besides the Abakundo, the chiefs of the Angbapio or Avurunaze lineage are mentioned in some traditions. The histories of the Auro — another section of the

Zande people — are also incomplete and fragmentary. Some of the Auro clans were formerly independent ethnic groups, which were later assimilated by the Zande. Certain of the Auro peoples lived in separate chiefdoms before the coming of the Mbomu and Vongara. The traditions also record that the clans were localized and headed by elders in those days. It seems that in the process of 'Zandeization' they abandoned their own traditions, provided they had any, in favor of those of the Vongara-Mbomu. There are no histories concerning the origin of the Zande clan totems and no credible accounts of the origin of Zande clan names (Mecklenburg 1912: 310; de Schlippe 1956: 7; Evans-Pritchard 1956a: 69–71, 1956b: 116–121, 1957d: 322–326).

Contrary to this, the history of the ruling Vongara clan is commonly known, and its genealogies are traced back as far as the middle of the eighteenth century. These Vongara traditions have been preserved by the Vongara themselves, as also by their Zande subjects. Evans-Pritchard remarks that the Zande know the Vongara genealogies better than they do their own. The traditions speak of a ruler called Ngura (1750–1780?) who consolidated his domain along the Lower Mbomu River. He sent his sons Mabenge and Tombo to conquer kingdoms of their own. Mabenge went in the direction of the Uele River and Tombo to the southwest. Tombo had four sons (in all likelihood the genealogies are schematic), who continued the expansion of their domains to the southwest; Mabenge also had four sons, who spread to the east. From these personages the genealogies lead to the chiefs and members of the Vongara clan of the 20th century. In principle there were seven Vongara 'ruling houses', which traced their origin from Tombo and Mabenge, viz.:

(1) Yakpati (son of Mabenge) — ruler of Zande Mbomu;
(2) Nunga (son of Mabenge) — ruler of Zande Nunga;
(3) Ngindo (son of Mabenge) — ruler of Zande Auro;
(4) Yatwe (son of Tombo) — ruler of Zande Podiyo;
(5) Mange (son of Tombo) — ruler of Zande Mokuma;
(6) Ngeni (son of Tombo) — ruler of Zande Abele;
(7) Ezo (son of Tombo) — ruler of Zande Embili.

(Baxter and Butt 1953: 21; Evans-Pritchard 1958: 1–15).

The origin of both the Mbomu and the Vongara is obscure, the traditions going back only to the eighteenth century. There are some myths concerning a hero who was an ancestor of the ruler Ngura. His name is different in different myths, viz. Kurangbwa, Kliso or Baseninonga. This man attained power and high rank due to personal abilities — he was a good host and judge, and introduced the custom of distributing spears among his followers, etc. The traditions emphasize the political abilities of this mythical hero; there are no traditions speaking of any kind of supernatural origin with respect to his (and consequently Vongara's) power. In point of fact, these myths lay down the rules for correct behavior for Zande rulers, their real historical value being questionable (Seligman 1932: 501–502; Baxter and Butt 1953: 54; Evans-Pritchard 1957d: 322–343).

2. ECONOMY

The main means of subsistence of the population were agriculture supplemented by hunting, fishing, and food-gathering. Due to the occurrence of the tse-tse fly it was not possible to keep cattle in the region. Agriculture was of the shifting cultivation type. After two or three crops the exhausted plots were invariably abandoned, the peasants who had tilled them returning to them after the lapse of six or seven years. The Zande worked the soil with hoes and digging-sticks, also using axes, hatchets and knives as agricultural implements. Fertilization and irrigation were unknown (Baxter and Butt 1953: 42–43; Baumann 1927: 33–48; de Schlippe 1956: 15, 79–80).

On the whole, the Zande grew about sixty-eight different kinds of crop, the most important being sorghum, manioc, groundnuts, maize, sweet potatoes, various kinds of marrows and gourds, vegetables and spices. In the southern regions bananas were cultivated. They, furthermore, raised fowls, dogs and, in smaller numbers, also goats (Baxter and Butt 1953: 43–44; de Schlippe 1956: 15, 48–77; Evans-Pritchard 1960c: 309–324).

Handicraft production was developed to only a very low degree, mostly taking the form of home production, in which the division of labor was determined by sex. Basketmaking, wood and ivorycarving, matweaving, ropemaking and netweaving were the men's domains, with pottery being part of the women's work. Only smiths were fully specialized, their craft being hereditary in certain families. They enjoyed a number of privileges, being excluded from the periodical collective labor for chiefs, and were held in honor by the people. A regular internal exchange of handicraft products and agricultural produce did not exist. According to de Schlippe, regular markets were introduced among the Zande only in the course of colonial rule. On the other hand, traditional trade with neighboring ethnic groups was widespread. The Zande traded in spears and skins and, from the middle of the last century, also in slaves, whom they sold to Arab merchants from Darfur. Before the arrival of the Europeans, iron knives and spears were widely used as a form of currency or a standard by which the value of other commodities was assessed. They were commonly used also for bride-price payments (Mecklenburg 1912: 268; de Schlippe 1956: 80, 146; Evans-Pritchard 1934: 172–175; 1967: 26, 28–30).

Land tenure and, following from this, the existence of rents are two of the problems most generally discussed with respect to the Zande. Evans-Pritchard (1963: 140–141) expressed the following opinion:

> ... in discussing the ruler–subject relationship Azande place the emphasis on personal allegiance rather than on tenure. It is true that in a sense the king owned the land and could order a subject off it, and in that sense anyone who lived on land over which he held dominion was *ipso facto* his subject. But no one was tied to any particular piece of land or district. The country was thinly populated, perhaps ten to the square mile, or even fewer, and people settled very much where they pleased, frequently moving their homes from one place to another. Landed property had little importance in a political context. There was no suggestion of tribute and services being paid as rent. Furthermore, if a Zande was dissatisfied with his lot in one kingdom, he could move to another. He might have to use discretion in doing so, but it was done; and he then transferred his allegiance to the ruler in whose territory he went to live. That the relationship was thought of in terms of personal allegiance rather than of tenure, of leadership rather than of possession, is illustrated by the fact that the people of a kingdom were designated by reference to a person rather than to a territory.

The Zande depended mostly on agriculture, and the ruler or chiefs controlled the use of the land. The nominal owner of all the land in the state was the ruler who also had the disposal of all plots in the frontier areas. He exercised the immediate right of disposal only jointly with the chief under whose administration he had placed the province in question as a whole. The provincial chief then bestowed the right to cultivate the land on individual cultivators, i.e., commoners (the use of all land was subject to his — though only formal — approval). Hence, the person possessing the actual right of disposal over land was the provincial chief; in the central province this was the ruler himself. In the border areas of his province he enjoyed complete freedom in the allocation of uncultivated land, while he might also take land away from a peasant. Commoners could not abandon their land/province with impunity, furthermore. If they left their province and returned later, they were punished by the chief (Baxter and Butt 1953: 42; Junker 1949: 186–193; Guttmann 1956: 51–53; de Schlippe 1956: 13, 104; Evans-Pritchard 1957a: 363; 1958: 12; 1963: 142–143).

The chiefs and ruler occupied a monopolistic position, and in them was vested the control of political as well as economic activities. The position of landowner coincided with that of office-holder, and thus a member of the state administration, in which capacity subordinate individuals could be prevented from gaining a share in one of the main sources of the office-holders' power and income — monopoly of land. This, then, was the case among the Zande, where the position of office-holders as landowners and bearers of the right of disposal of the surplus product (i.e., tribute) was protected and reinforced by their position in the political administration. The performance of political and ritual activities contributed to the strengthening of their economic position. They derived income from the consultation and manipulation of oracles, from jurisdiction, from conducting raids, etc. Besides, they received regular and irregular tribute in consequence of their economic position — mostly agricultural and handicraft products (Evans-Pritchard 1957a: 687–700; 1963: 146–147).

The Zande were not conscious of the connection between the performance of economic and of political functions and were likewise not aware of the actual source of the power and privileges of the chiefs and ruler. It was partly for this reason that they suggested that tributes were paid as a token of respect for the chiefs, in recognition of their great wisdom, etc. This Zande explanation was accepted by, among others, Evans-Pritchard (1963: 148). However, it appears to be an idealistic rather than a realistic explanation.

The income from tribute, which included not only foodstuffs but also handicraft products and all crops from fields cultivated with the public labor of commoners, was allocated to cover the chief's or ruler's entertainment expenses. The chiefs or ruler and their principal wives themselves were forbidden to eat of meals made from tributary food. This prohibition did not extend to the other wives of the chiefs or ruler, who hence prepared meals from this food. In theory they compensated the producers — i.e., the commoners who paid tribute and performed statute labor — for such tribute. They might do so in the form of gifts or hospitality. Of course, this 'exchange' or 'reciprocity' was regarded as a duty for commoners and a favor on the part of the chief/ruler. In actual fact this income — tribute — was consumed by the group of regular visitors to the chief's or ruler's court (members of military companies, envoys and certain ambitious private individuals, etc.). Most ordinary commoners

> ...tended to keep away from court, taking the view that though it might offer rewards — office, gifts, being-in-the-know — it also had its hazards: accusations of witchcraft, sorcery, and adultery with the king's wives, and the danger of being bewitched by jealous rivals for royal favours. Most people, especially the foreign elements, preferred to stay at home and mind their own business. (Evans-Pritchard 1963: 149).

From the point of view of ethnic origin, for instance, the Mbomu visited the chief's court more frequently than other commoners, as they, together with the Vongara, represented the ruling class in the province (Evans-Pritchard 1957a: 692, 696; 1960d: 101).

The implication of this is, that what looked like a form of reciprocity (tribute and statute labor versus gifts and hospitality on the chief's part) constituted in fact a one-sided advantage, as well as an important source of wealth for the chiefs and ruler and the narrow circle of their officials, trusty followers and court members. The rest of the population did not share the advantages of this relationship of 'reciprocity' with them.

3. KINSHIP

The descent groups which existed among the Zande were characterized as clans. There were more than 188 such clans among the Zande. Every clan was patrilineal, and, a few exceptions aside, was non-localized. All the members of one clan used a common clan name and claimed descent from the same mythical ancestor. Not necessarily all members of the clan had the same clan totem; on the other hand there were some clans which had the same totem. Totems were mostly animal. In many cases the members of a given clan were unable to specify the kinship relations between themselves, or had only a very slight knowledge of these. With the exception of those of the Vongara, genealogies had a depth of four to five generations at most. In view of the wide dispersion of members of any particular clan, it was difficult for them to keep in contact, and hence kinship ties beyond the family did not play a significant role in the life of the individual (Baxter and Butt 1953: 65–66; Evans-Pritchard 1956a: 169, 1961: 116–121).

The clan organization was of significance mainly in connection with the regulation of marriages. All clans, apart from the Vongara, were exogamic. Marriage prohibitions also applied to the members of mother's clan, and likewise extended to the members of father's mother's clan. Failure to observe this prohibition was threatened with supernatural punishment. Theoretically marriage between two persons having the same totem was also forbidden, but in practice this prohibition had no significance (Seligman 1932: 501; Baxter and Butt 1953: 66).

Membership of a clan or set of clans had certain social implications for the individual, as will be demonstrated later. Evans-Pritchard (1960a: 171) writes:

> Azande tend to class their clans as (1) Akulongbo or Avongara, the ruling clan; (2) Ambomu, the original Zande clans who followed the Avongara in their conquests; (3) named foreign stocks, Adio, Abarambo or Amiangba, Amadi and Abangbinda, all considerable peoples now assimilated to the Ambomu; and (4) Auro, a heterogeneous collection of clans of unspecified foreign peoples, ... assimilated to the Ambomu, but regarded by them more as foreigners than are the named stocks.

The Zande family might be of the elementary type; extended families were not unusual, however. Every family formed a separate and independent residential unit occupying one homestead. These homesteads lay scattered all over the country. There existed a division of labor according to sex, women performing most of the lighter agricultural work, such as hoeing and planting, and also all of the domestic tasks, while the men did the heavier agricultural work (Baxter and Butt 1953: 45–47).

4. POLITICAL ORGANIZATION

Around the year 1880 there existed in the Zande territory about fifteen relatively large independent states. In addition to these larger states, there also existed independent units of the size of the province, or even smaller units. Schweinfurth recorded thirty-five independent chiefs. These small states were often annexed by more powerful neighbors. The entire Zande area, i.e., including the existing states, was divided between the seven 'ruling houses' of Vongara. The members of one 'ruling house' usually ruled over a continuous area distributed over several separate, mutually independent states. For example, in 1885, members of the 'house of Nunga' ruled over approximately five states (Schweinfurth 1927: 84; Evans-Pritchard 1958: 1–15, 1963: 140).

The state boundaries were usually of a natural kind, mostly rivers. There was usually an uninhabited zone along the borders for reasons of security. Each state was internally divided into provinces, whose number was not fixed. The central province was ruled over by the ruler himself, and was surrounded by the remaining provinces, headed by appointed chiefs, whose palaces, in turn, were usually located in the center of their respective provinces. There were a number of paths leading from the chiefs' palaces to the court of the ruler. A province might be divided into two or three smaller units headed by sub-chiefs, but this division was not found in every province. In any case every province was divided into a number of smaller, not precisely demarcated areas, comprising several compounds and headed by so-called deputies (Baxter and Butt 1953: 48–50; Evans-Pritchard 1957a: 363–364, 690; 1963: 140, 142). The ruler and chiefs possessed their own palace compounds. Such a compound usually contained huts for the ruler/chief himself and for his wives, children, female slaves, courtiers and guests, while there were also barracks for the bodyguard, etc. There was, in addition, an assembly hall, as well as an open space for daily gatherings. Evans-Pritchard reports that the Gbudwe's compound was divided into three parts: an outer court, an inner court and the private royal quarters. The outer court was open to the public; here cases were heard, wars declared, commoner guests entertained, and so on. The inner court was accessible only to members of the aristocracy and senior office-holders; here food was served them and the ruler also.

privately discussed state affairs. The palace compounds represented the largest residential units in Zandeland. For example, that of King Bakangai covered an area of roughly 1000 by 500 yards (914× 457 metres), while Gbudwe's was spread over a distance of five miles (eight kilometres). The ruler's court was the center of the state, and, with due recognition of the fact that there were no towns in Zande-land, it is justified to speak of his court as the capital. After the death of a ruler his old capital (ruler's compound) was abandoned and a new capital built in another place by the new ruler. The location of the capital also changed in accordance with the cyclical fission of Zande states (Junker 1892: 4, 7, 24, 26; Seligman 1932: 504; Evans-Pritchard 1957c: 241). The bureaucratic organization of every Zande state was hierarchical; the rights and duties of all office-holders corres-ponding with the rank occupied by them.

The ruler, as the bearer of supreme authority, had to ensure the safety of the inhabitants of his state. He ruled with the help of the lower office-holders. For the enforcement of his decisions he had ultimate means of coercion at his disposal (e.g., military troops, judiciary powers). By virtue of his simultaneous function as chief of the central province he possessed the necessary politico-economic basis for *de facto* supremacy over individual provincial chiefs. In the ruler were concentrated all important powers, viz.:

(1) He was supreme judge and, within the state which he governed, there was no appeal against his verdicts. He adjudicated all the more serious cases for the territory of the state as a whole, implying that he adjudicated mainly cases of murder, sorcery, and adultery. His oracles were accredited with the highest legal authority, which enabled him to override, through the prophecies conveyed by his oracles, the verdicts of lower office-holders, which was in fact also his duty. In theory, without the sanction of his oracle no death sentence could be carried out and no case of adultery could be punished. But as stated by Evans-Pritchard (1957b: 66), in reality, the ruler's authority was not quite so effective.

(2) He was the commander of all the armed forces of the state. The core of his army was made up of soldiers of his bodyguard at court, which was composed of volunteers, servants and slaves, who in peace-time acted as his palace guards, i.e., kept a watch over the paths in its vicinity (Gbudwe permanently kept twenty companies under arms). The number of men in a single unit varied from twenty to 100 warriors, more numerous ones being rare. Other warriors, i.e., chiefly married men either organized in the military forces or not so or-ganized, would take up arms only in the event of mobilization. Orders for the mobilization of all men capable of performing military service from the territory of the state as a whole could be given solely by the

ruler (the state ruled by Gbudwe had about 20,000 warriors at its disposal). These orders he would send by messengers to the individual provincial chiefs. In the event of a general war, the provincial chiefs, together with their troops, came under the direct command of the ruler. Only he could conclude peace with a neighboring enemy ruler. Two or more rulers could also form a military alliance, possibly further strengthened by the conclusion of a blood pact between them.

(3) The ruler appointed provincial chiefs, mostly from among his sons, younger brothers, or other members of the Vongara clan. After the death of a provincial chief the ruler could appoint anyone to the vacant position, in spite of the fact that it was generally assumed that the deceased's position would go to one of his younger brothers or sons. He might also appoint chiefs from the ranks of commoners, usually of Mbomu origin. The appointment of chiefs was not accompanied by any ceremonies. Often, in Gbudwe's state the ruler's sons, other Vongara, or commoners would not be directly appointed by Gbudwe, but would go and settle in some other area, usually quite remote from the court, and there endeavor to acquire their own followers. Usually, the ruler did not interfere with them, provided they recognized his sovereignty and paid him taxes. Commoners and Vongara might naturally also be sent by the ruler to govern new territories and become provincial chiefs. The ruler had the right to depose provincial chiefs — a chief of Vongara origins could theoretically be deposed on suspicion of disloyalty to the ruler, cowardice, or bad management and maladministration of his province. He could depose a commoner chief at any time, however, mostly by appointing his own son in his stead (Lagae 1926: 20; Seligman 1932: 504; Junker 1949: 213; Baxter and Butt 1953: 48, 62–64, 56–58; Evans-Pritchard 1932–1933: 292; 1955: 131; 1957c: 240–241, 251–152, 255, 364; 1960b: 6, 8, 10–11, 26; 1963: 142–145, 151).

The provincial chief was supposed to afford protection to the commoners living in his province. To the ruler the chiefs were responsible for the maintenance of the public order in their provinces and for the performance of their special duties, which could include, for instance, the implementation of a policy aimed at the assimilation of foreigners, i.e., subjected groups living in Zande territory. For these reasons the chiefs made regular tours of inspection of their provinces. Among the more important duties of the chiefs ranked the defence of the state borders. The chiefs kept in touch with the ruler through messengers. They also communicated with him by means of drums. In addition, they visited the ruler once every month or two months in order to report on events occurring in their provinces. They were further obliged to consult the ruler on current court cases (sentences) on the occasion of their visits to his court. In his contacts with them the ruler regularly emphasized the necessity of keeping a constant border watch and of getting reports on the activities of neighboring states. Chiefs could act as judge, while the deputies might adjudge minor cases, with only the more serious ones coming under the jurisdiction of the chief, who was obliged to send grave offenders direct to the ruler's court. Each provincial chief was the commander of all the military forces in his province. The core of his army was also composed of bodyguards (the chiefs as a rule kept five–six companies under arms), likewise supplemented by a force made up of married men. Each individual province was capable of supplying from 200 to 300 up to 2,000 to 3,000 men. In the first place, the chiefs organized the regular border raids, which took place more or less continually. They did not have to inform the ruler in advance of their intention to attack the territory of a neighboring state or consult him on this in any other way. In the event of an attack on a province it was the province so attacked, together with any neighboring one, which armed and mobilized their warriors in the first place. More distant provinces or the central province would not mobilize their armies to begin with, but would wait for more detailed reports on the force and direction of the attack, as well as for instructions from the ruler. Provincial chiefs could appoint subchiefs and deputies (i.e., chief's agents or trustees, to use Evans-Pritchard's term) in their respective provinces. In some cases a provincial chief might divide his territory into smaller units, usually two to three, and place his brothers or sons at their head as sub-chiefs. The ruler did not, as a rule, object to such a division effected directly by the chief concerned. Only chiefs of Vongara origins so divided their provinces; again, usually members of the Vongara clan being appointed as sub-chiefs, although the position of subchief could also be attained by a commoner. To the position of deputy, the chiefs appointed commoners who had served at their court for several years and whom they could therefore trust. In some cases they might appoint to this post, chiefs of subjugated ethnic groups. According to Lagae the office of deputy was hereditary, subject to the approval of the chief (the reports of other authorities contradict this). However, the provincial chief could depose deputies, though only for major offences such as sorcery, disloyalty to himself, the misappropriation of tribute or failure to hand it over, and adultery with wives of commoner subjects (Lagae 1926: 17–18; Seligman 1932: 503–504; Junker 1949: 191; Baxter and Butt 1953: 58, 63–64: Guttmann 1956: 51; Evans-Pritchard 1957a: 689–690; 1957c: 240–241, 247; 1960b: 6, 26, 28–29; 1963). 143, 145.

The deputies governed a piece of territory that had no precisely defined borders. They enjoyed complete authority here, and all the people living in their territory were subjected to them. At the same time, the deputies were obliged to protect the population, and if they failed to observe the norms in force with regard to their behavior, such as, for example, by maladministering their territory or committing adultery with the wives of commoners, they could be dismissed by the provincial chief. They were obliged to visit the latter's court regularly and to submit reports on all events that had taken place in their territory, as also on the loyalty of their subjects. Deputies could adjudge minor cases. They also led the force, composed of their commoner subjects, into war, which meant that the office of deputy merged with that of commander of a military force. This force was composed solely of married men living in the deputy's territory (Lagae 1926: 18; Seligman 1932: 504; Baxter and Butt 1953: 58; Evans-Pritchard 1957a: 365, 687, 689–690).

Among the duties with economic implications we should note the office-holders' obligation to organize the collection of both the regular and irregular taxes, to organize the commoner labor force and to maintain communications. The deputies, with the assistance of their subjects were responsible for the maintenance of all communication channels within their respective administrative domains, as well as of the paths leading to the provincial chief's court. The latter inspected the paths within his province and maintained those leading to the ruler's court (Evans-Pritchard 1957a: 365; 1963: 142, 146).

Outside this bureaucratic organization there were different dignitaries fulfilling various special offices. These included the commanders of the guard troops composed of young men, who were mostly recruited from among commoners. They were different from the deputies commanding the forces made up of married men. These military commanders led the guard troops in military campaigns and on other occasions. Their peacetime duties included among other things the supervision of the sub-chiefs and deputies. They were immediately subordinate to the ruler or chief. Besides the military commander, every military company had a deputy leader, the order of rank or seniority being determined by length of service. The chiefs also employed spies for military purposes (Baxter and Butt 1953: 63; Guttman 1956: 52; Evans-Pritchard 1957a: 499; 1957c: 240–241, 245; 1963: 144).

Both the ruler and the provincial chiefs had special people in their service for consulting and interpreting the oracles. Usually there were two or three such specialists at the court of a chief or ruler, who carried out their task in rotation. Throughout the period of their service they were forced to observe certain rules and prohibitions, such as that of celibacy, abstinence from certain kinds of food, etc. (Seligman 1932: 528; Baxter and Butt 1953: 57).

At the court of the chief or ruler also lived people who might be specified as courtiers. They included the ruler's/chief's sons and other kinsmen not occupying special offices; regular visitors to the court of the ranks of respected deputies and commoners; pages, and so on (Junker 1892: 3–4; Evans-Pritchard 1963: 146).

At the court of the chief/ruler also lived his numerous wives — principal wives, favorites, servants, female slaves, etc. But women played an insignificant role in Zande political life (Evans-Pritchard 1957a: 702–710).

There are no data on the making of new rules and laws. Seeing that the ruler and chiefs held justice in their own hands, it was presumably they who made any such new rules and laws. In any case, the existing legal norms confirmed the power of the office-holders.

In legal practice two kinds of offences were distinguished, namely so-called 'private offences' and 'public offences', according to who sustained the damage. 'Private offences', i.e., injuries to individual subjects, were punishable by a mere fine in knives, or by enslavement. The so-called 'public offences' included outrages against chiefs, the use of magic against a chief, adultery with a chief's wife, membership of secret societies that imposed restrictions on the power of office-holders, and so on. In the majority of cases punishment for these offences took the form of strangulation; for lesser offences the offenders might be pilloried or enslaved. Sometimes, in cases of adultery with a chief's wife, the relatives of the offender might be forced to become the servants of the chief's wives or enslaved. For some offences a commoner could be banished by his chief. Also liable to banishment were the relatives of an offender whom a chief or ruler had sentenced to death and executed, mainly from fear of reprisals on their part (Lagae 1926: 23, 47; Seligman 1932: 505, 507, 516: Baxter and Butt 1953: 51, 55–57; Guttmann 1956: 52; Evans-Pritchard 1957c: 241, 250).

In the administration of justice, furthermore, differences in legal punishment were made in accordance with the rank of the offender. A Zande commoner was liable to punishment for every offence against another commoner or an office-holder. On the other hand, quite above the law, at least as far as their relations with commoners were concerned, were all members of the ruling Vongara clan, who could not be punished for any offences against them. In the majority of cases they were punished only for offences against the ruler or any of the chiefs. It was furthermore quite unlikely for a commoner to dare to establish guilt on the part of even the most powerless Vongara. If a member of the Vongara clan were accused of sorcery, the accusation was normally kept secret, whereas a commoner was liable to be punished if a similar accusation was lodged against him. If a commoner deserted his chief and moved to another province he could not return without punishment. If an office-holder had fled to a neighboring state, he could generally return without punishment. If a chief caught his wife after fleeing with a commoner, he would kill them both. A member of the Vongara clan (e.g., a chief's son) guilty of the same offence was also punished, it is true, but his punishment took the form of maiming (Baxter and Butt 1953: 55, 59, 81; Evans-Pritchard 1932–1933: 312; 1957b: 73; 1960b: 11).

In the context of legal practices we should mention also the rule of succession, especially in relation to the highest position in the Zande state, namely that of the ruler. The position of ruler could only be attained by a member of the privileged and ruling Vongara clan. There was no accurately defined rule of succession, however, and theoretically any member of the clan could attain this position of supreme authority. Junker states that, in theory, the eldest son of a deceased ruler was supposed to succeed him, but that, in practice usually the most powerful son did so. Evans-Pritchard writes that a pretender to the highest office had, in the first place, to exploit the current political situation in order to attain it. In some cases the decisive factor was the successful seizure of the central province (Seligman 1932: 503; Lagae 1926: 16; Junker 1949: 222; Baxter and Butt 1953: 48–49; Evans-Pritchard 1960b: 21; 1963: 151).

When a provincial chief died it was generally assumed that the deceased's office would go to one of his younger brothers or sons. However, the ruler could appoint anyone else to the vacant position. With respect to the deputies Lagae reports that their office was hereditary, subject to the approval of the chief. It seems that in determining the succession, in theory the principle of seniority carried some weight. This accords with the senior son's role of 'second father' with respect to his younger brothers and sisters after their father's death, as also with the practice of paying the elder brother honor. It may also explain why Zande rulers were reluctant to give provinces to older kinsmen to govern in the early years of their rule and often appointed commoner chiefs instead (Lagae 1926: 17–18; Seligman 1932: 507–509; Evans-Pritchard 1963: 142).

Ritual played a relatively insignificant role in the life of Zande office-holders. Their only ritual function was administration of poison oracles in the course of criminal trials or on any other important occasion. As was mentioned above, the legal authority of oracles depended on the rank of the office-holder concerned; in other words, they were ranked in hierarchical order. There was no appeal against the verdicts pronounced by the ruler's oracle. No other ritual activities are mentioned in connection with office-holders. The only exception to this was the keeping of certain relics of a deceased person by his eldest son and the occasional offering of sacrifices to these among the Vongara. However, this duty is connected rather with his role as eldest son than that as ruler or chief (Junker 1892: 23–26; Baxter and Butt 1953: 68).

5. SOCIAL STRATIFICATION[2]

In evaluating the general social stratification we must take into consideration the two principal lines of division among the Zande, i.e., the division of the population on the basis of different roles in the performance of economic, political, and ritual tasks, and that based on membership of the Vongara clan on the one hand and all the other clans on the other. In principle we can distinguish three social strata, namely commoners, aristocracy, and slaves. In view of their differential relation to the basic means of production these strata possess the character of social classes (Kandert 1968: 126).

5.1. *Commoners*

As a whole, this class was concerned with agricultural production, did not have the disposal of land and was given the use of land by chiefs (members of the aristocracy). From their position as mere users of land who were dependent on their chiefs there flowed numerous economic and political obligations (payment of tribute, performance of statute labor, military service, etc.). Their subordinate position found expression in different ways (dress, respectful behavior, etc.), and more especially in the practice of jurisdiction, involving as it did especially severe punishments for offences against the aristocracy and differential punishment for commoners and members of the aristocracy for the same kinds of offence. Due to the fact that commoners originated exclusively from non-Vongara clans, membership of this class was mostly hereditary and permanent, in the same way as clan membership. The only exception was provided by commoner chiefs, who were classed among the aristocracy. A commoner citizen could never become ruler (Junker 1949: 215). It is possible to divide the commoners into two sub-strata: commoners proper and deputies.

There was little difference in position between the Mbomu and Auro commoners. The Mbomu took a more active part in certain activities of their rulers and occupied a relatively privileged position in society in comparison with the Auro. But there were no differences in their duties and rights in general. For that reason they may generally both be classified into the substratum of commoners proper.

The deputies were distinguishable from the commoners proper by their active participation in certain economic and political activities. They collected tribute, assembled and led commoners for purposes of both statute labor and war, and so on. Although the deputies were, in fact, office-holders, it was in only very few of their activities that they could take decisions. In the majority of cases they were no more than the executors of orders given by the chief. Like other commoners, they were given their land by the chiefs. Deputies were recruited exclusively from the ranks of commoners. According to the majority of the authorities (with the exception of Lagae) tenure of their office was not hereditary. Individuals were appointed as deputies by the provincial chiefs; they were not inaugurated into office. As office-holders of the lowest rank they were differentiated from the commoners proper by a number of outer marks of rank (the possibility to visit the chiefs in their outer palace, etc.).

Only very few data are available on the general status of political and religious experts (i.e., military commanders, oracle wielders). In view of the fact that they were recruited from among commoners and captives, and considering their complete dependence on the office-holders, in addition to the relative insignificance of their role in the performance of offices, it can be supposed that, despite their function, they continued to possess the status of commoners or even slaves.

5.2. The Aristocracy

The aristocracy as a whole differed from the commoners by their monopoly of the land as well as of political and ritual functions. This difference was reflected by a number of outer symbols: they performed no manual work, wore different clothing and adornments, and, on visiting the ruler's court, ate in the inner palace, etc. The aristocracy of Vongara origin was endogamic.

The highest position was held by the ruler, who was the nominal owner of all the land in the state and allotted it to the individual chiefs. In his hands were concentrated all the means of exerting power, and he was subject to no form of control. A lower position was occupied by the provincial chiefs from the Vongara clan. Within the borders of their respective provinces they occupied the same unique position as the ruler within the borders of the state. They were subject to the ruler's control (in theory) and rendered him services. The ruler and the chiefs of Vongara origin together formed a substratum of the aristocracy.

Another special substratum was composed by the commoner chiefs and later on also members of the Vongara clan without any official rank. Although their position was lower than that of the ruler and the Vongara chiefs, they should be classified in the aristocratic rather than the commoner stratum nonetheless.

Commoner chiefs carried out the same economic, political, and ritual functions as Vongara chiefs. They were more dependent on the ruler, by whom they were appointed and for whom they also per-formed special services not required of Vongara chiefs (namely, the dispatch of workers to the ruler's province, and keeping the peace in their respective provinces). They could hold office only through appointment by the ruler, being unable to attain to this through their own efforts. It was likewise impossible for them to become independent rulers after the ruler's death, whereas Vongara chiefs could often become independent on this occasion. Despite the fact that they performed practically the same functions, they were not integrated with the Vongara and were regarded as mere commoners by them. Nonetheless, because of their performance of identical functions, and on account of certain similar privileges, they can be classified in the aristocratic class.

In the same substratum can be classified Vongara who held no office. Due to their membership of the Vongara clan, they retained aristocratic status, nevertheless. Like other members of that clan, they were entitled by their very birth to occupy even the highest office. In this they differed also from the commoner chiefs. Their membership of the Vongara group was further manifest from the employment of the same modes of address towards them, their exemption from punishment for offences against commoners, the mildness of their punishment as compared with that of commoners for the same offences, and the mutual assistance between them. Although they did not differ from commoners even as regards their standard of living, they can be regarded as members of the aristocratic class nonetheless.

5.3. *Slaves*

Slaves formed the lowest class in Zande society. They were owned by both members of the aristocracy and commoners. They played no part whatever in the performance of economic and political functions, or participated only passively. They were entirely subordinate to their owners, and worked solely for the latter's benefit. Membership of this class was not hereditary, and the slave status was not unchangeable for its members.

6. CYCLICAL DEVELOPMENT AND THE STABILITY OF THE STATE

The death of the ruler or the period of his rule during his old age constituted a critical juncture for the stability of the state. At this time a period of continuous fighting, elimination of opponents and intrigues between the various descendants — potential future rulers — would set in. There was also a more peaceful solution to the problem of the succession. The ruler could divide the entire state into a number of smaller units, usually among his sons, still during his lifetime. But the result was the same as in the case of pretenders quarrelling after the ruler's death — the stability of the state was threatened after the splitting up of the existing state unit (Junker 1892: 8–9; Evans-Pritchard 1958: 12; 1960d: 6, 22; 1963: 144).

This cyclical splitting up of powerful Zande states, and especially the ensuing chaos of war, has attracted the attention of all scholars concerned with the Zande. For an explanation of the instability of Zande states one should look at the course of development of every individual Zande state as well as the Zande system as a whole.

As soon as a certain Vongara clan member succeeded in securing an independent area (whether by conquest or succession) he would introduce in it the usual administrative organization of the Zande state. He would reserve for himself the right of direct rule over the new central province, while appointing chiefs to govern the other provinces. During the early period of the ruler's reign, as long as he had no adult sons, commoner chiefs were most often appointed. The ruler was usually afraid of ambitious brothers or other kinsmen who might try to gain independence in a province of their own. This danger was not present in the case of commoner chiefs, who were usually rich and influential deputies, or sometimes also chiefs of conquered groups. In the later years of his rule the ruler might replace such commoner chiefs by members of the Vongara clan — above all his own sons. The situation then remained the same till the ruler's death (Evans-Pritchard 1932–1933: 292; 1957a: 688; 1960a: 6, 8; 1963: 142–143, 151).

This cyclical process of fission, whereby younger sons of rulers with surplus followers of commoner rank entered new areas to found new states and to take possession of the land and its resources, had its advantages during the period of expansion. But in a period where a certain stabilization had occurred and expansion had stopped, this policy led to continuous warfare and the splitting up of existing states. Vagueness of the rules of succession gave every Vongara an opportunity to secure the title of ruler. In combination with the numerousness of the Vongara, this led to the existence of a great many pretenders, and consequently to fighting between them.

This process of splitting up was further encouraged by the internal political situation in the state. Every state consisted of a number of provinces, every province and its chief having a certain autonomy. The province was regarded as a unit. Commoners called themselves not only by the name of the ruler but also by that of the provincial chief (the commoners from the province of chief Rikiti used to call themselves 'avuru Gbudwe' and in addition 'avuru Rikiti'). Chiefs also often organized border raids, not only against neighboring states but also against neighboring provinces within the state. On the one hand, the ruler had the power not only to dismiss chiefs, but also to transfer them from one province to another without their having the right to object, on the other hand, he never interfered in provincial affairs unless dissension arose or a provincial chief proved incompetent (Evans-Pritchard 1957c: 240, 244–245, 247, 255; 1963: 143, 145).

It is possible to characterize the Zande states as conquest states in a period of transition. Originally, wars and conquests helped to strengthen the existing states, since pretenders went to new areas. The assimilation policy of the Vongara/Mbomu was in harmony with this. But in the second half of the nineteenth century, when expansion stopped, the continuing wars and conquests caused the splitting up of state units. Certain tendencies towards centralization were inherent in the state organization — the aristocracy held the monopoly of all economic, political and ritual functions — but the states were as yet weak. The splitting up or segmentation of the existing Zande state units may thus be regarded as an important characteristic of the early state at a specific level of development.

FOOTNOTES

[1] The majority of the data for this paper were taken from the reports of Evans-Pritchard, who carried out field research in the Sudan region, particularly in the territory of the former state of King Gbudwe. I admit that my paper contains a number of errors and inaccuracies due to my supposing that a similar situation to that found by Evans-Pritchard in the Sudan area prevailed in other regions inhabited by the Zande, although his reports are supplemented by reports from other Zande territories. The purpose of the present study will be to ascertain the political organization of the Zande in the second half of the nineteenth century, up to the time when the individual Zande states were subjected to colonial rule.

[2] For a more detailed analysis of Zande social stratification see: Kandert, Josef (1968). Social stratification of the Zande, in: *Social stratification in tribal Africa*, ed. by L. Holý and M. Stuchlík, pp. 97–130. Prague Academia.

REFERENCES

Baumann, H. (1927), *Die materielle Kultur der Azande und Mangbetu.* Baessler-Archiv, Bd. 11.

Baxter, P. T. W. and Butt A., (1953), *The Azande and related peoples of the Anglo-Egyptian Sudan and Belgian Congo.* London: International Africa Institute.

Evans-Pritchard, E. E. (1932–1933), The Zande corporation of witchdoctors. *JRAI* 62/63: 291–336, 63–100.

— (1934), Social character of bridewealth with special reference to the Azande, *Man* 34: 172–175.

— (1955), Zande historical texts, *Sudan Notes and Records* 36: 123–145.

— (1956a), Zande clan names, *Man* 62.

— (1956b), Zande totems, *Man* 110.
— (1957a), The Zande royal court, *Zaïre:* 361–389, 493–511, 687–713.
— (1957b), Zande kings and princes, *Anthropological Quarterly* 30: 618–690.
— (1957c), Zande warfare, *Anthropos* 70: 239–262.
— (1957d), The origin of the ruling clan of the Azande, *Southwest. J. Anthrop* 13: 322–343.
— (1958), A historical introduction to a study of Zande society, *African Studies* 17: 1–15.
— (1960a), Zande clans and settlements, *Man* 213.
— (1960b), The organization of a Zande kingdom, *Cahiers d'Etudes Africaines* 4: 5–37.
— (1960c), A contribution to the study of Zande culture, *Africa* 30: 309–324.
— (1960d), The ethnic origin of Zande office-holders, *Man* 141.
— (1961), Zande clans and totems, *Man* 147.
— (1963), The Zande state, *JRAI* 93: 134–153.
— (1967), Zande iron-working, *Paideuma*, Bd. 13: 26–31.
Guttmann, E. (1956), Land tenure among the Azande people of the equatorial province in the Sudan, *Sudan Notes and Records* 37: 48–55.
Junker, W. (1892), *Travels in Africa during the years 1882–1886.* London: Chapman and Hall.
Junker, V. V. (1949), *Puteshestviia po Afrike.* [Travels in Africa.] Moscow: Nauka.
Kandert, J. (1968), Social stratification of the Zande, in: *Social stratification in tribal Africa*, ed. by L. Holý and M. Stuchlík, 97–130. Prague: Academia.
Lagae, C. R. (1926), *Les Azande ou Niam-Niam.* Bruxelles: Musée Royale.
Mecklenburg, Adolf F. Herzog zu (1912), *Vom Kongo zum Niger und Nil.* Leipzig: Brockhaus.
Porshnev, B. F. (1959), *Nástin politické ekonomie feudalismu.* [An outline of the political economy of feudalism]. Prague.
Schlippe, P. de (1956), *The Azande system of agriculture.* London.
Schweinfurth, G. (1927), *Im Herzen von Afrika.* Leipzig: Brockhaus.
Seligman, G. G. (1932), *Pagan tribes of the Nilotic Sudan.* London: Oxford University Press.

PART THREE:

Synthesis

Part Three of the volume is first an attempt to synthesize the data in the Part Two and second to contrast the findings to the background of the ideas and hypotheses suggested in Part One. Answers to the questions presented are sought through the employment of three different approaches. First, a structural analysis in chapter 25 makes it possible to see what common features are found in the early states and what their characteristics are. Chapter 26 presents a processual method which enables the reader to arrive at an understanding of the dynamic regularities in the development of the early state. This chapter is inspired by Marx's ideas and recent discussions on the character of the early state. Chapter 27 attempts to delimit the beginning and the end of the early state in evolutionary terms. It also moves toward a definition of the early state by pointing out its limitations as a distinct social organization. A final chapter summarizes the findings and results of the volume. Its goal is not to set forth unshakeable truths, but to provide a basis for further research on, and discussion of, the early state.

25

The Early State: A Structural Approach

HENRI J. M. CLAESSEN

1. METHODOLOGICAL REMARKS

The first part of this volume comprised the introductory chapter on theories and working hypotheses, three theoretical chapters (by Cohen, Khazanov and Krader) and an overview of the problems that would be dealt with in the further course of the work. Then, in the second part, twenty-one case studies were presented. The authors of these essays all tried to give as much specific information as possible.

This first chapter will present a survey of the differences and similarities between these twenty-one cases. In accordance with our comparative interest, the resemblances will receive rather more attention than the differences. It will not be possible, of course, to be exhaustive in this chapter. The body of data is so vast that we will be unable to cover even all of the relevant aspects. We have therefore made a selection of those findings that are — at least in our view — important for an understanding of the structures of early states.

Before proceeding, we should try to clear up one problem: we have brought together twenty-one case essays, but are these cases representative? Can they be taken as a fair sample of all early states that ever existed? In point of fact, we are unable to answer this question. We do not know how many early states have existed in world history, so that the sampling level remains unknown. We do not even know if at least all the major areas are properly represented. Our volume includes cases from many different parts of the world: two from America, two from Oceania, eight from Africa (though these are spread over an enormous span of time), three from Europe (which is very few indeed), and six from Asia (also spread over a long span of time). Viewed historically, the states in our sample range from the ancient kingdom of

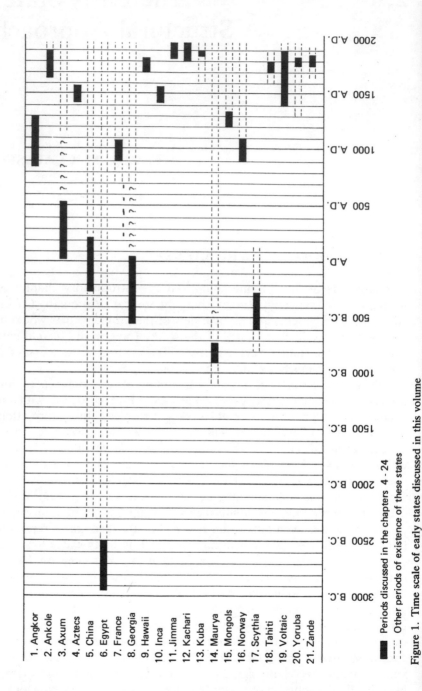

Figure 1. Time scale of early states discussed in this volume

Egypt, to Jimma, which came into existence in the 1830s. The only thing we know for certain is that there were *no direct* links between these states. Compared with the sample of Tuden and Marshall (1972), ours shows many differences. Their sample was based on Murdock and White's 'standard world sample' (Tuden and Marshall 1972: 436), which was taken according to different criteria, since it aimed to be representative for all world cultures. The same holds, in fact, for Naroll's *Permanent ethnographic probability sample universe* (1970: 921 ff.). We therefore feel obliged to fall back on Nadel's (old) idea that a number of carefully chosen and carefully studied cases should be sufficient to provide relevant data concerning the problem under study in general (Nadel 1969: 113 ff., 248 ff).

The above considerations have led us to the conviction that, in our case, complicated calculations would be a waste of time and energy: the representativeness of the sample is unknown, while, moreover, we will be bringing together in our analyses data of quite divergent origins, namely concerning the institutions and functions of states of widely different cultural backgrounds, and dispersed over long spans of time and distance.

Though the selection of data for the comparisons will inevitably contain an element of subjectivity, we nonetheless hope we have succeeded in making a satisfactory selection of the relevant data. This selection was based on:
—experience gathered in earlier studies of this kind (especially Claessen 1970);
—the relevance of the data as shown up by our case studies;
—the need for suggesting answers to the rather general questions and verifying the hypotheses put forward in the first chapter;
—the questions and problems raised in the theoretical chapters of the first part.

As the state is in the first place an organization, we are interested in the systematic aspects of this organization. The relations between the members of the state appear to be shaped by recurrent patterns; patterns that remain even after the original participants in the relationships long passed away. This view, in fact, is based on Radcliffe-Brown's concept of social structure (1952). The present chapter thus is concerned in the main with 'what it looks like', that is, with organizational aspects and institutions. However, we also believe in the possibility that 'behind' the surface structures, principles lie hidden and relations exist which, consciously or unconsciously, make the system as a whole *operate*, (and with these problems we are in the field of structuralism) (cf. De Josselin de Jong 1975).

To put a factual basis under our structural observations, we will *compare* the data of our case studies. To compare is, in fact 'to

consider two or more phenomena in relation to each other in order to
find differences and/or resemblances between them' (Kruijer 1959:
94). If the data to be compared belong to different cultural contexts—
as in our case—comparison becomes a difficult and most complicated
task (cf. Köbben 1967, 1970; Nadel 1969; Vermeulen and De Ruijter
1975). In the first place all comparison requires clear *definitions*. Only
if the categories are defined as clearly as possible will the risk of
wrongly bringing together different phenomena be reduced to an
acceptable minimum. The endeavor to use clear definitions does not
guarantee the total exclusion of error, however. Especially where the
data in the case essays are vague or inconclusive, an element of
arbitrariness in the categorization will be inevitable. The same holds
for the second problem, namely how identical are the phenomena
under consideration? Here again we are obliged to admit that in
cross-cultural studies the phenomena are seldom identical. In fact,
comparison in the social sciences invariably brings together
phenomena that are quite different. A solution to this problem may be
provided by '*facet*-comparison', whereby we do not compare complete
institutions, but only aspects of them. In this way it will be possible to
make valid comparisons of aspects of otherwise different institutions
(cf. the observations of Popper [1968: 420 ff] on the comparison of
different objects which always possess one trait in common). Of course,
this method demands a clear indication of what aspects will be compared. In view of the frequent elusiveness of the data, we will have to
make use many times of so-called *functional equivalents*. Functional
equivalents are phenomena which, though different in form, fulfil the
same functions (cf. Claessen 1975a). Viewed from a higher level of
abstraction, they are then comparable.

A third complex of problems is that relating to *intensity* and *frequency*. Certain phenomena may be found to exist in more than one
state, but may vary greatly in the number of times they occur, or the
influence they exercise. It is difficult, however, to find measures of
these factors, the more so since the essays do not provide quantitative
data on these variables. Only incidentally will we be able to include the
factors of frequency or intensity in our comparisons, therefore. The
data gathered will be grouped together in *tables*, divided according to
relevant aspects. In most cases it proved possible to identify the
characteristics on which information was asked. In these cases the
result will be indicated with an X-sign or a particular letter. Where no
data were supplied with reference to a specific characteristic, we will
use the 0-sign. Where the data furnished indicate that a certain
phenomenon was not found in one (or more) of the states studied, this
will be indicated with a dash.

We are aware that politics are a *process* (cf. Swartz, *et al.* 1966;

Swartz 1968). Our interest, however, goes primarily to organizational aspects. Processes here will therefore come only in the second place.

The structural analysis of our data will be arranged according to the following plan: the data furnished by the case-studies will be grouped around a number of *key concepts* (e.g., territory, sovereignty, stratification, etc.). In each of these *clusters* we will distinguish a number of *aspects*, from which aspects as many *characteristics* as we were able to find will be extracted and included in the tables. In some cases the aspects and characteristics were quite obvious. In others they were arbitrarily chosen, though always with close reference to the factual material. Some characteristics that may have been important could not be included for lack of data.

Incidentally, we were able to add certain missing data from other sources. Where we did so, the source has been explicitly mentioned. In the tables the states are arranged alphabetically. It goes without saying that '*China*' refers to the early state of China, as discussed by Pokora in his particular chapter. '*Egypt*' refers to the Old Kingdom. We will use the name *Iberia* for the Georgian states as discussed by Koranashvili in chapter 12, and *Mongolia* for the nomadic states dealt with by Krader in chapter 4. Furthermore *Tahiti* and *Volta* are shorthand forms for the Tahitian and Voltaic states respectively. *Yoruba* is used to designate for the greater part the Oyo state.

Where possible, we will try to formulate certain *structural characteristics*. To be so declared, specific characteristics will have to be present in at least sixteen cases, and absent in no more than two cases, while in the remaining three cases it will come under the heading 'no data', but its presence will be at least probable in view of the general pattern of the state concerned.[1]

2. STRUCTURAL COMPARISONS

2.1. *Territory*

In the first chapter we said that the presence of a certain territory is one of the main characteristics of the state. It would be superfluous to observe that each of our states possessed a territory if we were unable to add a few further qualifications. Every corporate social group in fact has a territory (cf. Schapera 1956). However, in the case of the early states under discussion it was found that this territory was occupied by people from different clans, or family groups, recognizing the presence of some sort of political unity extending to the boundaries of that territory.

In addition, the political organization appeared to be divided into territorial segments with regional or local functionaries at their head (for this see Section 2.12 and structural characteristics (S.C.) numbers 44 and 45).

In most cases in our sample there were natural boundaries delimiting the territory (for the *Aztecs* and *Norway*, no data were provided). In *Axum*, a distinction can be made between the center and the periphery, the latter part being ruled only nominally by the lord of *Axum*.

Nowhere was any kind of formal citizenship of the state mentioned. People seem to belong to a state by the sheer fact of being born, or permanently residing in its territory (cf. Trouwborst 1973). For details see Table I. The structural characteristic we are able to formulate here is:

(1) *The early states in our sample had a definite territory, divided into territorial divisions, which is usually loosely demarcated. The people permanently residing in them (with few exceptions) were considered as subjects or citizens of these states* (significant at the 99% level).

Table I. *General data*

	Territorial boundaries	Independence	Population density	Kind of capital	Urbanization	Kind of center	Type of infrastruct
Angkor	0	X	L	C	U̇	st	E
Ankole	N	X	H, P	K	—	M	—
Axum	N	X	L	C	U	st	Li
Aztecs	0	X	H, P	C	U	st	E
China	N	X	H, P	C	U	st	E
Egypt	N	X	0	C	–	st	E
France	S	X	H, P	C	U	st	E
Hawaii	N	X	L	K	—	M	0
Iberia	N	X	H	C	U	st	0
Inca	N	X	H	C	U	st	E
Jimma	N	X	L	C	—	st	E
Kachari	S	X	L	C	U	st	Li
Kuba	N	X	L	C	—	M	E
Maurya	N	X	H, P	C	U	st	E
Mongolia	S	X	L	C	—	st	0
Norway	N	X	H, P	K	U	M	0
Scythia	S	X	0	C	U	st	Li
Tahiti	N	X	H	K	—	st	Li
Volta	S	X	L	K/C	—	st/M	—
Yoruba	S	X	L	C	U	st	E
Zande	N	X	L	K	—	M	Li

Abbreviations: 0 = no data supplied; N = natural; S = not specified; P = population pressure; L = low density; H = high density; K = only a governmental center; C = capital city; U = existence of other towns; st = stable; M = moving; E = extensive infrastructure; Li = limited infrastructure.

2.2. Independence

The data of the case studies show that all twenty-one cases were independent; at least for the greater part of their existence. By this we mean that they were not answerable or in any other way subordinate to other states or rulers. *Ankole* was twice defeated in war, and was occupied for short periods of time as a consequence of this. It afterwards regained its independence, however. *Yoruba* presents the complication that most of the city-states in the end were subjected by the city-state of Ọyọ. This state at least preserved its independence a very long time. If *Yoruba* is taken to refer specially to Ọyọ, we feel that this state can be accepted as a positive case. *Jimma*, after a totally autonomous period of more than fifty years, began paying tax to Ethiopia. This did not in any way affect its internal autonomy. The same holds true for one of the *Voltaic* states, Dagbong, which paid a tribute to Asante. We therefore deem it justified to formulate as structural characteristic that:

(2) *An early state is an independent organization.* (Significant at the 99% level).

2.3. Population

In the introductory chapter we remarked that 'a sufficient population' is found in all states. This is a rather vague statement. Is it possible to give this phrase a more specific content? A possible modification is density of population. Since the publication of *African political systems* (1940) the problem of population density in states has been frequently discussed. Stevenson (1968) demonstrated that generally the density of population was higher in states than in non-state organizations, although he was unable to specify any degree of density. Neither, in fact are we.

Some authors argue that a state will always have a large population, and that a growth in population, leading to population pressure, in fact played a decisive role in the development of the state (cf. Carneiro 1970). However, Wright and Johnson (1975) have demonstrated, in the case investigated by them, the occurrence of a *drop* in population prior to state formation (cf. Cohen in the present volume). The role of population pressure in the process of state formation will be discussed in chapter 27. Here we will restrict ourselves to a general remark on data on population size or pressure. In our opinion all data on size will have to be related to the means of subsistence. This implies that 'high' or 'low' density are by no means absolute qualifications. The indication 'low' will therefore be used in the present volume in cases where the territory of a given state could easily have sustained a larger population. The mention that not all arable land was in use, or that there was a shortage of people to work the available land will be taken as an indicator of this. Where all available land was in use, where food had to be imported or where large-scale technical projects were needed for the expansion of food production, the density will be indicated as *high*. The results of this particular investigation are also shown in Table 1. In two cases no data were available on this. Here it appears that ten of our other cases had a low relative density, and nine of them a high one. For six of the cases of this latter group (*Ankole, Aztecs, China, France, Maurya and Norway*) either a temporary or a permanent population pressure was reported. In *Norway* this led to emigration. In the case of the *Aztecs, China* and *Maurya* it stimulated conquests, while it led to intermittent famine and misery in *Ankole*, and to an intensification of cultivation in *France*. No structural characteristic can be formulated here.

2.4. Urbanization

It is generally assumed that every state must have a capital, or at least a center of government. In order to be able to discuss this subject we will first have to define the concept of capital. The problem here is that none of our case studies are very specific on this point. In most cases solely the existence or nonexistence of a capital is mentioned. For our present purposes we will define 'capital' as a governmental center where the ruler had his residence, and where also live people who are not directly connected with government or the court, but who do not have agriculture as their main occupation, thus forming an urban center. Here we have in mind such people as artisans, merchants, scholars, etc. In Table I we have brought together data on the following aspects:
— the existence of only some kind of governmental center (K);
— the existence of a capital city (C);
— the existence of other towns or cities (U);
— stability (st) or mobility (M) of the center.
For *Mongolia* data have been added from another source (Haenisch 1948: 139).
    The results of the comparisons are:
A stable capital city was found in fifteen cases, in eleven of which other urban centers were also found, while in four cases there was only a stable capital. *Kuba* had a 'real' capital, but this city was regularly replaced. The remaining six cases had only some kind of govermental center, which usually was not confined to one place, but was regularly

on the move. In *Volta* these centers developed, in the course of time, into stable capital cities.

Only the following can be formulated by way of structural characteristic:

(3) *The early state has at a specific stage only one governmental center* (significant at the 99% level).

These results show that urbanization is not necessarily a characteristic of the early state, as was suggested by, for instance, Childe (1950) and Adams (1966). On the other hand it is clear, as Khazanov (Section 9, Chapter 3 of this volume) also argues, that, when the early state develops, the importance of urbanization becomes more and more evident. The existence of the state, however, does not depend on urbanization (cf. Crumley 1976).

2.5. *Infrastructure*

By this term we mean the system of roads, bridges, waterways, etc., which facilitates communication within the state. The data on the infrastructure were in several cases rather scanty, while sometimes no data were given on this at all. With regard to *Ankole* and *Volta* it was mentioned that no infrastructure at all existed. Some other states had only a few paths or caravan routes. Table I also sets out the relevant data in this connection, broken down into the categories:

— extensive infrastructure (E), and

— limited infrastructure (Li).

It appears that in ten cases there is question of an extensive infrastructure and in five cases of a limited one. In two cases there was none, while in four cases no data were given on this subject.

In this particular instance no structural characteristic can be formulated.

2.6. *Trade and Markets*

We will define *trade* as the exchange of commodities by barter or sale, and *markets* as places where traders and customers meet. In trade it is possible to distinguish between local and *long-distance trade*. We will be speaking of the latter where the trade extends beyond the boundaries of the state. We will also give attention to the existence of *professional traders*, who in some cases are mentioned explicitly. In a few cases (*Maurya, Scythia*) their existence was inferable from other data.

Directly connected with trade and markets is the use of currency. This currency sometimes consisted of coins and paper, and sometimes of cowry shells (*Kachari, Kuba, Volta, Yoruba*), arrow heads (*Scythia*), or knives (*Zande*).

As it is likely that the government will be interested in trade and commerce, we will use the term '*government-conducted*' where at least a considerable portion of the trade was organized by government agents. Where the government only levied taxes, made provisions for market places, or laid down rules and regulations for trade and markets, we will use the term '*government-controlled*'.

We have brought together the data on trade and markets, broken down into the following aspects, in Table II:
— the existence of a limited trade (t), or of trade of some importance (T);
— the existence of professional traders;
— the existence of markets of only limited, or local, importance (m), or of important markets (M);
— the existence of government-controlled (g), or government-conducted trade (G).

The data in Table II show that *trade* played a definite role in all the states. In thirteen cases it appeared to be of great importance, and in eight cases was found to be of minor importance. The two Polynesian states proved to be the least developed in this respect. None of the other characteristics were found here. For *Iberia* and *Egypt* we had no data. The existence of trade, markets and governmental influences nonetheless cannot be excluded here, expecially in the case of *Egypt*. The sources do not permit us to be more positive, however (cf. Janssen 1975: 161 ff.).

Long-distance trade was mentioned in seventeen cases, while professional traders were found in nine cases. It is probable that in *Kachari, Scythia* and *Maurya* professional traders were also found; the data were insufficient for us to take this for granted, however.

In seventeen cases *markets* were found, and in all of these governmental influence on trade and markets was mentioned. Only in *Axum*, the realm of the *Incas* and the *Yoruba* states was trade actually conducted by government agents. The structural characteristics one may formulate on the basis of these data are:

(4) *Trade is commonly practised in early states* (significant at the 99% level).

(5) *Markets are generally found in early states* (significant at the 99% level).

And, with the reservation that in some cases no data were available:

(6) *Long-distance trade is generally found in early states* (significant at the 99% level).

(cf. Adams 1974).

Table II. *The economy*

	Trade	Long-distance trade	Professional traders	Markets	Currency	Governmental influence	Specialists	Full-time specialists	Organized specialists	Main type of food production	Implements	Irrigation	Surplus
Angkor	T	X	0	M	X	g	X	X	X	A	0	X	X
Ankole	t	X	–	m	–	g	X	0	–	C/A	H	–	0
Axum	T	X	X	M	X	G	X	X	X	A	P	X	X
Aztecs	T	X		M	X	g	X	X	0	A	H	X	–
China	T	X	X	M	X	g	X	X	X	A	H	X	X
Egypt	t	0	0	0	0	0	X	X	X	A	P	0	X
France	T	X	X	M	X	g	X	X	X	A	H	–	X
Hawaii	t	–	–	–	–	–	X	0	0	A	P	X	X
Iberia	T	0	0	0	0	0	X	X	X	A	D	0	X
Inca	t	X	0	M	–	G	X	X	X	A	P	X	X
Jimma	T	X	X	M	X	g	X	X	X	A	H	–	X
Kachari	T	X	0	m	0	0	X	X	–	A	H	X	X
Kuba	T	X	X	M	X	g	X	X	X	A	P	–	X
Maurya	T	X	0	M	X	g	X	X	0	A	P	X	X
Mongolia	T	X	0	M	0	g	X	0	0	C	0	–	X
Norway	t	X	X	m	X	g	X	X	0	A	P	0	X
Scythia	T	X	0	M	–	g	X	X	0	C	H	0	X
Tahiti	t	–	–	–	–	–	X	X	–	A		–	X
Volta	t	X	X	m	X	G	X	X	X	A	H	–	X
Yoruba	T	X	X	M	0	G	X	X	X	A	H	–	X
Zande	t	X	–	m	X	g	X	X	0	A	H	–	X

Abbreviations: t = limited trade; T = important trade; m = minor markets; M = important markets; G = government-control; g = government-conduct; A = agriculture; C = grazing; P = plow; H = hoe; D = digging-stick.

Professional traders were not found to be a common characteristic of early states. As was the case with urbanization, this phenomenon evidently developed only after the state came into being. The same holds true for the use of money (cf. Kurtz 1974).

The rulers of most early states were well aware that trade could provide a lucrative source of income. In sixteen cases the influence of this was demonstrable while for *Egypt* it was highly probable. Only *Hawaii* and *Tahiti* yielded a negative result in this respect. So another structural characteristic we may formulate is:

(7) *Trade and markets form a source of income for the ruling hierarchy of the early state* (significant at the 99% level).

2.7. Division of Labor

Specialists are people possessing a special knowledge or special skills for the performance of certain tasks. The existence of this kind of specialists is mentioned for all of our cases—with the exception of *Iberia*, for which state no data were supplied on this, and *Norway*, where specialization seems to have begun only in later times. However, this probably applies only to full-time specialists, or professionals. Table II sets out, among others, the data relating to this aspect. For *Mongolia* the relevant data were derived from Dawson 1966.

Full-time specialists were mentioned in eighteen cases. In the other cases no explicit data were supplied. Still fewer data were furnished with regard to the organization of specialists. In three cases (*Ankole, Kuba* and *Tahiti*) the existence of this kind of organization was denied. However, the social context of *Kuba* makes some kind of organization not improbable, at any rate. For six cases no data were available. In twelve cases some form of organization of specialists was referred to. The combination full-time specialist/organizations seems to be found only in the more developed states. The structural characteristic here therefore can be expressed as:

(8) *In early states full-time specialists are generally found* (significant at the 99% level).

2.8. The Means of Subsistence

Except in the case of *Mongolia* and *Scythia* the principal means of subsistence was *agriculture*. This statement can in some cases be specified a little further. So in *Ankole* and *Tahiti* it took place on only small plots of land, so that here the term horticulture would perhaps be more appropriate. The *Yoruba* practised agriculture in the form of shifting cultivation.

In the case of the *Scythians* agriculture was second in importance, coming as it did after *cattle-herding*. The *Mongols* however, practised almost no agriculture at all. They obtained agricultural products mainly in exchange for animal products and often supplemented these with tribute or booty. In Table II are set out not only the data concerning agriculture, but also those regarding additional means of subsistence. They permit us to formulate as structural characteristic:

(9) *The most prevalent means of subsistence in early states is agriculture* (significant at the 99% level).
For *Ankole* (Doornbos 1975: 18) and *France* (Slicher van Bath 1960: 74 ff.) supplementary data were used with regard to this aspect.

In chapter I we already hinted at the fierce debates that have been provoked by the use of the concept of *surplus*. Therefore we defined surplus as a portion of the (agricultural) produce in the broadest sense reserved (voluntarily or compulsorily) for people who did not take part in actual production. A surplus of this kind was mentioned in eighteen of our cases. In two cases it appeared that no surplus was produced. Regarding *Norway*, Gurevich tells us that people repeatedly migrated, or went on long-distance voyages of trade or plunder because of shortages and scarcity. The shortages were apparently partly neutralized by the yields of these voyages. In the case of the *Aztecs*, imports of food, obtained by way of trade or tribute, met the needs. In both these cases one can assume that some sort of surplus outside of the boundaries of the state concerned was drawn on. Therefore we believe that we can state another characteristic to be:

(10) *The production of a surplus is characteristic of the economies of early states* (significant at the 99% level).

In only eight cases is *irrigation* known to have been used, or are at least some kind of hydraulic works to have been present. In four cases no data were available. There is no reason therefore, to include irrigation or hydraulic works in the group of general characteristics of early states. The same holds for the use of the plow. An interesting point to note in this context is that no correlation exists between the use of the plow and the existence of hydraulic works. In only two cases did the two appear together (*Axum, Maurya*) (see Table II). Possibly the inclusion of other cases would have changed the picture.

2.9. Social Stratification

This is so complex a subject that a number of comparisons will be necessary to give a picture of the phenomenon that is at all satisfactory. Here we will investigate first the presence of social stratification, and subsequently the way in which it finds expression.

2.9.1. *The Existence of Social Stratification.* Even a superficial perusal of the chapters describing specific early states will make it clear that a division of the population into '... rather broad, more or less stabilized categories showing a hierarchical order, and based on property, status and/or power' (chapter 1) was found everywhere. The wealth of data regarding this in the case studies enables us to be slightly more specific, moreover. With the use of these data, it is possible to distinguish at least twelve social categories, viz:

(1) *the sovereign and his kin* (instead of 'sovereign' we will also use the word 'ruler'); (2) an *aristocracy* (also referred to as nobility, princes, notables); (3) *priests* (or religious specialists, diviners, etc.); (4) *military leaders* (insofar as they formed a separate social category at all); (5) *ministeriales* (by which term, borrowed from European mediaeval history, we refer to people who, though *unfree*, were appointed to high offices; cf. Bloch 1967: 337 ff., especially 343, 343); (6) a *gentry* (i.e., people forming a kind of lower aristocracy, landowners of some status, minor chiefs, clanheads, etc., to which category usually also belong the traditional 'pre-state' dignitaries); (7) *smallholders* (i.e., people who work their own land, or land possessed communally by them as members of a clan or lineage. In the latter case they are nevertheless included in this category because they have an unalienable right to the land. In the case of pastoral nomads we have taken the term to refer to the owners of cattle, or those with access to the lineage herd); (8) *tenants* (i.e., people who possess neither their own land, nor any effective claims to clan or lineage land or cattle, but may have the usufruct of a plot of land in return for payments and services); (9) *traders* (as far as they are mentioned as forming a separate category, which usually is the case with professional traders); (10) *artisans* (again, only where these are mentioned as forming a separate category); (11) *servants* (ditto. Often these are members of subdued tribes or war captives); (12) *slaves* (this is always a difficult category to define, since the word 'slave' is often used without there being any precise evidence as to the status of those concerned. A useful definition here still is that of Nieboer (1910:9), viz. 'a slave is the property of somebody else', meaning that he can be purchased or sold. As the data furnished in this respect are seldom capable of being checked as to validity, we will have to accept them at face value, though with some reserve).

We have set out the data on this as provided by the case essays divided according to the categories outlined above, in Table III. Here it can be seen at a glance that the categories *sovereign and kin* and *aristocracy* are found in every case. An interesting point is that the category *smallholders* was found to be present in eighteen cases. In only two, (*Hawaii* and *Zande*) were they not found. With regard to

Table III. *Social categories*

	Sovereign and kin	Aristocracy	Priests	Military leaders	Ministeriales	Gentry	Smallholders	Tenants	Traders	Artisans	Servants, serfs	Slaves	U	M	L
Angkor	X	X	X	O	—	—	X	X	—	X	X	O	X	—	X
Ankole	X	X	O	X	—	X	X	X	—	—	X	—	X	X	X
Axum	X	X	O	X	X	—	O	O	X	O	O	X	X	O	X
Aztecs	X	X	X	X	—	X	X	X	X	X	X	X	X	X	X
China	X	X	—	—	—	X	X	X	—	O	—	X	X	X	X
Egypt	X	X	X	O	—	—	X	X	—	X	O	O	X	—	X
France*	X	X	X*	—	—	X*	—	X	—	—	X	X	X	X*	X
Hawaii	X	X	X	X	—	—	X	O	—	—	X	O	X	—	X
Iberia	X	X	X	—	—	—	—	X	—	—	X	X	X	—	X
Inca	X	X	X	—	X	X	X	X	O	X	X	O	X	—	X
Jimma	X	X	—	O	X	X	X	X	X	X	X	X	X	X	X
Kachari	X	X	X	—	—	X	X	X	O	X	X	X	X	X	X
Kuba	X	X	—	X	—	X	X	X	X	X	X	X	X	X	X
Maurya	X	X	X	—	—	X	X	X	X	—	X	X	X	X	X
Mongolia	X	X	—	X	—	X	X	X	O	—	X	X	X	—	X
Norway*	X	X	X*	—	O	X	X	X	X*	X*	O	X	X	X	X
Scythia	X	X	X	X	X	X	X	X	—	—	X	X	X	X	X
Tahiti	X	X	X	—	—	X	X	X	—	—	X	X	X	X	X
Volta	X	X	X	X	X	X	X	X	X	X	X	—	X	X	X
Yoruba	X	X	X	—	X	X	X	X	X	X	—	X	X	X	X
Zande	X	X	—	X	—	X	—	X	—	X	—	X	X	X	X

Abbreviations: * For France and Norway in a *later* period.

Axum it is only mentioned that the majority of the population enjoyed 'personal freedom'. It is not clear what exactly is meant by this. The data supplied enable us to formulate the following structural characteristics:

(11) *In all early states a sovereign and kin and an aristocracy are found* (significant at the 100% level).

(12) *Smallholders appear to be commonly found in early states* (significant at the 99% level).

Tenants also scored quite highly, being definitely present in nineteen cases, while in two (*Axum* and *Iberia*) insufficient data were available. So we can formulate as structural characteristic:

(13) *Tenants are generally found in early states* (significant at the 100% level.

Slaves were found to be positively present in fifteen cases and absent in two (*Ankole* and *Volta*) while for four there were insufficient data. Neither this nor any of the remaining categories could be demonstrated to constitute a general characteristic. It is interesting to note that *military leaders* appeared to form a separate category in only eight cases. In most cases they were reckoned with the aristocracy.

When trying to group the several categories into a limited number of broader social *strata*, we were able to distinguish three such strata, namely an *upper, middle* and *lower* one. To the upper stratum we reckoned as belonging the ruler, aristocracy, priests and military leaders, to the middle stratum the ministeriales and gentry, and to the lower stratum the remaining categories. The definition of the upper and lower strata generally posed no problems. However, the definition of the middle one was less easy. We therefore combined the opinions of the authors of the case essays with our own data. In the case of *Ankole* the lineage heads and the chiefs of the Iru appeared to possess something of a medial status. The members of the landed nobility in the case of the *Aztecs* also formed a kind of gentry. For *China* we reckoned the *Shih* as belonging to the middle stratum. In the case of *France* we felt that the lower nobles and certain categories of functionaries could be considered as belonging to the middle level, at least in a later period. In the state of the *Incas* the *curacas* formed a middle-level group. With regard to *Jimma* we would refer the reader to Lewis' remark that here a 'continuous series of distinctions' was found. Also in the case of *Kuba* it was possible to class several groups of office-holders in this category. Among the *Mongols* the clan and lineage heads (according to Krader 1968: 88) formed a middle stratum, the same holding for the chiefs of the junior clans of the *Kachari*. The complex social structure of the *Scythians* also suggests the existence of a group of this kind (viz. heads of dependent tribes, government functionaries). In *Tahiti* the *raatira*, in *Volta* the village chiefs, priest chiefs and even the earthpriests, and in *Yoruba* the *bale* are classifiable as middle strata, while in the case of *Zande* we are inclined to consider the lower-status members of the Vongara clan as well as the commoner chiefs and deputies as forming such a stratum. The upshot of all this is that in fifteen cases the social stratification was found to comprise at least three strata. In view of the five negative cases and of the one for which there were no data, however, we cannot regard this as a structural characteristic. We can only formulate the less rigid qualification, that:

(14)   *The social stratification of early states always embraces at least two strata* (significant at the 100% level).

2.9.2. Forms of Social Stratification. Data on the way in which social stratification finds expression are brought together in Table IV. The twelve social categories distinguished above here will be related to the means of production. It is to be regretted that in several cases the data presented in the case essays were not sufficiently clear to permit a precise evaluation of the situation. This was especially true for the categories *priests, military leaders, ministeriales, artisans* and *slaves*. Often priests and military leaders were simply reckoned with the 'aristocracy' without any further specification of their actual position. The economic categories distinguished in Table IV are the following:
(a) *Landownership.* Here we distinguished the following possibilities. Theoretical ownership (T), usually associated with the sovereign, which we gave a positive evaluation where the ruler was mentioned as the (nominal) owner of all land or livestock. Communal ownership (C), which is the case where the land (or livestock) belongs to the clan, the lineage, the temple community or the village as a whole. Membership of such a community entitles one to the usufruct of the land. Personal ownership (P) was assumed where the sources indicated that ownership was based on a personal claim, not connected with any specific function or the membership of a particular group. Feudal ownership (F) exists where land is granted in return for services rendered in a specific capacity (cf. Wolf 1966: 50, who distinguishes several types of domain a.o. the feudal one). Non-owners are indicated by the letter (N).
(b) *Productive activities.* These can be divided into *direct* (D) and *indirect* (I).
(c) *The source of the main part of the income of those having only indirect connections with food production through tribute* (tr). The various sources are specified in only very broad terms. They may include taxes, land-rent, booty, etc. Generally speaking, this category embraces all those cases in which the direct producers are obliged to hand over a portion of their produce.

Table IV. *Relations to means of production*

	Sovereign	Aristocracy	Priests	Military leaders	Ministeriales	Gentry	Small-holders	Tenants	Traders	Artisans	Servants	Slaves
Angkor	CItr	CI(g trAS	CI(g trAS	0	—	—	CDAS	NDAS	—	NIrAS	(C NDAS	0
Ankole	TItr	FItrAS	0	FItr0S	—	FItrAS	FDAS	NDAS	—	0	CDAS	—
Axum	0Itr	FItrAS	0	0	00r0S	—	CDAS	0	NIbA0	0	0	0
Aztecs	-Itr	(CI r/P tr)AS	0Ir0S	0	—	(CI r AS/P tr)	(C/P DAS	NDAS	NIbAS	NI(g/b AS	0CAS	NDrS
China	TItr	F/P -Itr0S	—	—	—	0Ir0S	(C/P DAS	NDAS	—	0	—	N0rS
Egypt	TItr	0ItrAS	CItr-S	0	—	—	ODAS	NDAS	—	NIrAS	0	0
France	TItr	FItrAS	FItrAS	0	—	FItrAS*	PDAS	NDAS	—	—	NDAS	ND0S
Hawaii	TItr	0ItrAS	CIg-S	—	—	—	—	NDAS	—	—	NDAS	0
Iberia	0Itr	-Itr00	CItr0S	0	—	—	PDPS	0	—	—	NDAS	0
Inca	TItr	(C/F I(tr-S/r	CItr-S	—	NIr-S	CItrAS	CDAS	NDAS	0	NIrAS	NDAS	0
Jimma	PItr	PItrAS	—	—	PItrAS	PItrAS	PDAS	PDAS	PIbA0	NIb-S	PDAS	NDAS
Kachari	(T/0 Itr	CItr0S	0	0	0	0	CDAS	NDAS	0	0	C-r-S	ND0S

Kuba	PItr	$\mathrm{PI}\left(^{r}_{tr}\mathrm{AS}\right)$	—	—	—	$--\left(^{r}_{b}\mathrm{AS}\right.$	CDAS	NDAS	NIbA0	NIbAS	NDAS	NDAS
Maurya	0Itr	$\left(^{F}_{P}\mathrm{I}^{r}_{tr}\mathrm{AS}\right.$	$\left(^{C}_{P}\mathrm{I}\left(^{r}_{tr}\text{-S}\right.\right.$	00r0S	—	—	PDAS	NDAS	NIbAS	NIr-S	NDAS	ND0S
Mongolia	TItr	$\left(^{C}_{0}\mathrm{I\,tr\,AS}\right.$	—	—	—	CI tr AS	CDAS	NDAS	0	—	NDAS	0
Norway	CI^{g}_{tr}	$\mathrm{CI}\left(^{r}_{tr}\mathrm{AS}\right.$	CI* tr-S	0	0	C00AS	CDAS	NDAS	NIbA0*	0	CDAS	NDAS
Scythia	CItr-S	CItr-S	0I 00S	—	00r-S	CI tr-S	CD-S	NDAS	—	—	$\mathrm{CDAS}\left(^{C}_{N}\right.$ | $N^{D}_{r}\big)\mathrm{0S}$
Tahiti	CItr	CI tr AS	CI tr AS	CI tr AS	—	CI tr AS	CDAS	$\left(^{C}_{N}\mathrm{DAS}\right.$	CDAS	$\left(^{N_{C}}\mathrm{IrAS}\right.$ | $N^{D}_{r}\big)\mathrm{AS}$	$N^{D}_{r}\big)\mathrm{0S}$
Volta	TItr CDg	$\mathrm{PD}\left(^{tr}_{g}\mathrm{AS}\;\mathrm{I}\right.$ | $\mathrm{P}^{D}_{I}\mathrm{I}^{r}_{g}\big)\mathrm{AS}$	0	PI tr AS	PD tr AS	PDAS	NDAS	$\mathrm{P}\left(^{D}_{I}\mathrm{bA-}\right.$	$\mathrm{P}\left(^{I}_{D}\mathrm{bA0}\right.$	PDAS	—
Yoruba	$\mathrm{FI}^{tr}_{r}\big)$	CI tr AS	00 r 0S	—	00 tr 0S	CI tr 0S	CDAS	NDAS	NIbA0	NI0AS	—	ND0S
Zande	TItr	FI tr-S	—	00 r 0S	—	FI tr-S	—	NDAS	—	NIr0S	—	ND0S

Abbreviations: N = non-ownership; C = communal ownership; T = theoretical ownership; P = private ownership; F = feudal ownership; I = indirect connection with food production; D = direct connection with food production; r = remuneration; tr = tribute; g = gift; b = barter; A = obligation to pay some form of tax; S = obligation to fulfil some kind of service; * = for France and Norway in a *later* period.

There is question of barter (b) where traders or craftsmen give other persons certain goods in exchange for food or other commodities.

Remuneration (r) takes place where services are rewarded either in kind or in coin.

As gifts (g) are considered food or money which people may receive without rendering any immediate services in return.

(d) *Obligations.* These have been divided into: taxes, rents or tribute, and gifts (A) and services (S). This item includes all kinds of obligatory services, ranging from compulsory labor on the land of notables and on the construction or repairs of houses or palaces, to the obligation to fulfil certain functions at court or in the governmental organization.

The data concerning the above-mentioned aspects are brought together in Table IV. Here it appears that the relations to food production are *indirect* for the following categories: the ruler, aristocracy, priests, military leaders, gentry, ministeriales, traders and artisans. *Direct* relations were found for the categories of small holders, tenants, servants and slaves. The structural characteristic here seems to be as follows:

(15)   *The direct participation in food production is limited to specific social categories (mostly at the lower end of the scale of social statuses). All the other categories have only indirect relations to it* (significant at the 99% level).

Another structural characteristic seems to be that, with the exception of traders, all social categories have to render services of some kind to the state. With regard to the aristocracy only the data for *Iberia* were insufficient. The duties of the ruler will be discussed in Section 4. The structural characteristic here is:

(16)   *With the exception of traders all social categories have the obligation to perform services for the state* (significant at the 99% level).

Table V.   *Taxation**

	Number of cases	Positive	Negative	No data
Aristocracy	21	15	3	3
Priests	14	4	5	5
Gentry	15	10	2	3
Smallholders	19	18	1	—
Tenants	19	19	—	—
Traders	8	8	—	—
Artisans	11	8	2	1
Servants	15	14	1	—

* In this table the social categories on which there were very limited data are not included.

In Table V the data concerning the obligation to pay taxes are compared. That taxation in one form or another is found in all states is clear at first sight. An interesting fact is that this obligation is by no means restricted to only the lower- and middle-level categories. In no less than fifteen of the twenty-one cases the aristocracy also had to pay taxes, while in ten out of the fifteen cases in which a gentry was mentioned this was found to apply to them as well. In view of the limitation we ourselves have imposed with regard to the 'structural characteristics', we should formulate the one in question as:

(17) *In all early states the obligation to pay taxes existed, which obligation in most cases the aristocracy also had to fulfil* (significant at the 99% level).

The data relating to ownership of land in Table IV are grouped together in Table VI. Two aspects are very obvious: (1) in early states the overwhelming majority of forms of landholding in all of the categories mentioned still are based upon communal rights; and (2) there are several categories mentioned as having no rights or virtually no rights to land at all, viz. *tenants, traders, artisans, servants* and *slaves*. These conclusions prompt the formulation of the following structural characteristic:

(18) *Access to the basic means of production, in casu land, in early states is unequal* (significant at the 99% level).

In chapter 1 we quoted Fried (1967: 191) where he argued that stratification appeared the moment that 'communal property' is replaced by 'private property'. Tables IV and VI demonstrate, however, that in early states communal ownership is still the most common form of control over land. We therefore believe that private ownership should not be regarded as the exclusive factor responsible for stratification. Feudal landownership also appeared to be an important type, while personal ownership was underdeveloped. The unequal access to resources therefore does not appear to be based on differences in the

Table VI. *Ownership of land*

	Number of cases	Theoretical ownership	Communal ownership	Feudal ownership	Personal ownership	Negative	No data
Ruler*	21	9	5	1	2	1	4
Aristocracy**	21	—	8	7	6	1	4
Priests†	14	—	8	1	2	—	4
Gentry	15	—	7	3	3	1	2
Small owners††	19	—	12	1	7	—	1

Abbreviations; * Volta had both nominal and communal ownership; ** combinations of forms of landholding were found for the *Aztecs China, Incas, Maurya,* and *Mongolia*; † in *Maurya* two types of ownership were found; †† among the *Aztecs* and in *China* two types existed.

relation to control of the means of production but on differential positions in the clan and lineage systems and in the socio-political organization of the early state. We will return to this problem in Section 2.11.

To come back to the data of Table IV the principal source of income of the ruler there is seen to be tribute. Only in *Norway, Volta* and *Yoruba* is it supplemented by certain kinds of gift (tributary gifts). The same is true for the aristocracy. Their basic income from tribute was supplemented by remunerations and gifts in seven cases. So the structural characteristic here will be:

(19) *Tribute is the main source of income of the sovereign and aristocracy* (significant at the 100% level).

It is interesting to note in this connection that in no less than fifteen cases the *aristocracy* was at the same time obliged to pay some kind of taxation itself. Another structural characteristic may be formulated concerning the sources of income of *smallholders* and *tenants.* Their main source of income lay in the direct production of food, which entailed the possibility of exchange and barter of part of their produce for other commodities.

(20) *The main source of income of smallholders and tenants is primary production* (significant at the 100% level).

The relation between landownership, the obligation to pay taxes and render services, and the principal source of income can be seen in Table VII. In this table we have not broken landownership down into the types set out in Table VI. The fact that in some cases there was question of several sources of income or of various obligations is responsible for the percentages sometimes appearing to be higher than a hundred per cent. This table quite convincingly demonstrates that it is impossible to ascribe uniform sources of income, or uniform kinds of obligation to the different social categories.

Table VII. *Rights and obligations*

	No. of cases	Landowner-ship*			Obligation to pay tax			Obligation to render services			Source of income			
		pos.	neg.	no data	pos.	neg.	no data	pos.	neg.	no data	trib.	own prod.	bar-ter	remun-era.
Aristocracy*	21	17	1	3	15	3	3	19	—	2	20	1	—	7
Priests	14	10	—	4	4	5	5	13	—	1	8	1	—	6
Gentry	15	12	1	2	10	2	3	14	—	1	11	1	1	3
Smallholders	19	18	—	1	18	1	—	18	—	1	—	19	—	—
Tenants	19	2	17	—	19	—	—	19	—	—	—	19	—	—
Traders	8	2	6	—	8	—	—	2	1	5	—	1	8	—
Artisans	11	2	9	—	8	2	1	10	—	1	—	1	4	7

Abbreviations: * 'No data' indicates that there is no information on the type of ownership in question; ** For Mongolia only the known fact of communal ownership is included.

2.10. *Legitimation of the Sovereign*

Up until now, the position of the ruler has been left out of most of the comparisons. We only noted his claims to land, and the fact that his main source of income was tribute. In the present section we will not only consider his rights and obligations in more detail, but also investigate on what his exalted position was based, or how it was *legitimized* (for a discussion of this concept see chapter 1). An analysis of this last-mentioned concept is of relevance not only for a study of the ruler's position, but also for that of the legitimation of the other ruling categories—in fact it is essential for an insight into the entire network of rights, duties, obligations and loyalties that knits together the social structure of the early state, since all these rights and duties and ties derived from one basic relationship, namely that between the ruler(s) and the ruled.

Although legitimation, as Kurtz has most convincingly demonstrated in his chapter on the *Aztecs*, is a process (and as such will be discussed in the following chapter), we will nevertheless analyse it strictly from the point of view of *structural* aspects in the present context.

In all of our cases the sovereign appeared to be elevated high above his people in several ways. His elevated position, as well as the socio-political repercussions of this, seem to have been accepted by all, or at any rate most of the citizens of the early state. Below we will investigate how the relationship was structured, as also in what ways it had become accepted by the population. Though we are well aware that the relationship is a complex whole, for purposes of analysis we will distinguish especially the following four aspects of the ruler's position: the ideological basis, the legal aspects, the sovereign as protector, and the sovereign 'benevolent lord' (cf. Claessen 1970: 220-223).

2.10.1. *The Ideological Basis: Sacrality and Ritual.* We shall have to take as our point of departure here any existing types of *mythical charter*, in which the basic relationship between the sovereign and his people is explained. Such charters usually take the form of *myths* containing the ideological foundation for the relationship. Then we will also have to clarify the (ascribed) supernatural status of the ruler. Is he considered as a god (G), or is he regarded as sacral (S). In other words, has he any supernatural qualities or mystical power (e.g., *mana, mahano*, etc.; cf. Evans-Pritchard 1948; Claessen 1974: 67 ff.; Beattie 1971: 118 ff., 239)? Or is the ruler simply a human being (B)? An important question then is how the ruler is ultimately connected with the supernatural forces. As this particular relationship is often explained in the form of *genealogies*, we will look for these. Finally we

Table VIII. *Ideological position of sovereign*

	Mythical charter	'Divine' status	Genealogies	Relationship to super-natural forces	Acquisition of sacral status	Ritual upon ruler's death	Human sacrifices	Ritual duties	Taboos
Angkor	X	S	X	M	I	G	0	R	X
Ankole	X	S	—	M	0	A	0	R	0
Axum	X	S	X	M	0	G	0	R	X
Aztecs	X	S	X	M	I	G	X	H	X
China	X	S	X	M	I	G	X	R	X
Egypt	X	S	X	0	I	G	X	H	X
France	X	S	X	M	I	G	—	R	X
Hawaii	X	S	X	M	C	A	X	R	X
Iberia	0	0	0	0	0	0	0	H	0
Inca	X	S	X	M	I	G	X	R	X
Jimma	—	B	—	—	—	0	—	R	0
Kachari	0	S	0	0	0	0	X	R	X
Kuba	X	S	X	M	I	A	X	H	X
Maurya	X	S	X	M	I	0	—	0	0
Mongolia	X	S	X	0	0	0	0	0	0
Norway	0	S	X	M	0	G	—	R	0
Scythia	X	S	X	0	I	G	X	R	0
Tahiti	X	S	X	M	C	A	X	R	X
Volta	X	S	X	M	I	A	—	0	0
Yoruba	X	S	X	M	I	G	X	H	X
Zande	X	0	X	—	I	G	0	R	0

Abbreviations: S = sacral ruler; B = non-divine human being; M = middleman; I = only through ritual inauguration; C = sacral already before inauguration; G = mourning only; A = ritual anarchy; R = performs rites; H = ruler is high priest as well.

will investigate the (sacral) ruler's services to his people in this capacity. Is there a direct connection between his activities and the fertility of the land and the people — as, since Frazer (1911), has often been assumed (D)? Is the ruler, in consequence of his relationship to the supernatural forces, a *middleman* between them and his people (M)? Or is his rule devoid of connections with the supernatural? Table VIII sets out the data relating to these aspects.

A *mythical charter* was found in seventeen cases, while in three the data were inconclusive. Only *Jimma* yielded a negative result. An interesting point is that in several cases this charter was probably evolved only after the state came into being. This was found to be definitely the case in *Ankole* (cf. Doornbos 1975: 17), *Angkor*, *Yoruba* and *Volta*. *France* poses the problem that many details of the charter are not 'mythical' but historical. In view of the role of this particular tradition, however, we do not consider it necessary to exclude this state from the positive cases. For the *Mongols* data were added from Krader (1968: 91), and for the *Incas* from Claessen (1970: 144 ff.). All this culminates in the following structural characteristic:

(21) *A mythical charter on which the relationship between the sovereign (ruling group) and his subjects is based is generally found in early states* (significant at the 99% level).

The '*divine*' *status* of the ruler appeared in most cases to be *sacral*. Only for *Jimma* was it stated that the ruler was not sacral. For *Iberia* and *Zande* the data were inconclusive. There was found to be a considerable difference in degree between, for instance, *Ankole*, where the relevant concepts were rather vague, and *Angkor*, where the sacral position of the ruler seemed to be the most elaborated. The Christian ruler of *France* displayed so many sacral features (cf. also Schramm 1966: 22 ff.) that we have no difficulty in classifying him as sacral. For the *Mongols* data were added from Haenisch (1948) and Krader (1968), and for the *Aztecs* from Soustelle (1958: 109). The structural characteristic we may formulate here is:

(22) *The basic characteristic of the sovereign is his sacral status* (significant at the 99% level).

In seventeen cases *genealogies* played a role of quite some importance. In the majority of cases they were mentioned not only in connection with the assumed divine descent of the ruler, but also as the normal document prescribing the forms of relation between the sovereign, aristocracy and commoners: in point of fact, a rationalization of the prevailing social situation. In only two cases (*Ankole* and *Jimma*) were genealogies reported not to play a role. For *Iberia* and *Kachari* no data were given. The data concerning the *Incas* were supplemented from elsewhere (Claessen 1970: 145 ff.).

The structural characteristic one may distil from these data is:

(23)   *The sovereign's exalted position is explained by his genealogical status. The aristocracy often bases its privileged position on its connections with the sovereign's lineage* (significant at the 99% level).

The ruler's *relationship to the supernatural forces* in fourteen cases appeared to be a *middleman* kind of one. In *Jimma* he was regarded as a 'defender of the faith', and for *Zande* no relations of any kind were mentioned at all. In five cases no data were available. Data from other sources were added for *Ankole* (Doornbos 1975: 32), *Aztecs* (Soustelle 1958: 111) and *Incas* (Claessen 1970: 173).

The sacral aspects of sovereignty seem to be so important and have so many far-reaching implications that we deem a more detailed examination of the way in which this sacrality finds expression entirely justified. For reasons of space the examination will be restricted to only a number of features. We have therefore brought together in Table VIII, among others, data on the following aspects:

— The way in which the sacral status is passed on to the new sovereign; here we have distinguished between the possibilities that (a) the successor was sacral before his accession to the throne (C), and (b) sacrality was conferred upon him during some ceremony in the course of his inauguration (I).

— The customs observed immediately after the death of the sovereign; the two possibilities here are (a) general mourning (G), (b) ritual anarchy (A).

— Human sacrifices in connection with the rites surrounding the sovereign.

— Ritual duties of the ruler; here we have distinguished between the following possibilities: (a) the ruler is mentioned as being a high priest, or some equivalent (H), and (b) he only performs rites without having the status of a priest (R).

— Any taboos surrounding the sovereign (Y).

Data were added for *Ankole* (Doornbos 1975: 32), *France* (Schramm 1966: 27 ff.), *Hawaii* (Davenport 1969), *Incas* (Claessen 1970: 146) and *Jimma* (Prof. Lewis: personal communication).

The data of Table VIII show that the ruler's sacral status was conferred on him by some rite during the inauguration ceremony in twelve cases. In only two cases (*Tahiti* and *Hawaii*) was the successor already sacral before his inauguration.

Mourning appears to have been the normal reaction to the ruler's death (eleven cases). Ritual anarchy was found in five cases. In some cases *political* anarchy followed upon the death of the sovereign, usually in the form of an interregnum of some kind, during which the various competing factions tried to gain support for their respective candidates (*Axum, Volta* and *Zande*).

Human sacrifices were mentioned in ten cases. For *China* this custom was mentioned only in connection with some of the Ch'ang rulers. Taboos were mentioned in twelve instances. In this connection no less than nine states had to be classified under the heading 'no data'.

In eighteen cases the ruler performed certain rites. The remaining three yielded insufficient data for us to form any judgement on this. In five cases these rites were performed in the capacity of priest or high priest. The structural characteristic here is:

(24)   *The sovereign performs rites* (significant at the 100% level).

2.10.2.   *Regulations and Laws.* In this section the organizational aspects of the making of laws and regulations will be discussed. We use both terms here, since it is not always clear whether the decrees of a sovereign have the force of laws. The definitions of the concept of law vary greatly (cf. Hoebel 1964: 28; Gluckman 1965: 178 ff.; Köbben 1966: 118 ff.), while, moreover, the data of the case studies do not permit us to draw definite conclusions about the effects of the decrees in question.

In theory the sovereign is the person who lays down the laws and maintains law and order. In reality lawgiving and the enforcement of laws are quite complex processes. In order to analyse these we have brought together in Table IX data concerning the following questions:

— How are *new laws* proclaimed? Publicly (pu) or to only a select few (Ch)?
— Is the sovereign considered as the (formal) *law giver*? This idea does not necessarily imply that *new* laws are constantly being devised. Often there only is question of the reformulation of existing laws and regulations, or the formulation of decisions made after long deliberation by a council.
— What *institutionalized bodies* exerting an influence on lawgiving are found (e.g., councils (C) or ministers (M)), and is the sovereign only a member of a lawgiving body (K)?
— Are there any people exercising an *informal* influence on law-making (members of the ruler's family (F), advisors (A), ministers (M), etc.)?
— Can one speak of any more or less *coherent body of laws*, or even a code of laws (S), or is jurisdiction dependent on customs, ad hoc decisions and incidental decrees (R)?
— Do *professional judges* (J) exist, or is the administration of justice a responsibility of more general kinds of functionaries (G) — or is there a mixture of both?
— Is *appeal* possible? Are there any courts of appeal?
— Is the ruler considered as the *supreme judge*?

— Is there a penal code (P), or is punishment based on arbitrary decisions (Z)?

— What kind of people *enforce the rules and laws:* a police force (Po), general functionaries (Se) or guards (Gu)?

— Does social inequality find expression in the *administration of justice?* Are members of the aristocracy (NO) or commoners (LM) punished more severely?

Data have been added for *Ankole* (Doornbos 1975: 33 ff.), *Hawaii* (Davenport 1969: 9), *Incas* (Claessen 1970: 159 ff., 169 ff.), *Jimma* (personal communication), *Maurya* (Thapar 1975: 82 ff.), and *Mongolia* (Krader 1968: 90 ff.).

The data of Table IX show that there are only three aspects that can be defined as structural characteristics:

(25) *The sovereign is the formal law giver in early states* (significant at the 99% level).

This was found to be the case in eighteen states. The only exceptions were *Kuba* and *Norway*, where laws were made by councils in which the ruler's voice was heard. For *Kachari* no data were given on this.

(26) *The sovereign is the supreme judge in early states* (significant at the 99% level).

This, too, was found to apply in eighteen cases. The data for *China*, *Norway* and *Axum* were inconclusive in this respect.

It was found in all cases that there were informal influences on lawgiving. Hence:

(27) *In early states one always finds informal influences on lawgiving* (significant at the 100% level).

The results regarding the other aspects showed marked diversity. Typically the *judicial system* was more developed in some states than in others. The most highly developed systems (at least by twentieth century standards) were found in *Angkor, Aztecs, China, France, Incas, Jimma, Kuba, Maurya* and *Yoruba*. In these states the presence of judges, a code of laws, a penal system and courts of appeal characterized the situation. In addition, institutionalized influences on lawgiving were found here.

The data on the existence of a police force are very scanty. In only four cases was such a force mentioned. In five cases royal servants or guards maintained public order. In the case of the *Incas* it was pointed out that no police was necessary. In eleven cases no data were given on this subject. The same vagueness was found in the data regarding the aspect of inequality; in eight states commoners were punished, more severely than aristocrats, while in three states (*Aztecs, Kachari* and *Zande*) the reverse was (sometimes) true.

Table IX. *Laws and regulations*

	Proclamation of law	Sovereign formal law giver	Formal inst. influence on lawgiving	Informal influence on lawgiving	Law as a system	Formal judges or gov. funct.	Court of appeal	Sovereign supreme judge	Formal punishment	Police force	Legal inequality
Angkor	Pu*	X	0	F	S	J	X	X	no ? cod.	0	LM
Ankole	0	X	C	A.F.	R	G	X	X	Z	0	0
Axum	0	X	0	F.A.	R	G	X	0	0	Po	N0
Aztecs	Pu	X	C.M.	0	S	J	X	X	P	0	0
China	Ch+	X	C	F.P.	S	G	0	0	P	0	LM
Egypt	0	X	0	A.F.	R	G	0	X	0	Se	LM
France	Ch	X	C	A.F.	S	GJ	X	X	P/Z	Se	LM
Hawaii	0	X	0	A	R	G	—	X	Z	0	0
Iberia	0	X	0	F.P.	R	G	0	X	0	—	0
Inca	Ch	X	C	F.A.	S	J	X	X	P	Gu/Po	0
Jimma	Pu	X	K	FAM.	S/R	GJ	0	X	P	Po	N0
Kachari	0	0	0	F.A.	0	GJ	X	X	P	0	0
Kuba	Pu	—	C.K.	A.P.	S	J	X	X	P	0	0
Maurya	Pu	X	C.M.	0	S	J	0	X	P	0	0
Mongolia	0	X	C	A.F.	R	G	0	X	0	0	0
Norway	Pu	—	C.K.P	A	R	G	—	—	0	0	LM
Scythia	Ch	X	C	F	R	G	X	X	0	Gu	LM
Tahiti	Ch	X	—	A.F.	R	G	—	X	Z	Se	LM
Volta	Ch	X	0	A	R	G	X	X	P	—	LM
Yoruba	0	X**	C.M.	F	R	GJ	X	X	P	Po	0
Zande	Ch	X	C	F	R	G	X	X	P	0	LM/N0

Abbreviations: Pu = public proclamation; Ch = proclamation to privileged groups only; C = influence of councils; M = influence of ministers; K = ruler as member of council; F = influence of ruler's relatives; A = influence of advisors; S = a coherent body of laws exists; R = no coherent body of laws exists; J = formal judges; G = administration of justice by general functionaries; P = a penal code exists; Po = a special police force exists; Gu = maintenance of law and order a general responsibility of guard; Se = maintenance of law and order a general responsibility of ruler's servants; LM = commoners are punished more severely; N0 = elite is punished more severely; * = edicts in the form of inscriptions; ** = interpretation of custom; + = secret.

Table X.   *Military aspects*

	Sovereign as supreme commander	Actual participation in combat	Bodyguard	Standing army	Type of military leader
Angkor	X	0	X	X	G
Ankole	X	0	X	X	G
Axum	X	0	X	X	S
Aztecs	X	X	X	X	G
China	X	0	0	X	S
Egypt	0	0	0	X	S
France	X	X	X	X	G
Hawaii	X	X	X	—	G
Iberia	X	0	X	0	S
Inca	X	X	X	X	G
Jimma	X	X	X	X	S
Kachari	0	0	X	X	S
Kuba	0	—	X	X	S
Maurya	X	X	X	X	S
Mongolia	X	X	X	0	G
Norway	X	X	X	X	S
Scythia	X	0	X	X	G
Tahiti	X	X	X	—	S
Volta	X	X	X	—	0
Yoruba	—	—	X	0	G
Zande	X	0	X	X	S

Abbreviations: G = general functionary; S = specialist.

2.10.3.   *The Sovereign as Protector.* A close connection is often assumed to exist between the sovereign and the military apparatus. Data
on this subject are compiled in Table X. The question we will analyse
here is: Is the sovereign regarded as supreme commander? A positive
answer to this question does not imply that this function will necessarily be exercised in practice. We will, therefore, also collect data on the
actual military leadership.

In order to be able to evaluate the effectiveness of the military
apparatus we will enquire into the existence of a *bodyguard* and a
standing army, and into the quality of the *military leaders.* Are they in
the first place military specialists or do they exercise command in
consequence of a more general kind of function (S. and G. respectively)?

The data of Table X make it clear that in eighteen cases the ruler
was considered as supreme commander. For *Egypt* and *Kachari* the
data were insufficient. In the case of *Yoruba* it is mentioned that the
supreme commander was a eunuch who bore the royal regalia, spoke
for the ruler and was entitled to every royal honor. This form of
representation had something in common with the situation in other
African states, where the sovereign transfers ritual responsibility for

war to his officials (cf. Claessen 1970: 264). The structural characteristic here is:

(28) *In early states the sovereign is considered as supreme commander* (significant at the 99% level).

Active participation in combat on the ruler's part was mentioned ten times.

A bodyguard was mentioned in nineteen cases. For *China* and *Egypt* there were no data on this point. Interestingly enough, in *Angkor* and *Maurya* this guard was formed by women. The structural characteristic in this connection is:

(29) *In early states the sovereign generally has a bodyguard* (significant at the 100% level).

In fifteen cases a standing army was mentioned; in three (*Hawaii, Tahiti* and *Volta*) a standing army was stated not to exist. Military specialists were found in eleven cases, while in nine cases the exercise of a military command was said to be the corollary of some more general kind of function (*Volta* no data).

2.10.4. *The 'Benevolent Lord'.* On the one hand, large quantities of food and other goods are collected on behalf of the sovereign, and numerous people are compelled to work for him. On the other hand, the sovereign expends and gives away virtually equivalent quantities— if only because of the fact that the food cannot be preserved, and the other goods are perishable as well. By means of gifts the ruler is able to bind people to himself even if these gifts constitute only a fraction of what they have given to the ruler. The sheer fact that a gift has been presented by the ruler compensates for everything the recipient has done for him. This is quite conclusively testified by Speke, who noted during a stay at the court of the ruler of Buganda in 1860 that:

> All acts of the king are counted benefits, for which he must be thanked; and so every deed done to his subjects is a gift received by them, though it should assume the shape of flogging or fine (1863: 255).

In order to be able to appreciate this statement at its true value we must bear in mind that it is made by Speke in the context of a discussion of the great misery and fear prevailing in Buganda during his stay there (cf. also Claessen 1970: 96–134, and the analysis of Buganda by Rusch 1975). On the other hand, in other African states as well, great joy is invariably aroused by, and deep gratitude shown for even only paltry gifts from the sovereign (cf. the comments by Forbes on Dahomey: 1851, II, 44 ff.). In Section 2.10.5 we will return to this complicated question. For the present we will confine ourselves to a classification of the data yielded by the case studies.

In most cases no distinction was drawn between expenditure of the state and of the ruler's household. There was seen to be a flow of food, commodities and labor to the top, and a flow of gifts, remunerations and payments from the top. It may be useful to divide the ruler's expenditures into three categories: direct expenses, indirect expenses and conspicuous consumption (a term borrowed from Veblen 1899). *Direct expenses* are all outlays on remunerations, salaries, gifts, and offerings for favorites, servants, functionaries, or gods. These direct expenditures imply a face-to-face relationship. *Gifts* are incidental donations and *remunerations* are incidental gifts in return for some service or other. *Salary* will be used to refer to regular payments in return for services. Offerings will be used with reference to *all* kinds of gifts to gods, priests or temples.

Indirect expenses are expenditures for the benefit of the people and state in general. These include the costs of (a) building and maintaining public works, such as irrigation systems, roads, etc., the existence of which will be taken as an indication of the existence of this kind of expenditure; and (b) all kinds of payments made on the lower levels of the bureaucratic hierarchy, e.g., salaries, remunerations, etc., paid by higher-level functionaries (out of their income from office or tribute) to lower-level functionaries, soldiers, etc.

Conspicuous consumption covers the expenses arising from the construction of palaces, tombs, etc., or the maintenance of a court, and so on. The presence of palaces, tombs or courts will be taken as evidence for such expenditure. Extra data were added for *Kuba* (Vansina 1964), *Maurya* (Thapar 1975) and *Mongolia*, Haenisch 1948).

In Table XI all the relevant data on this have been brought together. It is clear from this that the expenditures of early states show a marked uniformity. No less than five aspects can be formulated as structural characteristics:

(30) *In early states the sovereigns present gifts to their people* (significant at the 100% level).

This was mentioned as being the case seventeen times. In four cases no specific data were given on this, but it seemed most probable from the context. However, for the *Zande* it is stressed that only a very select group of people were the beneficiaries of the sovereign's benevolence, the same holding for *Scythia*, where only the warriors were given an annual feast. Remunerations were found to be paid in twenty cases (*Kachari* no data).

(31) *In early states the sovereign remunerates his people for services rendered* (significant at the 100% level).

Offerings in the broad sense indicated above were found to be present in seventeen cases, while in the remaining four (*Ankole, Axum, Kachari* and *Scythia*) no explicit data were provided on this subject.

Table XI. *Expenditures*

| | Direct | | | | Indirect | | | Conspicuous consumption | |
	Gifts	Remune-rations	Salaries	Offe-rings	Major works	Lower-level payments	Pala-ces	Tombs	Courts
Angkor	X	X	—	X	X	X	X	0	X
Ankole	X	X	—	0	—	X	X	—	X
Axum	X	X	0	0	X	X	X	X	X
Aztecs	X	X	X	X	X	X	X	0	X
China	0	X	0	X	X	0	X	0	X
Egypt	X	X	0	X	X	X	X	X	X
France	X	X	X	X	—	X	X	—	X
Hawaii	X	X	—	X	X	X	—	0	X
Iberia	X	X	0	X	X	X	0	0	X
Inca	X	X	X	X	X	X	X	X	X
Jimma	X	X	X	X	X	X	X	—	X
Kachari	0	0	0	0	X	0	X	0	X
Kuba	X	X	X	X	X	X	X	0	X
Maurya	0	X	X	X	X	X	X	0	X
Mongolia	X	X	—	X	—	X	0	—	X
Norway	X	X	0	X	—	X	0	0	X
Scythia	X	X	0	0	X	X	0	X	X
Tahiti	X	X	—	X	X	X	—	—	X
Volta	X	X	—	X	—	X	0	0	X
Yoruba	X	X	X	X	X	X	X	0	X
Zande	0	X	—	X	—	X	X	—	X

(32)   *In early states the sovereign generally pays offerings* (significant at the 100% level).

With the exception of *China* and *Kachari*, for which no data were given, lower-level payments were found everywhere. For *China* they are quite probable, moreover.

(33)   *The payment of salaries and remunerations and the presentation of offerings or gifts are found to be general, also on the lower levels of the government hierarchy* (significant at the 100% level).

(34)   *In all early states a royal court is found* (significant at the 100% level).

In only seven cases were data given that more or less pointed in the direction of the existence of *salaried* functionaries (*Aztecs, France, Inca, Jimma, Kuba, Maurya* and *Yoruba*). Seven cases yielded no data at all on this subject, and seven yielded negative results.

The organization of major works was mentioned in fifteen cases. As regards *Hawaii* and *Kuba* it should be added that these works were of limited importance. In the case of *China*, moreover, Pokora noted that the workers received no special remuneration: here they worked for their own benefit. The data on ruler's palaces were quite scanty, and those on tombs even extremely poor — in both cases mainly because of lack of information.

2.10.5. *Problems of the Sovereign's Legitimation.* In chapter 1 we already assumed the importance of this concept for an understanding of the way in which early states existed. Here we will concentrate mainly on the structural aspects of the concept. In the opinion of Swartz et al. (1966: 10), legitimacy is

> The type of support that derives not from force or its threat but from the *values* (our italics) held by the individuals formulating, influencing, and being affected by political ends.

Swartz, in a later study, adds to this the idea of the 'degree of legitimation' (1968: 32 ff.). By this he means that in reality a political system that is based on either coercion only or on consensus only is found nowhere. There will always be a combination of both, the degree of legitimacy representing the relative proportion of each. In an earlier work I myself concluded that

> ... only where the majority of the population accepts the authority of the ruler and considers his laws and regulations acceptable will a sufficient degree of observance (of the laws and regulations) be found (Claessen 1970: 320).

It is not likely that everybody will always agree with all the rules, laws or norms of his society (cf. Wertheim 1971). A certain amount of enforcement will therefore always be found.

All this leads to the hypothesis that behind every government (whether tribal or more advanced) will be found a number of norms and ideas that are accepted by at least the majority of the population. This complex of norms, values, ideas and concepts we will call the *ideology*, or, in the words of MacIver (1965: 13, 58, 88) the '*myth of the society*'. So the ruler who rules in accordance with the myth of his society can be considered as *legitime* (cf. Weber 1964: 739 ff.). Now, political leaders are usually well aware of these facts, and will try to promote such an ideology as much as possible (cf. Claessen 1974: 72 ff.). This brings us to the question of ideology and legitimation in early states. Kurtz, in his chapter on the *Aztecs*, convincingly demonstrates how the legitimation of the state is promoted and elaborated in the course of the development of the state. The other case essays as well provided many data on legitimation. These appear to be concentrated mainly around the sovereign — the derivation of the legitimation of other ruling groups in the society from his position being generally found. Many of the structural characteristics are found to point in this direction, viz. the position of the sovereign is based on a mythical charter (S.C. 21); the ruler is sacral (S.C. 22), the most important manifestation of this latter point appearing to be the ruler's middle-manship between his people and the supernatural forces; he performs rites (S.C. 24), and in some cases is even high priest; he placates the supernatural powers with offerings (S.C. 32). The sovereign is also the law giver (S.C. 25) and supreme judge (S.C. 26). Being the supreme commander of the armed forces (S.C. 28), he is charged with the protection of his people. His benevolence is expressed in the gifts presented (S.C. 30) and the remunerations paid by him (S.C. 31). The essential aim of all these characteristics is *protection* — against supernatural forces, secular powers, poverty and anarchy. It is believed that wherever the sovereign is, there is safety, order and well-being. The relation between the sovereign and his people can therefore in principle be seen as a *reciprocal* one: the people supply food, goods and services, and the ruler provides protection. This mostly ideological view is found explicitly expressed in some of our case essays, and implicitly in the others. The point of view put forward here comes close to the results of Van Baal's analysis of reciprocity (1975: 65–69). In fact, some of the latter's conclusions actually confirm our own hypothesis. This is the case where, for instance, Van Baal says that reciprocity

> can be anything from balanced to unbalanced or muddled where social
> solidarity is strong and social differences are recognized (1975: 67),

or he explains, that, where the principle of 'generalized reciprocity' is replaced by 'trade', a *new* type of society develops, in which inequality becomes an evil that has to be fought with all might.

This type of situation creates the right climate for a class struggle, where labor gradually becomes a commodity and the object of hard bargaining. The result is strong economic inequality because of the imagined economic equality (cf. also Van Baal 1974). The state in a society of this type seems more in conformity with Krader's concept of the state, which he regards as being non-reciprocal (see chapters 4 and 28 of this volume), than with the early state as described in our case studies. It is a state based on another kind of ideology. With the ending of a reciprocity-based ideology, the early state also comes to an end.

2.11. *Inequality*

At first sight this subject seems fairly simple. In the aforegoing analysis we already concluded that the population of early states was divided into a number of basic social categories, viz. that of the *sovereign*, the *aristocracy*, *smallholders* and *tenants* (S.C. 11, 12, 13), while such contiguous categories as *priests*, *artisans*, *servants* and *slaves* were also found to be fairly common. The fact that all early states had an *upper population stratum* and a *lower population stratum* has also been established (S.C. 14). The relation to food production in a number of social categories (*sovereign, aristocracy, priests, gentry, traders* and *artisans*) was indirect, and in others (*smallholders, tenants, servants* and *slaves*) direct (cf. S.C. 15, 20). The access to the basic resources was found to be *differential* (S.C. 18). Taken altogether, an obvious degree of social inequality was found in our early states, sometimes reinforced by sumptuary laws (e.g., the *Aztecs*).

On closer scrutiny the situation appears to be more complex, however. There is *no* clear-cut division between the upper and the lower stratum on the point of control of the means of production. Many members of the upper stratum actually produce food in their own fields and do not live on tribute from smallholders. Conversely, not all lower stratum categories actually produce their own food. Last but not least, *all* categories are obliged to pay taxes and to perform services for the sovereign (S.C. 16). Inequality seems to exist not only *between* the social categories, moreover, but also within them (cf. Khazanov, chapter 3 of this volume). This compels us to investigate social inequality in more detail, therefore. We will confine our examination to the following categories: the *aristocracy* and *priests* as representing the upper stratum, and *smallholders*, *tenants* and *artisans* as representing the lower stratum.

2.11.1. *The Upper Stratum.* In Table XII we have brought together data on the composition of the *aristocracy*. With the aid of these we may gain some sort of insight into the composition and structure of this social category as also into the claimed status of the aristocrats.

With the exception of *Norway* (insufficient data), the sovereign's kin were invariably counted with the aristocracy. Hence the first structural characteristic here is:

(35) *In early states the sovereign's kin belong to the aristocracy* (significant at the 100% level).

In addition occupation of high office qualifies people for membership of the aristocracy. All our cases yielded positive results in this respect. This, of course, is due partly to the fact that in many cases only people of high birth were deemed fit for such offices to begin with. However, the reverse was also found to be true. The complexity of the situation rendered further distinctions impossible.

(36) *Tenure of high office renders one eligible for classification with the aristocracy* (significant at the 100% level).

In eighteen cases it was found that the heads of at least a number of clans (or lineages, or comparable groups) were classified with the aristocracy. In most cases these clan dignitaries were connected to the ruler's family by matrimonial ties, or even descended from junior branches of these. Here, too, the connection with high position was found (not included separately in Table XII). Two cases (*Egypt* and *Iberia*) yielded inconclusive results in this respect. *Jimma* scored negatively on this point (Prof. Lewis: personal communication). Hence

Table XII. *Membership of aristocracy*

	Sovereign's kin	Clan or lineage heads	Occupants of high offices	Landed proprietors	Internal stratification
Angkor	X	X	X	X	X
Ankole	X	X	X	—	X
Axum	X	X	X	0	X
Aztecs	X	X	X	—	X
China	X	X	X	0	X
Egypt	X	0	X	0	0
France	X	X	X	0	X
Hawaii	X	X	X	—	X
Iberia	X	0	X	—	0
Inca	X	X	X	—	X
Jimma	X	—	X	X	X
Kachari	X	X	X	0	X
Kuba	X	X	X	X	X
Maurya	X	X	X	X	X
Mongolia	X	X	X	—	X
Norway	0	X	X	0	X
Scythia	X	X	X	—	X
Tahiti	X	X	X	—	X
Volta	X	X	X	—	X
Yoruba	X	X	X	—	X
Zande	X	X	X	—	X

the structural characteristic here is:

(37) *In early states the heads of certain clans belong to the aristocracy* (significant at the 99% level).

In a few cases (*Inca, Zande*) *all* members of certain clans were counted with the aristocracy. In these cases, however, great internal status differences were found.

In only four cases did it appear that landed proprietorship by itself was a sufficient condition for inclusion within the aristocracy. In no less than eleven cases this seemed to be judged of less importance. For six states insufficient data were available. The conclusion we can draw from these findings must therefore be that membership of the aristocracy is based less on property than on *descent*, and/or the *occupation of high office*. In the case of *Ankole, Mongolia* and *Scythia* cattle was taken as a functional equivalent for land.

There were nineteen cases in which the aristocracy showed *internal stratification*. There often existed whole hierarchies, ranging from a category of people with a status close to that of the sovereign, to one of people whose membership of the aristocracy was only marginal. The criteria for the determination of a person's position in the hierarchy were mostly rank order of birth and the kind of function occupied. In some cases (*Tahiti* and *Volta*) it was explicitly mentioned that people of aristocratic descent might even, as a result of these factors, gradually lose their aristocratic status altogether, in the course of time. For *France* and *Kachari* this is also probable. By way of structural characteristic we can state that:

(38)   *In early states the aristocracy is internally stratified according to rank order of birth and function occupied* (significant at the 100% level).

The aspects of appointment versus heredity will be considered in Section 2.12.

The other upper-level group is that formed by *priests*. Contrary to the rather vaguely status-based aristocracy, the position of the priesthood is a very specific one, being based on clear requirements. Van Baaren (1960: 153) even speaks of the 'professional character' (ambtelijk karakter) of the priesthood (cf. Keesing 1958: 338). The data concerning priests in our case studies were, unfortunately, rather limited in scope as well as depth, while in the chapters on *Ankole* and *Mongolia* virtually none were given (for which the editors are to be blamed, since they did not ask for any particulars on priests). In our comparisons regarding priests we will therefore be working with nineteen instead of twenty-one cases. For *Norway* only the older period will be considered. For *Hawaii* data have been added from elsewhere (Davenport 1969: 7 ff.). The *Volta* data are restricted to the earthpriests. The total data are summarized in Table XIII.

Table XIII.   *Priests*

	The sovereign or close kinsman is high priest	Sovereign performs rites	Hierarch. organization	Training	Participation of commoners	Support of the society's myth	Special pol. functionaries
Angkor	—	X	X	0	0	X	X
Ankole							
Axum	0	X	X	0	0	X	0
Aztecs	X	X	X	X	0	X	X
China	—	X	X	0	0	X	X
Egypt	X	X	X	0	0	X	0
France	—	X	X	X	0	X	X
Hawaii	—	X	X	X	0	X	X
Iberia	X	X	X	0	—	X	0
Inca	X	X	X	X	X	X	X
Jima	—	X	—	X	X	0	X
Kachari	—	X	X	X	0	0	X
Kuba	X	X	0	0	0	X	X
Maurya	—	0	0	X	0	X	X
Mongolia							
(Old) Norway	—	X	—	0	—	0	—
Scythia	X	X	0	0	—	X	0
Tahiti	X	X	X	X	X	X	X
Volta	—	0	X	0	X	X	X
Yoruba	X	X	X	0	0	X	X
Zande	—	X	—	X	0	X	X

These rather limited data show that there are close connections between the sovereign and the clergy. In seventeen cases he performed rites himself (in fact, he also conducted rites in *Ankole*, which state has been left out of consideration in this table; cf. S.C. 24). In eight cases either he or a close kinsman was high priest.

Support by the priesthood for the ideological basis or mythical charter was found in seventeen cases, while no cases scored negatively on this point. This makes possible the formulation of the following structural characteristic:

(39) *In early states the priesthood supports the ideological basis* (significant at the 100% level).

In thirteen cases *priests* also fulfilled important political functions (seventy-two percent). On the other hand, in only four cases was there mention of any possibility for commoners to become priests. In evaluating this statement we will have to bear in mind, however, that in no less than thirteen cases no data were given on this. The professional character of the priesthood was confirmed by the existence of special training in nine cases. A hierarchical organization was mentioned for thirteen states. This latter fact points towards the existence of status inequality within the priesthood.

In Section 2.9.2 we surveyed the relation of the *aristocracy* and *priesthood* to the means of production. Both categories were only indirectly involved in food production. *Tribute*, in whatever form, was the principal source of income of the aristocracy (G.S. 19), while it formed at least the partial basis of the income of the priesthood in eight out of fourteen cases; the latter being at least partly dependent on gifts and remunerations in six out of the fourteen cases (Table VII).

2.11.2. *The Lower Stratum.* Like the upper stratum, the lower stratum also showed marked internal differences. The *smallholders* and *tenants* here are the direct producers of food (Table VII), with the production of which the *artisans* have only indirect connections; they, participate however, in material production. On the other hand, *smallholders* have certain rights to land, whereas *tenants* and *artisans* only seldom have land of their own. There are also many indications that such factors as age, individual capacities, lineage position, etc., give rise to status differences within the lower stratum.

Table XIV sets out the data concerning the *rights and duties of commoners*. Lack of relevant data has made it impossible to go into this in more detail. This does not mean that there is no information on this subject at all, as is demonstrated in *Van vorsten en volken* (Claessen 1970: 282–307), careful research may bring many details to light. However, as in the case of the priesthood, the blame for the lack of data falls in the first place on the editors, since they omitted to ask for more specific information on this.

In this connection we have brought together data on:

— *commoners' influence on government;* here we have not distinguished between direct, indirect, or institutionalized influence, etc., but have only noted its presence or absence;
— the *possibility of appeal* in judicial matters, as evidence for which was accepted the existence of a court of appeal;
— the *right to remuneration* for work done for the state, its functionaries, or the aristocracy;
— the *right* to some sort of *protection* in emergencies (e.g., food shortages, war, etc.).

More data were available on the *obligations* of commoners. We were able to obtain data on the following:

— the obligation to *pay taxes* and/or tribute or rent, or to make donations;
— the obligation to assist in the construction of *major works;*
— the obligation to perform *menial services* (e.g., to work on the land of chiefs, or other notables or functionaries, to help with the repair of houses, fences, etc.);
— the obligation to meet *sexual demands* (e.g., to supply girls for harems, to observe the *jus primae noctis,* etc.);
— the obligation to perform *military service.*

Data have been added for *Jimma* (Prof. Lewis: personal communication) and *Mongolia* (Krader 1968: 88 ff.). The positive scoring of certain aspects does not imply that all commoners always had to fulfil all the duties concerned, but simply indicates that they were performed. The degree or frequency of fulfilment is not analysed.

The data of Table XIV are fairly limited. The only right that is found frequently is the right to payment for services on which fifteen cases scored positively, while in six no data were furnished. The other rights were even less often mentioned; as regards influence on government only seven cases scored positively and six negatively, while for the right to appeal thirteen cases had positive and two negative scores. With respect to the right to protection six scored positively, while for fourteen there were no data.

The data on obligations were more plentiful. The obligation *to pay taxes* is found in all cases. It is therefore a structural characteristic that:

(40)   *In all early states commoners have the obligation to pay taxes, tribute, or comparable levies* (significant at the 100% level).

The obligation to perform *military service* was non-existent only once (*France*), while for *Egypt* the data were insufficient. The structural characteristic here is:

(41)   *In early states commoners generally have the obligation to perform military service* (significant at the 99% level).

Table XIV. *Rights and obligations of commoners*

	Influ-ence on govern. pol.	Rights			Obligations				
		Right to appeal	Right to pay-ment	Right to protec-tion	Oblig. to pay taxes	Supply labor for constr. works	Menial tasks	Sexual services	Milit-ary services
Angkor	0	X	X	0	X	X	X	X	X
Ankole	—	X	X	0	X	—	X	0	X
Axum	0	X	0	0	X	X	0	0	X
Aztecs	0	X	X	X	X	X	X	0	X
China	X	0	X	0	X	X	X	—	X
Egypt	0	0	X	X	X	X	X	0	0
France	—	X	X	0	X	X	X	0	—
Hawaii	0	—	X	X	X	X	X	0	X
Iberia	X	0	0	0	X	X	Se X	0	X
Inca	—	X	X	X	X	X	X	X	X
Jimma	X	X	X	X	X	X	X	0	X
Kachari	0	0	0	0	X	X	X	X	X
Kuba	X	X	X	0	X	X	Se X	0	Sl Vol X
Maurya	0	X	X	0	X	X	X	0	X
Mongolia	—	0	0	0	X	—	X	0	X
Norway	X	0	0	X	X	—	Sl X	0	X
Scythia	0	X	X	0	X Se	—	Se X	0	X
Tahiti	X	—	X	0	X	X	X	0	X
Volta	X	X	X	0	X	—	Se X	X Se	Se X
Yoruba	—	X	X	0	X	X	X Se	0	X
Zande	—	X	0	0	X	X	X	0	X

Abbreviations: Se = fulfilled by servants or subjected villagers; Sl = performed by slaves; Vol = performed by volunteers.

Menial tasks were obligatory in twenty cases, no data being furnished for *Axum*. Hence:

(42) *In early states commoners have the obligation to perform menial services for the state, the aristocracy or functionaries* (significant at the 100% level).

Less general was the obligation to provide labor for roads, irrigation systems or palaces. This aspect scored positively in sixteen cases, and negatively in five. The obligation to render sexual services was found only four times (*Angkor, Incas, Kachari* and *Volta*). However, only in the case of *China* was it explicitly stated that this obligation was *not* found.

The data from Table XIV show quite convincingly that the common people — i.e., the members of the lower stratum — had, generally speaking, only a few rights and many obligations.

2.11.3. *The Upper vs the Lower Stratum.* In this section we will discuss the general differences between the upper and lower strata. How do they differ, and what, if anything, do they have in common? This latter question can only be answered by very general statements, such as: both strata belong to the same political entity, or both strata are supposed to respect the same basic ideology. One of the few more specific common aspects is the obligation for all categories (with the exception of traders) to render services to the state (Table IX, S.C. 16). Obviously, the differences are more important.

To find a general principle, an underlying idea, upon which the differences between the upper and lower strata may be based is no easy task. A number of characteristics which seem obvious, or are often mentioned as dividing the upper from the lower level, such as power, land ownership or high status, are to be regarded as mere derivatives, or the outcome of the factors behind these characteristics. For the early state one may possibly suggest as first dividing principle the *distance from the sovereign's lineage.* A second dividing principle may be *the actual tenure of office* other than on the basis of descent. Functionaries of this type are often to be found among the courtiers, councillors, or office holders with specialist knowledge in the administration. Other authors, such as Sahlins (1958 passim) and Krader (1968: 87) have hinted at the possibility of the first of these principles as a dividing factor before us. Of our case studies, especially those on *Kachari* and *Tahiti* provided clear examples of this kind of situation. We consider the following observations as supporting our hypothesis. As regards the *aristocracy* it was found that the ruler's family constituted one of its main components (S.C. 35). In addition, the heads of certain clans or lineages and their immediate relatives were counted as belonging to the aristocracy (S.C. 37). These people were connected to the sovereign's family by descent or marriage. In this context it seems important also that internal stratification within the aristocracy (S.C. 38) was usually dependent on relative distance from the lineage of the founders of the clan or the rank order of birth. In some cases junior sons of junior branches even gradually lost their status as aristocrats altogether, as the social distance from the senior lineages became too great. Sometimes slaves, placed in high positions also formed a kind of aristocracy (*Yoruba*). The *military group* was always composed of members of the aristocracy, and often formed no separate category at all (cf. Table IV). The *priesthood* was often also seen to have close kinship connections with the sovereign (S.C. 24). This is underlined by the fact that in only four cases was there mention of commoners having the opportunity to become priests (Table XIII). Between the commoner categories and the ruler's family *no* kinship relations at all were found. The division is so marked in all cases that we even judge it to be a structural characteristic that:

(43) *In early states there are no kinship relations between the sovereign and his family on the one hand, and commoners on the other* (significant at the 100% level).

The fact that in some cases there existed some vague idea that the rulers and the ruled both belonged to one enormous clan, or ramage (as in *Tahiti*), did not have any practical repercussions.

So, from the perspective of this principle the more favorable position of the upper stratum, as manifest in:
— a high governmental and ideological position,
— an income based on tribute and remunerations, and
— a high social status,
is most often a corollary of close connection to the sovereign's lineage. The common people, having no connections with this lineage have to be content with their inferior position, as reflected in:
— a limited influence on government decisions;
— limited access to ideologically based positions;
— the obligation to pay taxes and tribute, to supply labor and to perform military service.

For the upper level the reciprocal principle, as outlined in Section 2.10.5, involves receiving more and better things from the sovereign in return for services to him and the state in positions of great responsibility. The labor and payments of the commoners are reciprocated less in the form of material goods than in that of spiritual benefits, protection (or tokens thereof), and gifts (cf. Kandert's comments on this situation among the *Zande*).

This system contains, from the very beginning, the seeds of its own destruction. When later developments place increasing stress on already existing material objects of desire, when private ownership of the means of production replaces communal possession, and when feelings of mutual obligation (whether actual or fictive) fade, then the basic principle of reciprocity of the early state will lose its force. Then a new type of state, the mature type, will develop, of which antagonism between the by then fully developed social classes will be a key feature. The state as outlined by Krader in the present volume (cf. also Van Baal's analysis 1975: 67 ff.) is more like the latter than the early state under study in this volume.

2.12. *The Structure of the Administrative Apparatus*

The administrative apparatus needed to make a state run smoothly is necessarily a complex one. There are numerous functions that have to be fulfilled, and often the activities connected with these are mutually overlapping or contradictory. In all states a system that was adapted to the specific situation was developed in the course of time. This makes the degree of similarity between our cases rather low. However, when one looks behind the numerous institutions, one can discern general patterns. The existence of similarities, functional equivalents and cor-

respondences can be explained by the fact that the problems that had
to be solved were nearly always the same, viz.
— how to evolve particular laws and regulations;
— how to make people observe these laws and regulations;
— how to enforce decrees;
— how, if necessary, to coerce or compel people to do certain things;
— how to protect the state against external threats;
— how to maintain the existing social order;
— how to finance the state apparatus.

The number of people involved in the early state and the extent of
its territory make a *delegation of tasks and powers* inevitable. Even a
superficial perusal of the case studies makes it clear that this is a
structural characteristic of all early states. Hence:

(44) *In all early states the delegation of tasks and power constitutes a
principle of political organization* (significant at the 100% level).

It is tempting to use such terms as 'bureaucracy' or 'political
machine' to qualify the organizational structure. However, when we
examine Weber's characterization of the concept of 'bureaucracy'
(1964: 703 ff.) we find so many features that are not found in the
organization of early states that we hesitate to use this term. The same
holds for the concept of 'political machine' as analysed by Bax (1975:
7 ff.). Therefore the more general term *apparatus* will be used.

With the aid of the governmental apparatus the ruler is able to fulfil
the many tasks mentioned above. A problem that increases as the
apparatus develops is: how to keep it in hand? What must be done to
prevent the apparatus taking over the entire function of the sovereign?

In the following passages the structure of the governmental apparatus will be discussed. The problems of delegation and preservation
of power will be discussed in the next chapter.

2.12.1. *Types of Functionaries and the Levels on which they are
Employed.* Speaking in terms of rather broad generalization, the functionaries making up the apparatus can be divided into:
— those immediately connected with the preparation and execution of
  laws and regulations; this category can in turn be divided into:
  (a) general functionaries, whose activities embrace a number of
      types of governmental function;
  (b) special functionaries, whose governmental activities are re-
      stricted to only one aspect of government administration;
  (c) others, who, as a result of special status or position, exercise an
      influence on governmental decisions, but whose principal occu-
      pations are not directly concerned with government (priests,
      courtiers, soldiers, etc.);

— those who are members of councils, courts, or committees, and as
  such are more or less anonymous;
—those with positions in controlling agencies.
Obviously, a considerable degree of overlap will not be excluded,
while, conversely, certain functionaries may occupy a place in more
than one of the categories mentioned.

First we will discuss the 'general functionaries' and 'specialists', or,
in other words, the more or less 'visible' functionaries. Then the
categories of members of councils and people exercising an 'influence'
only — both of which are more or less 'invisible'[2] will come up for
discussion.

In Table XV we have brought together the data concerning general
functionaries. Here we will distinguish between the following features.
— The level at which they are employed, viz. national (N), regional
  (R), or local (L).
— Mode of succession, viz by inheritance (H), appointment (A), or
  election (E).
— The receipt of a status income, i.e., a remuneration obtained by the
  functionary in *direct* connection with the exercise of his function (cf.
  Weber 1964: 698).
— The power to take independent action.
— The exercise of control by functionaries of the next level up.
— Participation in the administration of justice.
— Obligation to collect taxes or tribute.
— Military obligations ranging from the obligation to act as comman-
  der of an armed force to the mere obligation to levy a military force.

In a few cases we have inserted the letter 'l', meaning 'of limited
importance'. Furthermore, the following should be borne in mind:

In the case of *Egypt*, we have considered the governors of the *nomes*
as regional functionaries. The function of *vizier*, which came into being
during the reign of Djoser, is considered as a general one on the
national level.

As regards *France*, apparently the state started off with specialists.
The more general kinds of functionaries, such as *bailiffs, prévots* and
vicarii came into prominence, or rather were revived, somewhat later.

With respect to *Mongolia*, no data were furnished on this subject.
This state has therefore been left out of consideration, while for
Norway we have confined our analysis to the older period only.
For *Tahiti* some data have been added from Claessen (1970: 15 ff.).

In the nineteen cases under study we found national-level functionaries mentioned fifteen times, regional functionaries eighteen times
and local-level functionaries sixteen times. Negative scores were obtained for functionaries at the national level in *Angkor*, the regional

Table XV. *General functionaries*

	Level			Mode of succession			Employment of status income			Entitlement to independent action			Control by superior			Judicial activities			Tax collection			Military obligations		
	N	R	L	N	R	L	N	R	L	N	R	L	N	R	L	N	R	L	N	R	L	N	R	L
Angkor	—	X	X		A/H	A/H	0	0	0	0	0	X	0	0	X	X	—	—	—	—	—	0	—	—
Ankole	Xl	X	X	A/H	A/H	H	0	0	0	0	X	X	0	0		X	0	X	0	X	X	0	X	0
Axum	0	X	X	A/H	A/H	A/H	0	0	0	0	X	X	X	X	0	0	0	0	0	X	0	0	X	X
Aztecs	X	X	X	A/H	A/H	A	X	X	X	0	0	0	0	X	X	0	X	X		0	X	0	0	0
China	0	X	X	0	A/H	A/H	X	—	0	0	X	0	X	X	X	0	X	X	0					
Egypt	Xl	X	0	A/H	A/H	0	X	X	X	X	0	0	X	X	X	X	X	0	X	X	0	0	0	0
France	X	X	X	A/H	A/H	A/H	X	X	X	X	0	0	X	X	X	X	X	0	0	X	0			
Hawaii	X	X	X	A	H	H	X	X	X	0	X	0	0	0	X	0	0	0	0	X	X	0	X	X
Iberia	X	X	X	0	A/H	A	0	0	0	X	0	X	X	X	X	0	X	X	X	X	0	X	X	0
Inca	X	X	X	A/H	A/H	A/0	X	X	X	X	X	Xl	X	0	0	X	0	X		X	X	X	X	X
Jimma	Xl	X	X	A	A	A	X	X	0	0	Xl	0	0	X	X	X	X	X	X			Xl	Xl	Xl
Kachari	X	X	X	0	A	0	X	X	X	0	0	X	X	0	X	0	X	0	X	X		X	X	0
Kuba	X	X	X	A/H	A/H	E/H	X	X	X	0	Xl	0	0	0	0	0	X	X	X	X		0	0	0
Maurya	X	X	X	A	0	0	0	X	0	0	0	X	X	X	X	0	0	0	0	X	0	0	0	0
Mongolia (Old)																								
Norway	X	X	X	H/A	H/A	H/0	X	0	0	0	X	0	0	X	0	0	X	X	X	X	X	0	X	X
Scythia	Xl	X	X	H	H	H	X	X	X	X	X	X	Xl	Xl	X	0	0	X	X	X	0	0	—	—
Tahiti	—	—	X	A/H		A/H	X	0	X	0		X	X	X	X	X	X	X	X	X	X	X	X	X
Volta	X	—	X	A	A	A	0	X	X	0	X	X	X	X	X		X	X	X			X	X	X
Yoruba	X	X	X	A	A/H	A	X	X	X	0	X	X	X	X	X		X	X		X	X	0	0	X
Zande	0	X	X	A/H	A/H	A	0	0	0	0	X	X	0	0	X	0	X	X	0	X	X	0	X	0

Abbreviations; l = of limited importance; A = by appointment; H = hereditary; E = by election.

level in *Volta*, and the local level in *Tahiti*. The lack of general functionaries at the national level may be easily explained by the presence of energetic rulers, who, in fact, were general functionaries themselves. As structural characteristic may be suggested:

(45) *In early states usually a three-tier administrative apparatus is found* (significant at the 99% level).

(46) *In early states general functionaries are found mostly on the regional level, and slightly less frequently on the national and local levels* (significant at the 99% level).

In thirteen cases the system of succession showed a *mixture* of appointment and heredity. Usually this meant that a certain function was hereditary in a specific clan or lineage, but that achievement, personal capacities or competition (as in *Volta*) decided which particular clan or lineage members would be appointed. In other cases exclusively appointive and exclusively hereditary functions existed side by side. Generally, the sovereign tried to promote the appointment of functionaries, while, conversely, the functionaries strove to make their positions hereditary in their respective families. Only in *Jimma* and *Yoruba* was appointment markedly predominant. In *Hawaii* and *Tahiti* succession was predominantly hereditary.

The connection between income and function was rather vague, though only because of lack of data:

— On the national level nine cases scored positively, while in eight cases no data were available.

— On the local level six cases scored positively, and no data were available in six cases.

— On the local level six cases scored positively, and no data were furnished in eleven cases.

The same vagueness is found with respect to 'independence of action', and 'control by superior functionaries'. In only a few cases were unambiguously positive or negative data supplied on this. The only conclusion we seem justified in drawing seems to be that functionaries on the regional level enjoy the most powers, but at the same time are most subject to control.

Of their various tasks, the collection of taxes (levies, tribute) seems to be the most prominent one, judicial and military tasks being the more particular preserve of specialists.

Table XVI sets out the data concerning '*specialists*'. In this table we have confined ourselves to the same aspects as in the case of 'general functionaries'. A consequence of this restriction is that some interesting data have had to be omitted from the table. We will therefore discuss these in the present context.

— *Iberia, Incas* and *Maurya* had high-level specialists entrusted with the supervision of large-scale works (irrigation, roads, etc.).

Table XVI. *Specialist functionaries*

	Level		Mode of succession		Enjoyment of status income		Entitlement to independent measure		Control by superior		Judicial activities		Tax-collection		Military obligations	
	H	M	H	M	H	M	H	M	H	M	H	M	H	M	H	M
Angkor	X	X	A/H	A/H	X	X	0	0	0	0	0	X	X	X	0	0
Ankole	X	X	H	0	0	0	0	0	0	0	0	X	0	0	0	X
Axum	X	0	A/H	0	0	0	0	0	0	0	0	0	X	0	X	0
Aztecs	X	X	A/H	A	X	X	0	0	0	X	0	0	0	X	0	0
China	X	X	A/H	0	—	0	0	0	0	0	0	X	X	0	X	0
Egypt	X	0	A	0	X	0	0	0	0	0	0	0	0	0	0	0
France	X	0	A	0	X	0	0	0	0	0	0	0	X	0	X	0
Hawaii	X	X	0	0	0	0	0	0	0	0	0	0	X	0	X	0
Iberia																
Inca	X	X	A/H	A/H	X	X	0	0	X	X	X	X	X	X	X	X
Jimma	X	X	A	A	X	X	0	0	X	X	X	Xl	X	X	X	Xl
Kachari	X	0	0	0	0	0	0	0	0	0	X	0	0	0	0	0
Kuba	X	0	A	0	X	0	0	0	0	0	0	0	X	0	X	0
Maurya	X	X	A/H	0	0	0	0	0	0	0	X	0	X	0	0	0
Mongolia																
(Old) Norway	X	X	0	0	0	0	X	0	0	0	0	0	X	X	0	X
Scythia																
Tahiti	X	X	H	H/A	0	0	X	X	0	0	—	—	—	—	X	X
Volta	X	—	A/H		X		0		0		0		0		0	
Yoruba	X	0	A	0	X	0	0	0	X	0	X	0	X	0	X	0
Zande	—	X	0	A/H	0	0	0	0	0	0	0	0	0	0	0	X

Abbreviations: l = of limited importance; A = by appointment; H = hereditary.

— For the *Aztecs, China, Egypt* and *France* high-level functionaries entrusted with the care of the 'royal household' or the 'economy' were mentioned.

In the table we have had to leave *Iberia, Mongolia* and *Scythia* out of consideration because of lack of data. For the *Aztecs* a few data were added from Soustelle (1958).

The levels distinguished here are 'high' and 'middle'. The first comprises functionaries on the national level, such as ministers and the like. The middle-level functionaries are comparable in status to the regional general functionaries of Table XV.

Of the eighteen cases that were compared, no fewer than seventeen appeared to possess high-level specialists. This, therefore, still qualifies for formulation as a structural characteristic, viz:

(47) *In early states specialist functionaries are usually found at the top level of the admistrative apparatus* (significant at the 99% level).

The data on the *middle level* are less unequivocal. Only eleven cases scored positively. The mode of succession, as in the case of the general functionaries, comprised a mixture of appointment and heredity. However, appointment seems to be slightly more prominent than among the 'general functionaries'. At the high level, appointment was found in five cases, and a mixture in seven, and heredity in two; no data were furnished in four cases. At the middle level, there was appointment in two cases, heredity in none, and a mixture in four; no data were furnished in twelve cases.

This probably has some connection with the need for specialist knowledge or personal qualifications for functions of this type (cf. Claessen 1975b: 46).

The data on the enjoyment of a status income, independence of action, or control by superiors are too limited to give us any clear insight into these matters. In addition, the administration of justice appeared to be a specialist function in only a few cases. In Section 2.12.2 we will return to this. Tax collection was more often the responsibility of specialists. On the high level this was the case thirteen times, and on the middle level six times. Furthermore military responsibilities are seen to be regularly associated with specialists; this was so in ten cases at the top level, and in six at the middle level.

2.12.2. *Anonymous Functionaries.* The functionaries in this category are rather elusive. They either exercise specialist functions as priests, military leaders, or courtiers, and use their status as such to influence government policy, or are lost in collective bodies such as councils, courts or committees. Nevertheless, these persons really do play a role in the government of the early state. We will therefore bring together the limited information we have gathered on this subject just the same.

The members of collective bodies are not usually mentioned individually. Only the presence of the bodies in question testifies to their existence. We will therefore only discuss the activities of these collectivities.

The relevant data are collected in Table XVII. In the first column the number of crosses indicates the number of bodies that are found in a given case. The various tasks are divided into: advisory, the administration of justice, the preparation of laws and the taking of 'major decisions'. This latter involves that decisions of major importance (e.g., relating to the declaration of war) are dependent upon some council.

The table shows that *China* and *Zande* apparently had no collective bodies in the government organization. For *Axum, Egypt, Iberia* and *Kachari* no data were found concerning this. In the remaining fifteen cases it was found that advisory tasks were the most prominent, this being so fourteen times. The administration of justice was found to be one of the council's duties in ten cases. Influence upon legislation was mentioned in five cases. Only in two of our early states were major decisions left to a council. Of course, it is most probable that behind

Table XVII. *Councils*

	Number of councils etc.	Tasks			
		Advisory	Judicial	Law-giving	Major decisions
Angkor	XX	X	X		
Ankole	X	X	X		
Axum	0				
Aztecs	XX	X	XX		
China	—				
Egypt	0				
France	XX	X	X		
Hawaii	X	X			
Iberia	0				
Inca	XX	X	X	X	X
Jimma	X		X		
Kachari					
		0			
Kuba	XXXX	X	X	X	X
Maurya	XX	X		X	
Mongolia	X	X			
Norway	X	X	X	X	
Scythia	X	X			
Tahiti	X	X			
Volta	X	X	X		
Yoruba	XXX	X	X	X	
Zande	—				

'advisory functions' much influence upon major decisions lies hidden. However, this was mentioned explicitly in only two cases.

It is possible at this stage to say something more about the administration of justice. In Table IX formal judges are listed for *Angkor*, the *Aztecs, France, Jimma, Incas, Kachari, Kuba* and *Maurya.* Table XVI, however, seems to present quite a different picture, no specialists engaged in legal activities being mentioned for the *Aztecs, France* or *Kuba*, while this has furthermore been added for *China*. With the aid of the data of Table XVII we are now able to solve these seeming contradictions. The fact of the matter is that the judges of the *Aztecs* (partially), *France* and *Kuba* were 'concealed' in collective bodies, while the *Chinese* specialists of Table XVI only had supervisory tasks.

We will now consider the persons with 'informal' influence. A problem in this connection is that people of some importance are often already members of some council, and, by virtue of this, exercise formal, institutionalized influence on governmental policy. As the composition of collective bodies is far from clear, and the 'informal' influence of members of inner circles, personal friends, courtiers, etc., was an established fact in most of the case studies, we feel justified in giving some attention to these subjects. In Table XVIII we have

brought together data in this respect on:
— the court, divided according to whether such courts existed and the
influence they exercised on politics;
— the sovereign's relatives; in which category we have distinguished
between influences exercised by the ruler's consort, his other wives
(the harem), his successor or his brothers, cousins, etc., and general
influences where the data of the case studies do not permit any
distinction in the above mentioned categories;
— the priesthood; here, too, we have distinguished between influence
exercised by specific functionaries and 'general' influence';
— military leaders, between whom we distinguished in the same way.
Data have been added for the *Aztecs* (Soustelle 1958: 108 ff.), *Incas*
(Claessen 1970: 15 ff.), and *Tahiti* (Claessen 1970: 14 ff.).

A court was found to exist everywhere (cf. S.C. 34). Its influence on
politics was mentioned eighteen times. This is therefore a structural
characteristic.

(48) *Generally in early states the courtiers exercise an influence on
political affairs* (significant at the 100% level).

General influence of the ruler's family was mentioned no less than
twenty times (no data for *Kachari*).

(49) *The members of the sovereign's family exercise an influence on
political decisions in all early states* (significant at the 100% level).

More specific influence exercised by the ruler's consort was mentioned in ten cases, and that of the harem in eight cases. Sons,

Table XVIII. *Informal influences*

| | Court | | Sovereign's relatives | | | | | Priests | | Mil. | |
	Pres-ence	Infl.	Con-sort	Other wives	Succes-sor	Broth-ers	Gen.	Gen.	Spec.	Spec.	Gen.
Angkor	X	X	X	X	—	X	X	0	X	X	X
Ankole	X	X	X	0	0	X	X	0	0	0	X
Axum	X	0	X	0	0	0	X	0	X	0	X
Aztecs	X	X	0	0	—	X	X	0	X	0	X
China	X	X	X	X	X	X	X	X	X	0	X
Egypt	X	0	X	0	0	X	X	0	X	—	—
France	X	X	X	—	X	X	X	X	X	X	X
Hawaii	X	X	X	X	0	0	X	X	X	X	0
Iberia	X	X	0	0	0	X	X	0	X	0	X
Inca	X	X	X	0	X	X	X	X	X	0	X
Jimma	X	X	0	X	X	X	X	X	X	0	0
Kachari	X	0	0	0	0	0	0	X	0	0	0
Kuba	X	X	0	X	0	0	X	X	X	0	0
Maurya	X	X	X	X	X	0	X	X	X	0	X
Mongolia	X	X	0	0	0	X	X	0	X	0	X
(Old) Norway	X	X	0	0	0	0	X	—	—	0	X
Scythia	X	X	0	0	0	X	X	0	X	0	0
Tahiti	X	X	X	—	—	X	X	X	X	X	X
Volta	X	X	0	X	—	0	X	X	X	0	X
Yoruba	X	X	0	X	—	X	X	X	X	—	X
Zande	X	X	—	—	—	X	X	X	—	X	0

brothers, etc., exercised an influence fourteen times. Only five times was there mention of the ruler's successor playing a role in political decision-making, while in no less than six cases his influence was non-existent. This is a result of the fact that it is often not known in advance which of the ruler's sons will be his successor.

Priests had a *general* influence upon decision-making in seventeen cases, while in two cases no data were provided (*Ankole* and *Kachari*). For (old) *Norway* and *Zande* the evidence was negative. As it was found in the case of the *Kachari* and *Zande* that the influence of specific priests did play a definite 'role', we feel justified in formulating as a structural characteristic:

(50)   *Priests exercise an influence on decision-making in early states* (significant at the 99% level).

The influence of military leaders, even from an informal point of view, is fairly weak. In fourteen cases some general influence was mentioned, and in five cases that of a specific functionary was mentioned.

2.12.3.   *The Surveillance Apparatus.* We have already alluded to the problem of control in the preceding sections. How does the central government enforce its decrees, regulations and laws? And how is the administrative apparatus itself kept under surveillance? The data of our case studies suggest several solutions to this problem, viz.:

(a) Extensive *travels* through the state on the sovereign's part. This gives him an opportunity to participate directly — though only incidentally — in regional or local government, to interfere where necessary, and to impress on his representatives the idea of his omnipresence. Only where this kind of 'inspection tour' exists will such interference be tolerated. Where the sovereign travels on only a limited scale, there is no reason to assume the latter to be the case (in Table XIX, E. indicates extensive and L. limited travelling). While on tour, the sovereign and his followers have an opportunity of consuming on the spot the unstorable tribute in kind.

(b) The use of special *messengers*, envoys, plenipotentiaries, etc., which gives the central government the opportunity to exercise direct influence on local or regional policy.

(c) The employment of *spies*, couriers or messengers by means of which the central government keeps informed on what is really happening in the outlying provinces and on the behavior of the many functionaries in remote areas. There is considerable overlap between the functions of this and the former category.

(d) The *forced entertainment* of relatives of regional and/or local functionaries in the capital and the prescription of regular visits of homage, which enable the central government to force functionaries to remain faithful.

The relevant data are grouped together in Table XIX. Only the rulers of *Yoruba* did not go on tour. For *Iberia, Kachari* and *Zande* no data are available on this subject. Extensive tours on the part of the ruler were found in thirteen cases. In *Volta* this changed from extensive to limited in the course of time. In four states only, limited travel was mentioned (*Jimma, Kuba, Ankole* and the *Aztecs*). The control here seemed to be exercised, for the greater part, through the medium of messengers and spies (for *Ankole* no data were supplied). In thirteen cases messengers of several different types were mentioned, and in ten cases a network of spies of some kind was found to exist. All in all, there are no reasons for us to assume the existence of a well-developed surveillance apparatus in early states. The practice of keeping hostages was mentioned in four cases only. In two cases (*China* and *Zande*) it was found that regional or local functionaries were obliged to appear regularly at court. The only kind of structural characteristic we can formulate here is:

(51)   *In the early state the sovereign travels through his realm in order to exact allegiance and tribute* (significant at the 99% level).

Table XIX.   *Methods of exercising control*

	Tours by sovereign	Through messengers	Use of spies	Entertainment
Angkor	E	X	X	0
Ankole	L	0	0	0
Axum	E	0	0	0
Aztecs	L	X	X	X
China	E	0	0	R
Egypt	E	0	0	0
France	E	X	X	0
Hawaii	E	0	0	—
Iberia	0	0	0	0
Inca	E	X	X	X
Jimma	L	X	X	X
Kachari	0	X	0	0
Kuba	L	X	X	0
Maurya	E	X	X	0
Mongolia	E	X	X	0
Norway	E	0	0	—
Scythia	E	X	0	0
Tahiti	E	X	X	—
Volta	E/L	0	0	—
Yoruba	—	X	X	X
Zande	0	X	0	R

Abbreviations: E = extensive   travelling;   L = limited   travelling;   R = obligation to report.

2.13. *Some Conclusions Concerning the Structural Characteristics of the Early State*

In the preceding sections we brought together the results of a great many comparisons based on the data furnished by the case essays. Incidentally, where necessary or useful, we added data from other sources. We grouped the relevant data together in nineteen tables, and were able to distinguish fifty-one structural characteristics. With the aid of these data we will now try to test, within the limits of the above structural analysis, some of the hypotheses put forward in the first chapter.

2.13.1. *The Seven Criteria.* In the first chapter we evolved seven criteria for the early state. As these are supposedly generally valid, we will test them only by reference to the structural characteristics.

(1) *A sufficient population to make possible social categorization, stratification and specialization.* This appeared to be too vague a criterion. We replaced it with that of population density. Our analysis of this aspect (Table I) showed that a high population density (in the absolute sense) was found in nine cases. There is reason to suppose that states will have a higher population density than non-states under comparable geographical or ecological conditions. However, this statement is still too vague. Birdsell's study on the 'basic demographic unit' makes it clear that face-to-face relations are possible only in groups of maximally 500 people (1973). As soon as there is a growth of population, fission or the development of a complex social organization seem to be the only two alternatives. In view of the rather complex social structures of the states studied by us, their populations must certainly have exceeded 500, though even this still remains rather vague.

(2) *Citizenship of the state is determined by residence or birth in the territory.* We found that all those permanently living in the territory of a state, as marked by certain boundaries, were considered as citizens or subjects of that state (S.C. 1). This usually found expression in certain obligations and duties toward the state.

(3) *The government is centralized and has the necessary power for the maintenance of law and order through the use of both authority and force, or the threat of force.* In all of the cases studied we found a center of government (S.C. 3) where the sovereign resided for the greater part of the year and where the court was located (S.C. 34). From this center, laws and regulations were issued by the sovereign (S.C. 25), upon which activity a number of groups or individuals exercised an influence, formal or informal (S.C. 27, 48, 49, 50). The sovereign was the head of a complex three-tier administrative apparatus, to which certain duties and powers were delegated (S.C. 44, 45) and which

always comprised regional and mostly also national- and local-level functionaries (S.C. 46). Top-level specialists were always found in the center (S.C. 47). Though controlling agencies were found everywhere, this aspect was too diversified for us to formulate more than one structural characteristic in connection with it (S.C. 51).

Codified laws were found in only eight cases. Less coherent systems were found in twelve states (Table IX). The maintenance of law and order seems to have been based for the greater part on authority, and much less on force. In only eight cases was some form of police force found (Table IX), while the controlling apparatus as was mentioned above, was not well-developed. The administration of justice was in the hands of formal judges in only nine cases. Elsewhere it was a side-function of certain other functionaries.

(4) *The state is independent, at least de facto, and the government has sufficient power to prevent separation, as well as the capacity to defend its external threats.* The independence of the state is a general characteristic (S.C. 2). The fact that all of our states had existed for a considerable length of time testifies sufficiently that their defensive mechanisms were adequate. Military aspects, however, did not figure very prominently in the list of general characteristics. Of these we would mention: the sovereign is supreme commander (S.C. 28), there exists a bodyguard (S.C. 29), and commoners are obliged to perform military service (S.C. 41). Military groups with explicitly in-stitutionalized influence on state policy were not found as a structural characteristic. Military functions were often side-functions (Table XV) of general functionaries or of members of the aristocracy. In a number of cases special functionaries were in charge of military affairs (Table XVI). In only a few cases did military leaders, as a group, play an openly recognized role (Table IV). A standing army was found in fifteen cases (Table X). Some informal influence on government was found in sixteen cases (Table XVIII). The question of separation or fission will be dealt with in the next chapters.

(5) *The population shows a sufficient degree of stratification for emergent social classes (rulers and ruled) to be distinguishable.* Our data show that social stratification in early states was a fairly complex matter. Several social categories with differential access to material and other resources were generally to be found. We distinguished between two basic social strata, an upper and a lower one, and moreover discovered that in the majority of cases a middle stratum also existed (Table IV). The upper stratum we took to comprise the sovereign, the aristocracy (S.C. 11) to which belonged a.o. the sovereign's kin (S.C. 35), holders of high offices (S.C. 36) and clan and lineage heads (S.C. 37)), and the priesthood. The middle stratum was composed of such categories as ministeriales and gentry (Table IV). To the lower stratum

belonged a.o. smallholders (S.C. 12) and tenants (S.C. 13), and less frequently such categories as artisans, traders, servants and slaves. The members of the upper stratum had only indirect connections with food production (S.C. 15). In the lower level only smallholders and tenants were mentioned as having a direct connection with food production (S.C. 20). To avoid misunderstanding it should be noted that we have not included the categories of slaves and servants in the comparisons concerned. The income of the sovereign and aristocracy was based on tribute, in whatever form (S.C. 19). The commoners were obliged to pay taxes — which appeared, in fact, to be obligatory for most categories (cf. S.C. 17) — and to perform menial services (S.C. 42). The obligation to render services was also found to apply to all social categories (S.C. 16). Our data showed that the term aristocracy referred to a category that was not composed of equals. On the contrary, large differences in status and position were found everywhere (S.C. 38). Whether or not the strata distinguished by us should be labeled 'social *classes*' depends on the definition of 'class'. The upper and lower social strata can be equated with emergent social classes. However, no classes based on the control of the means of production — supposed to be a typical feature for societies with a mature state organization — were found. A class struggle, or overt class antagonism, was not found to be characteristic of early states.

(6) *Productivity is so high that there is a regular surplus, which is used for the maintenance of the state organization.* In all cases a surplus was found (S.C. 10), which reached the ruling groups in the form of taxes, tribute or tributary gifts (S.C. 17, 19). This surplus was spent for the greater part on the maintenance of the administrative apparatus: the sovereign gave gifts (S.C. 30), remunerations (S.C. 31) and offerings (S.C. 32), while this kind of expenditure was also found on the lower levels (S.C. 33).

(7) *A common ideology exists, on which the legitimacy of the ruling stratum is based.* This characteristic appeared to be highly elaborated in all of our cases. Here, invariably, a mythical charter was found (S.C. 21) and the ruler legitimized his position by his divine descent (S.C. 22, 23), with which most of his activities were connected: he performed rites (S.C. 24), established law and order (S.C. 25, 26), as supreme commander was the protector of his people (S.C. 28), and gave gifts, remunerated his 'servants' (S.C. 30, 31), and made offerings to the supernatural forces (S.C. 32). Hence the early state had a basic ideology of *reciprocity* (cf. Section 2.10.5). In conformity with this mode of legitimation, social status was correlated with distance from the ruler's lineage (Section 2.11, cf. S.C. 35, 43) and the kind of office occupied. The state ideology was found to be upheld by the priesthood everywhere (S.C. 39, 50).

As this survey shows, the characteristics of early states put forward in chapter 1 are firmly supported by the structural data. The only aspect whose discussion had to be put off till the next chapters was that of fission and force.

2.13.2. The Three Types of Early State. Another task we set ourselves was the testing of the validity of the distinction of early states into three types: *inchoate, typical* and *transitional.*

The inchoate type we associated with dominant kinship, family and community ties in the field of politics, a limited existence of full-time specialists, vague and *ad hoc* forms of taxation, and social contrasts that were offset by reciprocity and direct contacts between the ruler and the ruled.

As the typical early state we considered the kind of state in which ties of kinship were counterbalanced by those of locality, where competition and appointment counterbalanced the principles of heredity, where non-kin officials and title-holders played a leading role in government administration, and where redistribution and reciprocity dominated the relations between the social strata.

As the transitional type, we considered the early state in which the administrative apparatus was dominated by appointed officials, where kinship affected only certain marginal aspects of government, and where the prerequisites for the emergence of private ownership of the means of production, of a market economy and of overtly antagonistic classes were already found.

At first glance the classification outlined above seems to be quite plausible. We will therefore try to find out in the present section whether our cases are classifiable along these lines, and the suggested criteria are applicable in practice. Those that show too much overlap or are incapable of being tested we will have to discard. Conversely, the possibility of adding other criteria will also be considered.

Clearly, not all of the criteria will apply specifically to only one or other of the types. Between heredity and appointment there exists an entire scale of gradual degrees of transition, from the dominance of kinship ties to the dominance of appointment, while in all of our cases both heredity and appointment played a role. The same holds more or less true for such aspects as the presence of full-time specialists or taxation systems, or the influence of reciprocity. The only really distinctive criteria seem to be those of the emergence of a market economy, private ownership of land or cattle and overt social antagonisms of the transitional type. When applied to our data, the following picture emerges. Our analysis showed the existence of markets to be a general characteristic (S.C. 5), excepting that in two cases (*Tahiti* and

Hawaii) no markets were found, while in *Ankole, Kachari, Norway, Volta* and *Zande* they were of limited importance only. Moreover, no data were supplied on this for *Egypt* and *Iberia*. Some additional confirmation may be found, provided by the existence of professional traders. In the case of *Ankole, Hawaii, Tahiti* and *Zande* they were not found to exist. In *Norway* and *Volta* professional traders were present, though only at a later stage of development. Again, no data were available for *Egypt, Iberia* and *Kachari*. At the other end of the scale, we assume that important markets and professional traders are found. Only the *Incas* seemed to have a less developed system. This enables us to make the following preliminary division of our states into the above mentioned three types:

INCHOATE—   *Ankole, Hawaii, Norway, Tahiti, Volta, Zande.*
TYPICAL—   *Iberia, Incas, Kachari.*
TRANSITIONAL— *Angkor, Axum, Aztecs, China, France, Jimma, Kuba, Maurya, Mongolia, Scythia, Yoruba.*

Modification of this preliminary division with the aid of the criterion of the presence of full-time specialists is impossible, for full-time specialists were found to be present nearly in all cases (S.C. 8). So we will have to exclude this particular criterion.

The presence of a well-developed taxation system is not very useful as a structural criterion. The levying of taxes happened to be a general characteristic (S.C. 17). The presence of top- and middle-level specialists as tax gatherers (Table XVI) was found in the case of *Angkor, Incas, Jimma, Maurya* and *Norway*. Only *Tahiti* scored negatively here. Tax collection by mainly general functionaries of the national and regional levels was found in the case of *France, Inca, Kachari, Kuba, Scythia* and *Tahiti*. All yielded rather mixed results. Besides, the existence of certain functionaries in itself provides little information on the way in which tax collection functioned. Hence we will leave the testing of this characteristic to the next chapter.

Application of the criterion of kinship versus heredity shows that:
For general functionaries: heredity (in the clan, lineage or family) was more or less dominant in *Ankole, Hawaii, Scythia* and *Tahiti*. No data were available for *Kachari, Mongolia* and *Norway*.
For special functionaries: heredity was dominant in *Ankole* and *Tahiti*. No data were supplied for *Hawaii, Iberia, Kachari, Mongolia, Norway* and *Scythia*.
Greater or lesser dominance of appointment of general functionaries was found in the case of the *Aztecs, Iberia, Jimma, Maurya, Yoruba*, and of special functionaries in that of the *Aztecs, Egypt, France, Jimma, Kuba* and *Yoruba*.
In the other cases a mixture of both systems was found.

In view of these findings our preliminary division may be modified as follows:

INCHOATE —   *Ankole, Hawaii, Norway, Tahiti, Volta* and *Zande.*

TYPICAL —   *Angkor, Axum, China, Egypt, France, Iberia, Inca, Kachari, Mongolia, Scythia.*

TRANSITIONAL — *Aztecs, Jimma, Kuba, Maurya, Yoruba.*

Personal ownership of land appeared to be a rather complex matter. As the data of Table IV show, personal ownership of land (or cattle) was found among members of the aristocracy in: *Aztecs, China* (sometimes), *Jimma. Kuba, Maurya* and *Volta*, and among smallholders in: *Aztecs, China, France, Iberia, Jimma, Maurya* and *Volta*. In the other cases various forms of collective ownership predominated. It is quite possible that the development of personal, and, later on, private ownership of the means of production would stimulate the emergence of mutually antagonistic classes. For the early states we studied there were no data pointing to the existence of this situation already, however.

Clearly, in view of the arbitrariness of our above divisions, the introduction of additional criteria will be useful. We would consider the following:

(a) the existence of salaried functionaries versus those receiving remunerations; and

(b) the degree of development of the legal system and the administration of justice.

Table XI sets out the data on the way in which functionaries were rewarded. Only in the case of the *Aztecs, France, Incas, Jimma, Kuba, Maurya* and *Yoruba* were salaried functionaries found. Negative results were yielded by *Angkor, Ankole, Hawaii, Mongolia, Tahiti, Volta* and *Zande.* The states at either end of this scale show a close correspondence with the division already made above.

For an investigation of the degree of development of the legal system and the administration of justice the following aspects will be relevant (Table IX): the existence of codified laws, formal judges and codified punishments. The existence of codified laws was found in the case of *Angkor, Aztecs, China, France, Incas, Jimma, Kuba,* and *Maurya.* For *Kachari* no data were provided on this.

The existence of formal judges was found in the case of *Angkor, Aztecs, France, Incas, Jimma, Kachari, Kuba, Maurya* and *Yoruba.* Codified punishments were mentioned for: *Aztecs, China, France, Incas, Kachari, Kuba, Maurya, Yoruba* and *Zande.*

In Table XX we have brought together the results of the above survey. The main conclusion seems to be that by applying structural

Table XX. *Degree of development*

	Markets	Professional traders	Mode of succession general functionaries	Mode of succession special functionaries	Salaries	Codified law	Formal judges	Codified punishment	Personal property of land aristocracy	Personal property of land commoners
Angkor	X	X	M	M	–	X	X	0	–	–
Ankole	1	–	H	H	–	–	–	–	–	–
Axum	X	X	M	M	0	–	–	0	–	–
Aztecs	X	X	A	A	X	X	X	X	X	X
China	X	X	M	M	0	X	–	X	X	X
Egypt	0	0	M	A	0	–	–	0	0	0
France	X	X	M	A	X	X	X	X	0	X
Hawaii	–	–	H	0	–	–	–	–	–	–
Iberia	0	0	A	0	0	–	–	0	0	X
Inca	X	0	M	M	X	X	X	X	–	–
Jimma	X	X	A	A	X	X	X	X	0	X
Kachari	1	0	0	0	0	0	X	X	–	–
Kuba	X	X	M	A	X	X	X	X	X	X
Maurya	X	X	A	M	X	X	X	X	–	–
Mongolia	X	X	0	0	–	–	–	0	X	X
Norway	1	1	0	0	0	–	–	0	X	–
Scythia	X	X	H	0	0	–	–	0	–	–
Tahiti	–	–	H	H	–	–	–	–	–	–
Volta	1	1	M	M	–	–	–	0	–	–
Yoruba	X	X	A	A	X	–	X	X	X	X
Zande	1	–	M	M	–	–	–	X	–	0

Abbreviations: 1 = of limited importance; H = hereditary; A = by appointment; M = mixture of hereditary and appointment.

criteria the early states under study can, in our view, be classified into the following types:[3]

INCHOATE — *Ankole, Hawaii, Norway* (old), *Tahiti, Volta, Zande.*

TYPICAL — *Angkor, Axum, Egypt, Iberia, Incas, Kachari, Mongolia, Scythia, Yoruba.*

TRANSITIONAL — *Aztecs, China, France, Jimma, Kuba, Maurya.*

We deem a structural division of early states into three types feasible and useful. The criteria we suggested in chapter 1, however, appeared to be in need of some modification. We dropped that of the presence of full-time specialists, left the discussion of that of taxation systems to the next chapter, and added those of the development of the legal system and the presence of salaried functionaries.

The implications of this classification for the study of the evolution of the state will be discussed chapter 27.

FOOTNOTES

[1] The reliability of the evaluations of the data for the formulations of the structural characteristics has been double checked, binomially with, as sample size, the sum of the explicit judgements (positive + negative) regarding the respective characteristics. The actual checking was done by our colleague Piet van de Velde.

[2] Weber (1964: 700) pointed out long ago that many governmental activities have secret aspects, and that this is even essential for an efficient performance of a government's tasks.

[3] Some of the political organizations to which we, on the basis of *our* criteria, have attached the epithet 'inchoate' (early state) have been classified by other authors, basing themselves on partly different criteria, as *chiefdoms* (cf. Service 1971: 144 ff., 1975: 150 ff.).

REFERENCES

Adams, Robert McC. (1966), *The evolution of urban society.* Chicago: Aldine.
— (1974), 'Anthropological perspectives on ancient trade', in: *Current Anthropology* 15: 239–258.
Baal, J. van (1974), *De agressie der gelijken* [The agression of equals]. Assen: Van Gorcum.
— (1975), *Reciprocity and the position of women.* Assen: Van Gorcum.
Baaren, Th. P. van (1960), *Wij mensen. Religie en wereldbeschouwing bij schriftloze volken* [Religion and the philosophy of life of primitive peoples]. Utrecht: Bijleveld.
Bax, Mart (1975), 'The political machine and its importance for the Irish republic', in: *Political Anthropology* 1: 6–20.
Beattie, J. H. M. (1971), *The Nyoro state.* Oxford: Clarendon.
Birdsell, J. (1973), 'A basic demographic unit', in: *Current Anthropology* 14: 337–356.

Bloch, M. (1967), *Feudal society*. London: Routledge

Carneiro, Robert L. (1970), 'A theory of the origin of the state', in: *Science* 169: 733–738.

Childe, V. Gordon (1950), 'The urban revolution', in: *Town Planning Review* 21: 3–17

Claessen, Henri J. M. (1970), *Van vorsten en volken* [Of princes and peoples]. Amsterdam: Joko.

— (1974), *Politieke antropologie*. Assen: Van Gorcum.

— (1975a), 'Comment', in: *Current Anthropology* 16: 38.

— (1975b), 'From rags to riches — and the reverse', in: *Rule and reality. Essays in honor of André J. F. Köbben*, ed. by Peter Kloos and Klaas W. van der Veen, pp. 29–49. Amsterdam: University of Amsterdam Press.

Crumley, Carole L. (1976), 'Toward a locational definition of state systems of settlement', in: *American Anthropologist* 78: 59–74.

Davenport, W. (1969), 'The Hawaiian cultural revolution', in: *American Anthropologist* 71: 1–20.

Dawson, Christopher, ed., (1966), *Mission to Asia*. New York: Harper and Row.

Doornbos, Martin R. (1975), *Regalia galore. The decline and eclipse of Ankole kingship*. Nairobi, etc.: East African Literature Bureau.

Evans-Pritchard, E. E. (1948), *The divine kingship of the Shilluk of the Nilotic Sudan*. Cambridge: Cambridge University Press.

Forbes, F. E. (1851), *Dahomey and the Dahomans*. London: Longman, Brown, Green and Longmans.

Fortes, M. and Evans-Pritchard, E. E. eds. (1940), *African political systems*. Oxford: International Africa Institute.

Frazer, Sir James (1911), *The golden bough*. London: Maxmillan.

Fried, Morton H. (1967), *The evolution of political society*. New York: Random House.

Gluckman, Max, (1965), *Politics, law and ritual in tribal society*. Oxford: Blackwell.

Haenisch, Erich, ed. (1948), *Die Geheime Geschichte der Mongolen*. Leipzig: Harallowitz.

Hoebel, E. A. (1964), *The law of primitive man*. 3rd pr. Cambridge Mass: Harvard University Press.

Janssen, Jac. J. (1975), 'Prolegomena to the study of Egypt's economic history during the New Kingdom', in: *Studien zur altägyptischen Kultur* 3: 127–185.

Josselin de Jong, P. E. de (1975), 'Structuralism in cultural anthropology', in: *Current anthropology in the Netherlands*, ed. by Peter Kloos and Henri J. M. Claessen, pp. 114–131. The Hague: Staatsuitgeverij.

Keesing, F. M. (1958), *Cultural anthropology*. New York: Holt, Rinehart and Winston.

Köbben, A. J. F. (1966), 'Law at the village level', in: *Law in culture and society*, ed. by Laura Nader, pp. 117–140. Chicago: Aldine.

— (1967), 'Why exceptions? The logic of cross-cultural analysis', in: *Current Anthropology* 8: 3–28.

— (1970), 'Comparativists and non-comparativists in anthropology', in: *A Handbook of method in cultural anthropology*, ed. by R. Naroll and Ronald Cohen, pp. 581–596. New York: Free Press.

Krader, Lawrence (1968), *Formation of the state*. Englewood Cliffs: Prentice Hall.

Kruijer, G. J. (1959), *Observeren en redeneren* [Observation and reasoning]. Meppel: Boom.

Kurtz, Donald V. (1974), 'Peripheral and transitional markets: The Aztec Case', in: *American Ethnologist* 1: 685–706.

MacIver, R. M. (1965), *The web of government.* Revised edition. New York: Free Press.

Nadel, S. F. (1969), *The foundations of social anthropology.* 5th pr. London: Cohen and West.

Naroll, Raoul (1970), 'Cross-cultural sampling', in: *A Handbook of method in cultural anthropology,* ed. by R. Naroll and Ronald Cohen, pp. 889–926. New York: Free Press.

Nieboer, H. N. (1910), *Slavery as an industrial system.* 2nd pr. The Hague: Nijhoff.

Popper, Karl R. (1968), *The logic of scientific discovery.* 5th pr. London: Hutchinson.

Radcliffe-Brown, A. R. (1952), *Structure and function in primitive society.* London: Oxford University Press.

Rusch, Walter (1975), *Klassen und Staat in Buganda vor der Kolonialzeit.* Berlin: Akademie Verlag.

Sahlins, M. D. (1958), *Social stratification in Polynesia.* Seattle: University of Washington Press.

Schapera, I. (1956), *Government and politics in tribal society.* London: Watts.

Schramm, P. E. (1966), 'Mythos des Königtums', in: *De Monarchie,* pp. 21–36. Amsterdam: Polak en Van Gennep.

Service, Elman R. (1971), *Primitive social organisation.* 2nd edn. New York: Random House.

— (1975), *Origins of the state and civilization.* New York: Norton.

Slicher van Bath, B. H. (1960), *De agrarische geschiedenis van West Europa* (500–1800) [The agrarian history of Western Europe, 500–1800]. Utrecht: Aula.

Soustelle, Jaques (1958), *Zo leefden de Azteken bij the invasie van de conquistadores.* (The daily life of the Aztecs before the coming of the conquistadores). Baarn: Hollandia.

Speke, J. H. (1863), *Journal of the discovery of the source of the Nile.* Edingburgh: Blackwood.

Stevenson, Robert F. (1968), *Population and political systems in tropical Africa.* New York: Columbia University Press.

Swartz, Marc J., ed. (1968), *Local-level politics.* Chicago: Aldine.

Swartz, Marc. J., Turner, V. and Tuden, A., eds. (1966), *Political anthropology.* Chicago: Aldine.

Thapar, Romila (1975), *Ancient history of India.* Harmondsworth Middx: Penguin Books.

Trouwborst, A. A. (1973), 'La base territoriale de l'état du Burundi ancien', in: *Revue universitaire du Burundi* 1: 245–254.

Tuden, A. and Marshall, Catherine (1972), 'Political organization: cross-cultural codes', in: *Ethnology* 11: 436–464.

Vansina, Jan, (1964), 'Le royaume Kuba', *Annales, serie in 8° Sciences humaines,* no. 49. Tervuren: Musée royal de l'Afrique Centrale.

Veblen, Th. (1899), *Theory of the leisure class.* New York.

Vermeulen, C. J. J. and de Ruijter, A. (1975), 'Dominant epistemological presuppositions in the use of the cross-cultural survey method', in: *Current Anthropology* 16: 29–52.

Weber, Max (1964), *Wirtschaft und Gesellschaft.* Sudienausgabe. Köln: Kippenheuer und Witsch.
Wertheim, W. F. (1971), *Evolutie en revolutie. De golfslag der emancipatie* [Evolution and revolution]. Amsterdam: Van Gennep.
Wolf, Eric (1966), *Peasants.* Englewood Cliffs: Prentice Hall.
Wright, Henry T., and Johnson, Gregory (1975), 'Population, exchange, and early state formation in southwestern Iran', in: *American Anthropologist* 77: 267–289.

26 The Early State as a Process

PETER SKALNÍK

1. METHODOLOGICAL INTRODUCTION

The mutual separation of the structural, functional and developmental aspects of the early state, even for strictly analytical purposes, appears to be fraught with no few difficulties. The aim of the present chapter is to transcend the obvious limitations of the treatment of each of the three in strict isolation from the others. This is in keeping with the adoption of the historical approach as a basis for the discussion of the phenomenon of the early state as representing a process whose developmental dynamics possess certain universal features, reflected by certain common characteristics of each of the concrete examples of the early state. Here the discussion is concentrated mainly on the early state as a processual model improved with the aid of the data provided by our sample of twenty-one cases. Comparative material from elsewhere will be added only as a secondary resort.

Thus, our task there is clear. It is to give a synthesized characterization of the dynamic aspects of the early state.

Before proceeding with the discussion, we will need to give a brief recapitulation of our preliminary hypotheses, which were outlined in the introductory chapter (chapter 1). There we launched the idea that each state is:

the organization for the regulation of social relations in a society that is divided into two emergent social classes, the rulers and the ruled.

We also pointed out that the functioning of the state had much to do with the exercise of power which in its turn again served as a backing for the government. It was supposed that a government invested with power controlled the division into strata and emergent social classes, and saw to the maintenance of the integrity of the state against the threat of separatism from within and aggression from without. Such, very briefly, was the view we expressed in chapter 1.

Political power works in cooperation and is interconnected with economic, ideological and kinship relations. An insight into how it is related to the production of material goods in a given society seems to be crucial for an understanding of the character of what we have called 'the early state'. For from this point one may proceed to make a useful comparison of the characteristics of the pre-state and early-state society on the one hand, and of the early-state and the successor society on the other. In my view, the early state can best be considered as a complex of interacting social *processes*, rather than as a static phenomenon. Therefore, the discussion in this chapter will concentrate on the processual aspects of the early state (cf. Vansina 1964) from two different perspectives. Firstly, the main points of a concrete *model of functioning* will be suggested by reference to the data of our case essays. Secondly, the *functional principles* as abstract dynamic correlates will be formulated on the basis of the preceding analysis. Our conclusions about the general significance of the early state will follow at the end of the volume.[1]

2. MODEL OF FUNCTIONING

Formally we are able to distinguish five *functional spheres*, viz. the administrative, economic, ideological, military, and political spheres. This division seems useful to us for analytical purposes, but can hardly be regarded as a goal in itself.

2.1. *The Administrative Functional Sphere*

The data of our sample show that all of the early states analyzed had an *administrative apparatus*, which was, in fact, the executive arm of the government (cf. Smith 1960: 15–20). Although forms of government are far from being restricted exclusively to states (Mair 1962), forms of administrative apparatus did originally develop only in early states. They were practically non-existent before the formation of the early state. To be more precise, administrations of one form or another began to develop only after the emergence of the state. Theoretically, proto-administrative functionaries may, in some cases, have been religious specialists, who existed well before the emergence of the state. Of course, they were not specialized in administration, but performed some administrative duties next to their principal functions in religio-political types of chiefdom (Evans-Pritchard 1962: 66–86).

In addition, a few persons from among those who were personally dependent on local headmen and religio-political chiefs can be considered as proto-administrative functionaries (*Yoruba, Volta* and *Zande* during their pre-state periods). For the inchoate level, when the early state was only just leaving its infancy, we discovered that sovereigns had only a small body of people from among their following at their disposal for the performance of administrative tasks (*Scythia, Tahiti, Hawaii*). In most cases there were no fixed courts, and the sovereign himself had to travel all over the state to ensure the allegiance of his subjects. This travelling government body, especially before it had a fixed seat or capital, was either maintained materially by means of 'booty production' (Goody 1971), or practised on-the-spot consumption of tribute or tributary gifts presented to the sovereign and his following.

The emergence of administrative tasks in connection with the collection of tribute took place comparatively soon after this. There are only a few rare examples of local elders, chiefs or other dignitaries of pre-state types of community assuming supra-local administrative functions created by the ruling hierarchy. In fact, it was impossible to create an efficient central administration until a 'new' group of people, who were free from obligations within their village communities and completely loyal to the central power, had become firmly established.

Gurevich's characterization of the situation in Norway (viz. his chapter, p. 408) seems quite typical for this particular stage of the development of administrations in early states in general. He says:

> It is evident that the royal power in Norway during the ninth and tenth centuries was relatively ineffective and hardly capable of strongly influencing the internal situation. The king had so far no administration at his disposal. All special tasks were carried out by his retainers or the stewards of his estates. The king was not yet able to organize his own power machine, and all mentions in sagas of such a bureaucracy are anachronistic.

Aside from its factual content, this quotation is valuable in that it also accentuates the processual and historical dimensions of the early state. It affords an insight into the functioning of the early state and its agencies in the process of their development during the primitive period of state formation.

What kind of people were engaged in the administration of early states?

They were those members of the ruling stratum (*emergent class of rulers*) who carried into effect the various decisions taken by the sovereign or by regional political functionaries. In fact, they formed a body of executive officials. Often there existed no kinship relation of any kind between them and the political decision-makers. They were of varied rank and status, subordinate to higher office-holders, and recruited in a situation of political rivalry and competition. This implies that the apparatus in early states usually had no connection with 'party-political' competition of any sort. Each member of the various administrative agencies had a personal link with the sovereign or with some other political functionary of lower status, and was usually appointed to serve him. He may also have been directly answerable and subordinate to some higher member of the administrative hierarchy. Succession to specific administrative offices was usually vested in particular families. In our sample, administrative offices were usually conferred on persons who were not in a position to put forward any legal kinship-based claims to political offices. The administration thus could play a key role in the maintenance of the balance of power between those members of the nobility who held political offices and those who did not, or who aspired to higher ones (see below). At best such persons might be entrusted with the 'administration' of a number of villages under the direct supervision of the sovereign. They did not have any right to the political title of village chief (*Volta*), however.

An important point is that, whatever administration as a set of activities involved, it was never so much concerned with territory, land or objects as with *people* as principal objects of value reference. It was first, and foremost the administration of people (a certain number, or a certain category of people in terms of ethnic or professional division) that counted in the early state. In this sense administrations followed the pattern of the political sphere, where 'power' also meant power over people. Only with the gradual growth of the complexity of that early state can we observe the beginning of a process whereby the administration of (productive) land, objects or other inanimate sources of material wealth gained prominence. This process usually had some connection with the definite establishment of a central seat of government, or a fixed capital. The tendency toward bureaucratization was the outcome of this.

As we saw in the preceding chapter, the political and administrative center of the early state was not necessarily an urban center, although in some of the typical and all of the transitional early states an urban capital was present. The capital, whatever its pattern of settlement, had to include the *court*. Regional political representatives had their smaller courts constructed on the model of the central one, in which local administration was exercised. As we have already mentioned in passing above, the expansion of the administration, and more especially the trend towards bureaucratization in the early state were closely connected with centralization. This was a result of the strengthening of the sovereign's power over possible claimants of political power among those with certain dynastic (kinship) rights to power. Thus the administrative apparatus served as a protective device against potential usurpers. This inevitably led to the participation of administrative officials in political decision making. Bureaucratization, in fact, involved the delegation of a certain amount of political power to the incumbents of administrative offices. This was the case in all the states in our sample. Cases of usurpation of high office by councillors or other members of the administration (or army) represented only extreme instances of exploitation of the new opportunities which had arisen in the realm of political power. The usurpers were often tacitly included in the dynastic genealogies (*Volta, Yoruba*). Members of administrative bodies who were formally of captive, 'slave', commoner, or even foreign origin could attain to fairly high positions in the state, and even to rule in the sovereign's place. In some states these people formed *state councils*, and there was little distinction between higher political and administrative offices. Government is, in fact, a junction of politics and administration, which serves to illustrate the limited usefulness of our arbitrary division into different functional spheres.

As the concrete data from the essays testify, it is typical of the early state that the 'state life' and 'political culture' involved only the rulers, i.e., the *members* of the state hierarchy. The latter would engage in competition for political offices and the cultivation of court customs, or concern themselves with rites or entertainment. Wars were fought by the state hierarchies. Fighting between villages of different states did not lead to a state of war between these states or even provinces.

However — and the data of our sample attest this with a uniform degree of force — this 'one-sidedness' was possible only thanks to the existence of a dialectical relationship, whereby the rulers were able to command material (economic) and ideological support for the state organization from the common producers, the members of the agricultural communities, who, willy-nilly, also were citizens of the early state. These communities, making a living by agriculture combined with the part-time exercise of crafts and trades, were more or less self-sufficient. Their links with the ruling state hierarchy ran via the administrative apparatus. It was mainly tribute- and tax-collecting which formed an at least comparatively regular point of contact between the communities and the rulers, and thus constituted a basic link in an otherwise divided society. The state as a functioning organization was possible, thanks to the material support of the primary producers and members of the communities. We will return to this point later, namely, in the discussion of the economic sphere of functioning of the early state.

Karl Marx and various other writers after him, have suggested that the state took over a considerable proportion of the functions which were previously fulfilled by the independent communities themselves.

The data of our sample support the idea of the duality of the early
state as expressed by Krader in his chapter in this volume (p. 94),
viz.:

> The agencies of the state, when established, took over these same tasks of the
> administration of justice, the conduct of war and diplomacy [previously all
> carried out within the communities — PS]... The agencies of the state now
> defended, warred, both in the interests of the state and that of the social
> whole. It is a double interest conflicting internally within itself; on the one
> side it is the interest of the state as the representative of the social class in
> whose interest it is organized, on the other, the interest of the social whole.

Let us now see what happened in the field of the 'administration of
justice', which is to be considered as an element of government in the
broadest sense. As the data provided by the twenty-one sample states
suggest, the judicial activities of the rulers were neither very comprehensive nor very frequent. Only cases in which the sovereign's
integrity was at stake (e.g., lese majesty) or the foundations of the state
were threatened (e.g., treason) were invariably adjudicated by state
judicial functionaries. The sovereign or other holders of government
functions acted as judges. Only in the *Aztec, Inca, Kuba,* and *Mauryan*
states were formally specialized, judicial functionaries found (see Table
IX in the previous chapter). In the other early states of our sample the
administration of justice was carried out either exclusively by general
functionaries or by the latter type of functionary together with formal
judges of some sort.

Characteristically, the growth of the state administration and the
subsequent bureaucratization were dependent on the sovereign's military following and on military power in general (cf. Danilova 1968).
Bodyguards, sometimes together with prisoners-of-war, privileged
'slaves', etc., appeared at first as individuals who had been alienated
from their own native communities (Marx's term 'Losreissung'). They
were personally dependent on the sovereign, and thus fully devoted to
his service. The exercise of administration was closely connected with
the political and military power of the sovereign (*Scythia*). In fact,
administrative functionaries derived their executive authority from the
political sphere. Administrations themselves, however, tended gradually to become active political (and military) powers, this process
running parallel to that of the gradual centralization of power in early
states. This had its roots in the process of bureaucratization, and was
an important index of the level of development of each individual early
state.

2.2. *The Economic Functional Sphere*

The early state, personified by the (emerging class of) rulers, forming a
ruling hierarchy, was possible as a result of, and practically defined by,

the relation of the communities of producers of food and other consumer goods to that hierarchy. This relation provided for the material maintenance of rulers, thus enabling the running of the state as an organization. The relationship was an unequal one, since it involved that the ruling hierarchy, with the sovereign at the top, though not participating in productive activities received a considerable portion of the communities' surplus product (or surplus labor) in exchange for protection and general assurances of peace and order in the territory of the state. The concrete mechanism was usually as follows: the communities passed their surplus product, in the form of irregular or regular tributary gifts, tribute or tax, on to the state hierarchy through its administrative agencies, with each court keeping a portion and the remainder (usually the larger portion) going to the court of the sovereign.

Moreover, the state hierarchy organized the construction of public works of three different kinds: irrigation systems, the infrastructure and ideological monuments such as pyramids, temples, etc.. However, only a few early states (*Angkor, Aztecs, China, Egypt,* and *Mauryan India,* cf. Table II in the previous chapter) were efficient and systematic in the organization of these works. All the other early states in our sample had only a small proportion of such works, or had only one or another of the different kinds. A few, namely, the inchoate states of the *Voltaic basin, Zande* and *Norway,* had none.

The state had a direct stake in the returns from interregional trade, which developed in proportion with the growing demand for luxury objects and foreign goods. Taxation of traders and merchants brought in considerable revenues for the state hierarchy. It is doubtful, however, whether the emergence of interregional trade and especially the creation of the necessary conditions for its safe functioning, in other words, the control of trade and markets, has any causal connection with the rise of the early state.

Of course, much of the justification for the unequal politico-economic relationship was produced in the ideological functional sphere of the early state, which will be discussed below. In the present sample of early states the relations of economic inequality were of varying degrees. They reflect a number of different levels of the early state of development, but are always present as a universal feature in every type of early state.

The development of inequality begins with the offering of 'voluntary' tributary gifts and occasional labor to sovereign or local state functionaries, as well as simple forms of appropriation (pillage or 'booty production'), the yields from which were neither very regular nor precisely defined as to quantity or quality. The middle phase in the development is represented by the imposition of a compulsory regular tribute and labor for the benefit of the state, supplemented by various sorts of levies and taxes, and the confiscation of spoils (as scrupulously enumerated by Kochakova in her essay on the *Yoruba*, for instance). The final stage of development of inequality within the early state is represented by the more or less well-defined and obviously exploitative concentration of state revenues with the aid of a fiscal and taxation machinery, not infrequently bolstered by the threatened or actual use of physical (military) force (*China, Mauryan India, Aztecs, France, Jimma, Kuba*).

Tributary relations emerged as the most characteristic form of relation of dependence in the early state. They define the unequal relationship between the *rulers* and *ruled* as one between two basic emergent classes in the early state (this corroborates and supplements Khazanov's discussion on forms of dependence, see p. 86).

The way in which the rulers exploited the ruled was mostly by extra-economic coercion. The dominance of the ruling hierarchy was more political and ideological than economic in character. The communities of direct producers did not, in principle, lose their rights to the land. Only in the case of *Zande* does Kandert assert that there existed a class division based on a 'differential relation to the basic means of production'. At the same time he admits that the sovereign's rights to the land in the realm were 'nominal'. This lends, in my view, only dubious support to the idea of private ownership of land in the *Zande* states. In most areas the majority of the land was subject to 'perpetual' tenure by the communities. However, as a counterweight, *state lands* emerged from the fusion of land belonging to the sovereign's kin with uncultivated land. This was worked by dependents and clients of the sovereign and other officials of the state. Through a long crystallization process, the state lands might pass into the private ownership of the sovereign and his kinsmen as well as of other high functionaries of the state.

In the inchoate types of state the sovereign together with the entire stratum of rulers, had to content themselves with the use of certain plots of land of their own and some form of tribute from a population which enjoyed its own land rights in the communities. In the typical and transitional types of early state the sovereign was usually able to secure control over an ever expanding area of land, in part through control over his courtiers, and more especially through dependent persons (tenants, captives, 'slaves', servants, clients) leaving their communities for some reason and asking the sovereign or another high political functionary for protection. This paved the way to state 'ownership' of land, which in turn might serve as a basis for appropriation for private use. However, also tenure of an office itself might provide its incumbent with an opportunity of extending his full private unconditional ownership of land. Nevertheless, it would be premature to speak of a distinct, fully developed influential sector of private owners of the means of production within the framework of the present sample of early states. It would be even less defensible to assert that economic inequality was the result of proprietary relations and of the role of private ownership of the means of production within their framework.

The process of class formation seems to near completion only where the possibilities of the early state are exhausted and the mature state takes its place. In the mature state class division is extremely clearly expressed in the forms of antagonism, and private ownership plays a key role in the development of patterns of inequality. In Europe more particularly, the case of *France* illustrates this transition to the mature state of the feudal epoch. It is hardly possible, in conclusion, to defend the idea that the early state was based on an accomplished process of class cleavage. Social division will result from such cleavage where two basic social strata already have a differential relation to production and hence may be called 'emergent classes', but where the antagonism that characterizes a fully developed class society has developed only gradually. The essential relation of the state versus the community, which also encompasses the main axis of exploitation, as was explained above, in the mature state is substituted by a plurality of relations of inequality, in which the state functions solely as the public sector overarching competition between the classes. The state as an organization here may appear marginal to the principal relations of inequality, dependence and even power, whereas in the preceding phase (that of the early state) it had unlimited, unconditional and unique powers at the supra-community level. There was, in fact, no supra-community organization other than the early state.

It was not as a result of the power of the state (though with its connivance) that a considerable proportion of the Norwegian peasantry was seen to be landless in the twelfth century, and subsequently became tenants on the private lands of the sovereign, but especially in consequence of that of the church and private landlords (cf. also Wolf 1966: 70 ff.). Similar developments are found in other, non-European, transitional early states, though to a less dramatic degree. They mark the end of the early state. It must be observed at this point that the majority of early states which existed until recently were cut short in their development by European conquest or induced 'modernization'.

To conclude this part of our discussion, we would like to stress once more that, although the early state, personified by the ruling hierarchy or emergent class of rulers, was economically dependent on the exploitation of agrarian communities, it was at the same time all but concentrated on economic matters in its overall functioning. Its economic basis, in fact, served as a condition for its implementation of its 'genuine', subjective strategies, or policies. Ideology, like the economy, created the necessary conditions for the performance of political activities, both by making possible and justifying social division in the community as a whole and among the rulers themselves.

2.3. *The Ideological Functional Sphere*

In the early state communal and tribal systems of faith ('pagan' religions) coexisted with an emerging state ideology. Particularly in the communities, the influence of a pre-state ideology was strong. Therefore, as in the cases of the state economy, the state ideology in early states represented only part of the total ideological life of the society. It was that part of which the state hierarchy, instead of the communities, took charge and which it promoted both for its own purposes and for those of the communities, and subsequently the social whole (though rather more ostensibly than actually so). State ideologies, as our sample data attest, were obviously designed for the justification and perpetuation of the early state and of the basic division of the society into two main strata or emergent classes. There was no teleological element in this. A mythical charter, belief in the supernatural qualities of the sovereign, and elaborate state rites all developed simultaneously with the other aspects of the early state.

The legitimation of the early state (cf. Kurtz's chapter on the *Aztecs* in this volume) was a complicated process which was attended to mainly in the religious sphere. By the creation of a myth of origin of the royal house, which was sometimes 'improved' on in the course of the state's existence, the basis for a state-wide religion was laid. Powerful religious systems imported from abroad, as in the case of European Christianity (*Norway, France*) strengthened these trends towards the development of state religions, and eventually encouraged drastic changes in the social structure of early state besides. In the case of only a few states (e.g., *France* and *Norway*), however, can we speak of the development of an independent, powerful group of religious specialists (priests, clergy) which eventually undermined the dominance of the state in the society. This marked the final, transitional, stage in the development of the early states in question.

The most important element in the legitimation of the state and the eventual establishment of its ideology was the belief in the supernatural qualities of the sovereign. It was believed by the masses, which belief was further strengthened by the religious specialists, that the sovereign was endowed with supernatural powers, and that thus the functioning of the society as a whole depended on him. In conformity with the natural conditions of the epoch, not so much the abstract idea of kingship, as the person of a specific monarch was of importance (Gurevich, p. 408, this volume).

As the case essays in our sample of early states show, there was typically more question of relevance for and belief in the divine powers of the sovereign than of his actual identification with some god in the early states under study (Chapter 25, S.C. 21, 25).

Another process of an ideological nature that was closely connected with that of legitimation in early states was ethnic integration. In a number of cases (cf. *Ankole, Axum, Aztecs, China, Inca, Scythia, Volta*) the state organization was seen to overarch two or more ethnic groups, while sometimes social division ran along the lines of ethnic division. The process of ethnic integration was only partly completed in the phase of the early state, and in most of the early states of our sample, it was the power of the state organization which kept a number of different ethnic groups together. The general trend was for the state hierarchy to try and overcome any ethnic differences in the total society.

The emergence of a common language was possible only where the state also controlled the educational and communication systems. Training for state service, as in the case of the *Yachahuasi* or boys' schools of the Inca and of the Aztec educational system (which extended to both members of the aristocracy and commoners) took place where the state was able to take advantage of the existence of a script and at least a small degree of literacy. Here it was possible for the legitimation process to become more effective (e.g., *Angkor, Axum, China, Mauryan India, Egypt*). However, with the possible exception of the *Aztecs*, there is no example of organized socialization or education for citizenship on a state-wide scale on the part of any early state in our sample. Only religion fulfilled the role of disseminating state propaganda and inculcating in the common people a sense of loyalty towards the state and its sovereign, and even then only partly so.

Next to the tributary relationship, the ideological relationship was the most common ever present relationship between the groups of the *ruled* and the *rulers*. In fact, it afforded the chief compensation for the economic burdens resulting from exploitation. Some early states respected the prevailing pre-state religious beliefs (as in the case of the earth cult in West Africa). Their ruling hierarchies adopted these and so a political–religious dualism, a 'ritual pact' between the religious specialists of the subdued communities and the rulers, came about. The latter then developed the state religion from a mixture of these beliefs and their own ancestor cults connected with political power (*Kuba, Volta, Yoruba, Zande*). The members of the communities, like the members of the ruling hierarchies, including the sovereign himself, were here taught to believe in the divine powers of the sovereign.

2.4. *The Military Functional Sphere*

One of the distinguishing features of the early state as represented by
our sample is that it monopolized the legal use of physical force. This
use of force, which was military in character, was exercised by groups
that were rather weak as specialized agencies of the early states in
question. Nevertheless, the early state hierarchy did manage to ensure
that no persons, or body of persons, other than those authorized by the
sovereign or his subordinates, resorted to physical force for the pursuit
of their individual goals. In the early state all military power, whether
resorted to to serve public or private interests, was deployed in the name of
the ruler, and consequently in that of the state. Military protection against
foreign or internal aggressors was often extended in 'exchange' for the
surplus products of the primary producers. At the same time it was easy for
pre-eminently private interests to manipulate this military power. This
kind of abuse was not common, however; at any rate there is insufficient
evidence of this, except for the fact that the *rulers*, as, for example, the
younger members of the aristocracy in the *Voltaic states*, could commit acts
of looting and pillage in the communities with the tacit consent of the state
sovereign and his councillors. This was tolerated because these forms of
plunder were considered as not curtailing the power of the top of the
hierarchy in any way.

It was in the military sphere that the dual character of the state in its
early phase becomes manifest. On the one hand, the *rulers* were
supposed to, and often actually did, create the necessary conditions of
peace and security vis-à-vis other states or any other kinds of external
force. This did not exclude the use of military force in the interest of
certain individuals of the ruling hierarchy, however. Although this was
not an everyday practice, it did sometimes occur in some of the early
states of our sample; it may be taken as an indication of the presence
of certain non-reciprocal aspects of the early state. Moreover, a
situation of internal security as created by the state organization was
an important condition for the undisturbed continuation of the unequal
division of the surplus product in favor of the ruling hierarchy.

Generally speaking, the military strength of early states was not
great. If there was little danger from without, the social order within
was quite stable. The ideological power was great enough to legitimize
and guarantee the continuance of the (unequal) redistribution of
wealth between the *ruled* and the *rulers*. In those early states whose
military strength was great enough for them to wage wars abroad, the
likelihood of an increase in inequality as well as of abuse of this
strength for unilateral or private ends was quite real (*Angkor, Aztecs,
China, France, Inca, Maurya, Mongolia, Norway, Scythia, Yoruba*).

The actual situation was not quite so simple, however. Aside from external threats to the integrity of early states, the internal threat of separation constantly kept sovereigns and their armies active. Such a situation of internal weakness was invariably a consequence of under-development of the infrastructure, and more especially of the distance between the center of power and the provincial sources of power. Regional government officials and administrators might use their *de facto* autonomy and their personal guard or armies to gain their independence and found their own states (especially, *Volta, Zande*). One of the most important tasks of the central government, therefore, was to prevent fission and to quell all attempts at separation. Further-more, local chiefs, or the pre-state aristocracy, had to be either eliminated or integrated by the central power to avoid fission. In some cases, as, for example, in that of *Norway*, conflicts between several groups or centers of power might culminate in civil war, which, in turn, might bring about a basic structural change or the end of the early state (cf. Claessen 1975a).

Though the military mode of state formation was common and efficient, it is also a fact that only a very few early states in our sample had standing armies. The sovereign either acted as military leader himself, or appointed a member of the council who was close to him as leader of the army. The sovereign, as the center of the state, was protected by a guard, but did not need an army for his personal security. The army was originally formed in an *ad hoc* way. In fairly isolated early states like *Egypt*, no army in fact existed. In most of the early states of our sample military actions were directed by persons involved in decision-making in other spheres of state activity. The military sphere was closely interrelated with the other spheres.

2.5. *The Political Functional Sphere*

From the data of our sample of early states, politics emerged as the decisive component of government, determining the entire character of the early state as a social reality as well as a concept. The early state functioned first and foremost as an organization of an emergent political society, a society characterized by the presence of political economy. Political power apparently was the primary object of the members of the emergent class of *rulers*. The sovereign and other persons possessing power had a decisive say in the running of the administration, the economy, and of military and ideological affairs. They also exercised great influence on vertical mobility in the society in general. Therefore, competition for political office was a key politi-cal concern in early states.

Succession to high office, however, soon became restricted to the members of only one or several kinship groups within the ruling hierarchy. At the same time in most early states the rules of succession were inadequately defined. It was usually open to competition between a number of people, such as the members of a specific (e.g., royal) clan, lineage or family. This principle is observable also in the succession to lower political offices, such as those of regional or local chief. As these political functionaries were usually appointed either by the sovereign himself or with his consent, it was usual for several candidates to compete for the sovereign's favor. The general impression is that, in most cases, political activity in the early state was restricted to the ruling hierarchy. In the political sphere the division between the state and the community, the rulers and the ruled was complete. This was a complementary sort of opposition, tending towards one-sidedness on the part of the rulers.

Despotic traits developed rather in the ideological sphere than in actual reality, although they could be very marked in the latter as well, especially in the case of some of the transitional types of early state (*Aztecs, Jimma, Maurya*, though also in *Angkor, Incas* and *Mongolia;* cf. Krader 1975: 290–291).

The economic surplus acquired from the direct producers was used by the ruling hierarchy not so much for simple consumption as to serve political ends. The hospitality extended by rulers and political functionaries constituted a means of gaining a following, which was expected to support the functionary or to help him reach a higher position. In fact, this lavishness, a conspicuous form of distribution of wealth as it was, served as a kind of mechanism for rewarding those members of the free population who supported the ruling group.

This kind of situation contained a clear element of reciprocity: all aid and support lent was rewarded, and both parties had obligations towards one another. Especially the coercive aspect of the ruler's position of power became accented this way. The holders of political offices thus accumulated power through redistribution in the widest sense of the word. The relation of reciprocity was not a balanced one, however, and moreover our data show that reciprocal tendencies gradually waned in the further course of the development of the early state. A situation of non-reciprocity, however, was only achieved in the phase of the mature state (cf. Krader, this volume).

In each of the early states of our sample one can observe that the central government, the ruler and his top officials, were protected by the administrative apparatus, often reinforced by a special group of guards, against attempts at supplantation by other pretenders to the supreme power. Thus a *balance of power* of sorts was fairly typical of the early state. This policy of achieving and maintaining a balance of power assumed considerable proportions in the course of time (cf.

Claessen 1978). Lewis, in his chapter on *Jimma*, states that here no real balance of power was found; this may well be an exception, however. One may point to certain phenomena in *Jimma*, however, which suggest that the ruler of this early state also knew how to divide — and hence to rule (the presence of a bodyguard, regional functionaries who were more or less strangers in their own provinces, etc.). In the other cases, the above-mentioned policy was often more explicitly enunciated (cf. *Angkor, Kuba, Tahiti*). The rulers of these states tried to play off appointed functionaries against hereditary ones, their kinsfolk against the official apparatus, military functionaries against courtiers or religious specialists, and so on. Even for states for which this is not explicitly mentioned, the data suggest that this kind of policy was pursued here, too.

In some early states, however, certain forces eventually developed which could no longer be contained in this way; one of these was the growing importance of private ownership. In part such private ownership was called into prominence by the state organization itself. The practice of distributing economic (and political) positions among the ruler's followers in the long run gave rise to the development of private ownership of land as the basic means of production. Landlords and 'state churches' in this way accumulated vast possessions and became independent of the state. This clearly marks the end of the phase of the early state.

It can be said that generally the competition for power resulted in upward mobility for only relatively few persons, and downward mobility for many. This is clearly apparent in the case of the aristocracy, whose privileged position was originally determined by genealogical distance from the ruler. The greater the distance between their respective lineages grew, the more junior sons of junior sons dropped from the ranks of the aristocracy, eventually to become commoners. In most cases (*France, Incas, Tahiti*) this decline took place most inconspicuously. Only in the case of the *Aztecs* did the sovereign demote certain recently created nobles (Kurtz). In all cases a process of commonerization in the junior ranks of the aristocracy was found, however. Conversely, other persons might climb to the top of the social hierarchy: where appointment of functionaries was possible, gifted commoners had an opportunity of rising sometimes to the highest positions, such as that of seal-keeper and vizier in *Egypt, höldar* or *veizlamen* in *Norway, bailiff* or *vicarius* in *France*, provincial chief in *Zande* states, or *kalaimoku* in *Hawaii.* Even slaves or eunuchs could rise to top positions (*Axum*, the *yanacona* of the *Incas, Jimma, Volta*, and *Yoruba*). Sometimes entire groups could be promoted to a higher rank: the Incas-by-privilege are a good example of this, as are also some clans in *Angkor*. The interplay of appointment versus heredity is seen by Peter Lloyd as one of the principal agencies of change of the structure of early states (cf. Lloyd 1965; Claessen 1975b).

The *Losreissung* or alienation of members of the ruling group from the village communities, as pointed out by Marx, thus seems to counterbalance the reverse trend of the return to the communities of former aristocrats. The growing cleavage between the rulers and populace is also reflected in the unbridgeable kinship gap between both groups. This, in fact, excluded commoners from serious competition for power in the early state. Only when a new ideology is evolved will this barrier disappear.

The despotic traits of the ruling group seem to be restricted to the ruling hierarchy in the broadest sense. Our data support the thesis that the lives of the population at large were hardly affected by the rulers — with the exception of those living in the vicinity of a court (cf. Kandert's comments). The sovereign travelled about, and, in so doing, personally reached many of his subjects (cf. Kendall 1971). However, once the royal party had departed again, life resumed its 'normal' routine. All this seems to support Krader's conclusions where he characterizes the type of society in which the Asiatic mode of production prevailed as follows:

> The monarch is a despot who has absolute power over his courtiers, clients, retainers and slaves; he regards them as his property; he enriches and confiscates, holding all the property of his kingdom in his power. But *his reach does not extend very far*, and, historically, the villages have their own lives. Once the tax has been collected from them, they utterly ignore the *gestes* of the court, the wars and the dynastic changes, and are in turn ignored by the sovereignty. (1976: 114; our italics).

The political life in the early states seems, for the greater part, to have been the exclusive concern of the ruling hierarchy, which identified itself with the state as such. The early state, in the sense of the organization, the power and the glory, seems to have existed solely for their benefit and their advantage. Only the payment of tribute and, from time to time, military actions affected the entire society of the early state. This is only one side of the picture, however. The necessity of the state for survival, the need for its protection against foreign invaders, and the inevitable necessity of organization in consequence of increased population should not be left out of this picture. An ideology and administration, and to a lesser extent also some form of military protection, were the instruments of legitimation, and, at the same time, of 'reciprocal exploitation'. It was in this that the existence of the ruling group found its justification — even if only in the latter's own eyes, though most probably also in the eyes of the people.

The whole of the society concerned, encompassing the rulers as well as the ruled, seems to have believed that the early state organization represented the only possible form of organization. The early state society was one of consensus — though this consensus was actively promoted by the bearers of its ideology.

The growth of private ownership, the expansion of the political sphere, the development of an independent state church, and so on, will, in the course of time, have led to a situation whereby it became impossible for the state to retain its dominant position in all spheres of activity above the community level. This then, marked the end of the early state, or rather, the beginning of a new type of state which may be designated the mature one.

3. FUNCTIONAL PRINCIPLES

The above presentation of a model of the functioning of the early state revealed:
(1) the necessity of a historical, processual way of looking at the agencies of the early state (cf. Swartz et al., 1966; Swartz 1968; Lloyd 1965: 73 ff., and 1968); and
(2) that the five functional spheres distinguished here for analytical purposes are, in fact, so intertwined, that it is hardly possible to speak of strictly 'economic' or 'political' functions of the early state.
I will now try to formulate, on the basis of these findings, some general *principles of functioning*. In so doing I will reintegrate, on a higher level the processes earlier separated.

3.1. *The Functional Principle of Syncretism*

Generally, the governmental agencies of the early state, as well as their representatives, are so interdependent and show so much overlap that it is hardly possible to discern specialists here. Only on the higher level of the early state organization were some specialists found. The dominant type of functionary, however, is the 'general' one fulfilling plural roles. These roles are not necessarily all formal. So religious specialists, for instance, were found to exercise informal influences on political decisions. Furthermore, functional spheres overlap each other, with, for instance, ideology bolstering politics, politics the economy, etc.. For the citizens of the early state, the ruling stratum included, there was apparently no distinction between these spheres. A syncretic view of society predominated.

The more specialization increased, and the greater the tendency became for salaried functionaries to be appointed, for a bureaucratic apparatus to come into prominence, and for private ownership of land to evolve, however, the more the character of the early state vanished.

Where independent class agencies came into being beside the state, a new type of state evolved. This was a non-reciprocal instrument of the class of persons controlling the means of production. It was the mature state.

3.2. *The Functional Principle of Redistributive Exploitation*

The early state retained a more or less reciprocal character throughout the period of its existence. This was based mainly on specific ideological convictions, as well as the extension of certain political and/or military services by the governmental apparatus to the common people, for which the populace paid with different kinds of tribute, levies, labor, etc.. In part, these contributions were used 'for the common good', such as major public works, the administration of state affairs, etc.. The members of the ruling hierarchy, for the greater part, drew their incomes from these contributions; these were then partly supplemented by the surplus from their own lands. The mechanism of exploitation represented, in fact, an *unbalanced* reciprocal system. It was a fairly smooth-running machine as a result of extra-economic, politico-ideological coercion. This mode of exploitation did not yield much income for the ruling stratum, which implies that the standard of living of the latter did not differ too greatly from that of the common people. It did not provoke much protest on the part of the exploited majority, either. That is why it is impossible to speak of any sort of class struggle in the early state. Mutually antagonistic social classes were not yet fully developed. Hence, we can only speak of 'emergent' social classes. Exploitation was covert, and was compensated for by a common ideology of reciprocity and mutual aid. Nevertheless, the society of the early state was already divided into the group of those who produced tribute, and those who received it. The dynamics of social inequality were fully operative, though it could, and usually did, take centuries before the class character of the fully developed state was finally established.

3.3. *The Functional Principle of Centralization*

In the early state generally a struggle for stabilization can be observed (cf. Claessen 1978). By evolving a balance of power between the central government and the centrifugal forces, however, it was possible for a fairly stable structure to be preserved for a fairly long period of time. This becomes especially manifest in the early state's capacity to prevent fission (cf. Cohen in the present volume). By this capacity the early state basically distinguished itself from the pre-state chiefdom.

The early state was centralized, and at the same time had only a single center of government. The central government continually strove to achieve centralization of all important social activities in the economic, ideological and even kinship spheres (e.g., the *Aztecs, Incas, Jimma*), and in so doing considerably strengthened its own position. In the inchoate phase of the early state many relations were based chiefly on kinship (*Ankole, Hawaii, Norway, Tahiti, Volta, Zande*), which accounts for their somewhat segmentary and tribal structure (cf. Southall 1956). Once this phase has been passed — gradually, by strengthening the central power and increasing the number of appointed functionaries — tribal and kinship factors begin to lose in importance, in favor of loyalties to the territory and state as a focus of loyalty in its own right. A gradual process of bureaucratization is characteristic of all early stages (perhaps with the exception of *China*) — though the qualities of the governmental apparatus here still fall far short of the proper ties defined by Max Weber (1964).

3.4. *The Functional Principle of Legitimation*

Mostly ideological persuasion is predominant in the legitimation of the early state. The state has to be justified to the members of both the communities and the pre-state tribal aristocracies which have lost their independence as a result of the annexation of their groups. The latter process involves ethnic as well as professional integration into the state organization. At the same time also, the far-reaching penetration of ideas of the dominant religion, i.e., that of the ruling stratum takes place. This legitimation was accompanied in some of the early states of our sample by the development of an official language, and the formal education of at least the sons of the former local aristocracy in the new values. This might take place in the form of compulsory enjoyment of 'hospitality' at the court (*Aztecs, Incas, Jimma, Yoruba*), or with the aid of a school system. In the *Aztec* case this formal education was also given to the children of commoners (Kurtz).

The state is also legitimized through repeated actions of a military nature, which serve to show that protection by the state is indispensable. Economic activities, such as the organization of irrigation schemes, lend support to the idea of legitimation(*Angkor, Axum, Aztecs, China, Hawaii, Inca, Maurya*).

3.5. *The Functional Principle of Sacral Sovereignty*

The sovereign was the very pivot of the early state. Sometimes he was even identified with the state. Usually, he was considered as sacral.

This is the most important feature of his leadership, reinforced by his connections with the supernatural forces. The sovereign actually decided all the most important issues in the early state, or at least decisively influenced decision-making by the councils. Early states, thus, are monarchies under more or less absolute, sometimes even quite despotic sovereigns with broad executive powers. We should remember here, however, that this applies mostly to the ruling hierarchy — more so than to the common people, at any rate. Our sample included no example of a democratic, republican type of early state, which does not, however, exclude the possibility that such kinds of early state may have existed (e.g., the Tswana city-states in South Africa were non-monarchist).

3.6. *The Functional Principle of Self-Oriented Political Strategy*

The ruling stratum of the early state seems to have been completely concentrated upon its own internal political life. This means that the pursuit of political power was mainly confined to the ruling group. It does not seem to have been of any importance to the society at large in which the early state developed.

The society at large was not affected by, and was, in fact, for the greater part excluded from the competition for and exercise of power. The lives of the commoners engaged in material production were lived separately from the state as such. They only kept the state organization alive by supplying it with energy (food, labor). Vertical social mobility was limited, though in the course of time members of the administrative apparatus, who were personally dependent on the bearers of political power themselves, came to exercise *de facto* power, and attained to ranks which enabled them to become active members.

3.7. *The Functional Principle of the Suppression and Transformation of Pre-State Patterns*

All agencies of the early state had to pass a test of endurance and vitality in their confrontation with institutions from previous levels of development. Kinship loyalties played a role throughout the entire period of the early state, but gradually lost in importance. They were gradually integrated and utilized by the agencies of the state. The same holds true for earlier cults, values, beliefs, and economic institutions.

Hence the organization of the early state evolved the power to convert existing institutions into agencies which it could use for its own ends. This capacity increased with the increasing perfection of political strategies and elaboration of ideological and military features. By the same token, the communal principle, which is characteristic of pre-state primitive societies, was suppressed together with the institut-ions coupled with it.

FOOTNOTES

[1] By the 'significance' of the early state I mean its objective role in society and history. The data at our disposal gives us reason to reject all 'plot' hypotheses concerning the origin of the early state, but, on the other hand, do enable the formulation of as general as possible characteristics of the early state as a distinct type of socio-political organiza-tion in the evolution of mankind.

REFERENCES

Claessen, Henri J. M. (1975a), 'Circumstances under which civil war comes into existence', in: *War, its causes and correlates*, ed. by M. A. Nettleship, R. D. Givens, and A. Nettleship, pp. 559–571. The Hague: Mouton.
— (1975b), 'From rags to riches — and the reverse', in: *Rule and reality, essays in honor of André J. F. Köbben*, ed. by Peter Kloos and Klaas W. van der Veen, pp. 29–49. Amsterdam: Universitaire Pers.
— (1978), 'The balance of power in primitive states', in: *Political anthropology and the state of the art*, ed. by S. Lee Seaton and H. J. M. Claessen The Hague: Mouton.
Danilova, L. V. (1968), 'Diskussionnye problemy teorii dokapitalisticheskikh obschestv', in: *Problemy istorii dokapitalisticheskikh obschestv* I. Moscow: Nauka.
Evans-Pritchard, E. E. (1962), 'The divine kingship of the Shilluk of the Nilotic Sudan' (1948), in: *Essays in Social Anthropology*, pp. 66–86. London: Faber & Faber.
Goody, Jack (1971), *Technology, tradition, and the state in Africa*, London: Oxford University Press.
Kendall, P. M. (1971), *Louix XI*. London: Allen & Unwin.
Krader, Lawrence (1975), *The Asiatic mode of production*. Assen: Van Gorcum.
— (1976, Social evolution and social revolution, in: *Dialectical Anthropol-ogy* I: 109–120.
Lloyd, Peter (1965), 'The political structure of African Kingdoms', in: *Political systems and the distribution of power*, ed. by M. Banton, pp. 63–109. ASA monographs 2. London: Tavistock.
— (1968), 'Conflict theory and Yoruba kingdoms', in: *History and social anthropology*, ed by I. M. Lewis, pp. 25–62. ASA monographs 7. London: Tavistock.
Mair, Lucy P. (1962), *Primitive government*. Harmondsworth: Pelican books.
Smith, M. G. (1960), *Government in Zazzau*. London: Oxford University Press.
Southall, A. W. (1956), *Alur society*. Cambridge: Heffer.
Swartz, Marc J., ed. (1968), *Local-level politics*. Chicago: Aldine.
Swartz, Marc J., Turner, V., and Tuden, A., eds. (1966), *Political anthropology*. Chicago: Aldine.

Vansina, Jan (1964), 'The use of process-models in African history', in: *The historian in tropical Africa*, pp. 375–386. London: Oxford University Press.

Weber, Max (1964), *Wirtschaft und Gesellschaft*. Köln: Kippenheuer und Witsch.

Wolf, Eric (1966), *Peasants*. Englewood Cliffs: Prentice Hall.

27 Limits: Beginning and End of the Early State

HENRI J. M. CLAESSEN and PETER SKALNÍK

In the foregoing two chapters we discussed, on a comparative basis, the structural and the processual aspects of the early state. Here we will make some general observations on the conditions under which the early state originated. As in the preceding chapters, we will base ourselves in the present one also on the data of our case studies.

In spite of the fact that we will be generalizing here, we are well aware that the historical process in each individual case was unique. Unique in the sense that the specific circumstances under which a given people acted in given ways will not be found recurring anywhere else.

However, when one brings the discussion to a higher level of abstraction, it will be possible, nonetheless, to discern a number of general patterns, or regularities in the total range of historical processes. This will enable us to place the early state more unequivocally within the general framework of the development of human society. After characterizing the above-mentioned regularities, we will undertake to answer the questions, earlier formulated on this subject, in chapter 28.

1. GENERAL ASPECTS OF THE ORIGINS OF THE EARLY STATE

Insofar as our case studies provide any data on the origins, the general picture appears to be that early states developed gradually from earlier-existing organizational forms. The early state certainly was not just 'invented, or discovered by somebody' (Krader, in this volume, p. 104). Only two cases require more detailed discussion in this respect, namely *Egypt* and *Jimma*.

With regard to *Egypt*, Janssen points out that virtually nothing is known about the pre-state situation. He even uses the expression: 'a foundling without parents' with reference to the Egyptian state. Influences from abroad, such as, for instance, from Mesopotamia, were very limited, if they were present at all, and do not seem to have had any noticeable impact upon the formation of the state. In fact, the only thing that is known with certainty is that the unification of Upper and Lower Egypt was a fairly slow process, in which war *may* have played a role. The data appear to be too scant to allow of any more definite conclusions. The conditions in pre-state *Egypt*, for the time being, remain an unsolved puzzle.

For *Jimma*, on the other hand, the data are abundant. Lewis tells us that the state of *Jimma Abba Jifar* was founded in the first half of the nineteenth century, and 'rapidly developed its own distinctive characteristics in terms of political structure and culture' (Lewis, this volume, p. 321). This development took place in an area in which state forms had come into being many times previous. Additionally, the rulers of *Jimma* had already, at an early stage, enlisted the assistance of councillors and political experts from abroad. These circumstances, we believe, explain sufficiently the rapid development of *Jimma* to the transitional type of early state. Besides, several 'transitional' characteristics, viz. a non-kin-based form of social organization, in which territorial, neighborhood, friendship and voluntary association principles underlay group activities, and where land was *not* owned by descent groups, were found already in the pre-state situation.

We agree with Khazanov (chapter 3, this volume) where the latter, following Fried (1967), distinguishes between *pristine* and *secondary* types of early states. Indeed, *Egypt*, *Tahiti*, and probably *Ankole*, *Hawaii* and *China* were examples of pristine early states. The others were most probably all of the secondary type, which implies that they developed under the influence of similar social structures preceding them, or existing in the same area. This latter implies that their material conditions differed from these of pristine early states (cf. also Lewis 1966: 402 ff, on secondary states, and Cohen, this volume, pp. 45–49). However that may be, both the pristine and the secondary early states enjoyed a gradual development, and many institutions of the pre-state period continued their existence within them. To realize this is to realize that it is impossible to pinpoint the precise moment of the birth of the state. We simply do not know when or where the decisive step — if there is justification for speaking of any decisive step — was taken in each individual case. The notion of a gradual development gives us more reason to think in terms of fairly inconspicuous processess. These took place very slowly and unnoticeably, until the anthropologist or historian is able, in the retrospect, to

observe the sudden presence of specific institutions that are characteristic of the state (cf. Smith 1977: 13). No one knows exactly when
they came about, but in some cases contemporary leaders must have
realized that a new situation had developed, or that the time was ripe
to create new, or reorganize existing institutions. When they did so
(professedly or really), through the introduction of new laws, new
forms of organization, or new mythical charters, they came to be
represented in history as the creators or founding fathers of the state in
question, though most probably they only *made explicit* certain already
existing trends; which is not denying their importance or genious.
Rulers like Ntare IV of *Ankole*, the Chou potentate WuWang of
China, the great law giver Montezuma I of the *Aztecs* the organizer of
the state religion in *Angkor*, Jayavarman II, the *Mongol* ruler Chingis
Khan, who tried to subdue a whole continent, Warga or Kango of the
Voltaic states of Moogo and Yatenga, the *Mauryan* organizer Aśoka,
the great *Inca* Pachacutec, and Kamehameha of *Hawaii*, all made
explicit specific existing trends or found solutions to certain urgent
problems. And, in doing so, they left their 'footprints in the sand of
time'.

The question of the 'Great Man' versus the general trends of history
has been the subject of numerous debates and polemics (cf. White
1949: 233–281; Claessen 1970: 198, and notes 1104, 1105; Harris
1968: 328). We do not believe that the place we have allocated the
'Great Man' in the evolution of mankind will end this discussion.
However, by stating that his influence on the course of history is
undeniable, but that he was able to exert this influence only under
especially favorable conditions, we feel we are doing justice to the
'Great Man' as well as to evolution.

There is a marked continuity in the development of the early state.
A complex social structure is already found in the chiefdom, where
there are likewise already, aspects of legitimation enhancing the
chief's position. Centralizing tendencies are found long before the
emergence of the state, while earlier phases of development, too, are
characterized by social inequality. The works of Fried (1967), Service
(1971, 1975), Goldman (1970) and Carneiro (1970b) all convincingly
demonstrate that these tendencies were to be found long before the
early state came into being. To this we must add here that many
tendencies that are characteristic of pre-state phases (such as, for
instance, communal ownership of land, allegiance to family or clan
heads) did not disappear after state formation. To describe this,
Natalia Kochakova, in her chapter on the *Yoruba* uses the felicitous
term 'dualistic character' with reference to the early state, indicating
that aspects of both a tribal and a class society are to be found here.
Koranashvili says the same about the early states of *Georgia*, while

Gurevich, in his analysis of *Norway*, rightly points out that it is virtually impossible to make an accurate division into types or phases on account of the fact that the institutions of an earlier phase do not disappear in the next. Estellie Smith expresses the same view, but adds: 'the simpler forms of sociocultural organization have not vanished, or merely maintain in fossil form, but have *adapted* so as to become specialized parts of the larger configuration'. (f.c.: 12; our italics). This formulation may be helpful in drawing a sharper distinction between the pre-state and the state level.

2. FACTORS RESPONSIBLE FOR THE ORIGIN OF THE EARLY STATE

In chapter 1 we discussed at length, a number of theories on the origin of the state. Now, after considering the origins of the early state in broad generalization, we will be more specific about this. To give our discussion a factual basis, we will outline here the 'case-histories' of those states of our sample on whose formation details are given in the essays.

With regard to *Angkor* new ideas and techniques coming from India provided the impetus for the introduction of more developed modes of agricultural production and methods of trading, warfare and conducting raids. These in turn stimulated a more intensive and effective organization of government, which was given a more effective legislation by Jayavarman II.

In *Ankole* groups of pastoral Hima settled a specific region of marshlands in the fifteenth century. This area was mostly devoid of population. Only a few scattered agriculturalists lived here. There were virtually no contacts between the two groups. In the eighteenth century droughts and famines set off a chain of battles and wars. Defeat in war and the fear of new wars led to the organization of a defensive apparatus. Marriage with foreign women set the ruler apart from the aristocracy. The cult of the drum was imported. Famines and wars continued to mould *Ankole* society, in which relations between the Hima and the agricultural Bairu gradually became more developed.

The *Aztecs* tried to find a solution to the problem of growing population pressure by levying tribute in kind from the surrounding population groups. This led to war and conquest which in turn gave rise to the necessity of greater organization, increased taxation, and more effective legitimation.

In *France* as well a growing population pressure seems to have triggered off numerous developments, such as agricultural expansion, changes in land tenure practices, the necessity to produce a greater surplus, an increase in political power on the basis, especially, of the aristocracy's higher incomes from taxes and tribute. War also strengthened the need for more and better organization. In addition reminiscences of former state structures played a role in the formation of the state under discussion here.

The *Hawaiian* states could only come into being after the conclusion of some kind of treaty between the various paramount chiefs, which curbed the endless wars for a sufficiently long time to enable some chiefs to evolve a more stable organization, which in turn was stimulated to expand after the recommencements of hostilities. A series of conquests and reconquests characterizes the period of the early state here.

The *Iberian* (Georgian) states seem to have developed as a result of the need to defend themselves against foreign invaders. Alliances were formed, and leaders rose to greater power. Furthermore, population growth required a more complex organization.

The *Incas* for a long time ruled only one of the many Andean chiefdoms. However, a victory in a war with their most important rival opened up the way to statehood. Annexation, and increased production stimulated by the pressure exerted by the governmental apparatus, made possible the more extensive and complex form of organization called into existence by war and conquest.

In the case of *Jimma*, a number of Galla groups, having apparently largely displaced earlier inhabitants, settled in their new homeland as mixed agriculturalists. Surrounded by previously existing states, they warred against these as well as among themselves, and competed for the control of land, trade routes and markets. The state arose as the result of a succession of local conquests, as one Galla group defeated and began to impose its rule over the others (Lewis: personal information).

The *Kachari* state originated in the hill districts of the northeastern part of the Indian subcontinent. Even before the state came into being, a disintegration of the clan system had occurred. The genealogical group gradually made way for a socio-professional type of group, which initiated growing social inequality. As the population grew the number of these groups also grew. Incessant warfare consolidated the position of the notables. The influence of military leaders was considerable. Technical as well as socio-political concepts were borrowed from surrounding states; these had a substantial impact upon the formation of the *Kachari* state.

The *Kuba* state shows how the production of a surplus, stimulated by the pressure exerted by chiefs, made possible a more complex governmental apparatus. This additionally made possible the production of luxury articles which were used to reward faithful servants.

Vansina points to the dialectical character of the process: bureaucracy and production mutually stimulated each other's development, and both fostered the development of a more complex ideology.

The same applies to *Maurya*: the production of a surplus made possible the development of the state organization, which in its turn boosted the production of the surplus, with, as a consequence, the development of trade and markets. This gave rise to the need for law and order, and led to the emergence of new social categories.

Developments in *Norway* seem to have been triggered off by the disintegration of the extended family. This may have been a result of the scarcity of resources in this country (cf. Wolf 1966: 72). This disintegration led to a lessening of the influence of the *bönder*, which made possible the gradual rise to power of a particular ruling family, who in the course of time succeeded in subduing several regions.

In *Scythia* the relationship between the nomadic Scythians and a number of the agricultural tribes formed the point of departure for state formation. The dominance of the nomads over the agriculturalists made some form of organization necessary, and gradually the state system developed (cf. also Khazanov 1975: 340). In point of fact, *Scythia* is a classical illustration of Oppenheimer's Conquest theory.

Tahiti shows how population growth made for an increasing social distance between the members of senior and those of junior descent lines. A distance that became so great that both groups became endogamous. Ownership of land and social status were dependent on position in the descent system, the division of the population into a group of rulers and a group of ruled being the consequence of the resultant configuration.

In the *Voltaic* area the presence of permanent threats of assault and pillage seems to have induced people to look for more effective protection and leadership. The increase in the political unity created by these circumstances was accompanied by the growth of a supra-village ideology. In the course of time this led to the stabilization of internal relations, greatly influenced by continuing external (political) pressures.

These condensed case histories of our states facilitate the search for certain patterns or regularities. The principal general characteristic, in our view, is the fact that the development into statehood, in all cases, was triggered off by some action or event which took place a long time before, and was *not directed especially* towards this goal. The other obvious characteristic of the development to statehood is that it always shows something of a snowball effect: once it comes into motion, it grows faster and faster. This is a consequence of *mutual reinforcement* in all of the developmental processes studied between the phenomena and their effects. Thus we can speak of a *positive feedback*. This seems to confirm Sahlins' suggestion that economy and politics grow together (1972: 140). Likewise, our data seem to corroborate Cohen's observation (chapter 2, p. 32) that:

Each set of factors, or any particular factor, once it develops, stimulates and feeds back onto others which are then made to change in the general direction of statehood. Although its roots may be multiple, once a society or group of them start developing toward early statehood, the end is remarkably similar, no matter where it occurs.

Aside from *historical progression* a set of mutually corresponding factors appeared to play a role in several cases. It is possible to isolate these factors and consider the relative importance of each. In so doing, we must emphasize that in the actual historical process their order was seen to vary, while not all factors necessarily always occurred.

These factors are:

(1) Population growth and population pressure;

(2) War, the threat of war or conquest, raids;

(3) Conquest;

(4) Progress in production and the promotion of a surplus, tribute, affluence;

(5) Ideology and legitimation;

(6) The influence of already existing states.

(1) *Population Pressure* — occasioned by population growth, may stimulate raids to obtain food, or to effect the payment of tribute by some population group living outside the territory to supplement production shortages within it (*Ankole, Aztecs*). This involves war, or the threat of war, which in turn stimulates the emergence of stronger leaders and a better organization, which in its turn makes conquest possible (*Incas, Scythia*). Alternatively, it may stimulate production, which (as in the case of *France* or *Kuba*) may in the end bring about affluence, which makes possible the development of a complex state apparatus — which, in its turn again, will stimulate increased production. Population pressure may bring about the disintegration of the institution of the extended family (*Norway*) which may enable the ruler to form a central government (cf. Wolf 1966: 70 ff.). Conversely, population growth may stimulate the growth of such families, in which the social distance between senior and junior lineages may then become unbridgeable (*Kachari, Tahiti*).

Population growth is an internal development, which has repercussions not only for the home community, but also for surrounding peoples. Our data appear to corroborate Carneiro's ideas on the influence of environmental or social circumscription (1970a). Webster's hypothesis (1975) that war, or the threat of war, calls into being stronger leaders and a better organization also finds confirmation in the data collected by us. Moreover, the views of Fried (1967) and

Kottak (1972) on the role of population growth or population pressure are supported by our findings.

How are we to square these results with the findings of Wright and Johnson on the basis of their analysis of Iranian data (1975), however? These show 'that there was a period of population decline prior to state formation'. (1975: 276). A possible explanation for this may be that the existing balance between the socio-economic structure of the society and the potentials of the territory and/or the cultural setting was upset (cf. Van Bakel 1976: 22 ff.). A new form of social organization was needed to create new conditions of life. As long as such a new form of organization remains ineffective the population will show a tendency to migrate, or be subject to conflicts, food shortages, etc. These latter factors may cause a decline in population. The social forces stimulating the development of a new organizational pattern may continue to be active at the same time. Once the new structure crystallizes, the population receives a renewed stimulus to grow. This hypothesis seems to find some corroboration in Polgar's assertion that socio-political changes occur before population growth starts (1975: 10).

(2) *War, or the Threat of War, and Raids* — or the need to conduct raids and collect tribute — their reasons or causes aside, all have the same consequences, viz. the emergence of stronger leaders and a better or stronger organization, be it for purposes of defense or attack (*Ankole, Aztecs, Hawaii, Iberia, Incas, Jimma, Kachari, Volta*). Such forms of organization create a permanent need for regular supplies of food and other commodities for the maintenance of the armed forces, the remuneration of warriors, and the establishment of communications by means of roads, boats, spies, messengers, etc. The payment of tribute as well as the exertion of pressure on the producers of a surplus are invariably found here. Here again, the condensed histories set out above corroborate Webster's hypothesis. State formation is *not* caused by war, but is greatly *promoted* by war, or by the threat of war and by social stress (cf. Nettleship 1975: 82 ff.; Corning 1975: 375 ff.). This further endorses Service's view (1975: 299) that 'the benefit of being part of the society (which) obviously outweighed the alternative'. The need for protection under these circumstances is obvious; as a result of this it was better to be a member of the state than not to be one. We, moreover, believe that Lowie's idea that the voluntary association was *one* of the roots of state formation is confirmed by some of the data of our case studies.

(3) *Influence of Conquest* — The origin of many of our states demonstrated the decided influence of conquest. However, only the

Mongol, the *Scythian*, and possibly the *Voltaic* states and *Zande* appeared to owe the formation of their state organization to conquest in the sense of Oppenheimer. Only in *Scythia* and *Mongolia* was the domination of agricultural peoples by pastoral nomads found. *Ankole* was *not* originally based upon the subjection of the group of agriculturalists. This took place in only a much later period, and even then to a rather limited extent. Relations between pastoralists and agriculturalists, living in the same area as they did, remained marginal there till the very end. Data furnished by Cohen (in the present volume, but also 1974, 1977) show that there are other cases in which the domination of pastoralists over agriculturalists led to state formation, however.

In the other cases in which conquest was mentioned as a factor in the formation of the early state (*Angkor, Aztecs, Hawaii, Incas, Jimma, Maurya*), such conquest appeared to be of peoples possessing the same mode of subsistence.

It is not very clear whether conquest leads to the formation of the early state, or, conversely, the formation of the early state leads to conquest. If conquest is interpreted as the occupation of territory and the integration of peoples into a given (foreign) political organization, then, in our view, the necessary institutions to make this possible will be found only at the state level. If, however, conquest is taken to refer to a situation in which two groups, each possessing different (or sometimes the same) modes of subsistence, are merged, with in the end the development of a political structure that stimulates the domination of one of the two by the other, then plainly it will be possible for conquest to have already started at a much earlier stage. At any rate, only few of the cases in our sample seem to corroborate the 'Ueberlagerungs' theories of Gumplowicz and Oppenheimer.

(4) *The Production of a Surplus* — seems to be a rather complicated matter. Without any doubt it is a necessary condition for the existence of the state. However, the production of a surplus is found already in the chiefdom, and possibly even before that. Nevertheless, the production of a surplus and the development of a more complex form of socio-political organization are closely correlated. This is clearly demonstrated by all of the above 'case histories'. An expanding government apparatus, the need for some kind of military force (for offensive as well as defensive purposes), a developing state religion — all these developments demand increased production, and increased production in its turn makes possible the further development of these institutions. This is also a most favorable situation for the stimulation and the promotion of the growth of (already existing) trade and markets (*Axum, Aztecs, France, Kuba, Maurya, Yoruba*).

On the one hand, a growing surplus makes for opulence and

conspicuous consumption, with a growing number of people (from aristocrats to artisans) having only an *indirect* relation to food production. On the other hand, it causes an increasing number of people to become exclusively committed to food production, with the obligation to hand over an ever increasing proportion of their produce. Social statuses become more and more rigidly structured. Economic inequality gradually becomes a permanent feature of the institutions of the social organization. The consequence of these developments in the early state is a clear-cut division of the population into a category of *rulers* and *ruled*, linked together in practice mainly by the taxation system.

In the formation of the early state, the production of a surplus constitutes the pre-eminent factor enabling the development of a governmental apparatus as well as the institutionalization of social inequality: a dialectical process (cf. Sahlins 1958, 1972: 140).

The discussion so far would lead one to conclude that social inequality already existed in some form or other before the formation of the state (cf. Maretina, in this volume), and moreover its elaboration is rather a consequence than a cause of state formation. Social inequality, indeed, is one of the characteristics of the (early) state, but for its origin was probably of only minor importance.

Kottak's hypothetical frame (1972) can easily be brought into agreement with this view. Our results do seem to be rather far removed from the theories of Fried (1967), however, who made social inequality the cornerstone of his argumentation. It seems to us that Fried, in fact, investigated, in the first place, the origin of social inequality, and only in the second place the evolution of political organization.

(5) *The Role of an Ideology* — or myth of the society in question, or of legitimation — all of them closely related concepts — is mentioned in almost all our 'case histories'. Everywhere a basic myth of the society concerned (cf. S.C. 21), which legitimized the position of its leader, chief or sovereign, was found. At the point where the development towards the early state was triggered off, this myth may have been in need of adaptation to account for, or justify, the growing social inequality, the increasing power of the sovereign, the necessity to defend the home territory, or the exalted duty to raid the territory of neighboring peoples. This seems to suggest that, generally speaking, the role of the state ideology is one of legitimizing, explaining or justifying. This sort of activity may lead to the elaboration of existing institutions, or the making explicit of existing tendencies. We are inclined to believe, however, that ideological activities have no more than a secondary influence upon the formation of the early state —

though its further development could not have been effected without it.

(6) *The Influence of Already Existing State Systems* — is mentioned in the case of *Angkor, Jimma, Kachari* and *Maurya*. In *France* there were not only other state systems surrounding the country, but there also existed an extensive knowledge of earlier periods of state formation. This was probably also the case in *Iberia*, and possibly also *Scythia*. The degree of influence of such earlier existing states varies per state. It provided at least some kind of framework for the developments to come in all cases, however. This would have been the position in most of the secondary states.

Summarizing the above, the existence of an ideology, as well as of a surplus, appears to have been a necessary condition for state formation. The elaboration of social inequality was found to be a consequence rather than a cause of such formation. This leaves us with the factors of population growth or pressure, war or the threat of war and raids, tribute, conquest and borrowed ideas as those which seem to have exercised a primary influence on the formation of the state. How these factors operated, influenced one another, and were interlinked with those of the existence of an ideology, a surplus, trade and social inequality in each individual case it is impossible to express in mere generalizations. Whatever the specific order of their appearance may have been, in each case, the result was the same in all of our cases, namely, the emergence of the early state.

With this conclusion we find ourselves in basic agreement with the ideas of Cohen and Khazanov as expressed in the theoretical part of this volume (cf. also Cohen 1977). There are some substantial differences between our and Krader's views, however. The reason for this, to our mind, is mainly that Krader concentrates more on the characteristics of the mature state than on the specific conditions of the early state.

3. THE INCHOATE EARLY STATE

The discussion up to this point gives rise to the question of how to distinguish the early state from earlier forms, in particular the chiefdom form. In chapter 1 we suggested a number of characteristics of the state, which we tested in chapters 25 and 26. However, as many of these characteristics are already found in one form or another in earlier stages of development, they are not very helpful in drawing a 'borderline'. Useful though such qualifications as 'more', 'better', or 'more complex' may be to denote a certain progress, the crystallization of a new system can only be demonstrated where the cumulative process finds expression in the emergence of specific traits that are *not* found in chiefdoms, or even *could never* be found here because of particular qualitative differences. To quote Estellie Smith once more: 'Such a plateau is recognized, however, seems to be reached, when the weight of 'trivial' accretive changes causes facilitative adjustment throughout the system' (f.c.: 13).

Qualitative changes, or the development of new traits, occur, we believe, in the development of *legitimized power* as manifest from: (a) the power — whether consensual or coercive — to enforce the decisions of the central government; (b) the power — whether consensual or coercive — to prevent fission. These two kinds of power, of course, are no more than the top of an iceberg. They are *indicative* of the development of a complex form of socio-political organization, of centralized government, of social inequality, of balances of power, of sufficient legitimation, of adequate state resources, and so on. We stressed the aspect of legitimation in the above, because our analysis made it clear that the consensual type of power was more highly developed than the coercive one (cf. Service 1971: 150 on chiefdoms, and idem 167 on the state). The power to push the decisions of the central government becomes manifest especially in the introduction and enforcement of laws and regulations. As in the typical and transitional types of early states this problem seems to have been definitely solved, we will restrict our analysis here to the situation at the inchoate level. Let us look at the relevant cases in our sample.

With reference to *Ankole* it is mentioned that the sovereign and his court made important decisions. There was, however, a large measure of local self-government. In a number of cases crimes were judged by the ruler and his court. For the enforcement of decisions there were a number of armed retainers kept at court. The Bairu seem to have lived their own lives, and were affected by the Hima in only some respects. All citizens of the state are mentioned as having had the obligation to pay taxes and perform military services. In the *Hawaiian* states the sovereign made all important laws and decisions. A group of armed retainers was found at the court. People could be called up for corvée labor, and had to pay taxes in kind. In addition military services had to be performed by all men. The obligations to pay tax and to perform military services affected the populace directly. The sovereign and his court travelled about the state partly for economic reasons, partly for political ones. The ruler's judicial duties were concentrated on the maintenance of the all-embracing *kapu*-system.

Norway constitutes an extremely interesting case, for Gurevich has not restricted himself to a single period of the early state here, but has described the development of the early state in *Norway* from the inchoate to the transitional stage. At the inchoate stage the role of the sovereign or the central government was only weakly developed. He had to travel extensively in order to impress his sovereign status upon the local *things*. This seems to have been underscored by the fact that he was usually accompanied by an armed retinue. The *bönder* accepted the obligation to *give* to the sovereign, as well as to perform military services. The ruler exercised some influence on the administration of justice. It was his personality that kept the political organization together. The abstract idea of legitimation of the state occurred only at the initial stage of development. The ruler's influence is seen gradually to have augmented, while the local community's power grew weaker.

In the case of *Tahiti* it was found that the sovereign had the right to make laws and regulations, which were proclaimed by heralds. The necessary control was exercised by special functionaries, and where required, their directives were enforced by the ruler's guard. The sovereign incidentally acted as supreme judge.

The *Voltaic* states showed some sort of a balance between the central government and the village chiefs. The judicial system was more or less centralized: the right of capital punishments was reserved for the sovereign. The court moved often in order to keep control over the village chiefs. An armed following of the ruler had powers to enforce his decisions. The people had to pay taxes and perform military and other services.

In the *Zande* states contacts between the center and the people were indirect: the sovereign's decrees were proclaimed by messengers. The sovereign was supreme judge in important cases; defendants might appeal against the decisions of lower functionaries with the ruler. Corvée labor, military services, and the obligation to pay taxes were found here, too. The ruler had an armed guard at his disposal.

In our view these data amply testify that in the inchoate types of state the sovereign, or the central government, had the necessary power to make and to enforce decisions. The existence of armed retainers, who were used to prevent opposition, is mentioned in every case. The number of cases in which physical force was actually used to compel obedience was limited.

With the possible exception of *Norway*, the sovereign was the apex of the judicial apparatus — though in some cases the ruler's actual activities in this field were limited.

The fact that commoners paid taxes and performed labor and military services in all cases, is clear testimony that the position of the central government was sufficiently strong to compel obedience.

In an evaluation of the above data, the *inchoate* character becomes plainly apparent: the states in question were still at the initial phase of their development. Their administrative apparatus showed certain deficiencies, and had difficulties in fulfilling its various tasks. The people's expectations, based as they were on an ideology of reciprocity — which was evolved during the chiefdom phase — had not yet been brought into line with the actual facts: a greater distance from the ruler, a less balanced form of reciprocity, and heavier taxation (cf. Sahlins 1972: 140–148). The underdevelopment of the governmental apparatus made *ad hoc* decisions inevitable, and the personal presence of the sovereign often essential. Force, and more often the threat of force, sometimes had to supplement persuasion, or to compensate shortcomings in the organization (cf. Service 1975: 295).

The other new trait we suggested was the power to prevent fission. Cohen (Chapter 2, this volume, and 1977) has given much attention to this question. In his opinion it even constituted the sole criterium for distinguishing the early state from the chiefdom. Though we fully agree that this power is of a prime importance, we consider the central government's power to enforce its decisions of equally great importance. To the 'capacity to prevent fission' we would add the words *for a considerable length of time* — at least exceeding the period of ordinary succesion problems. For there were many early states which, after a certain period of time, lost their cohesive force and disintegrated. With this provision in mind, we would suggest that the fact that the cases studied by us *existed* for a certain period of time, and often developed considerably during that time, is in itself proof that they were able to overcome separatist tendencies. For each early state was, in fact, composed of a number of previously structured bodies (villages, chiefdoms, etc.), which could easily survive *without* the overarching structure of the state. However, in the case of *Zande*, Kandert suggests that fission was found.

The prevention of fission has two aspects. The one involves the capacity to keep the parts together by means of force or the threat of force. The other involves the fact that for many people it is more advantageous to belong to a given state than not to belong to one (cf. Service 1975: 299, 301). Both these aspects were observable in our cases, sometimes even concurrently. An example of the latter situation is provided by the state of the *Incas*, where people living in the vicinity of Cuzco were promoted to be 'Incas-by-privilege', and greatly profited by the fact of their belonging to the Inca state, while at the same time numerous other groups were subjugated by the well-organized Inca armies, and were kept within the boundaries of the state only by means of force or the threat of force. The same situation most probably prevailed also in the states of the *Aztecs, Jimma, Kachari, Kuba, Maurya, Mongolia, Scythia, Volta, Yoruba-Oyo* and *Zande*, where groups of subjugated people were joined to the original population core.

The further survival of the early states does not seem to have depended primarily upon the exertion of physical force or military organization. Rather such factors as *legitimation* on the basis of consensus and the pursuit of a *balance of power policy* seem to have been decisive. This was manifest not only from the maintenance of inequality or the upholding of regulations and laws, but also from the cohesion of the different parts of the state.

4. THE END OF THE EARLY STATE

The structure of the early state appeared to have been based principally upon the concepts of reciprocity and genealogical distance from the sovereign. The more the early state developed, however, the weaker the role of these ideological components grew. The managerial and redistributive aspects became more and more dominant. The efficient governmental apparatus that developed after some time was quite capable of maintaining the state organization without the necessity of recourse to the ruler's supernatural powers, or perpetuating reciprocal obligations. We shall therefore consider the period of the early state as having terminated as soon as the ideological foundation of the state no longer is based upon *these* concepts. In several of our transitional types of early state the gradual disappearance of the old concepts is demonstrable, though many traces of them still remained.

In the state of the *Aztecs*, sacral legitimation was gradually replaced by 'legalistic' legitimation, whereby the sovereign shed most of his sacral obligations, and reciprocity became only a formality. Here the bureaucratic organization which had evolved captured a place of its own, and all interests and activities became state-centered.

This development is to be seen also in *China*. At a particular stage legalistic traits became noticeable, and personal and private ownership began to play a role. The sovereign's function changed in the direction of general managership, and such traits as genealogical distance and reciprocity remained important only in theory.

The case of *France* also illustrates the beginning of the end of the early state. Shortly after the period discussed in the present volume the position of the sovereign definitely changed from a ritually to a legally based one (cf. for this development: Teunis 1973).

In *Jimma* the transitional stage was reached very quickly. The sovereign based his position upon power. Genealogical distance almost never played a role. From the beginning, legalistic legitimation stood central, and personal ownership of the means of production was already developed to a high degree. There was virtually no sacral basis to sovereignty.

The same holds for *Kuba,* where in the period described by Vansina ritual aspects were very limited in scope, but trade and markets dominated the daily life, and complicated balances of power provided a legal basis for the state system. The degree of relationship to the sovereign was of limited importance, and personal ownership of land was prominent.

Maurya presents a similar picture. Here a complex governmental apparatus, a balance of power policy, a well-developed judicial system, efforts to create new ideological cohesive forces, the full development of personal ownership of land, and a search for new legal concepts are the signs of the approaching end of the early state. However, here the sovereign continued to exert a strong personal influence till the end, and the early state of *Maurya* only collapsed when the last sovereigns were no longer able to meet the many demands made on them.

The association of the early state with the concepts of reciprocity and genealogical distance enables us to indicate the end of the early state. Thus, the solution to Khazanov's question of how to demarcate the end may be provided. When the basic ideological concepts become empty of meaning, then the end is near. An efficient governmental apparatus will be able for some time to conceal this, but the need for new concepts, new rationalizations, or a new myth of the society nevertheless becomes apparent. An important point to note in this respect is the state hierarchy's increasing orientation towards property. Land as the basic means of production becomes an object of private ownership and the state organization becomes an instrument in the hands of the members of that social class which is defined by its monopolistic control of the means of production. The mature state thus supplants the early state. Reorganization will then enable the new ideological foundations to become explicit, as happened in *France,* where the early type of state was transformed into a legalistic one; or it will be no longer possible to prevent fission, as was the case in *China* and *Egypt,* where a period of chaos and anarchy separated the end of the early state from the beginning of a new type. Other early states never attained a subsequent stage, because they were destroyed or subjected by others — a fate which befell the *Aztecs* as well as the *Incas.* The development of other early states, such as *Kuba, Tahiti* and *Zande,* to mention but a few, was interrupted by colonialism.

REFERENCES

Bakel, M. A. van (1976), *Bevolkingsdruk en culturele evolutie* [Population pressure and cultural evolution]. Ms., Leiden.

Carneiro, Robert L. (1970a), A theory of the origin of the state, in: *Science:* 169: 733–738.

—— (1970b), 'Scale analysis, evolutionary sequences, and the rating of cultures', in: *A handbook of method in cultural anthropology*, ed. by R. Naroll and Ronald Cohen, pp. 834–871. New York: Natural History Press.

Claessen, H. J. M. (1970), *Van vorsten en volken* [Of princes and peoples]. Amsterdam: Joko.

Cohen, Ronald (1974), The evolution of hierarchical institutions: a case study from Biu, Nigeria, *Savanna* 3: 153–174.

—— (1977), 'State foundations: a controlled comparison'. in: *Origin of the state: a symposium*, ed. by Ronald Cohen and Elman R. Service. Philadelphia: ISHI.

Corning, Peter A. (1975), 'An evolutionary paradigm for the study of human aggression', in: *War, its causes and correlates*, ed. by Martin A. Nettleship, R. D. Givens and A. Nettleship, pp. 359–387. The Hague: Mouton.

Fried, Morton H. (1967), *The evolution of political society*. New York: Random House.

Goldman, Irving (1970), *Ancient Polynesian society*. Chicago: Chicago University Press.

Harris, Marvin (1968), *The rise of anthropological theory*. London: Routledge and Kegan Paul.

Khazanov, Anatolii M. (1975), *Sotsial'naia istoriia skifov. Osnovnye problemy razvitiia drevnikh kochnevnikov evraziiskikh stepei* [Social history of the Scythians. Main problems of the development of ancient nomads of the Eurasian steppes]. Moscow: Nauka.

Kottak, C. P. (1972), Ecological variables in the origin and evolution of African states. *Comparative studies in society and history* 14: 351–380.

Lewis, Herbert S. (1966), The origins of African kingdoms, *Cahiers d'études africaines* 6: 402–407.

Nettleship, Martin A. (1975), 'Definitions', in: *War, its causes and correlates*, ed. by M. A. Nettleship, R. D. Givens and A. Nettleship, pp. 73–93. The Hague: Mouton.

Polgar, S. (1975), 'Population, evolution and theoretical paradigms,' in: *Population, ecology and social evolution*, ed. by S. Polgar, pp. 1–25. The Hague: Mouton.

Sahlins, Marshall D. (1958), *Social stratification in Polynesia*. Seattle: University of Washington Press.

—— (1972), *Stone age economics*. Chicago: Aldine.

Service, Elman R. (1971), *Primitive social organization*. 2nd ed. New York: Random House.

—— (1975), *Origins of the state and civilization*. New York: Norton.

Smith, M. Estellie (f.c.), *Questions of urban analysis*. In press.

Teunis, H. B. (1973), *Crisis. Studie over een structur en normverandering in het Frankrijk van ±1150–±1250* [Crisis. A study of changes of structure and norms in France from ca. 1150–1250]. Groningen: Tjeenk Willink.

Webster, David (1975), Warfare and the evolution of the state: a reconsideration, in: *American Antiquity* 40: 464–470.

White, Leslie A. (1949), *The science of culture*. New York: Grove Press.

Wolf, Eric (1966), *Peasants*. Englewood Cliffs: Prentice Hall.

Wright, Henry T. and Johnson, Gregory (1975), Population, exchange and early state formation in southwestern Iran, *American Anthropologist* 77: 267–289.

28 The Early State: Models and Reality

HENRI J. M. CLAESSEN and PETER SKALNÍK

1. CONCLUSIONS

In this volume we have brought together twenty-one case studies of early states with the aim of finding the answers to a number of questions formulated in chapter 1. Towards this end, Claessen, in chapter 25, first made a careful analysis of the structure of the early state. With the aid of the results of numerous comparisons, grouped together in twenty *tables*, he was able to distinguish no less than fifty-one *structural characteristics*, all of them significant at the 99% level. Together these will form a kind of structural model of the early state.

1.1. *The Structural Model*

The early state is an independent socio-political organization with a bounded territory and a center of government. Its economy is characterized by agriculture (and in some cases by pastoralism or a mixed economy), supplemented by trade and a market system, and the presence of full-time specialists. The surplus produced in agriculture, together with the taxes levied on trade and markets form an important source of income for the government, represented by full-time functionaries exempted from material production.

The population is divided into at least two strata: an upper stratum comprising the sovereign, his relatives and the aristocracy, and a lower stratum including, among others smallholders and tenants living in small communities.

The actual production of food is limited within only certain social groups, and the access to material resources is unequal. The upper stratum generally has tribute as its main source of income. Tax, however, is paid by all social categories, though varying from one category to another in quantity and quality.

The position of the sovereign is based upon a mythical charter and a genealogy which connects him with the supernatural forces. He is also considered as a benevolent figure, namely as a source of gifts, remunerations, and offerings. He is surrounded by a court as well as a bodyguard.

The aristocracy comprises members of the sovereign's family, clan or lineage heads, and the incumbents of high offices. Private ownership of land is a rare phenomenon, and does not seem to be of importance for the attainment of high social status in the early state.

The ideology of the early state appears to be based upon the concept of reciprocity: all categories of subjects provide the sovereign with goods and services (tribute and tax), while the sovereign for his part is responsible for his subjects' protection, law and order, and the bestowal of benevolence. The priesthood supports the state ideology.

Social inequality seems to be based first and foremost upon birth, with relative distance from the ruler's lineage constituting the dividing principle. No direct kinship relations exist between the sovereign and the common people.

For the government of the early state a system of delegation of tasks and powers is evolved. There are numerous functionaries fulfilling tasks in the governmental apparatus. 'General functionaries' are found especially on the regional and local levels, while 'specialists' are found rather more on the national level. Though, ideally, only the sovereign has the right to issue laws and decrees, many other people exercise a formal or informal influence upon affairs and developments.

In addition to the structural analysis, Skalník prepared a partial synthesis of the functioning of the early state (chapter 26). This chapter, in which the early state was approached from a different angle altogether, gave a representation of the early state as reflective of a process, a complex of changing relations with certain developmental dynamics inherent in it. The seven *functional principles* distilled in this chapter can be summarized as follows:

1.2. *The Functional Model*

The organization of the early state reveals a tendency to function syncretically, implying that most of its functionaries fulfil more than one task. These 'generalists' dominate the state appparatus. Most state activities appear to be multi-purpose.

Though the underlying principle of the early state is reciprocity, this reciprocity does *not* appear to be balanced: the flow of goods and labor is reciprocated mostly on the ideological level, and, in reality, a form of redistributive exploitation prevails.

The government is oriented towards centralization and the establishment of centralized power, which is frequently characterized by the pursuit of a 'balance of power' policy and competition for important offices. The centripetal forces are seen to prevail over the tendencies towards fission and separation. The central government's influence is decisive in all spheres of life. Moreover, the government devotes much of its attention to its own legitimation. Many of its activities are directed towards this object, as well as to ethnic, professional and cultural integration and the development of a state ideology.

The sacral character of the ruler's position is the most important constituent of his leadership. He is considered as the guarantor of the state's prosperity. As a result he is the very pivot of the early state.

Connected with this, there is a tendency on the part of the emergent class of rulers or the ruling stratum to live more or less apart from the other citizens of the state. They are the only group who seem to take an interest in the state as such. For the commoners the state is far too remote to have much significance beyond the occasional call for tribute.

To provide for the survival of the early state, pre-state patterns will have to be either suppressed or converted into institutions of the early state.

The early state is thus illustrative of a continuous social process in its regulation of the relations between the emergent social classes of the rulers and the ruled.

1.3. *Answers to the Questions of Chapter 1*

(1) *The seven characteristics* of the early state defined by us there were discussed at length in chapter 25. Here we will restrict ourselves to giving only a brief summary of the results of that discussion.

(a) The characteristic of the presence of a number of people we discarded as being too vague.

(b) The characteristic of citizenship of the early state being determined by birth or permanent residence in its territory was confirmed.

(c) That of the government being centralized and possessing the power to maintain law and order by means of authority as well as force, or the threat of force, was corroborated also.

(d) The characteristic of the early state being independent — at least *de facto* — its government having sufficient power to prevent fission and to defend itself against external aggression also proved to be generally relevant, although the effects of defence sometimes appeared to be quite limited.

(e) The formulation of the characteristic of the population as displaying a complex social stratification, which can be simplified into a basic division into a level of rulers and of ruled, which two levels can be regarded as emergent social classes, with the dividing principle appearing in the majority of cases to be the relative distance from the ruler's lineage was slightly modified and supplemented here.

(f) The characteristic of the production of a regular surplus, which is used for the maintenance of the state organization was proved to be correct.

(g) Although the characteristic of the presence of a common ideology, which is used to legitimize the social structure, and whose basic concept is the principle of reciprocity between the ruler in the center and his subjects living for the greater part in agrarian communities, and also between the ruler and the other members of the upper stratum, was found to be correct in principle, it has been slightly elaborated and reformulated here.

(2) *The definition of the early state.* With an eye to the structural and functional models developed above, we feel justified in saying that the preliminary definition of the early state which we proposed in the first chapter seems to be correct in principle. However, some elaboration is necessary. We would therefore reformulate our definition as follows:

> The early state is a centralized socio-political organization for the regulation of social relations in a complex, stratified society divided into at least two basic strata, or emergent social classes — viz. the rulers and the ruled — , whose relations are characterized by political dominance of the former and tributary obligations of the latter, legitimized by a common ideology of which reciprocity is the basic principle.

(3) *The three types of early state.* In chapters 25 and 26 we tested the feasibility of the suggested division of the early state into the three types of the inchoate, the typical and the transitional early state. We found this division to be relevant, but also discovered that some of the criteria we wished to use for the division were too vague. So we discarded these and evolved some additional criteria for the division of our states into the said types. Eventually the following criteria were used:
— the degree of development of trade and markets;
— the mode of succession to important functions;
— the occurrence of private ownership of land;

— the method of remuneration of functionaries;
— the degree of development of the judicial system;
— the degree of development of the taxation system.

An early state was considered to be *inchoate* if:

trade and markets were of only limited (local) importance;

succession to high office, for 'general' as well as for 'specialist' functionaries was predominantly hereditary;

private ownership of land (or livestock) was found, but only exceptionally so, while communal ownership or possession was dominant;

functionaries only received remunerations (often in kind);

the judicial system did not have codification of laws and punishments, and there were no special formal judges;

taxes consisted for the greater part of voluntary tributary gifts and occasional labor for the state, neither of which were either very regular or accurately defined.

An early state was judged to be *typical* if:

trade and markets were developed at the supra-local level;

heredity as a principle of succession was balanced by appointment;

private ownership of land was still very limited, while state ownership was gradually becoming important;

salaried functionaries were found in it besides remunerated functionaries, or one and the same functionary was receiving a salary as well as remunerations;

a start towards codification of laws and punishments was found;

formal judges were present, besides 'general' functionaries;

regular tribute, partly in kind and partly in services, was exacted, and major works, organized by government functionaries, were being undertaken with the aid of compulsory labor.

An early state was judged to be *transitional* where:

trade and markets were of great importance;

appointment of functionaries was dominant;

private ownership of land was becoming of increased importance for the aristocracy as well as for the common people;

salaried functionaries were in the majority, and the governmental apparatus was gradually becoming a relatively independent political force;

the codification of laws and punishments was completed, and the administration of justice was for the greater part in the hands of formal judges;

taxation had developed into a well-defined system, with a complex apparatus to ensure its regular flow.

By applying these criteria, we divided our twenty-one cases as follows:

Inchoate: *Ankole, Hawaii, (Old) Norway, Tahiti, Volta, Zande;*

Typical: *Angkor, Axum, Egypt, Iberia, Incas, Kachari, Mongolia, Scythia, Yoruba;*
Transitional: *Aztecs, China, France, Jimma, Kuba, Maurya.*

(4) *The road to statehood.* We were unable in chapter 27 to define a general road to statehood. It did appear to be possible, however, to indicate a number of factors that had a relatively direct formative influence. These were:
(A) Population growth and/or population pressure;
(B) War, the threat of war or conquest, and raids;
(C) Conquest;
(D) The influence of previously existing states.
The actual historical sequence of these factors seemed to be of minor importance. It furthermore appeared that, in most cases, all of these influences were at work. Regardless which of these factors actually triggered off the development, the ultimate result was always very much the same, namely, the early state. The above four factors promoting the rise of the early state do not replace the essential conditions of a producing economy with a surplus and the consequent conditions of social inequality and the beginning of social stratification, without which the early state would be inconceivable.

Finally, we will try to formulate the answers to the specific questions put forward in the section on theories in chapter 1.
(1) *The existence of social classes and their role in the formation of the early state.* Our findings in this respect may be summarized as follows:
Social inequality, as evident from differential access to material resources and the existence of certain vague obligations to pay tribute in kind and services, existed long before the early state came into being. During the phase of the early state this social inequality came to be greatly elaborated and formalized. Though the obligation to pay taxes fell especially upon the common people, we discovered the upper-stratum categories to have an obligation to perform certain services as well, while the obligation to pay taxes in one form or another in the majority of cases was also binding on them (chapter 25: S. C. 16, and Table VII). When using the concept of class, we do so in the sense of class *an sich* and not *für sich;* in other words, we are speaking of *emergent* social classes, where class consciousness is not yet developed.

The maintenance of inequality was not found to be either an overt or a covert objective of the early state. Nor was social inequality found to be the sole prerequisite for the development of a state organization. The early state arose when other conditions were also present (see above, note 4). A state organization emerged only as a result of the concurrence of some of these conditions.

The rigidity of an elaborated system of inequality in the transitional type of early state is partly offset by the growing tendency to appoint functionaries, and by increased social mobility (chapter 25: Table XX).

(2) *The Asiatic mode of production.* The concept of the Asiatic mode of production (A.M.P.) as developed by Marx, and more especially by Krader (Krader 1972, 1975) was discussed by us in chapter 1. We took this mode of production to be characterized by a basic dichotomy between the state organization, invested with the political, economic and ideological power, on the one hand, and the agricultural or pastoral (village) communities, encompassed by a single overarching state system, on the other. However, the obligation to pay taxes and render services aside, the villagers were free to live their own lives. Where this mode of production prevailed, private ownership of land was practically non-existent. The imposition of taxes on the common people was based for the greater part on their allegiance to the sacral ruler, and justified by vestiges of reciprocity.

This mode of production seems to be generally found in the socio-political context of the early state, especially in the inchoate and typical early state. Only the transitional phase in the development of the early state displays certain traits superseding the characteristics of the A.M.P. and pointing towards the development of the mature class society; such as, for example, the feudal type of society. This is observable in the development of such early states as *France, Norway* in a later phase, and the private-property-based state of *Jimma*, and to a lesser degree in *China, Kuba* and *Maurya*. In addition the state of the *Aztecs* seems partly to have exceeded the limits of the A.M.P. (cf. chapter 25: Table XX).

These conclusions must be regarded as being strictly preliminary. It would seem to us that the use of the concept of the early state in a further analysis of the entire politico-economic setting of societies in which the A.M.P. is found, especially from the perspective of the producing communities, may yield interesting results. Only then will it be possible to provide more complete answers concerning the character of this mode of production. In the present volume only one aspect, namely, that of the organization of the state, has been dealt with.

(3) *The role of conquest (in the sense of Oppenheimer) in the formation of the early state*, according to our data, was limited. Only in the case of *Mongolia* and *Scythia*, and to some extent the *Voltaic* states and *Zande*, was the formation of the early state directly influenced by this factor (cf. also Cohen, this volume, and 1974, 1977; Lewis 1966).

(4) According to our findings, *the contacts between early states and their neighbors* were often dominated by *war*, raids, or attempts at conquest. War and its correlates had a positive influence upon the development of managerial and governmental institutions in all cases.

(5) The general effect of *population growth and/or pressure* was found to be that it exercised a direct influence on the development of more complex political organizations (provided there was no opportunity for migration). The drop in population *before* the emergence of the state, as demonstrated by Wright and Johnson, does not, in our view, affect this general conclusion. We looked for an explanation for this phenomenon in the increasing tension between the rising needs of a growing population and the limitations of the area. This could cause a temporary decline, which would be made up soon after the development of new social structures.

(6) Though *trade and commerce* were found to exist in all early states (chapter 25: S.C. 4, 5, 6), their influence appeared to be of importance only in the typical and transitional early state. We will therefore not include trade and commerce among the formative factors.

(7) The solution of *major internal conflicts* in early states was usually tackled with the help of the state judicial apparatus (chapter 25: S.C. 25, 26, 27). If necessary, its decisions might be backed by force (chapter 25: S.C. 28, 29).

(8) *Urbanization* was not found to play a decisive role in the formation of the early state. Several early states came into being without towns or cities being present at all; in others the role of urban centers came to be of importance only long after the emergence of the state (cf. Service 1975: xii).

In chapter 1 we divided the many theories on the origin and development of the state into two main categories, viz.
— theories based upon the idea that social inequality was the prime mover toward statehood;
— theories based upon the idea that the conclusion of some sort of social contract led to the formation of early states.
We have come to the conclusion since that the actual 'prime movers' — as far as these can be isolated at all — fall more or less outside the scope of this division. Population pressure, the threat of war, etc., cannot easily be fitted into one of these categories. On the other hand, we discovered that the development of the early state correlated with a considerable elaboration of social inequality, leading to a division of the society in question into at least two social categories (emergent social classes, superstrata), which division was at the same time concealed behind the notions of a 'social contract' ideology of which the idea of reciprocity was the key feature. The effort to overcome the problems posed by the growing cleavage of society resulted, under specific circumstances, in the development of the socio-political organization of the early state.

Each specific state emerged under a set of specific conditions, which is why the various early states differ so widely one from the other. We nevertheless believe it possible to distinguish the early state as a distinct basic category in the social evolution of mankind.

2. SOME COMMENTS ON THE THEORETICAL CHAPTERS (2, 3 AND 4)

After setting out our conclusions about the early state, we believe we are in a position to give some comments on a number of matters raised in the theoretical chapters by Cohen, Khazanov and Krader in Part One of this volume. We have no intention of discussing every aspect and every hypothesis put forward there. We will make comments only where our findings give us occasion to do so.

Cohen, in his chapter, advances quite a number of problems, hypotheses and questions, and we believe we can state at the outset that in the majority of cases our findings corroborated his views, or at least pointed in the same direction. We will follow here the main drift of his argumentation, condensed to a number of points, indicating each time our own findings in that respect.

Cohen, sees as one general characteristic of the state the capacity to prevent fission. We also found this to be so, in fact (chapter 25, Section 2.13.1, chapter 26, Section 2.4, chapter 27, Section 3).

The factor of 'personal acquisition' did not appear to be as general a characteristic as Cohen imagined. In several of our cases population pressure was mentioned, which seems to make personal acquisition rather superfluous (cf. chapter 25, Section 2.3).

Long-distance trade was mentioned by Cohen as both a cause and an effect of state formation. To our mind our findings are not incompatible with this view (cf. chapter 25: S.C. 4, 5, 6 and 7) though we are disinclined to attach too much importance to this factor as exercising a formative influence (cf. our discussion in chapter 27, Section 2).

The role of war in the formation of the early state suggested by Cohen appeared to correspond to what we found to be the case: it was both a cause and a result (cf. chapter 27, Section 2).

As regards the concept of property (or ownership) there is perhaps some discrepancy between Cohen's views and ours. This depends upon the definition of 'property'. We did not find private ownership of land as the basic means of production to be a general characteristic of early states. In the majority of cases land was owned, or possessed by communities of various types (cf. chapter 25: Tables IV and VI), the individual having, in fact, only rights of tenure or temporary occupancy. The upper stratum was generally seen to have certain rights to tribute or taxes, though these rights sprang but seldom from *ownership* of land. In most cases they were a consequence of specific *extra-economic* relations (chapter 25: S.C. 17, 18, 19, 20), in which especially the ideologically-based concept of reciprocity seemed to play a central role (cf. chapter 25, Section 2.10.5, and chapter 26, Section 2). In the course of the development of the early state from the inchoate to the transitional type, private ownership of the means of production appeared to increase.

Cohen's view that there are many roads to statehood, and that the formation of the early state represents, in fact, a systemic process, finds ample corroboration in the results of our analysis of the factors leading to the development of the early state (chapter 27 Section 2).

In addition, his view that the early state is not based upon (overt) class conflict, or sheer exploitation, finds some corroboration in our data. We tend to think, however, that actually this is in conformity rather with the pattern of social relations in the inchoate type of early state than with that in the transitional ones. The early state ends, in fact, when i.a. the ideology of reciprocity is replaced by a non-reciprocal system and an ideology reflecting class antagonism. However, this also is most probably a gradual process (cf. chapter 26).

Cohen's conclusion that the state religion provides sanctions for the legitimacy of the ruler, his duties to the people and theirs to him, and for his capacity to control and intercede with the supernatural forces for their benefit is fully corroborated by our findings (chapter 25, Section 2.10.5; chapter 26).

The data of our case studies did not enable us to collect much information on the subject of citizenship. That a state may have a multi-ethnic population appeared to be a correct, but not universally valid contention. Cohen's division of the population of the early state into two strata, namely the rulers and the ruled, is fully supported by our data.

Finally, Cohen's definition of the early state at the end of his chapter has, in our opinion, one weak point: although it draws a clear borderline between the early state and the chiefdom, it does not do so between the early state and other types of state, more especially the mature state.

This brings us to the theoretical chapter by *Khazanov*. In this case as well we can state at the outset that we are basically in agreement with him on most of the points he raises. As we did with respect to Cohen's chapter, we will limit our discussion mainly to those points on which our findings gave us occasion to make comments.

Khazanov opens his chapter with the question of when an early state ceases to be *early*. He proposes the answer: when it discards its primitive inheritance. He suggests that this takes place with the gradual strengthening of governmental structures, the stabilization of the social organization, and the development of new types of dependence. Our findings, as presented in chapter 27, seem to confirm this view. However, the above changes are, in fact, only quantitative, while the transition from the early to the mature state is a qualitative change. In our opinion this will only occur where there are changes in the ideological base (cf. our above comment on Cohen). As soon as a different ideology is evolved another phase of statehood is definitely reached. Signs of a changing ideology — under the strong influence of a growing trend towards private ownership of the basic means of production and the introduction of a form of money economy — are already discernible in the transitional type of early state. The concept of reciprocity grows gradually devoid of meaning here (cf. chapter 27).

Khazanov's views on the level of economic and technological development of the early state find ample corroboration in our data (cf. chapter 25: S.C. 8, 9, 10, and our comments in chapter 25, Section 2.8). His idea that this level must have imposed limits on further development, however, calls for further research (cf. Goody 1971).

As far as the problems of the origin of the state are concerned (chapter 3, Section 4) we once more find ourselves in agreement with his careful formulations of these. Contrary to him, however, we are not inclined to believe that military leaders in general formed a separate, influential group (cf. chapter 25: Tables IV, X, XV and XVI; chapter 26). In several cases military matters were the responsibility of a particular notable who was either a specialist or a general functionary, and in many cases military duties constituted an inseparable component of kingship (cf. also Khazanov's view in chapter 3, Section 8). A better case in this respect can be put forward as regards priests, who were more often found to form a separate group (chapter 25: Table IV), and whose influence on the political life was acknowledged everywhere (cf. chapter 25: Table XIII, and S.C. 39, 50; chapter 26).

That many institutions of the early state were already to be found in one form or another in the pre-state phase (chapter 3, Sections 4, 5), and that the early state developed only gradually, is in complete agreement with our views (chapter 27, Section 1). We also found confirmation for Khazanov's view that these were gradually modified and adapted to the new situation (cf. chapter 26). In point of fact, though we may speak here of stages, phases and levels, historic reality always shows only a process, so that each demarcation used by the researcher has something artificial or arbitrary about it.

There seems to be some difference between Khazanov's and our interpretation of the Asiatic mode of production. We deliberately excluded the production relations that were typical of the classical

(slave) and mediaeval feudal (serf) forms of society from our characterization of the early state. If the early state should be seen as a
distinct type of political organization, then we do not think it possible
that a mixture of all possible kinds of relation of dependence and
exploitation was found here. On the contrary, as the analyses of the
case studies show, a distinct form of tributary relations was predominant in the early state, this form of dependence existing between the
state hierarchy (or the emergent class of rulers) and the communities of
primary producers (or emergent class of ruled). Precisely the same kind
of social situation characterizes the societies in which the A.M.P. is
found (cf. Krader 1972, 1975) — so that in this way the early state is
the political organization of this type of society. It is not its predececes-
sor, as Khazanov seems to think, but may, in some cases, be rather its
successor. Especially the transitional types of early state no longer
constitute the forms of political organization that are characteristic of
societies of the A.M.P. They are on the threshold of societies marked
by the mediaeval or classical mode of production.

Khazanov's remarks on the despotic character of the sovereign in
the early state are most interesting. Some sovereigns are described as
being, and others as definitely not being despotic. The results of our
analysis of the *structure* of the governmental apparatus of the early
state show that here several kinds of curb on the ruler's power, in the
form of councils, ministers, priests, courtiers, and many other institutionalized groups of persons exercising a formal or informal influence upon decision-making, had been evolved. On the other hand,
however, the analysis of the *functioning* of the early state showed that
the actual amount of power concentrated in the sovereign's person was
enormous. This implies that there were two opposing tendencies,
namely the tendency to acquire vast power, and the tendency to create
institutions to check its abuse. We believe that the individual
personalities of the rulers and the nature of their surroundings played a
decisive role here. If the sovereign was able to keep his functionaries in
check by pursuing some kind of balance of power policy (*divide et
impera!*), he was able to rule despotically. If he himself was counter-
checked by his functionaries, however, his rule could only be mild. We
are only putting this explanation forward by way of hypothesis, since
we did not analyse this particular problem especially.

That 'civilization', as defined by Khazanov, is a different and, in
fact, much broader concept than that of the early state seems to be a
correct claim. The word refers to the overall level of development of a
given society. If we adopt Khazanov's definition, then several of our
cases must be said not to have attained the level of civilization (cf.
chapter 25, Sections 2.4 and 2.5. Cf. also Service 1975, whose views
are comparable with Khazanov's). If we adopt Marx' definition of

civilization — or secondary social formation —, however, then the early state will be seen to be a typical form of political organization of the initial stage of civilization. Clearly this problem deserves further investigation.

That the construction of typologies solely for their own sake is a senseless activity (anthropological 'butterfly collecting', to use Leach's phrase, 1961) is an idea we heartily endorse. The typology we have evolved above (of the inchoate, typical and transitional early state) has already proved its use for the analysis of the phenomenon of the early state, however. We therefore trust that, even in Khazanov's eyes, the construction of at least this particular typology will not have been a senseless undertaking.

Krader's brief theoretical introduction to his exposition on the state in a nomadic kind of society was written at a time when his major work of 1975 was already due to be published. We do not disagree with Krader's basic statements on the nature of the state. We realize that his attempt to present a general picture of the state made it difficult for him to appreciate the unique character of the early state, even though his own research activities have always been focused on the latter. That is why he omits to mention that relations of real or fictive reciprocity may have been dominant at specific periods, and that tributary relations are characteristic of such (early) periods. We do agree with him that the society of the early state is divided into the two categories of rulers and ruled, but in addition assume that this *emergent* class division is characteristic only of the early state and the society of the Asiatic mode of production. The mature state as well as societies with more developed modes of production possess a different structure.

The data of the case studies support Krader's assessment of the role of the community in the early state. The data also support his view that the state

> is formed as the society is divided and internally opposed. It is not formed by the ruling class, for that class has to be established in the first place by the process of social division in order to fulfil its ruling function. It would be an error to take the interest of the ruling class to be the process of formation of the state itself. (this volume, p. 94).

Our data justify Krader's emphasis on the dual concern of the state agencies, namely, to promote the interests of the rulers on the one hand, and those of the society as a whole on the other.

As Krader explicity states, the existence of a state implies the presence of social mechanisms for bridging the gap between the social classes. In the early state this gap is overcome by means of the same reciprocal relations on which legitimation is based, and more especially their ideological aspects (chapter 25: 10.5).

The differences between the concept of the early state as presented in the Synthesis of this volume and that emerging from Krader's statement's on the theory of the state will appear in a different light as soon as one becomes aware of: (1) the stress Krader placed on rigorousness and universality in his brief description in chapter 4; and (2) the way he handles the reality of the early state among the nomads, especially the *Mongols*.

In broad generalization, the theoretical premises of Cohen, Khazanov and Krader appeared to be in agreement with our findings in Part III of this volume. They also formed a most useful supplement to chapter 1, in which the editor's theses and hypotheses relating to the theory of the early state were set forth. The data of the case studies, forming the Antithesis, partly corroborated them, though in several respects they gave cause for important reformulations. This was, of course, the aim of the entire undertaking, which set out to refine the existing theoretical tools through confrontation with generalized data on actual early states.

REFERENCES

Cohen, Ronald (1974), The evolution of hierarchical institutions: a case study from Biu, Nigeria. *Savanna* 3: 153–174.
— (1977), 'State foundations, a controlled comparison', in: *Origin of the state: a symposium*, ed. by Ronald Cohen and Elman R. Service. Philadelphia: ISHI.
Goody, Jack (1971), *Technology, tradition and the state in Africa*. London: Oxford University Press.
Krader, Lawrence (1972), *The ethnological notebooks of Karl Marx*. Assen: Van Gorcum.
— (1975), *The Asiatic mode of production*. Assen: Van Gorcum.
Leach, E. (1961), *Rethinking anthropology*. London: Athlone Press.
Lewis, Herbert S. (1966), 'The origins of African kingdoms', *Cahiers d'études africaines* 6: 402–407.
Service, Elman R. (1975), *Origins of the state and civilization*. New York: Norton.

Biographical Notes

CLAESSEN, HENRI J. M. (1930). Ph.D (University of Amsterdam). Associate Professor of Cultural Anthropology, University of Leiden, The Netherlands.

1970   *Van vorsten en volken* [Of princes and peoples] Amsterdam: Joko.

1973   Despotism and irrigation. *Bijdragen tot de Taal-, Land- en Volkenkunde* 129: 70–85.

1974   *Politieke antropologie* [Introduction to political anthropology]. Assen: Van Gorcum.

1975   From rags to riches—and the reverse, in: *Rule and reality*, ed. by Peter Kloos and Klaas van der Veen, pp. 29–49. University of Amsterdam Press.

1978   Co-editor of *Political anthropology and the state of the art*. The Hague: Mouton.

COHEN, RONALD (1930). Professor of Anthropology and Political Science at Northwestern University, Evanston, Illinois, U.S.A. Published numerous articles and books. Main Publications:

1967   *The Kanuri of Bornu*. New York: Holt, Rinehart and Winston.

1969   *Modernization in Africa*. M. J. Herskovits Memorial Lecture.

1971   *Dominance and defiance: marital stability among the Kanuri*. Washington D.C.: American Anthropological Assocation.

1967   in collaboration with J. Middleton: *Comparative political systems*. New York: Natural History Press.

1970   in collaboration with Raoul Naroll: *A Handbook of method in cultural anthropology*. New York: Natural History Press.

1973   'Political anthropology', in: *Handbook of social and cultural anthropology*, ed. by J. J. Honigman. Chicago: Rand McNally.

GUREVICH, ARON. IA. Doctor of Sciences. Professor and top research fellow in the Institute of World History of the U.S.S.R. Academy of Sciences. Moscow, U.S.S.R. Main publications:

1967   *Svobodnoe krestianstvo feodal'noi Norvegii* [The free peasantry of feudal Norway]. Moscow: Nauka.

1970   *Problemy genezisa feodalizma v Zapadnoi Ievrope* [Problems of the genesis of feudalism in Western Europe]. Moscow: Nauka.

1972   *Kategorii srednevekovoi kul'tury* [Categories of mediaeval culture]. Moscow: Nauka.

JANSSEN, JACOBUS J. (1922). Associate Professor of Egyptology in the University of Leiden, The Netherlands. Main publications:

1961   *Two ancient Egyptian ship's logs.* Leiden: Brill.

1975   *Commodity prices from the Ramessid period.* Leiden: Brill.

1975   Prolegomena to the study of Egypt's economic history during the new Kingdom, *Studien zur altägyptischen Kultur* 3.

KANDERT, JOSEF (1943). Ph.D. and Candidate of Science (Charles University, Prague, Czechoslovakia). Curator and head of the Ethnographic Department of the Náprstek Museum, Prague. Main publications:

1968   'Social stratification of the Zande', in: *Social stratification in tribal Africa,* ed. by L. Holý and M. Stuchlík. Prague: Academia.

1974   *Folk pottery of Nigeria.* Annals of the Náprstek Museum 7.

KHAZANOV, ANATOLII M. (1937). Doctor of Sciences. Senior research fellow in the Institute of Ethnography of the U.S.S.R. Academy of Sciences, Moscow, U.S.S.R. Main publications:

1971   *Ocherki voennogo dela sarmatov* [Essays on the history of Sarmatian warfare]. Moscow: Nauka.

1972   'Les grandes lignes de la formation des classes dans la société primitive', in: *Problèmes théoriques de l'ethnographie.* Moscow: Academy of Sciences.

1974   'Military democracy and the epoch of class formation', in: *Soviet ethnology and anthropology today,* ed. by Yu. Bromley. The Hague: Mouton.

1975   *Sotsial'naia istoria Skifov. Osnovnye problemy razvitia drevnikh kochevnikov evraziiskikh stepei.* [Social history of the Scythians. Main problems of development among ancient pastoral nomads in the Eurasian Steppes]. Moscow: Nauka.

KOBISHCHANOV, YURI M. Candidate of Sciences. Senior research fellow in the Africa Institute of the U.S.S.R. Academy of Sciences, Moscow, U.S.S.R. Main publications:

1966 *Aksum.* Moscow: Nauka.

1974 Afrikanskie feodal'nye obschestva [African feudal societies], in: *Afrika: vozniknovenie otstalosti i puti razvitiia.* Moscow: Nauka.

1976 'Die Dorfgemeinde in Afrika', in: *Afrika, gegenwärtige soziale Prozesse und Strukturen,* ed. by K. Ernst und L. D. Jablochkov. Berlin: Akademie Verlag.

KOCHAKOVA, NATALIA B. Candidate of Sciences. Research fellow in the Africa Institute of the Academy of Sciences, Moscow, U.S.S.R. Main publications:

1968 *Goroda-gosudarstva iorubov* [City states of the Yoruba]. Moscow: Nauka.

1974 'Dokolonialnaia epokha' [pre-colonial epoch] and 'Sotsialnaia struktura' [Social structure], in: *Sovremennaia Nigeria.* Moscow: Nauka.

1976 'Die Rätsel des heiligen Ife', in: *Afrikas Vergangenheit.* Leipzig: Brockhaus.

KORANASHVILI, GURAM (1940). Candidate of Sciences. Senior research fellow in the Institute of History, Archaeology and Ethnography of the Academy of Sciences of Georgia, Tbilisi, U.S.S.R. Main publications:

1975 *The role of the geographical environment in the development of society* (in Georgian). Tbilisi: Ganatleba.

1976 *The problem of pre-capitalistic socio-economic formations in historical materialism.* Tbilisi: Tbilisi University Press.

KRADER, LAWRENCE (1919). Ph.D. Professor of Ethnology at the Free University of West Berlin. Main publications:

1963 *Social organization of the Mongol Turkic pastoral nomads.* The Hague: Mouton.

1968 *Formation of the state.* Englewood Cliffs: Prentice Hall.

1972 Editor of *Ethnological notebooks of Karl Marx.* Assen: Van Gorcum.

1975 *The Asiatic mode of production.* Assen: Van Gorcum.

1976 *Dialectic of civil society.* Assen: Van Gorcum.

KURTZ, DONALD D. (1933). Ph.D. (University of California, Davis) Associate Professor of Anthropology, University of Wisconsin, Milwaukee, U.S.A.

1973   *The politics of a poverty habitat.* New York: Ballinger.
1973   The rotating credit association, *Human Organization* 32.
1974   Peripheral and transitional markets: the Aztec case, *American Ethnologist* 1.

LEWIS, HERBERT S. (1934). Ph.D. (Columbia University). Professor of Anthropology at the University of Wisconsin, Madison, U.S.A. Main publications:
1965   *A Galla monarchy: Jimma Abba Jiffar, Ethiopia 1830–1932.* Madison: University of Wisconsin Press.
1966   The origins of African kingdoms. *Cahiers d'études africaines.*
1970   'Wealth, influence and prestige among the Shoa Galla', in: *Social stratification in Africa,* ed. by A. Tuden and L. Plotnicov. New York: Free Press.
1974   *Leaders and followers.* Addison-Wesley Module in Anthropology 50.

MARETINA, SOFIA A. (1929). Candidate of Sciences. Senior research fellow in the Leningrad branch of the Institute of Ethnography of the U.S.S.R. Academy of Sciences, Leningrad, U.S.S.R. Published numerous articles, mainly on the social structure of Indian tribes.
1974   'Conversion of Indian Varnas in Bali', in: *The countries and peoples of the East,* ed. by Yu. V. Maretin and B. A. Valskaya. Moscow: Nauka.
1975   Co-editor of *Sotsialnaia organizatsia narodov Azii i Afriki* [The social organization of the peoples of Asia and Africa]. Moscow: Nauka.

POKORA, TIMOTEUS (1928). JUDr., Ph.D. Candidate of Science. Studied in Brno, Prague and Peking. Lives in Prague, Czechoslovakia. Main publications:
1967   *The emperor Chín-Shih-huang-ti.* (in Czech). Prague: Orbis.
1971   *Wang Chúng's critical disquisitions* (in Czech). Prague: Academia.
1975   *Hsin-lun (New Treatise), and other writings by Huan Tán,* (43 *B.C.* 28 *A.D.*). Ann Arbor: University of Michigan press.

SCHAEDEL, RICHARD P. (1920). Ph.D. (Yale University). Professor of Anthropology at the University of Texas at Austin. Main publications:
1966   The Huaca el Dragon, in: *Journal de la Société des Américanistes* 55.
1967   *Etude comparative du milieu paysan en Amérique Latine.* Paris: Centre National de la Recherche Scientifique.
1970   The city and the origins of the state in America, *Proceedings of the 39th Congress of Americanists,* Lima.

SEATON, S. LEE (1943). Ph.D. (University of Hawaii). Until recently Assistant Professor of Anthropology, Bowling Green State University, Ohio, U.S.A.
Main publications:
1974 The Hawaiian *kapu* abolition of 1819, in: *American Ethnologist* 1.
1978 Co-editor of *Political anthropology and the state of the art.* The Hague: Mouton.

SEDOV, LEONID. Candidate of Sciences. Senior research fellow in the Institute of Oriental Studies, U.S.S.R. Academy of Sciences. Moscow, U.S.S.R.
Main publications:
1967 *Ankorskaia imperia* [The Angkor empire]. Moscow: Nauka.
1969 'La société angkorienne et le mode de production asiatique', in: *Sur le 'Mode de production asiatique'*, ed. by R. Garaudy. Paris: Editions sociales.

SENEVIRATNE, SUDARSHAN D. S. (1949). M. A. in Ancient History (J. Nehru University, New Delhi, India). Is preparing his Ph.D. thesis on the early state systems in South India and Sri Lanka.

SKALNÍK, PETER (1945). M. A. (Leningrad State University), PhD. (Charles University, Prague). Senior Lecturer in the Institute of Cultural and Social Studies, University of Leiden, The Netherlands. Formerly Research Fellow in the Institute of Ethnology, Comenius University, Bratislava, Czechoslovakia.
Main publications:
1966 Beginning of the discussion about the Asiatic mode of production in the U.S.S.R. and the People's Republic of China, *Eirene V*: 179–187 (with T. Pokora).
1973 Engels über die vorkapitalistischen Gesellschaften und die Ergebnisse der modernen Ethnologie, *Philosophica. Zborník Filozofickej fakulty Univerzity Komenského* XII–XIII: 405–414.
1975 Monarchies within republics: early Voltaic states in the twentieth century, *Asian and African Studies* XI: 177–193.
1976 'Marx's excerpts on fetishism from 1842' (Slovak edition of Marx's manuscript), in: *K. Marx-F. Engels O ateizme, náboženstve a cirkvi.* Bratislava Pravda, pp. 394–413.
1978 'Dynamics of early state development in the Voltaic area' in *Political anthropology and the state of the art*, ed. by S. Lee Seaton and H. J. M. Claessen. The Hague: Mouton.

STEINHART, EDWARD I. (1942). Ph.D. (Northwestern University). Assistant Professor of History at the University of Texas at Austin. Visiting lecturer at the University of Kingston, Jamaica (1975–1976).
Main publications:
1967   Vassal and fief in three Lacustrine kingdoms. in: *Cahiers d'études africaines*
1973   Royal clientage and the beginning of colonial modernization in Toro, in: *International Journal of African Historical Studies 2.*
1977   *Conflict and collaboration: the kingdoms of Western Uganda 1890–1907.* Princeton: Princeton University Press.

TEUNIS, HENRI B. (1940). Ph.D. (University of Utrecht). Associate Professor of History at the University of Utrecht, The Netherlands.
1973   *Crisis. Studie over een structuur- en normverandering in het Frankrijk van 1150–1250.* [Crisis, a study of change in structure and norms in France, between 1150–1250]. Groningen: Tjeenk Willink.

VANSINA, JAN (1929). Ph.D. (University of Leuven/Louvain). Professor of Anthropology and History, University of Wisconsin, Madison, U.S.A.
Main publications:
1963   *Geschiedenis van de Kuba* [History of the Kuba]. Tervuren: Musée royale de l'Afrique Centrale.
1964   *Le royaume Kuba* [The Kuba Kingdom]. Tervuren: Musée royale de l'Afrique Centrale.
1965   *Oral tradition.* London: Routledge and Kegan Paul.
1966   *Kingdoms of the Savanna.* Madison: University of Wisconsin Press.
1973   *The Tio kingdom of the Middle Congo: 1880–1892.* London: Oxford University Press.

Index of Names

Page numbers in brackets refer to authorship of chapters in this book

Index of Subjects